THE
TUTOR'D
MIND

A VOLUME IN THE SERIES

Native Americans of the Northeast:
Culture, History, and the Contemporary

Edited by
Colin G. Calloway and
Barry O'Connell

THE
TUTOR'D
MIND

Indian Missionary-Writers
in Antebellum America

BERND C. PEYER

UNIVERSITY OF MASSACHUSETTS PRESS
Amherst

Copyright © 1997 by
The University of Massachusetts Press
All rights reserved
Printed in the United States of America
LC 96-51956
ISBN 1-55849-098-1 (cloth); 099-X (pbk.)

Designed by Dennis Anderson
Set in Sabon
Printed and bound by
Braun-Brumfield, Inc.

Library of Congress Cataloging-in-Publication Data
Peyer, Bernd.
The tutor'd mind : Indian missionary-writers in antebellum America / Bernd C. Peyer.
p.   cm. — (Native Americans of the Northeast)
Includes bibliographical references and index.
ISBN 1-55849-098-1 (cloth : alk. paper). — ISBN 1-55849-099-X (pbk. : alk. paper)
1. American literature — Indian authors — History and criticism.
2. American literature — Colonial period, ca. 1600–1775 — History and criticism.
3. American literature — 19th century — History and criticism.
4. Christian literature, American — History and criticism.
5. Indians of North America — New England — Historiography.
6. Missionaries — New England — Historiography.
7. Protestantism and literature.
8. Missionaries in literature.
9. Indians in literature.   I. Title.   II. Series.
PS153.I52P49   1997
810.9'897 — dc21
96-51956
CIP

British Library Cataloguing in Publication data
are available.

Lo! the poor Indian, whose untutor'd mind
Sees God in clouds, or hears him in the wind;
His soul proud Science never taught to stray
Far as the solar walk, or milky way;
Yet simple Nature his hope has giv'n,
Behind the cloud-topt hill, an humbler heav'n.

Alexander Pope, 1733–34

We don't want merely blankets to cover the body, —
we want Light! We want Education!

George Copway, 1850

Contents

Acknowledgments

ix

1

The Indian Writer and the Colonial Situation

1

2

Forest Diplomats, Praying Indians, and Savage Scholars:
Seventeenth-Century Beginnings

21

3

Samson Occom and the Vision of a New England
Christian Indian Polity

54

4

William Apess, Pequot-Mashpee Insurrectionist
of the Removal Era

117

5

Elias Boudinot and the Cherokee Betrayal

166

6

George Copway, Canadian Ojibwa Methodist and
Romantic Cosmopolite

224

7

The Transition of American Indian Literature from
Salvationism to Modernity

278

Notes

297

Index

393

Acknowledgments

PERHAPS IT TAKES a foreigner like myself, so far from the source, to appreciate fully the privileges of an American research grant. Work on this book was made possible in great part by an American Council of Learned Societies Fellowship to the Tecumseh Center, University of California at Davis, in 1979–80; a Ford Foundation Fellowship to the D'Arcy McNickle Center for the History of the American Indian at the Newberry Library, Chicago, in 1986–87; and a Gordon Russell Visiting Professor grant to the Native American Studies Program at Dartmouth College in 1995. A hearty thanks goes out to all the good people at these honorable academic institutions, many of whom have since become friends, and to their treasure-trove libraries. I was also fortunate to be able to participate in two research projects conducted at the Center for North American Studies (ZENAF), Johann-Wolfgang-Goethe-Universität, Frankfurt, which gave me a space to write in and allowed me to cross the ocean for several occasions: one on acculturation among American Indians presided by Wolfgang Lindig and funded by the Volkswagen-Stiftung, 1980–83; the other on early American Indian literature presided by Martin Christadler and funded by the Deutsche Forschungsgemeinschaft, 1991–93. I want to express my appreciation as well for the ever mindful staff of the small but surprisingly well-stocked Völkerkundliche-Bibliothek of the Institut für Historische Ethnologie at the same university, where my first "excursions" into the topic took place back in the late 1970s.

Barry O'Connell was kind enough to review the manuscript and render invaluable advice, and Barbara Palmer did a remarkable job of editing a text that undoubtedly challenged her patience as well as her trained eye. The enthusiastic response throughout from the University of Massachusetts Press has been highly motivating. Finally, I am sincerely grateful to the following individuals for having assisted me in this endeavor at some time and in one way or another, listed alphabetically because kindness is not a measurable entity: John Aubrey, Colin Calloway, Ken Cramer, Jere Daniell, Larry Evers, Melissa Fawcett, Christian Feest, Jack Forbes, Kerstin Herzog, Wolfgang Hochbruck, Fred Hoxie, Chris Jocks, Sergei Kan, Hartmut Lutz, John Moody, Gary Moulton, David Murray, Peter Nabokov, Anne Ostendarp, Berndt Ostendorf, Dorothy Parker, Dieter Riemenschneider, David and Barbara Risling, Wendy Rose, LaVonne Brown Ruoff, Neal Salisbury, Alice Schlegel, William Sturtevant, Helen Tanner, Gladys Tantaquidgeon, Lewana Trout, Jay Vest, Gerald Vizenor, Linda Welch, Rüdiger Wersich, Andrew Wiget, Terry Wilson, Raymond Wood. Of course, I alone remain responsible for any errors, omissions, or other weaknesses in the content.

THE
TUTOR'D
MIND

I

The Indian Writer and the Colonial Situation

THE LITERARY BEQUEST of Indian missionaries in antebellum America should be regarded as a historical testimonial to a conquered people's creative accommodation to social change. Their lives and works can only be fully appreciated in association with the extreme nature of the relationship between Indians and whites at the time, or what might be called their contact environment, which is understood here as the physical and philosophical space in which social encounters take place. Since the character of that relationship was determined by a colonial situation, the contact environment imposed unusually harsh conditions for their advancement as individuals, as writers, and as cultural brokers.[1]

Although it is highly problematic to make generalizations about American Indians — indeed, cultural and linguistic diversity could be said to be one of their most common attributes — their history since the outset of the seventeenth century is most accurately described by the term "colonialism," regardless of current academic fashion. Colonialism, in its broader context, is a form of intergroup domination, or control exerted by individuals or groups over the territory and/or social behavior of other individuals or groups.[2] Whereas the details of colonialism may vary depending upon the relative power and stability of the societies involved, the contact between American Indian communities and Euro-American society has brought about a uniform result: The original inhabitants of the area now comprising the United States make up less than 1 percent of the total population and retain a precarious hold on little more than 2 percent of their former territory. The postcontact experience of the American Indian has, therefore, been regarded by some historians as the very archetype of colonialism.[3]

According to one definition, colonialism is "that form of intergroup domination in which settlers in significant numbers migrate permanently to the colony from the colonizing power."[4] North America was permanently settled by what Darcy Ribeiro and others have referred to as a transplanted people, meaning Europeans who migrated to various parts of the world where they gradually displaced or killed off the indigenous population while maintaining their own previous ways of life, ethnic profile, language, and culture and eventually establishing themselves as independent nations. American Indians have thus been reduced to a position where they are culturally and numerically strangers in their own country.[5] The displacement of the native population in North America was accelerated by certain biological, technical, and cultural advantages enjoyed by the European immigrants at the time of contact: a surplus population prepared to emigrate; an acquired immunity to specific bacteriological infections; the availability of more sophisticated means of transportation, military implements, and domestic tools; and a philosophy of conquest that joined absolutist religious beliefs to a pragmatic mercantilist-capitalist view of the world. By the end of the nineteenth century the remaining Indian communities were confined to reservations situated within a nation that did not even recognize Indians as citizens.

The peculiar relationship that eventually developed between Indian reservation communities and the government of the United States has occasionally been described as "internal colonialism."[6] Contemporary reservations do in fact resemble conventional European overseas colonies in many ways: dependent governments with only partial control over lands and resources; isolation from industrial and transportation centers; lack of capital and professional expertise; deficiency in essential services such as schools, hospitals, water, electricity, housing; lower average wages and higher unemployment rates in relation to the metropolis; large-scale immigration to urban centers; dependence upon corporate interests or government agencies for income; massive drug and alcohol-related problems; and subjection to racial discrimination. Joseph Jorgensen further characterizes the particular colonial situation in the United States as "domestic dependency," an especially oppressive form of domination that has had devastating economic, social, religious, and emotional effects on American Indian communities.[7]

Internal colonialism distinguishes the contact environment in North America from the former European colonies in Africa, Asia, and Latin America. In most of the so-called Third World countries, the indigenous populations still make up the majority in what are now sovereign nations, without necessarily having liberated themselves from the yoke of colonialism. The prevalent form of indirect exploitation by the industrial nations there has been appropriately defined as "neocolonialism."[8] Even though both terms essentially describe a similar process of subjugation and the experiences of the colonized in either case remain mutually relevant, the concept of internal colonialism is useful in specifying the unique situation of tribal minorities like the aborigines in Australia, the Maoris in New Zealand, and the "First Nations" of Canada, whose territories are still occupied by the descendants of Europeans. These colonies within former colonies have been designated as a Fourth World, a notion which denotes not only a similarity in tribal life styles but also a shared political concern.[9] Domestic dependency creates additional existential hardships for contemporary tribal communities. Internal colonies like reservations (reserves, rancherias, plantations, colonies) are in a precarious position because the present-day contact environment still threatens to erode their remaining land base and traditions.

A critic of the internal colonialism concept has conceded that, as long as it is regarded as "the combination of influences and processes which operate upon people's hearts and minds," it remains relevant for anyone "concerned with religious studies, intellectual and cultural history, and the history of education."[10] Once this premise is accepted as being accurately descriptive of the kind of contact environment that has shaped Indian–white relations in America since the seventeenth century, basic social issues such as culture, communication, language, education, literacy, and ideology acquire a special meaning. The mechanics of internal colonialism and an indigenous tribal people's resistance to it are thus crucial to an understanding of the evolution of a decolonized personality, or "tutor'd mind," and its authentic voice in postcolonial American Indian literature.

Writers on the colonial situation invariably highlight the deculturative aspects of a dominated-dominant relationship and are thus highly sensitive to the problems of "place" and "displacement."[11] There is general agreement here that the colonizer purposely tries to manipulate the culture of the colonized. If one gives due consideration to Clifford Geertz's definition of culture as "an historically transmitted pattern of meanings embodied in symbols, a system of inherited conceptions expressed in symbolic forms by means of which men communicate, perpetuate, and develop their knowledge about and attitudes toward life," then the extent to which such an intrusion can disrupt any individual's sense of self and place in society becomes more apparent.[12] African writer Ngugi wa Thiong'o, for instance, considers this to be the single most devastating instrument of conquest used by the colonizer, referring to it as a "cultural bomb" that annihilates "a people's belief in their names, in their languages, in their environment, in their heritage of struggle, in their unity, in their capacities and ultimately in themselves."[13]

European colonizers arrived with a highly nationalistic weltanschauung that was based on their firm conviction of being culturally superior to all other humans on the face of the earth. Such institutionalized ethnocentrism left little intellectual room for the comprehension of, let alone sympathy for, ways of life that appeared to diverge so much from their own. Backed up as it was by the biological and technological advantages already spoken of, European cultural megalomania left American Indians with only two plausible routes of escape from the colonial situation: physical extinction or total assimilation. As Jorgensen has pointed out, the "underlying theme, the ideological motor that has driven this history, has always been a desire to transform Indian culture to White culture, to integrate Indians into the fabric of American life as it is perceived by business, and federal, and Christian interests."[14]

The complex subject of cultural interaction in North America has already been addressed in numerous psychologically oriented "culture and personality" studies produced from the 1920s to the 1940s, and these were in turn succeeded during the 1950s by treatises on "culture-change" and "acculturation." This kind of nonpartisan academic approach is sometimes criticized for its failure to give adequate consideration to the political sources of social oppression.[15] Acculturation has been defined as "those phenomena which result when groups of individuals having different cultures come into continuous first-hand contact, with subsequent changes in the original cultural patterns of either or both groups." According to this definition, the term implies a dialectical exchange at various levels between societies in contact which eventually leads to some concrete evidence of cultural bilateralism, or what Cuban sociologist Fernando Ortiz has designated as *transculturación*.[16] In a colonial situation, however, transculturation in the true sense of the word can only occur either during the initial stages of contact, when the colonizing population is still in the minority, or at a much later contact phase whenever an indigenous population emerges as a powerful mestizo majority. Once dominance has been established by the colonizers, they will immediately proceed to impose their own supposed superior culture without, however, ever really being prepared to grant the colonized full participation on any egalitarian terms. Studies of acculturation thus tend to deal almost exclusively with cultural transformations among colonized groups, that is to say, communities that have adopted cultural elements from Euro-American society, rather than the other way around. This unilateral exchange, which can be attributed to the overpowering dominance of the colonizers rather than the desire for transformation among the colonized, is actually a manifestation of assimilation.[17] When the conquest of a people has been as complete and irreversible as in the case of North American Indians, the dominant society may eventually even promote the retention of certain native practices as an expression of its "own" national folklore. As Frantz Fanon has observed with reference to the situation in Africa, at this point it "is the colonialists who become the defenders of the native style."[18]

Accepting the internal colonialism construct does not, however, mean that Indians have to be regarded as passive victims of injustice. On the contrary, the fact that they have maintained their ethnic distinctiveness in the midst of one of the world's most insistently uniform societies is a testimonial to the effectiveness of their survival strategies. Social change is not a postcontact phenomenon in North America, as can be readily deduced from oral history and archaeological finds. What is new is not so much the act of accommodation itself but the purpose and the degree of transformation that occurs in a colonial situation.

Any societal interaction presupposes some form of dialogue. Whether a certain mode of communication can promote or retard the process of transculturation depends, once again, upon the nature of the contact environment. So long as autonomous groups are sufficiently motivated to retain their cultural differences, communication between them can involve bilingualism, the development of a mixed or simplified language (pidgin), the adoption of a lingua franca, or the use of some sort of functional sign language.[19] Highly sophisticated communication networks existed among native societies in the Americas long before the advent of Europeans. Some 350 to 500 languages (not dialects) are estimated to have been in use north of present-day Mexico prior to 1492. Over the past hundred years linguists have developed various systems of classification for Indian languages that feature as many as sixty different language families. Due to extensive interaction between different groups in the way of marriages, adoptions, political confederacies, trade networks, and ceremonial events, Indian speech communities were as often multilingual as they were language-unique.[20] It is also assumed, though inadequately documented, that some Indian languages functioned as effective linguae francae in intertribal trade relations during the precontact era. Indian-European pidgin languages played an important role in the postcontact period as well, such as Mobilian Jargon (Choctaw-Chickasaw trade language), used throughout the territory now making up the southeastern United States up until the nineteenth century, and Chinook Jargon, which spread all along the northwest coast from California to the Alaska Panhandle and inland as far as Idaho and Montana during its heyday from 1860 to 1900. The Plains Indians, on the other hand, created one of the most sophisticated nonverbal sign languages ever known, which worked formidably as a means of communication between various highly mobile and interactive communities speaking several mutually unintelligible languages.[21]

In view of this evidence of previous linguistic versatility, it seems highly unlikely that learning how to speak a European language automatically effected a cognitive modification among Indian speech communities. The cross-cultural exchange — or what might also be described as the flow of communication between societies in contact — can involve learning on both sides (A $\rightleftarrows$ B), learning in one direction only (A $\rightarrow$ B or A $\leftarrow$ B), or no learning at all (A $\leftrightarrow$ B).[22] By and large, the direction of flow is also determined by the contact environment. In a colonial situation it will invariably become one-directional, from colonizer to colonized (A $\rightarrow$ B). This means that the colonized speech communities are constantly pressured toward total language shift. To quote Ngugi wa Thiong'o once again, colonial alienation "starts with a deliberate disassociation of the language of conceptualization, of thinking, of formal education, of mental development, from the language of daily interaction in the home and in the community. It is like separating the mind from the body so that they are occupying two unrelated linguistic spheres in the same person. On a larger social scale it is like producing a society of bodiless heads and headless bodies."[23]

In a more egalitarian linguistic environment, such as Switzerland, multilingualism can have an altogether different status as it will not imply extreme social stratification. That the act of learning a second language can produce some form of change in perception is plausible enough, but whether it results in the expansion or the reduction of an individual's cultural horizon will depend on other factors. Deculturation is more likely to occur whenever a "superior" language is imposed upon a conquered peoples as a means of further cementing their subordinate status. As Albert Memmi has written, "Possession of two languages is not merely a matter of having two tools, but actually means participation in two physical and cultural realms. Here, the two worlds symbolized and conveyed by the two languages are in conflict; they are those of the colonizer and the colonized."[24]

If language becomes an instrument of conquest, then the unidirectional flow of communication will tend to accelerate cultural alienation. Linguistic imperialism thus stands in marked contrast to the natural process of transculturation that would take place whenever two more or less equal speech communities interact. According to Joshua Fishman, language shift of any kind is already an indicator for dislocation, as it "implies the breakdown of a previously established societal allocation of functions; the alteration of previously recognized role-relationships, situations and domains, so that these no longer imply or call for the language with which they were previously associated."[25] Reversing this trend is extremely difficult because it basically entails the rechanneling of communication, and the greater the power disparity is between interacting societies, the more unlikely it becomes.[26]

The primary catalyst of linguistic imperialism is a particular kind of education. Referred to by Paulo Freire as the "banking concept of education," its main function will be to blunt, rather than sharpen, the "colonized mind."[27] In keeping with the ideology of the English conquest of Ireland in the sixteenth century, the colonization of North America was closely linked to the Protestant missionizing imperative in order to legitimize the appropriation of Indian lands.[28] It was a propagandist formula that reduced the purpose of education (moral and mental development through instruction) to a form of spiritual brainwashing whereby Indians were to be transformed into lower-class duplicates of Europeans. That colonial schoolmasters ever intended for Indians to gain an equal intellectual standing in Anglo-American society is unlikely, as this would have entailed a potential challenge to the irrational policies of colonialism. Instead of making constructive pedagogic use of bilingualism, or what Freire differentiates as "liberating education," colonial educational policy tends to traumatize the transcultural individual, giving rise to conflicts of identity and feelings of inferiority.[29] As late as 1969, a Special Subcommittee on Indian Education report presented to the Ninety-first Congress concluded that one of the main causes for the failure of U.S. educational programs was a "coercive assimilation policy," which had its roots in the continuous desire to exploit and expropriate Indian lands and resources, and a self-righteous intolerance toward tribal communities and cultural differences.[30]

Although Indian speech communities have been systematically pressured toward wholesale language shift since at least the eighteenth century, when missionaries began officially to promote an English-only policy, about two hundred native languages continue to be spoken within the territory of the United States.[31] As Uriel Weinreich argued some time ago, as long as a dominated group continues to feel equal or even superior to the dominant one, it may develop a strong sense of loyalty to its native language as an expression of cultural self-assertiveness.[32] Language loyalty can promote the maintenance of a native language or, as is currently occurring among several eastern Indian communities, even result in the attempt to revitalize an extinct native language. When language is thus associated directly with the preservation of a group's ethnic identity, it can also be said to have become part of its nationalist ideology.[33]

Language maintenance, however, is not the only linguistic manifestation of cultural perseverance in a colonial situation. Equally representative for the vitality of Indian speech communities has been the ability to cope with English spread through language accommodation, which has been defined in postcolonial theory as the process by which language is taken and made to bear the burden of one's cultural experience.[34] This entails a progressive shift to a socially accepted form of balanced bilingualism in which both languages have a definitive and secure intergenerational function for the community as a whole. Such linguistic "diglossia," according to Fishman's use of the term, can be achieved with the compartmentalization of the intruding language. By integrating English on a separate social level from the native language, an Indian speech community is able to maintain a binary system of communication in which both languages can coexist without displacing one another.[35] This particular way of coping with an intruding dominant language is evident among Pueblo Indian communities in the Southwest, for instance, where both English and Spanish are known to have been successfully compartmentalized.[36]

Another example of Indian language accommodation is "customized" English. Research on this topic is still in its infant stage, but it is well known that certain communities have developed colloquialisms in which the intruding language has been structurally modified by native syntax. American Indian English, which is said to be spoken by about two-thirds of Indian youths today, has been described as an aggregate of English varieties differing from standard English by virtue of their close association with their speakers' traditional language.[37] As Dell Hymes has observed in the context of religious practices, there is no plausible reason why an adopted language should not be productively incorporated by an Indian speech community as a vehicle of legitimate self-expression.[38] Simon Ortiz, the noted bilingual

Acoma poet and short-story writer with a marked affinity for colonial theory, has stated it most poignantly:

> (T)he indigenous peoples of the Americas have taken the languages of the colonialists and used them for their own purposes. Some would argue that this means that Indian people have succumbed or become educated into a different linguistic system and have forgotten or have been forced to forsake their native selves. This is simply not true. Along with their native languages, Indian women and men have carried on their lives and their expression through the use of the newer languages, particularly Spanish, French, and English, and they have used these languages on their own terms. This is the crucial item that has to be understood, that it is entirely possible for a people to retain and maintain their lives through the use of any language. There is not a question of authenticity here; rather it is the way that Indian people have creatively responded to forced colonization. And this response has been one of resistance; there is no clearer word for it than resistance.[39]

The issue of linguistic imperialism also brings to mind the academic debate over the social implications behind the transition from orality to literacy, especially the technological determinism advocated by Marshall McLuhan, Walter Ong, Jack Goody, and associates. Contemporary dictionaries (i.e., *Webster's Third International Dictionary*) continue to define "civilization" as a stage in society in which written records are maintained. Most scholars agree that the Indian speech communities of North America lacked a true system of writing before the advent of Europeans. Symbols used in winter counts, birchbark etchings, wampum belts, kiva murals, petroglyphs, pictographs, and other traditional media are generally regarded as mnemonic devices rather than manifestations of literacy.[40] If Indians do in fact represent primary oral cultures and writing is a "consciousness-raising" skill, as Walter Ong maintains, it still remains questionable whether any confrontation between these two supposedly antithetical forms of communication will automatically lead to complete cultural and/or personality transformation among one or the other.[41] Ruth Finnegan, for one, believes that this depends entirely upon the specific historical and sociopolitical circumstances under which the confrontation occurs, rather than on the medium itself.[42]

The colonial discourse in the so-called New World, where the encounter between Indians and Europeans also entailed a clash in weltanschauung, is replete with examples of linguistic imperialism involving the conscious manipulation of the written word by the colonizers.[43] Tzvetan Todorov even goes so far as to maintain that the conquest of America was made possible in large part because of Western civilization's superiority in human communication, albeit at the high cost of losing its ability to communicate with the world.[44] Among Indian communities diplomatic agreements were concluded verbally and usually in the presence of those concerned. The face-to-face exchange between speakers and listeners, which was often highlighted by obligatory gifts, made it difficult for Indian leaders to modify the facts at some later date without the community being fully aware of what was going on. Orally transmitted knowledge and truth are, as James Axtell has pointed out, "not an individual matter so much as a corporate possession," and promises that were thus made in public became a part of the community's collective memory.[45]

European colonists, on the other hand, grounded their legal ideology in the written word, tracing its source back to the Bible and Greco-Roman treatises on "natural law." According to Jack Goody, one of the essential steps in the "domestication of the savage mind" is the shift away from oral intercourse to a set of abstract rules listed in written codes, which results in a more impersonal relationship between the ruler and the ruled.[46] The rather ignominious history of treaty making in the United States is perfectly illustrative of this development. As long as peaceful relations with Indians were of vital concern to European colonists, they were at great pains to observe the traditional decorum of oral-ceremonial legal transactions. Once the balance of power had swung the other way and the colonists no longer felt the need to obtain the explicit agreement of Indians to enforce their policies, the treaty-making process changed into an impersonal bureaucratic routine imposed upon Indians by colonial (later American) administrators, who soon came to regard the bothersome practice as little more than the cheapest means of conquest.[47]

Contrary to the common assumption that the written word has more permanency than the spoken one, legal documents, which merely require the signatures of a handful of designated "chiefs" for ratification rather than the consensus of the community they represent, were usually subjected to "interpretation." Signed agreements between Indians and Euro-Americans have thus been freely amended or abrogated by the juridical apparatus without ever taking on the tinge of illegality in the eyes of the beneficiaries. On the basis of two extremely vague clauses written into the Constitution, American judge-made law has "interpreted" Indian communities out of most of their lands, resources, and sovereignty.[48] The moral discrepancies inherent in the colonizer's application of codified laws did not escape the notice of earlier generations of educated Indians. As Luther Standing Bear writes:

Then, too, his law was a written law; his divine decalogue reposed in a book. And what better proof that his advent into this country and his subsequent acts were the result of divine will! He brought the Word! There ensued a blind worship of written history, of books, of the written word, that has denuded the spoken word of its power and sacredness. The written word became established as a criterion of the superior man — a symbol of emotional fineness. The man who could write his name on a piece of paper, whether or not he possessed the spiritual fineness to honor those words in speech, was by some miraculous formula a more highly developed and sensitized person than the one who had never had a pen in hand, but whose spoken word was inviolable and whose sense of honor and truth was tantamount.[49]

This form of chirographic opportunism is also conspicuous in colonial real estate practices. Yet another widespread assumption concerning Indians is that they regarded land as communal property. Although certain individuals and families did have exclusive rights to lands, these were really understood as applying only to the things that were on the land, or a usufruct right, rather than to the land itself.[50] European colonists, following the precedents established by their sovereigns and international law, viewed land as a commodity that could be acquired or disposed of with the transfer of a written deed. Once again, as long as there was need for Indian allies, conscious efforts were made to obtain the latter's lands through legal means. Early transfers of property thus at least involved a tacit agreement on both sides, even though it is doubtful whether Indian leaders always fully understood the consequences of the transaction or had the authority to sell in the first place. Once the tables were turned, however, Indian property rights were severely curtailed by legal decrees, and the sale of lands was thereafter enforced whenever the need arose. Legitimizing its claims to all "public" lands within its domain on the basis of the highly imaginative but nevertheless codified European principles of "discovery" and "conquest," the government of the United States finally restricted the proprietary status of native communities to a "right of occupancy."[51] Ironically, this means that Indians have retained certain usufruct rights in a quasi-traditional manner, while being denied full ownership by a society which has been telling them for centuries that private property is one of the pillars of Anglo-Saxon civilization.

That Euro-Americans have successfully imposed their doctrine of codified law upon the conquered tribes of North America is a straightforward fact of reservation life. But, as a recent study of U.S. criminal law in Indian territory demonstrates, there is no evidence that it has ever fully permeated the legal consciousness of Indian peoples.[52] Traditional forms of government and land use continue to exist side by side with adopted socioeconomic conventions, even if these are frequently in open conflict with each other. Educated Indians did not take long to understand the subtleties of court battles—treaties and other written documents have also served as the legal basis for numerous land claims against the United States—and what Francis Jennings has ironically referred to as the "deed game."[53] Here, too, the process of accommodating to an extraneous legal philosophy has obviously not prevented the retention of diverging older ideals.

The disruptive potential of literacy over orality is evident as well in the Protestant drive to alter native religious beliefs in North America.[54] Indian spiritual knowledge could be acquired directly through dreams or visions, tended to be individualistic rather than institutional, was passed on from generation to generation by word of mouth, and apparently lacked any conception of an omnipotent deity. The legitimacy of any claim to spiritual power was largely dependent upon its practical manifestation in daily life.[55] European missionaries were quick to recognize the Indians' associations between technological advances and religious prowess and duly proceeded to promote the misconception that the permanence of the printed biblical word, which they contrasted to the supposed transitoriness of oral "fables," guaranteed the authenticity of its divine origins.[56] The verification of a conversion experience, usually limited to members of conquered communities who had already been severely affected by the colonial situation, was made entirely subordinate to the neophyte's ability to read and interpret biblical texts. In addition, missionaries believed for some time that teaching a selected few how to write in their native languages would also help to spread the Gospel into more remote regions. What Protestant schoolmasters obviously expected of their pupils in exchange for revealing the secret of "talking leaves" was a voluntary submission to spiritual brainwashing which, as Axtell sees it, was tantamount to cultural annihilation.[57]

Nevertheless, Indians have accommodated to Christianity better than in just about any other realm of societal interaction. On the one hand, many traditional religions have persisted and, as in the case of the intertribal sun dance, some are currently in the process of expanding.[58] At no other period in the development of Indian–white relations have Christians paid more respect to Indian spiritual ways than at present. On the other hand, Indians have been incorporating elements from Western religions for centuries, as can be readily gleaned from the abundant historical evidence of syncretism and compartmentalization all over North America.[59] It is also doubtful whether Christian Indians ever succumbed wholesale to the missionary imperative of total spiritual transformation. Biblical citations alone may not always have sufficed to displace all traditional religious ideals from the "hot plate of [an Indian] man's consciousness," which is the essential phase in any true conversion experience, according to William James's famous essay on the subject.[60] As the present study tries to demonstrate, not even the highly motivated and literate Protestant Indian missionaries were prepared to ignore the crass inconsistencies they encountered between religious theory and practice in the colonial situation, and consequently they had to re-form their adopted beliefs into what can be legitimately designated as a theology of liberation.

Yet another common manifestation of literary chauvinism in a colonial situation is the fabrication of racial stereotypes to set the proper mood for conquest. Enough has already been written on the sociocultural significance of the diehard noble/brute savage construct and need not be repeated here.[61] Of particular relevance to the topic at hand, however, are the more illusive negative images that surround many of those who try to find ways in which to adapt to the colonial contact environment. Labeled contemptuously as sellouts, apples, Uncle Tomahawks, or, in its kindest form, progressives, transcultural Indians often found themselves stigmatized as the bastard offspring of two incompatible societies. To the colonizer, for whom the aphorism "the only good Indian is a dead Indian" was a familiar credo (ergo, the pervasive infatuation in American literature with the cadavers of noble/brute warriors), any Indian "half-breed" who proved able to "make it" inevitably challenged the former's racist presumptions.[62]

Despite the massive cultural intrusions into Indian speech communities outlined above, it remains doubtful whether the mere technical process of learning a new skill such as writing could be said to have been instrumental in fashioning a new Indian consciousness. Like any spoken language, literacy can also be compartmentalized by a primary oral society.[63] Illiterate Indians have occasionally produced functional orthographies for their native languages — Sequoyah's Cherokee syllabary is only the most famous case in point — which were subsequently used by their communities for the preservation of traditional knowledge.[64] Others, such as the Algonquian-speaking Praying Indians of seventeenth-century New England, who were taught how to write in their own languages by missionaries for the express purpose of propagating the Protestant religion, also made effective use of their vernacular literacy for purely domestic purposes.[65] Writing has been put to efficient use by Indian communities in various other ways as well, such as the countless tribal newspapers established since the first quarter of the nineteenth century.[66] Last but certainly not least, American Indians have produced an impressive body of writing in English since the second half of the eighteenth century, in which they have joined elements from oral traditions with Western literary conventions to create something that might rightly be called Indian "orature." The late Cahuilla activist Rupert Costo, whose own contributions as journalist, publisher, and founder of the American Indian Historical Society have been a weighty factor in the development of modern Indian intellectualism, has expressed his contempt for the "great divide" theory in no uncertain terms: "Have we Indians received something from the Europeans, to make up for all those corrupt influences, lawless practices, and inhumane treatment? Yes. But I would not give one copper cent for the art of writing (which we would have developed anyhow, in our own way)."[67]

Before entering into a discussion of the specific role relegated to American Indian authors in a colonial situation, however, I would first like to clarify certain polymorphous terms which have been subjected to numerous semantic face-liftings on their stony way to academic respectability. To begin with, there has been continuous debate over the social implications of the misnomer "Indian," even though nothing said or written about it so far has succeeded in banishing it from Indian English vocabulary. Alternative terms like "Native Americans" do little more than possibly signal a certain vestige of historical sensitivity among their users. At any rate, the word itself became a political reality for the indigenous peoples of the Americas upon contact with Europeans, who came to regard them uniformly as a conquered race. It also seems very unlikely that the various native groups dealing with the colonists did not soon come to recognize certain sociocultural and biological characteristics that set them apart from the latter collectively, such as material culture, religious beliefs, social structure, military practices, uses of land, physical features, and so on. Five centuries of interaction between native communities and Euro-American society, on the one hand, and a continuous intertribal traffic, on the other, have ultimately given etymological gestalt to the semantic anomaly born out of Columbus's faulty sense of geography. Today, the self-designation "Indian" is as frequently used as any tribal names, whose origins are often no less controversial.

Indians, like all other human beings, have a stratified rather than homogeneous social identity. Being "Indian" is thus determined by individual, familial, generational, tribal, national, and international spheres of activity. When used to denote membership in a specific group (band, clan, tribe) with a common heritage (language, kinship, religion, history, customs, material culture) it becomes synonymous with the concept of "ethnicity," which Fishman describes as the "peopleness" of a collectivity living within a larger society with a distinct sociocultural background.[68] In this case, it functions as an expression of personal identification with a group that is distinct from and yet representative of the collectivity known as "Indians." But if it is applied in a broader geopolitical context to include shared supratribal characteristics, or what has been referred to as "pan-Indianism," it takes on all the trappings of a nationalist ideology. According to an earlier interpretation by Cherokee anthropologist Robert Thomas, pan-Indianism is an expression of a new ethnic identity, the American Indian, and the institutions and symbols that foster it.[69] In his introduction to a compilation of writings on Indian revolutionary thought in Latin America, Mexican anthropologist and activist Guillermo Bonfil Batalla maintains that the basis for what he calls *identificación panindia* is the mutual recognition of the condition of colonization. He also postulates that there is one unitary *civilización india* in America and that the existing differences between the various ethnic groups have only been accentuated by the colonizer as a strategy of conquest.[70] The concept of pan-Indianism, which is more often associated with the diffusion of Plains Indian material culture, has thus evolved into a complex political expression of Indian cultural sovereignty, or what Fishman and others have identified as "ethnic nationalism."[71] In a more recent treatise on Kahnawake Mohawk politics, Gerald Alfred further distinguishes between two forms of nationalist ideology: "Ethno-Nationalism (Statehood)," whereby a group living within an existing state seeks to achieve political independence and cultural distinctiveness; and "Ethno-Nationalism (Autonomy)," under which a group tries to attain some degree of sovereignty by making formal self-government arrangements with the cooperation of existing state institutions, rather than through the creation of a new polity.[72] It is the latter form, of course, that accurately characterizes contemporary Indian nationalist sentiments and the political drive for more self-determination. Finally, identification as an Indian can also denote a certain feeling of solidarity with other colonized tribal peoples throughout the so-called Fourth World, which has surfaced, for instance, in the modern usage of the older term "indigenism."[73] All of these related levels of identity are clearly manifest in the single word "Indian" and can thus be used interchangeably.

To survive in a colonial situation an ethnic minority needs to establish some form of internal balance mechanism to cope with social change. Conservative elements, or traditionalists, function both as the keepers of cultural heritage — the visible thread that ties the community to its own past —

and as a living barrier against uncontrolled innovation. Their importance for the maintenance of Indian cultural identity is unquestionable. Progressive elements, on the other hand, introduce changes that may be necessary in order for the community to adapt to new environmental or political situations. They provide the dynamic energy that prevents an ethnic minority group from stagnating culturally. In an ideal situation, the ideological tug of war between these two opposing forces results in a permanent stalemate in which the community itself is the sole victor. The progressive, however, has always been viewed with suspicion. Indian oral tradition is replete with enigmatic figures (strangers, orphans, tricksters, zoomorphic beings) who must first perform some trickery or supernatural feat before they are finally allowed to introduce their novelty (i.e., a new sacred object, a previously unknown tool, an additional source of food). As symbolic agents of social change, they always pose a threat to the false security of habitual norms and are thus seldom welcome. In this sense, the culture hero and the trickster might be regarded as the original "half-breeds" of Indian oral history. This kind of fragile balance between a tenuous hold on tradition and creative adaptability to a rapidly changing world distinguishes what we nostalgically refer to as "tribal peoples" from our own seemingly chaotic society. As one careful observer of cultural vitality in Taos Pueblo has stated so beautifully, "it is this dance with time — two steps forward one step back — which allows the Taos to gradually adapt to the new while retaining (or even inventing when necessary) the past."[74]

Whenever societies come into contact there will emerge a group of individuals who move back and forth between them and whose services as cultural brokers become essential for both sides. These will often be the children of mixed marriages, who are born with the potential advantages of a bicultural heritage. Their role as intermediaries often helps them to gain influence within their own communities. As the interaction proceeds, they may eventually form a new kind of leadership, an "ethnic proto-elite," which can either cooperate with or be in opposition to traditional leaders. If the indigenous peoples make up a substantial portion of the total population, as in the case of Mexico, an ethnic proto-elite may even rise to the leadership of a new cultural grouping altogether ("proto-ethnos") and found a sovereign nation ("national ethos").[75] But in a colonial situation, the colonizer will attempt to usurp any uncooperative traditional leadership by supporting a more amenable faction. This selected minority is enticed by the prospects of enjoying the material benefits and the social prestige proffered by the colonizer. More often than not, however, these enticements prove to be illusory. Coopted leaders might be allowed to absorb the cultural patterns of the dominant society ("behavioral assimilation") but then be refused membership in the social cliques, political organizations, institutions, and general civil life of that society ("structural assimilation").[76] It will usually not take long for individuals whose ambitions are thus frustrated to recognize the limitations imposed on them by the colonizer and react accordingly, either by succumbing to the status quo and attempting to become ethnically invisible (passing) or by reevaluating their own ethnic identity.[77]

In a colonial situation it can be absolutely vital for an ethnic minority to maintain or reestablish harmony between its conservative and progressive factions. As the total isolation of traditionalists from outside influence is practically impossible in later stages of the colonial encounter, the role of transcultural individuals as mediators becomes increasingly important. It can be likened to the semipermeable membrane of one-cell marine organisms, which permits the life-sustaining exchange between the inner cell and the surrounding ocean environment without direct contact. In a state of internal societal equilibrium, members of the proto-elite can turn back to their roots and consequently fulfill the dual function of introducing external cultural impulses selectively and transmitting to the outside any knowledge that the community holds to be necessary — in short, they may initiate a reversal in the unilateral flow of information. At the moment in which members of the proto-elite begin to question the advantages of Western civilization and to look to their native communities for a new sense of social relatedness, or what Victor Turner calls "communitas," their relationships with their offended "benefactors" will become strained.[78]

The widespread notion that transcultural individuals have schizoid personalities because they are caught in a limbo between two incompatible worlds does not always stand up to a more careful analysis of their life histories. As James Clifton has shown, they may become more complicated psychologically and thus be able to master the knowledge of both cultures sufficiently to function properly within different social contexts.[79] Rather than being incapacitated by a disturbed personality, the transcultural individual can, given the right social conditions, develop a "new multiracial consciousness" that is culturally complex and still psychologically sound.[80] This difficult step from deculturation to transculturation is a gradual process. Everett Stonequist, for instance, developed one of the earliest theoretical models for the personal evolution of "marginal man": a stage in which the transcultural individual is still unaware of any conflict, followed by a period in which he experiences a "moment of crisis" as he becomes aware of his marginality, and a final phase in which he does or does not manage to adjust to the situation. Similarly, when an indigenous community is subject to outside control there will first occur a process of Westernization, which is then superseded by a "movement of cultural differentiation and political nationalism."[81] Marcus Lee Hansen's concept of third-generation nationalism establishes a similar pattern for immigrants in the United States: Whereas the second generation tries to rid itself of the stigma of its foreign lineage, the third generation will attempt to reinstate its heritage.[82]

Colonial literature will also progress in stages, first reflecting the current styles of the metropolis and then gradually developing its own character to become a national literature. Fanon differentiates among three phases in the evolution of African writing: the period of "unqualified assimilation" in which writers give proof of having imbibed the dominant culture, the period of "creative work" in which they begin to feel their isolation and look nostalgically to the past, and the "fighting stage" in which they try to address their own people and stimulate them to take action against the colonizer. The final phase is, in his opinion, the precondition for the emergence of a national literature.[83] This rather restrictive definition of national or postcolonial literature overemphasizes the matter of reception and thus tends to ignore the liberating potential found in earlier works addressed to the colonizer.[84] As James Scott has shown in his study of covert resistance to social oppression, a conquered people can transform literacy into a "hidden transcript" in which criticism of the conqueror is expressed between the lines.[85]

Another important aspect of postcolonial literature is freedom of expression in the adopted language. One of the ways in which Euro-American cultural chauvinism asserts itself is by the creation of artificial barriers between its own artistic productions and those of a "primitive" society, placing one on a higher (classical, fine, universal) aesthetic plane than the other (folk, primitive, regional). There is a marked tendency in contemporary literary criticism to analyze works published by ethnic writers from the perspective of "authenticity," which places too much emphasis on ethnographic accuracy. Creativity apparently loses relevance when ethnic writers are relegated to the roles of "informants" by readers who are obviously more interested in the exotic nature of "otherness" than in the human side of the ethnic experience. In a way, then, the moment in which ethnic minority literature has disengaged itself from colonialism can also be gauged by the emergence of creative writing and the acceptance of ethnic writers in the "literary guild."

A relatively egalitarian contact environment is a precondition for genuine cultural pluralism. As long as this is not the case, I prefer to approach postcolonial American Indian literature (understood here as writings produced in response to, rather than after, colonialism) ethnohistorically. Ethnohistory, as Axtell has pointed out, makes use of "both historical and ethnological methods and materials to gain knowledge of the nature and causes of change in a culture" and thus seems particularly suited to the subject at hand.[86] In the context of early American Indian literature this basically entails combing the life histories and writings of the authors for evidence of a personal commitment toward decolonization, rather than a detached hermeneutical exegesis of textual material. Both published and unpublished works, or autoethnographic sources of expression, are thereby regarded with direct reference to available ethnographic and historical documentation of the contact environment in which the authors lived and wrote.[87] This rather straightforward and perhaps old-fashioned approach is still relevant for the early period in the history of American Indian literature in which creative writing — the richer pastures for literary criticism — is virtually nonexistent.[88]

This study deals with the personal histories of early American Indian authors and their situation in the space of colonial encounters, or what has been referred to elsewhere as the "contact zone."[89] It tries to establish to what extent each author assimilated the values of the colonizer, whether there was an ensuing period of uncertainty, or moment of crisis, and how the resulting personal conflict was resolved. In addition, it gives consideration to the nature of the contact environment in which the authors and their native communities existed, the circumstances under which they made a cultural transition (conversion experience, education, professional life), their relationships with their native communities thereafter, the views they expressed on Indian–white relations, and the personalities and/or cultural trends that may have influenced their lives and work. Rather than taking an apologetic approach, this study will proceed under the premise that these representatives of an Indian proto-elite consciously followed the paths they sincerely believed would lead their people out of the colonial situation.[90]

American Indian literature is made up of the writings produced by individuals of Indian descent who regard themselves as members of the Indian community and who reflect this sense of belonging in their work. The biological connection (blood quotas) is not ignored here altogether but is subordinated entirely to the actual historical part played by each Indian author. This definition purposely omits writings by Indians on non-Indian themes because of the intended focus on the colonial experience. The topical context is further limited to works written in English by Indians living within the present-day territory of the United States. Canadian Indian authors, who properly belong in the distinct field of Canadian Indian studies, are considered here only if their lives and works had a direct and substantial connection to the United States. Not considered either are Indian publications in vernacular or in European languages other than English. All of these legitimate examples of North American Indian literature are simply beyond the scope of this book.

The history of American Indian literature can be roughly divided into three phases that correlate with major historical trends shaping colonial and federal Indian policy: the salvationist period from the early seventeenth century to the beginning of the Civil War, the transitional period from the Civil War until the 1930s, and the modern period from the 1930s until the present. Each one encompasses a great number of transcultural individuals with unique life histories and remarkable contributions to the growing genre of American Indian literature — a subject that could, and undoubtedly will, occupy the attention of generations of scholars to come.[91] The writers of the salvationist period, which is the historical focus of this book, were educated by missionaries and, with few exceptions, trained by them to serve as ministers of the Gospel. Their pietistic writings consequently reflect their own overall acceptance of Protestant ideals and their sincere belief in the need for all Indians to adapt to the dominant society in order to survive. In most cases, however, these authors also made rational and critical assessments of contemporary Indian–white relations and expressed their own notions for improving their people's situation. The intellectual confrontation with the colonial situation, which still characterizes much of contemporary Indian literature, has its roots in the lives and writings of the Indian missionary-writers.

2

Forest Diplomats, Praying Indians, and Savage Scholars

SEVENTEENTH-CENTURY BEGINNINGS

ALONG WITH VIRGIN soil epidemics, superior weaponry, horses, and thousands of renegade Indians, Hernán Cortés's most formidable ally in the conquest of the powerful Aztec empire was his Nahuatl interpreter Malintzin (Doña Marina), better known today as La Malinche. First given to the Mayas as a slave by Aztec rulers and then passed on as a gift to the Spanish, the bilingual (she was fluent in both Nahuatl and Mayan) transculturite soon learned to speak the Spanish language and became a key figure in the opening dialogue between Europe and the New World. It is thinkable that, without her invaluable assistance as an intermediary, the usurpation of Moctezuma would have proven to be a much more difficult task for the conquistadores. In his philosophical exposition on the conquest of America, Tzvetan Todorov extols her role as a cultural broker: "I myself see her in quite a different light — as the first example, and thereby the symbol, of the cross-breeding of cultures; she thereby heralds the modern state of Mexico and beyond that, the present state of us all, since if we are not invariably bilingual, we are inevitably bi- or tri-cultural. La Malinche glorifies mixture to the detriment of purity — Aztec or Spanish — and the role of the intermediary."[1] To the predominantly mestizo population of present-day Mexico, however, the expression *malinchismo* connotes base female betrayal. Here Doña Marina is still widely regarded as *la puta* ("the whore") who sold herself and her people to the Spanish conquerors. The ambivalent nature of Malintzin's life history, which is currently in the process of being salvaged by feminist scholars, is representative for numerous North American Indians who ventured beyond their ethnic borders after contact.[2]

During the initial phases of contact European travelers and colonists found it more expedient to rely on Indian guides and interpreters than to undertake the more difficult task of learning one of the many Indian languages. That native bilinguals would be instrumental in the colonization of the New World was already obvious to Columbus, who captured several hundred Indians in 1493–94 and brought them back to Spain to be sold as chattel and, as he put it, *para que deprendan fablar* ("so that they may learn to speak").[3] One of his Taino prisoners, who was captured on Guanahani Island in the Bahamas and then taken to Barcelona to be baptized as Don Diego Colón in the presence of Ferdinand and Isabella, served Columbus well as guide and interpreter during his subsequent voyages to the Caribbean. America's "discoverer" thus set an example that would be emulated by leaders of numerous future expeditions up until the turn of the seventeenth century. At this point there were enough resident translators available so that the further impressment of Indians for this purpose was no longer necessary.

It has been estimated that by the time the Pilgrims landed in Massachusetts in 1620 perhaps as many as two thousand Indians had already traveled to the Old World.[4] The native inhabitants of the northeastern seaboard began to experience this involuntary form of transatlantic contact as early as 1500–1501, when Gaspar Cortereal kidnapped more than fifty Newfoundland Indians to be sold into slavery. Sebastian Cabot arrived in 1502 and captured three Newfoundland natives whom he took to England and presented to Henry VII. And so the practice continued into the next century: In 1508 Thomas Aubert took several Indians from the St. Lawrence River region to Paris; in 1520 Francisco Gordillo and Pedro de Quexós captured 150 southeastern Indians; in 1525 Estévan Gomez seized more than fifty Indians along the New England coast; in 1534 Jacques Cartier abducted two Iroquois, Taignoagny and Domagaia, and subsequently employed them as guides on his next journey to Canada in 1535; in 1584 Philip Amadas and Arthur Barlowe apprehended two southeastern Indians, Manteo and Wanchese, and brought them to England, where both were eventually enlisted as guides for the ill-fated Roanoke expedition commanded by Richard Grenville in 1585 (Manteo was christened as Lord Roanoke by Sir Walter Raleigh in 1587); in 1605 Captain George Weymouth seized five Abenaki Indians — Tahanedo, Skicowaros, Amoret, Sassacomoit (Assacomit), and Maneddo — who had innocently boarded his ship off the coast of Maine and forced them to accompany him back to Europe. Tahanedo (Dehamada) returned to New England in 1606 with Martin Pring, and Skicowaros accompanied the George Popham and Raleigh Gilbert expedition to Maine one year later. Just how many American Indians suffered similar fates and what ultimately became of them will probably never be revealed.[5]

Not all of those who made the transatlantic crossing during the sixteenth and seventeenth centuries were involuntary passengers. Some ventured into the unknown out of sheer curiosity, and others had diplomatic missions to fulfill. In 1528 Moctezuma's son accompanied Hernán Cortés to the court of Charles V in Toledo, taking with him a dozen Aztec jugglers and acrobats who thrilled audiences in various places in Europe. A remarkable event took place in Rouen in 1550, where about fifty Tupinambás from Brazil performed in a pageant in honor of Henry II. By the 1560s Indians had become a relatively common sight in France. Michel de Montaigne met with three Tupinambás who were visiting Charles IX in 1562, and later recorded his impressions in his famous essay "Des Cannibales." Other notable seventeenth-century Indian "tourists" included Savignon, a Huron from Canada who traveled to Paris in 1610 and returned that same year with Champlain; and Messamoet, a Micmac from Nova Scotia who sailed to France around 1580 and later became a successful intermediary in the northeastern fur trade.[6]

Nor were all Indian travelers intimidated by what they had experienced. Francisco de Chicora, a Yamasee from South Carolina who was captured by Gordillo and Quexós in 1520 and then taken to Spain (where he was interviewed by Peter Martyr), lost no time in making his escape when he returned in 1526 as guide for an expedition headed by Lucas Vásquez de Ayllón.[7] Luis de Velasco, or Don Luis, an Algonquian Indian from the York River region in Virginia whom Spanish explorers had abducted around 1561 and taken to Cuba and Spain to be educated, accompanied a group of Spanish Jesuits back to his homeland in 1570 where he and his fellow tribesmen quickly made martyrs of them.[8] Epenow, a Capawake sachem from Martha's Vineyard who had been kidnapped by Edward Harlow and Nicholas Hobson in 1611, invented stories about gold to be found on his native island and finally managed to get himself and two other captives (Assacomit and Wanape) enlisted as guides for an expedition to the Northeast under Hobson in 1614. As soon as the ship reached the harbor at Martha's Vineyard, he made his escape and became a staunch adversary of English colonization thereafter. He is thought to have been partly responsible for the deadly Indian raid on the Thomas Dermer party in 1619.[9]

Despite such occasional setbacks (from the English point of view), most Indians who had learned a European language eventually fulfilled an important role in seventeenth-century Indian–white relations. Their skills were invaluable not only for European settlers but also for tribal leaders who had to contend with colonial administrators. The true significance of Indian interpreters in American colonial history has yet to be fully documented and analyzed.[10] Even the life histories of Squanto and Pocahontas, both recently incorporated into Disney's pantheon of fantasy figures, remain enigmatic at best as their roles in the colonial encounter have been subjected to massive ideological distortion.

Squanto's biography, or what little is known of it, is exemplary for the experience of involuntary Indian voyagers to sixteenth- and seventeenth-century Europe. His nigh incredible odyssey was not unique, however, as it was preceded by the adventures of Assacomit (Sassacomoit), one of the five Abenakis abducted by Captain George Weymouth in 1605. Assacomit and his companions were brought to England, where they were taken up by Sir Walter Raleigh's associates, Sir John Popham and Ferdinando Gorges. En route to Maine as a guide and interpreter for another English expedition (probably with Henry Challoung in 1606), he was captured by the Spanish along with the rest of the crew and taken to Spain. Assacomit returned to England after being ransomed by Gorges and from there sailed again to New England in 1614 as a guide for the Nicholas Hobson expedition — the same one from which Epenow managed to make his spectacular escape.[11]

Nothing is known about Squanto (Tisquantum) prior to his kidnapping by Thomas Hunt in 1614, or of the three years he spent in Spain after he had been taken there by Hunt to be sold as a slave along with about twenty other Indian captives.[12] There is even some uncertainty about the exact date of his capture, as the aging Ferdinando Gorges reported that he was brought to England by Weymouth along with Assacomit and the other Abenakis in 1605, and Captain John Smith claims to have put a certain "Tantum" ashore at Cape Cod in 1614. If this is so, then he may have traveled to England repeatedly before he was captured by Hunt. He is thought to have been a member of a Pawtuxet community living in the vicinity of the Plymouth site and may have been twenty or thirty years of age at the time of his capture. Judging from his subsequent display of diplomatic talent, Neal Salisbury concludes that he may well have had some previous standing in his own community, perhaps as a spiritual war leader (*pniese*), before his involuntary transatlantic travels began.[13] By 1617 he had apparently also accomplished the astonishing feat of escaping slavery in Spain and making his way back to England, because he is reported to have been a resident at the London home of John Slany, treasurer of the Newfoundland Company.

In 1618 Squanto was sent on an English expedition to Newfoundland, where he became acquainted with Thomas Dermer and sailed back to England with him that same year. He gave such a glowing account of his homeland in New England that Dermer finally asked Ferdinando Gorges for a commission to explore the area. Upon his return to New England with Dermer in 1619, Squanto discovered that his native village had been devastated by a wave of smallpox epidemics in 1617–19. Those who had managed to survive were scattered among neighboring Indian communities. Then, when Epenow and his allies mounted their devastating attack on Dermer's party, Squanto found himself a prisoner of the Wampanoags (Pokanokets). The fact that he was not immediately dispatched by Epenow's men for being allied to the hated English and was turned over instead to Massasoit, the Wampanoag sachem, speaks for both his own skills as a diplomat and the political farsightedness of Massasoit.

At the time of the Separatists' arrival in Plymouth in 1620 the Wampanoags were in the humiliating position of tributaries to the Narragansetts, who had somehow managed to remain unaffected by the 1617–19 epidemics and consequently were able to dominate their decimated neighbors. Massasoit, himself the paramount leader of a once powerful confederacy of tribes, thus regarded the English as welcome allies against the Narragansetts. The presence of a bilingual Indian with knowledge of European ways was, of course, a most opportune coincidence, even if his status among the Wampanoags was merely that of a lowly captive. In keeping with tribal decorum and plain common sense, however, Massasoit first appointed Samoset, a trusted sachem from the Pemaquid River region in Maine who had been trading with the English for years and could also communicate in their language, to open up negotiations with the settlers. Only after contact had thus been officially established did Samoset introduce Squanto, who obviously had better command of English, allowing him to mediate in the conclusion of the first treaty of friendship between the Wampanoags and the Puritans. Massasoit thereupon released Squanto to the Pilgrims, perhaps as a reward for his services as mediator. Squanto soon proved to be of invaluable service to the English colonists. He taught them how to cultivate Indian staple foods like maize, instructed them in local hunting and fishing techniques, acted as guide for inland explorations, and functioned as interpreter in the colonists' subsequent endeavors to establish relations with other tribes of the area — in short, all of those services which have earned him a permanent place of honor at Thanksgiving celebrations.

Brushing aside all mythic-propagandistic fantasies, Squanto clearly had no moral obligations toward the Wampanoags or the English, both of whom had merely sought to impress his services to their own advantage. The fact that he "sought his own ends and played his own game," as William Bradford put it and which some historians have disparaged as manifestations of an "irrational" or a "childish" form of behavior that ultimately threatened the delicate peace between New England colonists and Indians, can also be interpreted as the survival tactics of a highly capable and well-traveled individual, who was as adept at the art of diplomacy as any of his adversaries.[14] Since Squanto's prestige among other tribes of the region was steadily increasing and he was also busy trying to establish good relations between the English and the powerful Massachusetts, Massasoit had very good reason to feel threatened by his former captive. In the summer of 1621 he sent another bilingual emissary to the Pilgrims, a ranking Wampanoag *pniese* named Hobbamock, who presumably had orders to keep an eye on Squanto's doings.

The strained relations between Squanto and Massasoit finally came to a head when general hysteria broke out among the colonists following the news of Opechancanough's insurrection in Virginia in 1622, and both men accused each other of intriguing against the Puritans. Massasoit demanded that Squanto be turned over to him for punishment, as was his prerogative according to one of the stipulations of the treaty of friendship, but the English, who obviously still had good use for his talents, simply refused to comply. As John Smith conceded, "he [Squanto] speaking our language we could not well be without him." On the other hand, by having thus invoked Massasoit's enmity, Squanto in turn became entirely dependent upon the colonists' goodwill as he now had to remain as close to their settlements as possible if he wanted to stay alive. When he did finally venture out again in the company of a trading expedition led by William Bradford to the remote southeastern shore of Cape Cod in October of 1622, Squanto suddenly took ill with what Bradford diagnosed as "an Indian fever" and died within a few days. According to Bradford, just before his death Squanto requested the governor "to pray for him that he might go to the Englishman's God; and bequeathed sundry of his things to sundry of his English friends as remembrances of his love; of whom they had a great loss." Whether his death was caused by some infectious disease (as is likely) or, as Bradford implied, induced by Indian witchcraft, it certainly occurred at a most op-

portune moment for Massasoit. With the assistance of the faithful Hobbamock, the Wampanoag leader resumed his diplomatic relations with the
Pilgrims and, after turning them against the Massachusetts with repeated
implications of an impending insurrection, temporarily restored the supremacy of his own confederacy.[15]

The conflict between Squanto and Massasoit can be regarded as an example of traditional competitive leadership among Coastal Algonquians,
with the incumbent Squanto representing a legitimate alternative to Massasoit as an intertribal leader because of his linguistic skills and intimate
knowledge of English ways. Since his native community had been disbanded
by the effects of disease while he was away in England, Squanto really had
no choice but to find an application for his newly acquired talents elsewhere.
Perhaps, as Salisbury has suggested, he even envisioned a reconstituted
Pawtuxet band with himself as its paramount leader.[16]

The role of Pocahontas (Matoka) in the colonial discourse was more
glamorous than Squanto's.[17] As favorite daughter of the principal leader of
a powerful confederation of nearly thirty Tidewater Indian communities in
the Chesapeake Bay area, she was in a prestigious position from the outset.
Her father, Powhatan, ruled over approximately twelve thousand subjects
in a centralized form of state that has been likened to a small monarchy.[18]
The arrival of English colonists in 1607 was viewed with mixed feelings
by village leaders in Powhatan's realm and in neighboring communities.
Some of them favored a policy of fraternization, whereas those who had
already had negative experiences with Europeans called for immediate action against the intruders. Powhatan, who sought to strengthen his own
position by gaining control of the local trade between Indians and the
colonists, tended to regard the English presence more pragmatically.

If there is any truth whatsoever to John Smith's famous account of his
rescue from death by Pocahontas early in 1608, then it is quite likely that
the entire episode was an orchestrated event.[19] It may have entailed an
official adoption of John Smith by the relatives of two Indians who had
been killed by him prior to his capture, an act which would not only have
been acceptable compensation according to custom but also have cemented
relations between Powhatan and the English. With his apparently very
attractive teenage daughter acting as emissary, Powhatan went about cultivating the colonists' friendship by helping them to overcome initial difficulties with generous gifts. This exchange did in fact increase Powhatan's
prestige at the outset, but it was a rather strained relationship with each
side trying to gain the upper hand and armed confrontations permanently

threatening to disrupt the delicate balance of power. Powhatan had little control over his younger warriors, many of whom wanted to earn a reputation by harassing the settlers, and colonial administrators were equally unable to prevent incursions into Indian territory or the frequent raiding of Indian supplies by new immigrants.

In 1609 Pocahontas is said to have saved John Smith's life a second time when she warned him of an impending attack by Powhatan's warriors. It may be that she even acted on her own account out of affection for Smith, as legend would like it, or because she wanted to avoid a war between her people and the colonists. At any rate, following Smith's unannounced departure for England that same year, Pocahontas did not resume contact with the colonists until 1613, and then only as a hostage. Sometime in the late winter of 1612 or early spring of 1613 Pocahontas was captured by Samuel Argall, supposedly to guarantee the security of men and equipment being held at the same time by Powhatan. If, according to Ralph Hamor's account, "she began to be exceeding pensive and discontented," when told she was a prisoner of the English, Pocahontas nevertheless soon adjusted to the situation. One biographer has intimated that she may not have been overly upset about her abduction because she regarded it as a chance to function as a peace emissary once again.[20]

It was precisely at this critical moment in the relationship between Powhatan's confederacy and Virginia that Pocahontas converted to Christianity and her celebrated marriage to John Rolfe took place. The professed intent to convert her to Christianity, as Rolfe maintained in his oft-cited letter to Sir Thomas Dale, can hardly have been the prime motive behind this very unusual instance of officially sanctioned mixed marriage in colonial history, especially in view of the fact that Virginia would prohibit mixed marriages by 1691. It was probably based on somewhat more pragmatic considerations on the part of all those involved in the arrangement. Powhatan concluded a new treaty of peace with the colonists shortly thereafter and, in the words of Captain John Smith, "ever since wee have had friendly trade and commerce, as well with Powhatan himselfe, as all his subjects."[21]

In 1616 John Rolfe and his converted Indian bride sailed on a promotional tour to England. It was of vital economic interest for the foundering colony to assure prospective investors at home that a peaceful coexistence with the Indians was possible. Pocahontas — now Lady Rebecca — was a smashing success at court and in the parlors of English society, and this certainly did much to rekindle public interest in the colony of Virginia. It probably even prompted King James I to give a second order (the first was in 1615) to the clergy of his realm to hold special collections for the salvation of the heathen Indians. Powhatan, on the other hand, took advantage of the occasion and sent a retinue of fellow tribesmen to ascertain the situation in England and, possibly, also to monitor his daughter's activities there.

Unfortunately, Pocahontas's diplomatic mission in England was cut short by some unknown illness, and she died in Gravesend in 1617, just five years before Squanto's career would come to a similar end. Whereas the fruit of John Rolfe's marriage to Pocahontas eventually generated what Vine Deloria, Jr., has designated as the "Indian-grandmother complex" in America, the peaceful interim in the relations between the colonists and Tidewater Indians came to an abrupt end shortly after her death.[22] Renewed hostilities culminated in March of 1622 with an Indian insurrection led by Powhatan's brother Opechancanough, who had little sympathy for the English and their ways.[23] Almost 350 settlers were killed during the short-lived uprising, but casualties would probably have been much higher if "friendly" Indians had not warned the colonists of an impending attack. The "Jamestown Massacre," as the first Indian revolt in North America came to be known, only added fuel to the rising anti-Indian sentiment and provided the colonists with a welcome ideological legitimation for their subsequent repressive actions against the native populations of Virginia and elsewhere in the New World.[24]

If the superficial veneer covering the popular images of Pocahontas as a love-sick Indian princess or a half-naked, cartwheeling, "well-featured but wanton young girl" is rubbed away, there will appear a more realistic portrait of a rational individual performing the necessary functions of an intermediary in the early stages of contact when there was still room and need for bilateral communication. Nevertheless, both Pocahontas's and Squanto's experiences as preliterate cultural brokers are already illustrative of the polar tension acting upon those who felt called upon to mediate between clashing societies in a colonial situation. The future direction of the exchange was accurately foretold in the Reverend Alexander Whitaker's promotional pamphlet titled *Good Newes from Virginia* and published in 1613, the same year he baptized Lady Rebecca: "If we were once the masters of their countrey and they stoode in feare of us (which might with a few hands imployed about nothing else be in short time brought to passe), it were an easie matter to make them willingly to forsake the divell, to embrace the faith of Jesus Christ, and to be baptized."[25] Toward the middle of the seventeenth century, as the balance of power began to shift in favor of the colonists, the role of intermediary fell to literate bilingual Indians who had been educated by Protestant missionaries for the express purpose of spreading the Gospel among their people.

The two great pillars of European civilization, church and family, provided the ideological foundations for educational policies in early Stuart England and its American colonies. For most pupils schooling entailed learning how to read religious texts along with some elementary exercises in grammar and arithmetic. In an ideal situation men were subsequently bound into an apprenticeship while women were expected to turn to domestic chores. Only a select few actually managed to attend a grammar school and then go on to study at a college, usually with the end in view of obtaining a ministry. This pedagogical concept was also applied by colonial schoolmasters in the education of Indians — at least in theory.[26] Despite the religious overtones expressed in some of the colonial charters, Protestant efforts at missionizing Indians during the seventeenth century were quite modest in comparison with Catholic endeavors elsewhere in North America.[27] The few short-lived educational experiments that were actually attempted at this time in Virginia and Massachusetts failed to produce the desired results because of Indian reserve and English arrogance.

In accordance with early instructions from the London council of the Virginia Company, the colonists first detailed Indian children to English homes under the assumption that they would automatically absorb European norms through the good examples of their hosts. In 1619 a law was passed requiring each town, borough, or plantation to obtain a certain number of Indian children to be instructed as missionaries to the "heathen race." Most Indian parents were not overly enthusiastic about sending their children away to be educated by complete strangers, however, and so the colonists soon resorted to the tactic of resettling entire families in or near English villages in order to obtain their quota of charges. When this measure did not produce the desired results either, they finally found it more expedient to rely on hapless children who had been captured in war or taken as hostages from subjugated tribes. Laws passed in Virginia in 1655 and 1658, which prohibited treatment of Indian youths as chattel, restricted their transfer from one household to another, and required that they be released at the age of twenty-five, suggest that Christian piety was not always the sole motive for English families to rear Indian children in their own homes.[28]

Pragmatism also appears to have been the driving force behind the plans for Henrico College, a special educational institution for Indians in Virginia.[29] Company orders to Governor George Yeardley in 1618 contained instructions for the establishment of a college for Indian youths (to be expanded into a university at a later date) at the settlement of Henrico. It was conceived as a kind of industrial school where Indian pupils would be taught the necessary skills for farming, while those with special aptitudes were to receive further training as missionaries.

The settlement of Henrico had been founded seven years earlier by Sir Thomas Dale as a bastion against foreign incursions into Virginia territory and as an alternative site to the older, but environmentally unsound, colony at Jamestown. Henrico did not flourish as expected, however, and was practically abandoned in 1618. But news of the plans to establish a college and university there brought Henrico back to the attention of those in England who were prepared to invest substantial sums in missionary work among the Indians of North America. Profiting from Pocahontas's promotional tour in 1616–17 — which was readily interpreted by English philanthropists to mean that all of Virginia's Indians were eager to be converted — and the second royal order to the English clergymen for semiannual collections over a period of two years for the express purpose of promoting Christianity among the "heathen," the Virginia Company managed to take in about £1,500 in donations for its Indian college scheme. After "borrowing" about £700 to pay off debts and to invest in other company business, the gentlemen appointed to allocate the funds decided that it would be more convenient for the time being to cultivate the acreage that had been set aside for the institution, allegedly to secure a more permanent source of funds for the college. In 1619 they proceeded to import tenants from England to do the required menial labor. Eventually most of the tenants were diverted to private plantations — much to the embarrassment of the Virginia Company administrators whose books were audited in 1621 as a result — supposedly because their supplies at Henrico had run out and lack of adequate housing would have left them at the mercy of winter. An additional £550 provided by an anonymous donor in 1620 for the express purpose of Indian education were used to build an ironworks that soon turned out to be a financial fiasco.[30] In 1621 the Virginians came up with an additional educational scheme, a public school in Charles City where English children (rather than Indian) could be primed for attendance at the yet imaginary Indian college in Henrico. The Reverend Patrick Copeland managed to stimulate the generosity of some of the East India Company's stockholders in 1622, with the end result that the institution was to be named East Indian School in their honor and the philanthropist was granted 300 acres of prime Virginia land.

Neither the Indian college nor the public school ever materialized, in spite of the substantial funds that had been gathered for that purpose. Opechancanough's attack on Good Friday interrupted the dubious plan, and the revoking of the Virginia Company's charter on June 16, 1624, permanently scrapped it. The rather questionable practice of rechanneling funds donated specifically for the education of Indians, not a penny of which had been collected from the colonists themselves, is grounds enough for the suspicion that the entire Henrico project was a ruse to save the Virginia Company from financial ruin rather than Indian souls. It was, as Francis Jennings concludes bluntly, all part of a profitable colonial "missionary racket."[31]

After Opechancanough's second futile rebellion in 1644 and another genocidal Indian war in 1676 known as Bacon's Rebellion, the power scales tipped permanently in favor of the English in Virginia, whose numbers increased dramatically from about 15,000 in the 1640s to about 80,000 in the 1680s, while the Indian population decreased at an even more rapid rate. Treaties concluded in 1646 and 1677 with Virginia tribes reduced them to the state of tributaries who had to pay the colonists an annual amount in furs and hides.[32] As the laws passed for the protection of Indian youths in 1655 and 1658 indicate, the practice of educating them in English homes continued and the remaining funds for Henrico College were used up for this purpose. Plans for an Indian college in Virginia did not materialize until the end of the century with the founding of the College of William and Mary in 1693, whose charter specifically mentions the christianization of Indians as one of its primary objectives.[33]

Part of the Robert Boyle estate, which had been invested in Brafferton Manor in England after his death in 1691 to generate further funds for the education of Indians in America, was allocated to the college, and it subsequently began to receive a modest number of Indian students after the turn of the century. Indian parents were still hesitant about parting with their children, so once again colonial educators had to resort to captives obtained from hostile tribes. After the Tuscarora War of 1711, Lieutenant Governor Alexander Spotswood hit upon the idea to require the leaders of the defeated tribe and other tributary Indian communities to turn over two children from each village as hostages, who were to be educated at the college. "The delivering their Children as Hostages will not only prove the most effectuall Security for their fidelity," Spotswood explained, "but may be a good step towards the Conversion of that whole Nation to the Christian faith, and I could not hope for a more favorable Conjecture to make this demand than now, when they are under great apprehensions of our

Resentment for the late barbaritys committed in Carolina, and the impression made on them by the appearance of so great a force as I then showed them."[34]

The numbers of Indian students at William and Mary rose accordingly from four to about twenty by 1712. In 1723 Brafferton Hall was erected, a special building to accommodate them, which they ended up sharing with an expanding library. The Boyle School, as it was sometimes called, offered an elementary education that may have included some Greek and Latin to an unknown number of Indian students until funds were cut off in 1776, and it was forced to shut down shortly thereafter. The names of a few students (William Cooke, Gideon Langston, John Langston, John Montour, Charles Murphey, John Sampson, Thomas Sampson, William Squirrel) have been preserved, but almost nothing is known of their fate after they left the institution.[35] The success of the institution in terms of converting Indians was probably marginal at best. As former professor Hugh Jones observed pessimistically in his *Present State of Virginia* (1724), many died as a consequence of illness, unaccustomed diet, and improper care, and others quickly reverted to "their own savage customs and heathenish rites" upon returning to their native communities. A few remained in Williamsburg where, according to Jones, they either worked as servants among the English or "loitered and idled away their time in laziness and mischief." William Byrd's opinion in *History of the Dividing Line* (1728) was even less flattering: "And some of them too have made the worst use of the Knowledge they acquir'd among the English, by employing it against their Benefactors. Besides, as they unhappily forget all the good they learn, and remember the Ill, they are apt to be more vicious and disorderly than the rest of their Countrymen."[36]

Despite the religious fervor in New England and frequent references to the sacred duty of bringing the Gospel to "Satan's brood" — the seal of the Massachusetts Bay Company depicted a smiling Indian requesting the English to "Come over and help us" — the Saints were apparently in no great hurry to begin with the task of converting the Indians.[37] This initial hesitation was probably due as much to Indian disinterest as it was to the Puritans' own existential problems. Concrete plans for missionizing Indians thus did not materialize until 1643, when the Puritans finally managed to establish dominion over the tribes living in the area. The first step in this direction was the Puritans' all-out war against the Pequots in 1636–37, which left this once powerful Indian nation destitute. Prior to this campaign, which Jennings has appropriately called the "First Puritan Conquest," contact between Indians and Puritans had been limited to trade and diplomacy. As in Virginia, interest in Christianity among New England Indians did not begin to surface until the colonists were in a strong enough position to impose their own notions of spirituality.[38]

The impetus to begin mission work actually came from London, where complaints about the Puritans' obvious neglect to christianize the Indians were growing louder, especially among the dissenters who were not favorably inclined toward Puritan religious hegemony in Massachusetts. This, together with the likely possibility that the financially shaken colony also vied with Virginia for its own share of English mission funds, prompted the Massachusetts Bay Company to mount a promotional offensive in England in the early 1640s to clear its tarnished reputation. Its efforts finally bore fruit in 1649, when the Long Parliament created a special corporation to take charge of missionary efforts in New England. The President and Society for the Propagation of the Gospel in New England, which eventually became known as the New England Company, was the richest source of funds for missionizing activities in North America up until the end of the colonial period.[39]

Conversion of Indians, from the Puritan point of view, meant nothing less than total and uncompromising spiritual transformation. As James P. Ronda points out, it called for the complete rejection of all other customs and traditions, or a kind of "cultural suicide."[40] The Puritans, a self-declared elect with little margin of tolerance even for their own countrymen who thought differently — not a few Europeans found Indian ways of life more appealing — were unwilling to attribute any value whatsoever to Indian cultures.[41] On the contrary, to them Indians came to represent the absolute antithesis to everything they were striving to accomplish in New England. In keeping with proverbial Puritan arrogance, their ways of life were considered "base," their forms of government likened to anarchy, their means of subsistence dismissed as "idleness," and their religious beliefs condemned as manifestations of "devil worship." Even the physical presence of Indians was interpreted as a biblical burden to test Puritan steadfastness in a spiritual "wilderness." In such a hostile contact environment, Indians were left with only two alternative ways of interacting with the Puritans: forming military and/or trade alliances with them if they still had the potential to do so; or finding some means of accommodating to their domination if they did not.[42]

Of the many Protestant missionaries who became active in New England in the early 1640s, none were as influential and have been given so much notice as John Eliot (1604–90) and, to a somewhat lesser extent, Thomas Mayhew, Jr. (1621–57). Even though both were uncompromising assimilationists and their experimental Christian Indian communities functioned along the same religious guidelines, their individual methods still varied somewhat and affected the long-term results of their proselytizing activities.[43]

John Eliot, whom Cotton Mather exalted as "the First Preacher of the Gospel to the Indians in America," actually began his missionary work after Thomas Mayhew, Jr. He may even have taken credit for some of Mayhew's earlier activities on Martha's Vineyard when the Massachusetts Bay Company was making its pitch for mission funds in England.[44] In 1643, while Mayhew was busy in the field, Eliot commenced his three-year task of learning the Massachusett language in the relative comfort of his study. His first attempt to preach in Massachusett occurred in the summer of 1646, at the village of Cutshamekin. The sachem and his followers were not much impressed by Eliot's exhortation and apparently let him know it.[45] Avoiding any further confrontations with the skeptical Cutshamekin and other traditional leaders of the Massachusetts for the time being, Eliot decided to concentrate his efforts on the village of a less reticent Indian by the name of Waban. Coincidentally (or perhaps not), the General Court of Massachusetts passed a law shortly after Eliot's fiasco that made blasphemy a capital crime and also prohibited traditional ceremonies (powwowing) under penalty of stiff fines.[46]

Waban, who was not officially recognized by the Massachusett community as a leader, had managed to catch the missionary's attention by announcing his own inclination to learn more about Christianity. A year later the General Court appointed Waban "Chief Minister of Justice" and thus made sure that he would attain a position within his community not ordinarily due to him. Eliot frequently applied similar subversive tactics to obtain additional converts, often promising ambitious individuals relief from their tributary duties to sachems if they chose to join the English. In time, the growing numbers and relative affluence of the neophytes — Christian Indians had direct access to European goods and funds — forced some traditional leaders to follow suit if they wanted to retain their own authority. Even Cutshamekin eventually converted to become first ruler of Natick, Eliot's model Praying Indian town.

Eliot confronted Indians repeatedly with the notion of sin and eternal damnation, with the ultimate end in view of creating an association between guilt and traditional ways of life. It was a form of spiritual interference which, as Neal Salisbury has pointed out, aimed at producing a complete "breakdown" in the neophyte's personality.[47] Another tactic of his was to segregate the converts in reservation-like communities where, under strict missionary supervision, every minute of the day was regulated by a codified set of rules. In 1646 the General Court set aside some land for Christian Indians, and Eliot thereupon founded the Praying Indian village of Nonantum near Roxbury, Massachusetts. It eventually proved to be situated too close to English settlements and was consequently moved in 1651 to a site on the Charles River, about eighteen miles south of Boston. Natick, as the new Praying Indian village was named, soon became the model for thirteen other Christian Indian communities Eliot founded between 1651 and 1674 with a total of about 1,400 inhabitants.[48]

The political system under which the Praying Indian villages functioned was made up of elected leaders at the top of the hierarchy who ruled over groups of a hundred subjects each, followed by two lesser rulers for every group of fifty and ten rulers at the lower level to watch over groups of ten.[49] The first election was held at Natick on June 6, 1651, and, as might be expected, the faithful Waban was elected as ruler of one hundred. The authority of Indian officials in the Praying Indian villages was limited, however, as English "Indian Magistrates" appointed by the Court could veto all their decisions, and they also had broad discretionary powers in all daily matters of the communities.[50]

Each village had a written legal code based on a decalogue that was supposedly developed under Indian initiative in the first Christian Indian community of Nonantum in 1646 and later expanded at Concord into a list of twenty-five rules for proper conduct.[51] It prescribed fines and corporal punishment for "uncivil" behavior and outward appearance such as idleness, vagrancy, adultery, wife beating, lice picking, nakedness, and long hair. At the same time, Christian Indians were required to wear European clothes, build European-style houses, erect fences, plow fields for farming, and maintain domestic animals. Some were still sent to live in English homes, where they were supposed to learn a "useful" trade like woodcutting, shingle splitting, broom making, or basketry. Their education basically consisted of reading and discussing biblical texts, which Eliot had translated into the Massachusett dialect with the help of Indian interpreters, as well as remedial English grammar (Eliot also published an "English Primer" in 1669) and some elementary arithmetic. Daily life was interrupted by an elaborate cycle of religious meetings at which prayers were read from another booklet that Eliot had translated for that purpose in 1665.[52]

Eliot's Praying Indian villages can be viewed as a utopian Protestant experiment that was not even practicable in the Puritan's own communities.

On the surface, at least, Praying Indians seemed to have undergone the cultural and spiritual transformation required of them. For a while they were even tolerated by colonists because they were kept at a safe distance from white settlements, and it was generally believed that Praying Indian villages might be useful as buffer zones against hostile tribes. There is little likelihood, however, of there ever having been any serious thought given to their possible integration into Puritan society, from which they were effectively barred, other than to perform menial labor in English households. But even this kind of "tolerance" turned out to be extremely limited. With the outbreak of King Philip's War in 1675, Christian Indians were immediately subjected to repressive actions by the colonists. Although a good number of Praying Indians fought and died on their side, the General Court passed an order in October of that same year requiring them to move away from their villages and resettle collectively on Deer Island, where they were left without adequate supplies for the coming winter. Two years later another act was passed that confined all Praying Indians to four remaining villages, prohibited them from entertaining strangers, and denied them the use of firearms. In 1681 these communities were reduced to three, and all Indians in Massachusetts were required to remain within their limits or face imprisonment.[53] The handful of Praying Indians who survived soon became entirely dependent upon the colonists for their livelihood and, at the same time, had to deal with increasing incursions upon whatever lands they had managed to retain. Natick, once the model Praying Indian village, was gradually broken down into small private holdings by the turn of the century and, beginning as early as the 1680s, non-Indians began to settle there in such numbers that they were finally able to take over the town administration by 1712. Disease, poverty, sales of private lots, and intermarriage finally dissolved Eliot's experimental Christian Indian communities by the end of the eighteenth century.[54]

The Christian Indian communities on Martha's Vineyard turned out to be more enduring than their mainland counterparts, primarily because they were established in a somewhat more liberal contact environment.[55] In 1643, shortly after his father had purchased Martha's Vineyard along with Nantucket and Elizabeth Island, Thomas Mayhew, Jr., began to missionize the Wampanoags living there. Five generations of Mayhews subsequently controlled Indian life on Martha's Vineyard until the nineteenth century. The initial tactics of the Mayhews were almost identical to Eliot's. While Thomas Mayhew, Sr., set out to declare his sovereignty over the local sachems, his son established close relations with a young social upstart named Hiacoomes and proceeded to undermine the position of the traditional religious leaders with his assistance. In 1645 they unexpectedly profited from the effects of an epidemic. When Mayhew, Jr., was able to cure a few individuals with an improvised ritual of Christian prayers and shamanistic theatrics and Hiacoomes somehow managed not to get infected, the Wampanoags were undoubtedly deeply impressed by what they interpreted to be a clear sign of spiritual prowess.

An important difference in their approach, however, was that the elder Thomas Mayhew made a distinction between political and religious matters. He allowed the local sachems to retain at least vestiges of their former powers, such as property and tributary rights, and thereby enlisted their voluntary cooperation in his son's missionary endeavors.[56] A more liberal code of rules established with the approval of the Indian community in 1652, which did not require them to cut their hair, wear English-style clothes, or give up all customary ceremonies, on the one hand, and still allowed community leaders a degree of autonomy in internal matters on the other, left much more room for Indian participation in the further development of Praying Indian villages on Martha's Vineyard. Above all, this permissive policy allowed the Wampanoags to maintain their kinship-oriented social structure and to transfer the traditional function of sachemship to members of leading Christian Indian families. By the end of the 1660s there were ten functioning Christian Indian villages on the island, which included several hundred fully converted individuals as well as an equal number of still undecided relatives. The Mayhews' slightly more sensitive approach to evangelism, aided by the fact that the Wampanoags on Martha's Vineyard were less exposed to the side effects of colonialism, resulted in a relatively stable Christian Indian community. This is best exemplified by the Gay Head Indians, who now try to missionize the "heathen" tourists flocking to their island each summer.[57]

Much has been written about the disruptive effects of seventeenth-century New England missions on the life styles of local Indian communities, particularly those which had already been devastated by virgin soil epidemics and colonial warfare. The changes that were required of Indian neophytes were indeed far-reaching and already foreshadowed assimilationist policies for centuries to come: change from pantheism to monotheism, recognition of primordial sin, new religious rites, monogamy, sexual prudery, European-style homes, plowed fields, fences, private property, profit, segregation in reservations, shift in gender roles, enforced separation between children and their families, manual labor disguised as a pedagogical measure, externally controlled community politics, and countless other measures intended to form Indians in the Protestant missionary mold — without, however, ever actually accomplishing their integration into colonial society other than as members of the lowest class.[58] The abrupt termination of traditional life styles and the enforced adoption of entirely foreign ways in conjunction with all the negative aspects of racial discrimination and economic exploitation undoubtedly did, as Salisbury has maintained, leave many of the converts in a kind of "cultural limbo."[59]

Nevertheless, as more recent scholarship on the subject has also made evident, this was only one facet of the seventeenth-century colonial encounter in New England.[60] Very little has been written, for instance, about the possible similarities between Coastal Algonquian religious traditions and the adopted ways of Praying Indians, such as the integration of the spiritual and the secular in daily life, theocratic forms of government, the belief in supernatural forces, the open expression of humility in prayer, the closeness between traditional dream-vision and Christian conversion experience, the strict codes of morality and individual deportment, the acceptance of material wealth as a standard of social prestige and spiritual "grace," generosity and sagaciousness as desired personality traits, or the appreciation of oratorical skills and active group participation (singing) in ceremonial activities.[61]

Furthermore, the choice to live in Praying Indian villages was also based on pragmatic considerations on the part of individuals and entire communities. It provided a permanent land base for the dispossessed, a steady influx of European goods and technology, protective alliances against traditional enemies, release from tributary responsibilities, social mobility, and other benefits over and above plain survival. Praying Indian communities were also a refuge for the scattered remnants of shattered tribes, who had the chance here to establish new social ties and adapt to the colonial situation with the assistance of a proto-elite knowledgeable in the ways of Europeans. By voluntarily integrating themselves on the fringes of the dominant society, Praying Indians were also in a position to retain partial sovereignty and to maintain and/or reintroduce elements from their traditions in their villages in ways that were not immediately obvious to their overseers, who did not live in these communities and thus could not always enforce their authority. In this way many communities managed to sustain traditional lines of political succession with the rise of Christian family lineages; to continue living in customary dwellings while using their European-style structures for specific purposes only; to go on supplementing their stores with age-old hunting, fishing, and gathering techniques; and, for a while at least, to ensure a degree of ethnic distinctiveness through the exclusivity of their living native languages, which were usually only partially understood by the missionaries and overseers.

Above all else, in choosing to live in settlements patterned after early New England townships, Christian Indians could not only gain the status of town proprietors and thereby hold on to at least a portion of their former lands but also maintain their closely knit kinship-based village life and a communally oriented economy. Before proprietorship was increasingly granted to absentee speculators in the 1770s, New England townships (thirty-six-square-mile blocks of land given to groups of settlers rather than individuals) had certain affinities with traditional native villages, which the Christian Indians probably recognized at once: a "town common" with public buildings where all local issues were settled at regular town meetings; the "common and undivided lands," which remained under the exclusive management of town proprietors; the "common field system" by which lands were set aside and used for common cultivation; and the collective rights to grazing, timber, and forest products.[62]

It is this kind of minority survival strategy that James Scott has designated as the "hidden transcript" in his study of forms of covert resistance, and which has also been described as the practice of "Mau Mauing" in the context of modern-day urban Indian existence.[63] Christianity can thus also be said to have served threatened seventeenth-century eastern Indian communities as a means of coping with the colonial situation—a religion of the oppressed, so to speak—rather than to have always fulfilled its intended function as a catalyst for total social change. As James Axtell has pointed out, through such creative adaptability "the Indians ensured the survival of native culture by taking on the protective coloration of the invader's culture."[64] Finally, not a few of the Praying Indians decided to reject European ways after a period of experimentation, as is made evident by the common missionary complaints about "backsliding" and the fact that some of their neophytes even decided to join King Philip's campaign to wipe out the colonists altogether.

The New England missionaries also devised their own Indian college scheme in order to get a share of English donations. The first proposal to establish a college for Indians in Massachusetts was made by the London philanthropist Dr. John Stroughton in 1635. John Eliot had also sent two "hopeful young plants," the Massachusett Indians James and Jonathan, to live with Harvard's first president, Henry Dunster, in 1645. Harvard's charter of 1650 expressly mentions that the college was organized in 1636 "for all accommodacons of Buildings and all other necessary prouisions that may conduce to the education of the English and Indian Youth of this Country in knowledge and godliness." Finally, in 1653, the United Colonies, functioning as trustees for New England Company funds, authorized the erection of a special building at Harvard College to house "six hopefull Indians youthes" at a cost not to exceed £120.[65]

The building itself was actually completed around 1655, at a cost of about £400, but was never really put to its intended use. By 1656 Harvard's second president, Charles Chauncy, was already proposing that its empty rooms be used to accommodate English students and, from 1659 to 1692, it ended up housing the college press. On November 6, 1693, the New England Company agreed that the building, which was still being referred to as the "Indian College" even though it had been renovated in 1665 for the sole benefit of non-Indian tenants, be torn down at a cost not to exceed five pounds.

Other than John Sassomon, who studied briefly at Harvard before the "Indian College" was constructed, only four Indians (Caleb Cheeshahteaumauk, Joel Hiacoomes, John Wompowess, and Eleazar) are known to have attended this educational institution, one of whom (Caleb) actually managed to graduate. About twenty Indian students may have attended Elijah Cortlet's and Daniel Weld's preparatory grammar schools in Cambridge and Roxbury between 1655 and 1672 with the intention of going on to study at Harvard, but diseases, more than anything else, again thwarted what may have been a sincere effort to get Indian students that far up the academic ladder. At least one more Indian student, Benjamin Larnell, did draw from the Boyle Fund and was accepted at Harvard in 1712. However, like so many of his predecessors, he also succumbed to illness before having had a chance to complete his studies.[66]

Whatever the true intentions of New England's first missionaries may have been, their activities were violently interrupted by the outbreak of King Philip's War (1675–76), or what Jennings designates as the "Second Puritan Conquest," the outcome of which finally broke down Indian military potential all along the northeastern seaboard and left the surviving tribes in a subjugated status under imperial rule.[67] General distrust of Indians then gained the upper hand and undermined any continuing public support for the establishment of Praying Indian towns. For most Indians who chose to remain in the colonies instead of withdrawing westward, this meant confinement to small reservation-like areas and a marginal existence in extreme poverty. In other words, they had now become victims of that phase of conquest which has been specified here as internal colonialism. Following King Philip's War, missionary activity among the Indians of New England declined markedly, probably in conjunction with a general ebbing of religious fervor throughout the British colonies, and would not be promoted again until the "Great Awakening" of the 1730s and 1740s.[68]

Just before the outbreak of King Philip's War there may have been more than twenty Indian preachers in Massachusetts presiding over as many as three or four thousand Indian converts, a handful of whom were literate in Algonquian, English, Latin, and even Greek.[69] Unfortunately, only a few of their biographies have been preserved. Those that have were invariably recorded by missionaries for the express purpose of documenting their own success as evangelists and must therefore be viewed with some skepticism in terms of authentic autoethnographic expression.[70] Nevertheless, in contrast to Virginia, early missionizing efforts in the more literate New England colonies did at least leave posterity with fragmentary but invaluable information on a number of seventeenth-century Indian converts, including a few samples of their own writings.

More is known about Hiacoomes than Waban. In a lengthy letter written in 1650 and published the following year in a promotional tract titled *The Light appearing more and more towards the perfect Day*, Thomas Mayhew, Jr., gave a fairly detailed account of Hiacoomes's life up until that time. He wrote that the Wampanoag was "a man of a sad & a sober spirit" when he first began to show an interest in the English in 1643 but "not without some thoughts and hopes of a higher good he might possibly gain thereby."[71] In his *Indian Converts*, written almost sixty years later, Experience Mayhew described Hiacoomes in less flattering terms: "His Descent was but mean, his Speech but slow, and his Countenance not very promising. He was therefore by the *Indian Sachims*, and others of their principal Men, looked on as a mean Person, scarce worthy of their Notice or Regard."[72] Once he managed to attract the interest of the Mayhews, however, Hiacoomes quickly rose from obscurity among his fellow tribesmen.

Obviously alarmed by the fact that the unknown upstart might successfully circumvent the proper channels of authority and establish connections with the colonists on his own, some of the local Wampanoag leaders soon began pressuring him to mind his place. A sagamore by the name of Pake Ponesso publicly struck Hiacoomes "a great blow on the face" for being obedient to the English and probably would have done worse if the latter had not intervened. But Hiacoomes would not be deterred by threats or ridicule and, after Pake Ponesso was almost killed by a lightning bolt in 1644 and Hiacoomes's family somehow managed to survive an epidemic that killed off many other Wampanoags in 1645, his prestige began to grow along with his self-confidence. At last, in 1646, one of the chief sachems of the island invited both Mayhew and Hiacoomes to preach to him and such of his people as would also be willing to listen. According to the account by Experience Mayhew, the Indians then began to wonder "that he that had nothing to say in all their Meetings formerly, was now become the Teacher of the all."[73] At a subsequent showdown with a religious leader who had threatened to kill all the Christian neophytes with his powers, Hiacoomes reportedly challenged "all the Pawwawes of the Island" to "do their utmost they could against him, and when they did their worst by their witchcrafts to kill him, he would without feare set himself against them, by remembering *Jehovah*." He also expressed his contempt for the man and his beliefs by concluding that "he did put all the Pawwawes under his heel" while pointing to it.[74]

For many years thereafter Hiacoomes worked successfully as interpreter and lay preacher in the pay of the New England Company, until he was finally ordained as a minister in 1670 by John Eliot and John Cotton. When he died around 1690, he was regarded by the Christian Indian community of Martha's Vineyard as a respected elder. His voluntary association with the English had thus enabled him to rise to a position normally not due to him by birth, and to found a new Christian lineage that was to provide the Wampanoags with political and religious leadership for many generations.

Although less is known about Waban's conversion experience, there is some indication that his motives were also of a practical nature. A few specimens of oratory attributed to Waban have been preserved, among them a confession published by John Eliot in 1653 in which this becomes quite clear. "Before I heard of God, and before the English came into this Country," he begins, "many evil things did work, many thoughts I had in my heart; I wished for riches, I wished to be a witch, I wished to be a Sachem; and many such other evils were in my heart."[75] Eliot himself described Waban as "a man of gravitie and chiefe prudence and counsell among them [the Massachusetts], although no Sachem."[76] In other words, like Hiacoomes, Waban had all the necessary qualities for leadership and may even have functioned as a minor counselor among his people but probably lacked the proper family connections for a higher position of authority. This soon changed, of course, when he established direct ties with the English and was appointed by them as "Chief Minister of Justice" and ruler over a hundred Praying Indians.

By converting to Christianity, resourceful individuals like Hiacoomes and Waban maneuvered themselves into the influential position of middlemen in the political, economic, and spiritual concerns of their communities, a role traditionally assigned to the sachems and shamans. Although these incumbents may have been hoisted to their new status by the colonial power play, the loyalty of their followers was strictly voluntary and could be maintained only as long as it served the community's ends. Their attempts to circumvent genealogical restrictions while climbing the social ladder was really no more or less a break in traditional decorum than, for example, the political and economic alliances worked out by respected and established leaders like Powhatan, Miantonomo, Massasoit or Metacom, who also sought to extend their own spheres of influence. These leaders' diplomatic activities also furthered social change in their communities since they were just as quick as any of the converted Indians to incorporate certain European ways and products as a means to enhance their personal prestige, on the one hand, and to protect their subjects from outside threats on the other. The main difference here was that, from the vantage point of their own elevated position as sachems, they could see no immediate gain for themselves in either converting to Christianity or submitting to English rule. This relatively fine distinction is not sufficient to assign either party a definite place in the popular traditionalist-versus-progressive scheme.

Neither Hiacoomes nor Waban left a written record. But the history of American Indian literature still has its antecedents in seventeenth-century New England, where Eliot's translators, the Harvard Indian College scholars, and other literate Indians produced writings in Algonquian, Latin, Greek, and English.[77] It is very likely that more material from this period still slumbers undetected in various archives or public record offices in England and the United States.

Eliot's first translator was the Montauk Cockenoe-de-Long Island (Cheekonov, Chickino, Chekkonnow, Cockoo).[78] Born around 1620, he was captured by the colonists during the Pequot War, taken to Dorchester, Massachusetts, and indentured to the family of Richard Collacot. The exact date when he was taken in by Eliot is unknown, but he was employed by the missionary as a teacher and translator until the summer of 1647, at which time he set out on his own as a free-lance interpreter and then returned to his former employment temporarily in the winter of 1649. At the end of his booklet on Indian grammar, Eliot writes of him as follows: "Then presently I found (by Gods wise providence) a pregnant witted young man, who had been a Servant in an English house, who pretty well understood our Language, better than he could speak it, and well understood his own Language, and hath a clear pronunciation: Him I made my Interpreter. By his help I translated the Commandments, the Lords Prayer, and many Texts of Scripture."[79]

Colonial records also show that he was instrumental in a number of land settlement cases between Indians and colonists as of 1648, which became one of the main venues for Indian literacy in both English and Algonquian.[80] On September 2, 1652, for instance, he appeared before the Commission of the United Colonies of New England and successfully defended an Indian claim on Menhansich Island. In a deed that was penned by him on October 27, 1661, he writes:

> I, Cockoo Sagamore by virtue of a full and absolute power and order unto him and intrusted by Mahamequeet Sagamore & Meamehett Sagamore & Mamamettchoach & Capt Wappequairan all Ingines living up Hudson River on the Main land for me to bargain & absolutely sell unto Thos Revell . . . and fardder more I doe promise and ingage myself in behalf of the prenemad Ingaines & ye date thereof, for to give unto Thomas Revels or his order quiet and peacable possion.[81]

This fragment is a good illustration of his command of written English, which was rough but obviously adequate for the purpose intended and certainly not much faultier than the writings of most of his non-Indian colleagues in the translating business. It shows further that his Indian clientele had complete faith in his mastery of the colonial "deed game." His claim to the title of sagamore (an additional indication of his value to the Indian community) was apparently legitimized by his marriage to a sachem's sister, who had advanced to the position of *sunksquaw* ("female sachem") following her brother's death. In a similar transaction his services are valued at "one coat, foure pounds of pouder six pounds of led, one dutch hatchet, as also seventeen shillings in wampum," which proves that his special skills earned him material as well as social benefits. Cockenoe's name last appears on record as an interpreter for the English on August 3, 1687.[82]

Job Nesuton, a Massachusett who joined Eliot in 1646, learned how to read and write English and Algonquian sufficiently well in three years to replace Cockenoe as interpreter and translator. Daniel Gookin writes that "he was a very good linguist in the English tongue."[83] Nesuton served briefly as schoolmaster at Natick and then worked for Eliot until 1675, when he joined a group of fifty-two Indians under the command of Gookin in King Philip's War, a demonstration of loyalty that was to cost him his life. His contributions to American Indian literature are represented by the first edition of the Massachusett Bible, which has been attributed solely to Eliot.

James Printer (Wowaus) was born around 1640, the son of an influential Nipmuck family residing at the Praying Indian village of Hassanamesitt (now Grafton) in Massachusetts.[84] When he was five, his father brought him to Cambridge to live in an English home, probably hoping that his son would obtain an education there. It is possible that he attended Elijah Cortlet's Cambridge Grammar School before apprenticing to Samuel Green in 1659 as "printer's devil," a profession he would subsequently practice for twelve years (hence his name). James Printer assisted Green, then director of the Harvard Indian College Press, and his journeyman, Marmeduke Johnson, in printing about a hundred books by 1672, when the press's production began to decline.

For some unknown reason James Printer temporarily offered his services as a scribe to King Philip in 1675 and then took advantage of a declaration offering amnesty to all Indians who voluntarily returned to the fold of the English to make his way back to Boston by the summer of the following year. While with Philip he became indirectly involved in the captivity tale of Mary Rowlandson, who had been kidnapped on February 21, 1676. In this connection, James Printer is probably the author of a letter written in the name of King Philip, which outlined the terms for her release:

> For the Governor and the Council at Boston
> The Indians, Tom Nepennoump and Peter Tatutiquima hath brought us letter from you about the English captives, specially Mrs. Rowlandson: the answer is that I am sorrow that I have don much wrong to you for when we began quarrel at first with Plimouth much trouble as now is! therefore I am willing to hear your desire about the Captives. Therefore we desire you to sent Mr. Rolanson and Goodman Kettil: (for their wives) and these Indians Tom and Peter to redeem their wives, they shall come and goe very safely: Whereupon we ask Mrs. Rolanson how much your husband willing to give for you she gave an answer 20 pounds in goods but John Kittels wife could not tell, and the rest captives may be spoken of hereafter.[85]

Sometime after his repatriation he began to work for Eliot and, among other projects, helped him to print the first (1661–63) and second (1680–85) editions of the Bible in the Massachusett language. He may have completed his apprenticeship and moved to Boston with Bartholomew Green by

1709, as he is credited along with Green for having printed an edition of the Psalter there. Just how important his cooperation was for Eliot's translating endeavors is evident from a letter the latter wrote to Sir Robert Boyle in 1683, in which he admits that "we have but one man (viz. the Indian Printer) is able to compose the press & correct the press with understanding."[86] Colonial records last mention him in 1698, as schoolmaster to five Indian families in his native village of Hassanamesitt.

Cockenoe, Nesuton, and James Printer deserve at least equal credit for Eliot's famous "Indian Library," which initiated American publishing history.[87] The importance of these three bilingual Indians becomes more apparent if one considers that, unless a translator is a balanced bilingual (truly literate in both languages), it is generally more effective in terms of the results for him/her to be a native speaker in the language being translated into, rather than the other way around. It would not seem far-fetched, therefore, to maintain that Eliot's Indian "assistants," who were fluent in their native Algonquian languages and obviously had a fair command of written and spoken English, were the principal creators of seventeenth-century American-Algonquian literature.[88]

The biography of Harvard's first Indian student, the Massachusett John Sassomon of Natick, whose murder in 1675 was regarded as one of the key events that touched off King Philip's War, is somewhat of an enigma.[89] He was apparently sent to Harvard in 1653 by Eliot after having assisted him for some time as translator and was subsequently employed as schoolmaster at Natick. He left the English temporarily in 1662 to join King Philip, acting as interpreter, witness, and scribe, but returned soon after to become an active member in one of the Indian churches. In 1672 Sassomon was sent among the Namaskets and other Indians of Middleborough to be their schoolmaster, and obviously he performed his duties to their satisfaction. One of the principal sachems of the area, Watuspaquin, offered Sassomon some land in Assowomset as an inducement for him to settle there permanently. He accepted and married a local sachem's daughter soon after.

It was because of his connections to Philip that he met his untimely end, for reasons that never became clear. A search party looking for the reported missing Christian Indian found his body under the ice in Assowomset Pond in the spring of 1675, where he had apparently been placed to make it appear as if he had drowned himself. Three Wampanoags, including one of Philip's counselors and his son, were arraigned for the murder of Sassomon in a mock court and duly executed. Contemporary accounts of King Philip's War gave conflicting interpretations of the case. Increase Mather and William Hubbard both maintained that he was killed for having warned the colonists of King Philip's intentions to attack them. Nathaniel Saltonstall argued that he was executed for having attempted to convert Philip, and John Easton believed that it was an accidental drowning. If it was a case of homicide rather than an accident, then Increase Mather was probably not far from the truth when he concluded that "one reason why the *Indians* murdered *John Sausamon*, was out of hatred against him for his Religion."[90]

Information on the brief careers of Caleb Cheeshahteaumauk (various spellings) and Joel Hiacoomes, both of whom left Martha's Vineyard in 1659 to attend Cambridge Grammar School and then enrolled at Harvard in 1661, is also scanty.[91] Caleb, the son of a petty sachem of Holmes Hole (Vineyard Haven), graduated from Harvard in 1665 and died shortly thereafter of tuberculosis. Joel, the eldest son of Hiacoomes, was considered by Daniel Gookin to have been an especially promising scholar. He either drowned accidentally or was murdered by Nantucket Indians while on a vacation to Martha's Vineyard just prior to his scheduled graduation in 1665.

Caleb and Joel are each credited with having written a complimentary address in Latin, which John Winthrop, Jr., then governor of Connecticut, sent to Sir Robert Boyle on November 3, 1663.[92] Caleb's one-page letter, which has been erroneously referred to by Walter Meserve as a "graduation address," is a rather effusive expression of gratitude to the great British philanthropist, written in a curious mixture of archaic and classical Latin. It contains the expected seventeenth-century scholarly references to Greek mythology and makes a fervent evangelical call for the conversion of "barbarians." The original letter, in very clean handwriting, has been preserved in the archives of the Royal Society in London:

> Most honored benefactors,
>   Historians tell about Orpheus the musician and outstanding poet, that he received a lyre from Apollo, and that he was so excellent on it that the forests and the rocks were moved by his song. He made huge trees follow behind him, and indeed rendered the most ferocious beasts tamer. Because of the lyre he accepted, he descended into the nether world, lulled Pluto and Proserpina with his song and led Eurydice, his wife, out of the nether world into the upper world. The ancient philosophers state that this serves as a symbol to show how powerful the force and virtue of education and of refined literature are in the transformation of the barbarians' nature. They are like the trees, the rocks, and the brute beasts, and a substantial change (metamorphosis) has to be expected of them. They have to be secured like tigers and must be induced to follow.
>   The Lord delegated you to be our patrons, and he endowed you with all

wisdom and intimate compassion, so that you may perform the work of bringing blessing to us pagans, who derive our life and origin from our fore-bears. We were naked in our souls as well as in our bodies, we were aliens from all humanity, and we were led around in the desert by various errors.

Oh threefold and fourfold most illustrious and most loving men, what kind of thanks, if not the greatest and most immense, should we give to you, for that you have supported us with an abundance of all things for our educa-tion and for the sustenance of our bodies. You have poured forth immense, the greatest, resources.

And we will especially give great thanks to God the most excellent and highest, who has revealed the sacred scriptures to us, and who has shown to us our Lord Jesus Christ, who is the way of truth and of life. Besides all this, another hope has been left us through the depths of divine mercy: that we may be instruments to spread and propagate the gospel among our kin and neigh-bors, so that they also may know the Lord and Christ.

Even though we can not commensurately reciprocate your kindness and that of our other benefactors, we do hope, however. We are not left alone praying before the Lord with importunate supplications for those pious and merciful men who are still in the old England, who disbursed so much gold and silver for us to obtain the salvation of our souls, and for you as well, who were instruments like aquaeducts in bestowing all these benefits on us.

Most devoted to your dignity:

Caleb Cheeshahteaumauk.[93]

The third Harvard Indian scholar on record, John Wompowess (various spellings), was a minor Nipmuck sachem from the Praying Indian village of Hassanamesitt (Grafton), who soon quit the college to lead a rather adven-turous life as a mariner.[94] At the close of King Philip's War he was jailed in Boston for debt, which prompted him to send a petition to King Charles I in order to obtain his release:

To the Kings most Excellent Ma[tie]
The humble Petition of John Wampas als White.
Sheweth

That yo[r] Pet[r] being a poore Indian having a certaine Parcell of Land in Massy Chussit Bay the w[ch] he hath held for many yeares he having received the oaths of Allegiance and Supremacy and being now reduced to great dis-tresse was cast into Prison about six months since for a debt of fifty shillings where he hath remained ever since to his utter Ruine.

Therefore yo[r] Pet[r] most humbly prayes that yo[r] Ma[tie] will be graciously pleased to grant yo[r] Pet[r] yo[r] Ma[ts] Royall Letter to S[r] John Leveritt Knight Governor of Massy Chussitt Bay whereby he may be restored to his said Lands or else that he may free liberty to make Sale thereof for his p[r]sent releife and towards paying of his debts

And yo[r] Pet[r] shall ever pray etc.[95]

Before the king's positive answer ever arrived, however, John Wompowess broke out of jail and signed on for a longer sea voyage, presumably hoping that the matter would eventually blow over. Upon his return he became a roving realtor with somewhat loose principles, as his transactions included the unauthorized sale of property belonging to others. According to Allan Forbes, by 1677 he had become a "very useless citizen" who led a vagrant's life until his death in England a few years later. Even if the petition cited above, which is also written in an extraordinarily clean hand, should turn out to have been dictated by Wompowess to some professional scribe, it still shows that he was quite versatile in his application of the written word.

The fourth Harvard Indian College student, who joined the class of 1679, is known only as Eleazar.[96] He was considered to be a highly promising scholar as well, but disease struck him down before he was able to complete his studies. Eleazar produced a respectable elegiac poem in Latin distichs commemorating the death of his former teacher, the Reverend Thomas Thacher, which Cotton Mather decided to include as "a Curiosity" in the third volume of his *Magnalia Christi Americana*. Appended to the twenty-five-line elegy, signed by "Eleazar, *Judus* Senior Sophista," is a poem in Greek:

> On the death of that truly venerable man
> D. Thomas Thacher
> who
> went to the Lord from this life, 18.8.1678
> I seek to commemorate this illustrious man with sad grief,
> Whom our times reclaim with tears, this man.
> Thus Memnon's mother, thus the mother wept for Achilles
> with justified tears, and with grieving pain
> the mind is stunned, the mouth silent. Now the hand refuses its proper
> service: What? Grieving Apollo refuses his help?
> Nonetheless, Thacher, I, one of yours, will try to speak praise
> praise of virtue, which ascends higher than the stars.
> To the men of high learning, and to the people of standing
> your virtue was known, also your holy faith.
> You live after the funeral, happy after fate; you lie [dead?]
> But among the stars you lie indeed as glory
> your spirit already returns to the heavens; victory has been achieved:
> Yours already is Christ, yours what he merited
> Here is the end of the cross [of life's sorrow]; here the end of great evil;
> Further than that there is nowhere whence he could proceed.

You, cross, already stand empty; the bones rest in the grave;
death dies; Blessed life returns to life
when the last trumpet will send its sound through the dense clouds.
With the Lord returning, you bear iron scepters.
Then you will ascend into the skies, where the home of the truly pious is
Jesus precedes you now on the way to this homeland.
There is true rest, there is delight without end;
joys human voices cannot describe.[97]

Only one other Indian, Benjamin Larnell of the class of 1716, is known to have been accepted at Harvard during the colonial period and to have been provided for by the Boyle Fund.[98] Larnell was taught Latin by the Reverend Grindell Rawson of Taunton and then turned over to Samuel Sewall in 1711, with whom he remained for two years while attending the Boston Latin School. He did so well that he was tentatively enrolled at Harvard in the winter of 1712 but was dismissed and sent back to Sewall only six months later for "misconduct." Larnell apparently reformed because he was readmitted in the spring of 1714. He was described by Harvard president John Leverett as having been a gifted Latin and Greek poet and an acute grammarian. In a letter dated June 1, 1714, Cotton Mather sent William Ashurst of London one of Larnell's poems in "three learned languages," which may still repose somewhere in an English archive.[99] As one might almost come to expect at this point, Larnell died before having had the chance to finish college.

The relatively polished Latin and Greek texts left behind by these seventeenth-century Harvard scholars, which contain only minor grammatical mistakes according to a recent study, differ markedly from the rougher English writings of their contemporaries. This seems to indicate that the Harvard texts were carefully edited — if not written entirely — by members of the faculty. The authenticity of Cheeshahteaumauk's "address" and Eleazar's poem has been questioned, as the texts may well have been dictated or simply ascribed for propaganda purposes. This suspicion is corroborated by the fact that both pieces were sent to Boyle in 1663, two years before the two Indian scholars were scheduled to graduate.[100]

The less polished English texts, which were produced for domestic Indian needs, can be regarded as legitimate examples of seventeenth-century North American Indian literacy. Just how important native interpreters and scribes had become by this time in the dialogue between Indian communities and the colonists is illustrated in a rather original way by a communication to Governor Prince written for King Philip sometime between 1660 and 1670: "King Philip desire to let you understand that he could not come to the Court, for Tom [Nepponit], his interpreter, has a pain in his back, that he could not travil so far, and Philip sister is very sick."[101] As in the case of contemporary Massachusett vernacular literacy, these scattered samples of Indian English writing also reflect both continuity and change among its users. The deeds and contracts written by Cockenoe-de-Long Island, for example, show that a certain reorientation in terms of property values had taken place and, at the same time, that the English language itself had been modified by certain patterns of speech, forms of address, and direct quotations which were incorporated from native styles of oral transaction. This is even more conspicuous in the letters written by James Printer, Peter Jethro, Tom Nepponit, and other scribes working for King Philip, which are heavily infused with native syntax and formal modes of council oratory.[102] Taken together, the seventeenth-century Massachusett and English writings are an early manifestation of the successful compartmentalization of bilingual literacy in New England's Christian Indian communities, which gave way to an English language shift by the 1720s only because of the increasingly oppressive nature of the contact environment.

Despite the fact that secondary information and autoethnographic data on seventeenth-century Indian cultural brokers are limited, the material available on early missionary efforts in Virginia and New England already reveals certain patterns of societal interaction that would persist well into the future. Most of the early Indian converts came from tribes that had been massively altered by the colonial situation. Frequently they were members of influential but secondary families whose voluntary/involuntary role as cultural mediators brought about their ascent to positions of leadership — a proto-elite — in newly formed Christian Indian communities. Caleb's complimentary address to Boyle, for instance, makes it clear that seventeenth-century colonists had already recognized the practicality of training Indian converts as "instruments to spread and propagate the gospel" among their own people. But there are also contrary cases, such as King Philip's scribes, where bilingual individuals remained faithful to traditional leaders. They thus made use of their literacy without disturbing the status quo in their own communities or radically changing their own ways and beliefs. Finally, the common phenomenon of backsliding also suggests that "moments of crisis" were not uncommon among Christian Indians during this early phase of the colonial encounter. That individuals like Caleb Cheeshahteaumauk, Joel Hiacoomes, Eleazar, or Benjamin Larnell should give up their ethnic identities entirely in the course of a few years of subjection to Puritan scholarship remains questionable, even if their premature deaths preclude any concrete statements about their acculturation.

At the same time, however, the history of early Indian–white relations in North America does show that almost all of the precepts later applied by the United States in its interaction with Indians were already present, in one form or another, in the seventeenth-century Protestant missions. On the one hand, colonial missionaries and educators embraced a theoretical policy of total assimilation which was to transform their charges into model Europeans. "Civility," regarded by Protestant schoolmasters as the absolute prerequisite for conversion, demanded the unconditional acceptance of European norms and values. This cultural transformation was to be accomplished primarily through education, preferably in special, practice-oriented institutions for children. On the other hand, colonial administrators, who had to take into consideration the expansionist drive of their constituents, tended to favor an official policy of racial segregation, which stood in open contradiction to all of the alleged goals of the missionaries. This incompatible approach to cross-cultural relations was carried over into the eighteenth century with only one obvious shift in methodology, namely, a more pronounced emphasis upon the assimilative potential of English as the lingua franca of the civilization process.

If the seventeenth-century missionary experiment of Praying Indian villages failed, as is usually maintained by historians, then it was only because of the blatant inconsistency of colonial policies. When the peaceful Christian Indians at Wamesit decided to flee after they had been attacked by a white Protestant mob from Chelmsford in 1675, they left the following message in English that speaks for itself: "We are not sorry for what we leave behind, but we are sorry the English have driven us from our praying to God and from our teacher. We did begin to understand a little of praying to God."[103] It is generally thought that, with the exception of the Mashpees of Cape Cod and the Gay Head Indians of Martha's Vineyard, all Praying Indian villages disappeared by the end of the eighteenth century.[104] Although the villages as such may have ceased to exist officially in colonial records and maps, there can be little doubt that the Christian inhabitants either joined other Indian communities or founded new ones according to ancient custom, where they passed on their adapted beliefs and their literacy to future generations.

3

Samson Occom and the Vision of a New England Christian Indian Polity

SAMSON OCCOM'S REMARKABLE life history spans a dark period in the evolution of Indian–white relations in North America, dominated by suspicion and hatred on both sides. In spite of severe health problems and permanent disillusionment with Anglo-Saxon ethnocentrism, the "Pious Mohegan" managed to establish a solid reputation as an ordained Presbyterian minister, best-selling author, accomplished hymnist, and widely acclaimed orator. In his difficult role as cultural broker during troubled times he never once veered from the missionary path he had chosen for himself and remained true to his personal vision of an evangelical revival among his colonized people. When he finally came to the realization that it was practically impossible for Indians to live in "civilized" society according to the principles he had been taught to believe in by Protestant missionaries, he chose instead to found a new nation of Christian Indians in the "wilderness."[1]

Throughout the eighteenth century North America was racked by violence resulting from repeated European imperial contentions, the events leading up to the fratricidal war between England and its colonies, and desperate armed Indian resistance against further European incursions. During this period most Indian tribes living east of the Appalachians either experienced permanent subjugation under a progressively centralized Indian policy, which was first implemented by the English crown and then expanded by the government of the young republic, or sought temporary relief from direct contact with Euro-Americans by migrating westward. The struggle among England, France, and Spain for predominance as world powers culminated in four major continental wars that were also carried out in

North America: King William's War (War of the League of Augsburg, or War of the Palatinate), 1689–97; Queen Anne's War (War of the Spanish Succession), 1702–13; King George's War (War of the Austrian Succession), 1740–48; and the French and Indian War (Seven Years' War), 1754–63. Alliances with Indian nations were sought by each of the contending European powers and the Indians themselves, who also tried to play the Europeans against each other to their own advantage. The first war was primarily fought in New England, and the remaining three involved Indians from Maine to Georgia and were particularly intensive in the Ohio Valley in the interim between King George's War and the French and Indian War. It was in this area that numerous previously displaced eastern bands and tribes had taken refuge, somehow accommodating themselves among those already settled there and thus having recourse to a formidable number of fighting men. Their involvement in these imperial wars, however, brought about the total collapse of eastern Indian military potential beginning around the 1750s, which finally climaxed with the subjugation of the powerful confederacies of the Iroquois in the Northeast and Creeks in the Southeast at the close of the century. Various Indian revolts — the Yamasee War in 1715 involving Yamasees, Creeks, Choctaws, and Cherokees; Pontiac's War in 1763 fought by Ottawas and Delawares; Lord Dunmore's War in 1774 against the Shawnees; the resistance movement of the Northwest Confederacy (including Miamis, Iroquois, Shawnees, Ottawas, Ojibwas, Delawares, Kickapoos, Potawatomis, and Wyandots) and the Southern Indian Confederation under Alexander McGillivray (Creeks) in the 1780s; and Tecumseh's heroic efforts to form a pan-Indian front during the first decade of the nineteenth century — made life miserable for frontier settlers and were very costly in terms of lives and property but ultimately failed to stem the tide of European conquest.[2]

The first Treaty of Paris terminated the French and Indian War in 1763 and left England in control of almost all of the North American territory east of the Mississippi. Aware of the potential for further trouble with Indians in the dramatic increase of land-hungry European immigrants (from about 250,000 in 1700 to 1.2 million in 1750) and the unscrupulous practices of many Indian traders, the British government began to centralize Indian policy in the second half of the eighteenth century. The Atkin Report and Plan of 1755 led to the creation of the Indian superintendency system with a northern and southern department. In 1761 colonial governors received instructions not to issue any more grants to Indian lands, and in 1763 the Royal Proclamation designated the Appalachian watershed as the fixed

Samson Occom. Mezzotint by John Spilsbury, reproduced from an oil painting by Mason Chamberlain, ca. 1766. This was painted while Occom was touring England. Courtesy of the Baker Library, Dartmouth College.

boundary between British settlements and Indian country. But the British government's delayed attempt to assume exclusive jurisdiction over Indian affairs in the colonies proved to be unenforceable as it met with staunch opposition from its subjects there, who regarded it as an "intolerable" infringement upon their "natural rights." By 1773 some 60,000 had already settled in the area between Pittsburgh and Ohio in open defiance of the Royal Proclamation. At the same time, several land companies that had been founded during the 1740s were now confidently counting on enormous profits from the sale of Indian lands as the population in the colonies rose to two million by 1776. Indians were aware of the expansionist ambitions of the colonists (British anti-American propaganda made sure of that), and — with the exception of Oneidas, Tuscaroras, and some Christian Indians — most of them resolved to fight on the Tory side when the Revolution finally broke out. Its outcome proved to be the same for both "hostile" and "friendly" tribes, however, for the independence of the United States also terminated the era of Indian sovereignty in eastern North America.

The second Treaty of Paris in 1783 gave no consideration to the fate of England's Indian allies, many of whom had not yet officially surrendered, and the victors were thus left free to deal with the tribes living within their acquired territory as they pleased. Most American national leaders felt that, by virtue of their alliance with the British, the Indians had waged and lost an "unprovoked" war and that this legitimized the United States' claims to all their lands, from the Ohio River north to Lake Erie, by "right of conquest." Nevertheless, faced with the very real danger of renewed Indian-European military alliances and conscious of its own weakness following the Revolution, the young republic saw itself in no position at the time to sustain further armed conflicts. Instead, its leaders first set about formulating an Indian policy that basically took up where the English had left off: establishment of boundaries between settlements and Indian territory, restriction of white incursion into Indian territory, management of the sale of Indian lands, regulation of Indian trade, control of the liquor traffic, provisions for punishment of crimes committed between the races, and promotion of the civilization of Indians.[3] In 1775 the Continental Congress inaugurated federal Indian policy by adopting the recommendations of a special committee on Indian affairs with the avowed intention of "securing and preserving the friendship of the Indian nations." Three years later it concluded its first official treaty with the Delawares, thereby recognizing Indian tribes as sovereign entities just as the European powers had done before. In 1779 it resolved that no Indian land could be transferred except by consent of

Congress and, in 1783, it also prohibited the settlement of territory outside state jurisdiction, including Indian lands. The ninth article of the Articles of Confederation gave Congress the "sole and exclusive right and power of . . . regulating the trade and managing all affairs with the Indians, not members of the states," a legal principle which, as pointed out earlier, was adopted into the Constitution as the so-called Commerce Clause and, together with the president's right to conclude treaties, formed the jurisdictional basis for all future federal Indian policies.[4] In its oft-cited Northwest Ordinance of 1787, Congress reaffirmed its "utmost good faith" toward Indians and, beginning in 1790, passed a series of laws known collectively as the Indian Trade and Intercourse Acts with which it hoped to fulfill its self-delegated regulatory role.

The step between formulating and actualizing Indian policy, however, proved to be as difficult for Americans as it had been under British rule. Congress depended on the sale of public lands to pay its national debt, and it also had tremendous difficulty enforcing unpopular federal policies in recalcitrant states — not to mention the hopeless task of controlling the ever-growing number of settlers (five million by 1800) who were swarming westward into Indian country, far away from any law-enforcing agencies. Indian wars finally flared up in the Northwest Territory (or Old Northwest) and the Southeast, fanned by British agents who still entertained the realistic hope of reestablishing colonial rule. The volatility of the period is made evident by transfer of federal responsibility over Indian affairs to the secretary of war in 1786. The situation finally culminated in the War of 1812, which changed little in the political relations between the United States and Great Britain but definitely broke the last vestiges of resistance among the eastern tribes and left the federal government in a sufficiently strong position to develop and enforce its Indian policies unilaterally.

The profitability, in terms of peace at last, of an adequate "civilization program" for Indians — providing them with the means to acquire farming implements, keep domestic animals, and obtain a rudimentary education — was also duly recognized by the incumbent U.S. government. In 1775, for instance, the Continental Congress appropriated $500 for the education of Indian youth at Dartmouth, and in 1794 the federal government concluded its first treaty containing specific provisions for education with the Oneidas, Tuscaroras, and Stockbridge Indians. Following a brief lull due to the events leading up to the second war with Britain, the House Committee on Indian Affairs issued a report in 1818 stating that Indians now had little choice but to be "moralized" or exterminated. "Put into the hands of their children the primer and the hoe," it went on to state in the accustomed manner, "and they will naturally, in time, take hold of the plow, and as their minds become enlightened and expand the Bible will be their book, and they will grow up in the habits of morality and industry, leave the chase to those whose minds are less cultivated, and become useful members of society."[5] Congress reacted on March 3, 1819, by establishing an annual "civilization fund" of $10,000, and financial support for educational programs became a regular feature of federal Indian policy thereafter. The task of formulating and carrying out educational policies, however, was left entirely in the hands of Protestant missionaries, who showed an increasing tendency at the turn of the eighteenth century to coordinate their activities in North America under financially powerful church organizations such as the New England Company (1649, 1661), the Society for the Propagation of the Gospel in Foreign Parts (SPG, 1701), and the Society in Scotland for Propagating Christian Knowledge (SSPCK, 1709).[6]

Public anxiety in reaction to continuous warfare and increasing political unrest primed the North American colonies for a massive religious revival, which began in Europe (Evangelical Revival) around 1720 and spread along the entire English-speaking Atlantic seaboard during the 1730s and 1740s. Generally known as the Great Awakening, this rekindling of Protestant spirituality in North America was to be a major factor in the development of educational policies applied to Indians and, as a direct consequence thereof, the emergence of the first authors of North American Indian descent.[7] Its foremost exponents were George Whitefield and Jonathan Edwards, both of whom introduced a number of fundamental innovations that greatly popularized religious life in the colonies: the promotion of itinerant preachers, or laymen with no other credentials than devotion and a sincere "calling" to spread the word of God; a new kind of impromptu preaching, which painted a grim picture of sin and eternal damnation but also promised salvation ("new birth") through a personal conversion experience ("inward religion"). Such radical practices obviously challenged the established ministry and resulted in a split among the clergy into New Lights, who advocated the principles of the Great Awakening, and Old Lights, who viewed these changes with suspicion or opposed them altogether.[8] Understandably, it was the former's populist approach to religion that attracted the masses of less privileged members of colonial society, including African Americans and Indians, who otherwise found themselves excluded from regular church services.

The Great Awakening also gave a renewed impulse to missionizing efforts and, in concordance with Enlightenment ideas on progress and universal human advancement from savagism and barbarism to civilization, brought about the establishment of a new kind of educational institution for Indians, the manual labor boarding school.[9] One of the earliest advocates of such an institution was John Sargeant, Sr., missionary to the Housatonic Valley Indians from 1734 until his death in 1749 and founder of the Christian Indian community at Stockbridge, Massachusetts. In a letter to Benjamin Coleman, which was published in Boston in 1743, he made a spirited proposal for "a more effectual Method for the Education of Indian Children."[10] Sargeant requested English funds to erect a school building on 200 acres of land to be purchased specifically for that purpose, in which Indian youth were to be housed and made to divide their time equally between study and labor, so "as to make one the Diversion of the other." Profits from their labor were to be used primarily for their own maintenance. These educated Indians, he believed, would someday help to spread Christianity to the remotest tribes.

Sargeant's plan basically echoed what John Eliot and the Mayhews had attempted a century earlier, with the notable exception that he stressed the importance of teaching Indians the English language in his formula for total cultural transformation: "What I propose therefore in general is to take such a *Method* in the Education of our *Indian Children*, as shall in the most effectual Manner change their whole Habit of thinking and acting; and raise them, as far as possible, into the Condition of a civil industrious and polish'd People; while at the same Time the Principles of Vertue and Piety shall be carefully instilled into their Minds in a Way, that will make the most lasting Impression; and withal to introduce the *English Language* among them instead of their own imperfect and barbarous *Dialect*."

The earlier policy of translating the Gospel into Indian languages was now regarded as counterproductive. As Cotton Mather had observed earlier, "They can scarce retain their language, without a Tincture of other Salvage Inclinations, which do but ill suit, either with the Humor, or with the design of Christianity."[11] Even Eliot seems to have had some doubts about his method as, with reference to the younger Daniel Gookin's English teaching sessions, he conceded that it "doth greatly further the Indians in learning law & government in the English Tongue, such is a point of wisdom in civilizing them."[12]

John Sargeant's proposal failed to draw sufficient interest to produce the funds needed to get it started, and his death just six years later put an untimely end to his plan. Therefore, the idea of a manual labor boarding school for Indians was not actually realized until 1754, when Eleazar Wheelock founded Moor's Indian Charity School in Lebanon, Connecticut. It remained in operation there for sixteen years and was then transferred to Hanover, New Hampshire, where it eventually became Dartmouth College.[13] Contrary to Sargeant, who wanted to set up his school within the Stockbridge Indian community (as the heterogeneous Christian Indian group came to be known collectively), Wheelock felt that Indian children should be removed from the "pagan" influence of their fellow tribesmen and taught some useful "industry" in a special coeducational boarding school in which Indian boys and girls would have the advantage of associating directly with English youths. To civilize Indians in this way, he prognosticated confidently with a wink toward prospective financiers, was the most effective way of overcoming the "great Impediment" of their "continual rambling about; which they can't avoid so long as they depend so much upon Fishing, Fowling, and Hunting for their Support," and also of keeping them from committing further "depredations" along the frontier.[14]

Like Eliot and the Mayhews before him, Wheelock also proposed that it might prove advantageous to train Indians as missionaries to work among the more remote tribes, arguing that they had the advantage over Englishmen because they could speak native languages, were accustomed to the "savage" ways of life, and would require only half the expenses.[15] In contrast to all of his predecessors, however, Wheelock maintained a fairly regular correspondence with his Indian charges in the field, whose letters he carefully preserved and thus left to posterity an invaluable source of eighteenth-century Christian Indian autoethnographic expression.[16] The main incentive for his "Grand Design," as he liked to refer to his educational experiment, came from his fruitful association with Samson Occom, a Mohegan who was to become one of the most illustrious Indian personalities of the century and who can be rightfully designated as the father of North American Indian literature.

By the first quarter of the eighteenth century the Mohegans of Connecticut had reached a low point in their curious historical evolution as a distinct tribe in symbiosis with European colonists.[17] It is generally assumed that the Pequots and Mohegans were a closely related group until the early seventeenth century, when the ambitious minor sachem Uncas openly challenged the leadership of the grand sachem Sassacus and was banned by the latter along with a small following.[18] Through clever and sometimes outright unscrupulous diplomatic dealings with the English colonists, Uncas managed to increase his own prestige and ultimately became the paramount leader of a growing independent Indian community that came to be known as the Mohegans. Uncas joined the English in their campaigns against the Pequots in 1637 and afterward took up many of the Pequot survivors in order to augment his own sphere of influence. Subsequent rivalries between him and Narragansett sachem Miantonomo, which only aggravated the already tense situation between the Narragansetts and the colonists, finally resulted in the latter's assassination in 1643 by Uncas's own brother, supposedly with the silent consent of the commissioners of the United Colonies.[19] In 1675 Uncas's Mohegans also helped the English defeat King Philip's Wampanoags and their allies.

By the time Uncas died (ca. 1683) and his son Oweneco succeeded him as sachem, the Mohegans had become a fairly powerful group through their alliances with the English and had gained control of three large tracts of land comprising about 800 square miles along the Connecticut River which, however, turned out to be a permanent source of contention between them and the colony of Connecticut. The Mason Controversy, as this long-lasting dispute became known, began in 1640 when Uncas allegedly ceded all Mohegan lands not under cultivation to the colonists in exchange for five yards of cloth and a few pairs of stockings.[20] Matters were further complicated when Uncas deeded the Mohegan lands to John Mason in 1659, who in turn signed another deed turning over a relatively large section of land then known as the Sequestered Lands back to the Mohegans in 1671 under the condition that it should remain inalienable for all time. The dispute eventually created two permanent factions within the Mohegan community: One side, led by Mason and several generations of his descendants, contended that the land had been given to him directly to do with as he thought best for his charges; the other side, supported by the Connecticut administration, claimed that Mason had received the lands as an appointed agent of the colony and officially transferred title to it in 1660. The matter came to a head in 1704 when the Mason faction sent a petition to Queen Anne requesting her help in a land dispute with the township of Colchester. A special commission met at Stonington and decided in favor of the Mohegans in 1705, but Connecticut refused to comply and the crown never attempted to enforce the decision. Instead, the colony appealed the case in 1706 and managed to obtain a compromise resolution in 1708 whereby 5,000 acres were to be set aside for the Mohegans in exchange for the lands settled by the colonists. The Mason party objected, however, and the controversy dragged on until 1721, when a special committee of the General Court of Connecticut reversed the 1705 decision in favor of the white settlers. This reversal was affirmed by a new commission which convened in Norwich in the summer of 1743. The Mason faction continued to challenge the outcome until it was permanently decided in favor of the colony by the lords commissioners on June 11, 1771. The Mason Controversy and the legal dispute revolving around it under the designation *Mohegan Indians vs. Connecticut* were both widely publicized events in their day as they clearly reflected the growing discord between colonial administrators and the crown regarding the disposition of Indian lands.[21]

Not long after Uncas's death the immediate effects of the land dispute, internal power struggles, and increasing white incursion began seriously to disrupt the Mohegan community. The once coveted allies of the British were now employed as household servants, hired field hands, or other menial laborers. By the turn of the eighteenth century disease, alcohol, poverty, and disorientation had taken their toll, reducing the Mohegans to about 350 people. In response to an act passed by the General Court of Connecticut requiring Indians to live in villages, they settled along the Thames River, in a small community situated between Norwich and New London, which was eventually divided into two antagonistic camps named Ben's Town and John's Town after the two rival contenders for the sachemship. In 1723, the year of Occom's birth, Major Ben Uncas usurped the position from Mamohet, the legitimate successor, with the support of the General Court. After the former's demise in 1726, Mamohet's claim was overridden once again as the sachemship passed to Ben Uncas II. When Mamohet died in England in 1737, where he had gone with John Mason to appeal the land case before George II, the majority of the tribe and the Mason faction turned to John Uncas, the grandson of Uncas, as their choice for the sachemship. A small group remained loyal to Ben Uncas II, however, who was officially recognized as sachem by the General Court on June 13, 1838.[22]

Despite the close cooperation between the colonists and the Mohegans, the latter remained indifferent to the former's religious overtures for some time. Even the wily Uncas, who had willfully tied his own destiny to the English, stubbornly opposed all their missionizing efforts as long as he lived, probably because he feared the loss of his own authority. In 1673, after the General Court informed him that it would regard with disfavor all Indians who "remained outside the fold," he solemnly promised to assist the Reverend James Fitch, minister of Norwich, in his attempt to spread the Gospel among the Mohegans. When the zealous minister presented his handful of converted Indians with 300 acres for their exclusive use for as long as they retained their faith, Uncas and several of his followers began to pay lip service to Christianity — that is, until King Philip's War broke out and their proven abilities as warriors were, once again, at a higher premium than their souls. In 1723 the General Court granted Captain John Mason permission to reside in the Mohegan community and to set up a school there, which he did for the ensuing seven years, until his involvement in the land issue forced him to abandon it. Jonathan Barber took over where he had left off in 1733, but it was not long before he too was embroiled in the controversy and had to resign. Thus Christianity and civility did not really make much of an impression among the Mohegans until 1736, when sachem Ben Uncas II made a public avowal of having converted. Three years later the Reverend David Jewett of New London commenced to preach regularly among them and thus paved the way for the imminent spiritual repercussions of New England's Great Awakening.[23]

According to an autobiographical sketch from 1768, the only available source on his early life, Samson Occom (Occum, Awkum, Aucom, Ockham, Mawcum) was "Born a Heathen" on some unrecorded day in 1723 and "Brought up in Heathenism" until he reached the age of sixteen or seventeen. His parents, Joshua Ockham and his second wife Sarah Sampson, a Mashantucket Pequot who was said to be a descendant of Uncas, "Liv'd a wandering Life, as did all the Indians at Mohegan; they Chiefly Depended upon Hunting, Fishing, & Fowling for their Living and had no Connections with the English, excepting to Traffic with them, in their small Triffles; and they Strictly maintained and followed their Heathenish Ways, Customs, & Religion, though there was some Preaching among them."[24] Jonathan Barber's proselytizing apparently had little effect upon him, even though he concedes that he may have learned a little spelling from the minister. His interest in Christianity did not manifest itself until 1739, when he "heard a Strange Rumor among the English, that there were Extraordinary Ministers Preaching from Place to Place and a Strange Concern among the White People." By this time the religious fervor kindled by Jonathan Edwards in Northampton and fanned by the recent arrival of George Whitefield from England had also made its way into Mohegan territory. Occom was obviously "Impressd" by the Edwardsian "fire-and-brimstone" exhortations of local itinerant preachers as he became a regular participant at revivalist camp meetings. On one of these occasions he was finally "awakened & converted" by none other than the eccentric James Davenport (brother-in-law to Eleazar Wheelock), whose bombastic way of preaching and religious excesses eventually brought him into conflict with the authorities and earned him the reputation of being mentally unstable.[25] Following his conversion, Occom spent six months "under Trouble of Mind" until, at the age of seventeen, the revelation of "Salvation through Jesus Christ" removed the "Distress and Burden" from his thoughts and granted him "Serenity and Pleasure of Soul, in Serving God." By this time he had also taught himself to "read in the New Testament without Spelling" and, in response to the more liberal norms of the Great Awakening, discovered his calling to instruct his "poor Kindred," which he proceeded to do of his own accord for the next two years. Finding that his own people were "perishing for lack of Vision," he undoubtedly saw Christianity as an alternative to the spiritual void left by the colonial situation and, most likely, a vocational means of escaping poverty and social degradation. On July 1, 1742, he was selected along with his father as one of twelve Mohegan councilors by sachem Ben Uncas II who, contrary to traditional practice, requested the Connecticut Court to approve his appointments. Thus, for a time at least, Occom also maintained his family's long-standing affiliation with the Uncas clan by accepting a position of responsibility with the anti-Mason faction of the Mohegans.[26]

Through his mother, who was probably employed as a household servant in Lebanon, he learned that Eleazar Wheelock kept a private school there for English youths preparing for college and, hoping to obtain some assistance in improving his reading ability, asked her to arrange a meeting with the Congregationalist minister. Thus, as William De Loss Love has already pointed out in his biography, it was Occom who "found" Wheelock and not the other way around.[27] Wheelock was obviously impressed by the twenty-year-old Mohegan's sincere desire for an education for, on December 6, 1743, the young Mohegan autodidact moved to Lebanon for regular school attendance. Occom remained under the tutelage of Wheelock until the winter of 1747, when he taught school briefly in New London, and then spent an additional year with the Reverend Benjamin Pomeroy in Hebron. He thus received about four years of instruction in basic English as well as Latin, Greek, and Hebrew, the usual curriculum for college preparatory schools at the time. Despite the fact that his studies were constantly hindered by health problems and deteriorating eyesight, Occom made such progress as a student (the Reverend Samuel Buell estimated that he would have entered Yale "upon his second Year, at his first Admission") that Wheelock began to consider seriously the prospect of training other Indians as missionaries.[28]

However, late in 1748, when he was finally forced to abandon his studies, during which he had at least received a modest stipend from the Boston

Board of Commissioners for the New England Company, Occom suddenly found himself cut off from any means of financial support. He failed to find work until the summer of 1749, when the Montauks of Long Island expressed their desire to employ him as their schoolmaster. With the approval of Wheelock and the Boston Commissioners, who still hoped that he could complete his studies as planned, he moved with his family to Long Island that same year and remained among the Montauks for the following eleven years. It is important to note at this point that, rather than having received any employment assistance from his mentors as he may well have expected, Occom found relief by tapping the ancient sociolinguistic network among Coastal Algonquian Indian communities to find a useful application for his newly acquired skills.

The Montauks now numbered less than two hundred people and were reduced to the marginal lifestyle that was typical for remnant Indian groups throughout eighteenth-century New England. Occom, who spoke a similar Algonquian dialect, had little difficulty integrating himself into their community, where he became the protégé of the influential Fowler family and quickly ascended to a leadership position. Two years after his arrival he perpetuated his bond within the Montauk kinship network by marrying Mary Fowler, with whom he eventually raised twelve children. At the same time, the Montauks were not slow to recognize the practical sides of his education, and Occom soon found himself serving them and other Indian communities in the vicinity as schoolmaster, minister, healer, scribe, counselor, and ceremonial host — in short, assuming many of the responsibilities normally ascribed to sachems. His school prospered as well, increasing to "near thirty scholars" within its first season, which enabled him to perfect his own pedagogical talents. He taught his students how to spell using alphabet cards made of cedar chips (a depiction of which is found in his autobiography), thereby inventing a teaching aid that foreshadowed the methods of Friedrich Froebel's famous kindergarten experiment in 1837. He also encouraged the older children to assist their younger schoolmates, long before this measure would become regular practice in American schools with the introduction of the British Lancastrian system in 1806. In addition, he began to develop his ministerial skills here by performing the duties of a pastor in the churches that had been organized previously by Azariah Horton among the Montauks, Shinnecocks, and Poosepatucks.[29]

Evidently Wheelock was quite impressed by Occom's accomplishments, citing his success among the Montauks in his first *Narrative* (1763) and concluding optimistically that he could find "No reason to regret our toil and Expense." However, while Occom obviously proved Wheelock's theory that an Indian missionary would be "at least four Times as serviceable" as any Englishman, the Boston Commissioners only grudgingly agreed to provide him with an annual salary of fifteen pounds after he had already been in the field for two years, a sum that was less than a quarter of what was normally paid to white missionaries. The commissioners' subsequent complaint that he was "too extravagant in his way of living" stands in crass opposition to Occom's own assessment of his situation at the time:

> I Dwelt in a Wigwam, a Small Hut with Small Poles and Covered with Matts made of Flags. . . . I was obliged to contrive every way to Support my Family; I took all opportunities, to get Some thing to feed my Family Daily. I Planted my own Corn, Potatoes, and Beans; I used to be out hoeing my Corn Some times before Sun Rise and after my School is Dismist, and by this means I was able to raise my own Pork, for I was allowed to keep 5 Swine. Some mornings & Evenings I would be out with my Hook and Line to Catch fish, and in the Fall of Year and in Spring, I used my Gunn, for we lived very handy for Fowl, and I was very expert with gun, and fed my Family with Fowls. I could more than pay for my Powder & Shot with Feathers; At other Times I Bound old Books for Easthampton People, Made wooden Spoons and Ladles, Stocked guns, & worked on Cedar to make Pails, Piggins, and Churns, etc.

Perhaps it was this kind of marginal existence that Wheelock had in mind when he enumerated the disadvantages of training English missionaries to the Indians, "who can't conform to their [the Indians'] Manner of Living, and who will have no Dependence upon them for any Part of it." Even though Wheelock tried on several occasions to procure funds and employment for Occom, his uncompromisingly ethnocentric views of the role to be played by Indian missionaries precluded any factual equality in the vocation. "Indian missionaries," he wrote further along in his *Narrative*, "will not disdain to own English ones, who shall be Associated with them, (where the *English* can be introduced) as elder Brethren; nor scorn to be advised or reproved, counselled or conducted by them; especially so long as they shall be so much dependent upon the *English* for their Support." Having thus established the proper hierarchy, Wheelock then goes on to say: "There is no likelihood at all that they [the Indian missionaries] will, though ever so well qualified, get into Business, either as School-Masters or Ministers, among the *English*; at least till the Credit of their Nations be raised many Degrees above what it is now, and consequently they can't be employed as will be honorable for them, or in any Business they will be fit for, but among their own Nation."[30] From the above citations it is quite evident that Wheelock and the Boston Commissioners had as little intention of integrating Indians into the church hierarchy as any of their seventeenth-century predecessors. Occom's memories of his experiences at Montauk were understandably bitter:

> I Can't Conceive how these gentlemen would have me Live: I am ready to Impute it to their Ignorance, and would wish they had Changed Circumstances with me but one Month, that they may know by experience what my Case really was; but I am now fully Convinced, that it was not Ignorance, For I believe it can be proved to the world, that these Same Gentlemen gave a young Missionary, a Single man, *one Hundred Pounds* for one year, and fifty Pounds for an Interpreter, and thirty Pounds for an Introducer; so it Cost them one Hundred & Eighty Pounds in one Single Year, and they Sent too where there was no Need of a Missionary. Now you See what difference they made between me and other missionaries; they gave me 180 Pounds for 12 years Service, which they gave for one years Service in another Mission. — In my Service (I Speak like a fool, but I am Constrained) I was my own Interpreter, I was both a School master and Minister to the Indians, yea I was their Ear, Eye & Hand, as Well as Mouth. I leave it with the World, as wicked as it is, to Judge, whether I ought not to have had half as much, they gave a young man Just mentioned which would have been but 50£ a year; and if they ought to have given me that, I am not under obligations to them, I owe them nothing at all; what can be the Reason? that they used me after this manner. I can't think of any thing, but this as a Poor Indian Boy Said, Who was Bound out to an English Family, and he used to Drive Plow for a young man, and he whipt and Beat him allmost every Day, and the young man found fault with him, and Complained of him to his master and the poor Boy was Called to answer for himself before his master, and he was asked, what it was he did, that he was so Complained of and beat almost every Day. He Said, he did not know, but he Supposed it was because he could not drive any better; but says he, I Drive as well as I know how; and at other Times he Beats me, because he is of a mind to beat me; but says he believes he Beats me for the most of the Time "because I am an Indian."

At the end of his somber reflections, Occom arrives at his own conclusions for why the Boston Commissioners failed to provide him with just compensation for a job obviously well done: "So I am *ready* to Say, they have used me thus, because I Can't Influence the Indians so well as other missionaries; but I can assure them I have endeavoured to teach them as well as I know how; — but I *must Say*, 'I believe it is because I am a poor Indian.' I Can't help that God has made me so; I did not make myself So."

By the time he was preparing to leave Montauk in 1760, Occom's "extravagances" had left him with a debt of about £100, the greater part of which was finally paid off by private donations. His negative experiences

with racial discrimination in the missionary field must have severely dampened whatever optimism he may have had regarding the possibilities of
social advancement for Indians in New England society. A fragment of his
journal with an uncertain date and the ominous title of "Temperance Han-
nabal" gives an indication of the profoundly disturbed emotional state in
which Occom occasionally found himself:

> I have been the most miserable wretch yet ever lived, yea (I thought) there was
> nothing in all the Noise of Religion, and I thought and Said that the Christians
> Lied; I thought it was for me to gratify my own Inclinations — Till the Last fall,
> I was sick for Some Time, and in my Sickness, I began to Quarry, what would
> become of my Soul, if I Should Die in this State and Condition, and these
> thoughts threw me into Fright, and was Concern'd for my Soul for Some
> Time, but as I got well of my Sickness my Concern wane a way — for till this
> late Religious Stir I bethought of my Self again and after I had been to few
> Meetings I found my Self a great Sinner, and an undone Creature before god,
> yea Saw my Self fit for nothing but Hell and everlasting Distruction — and as I
> was at one meeting and as I was amusing and considering my State and
> Condition, it threw me into Such Horror and guilt of Concience and Confu-
> sion of face, I fell into a Swoon, and immediately I found my Self into great
> Darkness, and while I was there I heard a voice before me, Saying follow me,
> and I went that way, and Immediately found my Self upon Something, I Cant
> Compared to nothing but to a Pole, but ever [crossed out] Put over a Deep
> Hole.[31]

Nevertheless, in 1761 Occom's prospects as a minister of the Gospel still
seemed bright. His talents as an evangelist had been acknowledged by the
Boston Commissioners as early as 1756, when they recommended him for
ordination. The following year he managed to pass an examination administered by the Windham Association of Connecticut, which thereupon affirmed the Boston Commissioners' recommendation. During the next two
years his future was tossed around between the Congregationalists, who
were prepared to grant him thirty pounds a year to remain among the
Montauks, and the Presbyterians, who proposed to send him on a mission
to the Cherokees. On August 29, 1759, the "ornament to the Christian
Religion, and the Glory of the *Indian* Nation" was examined a second time
by the Long Island Presbytery and ordained at long last as "minister at large
to the Indians."[32] The outbreak of a rebellion among the Cherokees just a
few days before his ordination, however, thwarted the SSPCK's original
plans for Occom. Thus it was not until the spring of 1761, after he had
already done some extensive traveling as itinerant preacher among the Indian communities of Long Island and southern New England on his own,

that the New York correspondents of the Scottish society finally provided him with a lucrative assignment as missionary to the Oneidas in New York. The fact that this mission was to take place at the height of the French and Indian War when the English colonies had a vital interest in maintaining good relations with the Six Nations of the Iroquois gives some indication of its political import and immanent risks. Here, then, was the great opportunity to put Wheelock's Grand Design to the test.

Occom departed on his first "errand into the wilderness" in June 1761 in the company of his brother-in-law, David Fowler, who had been a pupil at Wheelock's Charity School since 1759.[33] In New York he was warmly received by weighty political leaders like Cadwallader Colden and Jeffrey Amherst, who provided him with a special pass for assistance at military installations, as well as Sir William Johnson, who formally introduced him to the Oneidas. Collections were made at various religious meetings, which must have been a welcome source of income for the two Mohegans as the SSPCK was already having second thoughts about supporting the mission and the only other funds available to them consisted of smaller sums gathered by Wheelock and Samuel Buell. "I am sorry you couldn't get at Least Some Money for David," Occom complained to Wheelock; "it looks like Presumption for us to go on long Journey thro' Christians without Money, if it was altogether among Indian Heathen we might do well enough — But I have determined to go, tho no White Missionary would go in Such Circumstances."[34]

In the course of his long journey to New York, Occom was confronted with yet another disillusioning experience as he observed the crass discrepancy between theory and practice in the conduct of some Christian whites on the Sabbath. The encounter apparently gave him some second thoughts about the pretended exemplariness of English manners: "I have thought there was no Heathen but the wild Indians, but I think now there is some English Heathen, where they Enjoy the Gospel of Jesus Christ too, Yea I believe they are worse than ye Savage Heathens of the Wilderness, — I have thought that I had rather go with the Meanest and most Dispis'd creature on Earth to Heaven, than Go with the greatest Monarch Down to Hell, after a Short Enjoyment of Sinful Pleasures with them in this World — I am glad there is one defect in the Indian Language, and I believe in all their Languages they Can't Curse or sware or take god's Name in Vain in their own Tongue."[35]

In all, Occom made three journeys to the Oneidas between 1761 and 1763, when his endeavors there were interrupted by the outbreak of Pontiac's rebellion. Though some criticism was expressed concerning his occasional severity in attempting to enforce European outward appearances among the Oneidas, Wheelock still evaluated his mission as another great success.[36] In fact, he and David Fowler paved the way for the Reverend Samuel Kirkland, who is generally credited with having pioneered the Oneida mission. The Oneidas, who had also succumbed to colonial domination by this time, wanted Occom to remain among them as a missionary, which is all the more remarkable considering the cultural and linguistic barriers he had to surmount as an Algonquian-speaking Mohegan. He apparently took an Oneida youth home with him after his first journey in order to learn the language and is said to have become quite proficient at it. In a report to Wheelock he gave an interesting account of a council meeting that had taken place on September 18, 1761, the night before he was to return to Montauk; it is an indication of just what the Oneidas may have expected to gain from his presence among them:

> This Evening the Sachem and principal Men of three Castles came together at the Council-house, and a great Number of Indians besides, and I was called to be with them; and after about an Hour's Consultation, the chief Speaker rose up with a religious Belt of Wampum in His Hand, and delivered a Speech. When he had done, he gave the Belt to my Interpreter, and he interpreted the Speech to me, which is as follows:
>
> Father, We are very glad you have come among us with the good Word of God, or God's News: And we think we are thankful to God, and give you Thanks, and the good Men who assisted you up here.
>
> We will, by the Help of God, endeavour to keep the Fire which you brought and kindled among us; and we will take our old Customs, Ways, and Sins, and put them behind our Backs, and never look on them again; but will look straight forward, and run after the Christian Religion.
>
> Whenever we shall attempt to erect Schools among us, we beg the Assistance of good People your Way.
>
> *We intreat the great Men to protect us on our Lands, that we may not be encroached on by any People.*
>
> *We request that the great Men would forbid Traders bringing any more Rum amongst us; for we find it not good; it destroys our Bodies and Souls.*
>
> This Belt shall bind us together firm in Friendship for ever.[37]

After his return from the last mission to the Oneidas, Occom turned once again to the commissioners in Boston for assistance in securing employment. In February of 1764 they repeated their offer of thirty pounds per year if he would work as a missionary among the Niantics, leaving him with the option of ministering to the Mohegans and other Indian communities in the neighborhood as well. Occom agreed in April and left Montauk to return to his native community in Connecticut with the intent of building a permanent home there for himself and his growing family. Wheelock, however, had other plans for him. In order to have more leeway in promoting his Grand Design — his relations with the Boston Commissioners had always been strained on account of his dissenting views — he established a new commission under the SSPCK in Connecticut in March. During its first meeting Wheelock suggested that Occom be incorporated if the Boston Commissioners would agree to release him. This they did on July 25, but under the condition that he be employed on a mission westward rather than remain on "their" New England circuit. Even though Wheelock's newly constituted commission had no funds available to it at this time, it still decided to send the Mohegan preacher on a mission to Mohawk territory. Occom, who had not finished building his house, reluctantly complied and set off for New York late in August in the company of David Fowler. Wheelock apparently speculated that they would obtain financial assistance from George Whitefield, who was preaching in New York at the time, but the latter was incensed by the supposition and sent Occom and Fowler back to Connecticut empty-handed. Occom had had serious doubts about the project from the very beginning, considering his previous experiences, and the embarrassment before Whitefield must have exasperated him still further. He had practically been deprived of a paid ministry among his own people by Wheelock's irrational decision only to find himself thrown out of employment once again. Moreover, his reappearance at Mohegan was also fraught with problems.

As a result of his extensive missionary activities Occom had become a fairly well-known personality among both whites and Indians in New England and had also acquired substantial experience in his dealings with the English. Thus it was quite natural for him to resume the responsibilities of a councilor upon his return to Mohegan. Here he found the Mohegans and colonists embroiled once again in the age-old land controversy as a final decision was pending in England at just about that time. He tried to maintain a neutral stance at first but then gradually turned away from sachem Ben Uncas III, a reputed alcoholic and puppet of the Connecticut administration, to side with the Mason faction along with the majority of the tribe in support of the Mohegan demands for restitution. Occom had the Mohegans sign a petition to King George III in which the tribe expressed the desire to be placed under the immediate protection of the crown in exchange for the lands in question.[38] As a direct consequence of this involvement in the affairs of his own community, he also came into open conflict with the

Reverend David Jewett, pastor of the North Church of New London and supervisor of Mohegan education, and the official schoolmaster Robert Clelland, both of whom favored the anti-Mason faction. The ill feelings that developed between them were undoubtedly aggravated by the question of competence that automatically arose with Occom's return, whose expertise and reputation must have threatened their own authority in the educational and religious matters of the tribe. After all, here was one of their own flesh and blood who had the necessary, if not far better, qualifications to perform such missionary services among them. Occom soon drew an increasing number of parishioners away from Jewett and other white ministers operating in the vicinity, which obviously did not improve their relationship.[39] He was also openly critical of Clelland's incompetence as a teacher, which had already become apparent to the Boston Commissioners as well. On being questioned by them concerning the matter, Occom reported that Clelland had crowded out Indian students by taking in too many English youths, that his teaching methods were ineffective, and that he had failed to provide for the Indians as required. But, in accordance with Wheelock's earlier prediction, he was an Indian missionary "dependent upon the English" for his support and ultimately had to mind his place in the clerical hierarchy when matters finally came to a head.

The first reaction of the Boston Commissioners upon receiving letters of complaint from Jewett and Ben Uncas III was to cut off his pension. Wheelock, perhaps hoping to end the squabble before it caused further damage to Occom's "reputation," suggested that Jewett bring the matter before the Connecticut Board of Commissioners, who immediately responded by calling a special meeting at Wheelock's home to consider the dispute.[40] Although Occom was acquitted of all charges of "ill Conduct towards the Oversees in the Affair of leasing the Indian Lands, and some proud and houghty Threatenings to turn Episcopalian and Unsettledness respecting the Constitution of our Churches and Infant Baptism, and disrespectful Treatment of the Rev. Mr. Jewett," the commissioners nevertheless required him to submit the following written confession, which clearly delineated his political bounds as an Indian missionary:

> Although as a Member of the Mohegan Tribe and, for many years, one of their Council, I thought I had not only a natural & civil Right, but that it was my Duty, to acquaint myself with their temporal Affairs; Yet I am, upon serious and close Reflexion, convinced, that as there was no absolute Necessity for it, it was very imprudent in me, and offensive to the Public, that I should so far engage, as, of late, I have done, in the *Mason Controversy*:

(which Conduct I might, upon due Consideration, have known, wou'd not only give public Offence, as above, but nearly affect my ministerial Character & hurt my Usefulness. This, I confess, ought to have been of greater weight with me, than said Controversy; which I ought to have passed by in Silence, rather than, by engaging therein, to hinder my profitting in ye Ministry; which I had given my Self wholly to, & solemnly engaged to attend upon). For this imprudent, rash, and offensive Conduct of mine, I am heartily sorry, and beg Forgiveness of God — of this honorable Board of Correspondents, of whom I ought to have asked farther Advice — and of the Public; determining that I will not for the future act in that affair, unless called thereto and obliged by lawful Authority.[41]

At the close of this council (mock trial might be the more appropriate designation) Occom and Jewett were made to shake hands as a symbolic gesture terminating the dispute. For a number of English colonists with landed interests, including Jewett himself, however, the "Pious Mohegan" had abruptly become a persona non grata. As far as Occom was concerned, the entire affair can only have brought him one step closer to total disillusionment with dominant society. At some later date, probably when he had managed to distance himself somewhat from his mentors, he made a rational deduction from this moment of crisis. "The grand controversy which has subsisted between the Colony of Connecticut and the Mohegan Indians above seventy years," he wrote, "is finally decided in favor of the Colony. I am afraid the poor Indians will never stand a good chance with the English in their land controversies, because they are very poor, they have no money. Money is almighty now-a-days, and the Indians have no learning, no wit, no cunning: the English have it all."[42]

One of the highlights of Occom's career came on December 23, 1765, when he and the Reverend Nathaniel Whitaker departed on a fund-raising tour to England, Scotland, and Ireland for the benefit of the Charity School.[43] Wheelock was badly in need of finances to expand his Grand Design and therefore reconsidered an earlier suggestion by one of his associates to send an Indian minister to England where he "might get a Bushel of Money for the School."[44] Even though Occom was the most likely choice for this enterprise, there was still considerable opposition to his going, particularly from the Boston Commissioners. Rumors were circulated that he had but recently been converted for the express purpose of collecting funds, that he could not speak a word of Algonquian, and that he was not even a Mohegan. Friends of Wheelock's cautioned him about the prospect of sending Occom to England, expressing their concern over whether his recent "Medling in the Indian affairs" might not work to the detriment of the school.[45] One reason for the opposition to Occom's going on the mission was the tension between Wheelock and the Boston Commissioners, who felt that it was they who had financed the Mohegan's education and that the Congregationalist minister was going over their heads with this new project. But the main cause for objection was indubitably the suspicion that Occom might bring up the matter of the Mohegan land dispute in London, as Mason's descendants (Samuel and John) were still petitioning the Privy Council to reopen the case.[46] Occom's reception in Boston, where he and Whitaker were temporarily stranded due to protest against the Stamp Act, was expectedly cool and caused him to have second thoughts about the mission he was preparing to embark upon. "I have a Struggle in my Mind At times," he confessed to Wheelock, "knowing not where I am going, I dont know but I am Looking for a Spot of ground where my Bones must be Buried, and never to see my Poor Family again."[47] That transatlantic journeys were extremely hazardous ventures for Indians was evident in the numerous casualties that had occurred among Indian travelers since Pocahontas's fate in 1617 and would soon be proven again in the case of the Narragansett Tobias Shattuck, a former student at Wheelock's school, who died of smallpox in England in the spring of 1768 at about the time Occom was preparing to return. Occom's legitimate fears proved to be unwarranted, however, as, with the exception of a brief bout with a smallpox inoculation, he not only survived the journey but made such an impact on English society that it recalled the more positive sides of Pocahontas's celebrated visit nearly a century and a half before.

Occom's travels took him all over England and into parts of Scotland and Ireland, and in most places he was kindly received by leading religious and political personalities of the day, despite efforts by members of the Boston Board to undermine the mission. His visit attracted the notice of King George III, who presented him with a psalter in Latin and Syriac, and, as the protégé of George Whitefield and the countess of Huntingdon, he had access to London's elite. The deference shown to him by the higher echelons of British society may well have been a demonstration of eighteenth-century nobility's "fetishistic" affinity with the image of the "noble savage," as Hayden White has suggested in another context, their own natural order and *ancien régime* having been disrupted by the spreading forces of bourgeois society in America.[48] Nevertheless, an Indian who could preach effectively in the English language was apparently a public sensation of sorts in Great Britain — sufficient, at any rate, to make him an object of parody on London stages and a target for satirical attacks in Grub Street penny papers.

Occom delivered several hundred sermons in the course of his sojourn which attracted a multitude of listeners (estimated at over three thousand in one particular case). His style of preaching, described by one contemporary as "decent, and . . . in some degree eloquent," was certainly polished enough to produce the desired results because it was he, more so than his "pale" companion, who motivated his audiences to donate the incredible sum of £11,000 or more for Indian education.[49]

In addition to his previous achievements as missionary among the Montauks and Oneidas, Occom's great success abroad must have replenished his self-esteem and, at the same time, increased his frustration at not being able to advance accordingly in his "calling." Conversely, Wheelock and some of his associates regarded his uncommon reception in England with great skepticism and admonished him repeatedly to "keep clear of that Indian distemper, Pride."[50] Not even Samuel Buell, a longtime friend and supporter of Occom could refrain from pointing him toward his proper place: "[Y]ou are an Indian, who was born a Pagan — I trust your guardian God will keep you at his adorable Footstol."[51]

When Occum returned from England on May 20, 1768, his reputation had reached unprecedented heights. He was an ordained, balanced-bilingual, widely traveled and well-connected minister with an impressive twenty-year missionary record. But he was also forty-five years old now, continually plagued by health problems, and had about a dozen mouths to feed. As a respected elder in the Indian community he was always expected to demonstrate generosity and to entertain any guest who might knock on his door. In England he had procured a huge sum of money for the benefit of the Indians, and he had proven himself more capable in this effort than Whitaker, whose dubious dealings in Europe had brought him into disrespect with the English trustees and moved them to take over the management of funds in 1766. Occom now had the legitimate expectation of being able to settle down permanently at his home in Mohegan and to obtain at least a small fraction of the English fund in compensation for his ministering to the Indian communities in southern New England, whose situation and language he was obviously more familiar with than any of his white colleagues. Connecticut, however, was the New England Company's "turf," and the commissioners in Boston, who had not forgotten his part in the land case, simply refused to employ him. In addition, Occom's long-standing relationship with Wheelock was deteriorating rapidly at this time.

While in England he had received disconcerting letters from his wife with accounts of economic hardships, and he came to feel that Wheelock had not cared adequately for his family during his absence as he had promised to do. Furthermore, he had the growing suspicion — shared in part by the trustees in England and local missionaries like Samuel Kirkland — that Wheelock intended to use the funds he had gathered for purposes other than educating Indians. Wheelock, in turn, felt that Occom was being petulant and ungrateful and found himself absolutely incapable of understanding the full extent of Occom's plight. He sincerely believed that he was doing his best to promote Occom's welfare. On several occasions in 1772–73 Wheelock offered Occom the chance to go on a funded mission to the "remote tribes" (i.e., Iroquois), which he thought was the proper place for the Mohegan minister to apply his talents.[52] He regarded Occom's increasing assertiveness as a negative aftereffect of the respect shown to him in England which, as he wrote in one of his letters, made him "aspire after Grandure & ease."[53] In the comfortable position of relative affluence and a privileged social status, Wheelock was apparently unable to see far enough beyond the ethnocentric perspectives of his Grand Design to recognize that for Occom there was much more at stake than mere pride. To be Indian in New England during the latter part of the eighteenth century usually entailed living in abject poverty at the margin of society, a kind of existence he was obviously not anxious to return to and which he had undoubtedly hoped to circumvent with the help of his education and subsequent profession. Ironically, it took a wealthy businessman like John Thornton, one of the English trustees who never once doubted Occom's sincerity, to grasp the full meaning behind the Mohegan's seeming recalcitrance. In a letter to Wheelock he wrote: "Mr. Occom seems to me to have been hardly treated. . . . it should be remembered he has been taken from that scene of life that made labour & the greatest parsimony habitual to him & it is not in human Nature to return to it with that alacrity which is expected from him."[54] But Occom's lack of enthusiasm for Wheelock's proposal that he move his family to New York also had much to do with his close ties to his Mohegan and Montauk relatives. The prospect of having to live somewhere in the "Hidious Wilderness" (his own words) among a people as foreign to him as they were to Europeans was hardly enticing under the circumstances.[55] And yet, it is quite likely that he would have accepted the mission eventually, as he intimated in some of his letters, if it had not been for his legitimate doubts concerning the financial aspects of such a venture.

In the period immediately following his return from England Occom actually saw little of "Grandure & ease"; on the contrary, he was forced to lead a hand-to-mouth existence as an independent itinerant preacher in

direct competition with white ministers who were being paid by some missionary society. That he was able to bring himself and his family through
this difficult stage in his life was due in no small measure to the charity of
philanthropists and faithful friends in distant England, such as the countess
of Huntingdon and John Thornton. It was at this time also (1769) that he
wrote his dispirited autobiographical sketch and may have sought solace in
alcohol, as he immediately penned two letters of confession, one to the
Suffolk Presbytery and another to the SSPCK. The former presided over his
case in November and came to the conclusion that his intoxication came
not from intemperance "but from having Drank a small quantity of Spirituous Liquor after having been all day without food."[56] Wheelock chose
to magnify the issue, however, and sent off letters for years to come to many
of Occom's friends informing them — with apparent glee — that even the
"Pious Mohegan" had finally fallen prey to that greatest of all Indian sins,
intemperance. As Love has pointed out, the exaggerated reaction bordered
on hypocrisy as it held Occom to a standard of total abstinence observed by
no one else in the eighteenth-century New England missionizing business.
Wheelock, who could also appreciate a good vintage, probably regarded it
as an opportune excuse to initiate some fundamental changes in his Grand
Design. The charge stigmatized Occom for the rest of his life. "I dont remember that I have been overtaken with strong drink this winter," he wrote
to Wheelock in the spring of 1769, "but many white people make no bones
of it to call me a drunkard, and I expected it, as I have many enemies round
about here, yea they curse and damn me to the lowest Hell."[57]

Above all else, it was Wheelock's plans to move the Charity School to
Hanover, New Hampshire, that finally brought about a permanent break in
their relationship. The steadily decreasing number of Indian students in
attendance after William Johnson ceased to support the school and the
Oneidas withdrew their children early in 1769 only confirmed Occom's
suspicion that the English and Scottish funds were not going to be used for
their original purpose. Accordingly, in the summer of 1771 he penned an
unusually lengthy complaint to Wheelock in which he openly confronted
the aging minister with his misgivings on the matter. The text is reprinted
here at some length because it is a rare example of his authentic voice:

> I am very jealous that instead of your Semenary Becoming alma Mater, she
> will be too alba mater to Suckle the Tawnees for She is already aDorned up too
> much like the Popish Virgin Mary. She'll be Naturally ashamed to Suckle the
> Tawnees for she is already equal in Power, Honor and Authority to any
> College in Europe, I think your College has too much Worked by Grandeur

for the Poor Indians, they'll never have much benefit of it, — In so Saying I speak the general Sentiment of Indians and English too in these parts. So many of your Missionaries and School masters and Indian Scholars Leaving you and your Service Confirms me in this opinion — your having so many White Scholars and so few or no Indian Scholars, gives me great Discouragement — I verily thought once that your Institution was Intended Purely for the poor Indians — with this thought I Cheerfully Ventured my Body & Soul, left my Country my poor young Family all my Friends and Relations, to sail over the Boisterous Seas to England, to help forward your School, Hoping that it may be a lasting Benefet to my poor Tawnee Brethren, With this View I went a Volunteer — I was quite willing to become a Gazing Stocke, Yea Even a Laughing Stocke, in Strange Countries to Promote your Cause. . . . But when we got Home behold all the glory had Decayed and now I am afraid, we shall be Deem'd as Liars and Deceivers, in Europe, unless you gather Indians quickly to your College, in great Numbers and not to have so many whites in the Charity, — I understand you have no Indians at Present except two or three Mallatoes — this I think is quite Contrary to the Minds of the Doners, We told them, that we were Beging for poor Miserable Indians, as for my part I went, purely for the poor Indians, and I should be as ready as ever to promote your school according to my poor Abilities if I Coud be Convinc'd by ocular Demonstration, that your pure Intention is to help the poor helpless Indians, but as long as you have no Indians, I am full of Doubts. . . . the opinion of many white People about here is that you have been Scheeming altogether, and that it was a Pollicy to Send me over to England, for (Say they) now they dont Care anything about you, you have answer'd their Lords, now you may Sink or Swim it is all one to them, this makes me think of what that great man of god Said to me, Mr. Whitefield, just before I left England in the hearing of Some gentlemen — ah Says he, you have been a fine Tool to get Money for them, but when you get home, they wont Regard you, they'll Set you a Drift, — I am ready to believe it Now — I am going to Say Something further, which is very Disagreeable. Modesty woud forbid me, but I am Constrain'd So to Write, — Many gentlemen in England and in this Country too, Say if you had not this Indian Buck you woud not Collected a quarter of the Money you did, one gentleman in Particular in England Said to me, if he hadn't Seen my face he woudnt have given a tuppence but now I have 50 £ freely — This one Consideration gives me great Quietness.[58]

Wheelock had already toyed with the idea of removing the Charity School to Iroquois territory in the early 1760s but, as a direct consequence of his troubles with the Oneidas and a subsequent better offer by Connecticut, he decided instead to transfer the school to Hanover in 1770, just one year after he had established Dartmouth College. Here it continued operations alongside the college until 1785, when it was closed temporarily for lack of funds, and then reopened from 1800 to 1829 and again from 1837 to 1850.[59] That Wheelock was quite adept at tapping the "missionary racket" is evident in his manipulation of the phraseology of the college charter in order to placate the trustees of the English and Scottish funds. As Dartmouth historian Jere Daniell has shown, he simply changed the phrase "for the Education & Instruction of Youths of the English" contained in the original statement of purpose to its present form: "for the Education & Instruction of *Youths of the Indian Tribes in this Land* in reading writing & all parts of Learning which shall appear necessary and expedient for civilizing and christianizing Children of Pagans as well as in all liberal Arts and Sciences; *and also of English Youth* and any others."[60] He thus gained access to whatever remained of the English fund by 1775 and used it up for the construction of the college buildings. The SSPCK, however, kept a tighter hold on its fund until 1800, when it permitted Wheelock's son to draw from it to support Indian students at the reopened Charity School. Dartmouth, which had obviously been conceived and developed by Wheelock as an institution of higher learning for whites in spite of its altered statement of purpose, provided instruction for less than a hundred Indians up until the first half of the present century.[61]

Wheelock had obviously already given up his original plan of training Indians as missionaries by the time Occom had penned his misgivings to him. The reasoning behind his change of mind is contained in his 1771 *Narrative*. "The most melancholy part of the account which I have here to relate, and which has occasioned me the greatest weight of sorrow," he writes, "has been the bad conduct, and behaviour of such as have been educated here, after they have left the school, and been put into business abroad: and it is that from which, I think, I had the fullest evidence that a greater proportion of English youths must be fitted for missionaries; and enough of them to take the lead intirely; and conduct the whole affair of christianizing and civilizing the savages, without any dependence upon their own sons, as leaders, in this matter, or any further, than they are employed under the immediate inspection and discretion of English men." Of the approximately forty Indians he had educated, Wheelock adds, no more than half were able to "preserve their characters unstain'd, either by a course of intemperance or uncleanness, or both. . . . And six of those who did preserve a good character, are now dead." He also blames the Indians for want of fortitude, "fashionable vices," and proneness to "wicked dealings," all of which convinced him of the "absolute necessity of sending well-chosen English youths on this errand."[62] The Grand Design had thus run its course and, as one may infer from his assessment, the Indian students were the ones who had proved unworthy of it. To Occom, who queried his mentor on several other occasions about the future course of his school, he explained the entire situation in a somewhat different light just one year after he had published the above statements. "The Plan is such that all the Benefit done or proposed to be done to the English is Subservient in the Best Manner to the Indian Cause," he assured him, "and greatly adds to and increases my ability to help the Indians and that many ways in so much that I hope in God to be able to support a Hundred Indians and Youths designed for Indian Service on Charity in a little Time." Occom was not convinced by Wheelock's hollow assurances, however. "In my apprehension your present plan is not calculated to benefit the poor Indians," he responded, "it is in no ways winning to them and unless there is an alternative suitable to the minds of the Indians you will never do much more good among the Indians; your First Plan was much better than the last, you did much good in it and if you rightly managed the Indians your Institution would have flourished by this Time."[63]

It seems that Occom never managed to make his way to Hanover to obtain an "ocular Demonstration" of Wheelock's new institution, in spite of the latter's invitation to do so. They maintained a sporadic exchange of cordial correspondence up until 1774, in which Occom complained repeatedly about the minister's lack of interest in him, and then their thirty-one-year relationship apparently ended. Occom's grudge against Wheelock continued even after the latter's death in 1779, as the following excerpt from a very bitter letter he wrote to a friend in 1783 demonstrates:

> Doc^r Wheelock's Indian Academy or Schools are become altogether unprofitable to the poor Indians. In short, he has done little or no good to the Indians with all that money we collected in England since we got home. That money never educated but one Indian and one Mollatoe — that is part Negro and part Indian — and there has not been one Indian in that Institution this some Time, all that money has done is, it has made [the] Doctor's Family very grand in the World . . . for the College is become a grand College for the White People. . . . I have nothing to do to help that Institution; If I had Twenty Sons I would not send one to be educated, I would not do it that Honour.[64]

For the rest of his own life, he continued to believe in the necessity of training Indian missionaries. "I am now fully Convinced," he wrote late in 1791, "that the Indians must have Teachers of their own Colour or Nation, they have a very great and rooted Prejudice against White People, and they have too much good reason for it, they have been imposed upon."[65]

To make matters worse, Occom was still having to contend with severe problems among his own people. When Ben Uncas III died in 1769, the internal squabbles over the legitimate heir to the sachemship broke out once again. During the funeral sermon preached by Jewett, Occom and his followers, who still supported John Uncas, got up demonstratively and left the premises in protest against a faction of Mohegans that had formed around councilor Zachary Johnson and Isiah Uncas, the dull-witted son of the deceased sachem who was favored by the Connecticut General Court. Since the tribe could not agree upon a successor and Isiah Uncas died in the spring of 1770, the Mohegan sachemship became extinct at this time.[66] In the years that followed, Occom refused to recognize the authority of Zachary Johnson as regent and disagreed sharply with his faction's policies concerning the distribution of lease moneys from Mohegan lands which had hitherto belonged to the sachem. From a fragment of a document written by Occom in 1778, in which he formulates six resolutions for the Mohegan tribe, we get a clear indication of his views on this particular issue: "In the evening, the Tribe met together, to Consult about the Disposal of the Rent money, and it has been agreed Unanimously heretofore once and again, that We Shall look upon one another as one Family, and Will Call and look upon no one as a Stranger, but will take one another as pure and True Mohegans; and So at this Time, we unanimously agreed that the Money does belong to the Whole Tribe, and it Shall be dispos'd of accordingly for the Benefit of the whole." As late as 1782, the Johnson faction was still writing letters protesting the actions of "the Strange Indians headed . . . by a Certain Indian Minister," whom they blamed for the tribe's internal troubles and its deteriorating relations with Connecticut.[67]

Around 1771 Occom began to develop his own "Grand Design" which, curiously enough, would eventually take him to where Wheelock had wanted him to go in the first place, albeit under different conditions altogether. His permanent financial difficulties, Wheelocks' about-face, continuing factionalism within the Mohegan community, and his observation of the negative effects resulting from permanent white incursions into the Christian Indian communities in New England finally led him to the realization that Indians had to seek their own salvation without (rather than within) white society. The notion of segregating Indian and white communities for their mutual benefit, which had played a role in British Indian policy since the Royal Proclamation of 1763 and would become official U.S. policy in the early nineteenth century, was just then beginning to take hold in the colonies as a potential solution to the perennial "Indian problem."[68] Together with his young son-in-law Joseph Johnson (whose life will be discussed further on) and David Fowler, Occom began to work out a plan under which members of seven northeastern Christian Indian communities (Charlestown, Groton, Stonington, Niantic, Farmington, Montauk, Mohegan) were to move voluntarily to Oneida territory in New York and establish an independent settlement there. The community they envisioned was the previously mentioned early New England–style, agriculturally based township with communally owned lands and its own "body politick," much like the Praying Indian villages of the seventeenth century, but with one important difference — it was, from its inception to its realization, an all-Indian affair. Occom had been to Natick more than once since his first visit in November of 1748 and was thus quite familiar with Eliot's experimental communities, as well as contemporary Connecticut townships.[69]

Such an idea involving voluntary Indian "removal" was, of course, born out of an involuntary capitulation before Euro-American expansion, and it complied overtly with the colonists' greed for additional Indian land — it is thus no coincidence that the plan met with the full support of the General Court of Connecticut and the missionary societies. "The prospect you give me of a foundation being laid for much good to the savages in the wilderness," Wheelock wrote to Occom in a conciliatory letter, "is the very one I have been long waiting and hoping for."[70] At the same time, however, it represented a viable alternative for Christian members of northeastern remnant tribes to maintain at least a semblance of their traditional village life on their own lands and, perhaps, to live out their own conceptions of Christianity as well. For Occom, who had steadfastly refused to go out into the "wilderness" among the Iroquois alone, an exodus in the company of family, relatives, friends, and parishioners was a different matter altogether because it also entailed the prospect of an autonomous, Indian-supported ministry. As he would observe several years later in his journal, "It is high Time that we should begin to maintain of ourselves, and to Support our Temporal & Religious Concerns."[71]

During a general meeting held at Mohegan on March 13, 1773, the participating Indians from the seven New England communities decided to send representatives to the Oneidas in order to explore the situation there, and in October of that same year Joseph Johnson and Elijah Wampy of Farmington made their way to New York for that purpose. At their first council on January 21, 1774, the Oneidas promised them a ten-mile tract of land but, at a follow-up meeting on the next day, they agreed to give the New England emigrants a larger section and also officially adopted them into their "Covenant Chain" according to ancient custom: "Brethren, we look upon you, as upon a Sixth Brother. We will tell you, of all your elder

Brothers, the Onoidas, Kiyougas, Nanticuks, Tuskaroras, Todelehonas, these five are your Elder Brothers. But as for the Mohawks, Onondaugas, and the Senecas they are our fathers, and they are your fathers." The likely motivation behind the Oneidas' generosity, other than a timely intercession by William Johnson on the Christian Indians' behalf, was the advantage they expected from the latter's transcultural experiences in their own precarious dealings with the English colonists. "Brethren," they declared earlier in the same speech, "we shall expect that ye will assist us in advising us, concerning the Affairs, that may be brought under our consideration, when ye shall live side of us your Brothers."[72]

In the following summer Occom traveled to New York in the company of David Fowler once again in order to view the prospective site, writing down his impressions there in more detail than usual in his journal. The gift of land was recorded in a formal deed on October 4, 1774, and, in the spring of the following year, the first group of New England Christian Indians made the trek to their new home in Oneida territory. The outbreak of the American Revolution, however, temporarily interrupted the voluntary exodus. According to Love, the first group of emigrants, who had been forced to take refuge among the Stockbridge Indians in Massachusetts with the approach of British troops, were instrumental in keeping the Oneidas and Tuscaroras peaceful and may very well have been the authors of the celebrated Oneida "Declaration of Neutrality" dated June 19, 1775.[73]

Even though he openly sympathized with the republican side and several of his own relatives and friends served in the conflict, Occom himself was most emphatic about maintaining neutrality, viewing any Indian partisanship in the fratricidal war as detrimental to their own cause. In an oft-cited address to his "Beloved Brethren," he gave them his own interpretation of the "Family Contentions of the English":

> I will now give you a little insight into the Nature of the English Quarrils over the great Waters. They got to be rich, I mean the Nobles and the great, and they are very Proud and they keep the rest of their Brethren under their Feet, they make Slaves of them. The great ones have got all the Land and the rest are poor Tenants — and the People in this Country live more upon a leavel and they live happy, and the former Kings of England use to let the People in this Country have their Freedom and Liberty; but the present King of England wants to make them Slaves to himself, and the People in this Country don't want to be Slaves, — and so they are come over to kill them, and the People here are oblig'd to Defend themselves, they dont go over the great Lake to kill them. And now I think, if you must join on one way or other you cant join the oppresser, but will help the oppressed. But let me conclude with one word of

Advice, use all your Influence to your Brethren, so far as you have any Connections to keep them in Peace and quietness, and not to intermeddle in these Quarrils among the White People. The Lord Jesus Christ says, Blessed are the Peacemakers, for they shall be called the Children of God.[74]

At the close of the war the emigrants who had fled to Stockbridge returned to New York to carry on with the project and, in the spring of 1784, Occom led another group there from New England. On Monday, November 7, 1785, he made the following historic entry in his journal:

In the Evening we met on our Temporal and Religious concerns — we met once before but we did not come to proceed any business. *But now we proceeded to form into a Body Politick — we Named our Town by the Name of Brotherton, in Indian Eeyamquittoowauconuck —* J. Fowler was chosen clarke for the Town. Roger Waupieh, David Fowler, Elijah Wympy, John Tuhy, and Abraham Simon were chosen a Committee or Trustees for the Town, for a year and for the future, the committee is to be chosen Annually, and Andrew Acorrocomb and Thomas Putchauker were chosen to be Fence Vewers to continue a year. Concluded to have a Centre near David Fowlers House, the main Street is to run North and South & East and West, to cross at the centre. Concluded to live in Peace, and in Friendship and to go in all their Public Concerns in Harmony both in their Religious and Temporal concerns, and every one to bear his part of Public Charges in the Town. They desired me to be a Teacher amongst them. I consented to spend some of my remaining days with them, and make this Town my Home and center.[75]

The Stockbridge Indians of Massachusetts, undoubtedly influenced by refugees they had harbored during the Revolution, also decided to remove to New York between 1783 and 1786, where they set up their own community, New Stockbridge, within six miles of Brothertown. Occom extended his services to them as well, and on August 27, 1787, they presented a written request to "God's Ambassador into this wilderness" to settle among them. They volunteered to provide him with twenty shillings in the first year, a sum which was to be augmented as they increased in "Number and Substance" until they had acquired the means to support him fully. "Sir, This Church is the first Indian Presbyterian Church that ever was formed by Indians themselves," he wrote proudly in a letter just a few months before his death, "for we had no white man to assist us when we formed."[76]

Occom did not move permanently to New York until 1789, maintaining himself and his family in the interim from funds provided by John Thornton and what he was able to collect as an itinerant preacher. He traveled hundreds of miles back and forth between New York and Connecticut, preaching whenever and wherever he could find a congregation, and depended entirely upon the hospitality of the people he met along the way for food and lodging. His exhortations were underscored by "Christian Cards" inscribed with rhymed biblical texts, which he would pass around for individual "players" to recite. He fulfilled not only the usual functions of a minister (sermons, weddings, baptisms, burials) but also those of a lay physician, setting broken bones, bleeding patients, or prescribing special Indian remedies whenever the need arose.[77]

Occom's difficulties were still far from over, however, for poverty and ill health were to plague him for the rest of his days. Additionally, he was beset again by all-too-familiar problems as American expansionism soon engulfed the two infant Christian Indian communities in New York. Spurred on by white speculators, the Oneidas tried to revoke the 1774 deed in 1786. Claiming that the Brothertown Indians had not fulfilled the conditions of the grant, they first proposed to leave them with 640 acres in lieu of their claim and then urged them to live on the Oneida lands at large without a title. Matters became more complicated in 1788 when the Oneidas ceded almost all of their lands to the United States under the Fort Schuyler Treaty. Fortunately, Occom had been wise enough to record the Oneida deed on paper, and it was thus duly recognized by an act passed by the General Assembly of New York on February 25, 1789. Some of the members of the Brothertown community were then talked into leasing lands and timber rights to whites, and Occom, who claimed that this group led by Elijah Wampy was primarily composed of "Mulattoes & Strangers" who "did not come from the Tribes to whom this Land was Given" and thus had no right to dispose of lands or resources "which were designed to be reserved for the Use of the Whole Town," again petitioned the General Assembly to have the settlement officially incorporated as an independent town government. His wish was granted with the passage of "An Act for the relief of the Indians residing in Brothertown and New Stockbridge" on February 21, 1791. Finally, in May 1792, Occom succeeded in convincing the General Assembly to appoint a date for the forcible ejection of whites who had managed to finagle ten-year leases from some of the more naive Christian Indian residents. "Whenever we Shall be ripe for leasing," he concluded, "it must be done in union and good agreement of the Whole Town."[78] Just as had happened among the Mohegans in Connecticut and other Indians elsewhere in New England, the issue created a serious fissure within the two New York Christian Indian communities which was to persist after his death until 1794, when the prowhite faction apparently recognized its folly and the General Assembly was finally able to enforce its 1792 decision. For his efforts to maintain the Brothertown land base Occom once again incurred the enmity of both whites and Indians, the latter of whom blamed him for their "present unhappy divisions & animosities," according to Samuel Kirkland's journal. This internal squabble may well have been the reason why the ailing Mohegan minister at last decided to move away from Brothertown, where some land had already been cleared for his personal use, to settle in New Stockbridge shortly before his death.[79]

Another frustrating episode clouding his final years was Occom's confrontation with John Sargeant, Jr., who had been a minister to the Stockbridge Indians in Massachusetts since 1771 and showed up in New Stockbridge in 1787 with plans to continue his mission there. At first they held joint services, but the rather awkward situation soon led to tensions between them and eventually split the New Stockbridge community into two congregations, one remaining faithful to Sargeant and the other preferring to assemble under Occom. Sargeant, who had received a handsome sum in compensation when the New England Company ceased operations in the United States, managed to enlist the patronage of the newly established Society for the Propagation of the Gospel among the Indians and Others in North America, which nominated him as the "official" pastor of the New Stockbridge Indians. It is not difficult to imagine Occom's consternation; he had been performing the function of minister and schoolmaster for the past two years with little financial support and had just recently accepted the appointment signed by the leading members of both communities, when the younger minister practically took over his "flock" in an officially sanctioned and salaried position. "Mr. Sargeant Preach'd," he jotted down peevishly in his journal on July 18, 1788, "and it was in Indian and it was no Edification to me." Nevertheless, he was apparently prepared to settle his differences with the unwelcome "interloper," as can be inferred from another entry in his journal just two days later: "[A]bout 9 we met together to have a debate with Mr. Sargeant but he Chuse not to Debate, I desired him to point out the Errors he had Charged us with, but he declin'd and finally Concluded that everyone Should have full Liberty to Chuse and act in according to the Light and Understanding he has in his Religious Concerns, and So we parted in Friendship, Concluded to agree and disagree, and so we returned to Brotherton, got to my Daughters before night."[80]

Following his permanent move to New York in 1789, Occom was continually traveling between Brothertown/New Stockbridge and the Indian communities in New England. But, as Harold Blodgett has pointed out, his journal contains indications that his unceasing difficulties and disappointments were beginning to wear him out. One of his final entries, dated January 10, 1790, reflects a somber mood: "I have been to no meetings four Sabbaths, we had one very bad Stormy Sabb, and my Mind has been fill'd with Trouble so that I have had no peace, but Sorrow, grief and Confusion of Heart — and I am yet in great Trouble."[81]

Samson Occom died in New Stockbridge on July 14, 1792, at the age of sixty-nine. According to Samuel Kirkland, who delivered his funeral sermon the next day, "the Indians were so alarmed at the sudden death of Mr. Occum that they began to collect at Tuscarora from the various settlements.... many of the Indians came the distance of 10 miles ... we moved about a mile to a bower near the centre of town for the sake of convenience, there being no house sufficiently large to contain the one half of the Indians who were assembled on that occasion." More than three hundred Indians from various tribes gathered to attend his funeral service. Nevertheless, when Kirkland preached there again on August 3, he decided not to mention Occom as many expected of him because "the divisions among the Indians were such that [he] thought it not prudent to attempt it; and indeed was advised to omit it."[82] It was a telling epitaph for Occom's difficult path between cultures. His remains probably lie in an unmarked grave in an old Christian Indian cemetery in the vicinity of Deansboro, New York.[83]

Occom's English writings cover a period of nearly fifty years. The greater part by far of his literary output was never intended for publication, and some of the published pieces did not appear in print until long after his death. Nevertheless, he produced two very popular texts during his lifetime, a rather admirable achievement if one keeps in mind that more than half of the practicing Protestant clergymen in eighteenth-century New England never published anything and only a handful ever managed to publish more than one sermon.[84]

Occom began to keep a journal on the day he entered Wheelock's school, on December 6, 1743, and maintained it irregularly until March 6, 1790.[85] Its conspicuously impersonal language and lack of descriptive passages, which led Blodgett to lament that Occom had "no talent for gossip, no ear for sound, or eye for the sight and show of things," would not qualify it as a bona fide diary according to most definitions.[86] Occom's succinct and meticulous listings of places visited, persons met, services performed, compensation received, and funds expended indicate that we are dealing here with a straightforward "professional journal," as required by the missionary societies from their representatives in the field, rather than expressions of his inner thoughts and emotions as might be expected from a spiritual diary or conversion testimony.[87] Like other contemporary missionary journals (i.e., Samuel Kirkland's), its introspective passages are too few and far between to serve as an adequate basis for a meaningful interpretation of the text. Its merit lies more in the nature of a historical document, particularly the more detailed sections describing his travels to the Oneidas in 1761 and 1764, his journey to England in 1765–66, and his peregrinations between Mohegan and Brothertown from 1784 to 1790.[88] The lengthy section (actually a separate notebook with forty-six pages of text) describing the England voyage from November 21, 1765, to July 22, 1766, for instance, is a unique eighteenth-century Indian travelogue with interesting, though brief, descriptions of famous places and people. His account of his travels between Mohegan and Brothertown, on the other hand, is a singular autoethnographic documentation of the postcontact formation of a heterogeneous New England Christian Indian tribe in New York. Furthermore, in its function as an unadorned record of his activities as a missionary, Occom's journal could also be likened to traditional warrior stories, or "coup tales," which David Brumble has included as legitimate examples of "preliterate traditions" in his excellent study of American Indian autobiography.[89] These factual oral accounts of valorous deeds performed by an individual formed the basis on which, so to speak, his "professional" status and prestige within the community remained on "public record." In a similar manner, Occom frequently documented his "missionary coups" in the field. "After Sermon a Number of Young People stayd to have exercise with Texts of Scripture and it was very Solemn many were deeply affected," he noted on Tuesday, March 21, 1786, "and I believe they can't forget the night, the most careless of them will remember it as long as they live and long even to eternity they must carrie it."[90]

Occom's oft-cited autobiographical sketch, which is included among his journal entries, was written September 17, 1768, on a separate, twenty-six-page notebook. On the surface it is a typical example of salvationist literature — writings with an evangelical purpose — which predominated in eighteenth-century colonial America. The autobiography begins in conformity with the usual schema of Indian conversion testimonies collected during the previous centuries by missionaries like John Eliot or Experience Mayhew, describing the process of his spiritual transformation from "heathenism" to "civility" and continuing with the development of his career as a missionary. However, rather than closing with the expected transition from "Trouble of Mind" to "Serenity and Pleasure of Soul, in Serving God," as mentioned at the beginning of the sketch, it turns abruptly into an angry denunciation of racial discrimination within the missionary field that has, as far as I can tell, no precedent in conventional salvationist texts. In this case, at least, Occom is making effective use of the conversion narrative format, or "the voice of a dominant order" (to quote Arnold Krupat), as a platform for his own undisguised, authentic voice.[91] Occom undoubtedly had every intention of reaching the general public with his autobiographical sketch in order — as he explained in a much shorter, letter-format version of his life history written just before his departure for England on November 28, 1765 — to counter the rumors that were then being spread about him and to take the "opportunity to give the World in few words, the true Account of my Education."[92] Other indications of his desire to have it published are the fact that the text has been carefully separated and changed (edited?) in several places and that it is subdivided into sections (chapters?) with underlined headings. That neither Wheelock nor the missionary societies had an interest in having it circulated is not surprising. As David Murray has shown, as long as Indian literacy was not widespread, anything published by an Indian "was likely to reflect the tastes of a white audience, and conform to a large extent to what at least some of them thought it was appropriate for an Indian to write."[93] The authentic voice of early North American Indian writers is, therefore, often discernible only if published material can be compared with unpublished sources or, failing that, if the authors' life histories and works are viewed simultaneously in an ethnohistorical perspective. Control over the publishing business is, in effect, the precondition for the hegemony of a dominant voice in literature; but, as James Scott has also pointed out, there are ways in which the dominated authentic voice can infiltrate a text in a "guarded" or "disguised" way to create a "hidden manuscript" with a critical message.[94]

Before going on to discuss Occom's two published works, mention must first be made of the brief ethnographic account of the Montauks he penned earlier, in 1761, but which was not published until 1809.[95] It proves that he did have sufficient "ear for sound" and "eye for the sight and show of things" to make careful note of traditional Montauk marriage customs, naming ceremonies, religious beliefs, funerary practices, and conceptions of the afterlife. Even though he concludes that the Montauks have since "renounced all their heathenish idolatry and superstition," his field notes do not lack a certain sense of scientific distance worthy of a serious ethnographer. His assessment that the Montauks had a dualistic notion of "one great and good God" opposing "a great evil god" and that they believed in the existence of a life after death, "where the righteous, or those who behaved

themselves well in this world, will exercise themselves in pleasurable singing and dancing forever," suggests a preexisting affinity between Coastal
Algonquian spirituality and Christianity. This notion of a religious parallel-
ism, evident in New England Indian folklore since the seventeenth century,
would soon become a standard feature of American Indian literature.[96]
Also striking is his description of "Powaws" (shamans) and the "great mystery of darkness" surrounding them which, as he says with an unmistakable
touch of pride, "I don't see for my part, why it is not as true, as the English
or any other nation's witchcraft." A related curiosity that reveals his continuing interest in Indian lore is his collection of Indian herbal medicines,
which he jotted down in 1754 and probably experimented with — along
with occidental practices like bleeding — during his later services as a lay
physician. Some of the "prescriptions" he recorded at this time were printed
posthumously, in 1954, as a small booklet titled *Ten Indian Remedies*.[97]

The second highlight in Occom's career, which earned him moderate
literary laurels in his own day, came in the summer of 1772, when a Mohegan named Moses Paul requested that Occom deliver a sermon at his execution in New Haven the coming fall.[98] Moses Paul, a Christian Indian who
had first served in the army and then on a British man-of-war, committed a
senseless murder under the influence of alcohol on December 7, 1771, for
which he was duly tried and sentenced to hang. Criminal executions had
been major public events in colonial New England since the seventeenth
century and provided Protestant ministers with a welcome occasion to exhort the multitudes. In the so-called execution sermon, a preacher would
first berate the condemned criminal for his/her misconduct and present an
analysis of how he/she had come to fall so low, before turning to the general
audience with a warning that they, too, could be led astray in a similar
manner. The execution sermon thus fulfilled several social functions: In
conjunction with the execution itself it was expected to be an effective
deterrent for prospective criminals, it pointed out the association between
the miscreant's deeds and the general state of morality in society, and it
provided a moral justification for the execution itself. Beginning with Samuel Danforth's *Cry of Sodom Enquired Into* (1675), the execution sermon
was also made available to an absentee audience in published form and
soon developed into an autonomous genre which enjoyed as much popularity as that other unique New England literary creation, the captivity
narrative. Between 1639 and 1800 more than sixty execution sermons were
printed, and they continued to be widely read until the first quarter of the
nineteenth century, when public hangings were abolished in New England.

The approximately fifty authors of execution sermons ranked among the top intellectuals of New England and included religious eminences like Increase and Cotton Mather, Charles Chauncy, John Rogers, Andrew Eliot, and Nathan Strong.[99]

Moses Paul's execution on September 2, 1772, was a carefully orchestrated spectacle. Public executions of Indians per se were not that unusual in colonial New England — on the contrary, in Massachusetts, for instance, the cases involving Indians outnumbered those of whites.[100] But in this particular case, it was the first (and only) time that an Indian delivered the sermon at the execution of a fellow tribesman. The colonial authorities were well aware of the propagandist potential of this unique event: On the one hand, there was an ordained Christian Indian whose very presence and words would not only justify the execution but also serve as visible and audible proof for the success of their efforts to civilize Indians and, on the other, a fallen Indian to whom society had discharged its responsibilities by giving him the advantage of a Christian upbringing but who, in accordance with a widespread stereotype, still succumbed to the most ordinary of all Indian vices. Inebriety was commonly thought to be a main source of Indian violence, even though similar alcohol-induced criminal cases among whites received the most frequent treatment in execution sermons.[101]

The event drew the expected crowd, including Indians and African Americans, and Samson Occom's execution sermon turned out to be such a success that he was immediately pressed to have it published. After an appropriate delay for "modest" consideration, he finally gave in to public demand for reasons he explained afterward in the preface of the printed version, which, in his own words, was also "a little altered and enlarged in some places":

> It seems altogether unlikely that my performance will do any manner of service in the world, since the most excellent writings of worthy and learned men are disregarded. But there are two or three considerations that have induced me to be willing, to suffer my broken lines to appear in the world. One is, that the books that are in the world are written in very high and refined language; and the sermons that are delivered every sabbath in general, are in a very high and lofty stile, so that the common people understand but little of them. But I think they cannot help understanding my talk; it is common, plain, every day talk: little children may understand me. And poor Negroes may plainly and fully understand my meaning; and it may be of service to them. Again, it may in a particular manner be serviceable to my poor kindred, the Indians. Further, as it comes from an uncommon quarter, it

may induce people to read it, because it is from an Indian. Lastly, God works where and when he pleases, and by what instruments he sees fit, and he can and has used weak and unlikely instruments to bring about his great work.[102]

Despite all this overt demonstration of becoming Christian meekness and republican "plain talk" by an Indian who was about as erudite and well read as most other scholars of his age, Occom was quite correct in his estimation of possible public interest in such a piece coming "from an uncommon quarter."[103] The first edition of *A Sermon Preached at the Execution of Moses Paul* . . . was printed by the press of Thomas and Samuel Green at New Haven on October 31, 1772. Demand was so high that a second edition was printed in New London on November 13, followed by a third on December 4 and a fourth on January 22 of the following year. Love recorded at least nineteen editions printed in various towns in New England and in London, including a Welsh translation in 1789.[104] His sermon was also condensed into a sixteen-stanza broadside printed and sold in Boston and Newburyport in November 1772.[105]

At first glance Occom's execution sermon appears to be the replication of a current salvationist genre. Just how closely Occom patterned (and plagiarized in part) his version after previous execution sermons becomes clear if one compares it to Sylvanus Conant's *Blood of Abel, and the Blood of Jesus*, a sermon that was given in 1764 at the execution of a young African American for murder and printed the following year.

> Poor unhappy Bristol! The Day of your Death is now come, and you have but a very few Hours more to live. The Laws of the Land and the laws of God, call for the Destruction of your mortal Life; *Whoso sheddeth Man's Blood, by Man shall his Blood be shed.* This is the Decree of Heaven, and it is to be executed by Man, nor have you the least Ray of Hope that you shall escape; for the Sentence is past, not to be revok'd — the Day of Execution is come — the Guard is about you — the Instruments of Death are made ready — your Coffin and your Grave are open.[106]

> My poor unhappy brother Moses . . . the day of your death is now come; the king of terrors is at hand; you have but a very few moments to breathe in this world, — The just laws of man, and the holy laws of Jehovah, call aloud for the destruction of your mortal life; God says, "Whoso sheddeth man's blood, by man shall his blood be shed." This is the ancient decree of heaven, and it is to be executed by man; nor have you the least gleam of hope of escape, for the unalterable sentence is past; the terrible day of execution is come; the unwelcome guard is about you; and the fatal instruments of death are now made ready; your coffin and your grave, your last lodging, are open ready to receive you.

Like most execution sermons, Occom's is also composed of three parts: He first elaborates on the general nature of sin, then confronts the condemned man with his heinous crime, and finally addresses the general audience with the usual lengthy warnings about death, sin, the horrors of hell, and the possibility of salvation through belief in Jesus Christ, all reinforced by numerous biblical citations. The message to the condemned man is standard as well, reminding him of imminent death and the justice of his punishment, denouncing his horrible sin, adjuring him to repent, and promising him a place in heaven through the mediation of Christ. Even Occom's eloquent excursions on intemperance, the central theme of his sermon, closely echo Samuel Danforth's popular *Woful Effects of Drunkenness*, which was published decades earlier.[107] However artificial it may seem from a modern-day perspective, Occom's execution sermon, rated by a contemporary reader as "ingenious discourse," obviously found wide acclaim among late-eighteenth-century New England and British audiences as it outsold and outlasted all of its predecessors and successors.[108] It was a best seller of its day.

But there is more to Occom's execution sermon than its positive reception. Its essential message is contained in the unconventional section in which he directly addresses his "poor kindred" on the sin of intemperance. Once again he seems to be following the salvationist conventions of eighteenth-century execution sermons by placing the blame squarely on the shoulders of the condemned criminal—"it was the sin of drunkenness that has brought this destruction and untimely death upon him"—and then proceeding to use his impending death as a general warning, first and foremost, to all Indians in the audience. However, rather than focusing on the popular issue of intemperance and violence among Indians—Moses Paul had, after all, clubbed a respected white citizen to death—he goes on to illustrate how alcohol has been the main source of misery for his people:

> By this sin we can't have comfortable houses, nor anything comfortable in our houses; neither food nor raiment, nor decent utensils. We are obliged to put up any sort of shelter just to screen us from the severity of the weather; and we go about with very mean, ragged and dirty cloaths, almost naked. And we are half starved, for most of the time obliged to pick up any thing to eat.—And our poor children are suffering every day for want of the necessaries of life; they are very often crying for want of food, and we have nothing to give them; and in the cold weather they are shivering and crying, being pinched with cold—All this for the love of strong drink.

A drunkard, he goes on like Danforth before him, is an irrational being who, "if he has any money or any thing valuable, he may lose it all, or may be robb'd, or he may make a foolish bargain, and be cheated out of all he has." And then, inserted almost unobtrusively at the end of his lengthy discourse, comes the conclusion: "And here I cannot but observe, we find in sacred writ, a woe denounced against men, who put their bottles to their neighbors mouth to make them drunk, that they may see their nakedness; and no doubt there are such devilish men now in our days, as there were in the days of old." Although he clearly identifies the root of the problem here, he still refrains from merely shifting the responsibility for the effects of drunkenness from the individual concerned to colonial society. Moses Paul was not innocent in his eyes because he had "been brought up under the bright sun-shine, and plain, and loud sound of the gospel." Occom thus confronted him with the observation that "you have had a good education; you can read and write well; and God has given you a good natural understanding"; in other words, by acquiring knowledge he should have known better than to allow himself to be duped in this manner by the "devilish men now in our days." To the Indians in the audience he posed the following question immediately after establishing Moses Paul's guilt: "by this sin we have no name nor credit in the world among polite nations; for this sin we are despised in the world, and it is alright and just, *for we despise ourselves more; and if we don't regard ourselves, who will regard us?*" (italics mine). The tamed Christian "savage," who is thus overtly berating his renegade compatriot to appease New England Puritan self-righteousness, is also making a covert psychological appeal to his peers' self-esteem to resist one of colonialism's most effective agents. Overall, that section in Occom's sermon directed at the Indian (and African American) audience, which one might justifiably call the "hidden transcript" within the salvationist discourse, reflects his own belief in Christianity — and the educational process he directly associated with it — as a guiding force in the will to overcome the spiritual chaos inherent in the colonial encounter. He also makes the realistic (and very personal) connection here between social inequality among ethnic minorities and "this abominable, this beastly and accursed sin of drunkenness."[109]

Other than being the most widely read example of a typical early New England literary tradition, Occom's sermon is also the earliest concrete example of the confluence of Indian oral tradition and European literacy. "Indian monologues" have fascinated the Euro-American public since at least the second half of the seventeenth century, and this phenomenon obviously coincides with the fact that most of the early Indian authors were also successful public speakers. Written versions of public addresses thus make up a substantial portion of American Indian literary production well up until the 1920s.[110]

The success of his sermon enabled Occom to publish his *Collection of Hymns and Spiritual Songs* in 1774, which was never quite as popular but nevertheless went through at least two additional editions in 1785 and 1792.[111] Just how many of the 108 numbered hymns in the collection were his creation is impossible to ascertain. Love maintains that a considerable number of them are not found in earlier books or remain unassigned by hymnologists, concluding therefore that Occom was the author of such. Blodgett also believes that Occom probably did compose several of them on the basis of three handwritten hymns found in Dartmouth's Baker Library Special Collections, which "have the *naiveté*, the earnest simplicity, which is characteristic of his utterances." The greater part by far are by Watts, Wesley, Madan, and other noted hymnists and were thus collected from contemporary hymnbooks, several of which he had brought back from England.[112] Certain hymns that have generally been attributed to him, such as the two somewhat different versions of the same hymn titled "Awaked by Sinai's Awful Sound" or "Waked by the Gospel's Powerful Sound," which were not included in the original collection, became quite popular shortly after his death and have survived in present-day hymnals.[113] More important than the question of authorship, however, is Occom's avid interest in psalmody, which he shared with most Christian Indians since the days of Eliot and the Mayhews, and his successful incorporation of this Western tradition for Indian domestic purposes. Communal singing of spiritual melodies, especially the Anglo-American style of hymnody founded by Isaac Watts (1674–1748), continues to be a popular social activity among Indians today and may well be one of the most effective and permanent vehicles of cross-cultural communication ever applied by Christian missionaries throughout the world. In marked contrast to Blodgett's somewhat condescending evaluation of Occom's skills in hymnody, oral tradition among the Shinnecock Indians of Long Island, as recorded by one of their number in 1950, recalls his Gospel songs with unencumbered enthusiasm: "The words were so beautiful and the melodies so touching the Indians claimed they heard them in the skies."[114] It could be, then, that Occom's Christian hymnals exuded an authentic voice to Indian listeners, one that went beyond (or perhaps inside) the usual literary meaning associated with the term.

On April 2, 1786, Occom, who had observed earlier that Montauk shamans "get their art from dreams . . . or night visions," had a dream (or vision) that was apparently significant enough for him to record it in his journal with unusual attention to detail:

> Last Night I had a remarkable dream about Mr. Whitefield, I thought he was preaching as he use to, when he was alive, I thought he was at a certain place where there was a great Number of Indians and Some White People, — and I had been Preaching, and he came to me, and took hold of my wright Hand and put his face to my face, and rub'd his face to mine and Said, I'm glad, that you preach the Excellency of Jesus Christ yet, and Said, go on and the Lord be with thee, we Shall now Soon done, and then he Stretched himself upon the ground flat on his face and reach'd his hands forward, and made a mark with his Hand, and Said I will out doe and over reach all Sinners, and I thought he Barked like a Dog, with a Thundering Voice, — and I thought Some People Laugh'd Some were pleased, and Some were frightened, and after that he got up, Said to me I am going to Mr. Potters to preach, and Said will you go, and I Said Yes Sir and as we were about to Set out I awoke, and behold it was a Dream — and this Dream has put me much upon thinking of the End of my Journey.[115]

In this remarkable dream the late Whitefield, foremost voice of the Great Awakening, appears to him much in the manner of a powerful Indian spirit and, contrary to all the Clellands, Jewetts, Sargeants, and Wheelocks of his stony missionary career, assures him of the righteousness of the path he has chosen to follow just before he is transformed into a barking dog. According to Frank Speck, the Mohegans considered dreams to be messages from ancestors who are in the spirit world, which gives some indication of Occom's close spiritual ties to the New Light revivalist.[116] It is tempting, of course, to speculate on the possible symbolism of the physical transformation. The practice of sacrificing a dog after an ominous dream, for instance, was fairly common among Coastal Algonquians; and Daniel Brinton has established parallelisms between the Greek Cerberus, the three-headed dog who guards the passage over the river Styx, and similar canine spirits in Indian lore who challenge souls on their way to the other world.[117] Occom's careful description of his dream is thus very reminiscent of what Brumble refers to as traditional "power-quest narratives" which, in contrast to the more succinct "coup tales," were accounts of visions or dreams that needed to be told in great detail so that they might be interpreted properly by those qualified to do so and subsequently evaluated by them and the community as potential sources of spiritual power.[118] On the other hand, he may simply be making a straightforward association with revivalist "exercises," or neuromuscular seizures that sometimes befell converts during public worship (including the act of barking like a dog), which came to be an increasingly common expression of religious exaltation at the turn of the century.[119] Occom's dream, in which Christian and Algonquian spirituality are obviously fused together, could thus be interpreted as a form of visionary power legitimizing his own choice to initiate a religious revival among his people.

The accomplishments of a transcultural individual can be measured in part by an assessment of his/her reputation among the societies in which he/she functioned. Occom has had a pond, a bridge, an inn, and even a World War II Liberator vessel named in his honor. The Samson Occom Pooled Income Fund, which generated an additional half-million dollars in tax-deductible donations from Dartmouth's alumni in 1980–82, proves that his name is still good for credit. It is this kind of posthumous "fame" that must have prompted a Dartmouth scholar to refer to him ironically as "Big Chief Samson Quantum Wampum Occom."[120] Occom's legacy among the eastern Indian communities that were affected by his life's work, however, forces us to see the role of a Christian Indian in a somewhat more differentiated perspective.

Despite his many difficulties, there is no evidence that Occom ever wavered one iota from his chosen destiny. His moments of crisis, and there were not a few, thus had little to do with problems of identity, ethnic or otherwise. Instead, they were strictly of a socioeconomic nature, resulting primarily from the racial discrimination he encountered in his chosen professional field and straightforward poverty. In terms of psychology, they had more to do with a damaged self-esteem as a result of social oppression than with any culturally related personality conflicts. He never ceased to be an active member of the Indian community he had been born into, and he maintained both his native language and traditional kinship ties. At the same time, he voluntarily adopted new religious impulses from the Great Awakening and earnestly believed in the evangelical Calvinist reading of original sin and the terrible prospect of eternal damnation, which he ardently preached to his Indian and white convocations. But he also regarded Christianity as a substitution for the spiritual void resulting from the post-contact disruption of traditional Indian ways of life and sought to instrumentalize it as a means of cementing together scattered remnants of conquered New England tribes, who faced immediate biological and cultural extinction, into new and viable communities. In this process, he made effective use of English as the lingua franca for the distinct Indian speech communities involved in his experiment who, according to his own obser-

vations, at times represented as many as "ten different Languages."[121] Protestantism and European life styles, to which the Mohegans and other New
England Indian groups had been adapting long before Occom was born,
did not automatically displace deeply rooted social patterns, even though
dramatic changes were inevitable due to the repressive constellation of the
contact environment.

What, then, became of Occom's vision of a New England Christian
Indian "Body Politick"? As with the Gay Head Indians, conversion was also
a tactic for survival and, in this sense at least, history never proved Occom
wrong, for the Indians among whom he exerted his influence — Mohegans,
Montauks, Niantics, Tunxis, Shinnecocks, Mahicans, Pequots, Narragansetts, Oneidas, and others — did in fact survive, even though dominant society has since proclaimed them "invisible." The nature of his relations with
the Long Island Indian communities, for instance, was such that the memory of his sojourn there has been fondly preserved until the present day.
Both Montauks and Shinnecocks regard him as one of their great ancestors.
The Montauk Historical Society even made a proposal in 1969 for the declaration of a Samson Occom Day, which was celebrated during the summer
of the following year. On this occasion Peter Silva, Jr., son of the Shinnecock sachem, delivered a speech honoring the Mohegan missionary with
the following words: "[Occom] gave his fellow Indians hope, thought of
tomorrow, pride, and respect for the individual; he laid the foundation for
the coming together of minds."[122] Another testimonial to Occom's historical significance is the reference made by the Mohegans in the course of their
first petition for federal recognition in 1978 to his form of leadership (defined by their tribal historian as a "sociocultural authority" that need not
necessarily be embodied in an official sachemship and can arise during
periods of severe cultural conflict) as proof of the continuity of the tribal
political framework. That the approximately one thousand enrolled Mohegans of Uncasville, whose cultural identity has been tied to a Protestant
church erected in 1831, finally did achieve federal recognition on March 7,
1994, is due at least in part to Occom's life work.[123] Perhaps the greatest
tribute to Occom's efforts is the fact that the New England Christian Indian
community he founded in New York is currently seeking federal recognition as the Brothertown Indian Nation of Wisconsin.[124]

In retrospect, it can be said that Samson Occom is at least as significant
historically as Eleazar Wheelock's most famous pupil, the Mohawk Joseph
Brant (ca. 1742–1807). Brant adopted a similar policy of voluntary removal, leading his people to Ontario after the American Revolution in order

to establish an independent Indian township there, but—in contrast to Occom—he had the great advantage of having been born into a prestigious position within a powerful and still fairly autonomous Indian nation. In the realm of American Indian literature, however, Occom plays a much more important role than the equally literate Brant, who has been the subject of many English publications but the author of none.[125] To assess properly Occom's place in the history of American Indian literature—especially when the question of reception is raised—one must bear in mind his dual role as missionary and author and, in addition, make correlations among those of his writings that were published during his lifetime, those that appeared posthumously, and those that never made it into print. There can be little doubt that many of Occom's unpublished sermons were directed to members of ethnic minorities and the lower classes. "To all the Indians in this Boundless Continent," he begins in one of his undated manuscripts, "I am an Indian also, Your Brother and You are my Brethren the Bone of my Bone and Flesh of my Flesh."[126] Like many of his white counterparts in the Protestant revival, he did not refrain from expressing overt criticism on highly volatile contemporary social issues such as abolitionism. "If I understand the Gospel aright," he wrote concerning certain ministers who held slaves (i.e., Wheelock), "I think it is a Dispensation of Freedom and Liberty, both Temporal and Spiritual, and (if) the Preachers of the Holy Gospel of Jesus do preach it according to the mind of God, they preach True Liberty and how can such keep Negroes in slavery? And if ministers are True Liberty men, let them preach Liberty for the poor Negroes fervently and with great zeal, and those ministers who have Negroes set an example before their People by freeing their Negroes, let them show their faith by their Works." In another of his unpublished sermons he is even more vehement in his opposition to slavery: "[T]here is one Sort of open murther is now carried on allowedly by those who are calld Christian People and here some may (querry) again and Say, What is that, Why it is encouraging and carrying on Negro Slave Trade, this is a Murdorous Trade, it is the Worst Complicated Wickedness to Carry on this Trade, it is the most accused and most Devilish Practice that ever was found among the Children of men."[127] His abolitionist sentiments apparently influenced the famous African American poet, Phyllis Wheatley, with whom he maintained sporadic contact and whose oft-cited letter revealing her own critical views on the issue was originally addressed to him.[128] Occom's authentic voice thus breaks through much more frequently in his unpublished manuscripts, or "undisguised transcripts," and it is here, too, that his literary talents become most apparent. This is particularly evident in his autobiographical sketch, one of his most expressive pieces, and in a few of the letters that have been cited above.[129] Eighteenth-century New England was obviously not quite ready yet for this kind of writing coming from "an uncommon quarter."

Mastering the dominant voice, which Occom did, also enabled him to defend himself against colonial repression. His petitions to George III and the New York Assembly prove the point. An entry in his journal dated February 8, 1786, provides an additional, rather curious, illustration: "[A]n officer came to my House and attachd my oxen for a Small Debt I owed, and Thursday I went down to N London to see whether the Law, in the New Revised Law Book was yet in favour of the Indians, and I found it Strong in favour of us, — and I sent a line to one of the Men, and the next he came and Promisd to withdraw his action, and they did withdraw."[130]

Occom is more than just a statistical starting point in the history of American Indian literature, and not only because his writings display an unusual degree of versatility for an eighteenth-century salvationist author, including sermons, autobiographies, professional journals, tribal ethnography, and hymnody. Placed in its proper ethnohistorical context, his literary legacy enables us to take our first inside look at a representative of the Christian Indian proto-elite who chose creative adaptation as their tactic of survival in the colonial situation, and it thereby provides us with an important alternative perspective to the life histories of military leaders like Pontiac, Tecumseh, Black Hawk, and others whom we seemingly prefer to read about. The predicate "father" is thus applicable to the "Pious Mohegan" in more ways than one.

Two minor Indian writers of the eighteenth century deserve to be mentioned here as well, if only because their intellectual development was molded to some extent by Occom: his son-in-law and fellow tribesman, Joseph Johnson (ca. 1750–76); and his friend, the Mahican sachem Hendrick Aupaumut (1757–1830). Both had very similar educational backgrounds and were equally instrumental in founding the two Christian Indian communities of New York.

Joseph Johnson was the nephew of Zachary Johnson, the councilor and later regent of the Mohegans who tried to outlaw Occom in 1774.[131] His father, also named Joseph Johnson, apparently died while serving the British as a captain of Indian scouts during the French and Indian War. The younger Johnson was enrolled at Wheelock's Charity School on December 7, 1758, where he studied for about seven years. He must have been an extraordinary scholar because in 1766, when he was only fifteen, Wheelock sent him and David Fowler to New York to serve as schoolmasters to the Oneidas. In contrast to Occom, Johnson suffered from inner turmoil concerning his own role as a missionary, and this is in turn reflected in his morose, and frequently verbose, writings. After this highly promising start as a scholar and teacher, he suddenly fell into disgrace at Oneida when he joined a bacchanalian spree during the spring of 1768, in the course of which he supposedly drank nearly three gallons of wine and six to seven gallons of rum, according to Samuel Kirkland's report to Wheelock. "It seems," the indignant missionary concluded, "he is fond of Changes — weary w^h ye form of y^t old fashiond Thing calld puritanic Relig^n he turn'd pagan for about a week — painted, sung — danc'd — drank & whor'd it, w^h some of ye savage Indians he cou'd find — his name stinks from Kanajohare to Fort Stanwix — even every rode smells strong of his pride falsehood & diabolical Conduct."[132]

Johnson's teenage "crisis" had apparently been germinating for some time before this outbreak, however, for he had tried to convey his distress to Wheelock in several letters. In one of these, written exactly one year earlier than Kirkland's report, he already gave some indication of what was troubling him: "I would once more ask the Continuance of your prayers, that God keep me from pride, from Ingratitude, from dishonouring his great Name — from all the Temptations of the Divil, and from all the Temptations of my fellow Youth. That he would keep me from the Lusts of the Eye, and the Lusts of the flesh, and in short from Everything that is Displeasing to him."[133] But "Temptations of the Divil" were not the only causes for his shaken faith, as he also complained bitterly to Wheelock about the hardship of having to live among a strange and impoverished people without adequate financial support from the missionary society.[134] In addition, both he and David Fowler were experiencing difficulties with Samuel Kirkland, who demonstrated little sensitivity as he set about establishing his authority over them immediately after his arrival in 1768. Although their relationship mended in later life, Fowler's altercations with Kirkland over matters of competence ultimately led the frustrated Montauk convert to abandon his post in 1767. Thus it may well be that Johnson's fall from grace somewhat later was also a reaction to the racist patronizing that had already enervated Occom.[135] Denigrating himself repeatedly as an "Ignorant Pupil, and good for nothing Black Indian," Johnson tried in several subsequent letters to make up for his rash behavior, but Wheelock evidently did not have the time or inclination to answer him. Finally, after advising his stern mentor to "forgive what I have done and bury me in deep forgetfullness and Remember me no more," he made his way to Rhode Island where, like so many other displaced New England Indians, he decided to try his luck as a whaler.[136]

Unfortunately, nothing is known of Johnson's whereabouts and activities in the years between 1769 and 1771, when he made his way back to Mohegan, other than a few tantalizing scraps of information contained in a short and undated autobiographical sketch titled "Joseph Johnson to Inquiring Friends," which is attached to what appears to be a letter of solicitation. It reads:

> Would you know kind Sir, who the composer of this Discourse is. Be pleased to read following. I am an Indian of the Mohegan Tribe, known by the Name of Joseph Johnson. Educated by the Revd Eleazar Wheelock D.D. whose school I left when I was 14 years of age, and in the 3rd month of my 15th year, I was sent amongst the Six nations and I spent about 2 years in those Parts, keeping School. afterward, I left the school intirely Revd Eleazar Wheelock D.D. intirely. and from that time, I been wandering up, and down, in this Delusive World. Some of my time I Spent at Providence Town. keeping a School. Some of my time, I have spent on the Ocean wide. I have been down Eastward, as far as the Western Islands, twice Curvo, & florus, I have Seen . . . and to the Southward I have been as far, to the West Indies. Seen also the Islands between Antigua and Granades. and again from antigua I have Sailed down leward Sailed by the Virgin Islands, also by Sandy cruize, Portireco. down as far is to mona, and after So long time Even in my 21st year I Safely arrived to my Native place. their I Spent one year in working upon my farm.[137]

After returning to Rhode Island from his whaling odyssey on October 9, 1771, Johnson began to maintain a fairly detailed record of his experiences until March 7, 1772. In contrast to Occom's more cursory journals, his ninety-six-page account is a soul-searching spiritual diary describing his own gradual redemption in the most vivid detail.[138] After he landed at Providence he wandered about aimlessly for twenty days before finally finding his way back to his uncle's farm at Mohegan, suffering from what appears to have been some kind of venereal ailment contracted during an amorous encounter at Newport. "I long to be in health it seems to me to be a continual Imprisonment while I remain in this Case," he noted in his diary, "and now I may Reflect back upon my Folly and Repent it at my leisure. how Easy it is to buy harm Cheap. for the Sake of one minuits pleasure to lose so much precious time and undergo So much hardship. but who can help it — they that Dance must pay the fidler." While recovering at his uncle's farm, Johnson was gradually reintegrated into Mohegan communal affairs by his relatives, who had him partake in the daily work cycle as much as his health would permit and brought him along to religious meetings led by Samson Occom, who had initiated a spiritual revival among the Mohegans upon his return from England in 1769. He also spent much of his time reading the New Testament and Richard Baxter's *Saints' Everlasting Rest*, both of which inspired him to reflect upon his own recent fall and to write lengthy excursions on the nature of sin and endless supplications to God for a redemptive sign.[139] Then, on December 26, 1771, he recorded an apocalyptic dream that seems to have been a turning point in the process of his spiritual regeneration:

> Dreamt a Strange dream the night past, and I Suppose that I have in Small measure felt the terror, and Supprise which will seize on those upon whom the Lord Jesus will come Unawares, for I dreamt that the Earth was on fire, and the moon and the Stars were dropping from the heavens. and what was my greatest astonishment I was unprepared, and had never knew the Savior, but I stood a while Seeing many People crying or Praying I took Encouragement also and I began to Pray, looking, and Expecting Each moment to See Christ and all of the host of heaven Coming to Judgment, and amidst of the fire I did yet hope to be Saved and heard tho I trembled not knowing what my Sentance will Soon be, I thought alas is time now to be at an End with me, then time Seemed Precious indeed, and in this destraction of mind I awoke, and am yet a Probationer blessed be god who is Such a Merciful god.

The dream obviously heightened his state of anxiety about being caught "unprepared" before the certainty of death and uncertainty of life thereafter, as this eventually became the dominant theme of his exhortations. Following "a very powerful meeting" on March 1, 1772, Johnson expressed his resolution to keep away from "vain and unprofitable Company" and "from being intoxicated with strong drink." Shortly thereafter, on May 24, he evidently experienced his second conversion: "[A]fter a long time under the workings of gods holy spirit I humbly trust — I this day have concluded that by the help of god I'll endeavour to dedicate my Self to him."[140] He obviously wasted no time in redeeming himself in the eyes of his former employers because that same year he managed to obtain a commission from the Boston Commissioners to teach a group of Indians at Farmington. In December of the following year he married Occom's daughter Tabitha, who bore him a son. Finally, on August 25, 1774, the reborn Christian Mohegan was licensed as a minister at Dartmouth College.[141] He also resumed his regular correspondence with Wheelock in that eventful year, which is a certain indication that they had mended their relationship at some point after his recovery. "*I was 21 years in this World, before I was born,*" he summarizes in another brief autobiographical sketch, "and as Soon as I was born, & I had my Eyes Opened, I Saw the World, as it were full of Secure Souls. and I could not forbear, but I lifted up my infant voice directly, and Called upon my fellow mortals. disclosed unto them their great danger. and Endeavoured to direct them to him, who alone was able to join them." [142]

Joseph Johnson began to concentrate his efforts on the voluntary removal of New England's Christian Indians to Oneida territory — his "Great Undertaking," as he liked to refer to it — almost immediately after his redemption and, being much younger than Occom, he soon turned out to be the driving force behind its realization. His urgency to get the project started is evident in a public message titled "To the Indians Concerning Oneida Lands — To All, Who are truely Engaged in the Mohawk Affair," dated December 24, 1773:

> Our dear brethren, seeing that the time is nigh at hand. that those chosen men. or others in this room. should go forth. into the Western Country. according to the appointment of his Honour S.ʳ William Johnson. Baronet. and the desire of the Oneida Indians. We say that the time is almost Come. Seeing then it is so nigh. we thought proper. to send to you our dear Brethren this once more. humbly, and earnestly desiring that ye would consider of things. and by all means Let one out of each Town. or Tribe go up to the Mohawk Country. what can we say more. we have used all proper means yea we have been much concerned concerning you our dear Brethren. and we are Sorry. to See. So much Coldness. Lukewarmness. and indifferency. amongst you. as ye have discovered. since last march. 1773. what shall we think of you. if ye do not send one out of Each Town. or Tribe. Yea. what will General Johnson think of you, and what will the Indians under his Special Inspection think of you, who hath, by the Great Influence of his Honor Sir William given us great. and unexpected Encouragement. We pray you to consider of things Seriously.[143]

In the years between 1773 and the outbreak of the Revolution, he traveled repeatedly between Connecticut and New York in order to treat with the Oneidas for an appropriate tract of land, initiated several fund-raising ventures, and wrote numerous letters of solicitation to prominent citizens and colonial administrative bodies requesting their aid for the "grand Design" of teaching the western Indians "by our example the ways of industry, in the ways of husbandry, in the ways of civility, and above all in the ways of godliness."[144] That his second life as missionary was as beset with privation as the first in spite of his rekindled spiritual zeal is made evident in a letter he wrote to Occom in 1774. "I am most discouraged sometimes," he laments; "I am but young and I am but poor. I am an Indian. If I was the son of some Rich English man perhaps I should be able better to travel the country up and down at my charges — O that Indians were men."[145]

The Christian Indians from the seven tribes elected Johnson as their principal speaker for the Brothertown project. One of the speeches he delivered during his second meeting with Oneida representatives in January 1774 has been preserved along with the answers provided by the hosting party.[146] Taken together, these speeches are unique autoethnographic examples of a relatively popular contemporary genre that has been referred to as "treaty literature." There was a marked public interest in Indian treaties beginning in the second half of the eighteenth century, when many were published throughout the colonies and circulated as far as England, including thirteen printed by Benjamin Franklin between 1736 and 1762.[147] Johnson's Oneida speech distinguishes itself from most other transcriptions of Indian council oratory as it was originally written and delivered in the English language, which had served as the lingua franca in the dealings between the representatives of Algonquian and Iroquoian speech communities. Besides its political content — it includes a caustic denunciation of the English treatment of New England Indians — it is particularly interesting because of the kind of language he uses, which differs markedly from the style of his salvationist prose. Here he has purposely retained the ceremonial decorum and institutionalized verbal style of traditional council oratory. A segment of his speech illustrates the point:

> Our dear and well beloved Brethren it is with much pleasure that we see so many of you assembled together at this time and upon this Occasion, we give you our great respects and sincere love, we look upon you at present as upon an elder Brother as a Nation, and beloved Brethren, we pray you to consider of us and harken to us, as to a younger Brother, not only consider of us as two Persons, but view us to be speaking, or acting for all our Brethren in New England, or at least for seven Towns. We pray you to consider seriously of our Words, ye old men who are wise, also ye warriors, and stout hearted young men listen unto us, yea let Children harken, that what we say may not soon be forgotten.

Johnson thus establishes the proper genealogical-political relation between the Christian Indian petitioners and the Oneida hosts as that of younger to elder brothers, and then respectfully addresses the Oneida representatives by the correct order of rank before proceeding with his critical summary of past English-Indian relations in New England:

> Brethren in the first place we will acquaint you of the State and Circumstances of our New England Brethren, and also we will inform you of our proceedings hitherto. Brethren we in New England, or at least many of us are very poor, by reason of the Ignorance of our forefathers who are now dead. Brethren ye

know that the English are a very wise people, and can see great ways. but some says, that the Indians can see but very little ways. Brethren, ye also know that some of the English loves to take the advantage of poor, Ignorant, and blind Indians. Well so it was in the days of our forefathers in New England. but not to expose the unjust acts of our English Brethren I shall not say much more about them, least I cast a prejudice in your Hearts against the English Brethren, notwithstanding there are so many wicked, or unjust men, among the English, yet there are great many good, and Just men, among the English, who loves poor Indians, from the bottom of their hearts, and wishes us all, a well being in this World, and in the World to come Lifeeverlasting, but all I have to say about the English at present is this Whilst our forefathers were blind, and ignorant yea drowned in Spirituous Liquors; the English stripped them, yea they as it were cut off their Right hands; — and now we their Children just opening our Eyes, and having knowledge grafted, and growing in our hearts, and just reviving, or coming to our Senses, like one that has been drunk — I say that now we begin to look around, and Consider and we perceive that we are stripped indeed, having nothing to help ourselves, and thus our English Brethren leaves us and laugh. So now Brethren, we leave the English those who have acted unjustly towards us in New England, I say we leave them all in the hands of that God who knoweth all things, and will reward every one according to their deeds whether good or Evil.

After he has pointed out the causes for the intended migration, Johnson goes on to review all of the steps taken so far by the Christian Indians toward this end, not forgetting, of course, to remind them diplomatically that even Sir William Johnson, whose influence among the Oneidas was great, had favored the project. His address ends appropriately with an expression of gratitude for the Oneidas' generosity and the dramatic presentation of a reciprocal gift, a silver pipe "as a Sure token from our Several Tribes in New England that we are one and sincere in what we say and do."

The Revolution temporarily interrupted the migration shortly after Johnson, Fowler, and Elijah Wampy of Farmington had led the first group of immigrants to Oneida in March 1775. Johnson's views of the impending conflict, which he expressed in a letter to Sir William Johnson in 1774 imploring him to use his influence to keep Indians neutral, were identical to Occom's. "I feel Sorrow in this once Savage heart of mine," he noted, "when I Behold in my mind, not only a civilized, but a Christianized People Bleeding. — it would grieve me much to See the Christian People bleeding, before the Savage Nations of North America, or before the vain conceited French. — but think it grieves me much more, when I see a Brother taking up arms against a Brother. — and a Brother bleeding to death before a Brother. — is this the fruits of Christianity, what will the heathen Nations Say. O Britain!

O North America! can the heathen Say, Behold and See how those Christians love one another."[148]

During the early stages of the war, when the first group of emigrants was forced to leave its new settlement in Oneida by the advance of British troops, Johnson acted as the Americans' emissary of peace to the Six Nations. Just how much importance was attached to his role as mediator between the Iroquois and the new republic, whose future as a nation also depended upon the stance taken by the Six Nations and other Indian tribes beyond the frontier, is clearly discernible from the official papers and letters presented to him by the Provincial Congress of New York on June 22, 1775, and the New Hampshire House of Representatives on January 16, 1776. George Washington, with whom he had conferred personally before embarking upon his delicate mission, wrote him a letter of recommendation on February 20, 1776. "Their attention to you," Washington wrote, "will be a proof to us that they wish the same [friendship], we recommend you to them, and hope by your Spreading the truths of the Holy Gospel amongst them, it will Contribute to keep the Chain so bright, that, the malicious insinuations, or practices of our Enemies will never be able to break this Union, so much for the benefit of our Brothers of the Six Nations and of us."[149] The message of peace transmitted by Johnson and other northeastern Christian Indians acting as couriers was probably a decisive factor in the Oneidas' and Tuscaroras' final decision to remain neutral in spite of Tory anti-American propaganda and British political pressure which, after all, was massive enough to convince other Iroquois leaders like Joseph Brant to take sides against the revolutionaries.

Perhaps Johnson had something like a premonition in his previously cited dream when he felt that "time Seemed Precious indeed," for he died only five years after his reformation, at the tender age of twenty-six. The exact date and cause of his death remain unknown. During his short life Johnson had at least two "salvationist" pieces published, one of which, a letter of exhortation addressed to the imprisoned Moses Paul, has been preserved.[150] This piece, titled "Letter from *J——h J——n*, one of the Mohegan Tribe of Indians, to his Countryman, *Moses Paul*, under Sentence of Death, in New-Haven Gaol," was printed in New London, probably shortly after Samson Occom's popular sermon appeared. However, it is dated March 29, 1772, which means that Johnson must have been in contact with Moses Paul before the latter requested (on July 16, 1772) Occom to officiate at his execution. "My Spirit mourned within me," he wrote to the unfortunate Mohegan, "when I heard that you was unconcerned about your Soul's eternal welfare." He may thus have been the one who actually convinced Moses Paul to make a public show of repentance. Johnson's "letter," which was written before he was licensed to preach, is really an execution sermon. It also begins by justifying the death sentence itself, before proceeding to map out the terrible prospects of eternal damnation to the condemned man with all the expected biblical fanfare. "I mean to be sincere," he declares with the same (mock?) modesty that characterizes Occom's prelude, "But I am uncapable of expressing myself, or writing as some may who have been favoured with great learning, and have had great experiences, and those who know (the) arts and sciences, neither can I speak as those who are acquainted with the deep mysteries of the kingdom of God." And then follow cascades of salvationist verbosity. Similarly, he does not fail to take at least one covert stab at English society: "And be assured, if you fall short of heaven, into hell you must be turned: and I doubt not, but this is the earnest prayer and desire of many, who have a prejudice against the Indian nations, and with no better of your soul, than to endure God's eternal wrath, and even rejoice that one of the devilish Indians, (as many express themselves) are suffered to act such a part; and with that all were as nigh their end."

The unpublished material Johnson left behind also includes a number of handwritten sermons, or "discourses" as he preferred to call them, which do not diverge from the typical fare of Edwardsian exhortations with all their horrific illustrations of hell geared to arouse emotional outbursts of repentance among the audience. "My friends," he warned a mixed congregation at Farmington in 1773, "if prejudice is in the heart of any I beseech you to cast it out, and lay aside all manner of prejudice, for it will profit you nothing in this, nor in the world to come." In this twenty-four-page millennialist excursion on the Second Coming of Christ, the joy of those who are "prepared" is vividly contrasted to the terrors awaiting those who are not. Another sermon, which was addressed to his "Indian Brethren" at Oneida in 1774, contains an introductory passage asking forgiveness for his own failings six years before and expressing the hope that it would serve them as a deterrent for the future. Even though the audience here is probably all Indian, he still adheres to evangelist fire-and-brimstone language, with the possible exception that, rather than padding his argument with standard citations, he frequently turns to biblical stories in order to illustrate his point—perhaps as a small tribute to oral traditions.[151]

Joseph Johnson's manuscripts show him to be one of the most talented writers to emerge from Wheelock's Charity School, and perhaps also the most spontaneous, as they reveal a great deal more about his personal sentiments than those of his more illustrious but less communicative father-in-law. Eighteenth-century American Indian literature — and history for that matter — undoubtedly lost much on account of his premature death.

Hendrick Aupaumut (Arepaument, Umpoumut), a Hudson River Mahican, was born and raised in Stockbridge, John Sargeant's Christian Indian settlement in Massachusetts.[152] The Mahicans, who spoke a Munsee dialect and should not be confused with the Mohegans of Connecticut, had had close relations with Europeans for over a century and had been relatively successful in accommodating to the colonial situation. When the Dutch arrived in 1613, the Mahicans were still a powerful group residing in the area extending from Lake Champlain southward to the northeastern part of New York and eastward to south-central Vermont.[153] Under a treaty concluded with the Dutch in 1614, they agreed to the establishment of a trading post on Castle Island in close proximity to a Mahican village, which enabled them to monopolize the regional Indian fur trade. The resulting economic advantages in turn allowed them to become the dominant group in a loose confederation of tribes and also led to a vacillating, often bellicose relationship with the competing Mohawks, which finally ended in a permanent peace agreement between them in 1675. By 1700 Mahican society was already suffering from the negative side effects of its dependency on Europeans, especially after the British took over the territory in 1644 and various village communities were forced to disperse westward in order to make room for the steadily advancing settlers.

John Sargeant established the Christian Indian village of Stockbridge on the Housatonic River in 1735, an area where several Mahican families had already taken refuge among the Housatonics, and soon these and other linguistically related Indian groups of the region (Wappinger, Esopus) began to settle in or near the new community and to conform to European ways. The Mahicans' language and traditions, however, continued to dominate the heterogeneous Stockbridge community for some time. John Sargeant managed to convert the principal families with relative ease and then set about establishing a school and a New England–style town council. At the time Aupaumut was growing up, Stockbridge had already developed into a relatively prosperous Praying Indian community. But the subsequent participation of its men in the French and Indian War, Pontiac's rebellion, and the American Revolution quickly reduced its population to the extent that non-Indians were able to move into the community, entice many of the remaining residents to sell their lands, and finally displace them from the town government altogether.[154] Their long-standing loyalty to the English and Americans proved to be no deterrent to expansionism — nor did it prevent the massacre of ninety Moravian Mahicans in Gnadenhütten, Ohio, by the militia in 1782 — so that most of the Stockbridge Mahicans now saw themselves forced to immigrate to Oneida lands in New York in 1783. As mentioned previously, they then established the Christian Indian community of New Stockbridge in the neighborhood of Brothertown, where they prospered once again.

Aupaumut was born into a leading Hudson River Mahican family and is thought to have been the grandson of the renowned adopted Mohawk sachem "King" Hendrick (ca. 1680–1755), who had moved to Stockbridge around 1750.[155] He attended Sargeant's school for an unknown number of years during which he became literate in both English and Mahican.[156] In the summer of 1775, he enlisted in the revolutionary army along with numerous other Indians from Stockbridge and was promoted to the captaincy of his company in 1778 by George Washington. He is, therefore, frequently referred to as "Captain Hendrick" in historical documents. One year earlier he had also assumed the hereditary position of a Hudson River Mahican sachem at a very critical phase in the Stockbridge community's history.

After the Revolution Aupaumut played a significant diplomatic role — very much like Joseph Johnson and other Christian Indians had at the outset of the conflict — in the U.S. government's endeavors to pacify the remaining "hostile" tribes of the Ohio Valley. In 1791 he acted as the U.S. emissary of peace at a council of the Six Nations at Newton, New York, but his presence there was evidently of little consequence since various tribes continued to fight against the Americans, a situation that culminated in the defeat of Anthony St. Clair by Indian forces in November of that year. Peace negotiations were resumed the following spring, and Aupaumut once again attended meetings with several leaders of different Ohio Valley Indian tribes in 1792–93, trying to convince them to cease hostilities. Continuing trans-Appalachian incursions by the colonists, however, disrupted the negotiations, and frontier warfare persisted until the Indians of the Ohio Valley were decisively defeated by General Anthony Wayne at the Battle of Fallen Timbers in 1794, and the Americans consequently took possession of the greater portion of their territory in Ohio and Indiana after the conclusion of the Treaty of Greenville in 1795.[157]

Hendrick Aupaumut wrote a fairly detailed account of his activities as a peace emissary in 1792–93, which was published posthumously in 1827.[158] This unique historical document is, together with Johnson's Oneida speech, another rare example of eighteenth-century Indian "treaty literature." Aupaumut's grounds for writing this personal account were certain negative rumors ("I understand that my Character is darkened by envious Indians") concerning his supposed failures as an emissary, which had been spread by some Iroquois delegates and possibly had come to the attention of Henry Knox.[159] He begins his narrative with a prefatory outline of traditional northeastern Indian intertribal relations, which serves as a useful guide for the proper understanding of the subsequent diplomatic conventions and treaty dialogues he records, on the one hand, and legitimizes his own role as peace emissary on the basis of the respectful position accorded to Mahican sachems and counselors in past intertribal councils on the other. At the same time, it is indicative of the persistence and geographical extent of the socio-kinship network into which the New England Indians were integrated. The narrative contains several speeches by Aupaumut proffering peaceful relations with the U.S. government as instructed, followed by the responses from representatives of various northeastern tribes. Even though he also recorded them in English, the speeches retain a certain distinctiveness in style and content which results primarily from the frequent infusion of native syntax in the text. In one of his speeches to the Delawares, for example, Aupaumut displays his diplomatic finesse as he attempts, in accordance with traditional decorum, to smooth over past grievances prior to delivering the essential message. In this particular case he officially commiserates with the Delaware representative on the previous death of a brother, who had been recently killed by Iroquois warriors, and in so doing he demonstrates the necessary courtesy for the latter (whose grief would otherwise not permit him to answer publicly) to break his silence:

> Grandfather—
>   You have meet great losses; your great Sachem is fallen, and also some of your principal young men. The sound of which stopd your eyes and ears; your tears flowing down, and that continually; and for which reason you could not look up.
> Grandfather—
>   Having seen you in such a situation, I without delay arise and come, and now put my hand to your face and wipe off your tears and open your Eyes, so that you may now see the sun when it rises, also when it sets down, and also other things, and that you could see your Grandchildren in a clear light; also I clean your Ears that you may hear distinctly. And I clean your throat also, and losen your Tongue, that you now may speak, and that freely. And there is such

weight of sorrow causes your heart to hang upside down, but I now remove these burdens, and set your heart aright, that you may contemplate the welfare of your Children, and that with pleasure.
Six strings of wampom delivered.
Grandfather —

Many troubles has attended us. You have lost your great Sachem; also some honourable young men, who have fallen, and lay under the earth ever since last Spring. I now remember what our good ancestors used to teach us their Children. And I now gather the bones of these deceased, and put them together, and take up the lasting Plank and put it over the grave, that the heat of the Sun may not penetrated and that the rain may not flow into them. (Nunneh *this is all*.)[160]

After the Battle of Fallen Timbers, in which Aupaumut took an active part, he continued to render diplomatic service to the U.S. government in its further dealings with northeastern Indians. He functioned as mediator for the Treaty of Greenville in 1795 and assisted the federal government in the conclusion of the 1803 and 1809 Treaties of Fort Wayne, under which the Indian land base in the Old Northwest was reduced even further. In the period between 1805 and the outbreak of the War of 1812, Aupaumut was one of the most outspoken Indian adversaries of Tecumseh and his brother Tenskwatawa, the latter of whom he designated as "the emissary of Satan" in a letter to John Sargeant, Jr., and he voluntarily joined General William Harrison's successful campaign against them.[161] Considering that the Mahican community at Stockbridge was being ruthlessly displaced by racist Americans while he was busy conferring with "hostile" tribes of the Old Northwest and risking his life in the service of the United States, Aupaumut's faith in the integrity of the federal government's Indian policies is somewhat remarkable, if not naive. When a Delaware representative voiced his doubts about the sincerity of the U.S. peace proposal, Aupaumut countered:

If the great men of the United States have the like principal or disposition as the Big knifes had, My nation and other Indians in the East would been along ago anihilated. But they are not so, Especially since they have their Liberty — they begin with new things, and now they endeavour to lift us up the Indians from the ground, that we may stand up and walk ourselves; because we the Indians, hitherto have lay flat as it were on the ground, by which we could not see great way; but if we could stand then we could see some distance. The United States in seeing our situation they put their hands on us, and lead us in the means of Life untill we could stand and walk as they are. . . . the United Sachems [the U.S. representatives] will not speak wrong. Whatever they promise to Indians they will perform.[162]

That he was fully aware of the critical situation at Stockbridge at the time is evident just a few lines farther along in his account, however. "In all my arguments with these Indians," he goes on to say, "I have as it were oblige to say nothing with regard of the conduct of Yorkers, how they cheat my fathers, how they taken our lands Unjustly, and how my fathers were groaning as it were to their graves, in loseing their lands for nothing, although they were faithful friends to the Whites; and how the white people artfully got their Deeds confirm in their Laws, &c." His conclusion that "had I mention these things to the Indians, it would agravate their prejudices against all white people, &c," is certainly realistic.[163]

Aupaumut's belief in the necessity of Indian adaptation to the sociopolitical realities of his day was undoubtedly as sincere as that of his Mohegan friends. After all, he had personally experienced the positive sides of such a symbiotic relationship in the community where he had grown up as a third-generation Christian Indian. As Jeanne and James Ronda have observed, he probably regarded Christianity as the "fulfillment of earlier Muhheakunnuk religion" and hoped that the new teachings would help him to hold his people together.[164] This is also evident in a brief autohistoriography titled "History of the Muh-he-con-nuk Indians," which he wrote around 1790.[165] Here Aupaumut highlights the inter- and intratribal sociokinship network into which the Mahicans are bound once again and, in the subsequent descriptions of their ways of life, he shows an even more pronounced tendency to accentuate the affinities between Indian religious practices and Christianity than Occom did in his study of the Montauks. He maintains that his ancestors worshiped a Supreme Being long "before they ever enjoyed Gospel revelation" and outlines what he claims to be a traditional and orally transmitted moral codex that has obvious similarities to the Ten Commandments. "Our ancestors' Government was a Democratical," he maintains as well, and he bolsters his contention with a detailed description of the complex social responsibilities assigned to the sachem and his assistants. In contrast to Occom's account, however, Aupaumut gives no indication that he regards any of the practices he is describing as being mere "superstitions." This open manifestation of pride in Mahican traditions could be because, though as thoroughly christianized as Occom, he was a hereditary sachem of his community and not a Protestant missionary.[166]

His steadfastness in the face of adverse developments in Indian–white relations is most likely due to his willingness to regard Europeans and Americans in a differential manner, just as Occom did. In agreement with colonial and federal administrators, who often ascribed the "Indian problem" to the lack of adequate civil control along the frontier, he placed much of the blame on renegade white men, or "Big Knives," who "have lived at such a distance from the United States, that in these several years the Law could not reach them because they would run in the woods, and no body could find them." He was certain that "once the people of the United States settle among them," then "the Law" would bring order and justice to Indian Territory as well.[167] In an eloquent speech to the Delawares on April 15, 1803, Aupaumut maintained that "there is and has been two sorts of white people, who follow two different paths . . . the one has been endeavouring to civilize and christianize them, and the other has taught them to drink the poisonous liquor to excess, and many other wicked practices." It is in this same address, which was recorded by John Sargeant, Jr., that Aupaumut's political views are most clearly expressed. "Grandfather," he went on to say, "Be it known to you and your tribes, that all the nations who thus rejected civilization, and Christian religion, and embraced the wicked practices of the white people, were poor, and finally became extinct from the earth. But on the other hand all the Indians who accepted the offer of the good white people, were blessed. So far as they were faithful, they prospered, and the remnants of them remain to this day." Aupaumut recommended that the Delawares become acquainted with "what our white brothers call A.B.C., which is the foundation of learning." In concluding he promised them that if they heeded his "simple truth" they would also have numerous advantages in their future dealings with the colonists: "Grandfather, Be assured that by following this path I and my nation have found many advantages. Among other things, our white brothers cannot so easily cheat us now with regard to our land affairs as they have done our forefathers. . . . And further, you will be able to hold your lands to the latest generations; for this is the will of the great and good Spirit."[168]

The fate of the New Stockbridge community after the War of 1812, however, must have dampened Aupaumut's optimism considerably. Strained relations with the Oneidas, who were becoming more and more immersed in Handsome Lake's syncretistic religion, had already led the Mahican sachem to consider another removal as early as 1791. Based on an old covenant with the Miamis and Potawatomis, under which lands had been reserved for former members of the so-called River Indian Confederacy, he was able in 1808 to secure a grant from said tribes and thereupon began to work out a plan for a gradual move to Indiana. The realization of the exodus itself was postponed by the events leading up to the War of 1812, so that the first emigrants did not actually begin their trek until 1817. Once again, in spite of the substantial record of Stockbridge Indian services to the United States and a written confirmation signed by none other than Thomas Jefferson, with whom Aupaumut had conferred concerning the matter of the prospective migration in December of 1808, the emigrants found themselves confronted by American expansionism shortly after their arrival there because in the meantime the U.S. government had forced the Miamis to sell the land they had planned to settle on. Aupaumut sent his son Solomon Hendrick to Washington to protest the issue, but this proved to be of little avail with a new administration attuned to land speculation and in preparation for another war with England. In 1821 Solomon managed to purchase 6,000 acres from the Menominees in Wisconsin, and the frustrated White River emigrants moved to the alternative site the next year. In 1828 John W. Quinney led most of the remaining New Stockbridge residents to the new community on the Fox River, where he was joined by the aging Aupaumut in 1829. It is said that the disappointed Mahican sachem succumbed to alcohol in the last days of his life.[169]

As the Rondas have pointed out, Aupaumut was an Indian leader whose intentions and talents were not unlike Tecumseh's, except that he embodied a diametrically opposed strategy of survival.[170] Whereas Tecumseh urged the Indian nations to return to traditional ways of life and defend themselves militarily against further encroachments, Aupaumut regarded selective adaptation as the only fruitful way to deal with the colonial situation. Tecumseh's Indian confederacy was shattered at Tippecanoe in 1811, but his dream still finds widespread admiration; Aupaumut's (and Occom's and Johnson's) Christian Indian experiment has persisted but still attracts little public attention. His policy was perpetuated by his son and, above all, by John W. Quinney, who drafted a new constitution in 1837 establishing an electoral form of government under which he was elected grand sachem in 1852.[171] The Stockbridge Indians managed to withstand the continuing incursions into their territory in Green Bay and, in 1856, they concluded a new agreement with the Menominees allowing them to establish a separate reservation where they were eventually joined by their former neighbors of Brothertown. In 1938 the Bureau of Indian Affairs approved the tribal constitution of the Stockbridge-Munsee community and recognized its title to 2,250 acres in Bartelme Township, Wisconsin. The Stockbridge-Munsees of today are regarded as an acculturated Indian community with a distinctly Indian value system, a relatively stable economic level, and a viable community organization headed by an effective leadership — one in which Aupaumut's direct descendants continue to play a prominent role.[172]

4

William Apess, Pequot-Mashpee Insurrectionist of the Removal Era

WILLIAM APESS, PEQUOT, Methodist preacher, author, reformer, abolitionist, and rebel, is one of the most intriguing personalities in the history of American Indian literature. Other than a few newspaper articles and some scattered documents in public archives, all that is currently known about the life of this extraordinary man is derived solely from his own publications.[1] Thus, unless additional material is uncovered, any interpretations of his moving life will have to be based entirely upon what he has chosen to reveal about himself in autoethnographic expression. He is, to borrow N. Scott Momaday's oft-cited phrase, a "man made of words."[2] His personal experiences with deracination, poverty, and racism made him particularly receptive to the humanistic currents of thought in his day and, at the same time, outspokenly critical of Anglo-American treatment of Indians. His self-propelled rise from the marginal status of a "cast-off member of the tribe," as he designated himself, and an indentured servant to a noted public figure and leader of the only successful Indian "insurrection" in New England history is a classic illustration of the antebellum "ethnic success" story.

Apess lived during a period in which fundamental changes were occurring in the relations between the indigenous peoples and transplanted Euro-Americans. The battles of the Thames (1813) and Horseshoe Bend (1814) effectively broke down whatever military potential the more populous tribes of the Old Northwest and Old Southwest still had, even though armed Indian resistance would continue into the latter part of the nineteenth century. The Treaty of Ghent (1814) terminated the second fratricidal conflict with Britain and left the United States as the unchallenged sovereign over a vast territory that had been expanded with the Louisiana Purchase of 1803.

William Apess. Undated portrait, imprinted on a card with a ticket for his lecture "Eulogy on King Philip" (1836). Courtesy Edward E. Ayer Collection, The Newberry Library.

A burgeoning population and empty state coffers focused national attention on one major issue: the distribution of "western" lands, which were regarded as part of the "public domain." In the half-century that passed between the Northwest Ordinance (1787) and the 1840s, nearly five million settlers crossed the Appalachian watershed into Indian lands, a dozen new states were added to the original thirteen, and one of the greatest real estate transactions in American history was consummated. As Michael Rogin has observed, the realization of Manifest Destiny actually began in Indian territory to the west of the Appalachians immediately following the War of 1812, and not west of the Mississippi thirty years later.[3] Such massive migration inevitably brought about the displacement of tribes residing in the desired regions, and the legal and moral justification for the usurpation of Indian lands consequently became a topic of hot debate among American politicians and writers. In keeping with the contradictory trends already established during the British colonial era, the more conventional "civilization program" started by George Washington and Henry Knox after 1789 was quickly circumvented as federal Indian policy began to develop in direct opposition to most avowed national principles. Even though the young republic had been shaped by the Enlightenment maxim of the "natural rights of man," as expounded in the Declaration of Independence and the Constitution, the federal government soon found itself having to accommodate its legal framework to emergent American romantic nationalism and growing segregationist sentiments.[4]

The threadbare efforts to "civilize savages" were now officially coupled to the persistent allegation that direct contacts between Indians and whites had turned out to the detriment of the former. It was an opportunistic outlook that disregarded the numerous contemporary cases of successful Indian adaptation, especially in the Old Southwest where, ironically enough (but in this particular context only), the Cherokees, Creeks, Choctaws, Chickasaws, and Seminoles came to be popularly known as the Five Civilized Tribes. Under this artificial notion of irreversible mutual incompatibility, the most plausible conclusion was, of course, that only the "removal" of Indians to some remote area, far away from such "negative" influences, could forestall their immediate destruction and give at least some of them the necessary time to adapt gradually. The concept of removal itself was certainly not new: It was given brief consideration by John Adams, taken up again by Thomas Jefferson with reference to Indians and black freedmen, officially advocated by James Monroe in a special report to Congress in 1825, and pushed halfheartedly by John Quincy Adams before it was finally written into law (Removal Act, 4 U.S. Stat. 411–412) under the presidency of Andrew Jackson on May 28, 1830.[5] Jackson shared the highly popular view that all Indians had forfeited their sovereignty by participating in the war with Britain, even though some had fought on the American side and others had remained neutral, and he also regarded the established lateral treaty-making process as an obsolete political expediency. In other words, the power ratio was now such that the fate of Indians within U.S. territory could be determined and directed autonomously by the federal government, which decided that, in order to make room for American expansionism, Indians must "voluntarily" withdraw to territory west of the Mississippi or, for those remnant eastern tribes who were permitted to remain, become subject to the laws of whichever states they resided in. The legal foundations laid by the Indian Trade and Intercourse Acts, which had established federal control over Indian commerce and defined Indian territory, were supplemented by a Supreme Court decision in 1823 (*Johnson's and Graham's Lessee* v. *William McIntosh*) in which Indian claims on land ("right of occupancy") were subordinated to those inherited by the United States from Britain by virtue of "discovery" and "conquest."[6] In order to implement U.S. Indian policy more effectively, Secretary of War John C. Calhoun created the Bureau of Indian Affairs (then known as the Office of Indian Affairs) in 1824. It was regularized by Congress simultaneously with the creation of the post of commissioner of Indian affairs in 1832 and formalized with the last Intercourse Act of 1834, which also stated that American law would take precedence over Indian law in Indian–white relations.[7] Previous to this, in *Cherokee Nation* v. *State of Georgia* (1831), Justice John Marshall had defined the status of Indian tribes as "domestic dependent nations" who are "in a state of pupilage" and whose "relation to the United States resembles that of a ward to his guardian." Marshall partially reversed his interpretation the following year in *Worcester* v. *State of Georgia* (1832) — characterizing Indian tribes "as distinct political communities, having territorial boundaries, within which their authority is exclusive, and having a right to all lands within those boundaries, which is not only acknowledged, but guaranteed by the United States" — but the subordinate status of Indians was by then a juridical and political fait accompli, even though many western tribes were still independent and had never concluded an agreement with the United States.[8]

The ideological rationale for removal, which was to provide the moral guise necessary to make it more plausible to those who were still troubled about obvious incongruences with the egalitarian aspects of republicanism, got its impetus primarily from eighteenth-century European environmentalist theory and Scottish "conjectural history."[9] Environmentalism, with its focus on the physical surroundings as an explanation for human and social diversity, supplied the reason for the purported inability of Indians to "advance," namely, that the harsh North American environment had forced them to lead an unproductive nomadic life revolving around hunting and warfare. The progress theory expounded by eighteenth-century historians in France and Scotland, who viewed the social, technical, and moral development of humans as a universal sequence from savagism to barbarism to civilization, delivered the justification for appropriating Indian lands, namely, that the guided introduction to "civilization" proffered in return for these "unused" territories was a square political deal. The biblical principle embodied in Genesis 1:28 ("Be fruitful, and multiply, and replenish the earth, and subdue it") was further bolstered by the juridical constructs of European "natural law," especially John Locke's notions of property in the second of his *Two Treatises of Government* (1690) and Emerich von Vattel's *Droit des gens, ou Principes de la Loi Naturelle* (1758), which denied the right of nomadic hunters to prevent a more laborious and advanced people from taking over lands and putting them to more effective use (i.e., European agriculture).[10]

American literati of the early nineteenth century inevitably found themselves confronted with Indians in their explorations of national identity. Now that they no longer posed an immediate threat to the population of the eastern seaboard states, their tarnished image since King Philip's War could be polished in such a way as to make it more presentable for the premiere of American literature. Indeed, in the period between the close of the War of 1812 and the beginning of the Civil War, Indians were assigned the most prominent role they ever had in American letters, arts, and philosophy.[11] American poets, dramatists, and prose writers picked up on the tail end of European primitivist tradition, which had found its most recent literary expression in the romantic image of the sentimental (rather than rational) *bon sauvage* in the works of Thomas Campbell in England and René de Chateaubriand in France, and simply amplified the Indian's noble traits to match the breathtaking grandeur of the American wilderness — all this as a challenge to contemporary European environmentalists' (notably the French naturalist Georges Louis Leclerc, comte de Buffon) postulations on American decadence.[12] However, since they also basically shared the European conviction that civilization was bound to supersede savagism, they located their American-style *bon sauvage* beyond corruption's reach, in the innocent precontact past and/or in the pristine western "wilderness." The Metamoras, Uncases, and Hiawathas of the poetic imagination were then furnished with all the necessary noble trappings to make their lost cause a heroic one and their programmed demise the proper substance for tragic elegies. Those who still insisted on staying alive and remaining among the whites, such as the aging Chingachgook, succumbed to the terrible vices of civilization. Emergent American cultural identity thus took shape simultaneously with the creation of a new racial stereotype — the "vanishing Indian."[13] Set before the backdrop of the grandiose North American scenery, this New World image of the sentimental noble savage became the symbolic trump card with which American writers could finally make a fair bid against European literary biases. Pioneer American historians like Heckewelder, Schoolcraft, Drake, Gallatin, and others dedicated themselves wholeheartedly to the task of "salvage ethnology," recording for posterity all the information they could still gather about a uniquely "American" people bound for extinction. As Roy Harvey Pearce put it so poignantly, in the process of removing west of the Mississippi, Indians were also "forced out of American life into American history."[14]

At the very same time, however, the contrary image of the bloodthirsty savage was also carried over from previous centuries and remodeled to suit the times. Charles Brockden Brown's *Edgar Huntly* (1799), for instance, lent a certain literary format to the bloody scenes popularized in seventeenth-century captivity narratives, a particularly violent anti-Indian genre that continued to find audiences well into the second half of the nineteenth century, when it merged into the paperback "western."[15] Even the noble Indians in Cooper's widely read romantic novels were counterposed by sinister figures like Magua, whose cruelty was yet overshadowed by the murdering savages in Robert Montgomery Bird's equally popular *Nick of the Woods* (1836). Philip Freneau's and William Cullen Bryant's sentimental elegies on vanquished warriors were more than offset by the "Indian-hater" language of a James Kirke Paulding or James McHenry. All of these "vanishing Indian" constructs, whether noble or ignoble, simply functioned as a circumlocution for pragmatic American expansionism.[16]

As the obvious moral dilemma between racial discrimination and the republican principles of egalitarianism was brought to the fore in the increasing public debates over removal and slavery, racist theory acquired a more "scientific" outlook.[17] Although the Enlightenment view of humans as innately equal beings with the same capabilities for "improvement" was not abandoned during the first half of the nineteenth century, the number of those who believed (or wanted to believe) that Indians were incapable of being assimilated into American society because of racial handicaps grew steadily. Empirical "proof" seemed to be provided by the emergent theory of polygenesis, which challenged the universalist notion of a single human species (monogenesis) with the contention that distinct species of man with inherent abilities and/or disabilities had evolved separately. Basically, the polygenetic racist construct was a modern variant of the Aristotelian principle of "natural slavery," which Juan Ginés de Sepúlveda had already incorporated into his famous debate with Bartolomé de Las Casas in Valladolid in 1550–51, but underscored with the latest revelations from the budding fields of natural science (biology, zoology, anthropology) in order to add "scientific" weight to the prevalent assertion that "colored" peoples were inferior beings biologically and therefore not entitled to equal standing with whites in a democratic society. The polygenetic theories expounded earlier by European thinkers like Lord Kames, which were still being contested by the likes of Samuel Stanhope Smith at the end of the eighteenth century, received a tremendous boost in the United States during the 1830s with the publication of Charles Caldwell's *Thoughts on the Original Unity of the Human Race* (1830) and Samuel George Morton's *Crania Americana* (1839). Following the wide dissemination of polygenetic literature during the 1830s and 1840s, the notion of predetermined racial distinctions became a major topic of public discussion in conjunction with American expansionism and, of course, it also fueled the propagation of Anglo-Saxon racial superiority. As Reginald Horsman has pointed out, there is sufficient historical evidence that by this time (1830s) most American people and their political leaders had become convinced, for purely racist reasons, that Indians could not be integrated into American society.[18]

Although the racist line of thought obviously sat well with those who profited directly from the appropriation of Indian (and Mexican) lands and the institution of slavery, there were still many Americans who sincerely believed in the missionary imperative of bringing civilization and Christianity to Indians. Their source of legitimation was the biblical concept of universal human descent from one common progenitor, and they consequently sought to refute contemporary polygenetic contentions by revitalizing the "Ten Lost Tribes of Israel" conjecture of Indian origin that had sprung up in sixteenth-century Spain and Portugal and been widely discussed throughout Europe during the mid-seventeenth century.[19] It was expanded upon in James Adair's widely read *History of the American Indians* (1775) and came to the fore again during the first half of the nineteenth century in numerous publications that followed Elias Boudinot's *Star in the West* (1816), which had a direct influence on Apess.[20] The gist of their association between Indians and Hebrews was, simply, that a common biblical ancestry with Europeans was implicit "proof" for the feasibility of Indian advancement.

Of course, there was also pronounced public opposition to the policy of removal. The Indians themselves resisted militarily (Winnebago Rebellion in 1827, Black Hawk War in 1832, Second Seminole War in 1835) and, particularly in the case of the Five Civilized Tribes, applied other nonviolent tactics through the American legal system and the media. American politicians, too, were divided on the issue, as the records of the heated congressional debates on two proposed removal bills in the spring of 1830 and the close vote on the final version clearly show.[21] The loudest protest came, as might be expected, from Protestant philanthropic circles and organizations, such as the newly constituted American Board of Commissioners for Foreign Missions (ABCFM, 1810), which had been involved in a series of evangelical revivals since the turn of the century commonly referred to as the Second Great Awakening.[22]

In many ways, the religious revivals that occurred in New England and in the areas then known as the "West" (Tennessee, Kentucky, and Ohio in the Old Southwest; Illinois, Wisconsin, Minnesota, and Iowa in the Old Northwest) between the 1790s and the 1830s were but a continuation of the previous century's Great Awakening. The main emphasis was still on the Bible as the sole source of revelation, on personal and emotional conversion experiences, and on the missionary imperative of spreading the Gospel. Social issues such as intemperance, universal peace, or slavery had been broached by philanthropists earlier in America, especially the Quakers, but several changes (more in degree than in substance) had since taken place in connection with Enlightenment ideas and revolutionary ideology.[23] Along with the separation of church and state in the new republic there was also a marked tendency within religious bodies toward disestablishment in spiritual matters. Volunteer laymen began to assume the initiative in areas that had hitherto been the sole responsibility of clergy or civil administrators, and established denominational bodies gradually atomized into countless interrelated, but independent, religious-humanitarian organizations. Infused with current republican ideals, the missionizing spirit also took on a more pluralistic stance, allowing for the increased direct participation of women and ethnic minorities in daily religious affairs. African Americans and Indians joined the clergy in greater numbers than ever before, particularly among the Methodists and Baptists, who rose to prominence during the Second Great Awakening. They carried on the itinerant-preacher tradition with their system of "circuit riders," young men with more religious dedication than theological training, who went around designated districts preaching the Gospel. Their style of revivalism was most effectively introduced to the masses in week-long, summer religious happenings referred to as camp meetings, which became increasingly popular at the turn of the century and drew huge crowds of prospective converts with their singing, feasting, and emotional demonstrations of religious fervor.

These practical innovations were accompanied by fundamental changes in theological doctrine, as the Calvinist focus on depravity and original sin was being challenged by the belief in the human ability to do right according to God's will. Enlightenment rationalism, which began to dominate American thinking after the turn of the nineteenth century at the very latest, led to an emphasis on the individual's active role in salvation (Arminianism). It also stressed the importance of ethics, on the one hand, and a deemphasized doctrinairism on the other. This entailed a general shift of moral concern from individual vices to broader social issues in American life, which in turn led to an unprecedented surge of reformist activity during the first half of the nineteenth century and the creation of a myriad of so-called benevolent societies.[24] Based on similar organizations in England at the time, these nondenominational societies were made up of volunteers and generally obtained financial support from private businessmen. They were first organized on a local level and then quickly gained sufficient followers to coalesce into national bodies (i.e., American Bible Society, 1816; American Sunday School Union, 1824; American Tract Society, 1826; American Temperance Union, 1826; National American Education Society, 1826). The main purpose of this network of humanitarian societies, which came to be known publicly as the Benevolent Empire by the 1830s, was to spread the "true" religion and to prevent the "moral decay" of the nation. They proceeded to carry out this self-imposed obligation by producing an unprecedented mass of tract literature, promoting educational facilities, organizing public rallies with keynote speakers, and providing welfare services. The issues taken up by the humanitarian reformists were manyfold: peace, intemperance, prostitution, the handicapped, foreign missions, Sunday schools, women's rights, conversion of Indians, and so on. Beginning around the 1820s, they became increasingly concerned with the problem of slavery, which led to a controversy that eventually split the ranks of the reformist movement and, of course, ultimately disrupted the Union itself.[25]

Tied in closely with the abolitionist movement was the protest against Indian removal.[26] Connections between abolitionists and Indians can be traced on several levels. In the first place, the enslavement of Indians continued up until the Revolution and, it might be added, the common practice of "indenturing" Indian children was no less inhuman. At the same time, the Five Civilized Tribes, who had been active participants in the Indian slave trade, also turned to African American slave labor after the Revolution when they adopted southern white agricultural practices and instituted their own racist policies.[27] The question of slavery among the southeastern Indians was obviously a source of much embarrassment for most of the missionaries residing among them and abolitionists elsewhere who otherwise supported their antiremoval efforts.[28]

The resurgence of slavery in America after the War of 1812 was directly related to the defeat of the southeastern tribes and the subsequent availability of vast Indian lands in that area for the expanding cotton industry. The cotton boom of the 1820s was also responsible for the political pressure exerted by the southern states for the immediate removal of Indians from the fertile "Black Belt" area. Resistance to removal was thus coupled with the North's anxiety that the spread of the institution of slavery into new territories would potentially increase the number of proslavery states.[29]

Much of the opposition to removal came from leading abolitionists, such as Lydia Maria Child, Benjamin Lundy, James Russell Lowell, and Jeremiah Evarts, who incorporated the same line of argument in their publications criticizing this policy as they did against slavery: the moral-religious denunciation of racism as a public sin and the political call for basic human rights as guaranteed by the Constitution. Former abolitionists would eventually constitute the main body of advocates of Indian reform policies after the Civil War.[30]

Reformers and administrators also found an application for the policy of removal in their plans to send liberated slaves to a colony established for them in Africa. This outlandish proposition was actually carried out by the American Colonization Society, which was founded for that purpose in 1816. Although it proved to be a hopelessly impractical scheme in the long run, it still gained the temporary approval of several benevolent societies, who financed the first of several groups of African American "colonists" headed for Liberia in 1820.[31] As Brian Dippie has observed, the segregation of freedmen and Indians remained a primary white objective throughout the first half of the nineteenth century, "the one to be separated by an ocean, the other by a river."[32] By the 1830s, however, this "humanitarian" project and the American Colonization Society itself came under increasing fire from perfectionist reformers (immediatists), who called for immediate and unconditional emancipation.[33]

Lastly, there were various other forms of societal interaction between African Americans and Indians besides slavery.[34] Intermarriage was fairly common at the turn of the century, especially among the coastal New England tribes, and numerous runaway slaves were incorporated into Indian communities beyond the frontier. The First (1817) and Second (1835) Seminole Wars, the latter of which (Florida War) was covered extensively in abolitionist papers, were as much retaliatory raids against runaway slaves as they were military actions against "hostile" Indians.[35] Several states in the South made no distinctions among "colored persons" as far as their underprivileged legal status was concerned, and personal experiences with white racist attitudes as well as resistance against them were, of course, common to both Indians and African Americans. Substantial interaction occurred as well within Christian religious circles during the Second Great Awakening, nominally among the Methodists and Baptists, whose multiracial membership was also found at the vanguard of reformist-abolitionist activities.

Removal was particularly traumatic for the larger landed Indian communities of the Southeast (or Old Southwest) such as the Five Civilized Tribes, who had hitherto been able to assert their sovereignty to a great extent, and it was their plight that drew nearly all of the philanthropic concern (more on this in the following chapter). For the remnant Coastal Algonquian tribes of New England, however, who were not affected by the Removal Act of 1830, the new political trend brought little they had not already been confronted with in their relations with Euro-Americans over the past two centuries. For them dispossession, demographic shift, and socioeconomic dependency had long been a fact of life. Their survival strategy now entailed the daily struggle for existence on the fringes of Anglo-American society, the retention of whatever scraps of lands still remained in their possession, and — much more so than among the tribes of the Old Southwest or Old Northwest at the time — resistance against total annexation on a physical, cultural, and political level.

It will be recalled that, of all the New England tribes, it was the powerful Pequots who first experienced the full force of European aggression in 1637, when troops under John Mason and John Underhill massacred nearly all of the inhabitants, women and children included, at the village of Mystic.[36] One year later, the defeated tribe was officially dissolved under the Treaty of Hartford. Even the word "Pequot" was stricken from the Puritans' vocabulary by the stipulations of this treaty, which also rechristened the Pequot village New London.[37] Those who survived the Puritan campaign were either distributed as captives among the Mohegans and Narragansetts or shipped to the Caribbean as chattel. Before the war, nearly half of the estimated 10,000–15,000 Pequots had already succumbed to diseases; by the end of the war only about 2,500 still remained alive. As far as the colonists were concerned — and most Americans up to the present date for that matter — the Pequots had effectively ceased to exist. "*Pequod*, you will no doubt remember," Melville's Ishmael would comment in *Moby Dick* more than two centuries later, "was the name of a celebrated tribe of Massachusetts [*sic*] Indians, now extinct as the ancient Medes."

Nevertheless, the scattered survivors managed to consolidate again just a few years after the Pequot War under the leadership of sachem Robin Cassasinamon (d. 1692) and were eventually allowed to return and live in four Indian towns established by the Connecticut administration and supervised by two Pequot "governors." Continuing white encroachment soon reduced these to two small reservations, the Mashantucket (or Western) Pequots of Ledyard (Groton) and the Paucatuck (or Eastern) Pequots of the Lantern Hill Reservation in North Stonington. Despite tremendous hardships that confronted them over the next three centuries, the two remaining Pequot communities were able to hold on to a fraction of their land base in Connecticut and to maintain their tribal identity. The Mashantucket Pequots presently enjoy the status of a federally recognized tribe, while the Eastern Pequots have managed to be recognized as such only by the state of Connecticut. With the passage of the Mashantucket Pequot Indian Land Claims Settlement Act (Public Law 98-134, Title 25 U.S.C.A. 1751–1760) in 1983, the Mashantucket Pequot Nation, as they now refer to themselves, not only received federal recognition but were also awarded a $900,000 trust fund with which they expanded their land base substantially from 214 to more than 3,072 acres, built several modern housing complexes and a luxurious tribal headquarters, and set up a number of tribal enterprises, including an expanding mega-gambling operation, the Foxwoods High Stakes Bingo and Casino Resort, which has made them the wealthiest rural community in the entire state and a major local employer. The descendants of New England's Puritans now arrive in hordes each day (including the Sabbath) to dedicate themselves wholeheartedly to the "vice" of gambling in a casino run by a multiracial Indian group who supposedly disappeared more than three centuries ago — a situation that does not lack a certain tinge of "black" humor.[38]

In William Apess's days, however, the two remnant Pequot communities were facing serious existential difficulties. Casualties incurred during the American Revolution had greatly reduced the male population, and many of the survivors were forced to earn a living outside of the community as indentured servants, day laborers, basket makers, or whalers. After the Revolution a number of Pequots had moved to New York to join the other

New England Christian Indians at Brothertown. Such a drain on the male Pequot population obviously affected the social makeup of the two communities. The resulting increase in intermarriages with non-Pequots, for instance, put an additional strain on tribal coherence. As the ratio of women in the community increased, they gradually assumed more responsibility in local affairs. Such demographic irregularities in turn eased further white encroachment on Pequot lands and the illegal exploitation of natural resources such as timber. As a consequence of all this, certain core families who had taken up leadership positions in the Pequot communities had to expend much of their time and energy in litigation against the machinations of corrupt overseers. Finally, deracination and the effects of extreme poverty also opened the way for all of the other common accompaniments of the colonial situation. According to Apess's own estimation, the majority of New England Indians at the time were "the most mean, abject, miserable race of beings in the world" and their communities "a complete place of prodigality and prostitution."[39]

William Apess's life history is exemplary of the precarious existence of New England Indians at the turn of the nineteenth century. He was born on January 31, 1798, at Colrain, Massachusetts.[40] According to his own account his "grandfather was a white man and married a female attached to the royal family of Philip, king of the Pequod tribe of Indians." Their mixed-blood son (Apess's father) joined the Pequots as an adult and "married a female of the tribe, in whose veins a single drop of the white man's blood never flowed."[41] Apess's family tree, which qualifies him as a three-fourths Pequot according to conventional modern-day tribal membership requirements based on blood quotas, must nevertheless be viewed critically, even if one merely takes into consideration his erroneous assumption that King Philip was a Pequot. This error (Metacom was a Wampanoag) may well have been intentional on his part because, as will be discussed later, connection to "royalty" was a frequent claim in contemporary ethnic autobiographies and, additionally, the memory of the great Indian patriot was being resurrected in American literary circles at the time as the epitome of the tragic noble-savage hero. Because the story of King Philip had attained culture-heroic proportions, he could thus be legitimately "claimed" as a common ancestor by the various northeastern Algonquian groups who had participated in his unsuccessful rebellion. Lastly, as has been pointed out repeatedly, the extensive New England Indian sociokinship network forces us to be equally skeptical of postcontact "tribal" constructs. Even though Apes(s) was not an uncommon Pequot family name, his background still remains somewhat nebulous because the colonial census data available contain" contradictory information — a common occurrence in the case of New England multiracial communities during an era in which nonwhites were frequently listed as "colored" or "mulatto."[42] From the genealogical information he has managed to compile, Barry O'Connell surmises with caution that Apess was the eldest son of William Apes, who was probably a mixed-blood Paucatuck Pequot, and Candace Apes, who may possibly have been a former slave of African descent.[43] As mentioned previously, such a racial mix would certainly not have been out of the ordinary among the Pequots in the early part of the nineteenth century.[44] If O'Connell's assumption is correct, then Apess was either ignorant of his African American ancestry or purposely chose to ignore it in his writings for some unknown reason.

Absolute certainty concerning his descent will certainly not change anything as far as Apess's rightful place in the history of American Indian literature is concerned, but the fact that intermarriage between African Americans and remnant Coastal Algonquian groups was a fairly common phenomenon at the time may help to illuminate the marked affinities between his life and work and the abolitionist movement. The subject of Afro-Indian writers has been given far too little attention so far. Racial discrimination probably motivated some mixed-blood individuals to "pass" for Indians, particularly as in some cases this provided an escape from the status of slave.[45] A case in point, among many others, which illustrates the problems involved in tracing accurately the genealogy of some early Afro-Indian authors, is that of Paul Cuffee (1759–1817), the noted mixed-blood sea merchant and cofounder of the freedmen colony of Sierra Leone in Africa. Himself of mixed African and undetermined Indian ancestry, Cuffee is recorded as having married an Indian woman by the rather descriptive name of Alice Pequit, who was nevertheless said to be a member of the Wampanoag tribe. Their eldest son obviously identified himself as Pequot, however, because he titled his autobiography *Narrative of the Life and Adventures of Paul Cuffee, a Pequot Indian* (1839), even though it is a seafaring yarn with absolutely no references to that tribe other than in the title itself. Another curious example is that of Okah Tubbee, an ex-slave and traveling musician who became a "Choctaw Chief" in his "autobiographical" narrative, *A Thrilling Sketch of the Life of the Distinguished Chief Okah Tubbee* (1848). This otherwise typical slave narrative was probably written by his wife, Laah Ceil Manatoi Elaah Tubbee, whose own Indian origins also remain unclear (Delaware or Stockbridge). Yet another, more recent case is that of Sylvester Long, author of the very popular "autobiography" *Long Lance* (1926). He was actually of African-Catawban descent but first designated himself as a Cherokee and then claimed to have been adopted by the Blackfoot Indians to become "chief" Buffalo Child Long Lance.[46] The fact that there was much societal interaction between African Americans and eastern Indians at the time does not, of course, make Apess (or most of the other mixed-blood authors mentioned above) any less "Indian." It merely creates an additional ethnohistorical dimension that needs to be taken into account in order to do full justice to their multicultural backgrounds.

When William Apess was about three years old his parents separated and left their six children in the care of relatives. His maternal grandparents, as it turned out, were "wedded to the beastly vice of intemperance," and consequently Apess and his siblings had to endure a highly disturbed childhood.[47] At one point his intoxicated grandmother beat him so severely that he nearly died from the injuries. Acting upon the request of an uncle, the town selectmen subsequently removed him from his grandparents' care in 1802 and, as was commonly done then with orphans or the children of impoverished families regardless of race, bound him out to a local white Baptist family until he should reach the age of twenty-one.[48] Apess's situation was thus emblematic for the radical disruptions in the Pequot social network after the Revolution. His grandmother, who would normally have functioned as one of the primary mediators of tribal traditions in her grandchild's early life, in this case turned out to be nothing less than the agent of his cultural alienation. Ethnographic sources consistently show that child beating was universally abhorred in Indian society.[49] In marked contrast to Apess's account, Indian grandparents are almost always presented in a very positive light in later American Indian autobiographies and novels, in which they almost always function as the main reference point for an alienated protagonist's resurgent cultural awareness. Seen in this light, Apess's description of his negative childhood experience is highly significant. Thus deprived of his traditional birthright, he now had to establish a completely new identity for himself on the extreme fringes of an alien, racist society. As an adult he still managed somehow to regard this most traumatic moment of his life within the larger, more impersonal context of the colonial situation:

> I attribute it in a great measure to the whites, inasmuch as they introduced among my countrymen, that bane of comfort and happiness, ardent spirits — seduced them into a love of it, and when under its unhappy influence, wronged them out of their lawful possessions — that land, where reposed the ashes of

their sires; and not only so, but they committed violence of the most revolting kind upon the persons of the female portion of the tribe who, previous to the introduction among them of the arts, and vices, and debaucheries of the whites, were as unoffending and happy as they roamed over their godly possessions, as any people on whom the sun of heaven ever shown. The consequence was, that they were scattered abroad. Now many of them were seen reeling about intoxicated with liquor, neglecting to provide for themselves and families, who before were assiduously engaged in supplying the necessities of those depending on them for support. I do not make this statement in order to justify those who treated me so unkindly, but simply to shew, that inasmuch as I was thus treated only when they were under the influence of spirituous liquor, that the whites were justly chargeable with at least some portion of my sufferings.[50]

Whatever knowledge Apess managed to absorb about Pequot traditions in the four short years of his life before being bound out was subsequently corrupted by current American racist attitudes. His alienation progressed so far that at the age of six or seven he ran away, terrified, from a chance encounter in the woods with a group of white women whose sunburned complexion had caused him to mistake them for "wild Indians" who, as he had been taught by his guardians, "were in the habit of killing and scalping men, women, and children." For him the designation "Indian" was obviously charged with all the negative associations common to the racist term "nigger." "I thought it disgraceful to be called an Indian," he writes; "it was considered as a slur upon an oppressed and scattered nation, and I have often been led to inquire where the whites received this word, which they so often threw as an opprobrious epithet at the sons of the forest." But he was not beyond making a sardonic joke about the defamatory misnomer either, suggesting, as Voltaire had done indirectly with his Huron character L'Ingénu, that its origins might be found in the English word "in-gen-uity." Apess then proposed that "Natives" would be a more appropriate designation for the original inhabitants of America, even though he continued to use the more common "slur" in all of his subsequent publications.[51]

As an adolescent Apess sought solace from loneliness and degradation in the soothing messages proffered by the exponents of the Second Great Awakening. He had already been introduced to Protestant theology by the ministrations of his foster parent, Mrs. Furman, who had done her utmost to impress him with the usual evangelical illustrations of eternal damnation, but his religious interest was actually sparked "by a sect called the Christians [Methodists]," who had visited his neighborhood when he was about eight.[52] Apess attended their meetings on several occasions, and the notice taken of his interest had "a very happy influence on [his] mind."[53]

However, his budding affinity for Methodist teachings met with the disapproval of his Baptist foster parents, who prohibited him from further associating with the disreputable sect. At this time Apess was also severely affected by his second loss of a "grandmother" with the death of Mrs. Furman's mother, who had probably assumed the role of an ersatz parent. As he would write later, "She had always been so kind to me that I missed her quite as much as her children, and I had been allowed to call her mother." Shortly after this incident he fell into a kind of stupor and, following a severe flogging by Mr. Furman aimed at driving out the "devil," suffered what appears to have been a hysterical fit. It was from this moment on that a rift began to develop between him and the Furman family, which would ultimately open his eyes to the realities behind his situation as an indentured servant.[54]

Whatever shortcomings he may have had to contend with as a bound-out Indian child, Apess nevertheless seems to have developed a genuine feeling of familiarity with the Furmans who, according to his own assessment, treated him fairly well and even saw to it that he could attend school for six winters—the sole extent of his education. It is not difficult to imagine the shock he must have experienced when, in punishment for the ordinary adolescent prank of "running away" at the age of ten or eleven, his indenture was sold to another white family. This was, in effect, his first direct encounter with the gruesome realities of slavery, even though as an indentured servant he was purportedly the beneficiary of a humane social arrangement:

> But so it was; I was alone in the world, fatherless, motherless, and helpless, as it were, and none to speak for the poor little Indian boy. Had my skin been white, with the same abilities and the same parentage, there could not have been found a place good enough for me. But such is the case with depraved nature, that their judgment for fancy sets upon the eye, skin, nose, lips, cheeks, chin or teeth and, sometimes, the forehead and hair—without any further examination, the mind is made up and the price set. This is something like buying chaff for wheat, or twigs of wood for solid substance.[55]

Apess's sojourn with his new master, Judge William Hillhouse of New London, proved to be much less acceptable to him because he was not provided with adequate clothing or schooling as required by the stipulations of the indenture. After several attempts to run away, his indenture was sold once again, "as a farmer would sell his sheep for the slaughter," to another white man named William Williams, with whom he remained until 1813.[56]

Around 1809 he rediscovered his predilection for Methodist camp meetings. Their style of impromptu preaching, "which made the language of the speaker eloquent and sublime," was more appealing to him than those who "read off in an elegant style, which only seemed to please the ear and lull the people to sleep." He was drawn by the spontaneous outbursts of religious fervor among the participants, who "shouted for joy — while sinners wept" and caused him to be "affected even unto tears." And he also began to develop a deep feeling of solidarity with their negative image among the "sectarian bigots" in established religious circles. The Methodists, "a poor, despised people," he concluded, "were the true people of God."[57]

At the age of fifteen all of the horrors of hellfire were revealed to him in a moving dream-vision, and soon after, on March 15, 1813 (recorded precisely in both of his autobiographical accounts), he had a conversion experience in which he heard a voice calling on him to "go in peace and sin no more." Like Occom, Apess found "great peace of mind" in this revelation. Unlike his Presbyterian predecessors, however, he also became convinced that "Christ died for all mankind — that age, sect, color, country, or situation made no difference."[58]

Apess's third indenture brought little improvement in his situation, and shortly after his conversion experience he once again decided to escape, this time permanently. In the company of a fellow runaway, he made his way to New York City and eventually enlisted as drummer boy in an American militia unit on its way to fight the British in Canada. When he was involuntarily detailed to the infantry he attempted to desert. "I could not think why I should risk my life and limbs in fighting for the white man," he rationalized, "who had cheated my forefathers out of their land." He was soon caught, however, and promptly sent back to the Canadian front, where he witnessed several abortive American efforts to take Montreal and then participated in the more successful Battle of Lake Champlain in 1814. Here he was not only introduced to "all the horrors of war" but also began to "lose sight of religion and of God" and develop what would eventually become a serious drinking problem ("the shadows of spiritual death began to gather around my soul") by the time he obtained his release — or deserted again — from the army in the fall of 1815. "In a little time I became almost as bad as any of them," Apess concluded, "[I] could drink rum, play cards, and act as wickedly as any."[59]

After the war Apess wandered around aimlessly in Canada for about a year, trying his luck as baker's assistant, cook, farm laborer, and household servant but barely managing to sustain himself and his addiction to rum.

During this time he also had some contact with Canadian Indians, which made him feel "like home." Once, during a hunting trip to the Bay of Quinte, Ontario, he had a second vision that marked another turning point in his life, one that would eventually take him back to his own people and restore his sense of direction. Observing the beauty of the landscape before him, he had what amounted to a transcendental experience:

> On the very top of a high mountain in the neighbourhood there was a large pond of water, to which there was no visible outlet;—this pond was unfathomable. It was very surprising to me that so great a body of water should be found so far above the common level of the earth. There was also in the neighbourhood a rock, that had the appearance of being hollowed out by the hand of a skilful artificer; through this rock wound a narrow stream of water: it had a most beautiful and romantic appearance, and I could not but admire the wisdom of God in the order, regularity, and beauty of creation; I then turned my eyes to the forest, and it seemed alive with its sons and daughters. There appeared to be the utmost order and regularity in their encampment.[60]

Not long after this event he was drawn into a chapel by the sound of an exhorter's voice and, remembering his own "promises of reformation," concluded that it was time for him to return. "As I found I was friendless, without money, and without work, the desire of my heart was to get home."[61]

Sometime around the close of 1816 he began his return journey to Connecticut on foot, a trek that would take him several months as he had to find employment to maintain himself along the way. His "long way back" was arduous—in many ways it recalls Johnson's similar odyssey to Mohegan nearly a half-century earlier—and at least once he was lured by "bad company" to stray from his projected destination. He finally arrived at Groton in the spring of 1817, much to the surprise of his "kindred in the flesh" who regarded him "as one risen from the dead." With the help of relatives, Apess also experienced a spiritual rebirth shortly after his return to his native community, a "return from my backsliding state, to the worship of God." He then resolved "to go to work and be steady," started to attend Methodist meetings regularly, and began to wrestle with his own doubts. "Hour after hour, and day after day," he writes, "did I endeavor to lift my heart to God, to implore forgiveness of my sins and grace to enable me to lay hold of the promise to the vilest of the vile, through Jesus Christ our Lord." But when a white man threatened to withhold pay due to him for his labor, he also made another, more worldly resolution: "I served him faithfully, but when I wanted my pay, he undertook to treat me as he would a degraded

African slave, he took a cart-stake in order to pay me; but he soon found out his mistake, as I made him put it down as quick as he had taken it up. I had been cheated so often that I determined to have my rights this time, and forever after." Thus, at age nineteen, Apess cast off "the shadows of spiritual death" and became "steady." He joined the Methodists on a trial basis and, after spending a spiritually revitalizing winter season with his aunt Sally George, who personalized a successful blend of Christian piety and Pequot shamanism (a positive grandmother image), he was finally baptized by immersion during a camp meeting in December 1818.[62]

In the spring of the following year he went to Colrain to reunite with his father. Before he arrived, however, Apess got hopelessly lost as he attempted to take a shortcut through the forest and suddenly found himself in a dark swamp that seemed to embody all of the perils of his own spiritual journey:

> I was now amazed; what to do I knew not; shut out from the light of heaven—surrounded by appalling darkness—standing on uncertain ground—and having proceeded so far, that to return, if possible, were as "dangerous as to go over." This was the hour of peril—I could not call for assistance on my fellow creatures; there was no mortal ear to listen to my cry. I was shut out from the world, and did not know but that I should perish there, and my fate forever remain a mystery to my friends. I raised my heart in humble prayer and supplication to the father of mercies, and behold he stretched forth his hand and delivered me from this place of danger.[63]

Divine intervention thus enabled the disoriented "son of the forest" to surmount the one remaining obstacle in the "wilderness" and come to the completion of his circular journey from "cast-off member of the tribe" to both filial and spiritual recoupment. At Colrain he had yet another dream (or vision) in which he traveled "through a miry place in a dark and dreary way" to reach a large plain "on which the sun shone with perfect brightness," where an angel addressed him with "some extracts from St. John's Gospel, respecting the preaching of the word of life." Apess now became fully convinced that he had been "called to preach the Gospel of our Lord and Savior Jesus Christ."[64]

Apess began at once to practice his calling without the official "blessings" of a denominational body, exhorting wherever he could find an audience willing to listen to an Indian. Not infrequently his efforts met with racist aggression, and even his own father, who was a staunch Baptist, regarded his self-imposed mission with skepticism. As he continued to exhort without a license, he soon came into conflict with the local Methodist circuit rider, who promptly had him censured. This unexpected setback, which left him feeling once again like an "outcast from society," brought on a temporary relapse into intemperance.[65]

In the fall of 1820 he returned briefly to his native community, apparently seeking to regain composure by participating in religious activities there, and then moved on to Old Saybrook, where he eventually joined a group of "colored" Methodists. It was at this uncertain period in his life that he met Mary Wood of Salem, "a woman of nearly the same color as myself" with origins in the Spanish Caribbean, whom he married on December 16, 1821.[66] Though he never says so explicitly in his writings, his marriage may well have reversed his negative image of women, who had hitherto been the source of many of his problems, and provided him with the psychological stability he needed to persist in the difficult goals he had set for himself. In the years between 1821 and 1824 he was primarily occupied with finding some means to support his family, first setting himself up in the shoemaking business, which he had learned from his father, and later hiring out as a migrant laborer. But he also kept up his religious activities and, after moving with his family to Providence, Rhode Island, in 1825, he was appointed "class leader" of the local Methodist society. He held this position for almost two years and was then finally granted an exhorter's license. Consequently, from 1827 until the spring of 1829, he engaged in the regular activities of an itinerant exhorter throughout New England and New York — "crowds flocked out, some to *hear* the truth and others to *see* the 'Indian' " — and made some money on the side as colporteur, selling religious tracts (probably produced by the Methodist Book Concern).[67] Thus, by 1829 he had actually managed to gain a modest foothold in American society as a Protestant exhorter, no mean achievement for a "colored" indentured servant at the height of the slavery controversy. It was at this time that he also began to implement his latent talents as a writer and to develop his reformist ideas. That same year he deposited copyright title to *A Son of the Forest* in New York and had his first open confrontation with church authorities.

Apess made an application to the Methodist Episcopal Church at Albany for a preacher's license, which was reviewed at the quarterly conference in Utica in April 1829 and denied on the grounds that there was still some uncertainty concerning his "character." He agreed at first to accept an extension of his exhorter's license instead but reversed his decision only three months later and left the Methodist Episcopal Church to join the dissenting Methodist Protestant Church. He was ordained by this less discriminate religious body that very same year.[68] The issue at hand, however, was probably more complicated than is immediately apparent from the "doctored" information provided by Apess. As O'Connell has pointed out, the details concerning this particular incident were substantially deleted from the second, revised edition of his autobiography.[69] Apess's personal reasons for thus downplaying this humiliating experience are not known, but the denial may well be related to the fact that the Methodist Episcopal Church was then facing a major internal crisis. Two points of contention were threatening to split its own ranks: racism and hierarchical authority within the church. By the turn of the century, the Methodist Episcopal Church had moderated considerably its traditional antislavery stance as propagated by John Wesley, which alienated many of its reformist supporters.[70] Several of its prominent African American preachers, who had been involved with the rise of American Methodism from the outset, left the organization because of increasing racist incidents since the late 1780s and founded their own churches, such as the African Methodist Episcopal Church (1816) and the African Methodist Episcopal Zion Church (1821).[71] Apess's difficulties in obtaining a preacher's license, for instance, had been experienced previously by the Reverend George White, an African American Methodist exhorter whose application was rejected no less than five times before he finally succeeded in obtaining one in 1807. White described his frustrating struggle for recognition within the Methodist Episcopal Church in an autobiographical account published in 1810, a work Apess may very well have been aware of.[72] Racial discrimination within church ranks was thus a touchy subject when Apess applied for his license in 1829, at a time when abolitionist sentiment was becoming much more militant and beginning seriously to test the cohesiveness of Protestant organizations.

Another interdenominational controversy that developed at the turn of the century with the advent of the Second Great Awakening and came to a head in the 1820s concerned the question of episcopal authority and the right of lay people to representation in the policy-making and administrative conferences of the church. Exhorters had the lowest standing in church hierarchy and needed permission from an ordained minister just to speak before a congregation. To obtain a preacher's license was, therefore, not only an economic consideration but also a matter of social standing and professional autonomy in interpreting the Gospel. A "reform party" emerged during the 1820s advocating fundamental changes in the administration, such as elimination of the office of bishop, election rather than appointment of presiding elders, and equal representation of laity and clergy in conferences. This finally led to the expulsion of many members of the Methodist Episcopal Church in 1827, and these subsequently met in Baltimore to form a new organization in 1830, the Methodist Protestant Church.[73] Consequently, the Methodist Episcopals were particularly sensitive at this time about persons who showed any indication of not wanting to conform to established patterns of authority. Apess had, of course, already openly demonstrated his unwillingness to adhere to the established rules when he continued to exhort without a license, and the refusal to grant him a preacher's license on the basis of uncertain "character" is thus understandable from the religious organization's point of view. As far as can be gleaned from the information disclosed in the first edition of his autobiography, however, the denial itself was not the only reason that prompted Apess to leave the Methodist Episcopal Church. He writes:

> I feel a great deal happier in the *new* than I did in the *old* church — the government of the first is founded on *republican*, while that of the latter is founded on *monarchial* principles — and surely in this land where the tree of liberty has been nourished by the blood of thousands, we have good cause to contend for *mutual rights*, more especially as the Lord himself *died to make us free*! I rejoice sincerely in the spread of the principles of civil and religious liberty — may they ever be found "hand in hand" accomplishing the designs of God, in promoting the welfare of mankind. If these blessed principles prevail, sectarianism will lose its influence, and the image of God in his members will be a sufficient passport to all Christian privileges; and all the followers of the most high will unite together in singing the song of praise, "Glory to God in the highest," etc.[74]

Apess had evidently been swept along with the contemporary American reformist spirit as expounded by noted revivalist-abolitionists of the day like Charles Grandison Finney or Theodore Dwight Weld.

Almost nothing is known of Apess's activities from the time he was ordained by the Methodist Protestants in 1829, the precise point at which he ends his autobiography, until his involvement with the Mashpees of Massachusetts in 1833. As O'Connell extrapolates from Apess's other publications, he probably traveled extensively as a circuit rider, preaching sermons on "the soul-harrowing theme of Indian degradation" and his own brand of "color-blind" religion to racially mixed audiences and applying his multifarious talents to some other worldly means of support for his family.[75] In 1831 he was appointed by the New York Annual Conference of the Methodist Protestant Church to preach among the Pequots in Connecticut. He was also busy writing as he brought out the second edition of *A Son of the Forest* in 1831, followed by *The Increase of the Kingdom of Christ: A Sermon*, published in New York in 1831, and *The Experiences of Five Christian Indians of the Pequot Tribe*, which appeared in Boston in 1833.

The reason why Apess chose to leave his Pequot relatives in Connecticut, who were having their own serious contentions with corrupt overseers at the time, to champion a similar cause among the Mashpees of Cape Cod remains a mystery as well. It is likely that both Pequot communities were being effectively administrated by established leaders at the time and thus had no immediate need or room for his special skills.[76] Two letters attesting to his "character and standing among the whites and natives (the Pequot tribe), in Groton," which Apess probably included in his *Indian Nullification* to counter rumors of his having been expelled from the Pequot community at Groton for illicit activities, indicate that he did function in some official capacity for the tribe. The letters, signed by several Pequot representatives, confirm his appointment as an agent in the tribe's efforts to generate funds for the construction of a church and authorize him to deduct expenses from the collections. They mention as well his nomination as a tribal delegate to the conference of the Methodist Protestant Church in New York on April 2, 1831.[77] His departure could, of course, also be viewed in connection with his estranged relationship to the Pequots by virtue of his own mixed ancestry and his having been brought up outside of the community. In fact, at one point he describes himself as being only "somewhat connected with the tribe."[78] The most likely explanation, however, would be that neither of the Pequot communities had sufficient funds to provide him with a salaried position and, like so many other members of the tribe, he was consequently forced to seek some form of employment elsewhere.

Apess first visited the Mashpees in the spring of 1833. Their struggle for political autonomy had been going on since at least 1748, so that his arrival there did not actually initiate the events that were to follow. Instead, he seems to have added his own energy and, more important, his organizational and rhetorical talents to revitalize an ongoing process. Nevertheless, at the beginning of the nineteenth century the Mashpees were experiencing another critical point in their relationship with their American neighbors, and perhaps it required the assistance of an outsider to direct their century-old frustrations into politically productive channels.[79]

Mashpee was originally a Christian Indian "plantation" established by Richard Bourne in 1665 on lands granted to him for that purpose by the Wampanoags. Due to their relative geographical isolation on Cape Cod and wise decision not to get involved in King Philip's War, the Mashpees were one of the few New England Praying Indian villages to survive the seventeenth century. After Bourne's death, in 1685, the original Wampanoag deed was confirmed by the General Court of Plymouth Colony "to be perpetually to them & their children, as that no part of them shall be granted to or purchased by any English whatsoever, by the Court's allowance, without the consent of all the said Indians."[80] When Plymouth and Massachusetts Bay joined as Massachusetts Colony in 1692, the Mashpees were consigned to the protection of the new government, and their religious concerns were ministered to by the Society for the Propagation of the Gospel among the Indians and Others in North America. Later, in 1746, the General Court appointed overseers to manage all secular affairs of the community, a situation that did not please the Mashpees, who began almost immediately to protest against the imposed system. In 1760 they sent a resident Mohegan to England in order to appeal their case directly to King George III, as a consequence of which the colonial administration changed the status of the Mashpee "plantation" into a legal district and gave the Indian "proprietors" the right to elect their own overseers. However, following the American Revolution—in which the Mashpees lost about half of their male population fighting for the republican cause—the legislature of Massachusetts repealed all former laws pertaining to them in 1788 and granted three white nonresident overseers quasi-dictatorial powers over the community's inhabitants, lands, and resources. To make matters worse, their autonomy in religious matters was also encroached upon when Harvard appointed the Reverend Phineas Fish as their minister and, despite their repeated protests, insisted upon paying for his undesired services with trust funds that had been originally donated for the sole benefit of Indians. Fish, an Old Light conservative, outlawed all non-Congregationalists from the Mashpee meetinghouse, the community's own religious and civil center which had been built with Indian funds in 1684, and consequently alienated the growing Baptist congregation led by the popular Mashpee preacher, Joseph ("Blind Joe") Amos.

At the time of Apess's arrival, the Mashpees were a heterogeneous group, or what James Clifford designates as an "artificial community" rather than a tribe, made up of about three hundred primarily mixed-blood descendants of various New England Indian groups (Wampanoags, Mohegans, Montauks, Narragansetts), as well as Anglo-Americans, Hessians, Cape Verde Islanders, and African Americans.[81] Massachusett, the local dialect, was apparently no longer spoken among them at the turn of the century. Mashpee lands and resources, primarily timber, were being exploited by neighboring whites with the cooperation of corrupt overseers. Children were frequently bound out to white families because their own parents barely managed to sustain themselves, having to supplement subsistence agriculture with hunting and fishing, or hiring out as day laborers and whalers. Intemperance and prostitution were widespread and, at the same time, those who sought social and moral stability in Blind Joe Amos's Baptist revival were being barred from meeting in their own community center by an imposed white Congregationalist preacher. In short, it was the kind of contact environment with which the visiting Pequot Methodist missionary was most familiar.

When Apess accepted Phineas Fish's friendly invitation to preach in his stead at Mashpee, he was surprised to find the meetinghouse occupied almost exclusively by non-Indians. In his later account of the Mashpee affair he remarked wryly: "All the Indians I had ever seen were of a reddish color, sometimes approaching a yellow, but now, look to whatever quarter I would, most of those who were coming were pale faces, and, in my disappointment, it seemed to me that the hue of death sat upon their countenances. It seemed very strange to me that my brethren should have changed their natural color and become in every respect like white men." A few days later, as Apess was speaking before a Mashpee audience on the history of New England's Indians, they "requested [him] to hear their whole story and to help them," and he accordingly arranged a public meeting with them on May 21 to discuss the matter. After hearing their grievances, he suggested they apply to the governor and Council of Massachusetts for redress and, when they informed him they had already tried to do so without success, he offered his assistance on the condition that they adopt him as a member of the tribe:

> I began by saying that, though I was a stranger among them, I did not doubt but that I might do them some good and be instrumental in procuring the discharge of the overseers and an alteration of the existing laws. As, however, I was not a son of their particular tribe, if they wished me to assist them, it would be necessary for them to give me a right to act in their behalf by adopting me, as then our rights and interests would become identical. They must be aware that all the evil reports calumny could invent would be put in circulation against me by the whites interested, and that no means to set them against me would be neglected.

In an official document drawn up at the meeting and signed by about a hundred participants, Apess and his wife and two children were formally adopted into the Mashpee tribe of Indians "forever." It was further agreed to orally that he would be provided with a house to live in and with some means of support.[82]

Apess wasted no time in organizing a small-scale Indian insurrection that came to be known locally as the Woodland Revolt. At said gathering he helped the Mashpees to formulate (there can be little doubt that he was the author) two petitions, one to the governor and Council of Massachusetts and the other to Harvard College. Appended to both was a set of "resolutions," which were tantamount to a Mashpee "Declaration of Independence":

> *Resolved*, That we, as a tribe, will rule ourselves, and have the right to do so; for all men are born free and equal, says the Constitution of the country.
> *Resolved*, That we will not permit any white man to come upon our plantation, to cut or carry off wood or hay, or any other article, without our permission, after the 1st of July next.
> *Resolved*, That we will put said resolutions in force that date (July next), with the penalty of binding and throwing them from the plantation, if they will not stay away without.[83]

The petition to the governor listed their grievances concerning the illegal use of their resources by whites and charged the treasurer and overseers with having mismanaged their funds. The one sent to Harvard filed a complaint against the activities of Phineas Fish and demanded his discharge. Banking on the hue and cry that had been raised recently in the New England states in response to Georgia's treatment of the Cherokees, they cannily confronted the good citizens of Massachusetts with identical problems at their own doorstep: "Perhaps you have heard of the oppression of the Cherokees and lamented over them much, and thought the Georgians were hard and cruel creatures; but did you ever hear of the poor, oppressed and degraded Marshpee Indians in Massachusetts, and lament over them?" The same petition also contained an additional set of resolutions proclaiming the tribe's right to appoint its own minister, demanding free access to its meetinghouse, and — with due respect for the power of the written word — threatening to "publish this to the world" if these were not complied with.[84]

Following this memorable meeting Apess journeyed to New Bedford, lecturing along the way on Indian affairs and obviously causing some commotion with his radical opinion among "advocates of oppression" who, in his own estimation, "feared that an insurrection might break out among the colored people, in which blood might be shed."[85] The ensuing overreaction to the Woodland Revolt does in fact reflect the current phobia about slave insurrections, in which New England Indians and African Americans were known to have occasionally joined forces as early as the second half of the seventeenth century. The fear of a joint Indian–African American revolt is also evident, for instance, in the inclusion of Indians in many of the pre-revolutionary slave codes in New England.[86] Influenced in part by the relatively recent violent birth of a free slave republic in Santo Domingo in 1791, the number of attempted slave revolts in the United States had increased dramatically after the turn of the century. The most widely publicized of these, Nat Turner's rebellion of 1831, was still very fresh in the public mind. In view of the increasing population of freedmen in New England, the burgeoning controversy over manumission, and the related series of riots occurring in major northeastern cities during the 1830s, the hysteria produced by the nonviolent efforts of the tiny Mashpee community to obtain some vestiges of political autonomy is perhaps somewhat more understandable.[87]

On June 7, Apess accompanied a delegation of Mashpee proprietors to Boston to present the memorial to the governor. Even though they did not actually meet with him personally, they somehow came away with the erroneous assumption that Governor Levi Lincoln supported their resolutions. After Apess had been rejoined by his family in Mashpee on June 18, a meeting was scheduled for June 25 in order to elect a National Assembly of the Mashpee Tribe. Apess described the occasion with words that clearly recall Occom's republican sentiments: "We now, in our synagogue, for the first time, concerted the form of a government, suited to the spirit and capacity of freeborn sons of the forest, after the pattern set us by our white brethren. There was but one exception, viz., that *all* who dwelt in our precincts were to be held free and equal, *in truth*, as well as in letter."[88] The new tribal government then proceeded to issue a public notice to the effect that all resolutions made at the May 21 meeting (which, as has been pointed out, they mistakenly assumed to have been acknowledged by the governor) would be enforced by the tribe as of July 1, "firmly believing that each and every one of the existing laws concerning the poor Israelites of Marshpee was founded on wrong and misconception." It further dismissed the overseers, the treasurer, and the missionary. On said date Apess and a number of Mashpees confronted two whites who had been gathering wood in defiance of the tribe's resolution, unloaded their cart, and forced them to leave the premises empty-handed—the infamous Woodland Revolt had thus begun.[89]

Acting on reports filed by the overseers, Fish, and some neighboring whites, Governor Lincoln sent John Fiske as his representative to mediate in the Mashpee affair. On July 4, a date picked explicitly by the tribe for its obvious symbolic connotation, a meeting was arranged between Fiske and the Mashpee representatives, which was attended by about a hundred Indians as well as the overseers (under protection of the sheriff) and a number of "concerned" citizens. Fiske tried to convince the Mashpees that their actions were illegal and suggested that they trust instead in the goodwill of the state administration and allow it to regulate matters for them. Apess apparently delivered a spirited speech on this occasion in which he questioned the constitutionality of the previous laws and appropriately recalled Jeffersonian political philosophy (a people's inherent right to divest themselves of unjust laws) to legitimize the Mashpees' actions. As he had predicted, his right to speak for the tribe was immediately challenged by Fiske. He countered the charge by citing his official adoption, but this was promptly rejected as being illegal. Although there was some tension throughout the meeting, it was carried on in an orderly manner, even after Apess was arrested on the charge of "riot, assault, and trespass" for his actions on July 1 and duly sentenced to thirty days in jail and a fine of $100. Since he was regarded as the ringleader of the Mashpee protest movement, his arrest was no doubt calculated to reduce his influence within the community. He was soon released on bail, paid by a sympathetic white, and allowed to return to Mashpee. But the arrest apparently had the desired effect because the tribe posted a notice on July 6 in which it recalled its previous resolutions until the matter should be cleared by the General Court of Massachusetts.[90]

By this time the Mashpee affair was being followed closely by the New England press. The Mashpees' position was defended in abolitionist papers, particularly in Benjamin Hallett's *Boston Daily Advocate*, which also published editorials by Apess, as well as in William Lloyd Garrison's *Liberator*, which had hitherto dedicated little space to Indians because of the practice of slavery among the Five Civilized Tribes.[91] Bitter opposition was voiced in conservative papers like the *Boston Courier* and the local *Barnstable Patriot*, which also targeted Apess as the instigator. One such article in the *Patriot*, which Apess reprinted in his account, contradicts in a curious way the common assumption of the times that Indians were incapable of "improvement":

> At the time of Apes' coming among them, they were quiet and peaceable, and their condition, mentally, morally, and pecuniarily improving. At this time, and when this is the condition and situation of the Indians, comes this intruder, this disturber, this riotous and mischief-making Indian, from the Pequot tribe, in Connecticut. He goes among the inhabitants of Marshpee, and

by all the arts of a talented, educated, wily, unprincipled Indian, professing with all, to be an apostle of Christianity; he stirs them up to sedition, riot, *treason*! Instigates them to declare their independence of the laws of Massachusetts, and to *arm themselves* to defend it.[92]

Apess, who at one point remarks coyly that he is "not a man skilled in legal subtleties," filed a successful suit against a number of individuals following the publication of an especially defamatory letter in the *Daily Commercial Gazette* and eventually forced the authors to make a public apology for their libelous statements.[93]

Apess's activities at Mashpee throughout this difficult period were manifold: He was pastor of "The Free and United Church" he had organized together with Blind Joe Amos, with whom he also formed a temperance society, and he continued to use his "wily talents" to further the community's cause. Other than writing newspaper articles, he was instrumental in the formulation of "An Indian's Appeal to the White Men of Massachusetts," a leaflet dated December 19, 1833, which was probably inspired by Jeremiah Evarts's famous "William Penn" essays, especially his widely circulated antiremoval publication titled "Address of the Cherokees to the People of the United States." Once again the Mashpees pointed to the obvious discrepancy between public criticism of Georgia's infamous treatment of the Cherokees and their silence concerning the situation of New England's Indians:

> As our brethren, the white men of Massachusetts, have recently manifested much sympathy for the red men of the Cherokee nation, who have suffered much from their white brethren; as it is contended in this State, that our red brethren, the Cherokees, should be an independent people, having the privileges of the white men; we, the red men of the Marshpee tribe, consider it a favorable time to speak. We are not free. We wish to be so, as much as the red men of Georgia. How will the white man of Massachusetts ask favor for the red men of the South, while the poor Marshpee red men, his near neighbors, sigh in bondage? Will not your white brothers of Georgia tell you to look at home, and clear your own borders of oppression, before you trouble them?[94]

In cooperation with Isaac Coombs and Daniel Amos, two educated Mashpee leaders, Apess also presented a "Petition of the Marshpee Tribe of Indians" to the Massachusetts House of Representatives in which the tribe repeated its desire to manage its own property, be incorporated as a township, have the right to institute its own municipal regulations and to appoint magistrates, and effect the immediate abolition of the overseership.[95]

The Woodland Revolt was partially (if only temporarily) successful as, in

March of 1834, the Mashpees reacquired the status of a district. Thereby they gained the right to elect selectmen who could officiate over certain internal judicial, political, financial, and educational matters and were placed under the supervision of only one commissioner and treasurer appointed by the governor. Even though it was only a partial victory at best—the Massachusetts legislature reserved the right to repeal the act, and Mr. Fish continued on the premises until 1846—it was still an extraordinary feat because, as Kim McQuaid has properly observed, it stood as one of the very few substantial victories for Indian rights during the removal era when many other eastern Indian tribes were being ruthlessly pushed out of their territory.[96] William Apess, an adopted Pequot Methodist missionary, thus played a key role in the transformation of an "artificial community" into a homogeneous tribe. Despite numerous setbacks in their history, such as the frustrating denial of tribal status in a federal district court decision in 1978, the Mashpees now identify themselves as a Wampanoag Indian community and maintain an official tribal council.[97]

Included in Apess's account of the Mashpee episode is a letter signed by three Mashpee selectmen on March 19, 1835, in which they attest that "we love our red brother, the Rev. William Apes, who preaches to us, and have all the confidence in him that we can put in any man, knowing him to be a devout Christian, of sound mind, of firm purpose, and worthy to be trusted by reason of his truth."[98] Nevertheless, Apess's influence among the Mashpees began to decline sometime after 1835. Daniel Amos and other Mashpees had already published a letter in the *Boston Daily Advocate* in 1833 asserting that "we know something of our own rights without being told by Mr. Apes or any one."[99] Apess had apparently helped the Mashpees to bridge a moment of crisis and, once they had managed with his invaluable assistance to regain their stability as a tribe, they were able once again to rely entirely upon their own traditional leadership. He may have remained at Mashpee until 1838, during which time he published his *Indian Nullification* (1835); gave two oral presentations in Boston in January of 1836, which were published as *Eulogy on King Philip* in 1836 and reprinted in 1837; and brought out a second edition of *The Experiences of Five Christian Indians* in 1837. Three debt actions brought against him in the Barnstable court in 1836, 1837, and 1838 prove that his financial situation had also deteriorated further by then.[100]

Up until very recently, Apess's whereabouts after 1838 and the circumstances of his death remained unknown. According to an obituary recently discovered, Apess died in New York City in April of 1839 from the effects of alcoholism. It appears that his final years were beset with personal problems, as the obituary mentions further that his "conduct had been quite irregular, and he had lost the confidence of the best portions of the community," and that he was in the habit of going on "frolics that would continue for a week or two."[101] Drawing from what is known about the earlier part of his life history and comparing it with the experiences of his eighteenth-century predecessors, it is not difficult to conjecture what may have broken his spirit at the end.

Considering William Apess's social privations and his limited educational opportunities, the volume and scope of his literary output are all the more astonishing and invariably bring up the question of authorship. As no original manuscripts have been found to date and the practice of ghostwriting was far from uncommon in those days, the suspicion that Apess may have had some assistance is legitimate. Nevertheless, with the likely exception of some editorial cooperation in *Indian Nullification*, Apess can be regarded as the sole or primary author of his five known publications on the basis of his "wily talents": his reputation as an eloquent speaker, his function as a scribe for the Mashpees and "a consistency of voice and sensibility" in the writings published under his name.[102] In addition, it can be pointed out that the education enjoyed by Samson Occom and Joseph Johnson, whose literacy is confirmed by handwritten documents, was no more or less adequate for the task at hand than Apess's "six successive winters" of schooling. Much more important than the matter of possible editorial intervention in his writings is Apess's receptiveness to the cultural-historical trends of his times, especially those directly affecting the development of ethnic minority literature in the emergent American nation.

The public interest aroused by the issues of Indian removal and slavery on the eve of the Civil War opened up a marginal market for writings coming "from an uncommon quarter." Among other Indian publications to appear during the second decade of the nineteenth century, Apess's autobiography was preceded in 1824 by the widely read memoirs of Catherine Brown, a well-known Cherokee missionary whose tragic death at the tender age of twenty-three the year before had moved the public in New England.[103] Of particular relevance to Apess's work, however, is the blossoming of African American literature during the first half of the nineteenth century and the rise of the American abolitionist movement.[104] African American literature also had its beginnings in the eighteenth century (Jupiter Hammon, Lemuel Haynes, Phillis Wheatley) and was already well represented in the first decades of the nineteenth by various kinds of publications (treatises, tracts, appeals, poems, sermons) dealing primarily with religious and social issues. But the genre that experienced the widest circulation by far was the African American autobiography, particularly the accounts of ex-slaves, which began to appear with increasing frequency in the latter part of the eighteenth century and then boomed in the 1830s, when the abolitionist movement went into a more militant phase. At this point the slave narrative even began to surpass in popularity traditional American favorites like spiritual diaries and captivity narratives.[105]

Even though there are few direct references to African Americans in Apess's works and he makes a clear distinction between his own situation and slavery in *A Son of the Forest*, it is still very likely that he became aware of African American publications in the course of his relations with fellow Methodists, if not by virtue of his own concern with the issue of racism and obvious devotion to reading (as indicated by the numerous literary citations in his writings). At any rate, his autobiography shares many of the elements that are characteristic of contemporary African American autobiographies, some of which, of course, were due to common borrowings from current American literary trends. Contemporary African American and American Indian authors both borrowed freely from salvationist literature and were quite familiar with Enlightenment treatises on the natural rights of man. The schematic conversion-backsliding-rebirth story line of spiritual diaries, as exemplified by publications such as Jonathan Edwards's widely read edition of *Memoirs of the Reverend David Brainerd, Missionary to the Indians* (1822), was frequently imitated by ethnic minority writers. Apess's conversion experience, for instance, is wrought with the same emotional imbalance between ecstatic perception of divine love and tormented disbelief found in Brainerd's memoirs. In conventional spiritual autobiographies, including *A Son of the Forest*, these disturbances usually continue up until the moment of the protagonist's "rebirth." It is this final spiritual victory that qualifies the ethnic neophyte as a full-fledged member of the church.[106]

At the same time, early African American writers also conceived of themselves as members of an oppressed social group, what Arnold Krupat has designated as a "synecdochic sense of self," and antebellum African American autobiography thus usually has a sociopolitical motif tied in with its standard salvationist denouement, namely, the exposure of the social evils that worked against the fulfillment of a collective ethnic conversion experience.[107] African American writers thereby often appropriated the protest language of reformist-abolitionist literature, as well as the aggressive immediatism of Garrisonian rhetoric.[108] Apess also identifies himself with an oppressed group — "natives" in *A Son of the Forest* and "colored people" in his subsequent writings — and his autobiography is replete with illustrations of how white society made it extremely difficult for him to pursue his religious inclinations and develop the full potential of his talents. His concern with a synecdochic self is made evident, for example, by his addition of an appendix of nearly equal length to *A Son of the Forest* containing "some general observations on the origin and character of the Indians, as a nation," which he excerpted (and sometimes simply plagiarized) from current expositions by white authors like Elias Boudinot and Washington Irving.[109]

Another shared characteristic in early nineteenth-century ethnic literature is the frequent reference made to the Israelites and the Ten Lost Tribes as the origin for both African and Indian peoples.[110] Apess incorporates this revived sixteenth-century European theory in his autobiography — "It is my opinion that our nation retains the original complexion of our common father, Adam" — and makes it the central theme of his only published sermon, *Increase of the Kingdom of Christ*, to which he attached a separate essay titled "The Indians: The Ten Lost Tribes."[111] Other than providing him with a legitimation for missionizing Indians, the notion of a common biblical progenitor also serves him as an argumentative basis for his own personal commitment to egalitarian Christianity. In his later essay, "An Indian's Looking-Glass for the White Man," he confronts white bigotry with the frequently employed African American analogy of Christ as a "colored person."[112]

Finally, the slave narrative, like Apess's autobiography, is often a tale of perseverance in the face of seemingly insurmountable odds, an "ethnic success story," with obvious parallels to contemporary "self-made-man" literature such as Benjamin Franklin's immensely popular *Autobiography* (1817–18), which had already become a part of American vernacular culture by the time Apess began to publish his work.[113] Striving for advancement within dominant society in full compliance with the "Protestant ethic" — temperance, honesty, hard work, frugality, devoutness, and so on — is also a prevalent motif in African American and American Indian autobiographies well into the twentieth century.

The main affinity between Apess's works and early nineteenth-century African American literature, however, is his spirited campaign against racism. Like Olaudah Equiano, George White, William Grimes, and other writers of African descent before him, Apess extended the title of his autobiography with what amounts to a proclamation of literary emancipation: "written by himself."[114] For the ethnic writer of the 1830s, when "scientific racism" was making the rounds in proslavery circles, the technical act of writing was already tantamount to an expression of defiance because it contradicted contentions that "colored people" could not be educated. Like Occom and numerous earlier African American writers, Apess also incorporates ironic apologias for his personal "deficiencies," backed by signed letters of reference attesting to his sound "character." He seems to be employing the techniques of judicial oratory here to appease readers who might possibly feel called upon to sit in judgment over his "audacious" implications of racial equality, first luring them into dropping their racist guard with pretended modesty and sentimental appeals to their sense of piety, and then striking them unexpectedly with the full force of his caustic (and very literate) language before they have a chance to close the book in indignation.[115] Antebellum autoethnographic expression thus also functioned as an affirmation of the synecdochic sense of self (I write, therefore we are) and, furthermore, provided legible proof of the author's ability to "make it" in the White Man's most sacrosanct cultural realm. Its political portent is implicit, for instance, in the repressive laws passed in some southern states during the mid-1830s, which made literacy among "colored people" illegal.[116]

One of the most pervasive characteristics of the antebellum fugitive slave narrative is the protagonist's journey north, or quest motif, which represents multiple levels of spiritual and social evolution.[117] It entails the chronological account of a physical and psychological flight away from oppression and cultural alienation toward the promise of freedom and integration, as well as a spiritual rite of passage to salvation. Apess also reacts to alienation and bondage — "it was too much for one to bear, to call every man 'master' " — by escaping to New York and then heading northward to Canada to be, as he says, "out on the broad theatre of the world."[118] His "space" in society as an ordained Methodist minister, however, can materialize only after his return to his own native community in Connecticut. This circular plot is an underlying difference between Apess's "native" autobiography and contemporary African American slave narratives, as a "long way back" for the latter would have entailed the choice of embarking upon an uncertain voyage to Africa or regressing into bondage.

Yet another important common feature in African American and American Indian literature of the times is a special kind of humor that distinguishes itself from the diatribes commonly found in abolitionist writings.[119]

The former is a much more illusive sort of humor, a form of masked verbal defiance ("puttin' on ole Massa!"), which probably has its roots in the postcontact fusion of African and North American trickster stories. The trickster figure, who releases social tensions through his seemingly ludicrous antics, according to Jung's classic interpretation, often "fools" himself and his antagonists into a learning process.[120] Apess's writings, though often embittered and melodramatic, are also sprinkled with candid and covertly humorous passages. His comment on religious bigotry in Connecticut, "where they are so pious that they kill the cats for killing rats, and whip the beer barrels for working upon the Sabbath," for instance, contrasts markedly with his subtle confession that he began "to lose sight of religion and of God" immediately after having charged a pair of decent shoes to his master's account without permission as he was about to set off on his long march north to freedom. This particular incident leaves the critical reader wondering whether the confession of guilt is really as pious as it is made to appear, especially if one considers that when he finally starts on his "long way back" as a changed man who will no longer be cheated by the White Man he does so on a new pair of shoes he paid for with the fruit of his own labor. Perhaps his confession is really intended as an expression of defiance, as theft was one of the common covert ways in which slaves could get back at their masters.[121]

Apess's writings reveal a process of political maturation between 1829, the publication date of the first edition of *A Son of the Forest*, and 1836, when *Eulogy on King Philip* appeared.[122] His books thus seem to follow the chronological trend in abolitionist and African American literature from a milder moralistic appeal to the American conscience up until the 1820s to a militant protest rhetoric exposing the moral deficit of the American political ethos at the close of the decade, as represented by the hard-line antislavery statement in *Walker's Appeal, in Four Articles* (1829) and the editorials in Garrison's *Liberator* (founded 1831).[123] Apess's pietistic tone and guarded criticism in *A Son of the Forest* are gradually replaced by more explicit historical, social, and political concerns in his subsequent publications. His deletion of the lengthy passage referring to his break with the Methodist Episcopal Church in the second (1831) edition of his autobiography, after which he produced his most critical writings, and the omission of his caustic essay on racism in the second (1837) version of *The Experiences of Five Christian Indians* suggest a period of pronounced political assertiveness in his career as a writer corresponding approximately with the duration of his sojourn among the Mashpees from 1833 to 1836–37. Perhaps the reprints of his autobiographical pieces, which he first published on his own account, were financed by a conservative interest group or religious body who found these passages "objectionable," as Apess himself intimates.[124] It is telling, for instance, that William Grimes's critical autobiography was virtually ignored by the abolitionists and he had to finance the second edition himself as well, even though it appeared at the height of antislavery sentiment in 1855. Publications by early nineteenth-century ethnic writers who did not subscribe to the northern myth of individual triumph over corrupt southern institutions were apparently more difficult to market.[125]

Increase of the Kingdom of Christ is the sole surviving example of Apess's sermon rhetoric, but the occasion at which it was presented and the circumstances for its publication are not known. Its millennialist message and advocacy of egalitarian Christianity are, as may be expected from an exponent of Methodist revivalism, essentially as orthodox as Occom's or Johnson's exhortations tended to be. The only aspect that distinguishes it somewhat from the conventional evangelist fire-and-brimstone syllogisms is his justification for the effort to missionize Indians on the basis of the popular Ten Lost Tribes construct. "If . . . the Indians of the American continent are a part of the long lost ten tribes of Israel," he argues here, "have not the great American nation reason to fear the swift judgments of heaven on them for nameless cruelties, extortions, and exterminations inflicted upon the poor natives of the forest?" America's great "national sin," he concludes, is that it "has utterly failed to amalgamate the red man of the woods into the artificial, cultivated ranks of social life." Once again, he underscores his arguments with an appended essay in defense of the "Indian character" which, he feels, has been "grossly misrepresented and misunderstood." The appendage seems to convey a bilateral view of the Indian future. As "one of the few remaining descendants of a once powerful tribe of Indians," Apess "looks forward with a degree of confidence to the day as being not far distant when ample justice shall be done the red man by his white brother — when he shall be allowed that station in the scale of being and intelligence which unerring wisdom designed him to occupy." Yet, a few lines further he warns that only a "remnant of multitudes" remains to be converted, "and they are on their march to eternity." This closing statement, which appears to give in to current "vanishing Indian" sentiment, can — if the word "eternity" is related back again to the "increase" topic of the sermon — be interpreted as Apess's firm belief "that the soul of the Indian is immortal." Only then would Apess's statement toward the close of his sermon, in which he skillfully weaves evangelist and abolitionist language into a figurative frontier antithesis to screaming "wild savages," actually make sense: "Revivals follow revivals, and the deep brown wilderness is vocal with the shouting and songs of the delivered tribes, long slaves to error but now emancipated and brought out of the wilderness of sin into the Canaan of Gospel liberty."[126]

Apess's third publication, *The Experiences of Five Christian Indians*, marks his transition toward an increasingly authentic voice. The book is made up of an abbreviated version of Apess's first autobiography; a first-person account written by the "Missionary's Consort," Mary Wood Apess; three brief conversion biographies of Pequot neophytes (Hannah Caleb, Sally George, Anne Wampy) authored by Apess; and an additional essay titled "An Indian's Looking-Glass for the White Man."[127] Here he also blends revivalist-abolitionist rhetoric into a unique bifocally inverted assessment of Indian–white relations. The full impact of his unrelenting attack on white racism in the appended essay is actually carried by the pious tone of the personal narratives that precede it, which ostensibly conform to the traditional patterns of seventeenth-century Indian conversion testimonies. On the surface, this collection of life stories documents the success of Apess's mission among the Pequots in 1831 by counting souls saved, but the conversion experiences included here differ somewhat from their Puritan models in that each one exposes the contradiction between white Protestant morality and racism. Hannah Caleb (speaking through Apess's pen) attributes her initial reservation about Christian beliefs primarily to white bigotry:

> I saw such a great inconsistency in their precepts and examples that I could not believe them. They openly professed to love one another, as Christians, and every people of all nations whom God hath made — and yet they would backbite each other, and quarrel with one another, and would not so much as eat and drink together, nor worship God together. And not only so, the poor Indians, the people to whom I was wedded by the common ties of nature, were set at naught by those noble professors of grace, merely because we were Indians — and I had to bear a part with them, being of the same coin, when in fact, with the same abilities, with a white skin, I should have been looked upon with honor and respect.[128]

This "ingenuous" reversal of religious role models, "civil" Indians as opposed to "savage" whites, is also found in numerous contemporary religious tracts in which African American or American Indian converts turn out to be better Christians than whites could ever aspire to be. With the exception of his own account, Apess's book focuses entirely on the conversion experiences of women, perhaps as a subconscious tribute to his own recuperation from the female-induced traumas of his youth or simply as a conscious acknowledgment of the increasing importance of women in Christian Indian communities. Each of the four conversion experiences occurred on the very edges of despair and self-destruction—against all odds, so to speak—and is thus clearly intended as a statement of Indian moral and spiritual perseverance (the ethnic success story) rather than an appeal to white empathy. Apess's own "poor self-taught Indian youth" narrative, which he claims to have written "for the purpose of giving the youth a transient view between their condition and mine," is much more direct in its confrontation of the issue of racism than his lengthier autobiography.

In what appears by now to be a typical "Apessian" literary trait, any room for doubt concerning his intended message to the reader is precluded by an absolutely unambiguous postscript. "An Indian's Looking-Glass for the White Man" is an unrelenting diatribe on racism that reveals the full potential of Apess's incisive language and stands as a worthy prelude to later masters of Indian satire such as Alexander Posey, Vine Deloria, Jr., and Gerald Vizenor. Apess begins in an orthodox reformist manner by listing the usual sources of the "Indian problem" in New England: intemperance, absence of males at sea, treatment of Indians as minors, corrupt white agents, poor education, and lack of protection for persons and property. But the primary factor, as he sees it, is pigmentation:

> But, reader, I acknowledge that this is a confused world, and I am not seeking for office; but merely placing before you the black inconsistency that you place before me—which is ten times blacker than any skin that you will find in the Universe. And now let me exhort you to do away with that principle, as it appears ten times worse in the sight of God and candid men, than skins of color—more disgraceful than all the skins that Jehovah ever made. If black or red skins, or any other skin of color is disgraceful to God, it appears he has disgraced himself a great deal—for he has made fifteen colored people to one white, and placed them here upon this earth.
>
> Now let me ask you, white man, if it is a disgrace for to eat, drink and sleep with the image of God, or sit, or walk and talk with them? Or have you the folly to think that the white man, being one in fifteen or sixteen, are the only beloved images of God? Assemble all nations together in your imagination, and then let the whites be seated amongst them, and then let us look for the whites, and I doubt not it would be hard finding them; for to the rest of the nations, they are still but a handful.

Apess then expands his imaginative epidermal scenario to illustrate in a unique manner the summation of America's "national sins":

Now suppose these skins were put together, and each skin had its national crimes written upon it — which skin do you think would have the greatest? I will ask one question more. Can you charge the Indians with robbing a nation almost of their whole Continent, and murdering their women and children, and then depriving the remainder of their lawful rights, that nature and God require them to have? And to cap the climax, rob another nation to till their grounds, and welter out their days under the lash with hunger and fatigue under the scorching rays of a burning sun? I should look at all the skins, and I know that when I cast my eye upon that white skin, and if I saw those crimes written upon it, I should enter my protest against it immediately, and cleave to that which is more honorable.

Apess proffers his own brand of egalitarian Christianity in this essay as well, pointing out once again that Christ and his disciples were dark-skinned people and that consequently whites were "not indebted to a principle beneath a white skin for [their] religious services, but to a colored one."[129] Banking on contemporary abolitionist protest against laws prohibiting racial intermarriage in Massachusetts since 1705 (reinstated in 1786 with the so-called Solemnization of Marriage Act voiding all unions between whites and African Americans), he openly advocates "amalgamation," which, in his opinion, has produced people "of the first respectability" in Boston and elsewhere.[130] Indians have the same right to intermarry as all of the whites, he goes on to say after first assuring the reader that he is not looking for a wife himself ("having one of the finest cast"), who "have taken the liberty to choose my brethren, the Indians, hundreds and thousands of them as partners in life." Summarizing what he has learned so far about the nature of "white" principles, Apess concludes dryly, "I should say they were skin deep."[131]

In contrast to the pervading moralistic-pietistic tone in his previous publications, Apess develops a more straightforward legalistic approach to the subject of Indian political rights in his bulkiest work, *Indian Nullification of the Unconstitutional Laws of Massachusetts Relative to the Marshpee Tribe*. The language he appropriates here is the republican rhetoric of the American Revolution and the pamphleteering style of antiremoval writers like Jeremiah Evarts. "If, in the course of this little volume, I have been obliged to use language that seems harsh," he concedes at the end of his treatise, "I beg my readers to remember that it was in defense of the character of the people under my spiritual charge and of my own."[132] His chronological account of the Mashpee affair, which parallels the emancipatory struggle of the former English colonies in many ways, is underscored by an array of pertinent documents such as newspaper articles, letters, appeals, minutes, and resolutions. It is thus a complex ethnohistorical collage that presents the case from several points of view, both in concurrence and in opposition to his own. William G. Snelling, a contemporary writer and journalist, has been credited as its author, but, as has been pointed out earlier, consistencies in the main narrative with Apess's other publications make it more likely that Snelling functioned only as his editor.[133]

In juxtaposing the Mashpees' inherent right to oppose the oppressive laws of Massachusetts ("the boasted cradle of independence") to the American Revolution, Apess demonstrates a keen grasp of contemporary political trends. This is also evident, for instance, in the title he chose for his book, which is an obvious play on the "theory of nullification" formulated by John C. Calhoun during the nullification crisis of 1832, and the political connections between Georgia's annulment of Cherokee laws in 1828–30 and South Carolina's defiance of federal tariff regulations in 1828 and 1832.[134] The account itself is a well-documented and juridically sound plea in defense of the Mashpees and their ongoing controversy with the Massachusetts administration, as well as a valuable historical record of the case. Obviously, he does not let the opportunity pass by to make "a few general remarks" about basic colonialist modi operandi in New England's historical relations with Indians, particularly concerning the barter in "civilization" for Indian lands. His résumé of past legislative actions leaves little doubt as to which side has profited from the transaction:

> It is a sorrowful truth that, heretofore, all legislation regarding the affairs of Indians has had a direct tendency to degrade them, to drive them from their homes and the graves of their fathers, and to give their lands as a spoil to the general government, or to the several states. . . . From what I have been able to learn from the public prints and other sources, the amount annually derived to the American people from Indian lands is not far from six millions, a tax of which they have almost the sole benefit. In the meanwhile, we daily see the Indian driven farther and farther by inhuman legislation and wars, and all to enrich a people who call themselves Christians and are governed by laws derived from the moral and pious Puritans. I say that, from the year of our Lord, 1656, to the present day, the conduct of the whites toward the Indians has been one continued system of robbery.[135]

Apess then proceeds to make a critical assessment of the role played by missionaries in this unequal exchange and the kind of "civilization" they promoted among Indians. His lucid observations here seem to illustrate perfectly Paulo Freire's analysis of colonialist "banking education" and its systematic pedagogy of oppression. Apess writes:

It is the general fault of those who go on missions that they cannot sacrifice the pride of their hearts in order to do good. It seems to have been usually the object to seat the Indians between two stools, in order that they might fall to the ground, by breaking up their government and forms of society, without giving them any others in their place. It does not appear to be the aim of the missionaries to improve the Indians by making citizens of them. Hence, in most cases, anarchy and confusion are the results. Nothing has more effectually contributed to the decay of several tribes than the course pursued by their missionaries. Let us look back to the first of them for proofs. From the days of Eliot to the year 1834, have they made one citizen?[136]

His own conclusions on this matter in turn echo the sentiments expressed by Albert Memmi, who observes that the failure of colonial missions was inevitable because "the colonialist could not favor an undertaking which would have contributed to the disappearance of colonial relationships." In a similar vein, Apess argues that, "No doubt, many of them have done much good; but I greatly doubt that any missionary has ever thought of making the Indian or African his equal. As soon as we begin to talk about equal rights, the cry of amalgamation is set up, as if men of color could not enjoy their natural rights without any necessity for intermarriage between the sons and daughters of the two races."[137] At this point in his account Apess makes a connection between his negative historical summary of Indian–white relations and the current problem of racial discrimination in New England, perhaps still thinking specifically of the pronounced Anglo-Saxon distaste for miscegenation in Massachusetts, where legal restrictions on mixed marriages continued to hold sway until 1839 while similar antimiscegenation laws had already been revoked in New York in 1785 and Rhode Island in 1798. His own candid suggestions as to this particularly sensitive issue give a curious twist to the "vanishing Indian" theory in juxtaposition to puritanical sexual mores:

Were I permitted to express an opinion, it would be that it is more honorable in the two races to intermarry than to act as too many of them do. My advice to the white man is to let the colored race alone. It will considerably diminish the annual amount of sin committed. Or else let them even *marry* our daughters, and no more ado about amalgamation. We desire none of their connection that way. All we ask of them is peace and our rights. We can find wives enough without asking any favors of them. We have some wildflowers among us as fair, as blooming, and quite as pure as any they can show. But enough has been said on this subject, which I should not have mentioned at all, but that it has been rung in my ears by almost every white lecturer I ever had the misfortune to meet.[138]

At the same time, *Indian Nullification* is a plea against the "vilest calumnies" that were made public after his personal involvement in the Mashpee affair, in which he was "represented as an exciter of sedition, a hypocrite, and a gambler." His primary motive for writing the account, according to his own "concluding observations," was to vindicate his "reputation" which, as Occom had experienced earlier, was subjected to slander the moment he decided to take a defiant stand in a conflict of interest between Indians and whites. In contrast to Occom, however, Apess did not have to sign a public apology for his "imprudence." On the contrary, he wielded his pen in a most effective manner to help the Mashpees obtain at least a temporary victory and to clear his reputation in court. "Though an Indian," he states in the closing lines of his book, "I am at least a man, with all the feelings proper to humanity, and my reputation is dear to me; and I conceive it to be my duty to the children I shall leave behind me, as well as to myself, not to leave them with the inheritance of a blasted name."[139] Apess's remarkable steadfastness in this case must, of course, also be regarded in the context of the reformist sentiment during the Second Great Awakening, which was certainly more receptive to the issue of racism than the evangelical revival of the previous century. Occom's critical autobiographical sketch, it will be recalled, was penned in the same defiant spirit but did not make it into print.

Apess's last publication, *Eulogy on King Philip*, is his "valedictory performance."[140] In this written version of a public address he delivered at the Odeon in Boston on January 8, 1836 (with an encore by popular request on January 26), which was published that same year and reprinted in an abridged version in 1837, Apess's polyphonic literary voice seems to have reached its maximum force of expression. His skills as orator and writer are reinforced here by his growing knowledge of Anglo-American letters and his experience in Indian politics, allowing him to mount a lethal verbal assault on Puritan (mis)interpretations of American history. Some of the passages in this address anticipate the scathing tone of Francis Jennings's epochal study on the subject well over a century later. Here Apess demonstrates once again his awareness of current intellectual trends by pulling a variety of ideological strings—democratic republicanism, abolitionism, revivalism, romantic primitivism—in what can be considered one of the strongest pro-Indian statements in the history of American Indian literature. Even if the political climate in New England permitted a certain degree of social tolerance for a critical Indian voice, an oratorical thrashing such as this delivered by a "colored person" in Boston, where only three months earlier, on October 21, 1835, a mob had paraded William Garrison around the streets with a noose around his neck, was still a rather audacious act.[141]

American writers employing Indian imagery as an expression of national culture had already begun to salvage Metacom's "character" from the malignant stereotypes created by Increase Mather's and William Hubbard's biased seventeenth-century accounts of King Philip's War long before Apess delivered his erudite vindication of the Wampanoag leader in 1836. His own rendition of the historical event, for instance, closely follows Washington Irving's popular essay, "Philip of Pokanoket," in which Metacom is transformed into a quasi-legendary personality of American romantic nationalism.[142] Since Irving also included this particular piece in his *Sketch Book* (1819) along with "Traits of Indian Character," which is reprinted almost verbatim in the appendix of *A Son of the Forest*, there can be little doubt that Apess was very familiar with it. Perhaps he had also read James Wallis Eastburn's and Robert Charles Sand's epic poem, *Yamoyden, a Tale of the Wars of King Philip: in Six Cantos* (1820), which presents Metacom as a heroic leader fighting for the preservation of his people's independence. James Fenimore Cooper, too, manifests sympathy for Metacom in his *Wept of Wish-Ton-Wish* (1829); and Lydia Maria Child, an ardent opponent of removal policy, painted a grim picture of Puritan–Indian relations in her juvenile novel, *The First Settlers of New England* (1828).[143] But the most popular nineteenth-century image of King Philip was created by Edwin Forrest's portrayal of him as a tragic hero in John Augustus Stone's *Metamora; or, The Last of the Wampanoags*, which opened in New York on December 15, 1829 (the same year Apess's autobiography appeared) and held the stage consistently for about forty years.[144] Apess must have been aware of this Indian play (if not all of the above), which was a major cultural event of his day, and the favorable public mood it set in New England for his own appeal to the American conscience.

Apess's primitivist reinstatement of King Philip, whom he styles "the greatest man that ever lived upon the American shores, for natural abilities," and whose cause he considers to be "as glorious as the *American* Revolution," actually serves him as a platform from which to launch a much more complex résumé of early Indian–white relations in New England from an Indian perspective. His relatively detailed historical account of King Philip's War exposes the Puritans, whose conduct toward Indians was not always exemplary of Christian piety, as the actual aggressors in the conflict. With reference to Increase Mather's propagandist application of salvationist language to legitimize the wholesale slaughter of Indians, he remarks sardonically:

> It is true that this language is sickening, and is as true as the sun is in the heavens, that such language was made use of, and it was a common thing for all the pilgrims to curse the Indians, according to the order of their priests. It is also wonderful how they prayed, that they should pray the bullet through the Indian's heart and their souls down into hell. If I had any faith in such prayers, I should begin to think that soon we should all be gone. However, if this is the way they pray, that is, bullets through people's hearts, I hope they will not pray for me; I should rather be excused.[145]

Apess does not, however, expose Puritan bigotry in their relations with Indians during early colonial times in order to relegate the unpleasant memory to some immutable mythopoetic past, as is generally the case in contemporary literature catering to the "vanishing Indian" theme. Throughout his *Eulogy*, Apess takes every available opportunity to digress from the ostensible topic at hand to bring attention to some relevant issue. When, for instance, he recounts how Metacom's wife and children were captured and sold into slavery by the Puritans, he does not fail to establish a link between Indian resistance and contemporary abolitionist sentiment:

> Gentlemen and ladies, I blush at these tales, if you do not, especially when they professed to be a free and humane people. Yes, they did; they took a part of my tribe, and sold them, to the Spaniards in Bermuda, and many others; and then on the Sabbath day, these people would gather themselves together, and say that God is no respecter of persons; while the divines would pour forth, "he that says he loves God, and hates his brother, is a liar, and the truth is not in him"; and at the same time they hating and selling their fellow men in bondage. And there is no manner of doubt that all my countrymen would have been enslaved if they had tamely submitted. But no; sooner would they butcher every white man that come in their way, and even put an end to their own wives and children, and that was all that prevented them from being slaves; yes, *all*. It was not the good will of those holy pilgrims that prevented, no. But I would speak, and I wish it might be like the voice of thunder, that I might be heard afar off, even to the ends of the earth. He that will advocate slavery is worse than a beast, is a being devoid of shame; and has gathered around him the most corrupt and debasing principles in the world . . . —no, not excepting the head men of the nation. And he that will not set his face against its corrupt principles is a coward and not worthy of being numbered among men and Christians—and conduct, too, that libels the laws of the country, and the word of God, that men profess to believe in.[146]

For Apess, American racism thus had its roots in the "sins" perpetrated by the honored Pilgrim Fathers. "I do not hesitate to say that through the prayers, preaching, and examples of those pretended pious," he maintains, "has been the foundation of all the slavery and degradation in the American colonies, towards colored people." [147]

Moreover, Apess also detects duplicity in the Puritans' secular dealings with Indians. Reviewing Indian policy up until his own day in what amounts to an appeal to both reformist and patriotic sensibility, he maintains that the long trail of broken treaties leading up to removal policy actually begins at Plymouth Rock. With unusually (even for Apess) harsh words which, interestingly enough, were deleted from the second edition of the *Eulogy*, he pinpoints the chirographic machinations concealed behind the colonial treaty system:

> Our groves and hunting grounds are gone, our dead are dug up, our council fires are put out, and a foundation was laid in the first Legislature to enslave our people, by taking from them all rights, which has been strictly adhered to ever since. Look at the disgraceful laws, disfranchising us as citizens. Look at the treaties made by Congress, all broken. Look at all the deep-rooted plans laid, when a territory becomes a state, that after so many years the laws shall be extended over the Indians that live within their boundaries. Yea, every charter that has been given was given with the view of driving the Indians out of the states, or dooming them to become chained under desperate laws, that would make them drag out a miserable life as one chained to the galley; and this is the course that has been pursued for nearly two hundred years. A fire, a canker, created by the Pilgrims from across the Atlantic, to burn and destroy my poor unfortunate brethren, and it cannot be denied. What, then, shall we do? Shall we cease crying and say it is all wrong, or shall we bury the hatchet and those unjust laws and Plymouth Rock together and become friends? And will the sons of the Pilgrims aid in putting out the fire and destroying the canker that will ruin all that their fathers left behind them to destroy? [148]

And here, too, Apess makes a direct transition from a demystified Puritan past to the immediate present by adding an ironic paraphrase of Andrew Jackson's first presidential address to Congress on December 8, 1829, in which he listed the "benefits" Indians could expect from removal. [149] The parody recaptures perfectly the overbearing, paternalistic tone of Jackson's numerous orations to southeastern Indians who had their doubts about "his" policy:

> You see, my children, that our fathers carried on this scheme of getting your lands for our use, and we have now become rich and powerful; and we have a right to do with you as we please; we claim to be your fathers. And we think we shall do you a great favor, my dear sons and daughters, to drive you out, to get you away, out of the reach of civilized people, who are cheating you; for

we have no law to reach them, we cannot protect you, although you be our children. So it is no use, you need not cry, you must go, even if the lions devour you, for we promised the land you have to somebody else, long ago, perhaps twenty or thirty years; and we did so without your consent, it is true. But this has been the way our fathers first brought us up, and it is hard to depart from it; therefore you shall have no protection from us.[150]

At the beginning of *Eulogy*, Apess makes a statement that clearly foreshadows the spectacular protest acts of militant New England Indians during the 1970s:

> Let the children of the pilgrims blush, while the son of the forest drops a tear, and groans over the fate of his murdered and departed fathers. He would say to the sons of the pilgrims, (as Job said about his birth day), let the day be dark, the 22d of December, 1622; let it be forgotten in your celebration, in your speeches, and by the burying of the rock that your fathers first put their foot upon. For be it remembered, although the gospel is said to be glad tidings to all people, yet we poor Indians never have found those who brought it as messengers of mercy, but contrawise. We say, therefore, let every man of color wrap himself in mourning, for the 22d of December and the 4th of July are days of mourning and not of joy. Let them rather fast and pray to the great Spirit, the Indian's God, who deals out mercy to his red children, and not destruction.[151]

In view of all of the above, the expression of gratitude to the audience for listening patiently to "an unworthy speaker" and the conciliatory wishes of "a poor Indian" at the close of the address have the same sarcastic ring as did Occom's nearly identical apologia at the end of his autobiographical sketch three-quarters of a century earlier.

William Apess is the first Indian missionary-writer to identify clearly some of the fundamental colonialist mechanisms operating in the history of Indian–white relations in America. His political candor is expressed in a forceful style of language not to be encountered again in American Indian letters until Carlos Montezuma, the "Fiery Apache [*sic*]" whose own biography reveals many parallels to the life of the rebellious Pequot, aimed his sharp journalistic "Arrow Points" at the Bureau of Indian Affairs during the second decade of the twentieth century.[152] His singular achievement in the infant stage of American Indian literature is probably due to a combination of two mutually reinforcing factors that influenced his development as a writer: the involuntary separation from his own family and community, and the voluntary affinity with contemporary reformist-abolitionist ideology. The extremity of his deracination and degrading experiences on the lowest rungs of American society as a "colored" indentured servant undoubtedly whetted his sensitivity for the ongoing moral debate on racial discrimination, and Apess consequently developed a "synecdochic sense of self" based on a broader understanding of a collective ethnic identity.[153] Apess succeeded in appropriating the critical rhetoric of a dissenting faction (revivalist-abolitionist) within the dominant voice in order to project the authentic voice of the remnant northeastern Algonquian communities in the universal context of social justice. Regardless of his genealogy, his close ties to the African American struggle against slavery are undeniable. His writings meet every criterion of what James H. Cone has designated as a "Black Theology of Liberation," an interpretation of Christianity that unreservedly identifies it with the "divine character" of an oppressed community's struggle against its oppressors. "Black Theology," according to Cone, is a theology of survival expressed in "passionate language" and dealing with the "black experience," a life of humiliation and suffering as a consequence of white racism. It extols, as Apess clearly does, the liberation teachings of a "Black Christ," who is worshiped as the savior of the oppressed.[154]

In many ways Apess's socialization can be likened to the contemporary urban Indian experience, in which the frequent loss of direct tribal connections has been compensated in part at least by a consciously assumed "pan-Indian" identity. Like many Indians thus isolated in an urban ghetto setting, William Apess also became involved in the defense of the sovereignty of an Indian community into which he was not born but with which he could easily identify on the basis of ethnic solidarity. At Mashpee, where he was incorporated by the traditional process of adoption, he stepped into the activist role of an ethnic proto-elite and implemented his own brand of what could now be called an "Indian Theology of Liberation." It is precisely this activist standpoint — belief in improvement through personal involvement — that stands out in Apess's writings and distinguishes them from the fatalistic "vanishing Indian" literature dominating the nineteenth century. If Paul Brodeur's observation that Apess remains "a hero of almost messianic proportions" among the Mashpees is correct, and it is corroborated by their own tribal historian, then his accomplishments represent yet another contradiction to the common image of Christian Indians as sellouts.[155]

Cheated out of his cultural birthright by adverse circumstances and stranded in a society that advocated egalitarianism but implemented racial segregation, Apess chose to reestablish his personal integrity in universalist terms borrowed in part from Enlightenment notions of the natural rights of man and their manifestations in the American Revolution and the ensuing abolitionist movement. Thus his criticism was directed not against the moral, political, and religious precepts of the United States per se but rather against the hypocrisy of those who bend them to their advantage. Apess, like most of his Praying Indian predecessors, found little discrepancy between the fundamental principles of the Protestant ethic (as he understood it, of course) and what he still remembered of Indian traditions and consequently had little trouble adopting them as his own. Toward the close of his berating speech in Boston he stated:

> I say, then, a different course must be pursued, and different laws must be enacted, and all men must operate under one general law. And while you ask yourselves, "What do they, the Indians, want?" you have only to look at the unjust laws made for them and say, "They want what I want," in order to make men of them, good and wholesome citizens. And this plan ought to be pursued by all missionaries or not pursued at all. This is not only to make Christians of us, but men, which plan as yet has never been pursued. And when it is, I will then throw my might upon the side of missions and do what I can to favor it. But this work must begin here first, in New England.[156]

His "Indian problem" thus also had less to do with a personal quest for identity — "I choose to remain as I am, and praise my Maker while I live that an Indian he has made" — than with rejecting, by force if necessary, a negative one imposed by racist doctrines.[157] Apess's life history, "written by himself" entirely, is a permanent tribute to the creative adaptability of New England's "remnant" Algonquian peoples.

5

Elias Boudinot and the Cherokee Betrayal

THE TRAGIC FATE of Elias Boudinot, who is honored as the "Father of American Indian Journalism," on the one hand, and stigmatized as a "traitor" to the Cherokee Nation on the other, well illustrates the vicissitudes of transcultural experience in a colonial situation.[1] Additionally, his role in Cherokee history underlines the inadequacy of "traditionalist-progressive" constructs in the analysis of societal interaction and consequently calls into question the qualitative labels appended to either artificial category. The singularity of his experience is, of course, directly related to the unique postcontact situation of the Cherokees, who occupied a prominent place in the development of early United States Indian policy. Few indigenous groups in North America demonstrated such a remarkable propensity for creative culture change and, conversely, were so completely overwhelmed by the moral duplicity of "civilization" programs in the colonial encounter. The trauma of the Cherokee "Trail of Tears" is thus clearly reflected in Boudinot's life and work.[2]

By the beginning of the nineteenth century the Cherokees had already completed their first phase of postcontact cultural transformation, which had ranged in time from their first contact with Europeans in the sixteenth century to the signing of their first treaty with the United States in 1785, and subsequently initiated their second phase in an attempt to come to terms with American expansionism. Even though the Cherokees probably had contact with Europeans as early as the 1540s in the course of De Soto's expedition, it remained sporadic at best until the second half of the seventeenth century, when trade relations with Spanish, French, and, finally, English colonists began to intensify. The latter began with traders from Virginia and then, following the founding of Charleston in 1670, increased rapidly with the arrival of South Carolinians. At this time the Cherokees began to receive regular supplies of guns and other European products in exchange for deerskins, and by 1690 they started to make the transition from "a stable, hunting-gathering-farming society with a subsistence economy and an internally oriented, communal order to a mobile, free-trade, market economy."[3] The incorporation of the Cherokees into the transatlantic market in the course of the eighteenth century also triggered the usual disruptive colonialist mechanisms in their midst. Constant warfare with their Indian neighbors (Tuscaroras, Shawnees, Creeks, Chickasaws) and involvement in imperial conflicts (between French and English, 1744–48 and 1755–63; a brief but devastating border war with the British, 1759–61; and on the British side during the revolutionary war, 1776–85) led to great losses in population, territory, and resources. The population was further decimated by epidemics in 1738–39 and 1783, so that of an estimated 22,000 Cherokees in the 1600s only about 13,000 remained at the turn of the nineteenth century.[4]

Traditional Cherokee social structures remained fairly intact up until the first decade of the eighteenth century. The tribe still consisted of a number of independent towns, which were bound to each other linguistically and culturally but did not recognize any authority beyond the local town councils. As economic and political relations with the colonists progressed, however, the need for modifications in the Cherokee system of government increased and eventually led to the centralization and secularization of administrative powers. Increasingly called for were more specialized leaders with commercial connections and knowledge of colonial politics. The Cherokees themselves recognized the need for some instance of centralized control, if only to avoid reprisals by the colonists, who consistently made the entire tribe responsible for individual acts of violence committed against them. Around 1753 the "beloved old men" became more involved in tribal rather than local politics and created a loose form of administration modeled after traditional village organizations, which assumed the task of managing the tribe's external affairs until the 1780s.[5]

Decisions were still based on consensus, however, and the tribal council had no means of enforcing its policies other than the personal prestige and influence of its delegates. This executive weakness brought on a crisis during the turbulent years of the American Revolution, when a dissenting faction under young war leaders refused to recognize a peace agreement concluded with the Americans by the more conservative members of the council in 1777. The dissenters and their followers, who still refused to make peace with the United States as late as 1794, then moved to a more remote part of

Elias Boudinot, Cherokee leader. By permission of Western
History Collections, University of Oklahoma Libraries.

the Cherokee territory in present-day Tennessee, where they became known as the Chickamaugans (later the Five Lower Towns).[6] It was the first major crisis in a sequence of postcontact events that would lead to a permanent and consequential rift in the tribe. Toward the end of the eighteenth century the pressure upon the majority of the Cherokees to conform to the decisions of the tribal council increased as it gradually assumed control over internal affairs as well, under the initiative of a new generation of mixed-blood leaders. The Cherokees were thus well on the way to viewing themselves as a "nation" rather than as an autonomous village–ceremonial-center grouping when, on November 28, 1785, the tribal council (or National Council, as it became known at the turn of the century) concluded the first official treaty (Treaty of Hopewell) with the United States and thereby recognized its sovereignty.[7]

Thus, as the Cherokees entered the nineteenth century, they had already made several fundamental changes in their ways of life. They had joined the European fur trade as suppliers of raw materials (deerskins) in exchange for finished products, a commercial venture that had almost run its course because of the depletion of game and reduction of hunting territory; and they had created a centralized administrative apparatus to deal more effectively with the incumbent Anglo-American powers. But they had also experienced disruptive, traumatic changes in their social and cultural fabric: severe population decline and demographic shift due to warfare and disease; loss of substantial portions of their territory in numerous involuntary land cessions after 1765; permanent factionalism resulting in abhorred in-group violence; a marked reduction in traditional religious-ceremonial activities; and a progressive shift from a communal social ethos to individualistic entrepreneurship.[8]

The ensuing phase in Cherokee postcontact history (1786–1839), the one in which Elias Boudinot emerged as a crucial and controversial figure, can be characterized as a losing race between Cherokee acculturative survival strategies and the insatiable land greed of an expanding and increasingly aggressive American nation. During this period the Cherokees were once again confronted with several far-reaching changes in their cultural makeup, such as a relatively rapid economic shift from fur trading to farming, a partial transition from kinship- and clan-oriented social structure to patriarchal nuclear families, the displacement of traditional religious beliefs by Christianity among an influential segment of the population, the adoption of a republican form of administration modeled after the U.S. federal government, a changeover from a primary oral to a chirographic culture, and a language shift to English in key sectors of political life. These changes were effected by four interacting agents: the involvement of a newly emergent class of affluent mixed-bloods in Cherokee politics, the short-lived "civilization policy" promoted by early U.S. administrations, the resulting activities of Protestant missionaries in Cherokee territory, and the political pressure exerted in Congress by recently established southeastern "frontier" states to extinguish all Indian land claims within their boundaries.[9]

Intermarriage between whites and Indians was fairly common in the Southeast as of the 1790s, when the mixed-blood children of European (primarily Scotch, Irish, English, and German) traders, officials, soldiers, Tories, or adventurers also began to make their influence felt in Cherokee affairs. According to one source, no less than one-fourth of the Cherokee population had some white ancestry by 1825.[10] The incorporation of mixed-blood children as full-fledged members of the tribe was facilitated by the matrilineal orientation in Cherokee society and the fact that intermarriages occurred primarily between white males and Cherokee females. The mixed-blood generation born after the 1790s, particularly those who received an education and reached adulthood by the 1820s, profited most from the changes in Cherokee society.

The shift in the Cherokee economy to farming, which had practically been consummated by the first decade of the nineteenth century, thus brought about a separation of the population on two levels. In the first place, nuclear families began to reside in widely scattered farms, which automatically led to an inhibition of traditional town-centered communal life. Second, by the mid-1820s, it created a class society composed of a small group (ca. 10 percent of the total population) of mixed-blood landed proprietors and merchant-traders at the top, a larger group of small-scale farmers in between, and a majority of subsistence farmers at the bottom.[11]

The new generation of mixed-blood Cherokees, who were disproportionately represented in the upper and middle classes, became increasingly influential in the Cherokee administration as the pressure for removal was stepped up by the federal government after 1807. When a minority delegation headed by Doublehead and other Lower Town chiefs was bribed into signing away remaining Cherokee hunting territory in 1805, it resulted in the execution of Doublehead in 1807 and led to a revolt of the so-called young chiefs. Soon after, during the "first removal crisis" in 1808–11, when the Lower Town chiefs wanted to emigrate to lands in present-day Arkansas and a segment of Upper Town Cherokees favored separation, the same young chiefs took a decided stand for a unified nation, a more highly centralized form of government, and tribal ownership of land. Above all, they vehemently opposed removal and any further sale of Cherokee lands. As William McLoughlin points out, the group he refers to as "young chiefs" differentiated itself from the "old chiefs" by the policies it represented rather than age or distinction, and by the fact that most of those who joined the early stages of said rebellion were of mixed-blood ancestry. By 1809 mixed-bloods also dominated the National Committee, an administrative body created in September of that year to guide the nation during the intervals when the National Council was not in session. Henceforward, the mixed-bloods' policy of adopting white ways to counteract the growing political pressures for removal would shape the course of Cherokee sociocultural development.[12]

During the first twenty-five years of its existence, the federal government endeavored to protect Indian land rights by setting up "permanent" boundaries to Indian country, to control the sale of Indian lands and regulate Indian trade, to provide for the punishment of crimes committed by members of one race against the other, and to promote white standards of civilization with the end in view of absorbing Indians into the general stream of American society. As was mentioned in previous chapters, this policy was promoted by the administrations under Washington and Jefferson and codified by Congress in a series of Indian Trade and Intercourse Acts passed between 1790 and 1822. In exchange for such "services," the Indians were expected to give up some of their "excess" lands from time to time, and the Cherokees thus found themselves having to negotiate a total of twenty-five land-cession agreements with the federal government during the same period (1791–1819).[13] In 1819 Congress also authorized an annual sum of $10,000 for a so-called civilization fund, which was to be used at the president's discretion to promote the civilization of Indians by employing "capable persons of good moral character, to instruct them in the mode of agriculture suited to their situation; and for teaching their children in reading, writing, and arithmetic."[14] The program was implemented with the cooperation of missionary societies, who also supplemented the limited funds provided by the government. High on the priority list of the "civilization" campaign were the Cherokees and their neighbors, the so-called Five Civilized Tribes. Both Washington and Jefferson personally encouraged them to form a "United Cherokee Nation" and to adopt a new legal system patterned after the Constitution.[15] Their second compact with the United States, the Treaty of Holston (1791), had already promised the Cherokees "useful implements of husbandry" so that they could "be led to a greater degree of civilization and to become herdsmen and cultivators instead of remaining in a state of hunters."[16] In spite of early opposition from southeastern states, the federal government continued to promote such a relatively liberal policy among the Cherokees and other Indians until the 1820s, when proremoval sentiment began to make itself felt in Congress.

Protestant missionaries had been visiting Cherokee villages sporadically since about 1740 but had aroused little interest among the inhabitants. At the turn of the century, however, disruption in Cherokee religious practices in the course of the social upheaval outlined above and the rise of an influential mixed-blood minority in favor of acculturation made them more receptive to the missionary fervor of the Second Great Awakening, particularly in the realm of education.[17] The first permanent mission among the Cherokees was established by the United Brethren (Moravians) at Spring Place (near present-day Chatsworth, Georgia) in 1801. At the instigation of Upper Town mixed-bloods, the National Council had agreed the year before to let the organization proceed with its mission on the condition that it first establish a school for Cherokee children, which it was not actually able to comply with until November 1804.[18] This was accomplished earlier by Gideon Blackburn who, supported by funds from the Presbyterian General Assembly, opened the first Cherokee school on the Hiwassee River in February of that same year and then started another one on Sale Creek in March 1806. Even though Blackburn's educational experiment had a higher enrollment rate than the Moravians' more modest effort, the latter ultimately prevailed because the Presbyterian missionary fell under the suspicion of being involved in shady transactions with alcohol and had to close both his schools by 1810.[19] The most successful educational institution among the Cherokees before removal, however, was established at the Brainerd mission in March of 1817 by Cyrus Kingsbury and other missionaries affiliated with the American Board of Commissioners for Foreign Missions (ABCFM), an interdenominational organization that had been founded in New England by Congregationalists in 1810 in order to coordinate Protestant missionizing efforts.[20] The type of institution favored by the Moravians, Presbyterians, and Congregationalists corresponded to the manual-labor boarding school model established in the previous century by Sargeant and Wheelock.[21] Baptists and Methodists also began to establish missions among the Cherokees in 1819 and 1823, respectively. Even though they were latecomers initially, their egalitarian approach and willingness to train native exhorters and preachers soon enabled them to outstrip the other denominations in terms of Cherokee congregations. By 1826 the number of mission schools in Cherokee territory had already risen to eighteen.[22] Thus, in spite of a revival of traditional religion known as the "ghost dance movement" among the Cherokees in 1811–13, Christianity had taken a firm hold in the upper echelons of Cherokee society — many of whom had been educated in Protestant mission schools — and consequently became a guiding force in the rise of Cherokee nationalism.[23] The extent of Christian influence at this time is made evident by a National Council resolution passed on October 13, 1826, which excluded from office anyone "who disbelieves in the existence of the Creator, and of rewards and punishments after death," and was later qualified as Article VI, section 2, of the Cherokee Constitution to the effect that "No person who denies the being of a God, or a future state of rewards and punishment, shall hold any office in the civil department of this Nation."[24]

The integrationist policies advocated by the federal government and the positive Cherokee response to them obviously did not harmonize with the loud clamor for Indian lands among an exploding frontier population and administrators of western territories, whose demands would eventually set the political tone in the approaching era of "Jacksonian democracy," nor could they be reconciled with the profit-mindedness of large-scale speculators, whose ranks included none other than Andrew Jackson himself. The mere possibility that Indians could become proprietors of their lands already posed a practical and legal impediment to American expansionism. The few who gave any thought at all to Indian rights in a historical process now equated with Manifest Destiny became firm believers in the removal idea as the most "humanitarian" solution to the "Indian problem."[25] With his customary insight into American idiosyncrasies, Alexis de Tocqueville observed that, as far as the policy of removal was concerned, "It [was] impossible to destroy men with more respect for the laws of humanity."[26]

As pointed out in the preceding chapter, the idea of removal had already surfaced during the late eighteenth century, but it was Thomas Jefferson who, in anticipation of the Louisiana Purchase in 1803, made the first official recommendation for its realization in a draft for an amendment to the Constitution proposing to grant Congress the power "to exchange the right of occupancy in portions where the U.S. have full rights for lands possessed by Indians within the U.S. on the East side of the Mississippi."[27] It was also Jefferson who engineered the fateful (for the Cherokees) Georgia Compact of 1802, in which the state's administrative body agreed to cede its western claims to the United States for a certain sum and the guarantee that the latter would "extinguish, at their own expense, for the use of

Georgia, as early as the same can be peaceably obtained, upon reasonable terms, the Indian title to the lands lying within the limits of that state."[28] Despite the vast land cessions already made by the Cherokees during the first quarter of the nineteenth century in order to accommodate the flood of squatters in their territory and the voluntary participation of about six hundred of their men in Jackson's campaign against the Creeks (Creek War, 1812–14), lobbying for total removal began to take effect during Madison's presidency (1808–12) and was officially endorsed by Monroe at the close of his administration in 1824–25.[29]

At the same time, the Cherokees had to contend with removal problems within their own ranks. Chief Bowles had already led a group of voluntary exiles to Arkansas territory in 1794. In 1808 they were followed by about a thousand Chickamaugans, and in 1817 another two to three thousand Cherokees agreed to give up their lands in exchange for new territory on the Arkansas and White rivers in a dubious treaty with the United States that had been signed by only a minority of chiefs. During the so-called Creek Path Conspiracy of 1819–22, chiefs of the Creek Path town located in northeastern Alabama also tried to negotiate a separate removal without the official consent of the National Council. In all, approximately five thousand Cherokees had moved west of the Mississippi by 1828, where they became known collectively as the Arkansas Cherokees, or "Old Settlers." As a consequence, it became of the utmost concern for Cherokee leadership in the 1820s and 1830s to maintain a united front against both internal and external pressures for removal.[30]

Instead of "taking up the hatchet" against their oppressors, which would have conformed to prevalent notions of "savagism," the Cherokees chose a tactic which one author has appropriately described as nonviolent action.[31] Other than their shift from hunting and subsistence farming to market agriculture, the most remarkable transformations to occur among the Cherokees during the first third of the nineteenth century were in the realms of jurisprudence and communication. These turned out to be so successful that the designation "civilized tribe" was permanently affixed to the Cherokee people thereafter. In 1808, when the National Council created an internal police force called the Lighthorse Guard, the Cherokees began to maintain a legal code which was first recorded in English (the official language of the government) and later translated into Cherokee. Between 1817 and 1828, it passed more than a hundred resolutions, the majority of which either provided for the organization of the administration itself or regulated commerce in Cherokee territory.[32] During these two decades the Cherokees practically revolutionized their form of government: In 1817 the National Council created a bicameral system with an executive arm (Standing Committee, later changed to National Committee) to assume jurisdiction over relations with the United States; three years later, in 1820, it divided Cherokee territory into eight districts with a district court in each; in 1822 it modified the judiciary into a three-tiered system similar to the American model, including district courts, circuit courts, and a supreme court; and in 1825 it created a new administrative capital at New Town and rechristened it New Echota. These administrative reforms were more or less adopted and then expanded in the Cherokee Constitution, which was proposed by resolution on October 13, 1826, incorporated in July of the following year, and modified somewhat in 1829 to conform more closely to the U.S. Constitution. The Cherokee Constitution established three branches of government: an executive headed by a principal chief, an assistant chief, a treasurer, and a national marshal; a dual legislative body (General Council) made up of the National Committee and National Council; and a judiciary that remained just about as it was. In addition, it created a three-member council, jointly elected by the Committee and Council, to meet with and advise the principal chief.[33]

The Cherokee government also passed resolutions at this time that fundamentally changed traditional social patterns. It abolished clan revenge (*lex talionis*), prohibited polygamy and infanticide, established rules that amounted to compulsory education for children already enrolled in school, reformed inheritance policies in favor of a paternalistic nuclear family structure (although it also recognized property titles along maternal lines), and proclaimed that Cherokees who voluntarily left the nation would forfeit all claims to property. Thus, as McLoughlin indicates, the Cherokees made a major transition during this period from an "ethnic nation," in which being a Cherokee was defined primarily by clan membership, into a "nation-state" (Cherokee Nation), in which membership was established by residence within a defined territory and loyalty to a governing body. Of course, there was also resistance among the Cherokees against the progressive leaders and their constitutional government, which culminated in what has become known as the White Path Rebellion in 1827.[34] However, opposition was not pronounced enough to reverse the course of the administration, and its uncompromising stance against removal ultimately offered a common political platform with which the more conservative segments of the Cherokee population were also able to identify. In order to protect itself further from the negative effects of removal policies, the Cherokee government also proclaimed that all lands within its jurisdiction would remain common property of the nation and could not be disposed of (other than improvements on such lands) by any individual. On July 7, 1818, the National Council passed a law determining that any Cherokee who agreed to sell land belonging to the nation without the consent of a full council would be subject to the death penalty.[35]

The advances in the field of communication, which entailed a complete transition of the Cherokee speech community from orality to literacy, were made possible by the remarkable achievement of an illiterate mixed-blood Cherokee, George Gist (Guess, Guest), better known as Sequoyah. Little is actually known about Sequoyah's background, but it has been suggested that he was probably born around 1773 in the Overhills Cherokee village of Tuskegee, the son of a Virginian by the name of Nathaniel Gist. He began to work on a writing system for the Cherokee language sometime around 1809 and completed his famous eighty-six-symbol (each representing a sound in the Cherokee language) syllabary by 1821 while he was residing among the Arkansas Cherokees, with whom he had emigrated three years before. That same year he returned to the Cherokee Nation to introduce his invention to the General Council which, after some initial skepticism, became convinced of its functionality and quickly adopted it. In 1824 it awarded Sequoyah a special medal for his syllabary and began to promote its implementation throughout the nation.[36] It is said that by the end of the decade a substantial portion of the Cherokee population became literate.[37]

The rapidity with which the Cherokees accepted Sequoyah's syllabary was due not only to its promotion by the progressive faction and missionaries but also to the interests of the conservative majority, who found it practical for their own specific purposes. For the latter it was a welcome way to communicate with relatives in other Cherokee villages and in distant Arkansas, as well as an effective system for recording orally transmitted traditions (i.e., secret ceremonial formulas) for generations to come.[38] Curiously enough, most missionaries were loath at first to accept Sequoyah's syllabary, preferring an earlier orthography developed by John Pickering of the ABCFM. But, as a result of the Reverend Samuel Worcester's efforts to popularize its use in 1826, when he sent the first five verses of the Book of Genesis in Cherokee to the *Missionary Herald* for publication, many came to recognize its practicality as an instrument with which to spread the Gospel among monolingual Cherokees.[39] Soon after, they began translating biblical texts into the syllabary regularly in collaboration with two Cherokee bilinguals who had attended the Brainerd school, John Arch and David Brown.[40]

As far as the Cherokee government was concerned, Sequoyah's writing system enabled it to legitimize the introduction of a foreign legal system by having its English resolutions translated into Cherokee and distributed to all parts of the nation. Accordingly, during a fall session in 1825, the General Council appointed Elias Boudinot "to solicit and receive donations in money from individuals, or societies throughout the United States, for the object of establishing a national academy, and for procuring two sets of types to fit one press, to establish a printing office at New Town, (C.N.) one set of types to be composed of English letters, the other of Cherokee characters, the invention of George Gist, a Cherokee."[41] At its next annual meeting, on October 18, 1826, it approved the founding of a national newspaper and the hiring of an editor with the ability to "translate matter in the Cherokee language for the columns of said paper as well as to translate all public documents . . . submitted for publication."[42] On November 2, the Council further agreed to have a building erected in New Echota to house the Cherokee press and, two days later, it also decided to have eight copies of its laws printed in the Cherokee syllabary. With the aid of Samuel Worcester and the ABCFM, who forwarded the necessary funds (later reimbursed by the National Council), a Cherokee press was finally installed at New Echota sometime in January 1828.[43] On February 21, the press produced the first issue of the bilingual *Cherokee Phoenix* (*Tsa-la-ge-Tsi-le-hi-sa-ni-hi*) under the editorship of twenty-four-year-old Elias Boudinot.[44]

Elias Boudinot, or Gallegina ("The Buck"), was born around 1804, the eldest son of Oowatie and Susanna Reese. Boudinot's paternal grandmother is thought to have been of Scotch-Cherokee ancestry and, according to an account given by his granddaughter, his paternal grandfather was the descendant of a member of the De Soto party who had married a daughter of the noted Cherokee peace chief, Attaculcullah ("Little Carpenter," formerly Oukanaekah). Much more revealing than his actual blood quota, however, is the fact that Boudinot was raised in the progressive settlement of Oothcaloga, which was founded about 1800 in the northwestern part of Georgia by Cherokees like Oowatie and his elder brother, Kahnungdatlageh, who had left the conservative town of Hiwassee in order to live on scattered farms according to the stipulations of the federal "civilization" program. Here they cleared the land, tilled the ground, kept domesticated animals, built log houses, erected fences, and gradually transformed Oothcaloga Valley into the "garden spot" of the Cherokee Nation. Oowatie eventually became David Watie, and his more illustrious brother made history under the name of The Ridge (or Major Ridge).[45]

The Ridge (ca. 1770–1839) and his son John Ridge (Skahtlelohskee, 1803–39) played a central role in Boudinot's life, probably more so than any other members of his immediate family. The Ridge became not only one of the wealthiest men of the Cherokee Nation but also one of the most influential individuals to figure in the Cherokee nationalist movement. Entering tribal politics around 1796, he soon joined ranks with James Vann, Charles Hicks, and other mixed-blood leaders of the young-chief faction. He actively participated in the execution of Doublehead in 1807 and the subsequent rebellion of the young chiefs in 1808. That same year he was appointed as head of the Lighthorse Guard and, in 1809, elected as one of the thirteen members of the original National Committee. In 1813 he raised a volunteer army of Cherokees to fight on the American side in the Creek War, from which he emerged with the rank of major. Finally, in 1828, he was nominated as one of the three counselors to the principal chief. The Ridge, who also joined numerous Cherokee delegations to Washington, proved to be one of the most adamant advocates of land retention policies and an equally strong opponent of removal — that is, until he signed the Treaty of New Echota in 1835 along with his son and nephew.[46]

In keeping with their progressive outlook, both David Watie and The Ridge took pains to provide their numerous offspring with an education. At the instigation of The Ridge, David Watie sent his eldest son to the Moravian mission school at Spring Place in 1811, where he joined his cousins John and Nancy Ridge, who had been enrolled there by their father in November of the previous year. Other than a brief interruption during which he was taught by a private tutor hired by his uncle, Boudinot remained at Spring Place under the tutelage of the Reverend John Gambold and his wife, Anna, until the spring of 1818. It appears that by then he already manifested the right sort of attitude, or "piety," that eventually made him a likely candidate for missionary work in the eyes of his schoolmasters. That same year Elias Cornelius of the ABCFM chose him and other promising Cherokee students like David Brown to attend the Foreign Mission School in Cornwall, Connecticut. On his way to Connecticut he met the elderly philanthropist, Elias Boudinot, who must also have been impressed with the young Cherokee because he bequeathed him his Christian name and made him his beneficiary.

The Foreign Mission School was an academy specializing in the instruction of "heathens" from all over the world—its student body included Malays, Polynesians, Chinese, East Indians, Indians, and a few whites. It was established in 1817 with the assistance of the late Henry Obookiah, a young Sandwich Island convert whose popular *Memoirs* were published posthumously in 1819.[47] The purported goal of the institution was an expanded version of Sargeant's and Wheelock's earlier pedagogical models: "the education in our country, of Heathen youths, in such a manner, as, with subsequent professional instruction, will qualify them to become useful Missionaries, Physicians, Surgeons, School-masters, or Interpreters; and to communicate to the Heathen nations such knowledge in agriculture and the arts, as may prove the means of promoting Christianity and civilization."[48] Boudinot and John Ridge, the latter of whom had followed his cousin in 1819, were thus the recipients of a somewhat more diverse curriculum corresponding to a secondary education, which included studies in geography and natural science as well as the usual courses in theology, English, Greek, and Latin.

It was here that Elias Boudinot and John Ridge made their first attempts at writing which, among other things, already reveal some fundamental distinctions in their characters. When the baron de Campagne sent the school two substantial monetary contributions from his residence near Zurich in 1820 and 1821, Boudinot and David Brown were selected to write letters of appreciation, which were subsequently published for propaganda purposes in the ABCFM's own journal, the *Missionary Herald*. Boudinot's short letter shows that he was already seriously contemplating missionary work among his people just one year after he had joined the First Congregational Church. "I sometimes feel an ardent desire to return to my countrymen and to teach them the way to salvation," he confided to the generous baron, but then added modestly, "Pray for me that my faith fail not, and that I may not finally prove insincere."[49] In a subsequent letter of his that was published that same year in the Philadelphia-based Presbyterian weekly, the *Religious Remembrancer*, Boudinot began to have doubts about the practicality of his plans because of serious health problems that would eventually force him to abandon his studies:

> I feel myself relieved from the many complaints to which I was subject, which hindered me from my daily pursuits; I can now study without being molested by headache, weakness, dizziness, &c. But what shall I say concerning my spiritual interest? I cannot but blush, whenever I turn my pen to write upon this subject. There is great leanness in my soul. Perhaps I must at least be cast away and dashed to pieces, when the storm shall arise which will sweep away

the wicked from the earth. You know that many are called, but that few are chosen. . . . Perhaps my profession is unsound; for the evidences of true piety do not consist in the outward performances of the duties required. I have been lately doubting what course to take when I leave this institution. When you was here, you know that I proposed studying Theology. But it is not certain whether I shall. I feel myself deficient in those important Christian graces which constitute a true preacher of the gospel. But let the earth rejoice, the hearts of the children of men are in the hands of God, and he can turn them whithersoever he pleases. I have now opened my heart to you, that you may pray for me, that I may not be shaken by every wind.[50]

In yet another of his letters from Cornwall, Boudinot concludes that, even though Indians do believe in a Supreme Being, the immortality of the soul, and future rewards and punishments, they have never heard a word of Christ, and therefore "the whole Heathen world of 600,000,000 souls will, ere long, sink into the bottomless pit!" Shortly after this letter was written, Boudinot apparently decided that his services as a missionary were needed and enrolled at the Andover Theological Seminary near Boston in the fall of 1822 together with David Brown. His poor health, however, forced him to leave the institution before the year was over and return to the Cherokee Nation.[51] On his way home he first joined John Ridge and a group of Cherokee youth for a fund-raising tour to Charleston, South Carolina. In the spring of 1823, after having recovered from a severe relapse at home, Boudinot traveled around the Cherokee Nation, visiting the mission schools at Creek Path and Brainerd, and also crossed the border into Alabama. During this journey he described some of his experiences in letters published that same year in the *Religious Remembrancer*.[52]

John Ridge, who would turn out to be as accomplished and prolific a writer (he even tried his hand at poetry) as Boudinot, apparently had a much more pragmatic outlook on life.[53] Whereas Boudinot's Cornwall letters reveal a sincere concern with spiritual matters, John Ridge's early correspondence indicates that he preferred to deal with Indian politics. While at Cornwall, for instance, he wrote a letter to President Monroe relating his views on the present situation of the Cherokees. The letter, dated March 8, 1822, and supposedly left unedited by his tutors, enumerates the advances made in "civilization" by the Cherokees and expresses the hope that "Congress will encircle them in the arms of love, and adopt them into the fond embraces of the *Union*."[54] He readily concedes that the presence of missionaries among the Cherokees has helped them to take "faster steps to civilization," but he still leaves no doubt as to his own more worldly definition of progress: large farms, domestic animals, manufactured articles, and, of course, education. In contrasting the advances made by Cherokees still living east of the Mississippi to the less propitious situation of their fellow tribesmen "who have been enticed by their foolish imaginations, and particularly by the allurement of the white men, to remove to the Arkansas," he transmits a typical young-chief antiremoval statement to the highest office in the American government. Thus, at age nineteen, John Ridge had evidently incorporated the policies promoted within the Cherokee government by his father and the other progressives and had also discovered his own talent for political exposition. This is particularly evident in a speech he delivered at the Circular Church in Charleston on November 15, 1822, in which he stressed that Indians, especially the Five Civilized Tribes, were capable of making "great advances" toward civilization. In response to the question of whether Indians would be better off continuing as distinct, independent governments from the United States, he stated: "It is one of my greatest desires, to live long enough to see the Cherokees adopted into the United States. However, this proposition for such an union, must be made by their own sons in whom they can confide."[55] In view of his later involvement in Cherokee politics and close cooperation with Elias Boudinot in that field, it seems reasonable to assume that he also had substantial influence on the development of his cousin's political consciousness.

During their sojourn at Cornwall the two teenage Cherokees shared an emotional experience which, if it had not been for the fact that both were Indian, would undoubtedly have been relegated to the pages of historical trivia. Sometime in 1821 the convalescent John Ridge, who had developed a severe hip problem due to the cold Connecticut weather, fell in love with Sarah Bird Northrup, the fourteen-year-old daughter of the school's steward, and determined to marry her. The parents acquiesced after Sarah had what probably amounted to a hysterical tantrum, and then only under the condition that he return in two years from the Cherokee Nation without his crutches. When he did make it back without them and the marriage was finally consummated on January 27, 1824, many of the pious people of Cornwall and beyond were appalled by the union and held the missionaries at the school accountable for the "disgrace." Opponents of miscegenation published racist diatribes in local papers, and well-intentioned sentimentalists produced rhymes that were in nearly as poor taste. The hypocritical furor had hardly begun to subside when the news leaked out that Harriet Ruggles Gold, daughter of the agent for the school, had consented to marry Elias Boudinot despite similar resistance from her parents. Their wedding on March 28, 1826, created such a storm of protest within the Congregationalist community that the famous Foreign Mission School was forced to close its doors permanently in the autumn of that same year.[56]

Theda Perdue's contention that the episode must have traumatized Boudinot is undoubtedly correct, and her conclusion that he thereafter abandoned all notions of integration in favor of a policy of adaptation in segregation — a separate but "civilized" Cherokee Nation — is also very plausible.[57] Unfortunately, no comments by Boudinot on the affair have been brought to light so far. It is quite likely, however, that his feelings on the matter were similar to John Ridge's, who did express his bitterness in a letter dated July 8, 1822, which was published in the *Christian Herald*:

> Prejudice is the ruling passion of the age, and an Indian is almost considered accursed. He is frowned upon by the meanest peasant, and the scum of the earth are considered sacred in comparison to the son of nature. If an Indian is educated in the sciences, has a good knowledge of the classics, astronomy, mathematics, moral and natural philosophy, and his conduct equally modest and polite, yet he is an Indian, and the most stupid and illiterate white man will disdain and triumph over this worthy individual. It is disgusting to enter the house of a white man and be stared full in the face with inquisitive ignorance. I find that such prejudices are more prevalent among the ignorant than among the enlightened, and let a received opinion be counteracted by solid facts, the ignorant will still hold to it and carry it with him to his grave.[58]

Indeed, little is known of Boudinot's activities from the time he left Cornwall in 1822 until his marriage four years later. It has been intimated that, as a possible reaction to threatening letters he had received from New England in conjunction with his intended marriage to Harriet Gold, Boudinot had a brief phase of "backsliding." He apparently attended a "heathen" Cherokee ball game during the summer of 1825 and thereby tarnished his golden-boy reputation among the missionaries, that is, until Samuel Worcester, who required his assistance to work out a Cherokee grammar and translate biblical texts, reinstated him soon after.[59]

Boudinot's backsliding — if it really was that, considering the popularity of ball games among all classes in the Cherokee community — can have been only a momentary lapse at best, as both he and John Ridge were quite active in promoting "civilization" among the Cherokees at the same time. Ridge served as interpreter during the annual council in 1823 and was elected to the National Committee the year following. During the 1824 fall meeting at New Town, the same one in which Sequoyah was awarded a silver medal for his syllabary, the General Council resolved to establish a national academy for Cherokee students and, in association with it, a national museum in which samples of traditional Cherokee material culture were to be kept under the care of Elias Boudinot. Although parts of this particular plan did not materialize until a later date, the resolution never-theless shows that the Cherokee administrators had uses for Boudinot's talents, who also served the General Council as clerk from 1825 to 1827.[60] This became more concrete during the fall council of 1825 when the deci-sion was made to establish a national press and newspaper and to send Boudinot north as an agent to generate funds for the project. Before that, on November 5, 1824, Boudinot, John Ridge, David Brown, John Ross, and other Cherokee intellectuals had also been busy founding the Moral and Literary Society of the Cherokee Nation. Boudinot was appointed as its corresponding secretary, and John Ridge was assigned the task of writing down and publicizing its constitution. Its goals, which were outlined by John Ridge in the *Boston Recorder and Telegraph* in 1825, were "the sup-pression of vice, the encouragement of morality, and the general improve-ment of this Nation," as well as "to unite in fidelity the citizens of this Nation to the true interest of their country, and for supporting the govern-ment and laws thereof." In a public call for financial support published in the same journal, Boudinot repeated these goals and added that "Books on Travels, Histories, both ancient and modern, Maps, and in fine, books of all descriptions tending to the objects of the Society, will be gratefully received and acknowledged."[61]

While John Ridge was trying to further his political career by hiring out his literary talents to the Creeks for hard cash during their treaty negotia-tions with the federal government — an activity that earned him enough money to go into business for himself as a lawyer in the Cherokee Nation — Elias Boudinot embarked upon his tour to solicit funds for the Cherokee press with the promise of the General Council that he could keep 8 percent of the amount he took in.[62] Departing in the spring of 1826, he made his way to Charleston, New York, Salem, Boston, and Philadelphia, where he delivered his famous speech on Cherokee progress that was published as a pamphlet that same year. Along the way he stopped off long enough at Cornwall to marry Harriet Gold, with whom he finally returned in the winter to live at Hightower in the Cherokee Nation, where he temporarily taught at the mission school for a meager salary of twenty dollars a month. His appeals to the generosity of white audiences had their effect as the General Council agreed that very fall to appropriate $1,500 for the estab-lishment of a press.

When the editorship for the projected national paper was offered to

Boudinot during the fall session of the General Council in 1826, he was at first reluctant to accept the position on the grounds that the chiefs wanted to grant him less pay than the white printer.[63] It was at this point that Worcester interceded for him and arranged for an additional salary to be paid by the ABCFM, in return for which he counted on Boudinot's assistance in publishing religious literature in Sequoyah's syllabary. Even though Boudinot had not even been aware of the existence of Sequoyah's writing system prior to 1824, when the General Council officially honored its inventor, he nevertheless became fairly proficient in its use shortly thereafter.[64] The association between Boudinot and Worcester, who would soon refer to the former as his "right hand," was obviously a fruitful one as together they produced, among other things, a book of Cherokee hymns, which Boudinot claimed to be "the first Cherokee book ever published," and translations of several biblical texts.[65] In addition, they joined efforts in bringing out the weekly issues of the *Cherokee Phoenix*. Boudinot's close relationship with Samuel Worcester on a professional as well as private level undoubtedly reinforced the Protestant ideals he had absorbed previously from the Moravians and Presbyterians.

In the latter part of 1827, Elias Boudinot and his wife moved from Hightower to New Echota, where they occupied a two-story house adjacent to the Worcester home. The press and type, which had been shipped from Boston by the Prudential Committee of the ABCFM in November of that year, did not arrive at New Echota until late January 1828. During the foregoing October, Boudinot had already had a broadside printed elsewhere titled "Prospectus for Publishing at New Echota, in the Cherokee Nation, a Weekly Newspaper to Be Called the *Cherokee Phoenix*," which synchronized the paper's purported goal and content with the Protestant principles taken over from the missionaries and incorporated into the Cherokee Constitution of 1827:

> As the great object of the Phoenix will be the benefit of the Cherokees, the following subjects will occupy its columns.
> 1. The laws and public documents of the Nation.
> 2. Account of the manners and customs of the Cherokees, and their progress in Education, Religion and the arts of civilized life; with such notices of other Indian tribes as our limited means of information will allow.
> 3. The principal interesting news of the day.
> 4. Miscellaneous articles, calculated to promote Literature, Civilization, and Religion among the Cherokees.[66]

Boudinot's editorial policy, or what he called his great aim, was outlined in a much more detailed statement addressed "To the Public" in the first issue of the *Cherokee Phoenix*, which appeared on February 21, 1828. Here he once again acknowledges the importance of white charity in the establishment of the paper, but he also points out to the public with unmistakable pride that it "is the property of the Nation . . . patronized by, and under the direction of, the Cherokee Legislature." He then goes on to give his interpretation of the ties between himself as editor of the *Phoenix* and the policies of the Cherokee government, which would one day prove to be untenable:

> As servants, we are bound to that body, from which, however, we have not received any instructions, but are left at liberty to form such regulations for our conduct as will appear to us most conducive to the interests of the people, for whose benefit, this paper has been established.
>
> As the Phoenix is a national newspaper, we shall feel ourselves bound to devote it to national purposes. "The laws and public documents of the Nation," and matters relating to the welfare and condition of the Cherokees as a people, will be faithfully published in English and Cherokee.
>
> As the liberty of the press is so essential to the improvement of the mind, we shall consider our paper, a *free paper*, with, however, proper and usual restrictions. We shall reserve to ourselves the liberty of rejecting such communications as tend to be evil, and such as are too intemperate and too personal. But the columns of this paper shall always be open to free and temperate discussions on matters of politics, religion, &c.

As editor he also proposes to avoid sectarian topics, not to intermeddle with the politics and affairs of neighbors, and to refrain from commenting on the current presidential campaign between John Quincy Adams (whom the Cherokees favored) and Andrew Jackson. But he also makes an additional promise that he would eventually feel forced to break:

> In regard to the controversy with Georgia, and the present policy of the General Government, in removing, and concentrating the Indians, out of the limits of any state, which, by the way, appears to be gaining strength, *we will invariably and faithfully state the feelings of the majority of our people.* Our views, as a people, on this subject, have been sadly misrepresented. These views we do not wish to conceal, but are willing that the public should know what we think of this policy, which, in our opinion, if carried into effect, will prove pernicious to us.

Boudinot concludes his editorial message with an affirmation of the universalist notion shared by nineteenth-century American humanitarians "that

Indians can be reclaimed from a savage state, and that with proper advantages, they are as capable of improvement in mind as any other people," and expresses his own longing for the advent of "that happy period, when all the Indian tribes of America shall arise, Phoenix like, from their ashes."[67]

As he readily conceded in both the "Prospectus" and lengthier address "To the Public," Boudinot had no previous experience as editor and had to learn the trade on the job. The success of the *Phoenix*, which soon had accredited agents selling it all over the United States and subscribers as far away as Europe, is therefore all the more remarkable, even if one takes into consideration the assistance of Worcester and the hired white printers. In the four and one-half years that Boudinot was editor of the *Phoenix* he read proof, prepared most of the material to be published in Cherokee, selected articles from other periodicals for reprinting, corresponded with readers, and served as the paper's business manager. In addition to all this and his translating work with Worcester, he also wrote a weekly column under the heading "New Echota" on various subjects pertaining to the Cherokees and their nation, which were widely read and frequently reprinted in other newspapers. Just how heavy his work load was is indicated by the fact that he threatened to resign at the end of his first year as editor because the Council refused to grant him funds to hire an assistant.[68]

Other than the politics of removal, Boudinot was primarily concerned with moral and religious issues. He thus covered Cherokee domestic affairs with special reference to "progress in Education, Religion and the arts of civilized life" rather than "manners and customs" as originally promised in the "Prospectus." One of the main purposes of the *Phoenix* was, as its editor and sponsoring body both understood it, to convey Cherokee adaptation to the outside world in progressivist terms, whereby it was hoped that the exemplary advances made by the Cherokee people would eventually stifle proremoval contentions that Indians could never be civilized. As Boudinot wrote in one of his early editorials, "We do not expect ever to be a great nation, in the common sense of the word, for our population is too trifling to entitle us to that appellation. We may, nevertheless, by our improvement in the various departments of life, gain the respect and esteem of other nations. Or, should we blended [*sic*] with the United States (which perhaps may be the case,) we shall enjoy the privileges of her citizens and receive in common, the regard due her from abroad."[69] His orientation toward a non-Cherokee reading public is also indicated by the fact that nearly all inclusions other than new Cherokee laws and removal issues were written solely in English even though no more than 18 percent of Cherokee households had members who could read that language, according to a census taken in 1835.[70]

Though Boudinot did occasionally write sketches on Cherokee traditions, usually in response to external inquiries or information published elsewhere, he tended to treat them as obsolete curiosities. "Traditions are becoming unpopular," he maintained in one case, "and there are now but a few aged persons amongst us who regard them as our forefathers did." In a brief account of the social and legal functions of Cherokee clans, for instance, he concludes "with pleasure, that they are all repealed, and are remembered only as vestiges of ignorance and barbarism."[71] To what extent Boudinot had incorporated the ethnocentric views of his Protestant mentors is made evident in an editorial he wrote on "those days of ignorance and heathenism" as a postscript to a fellow progressive's critical description of a Cherokee dance:

> If he had visited this Nation *thirty years* ago, and witnessed the practices of the inhabitants in their full extent, his tears would have flowed more freely, and the consideration of their wretchedness would have been without a redeeming thought. — At that period the Cherokees resided in villages, in each of which was a "Townhouse," the head quarter of frivolity. Here were assembled almost every night (we are told, we speak from hearsay for we are born under an era of reformation,) men and women, old and young, to dance their *bear dance, buffalo dance, eagle dance, green-corn dance,* &c. &c. &c. and when the day appeared, instead of going to their farms, and labouring for the support of their families, the young and middle aged of the males were seen to leave their houses, their faces fantastically painted, and their heads decorated with feathers, and step off with a merry whoop, which indicated that they were *real men*, to a ball play, or a meeting of similar nature. Such in a word was the life of a Cherokee in those days during spring & summer seasons. In the fall and winter seasons they were gone to follow the chase, which occupation enabled them to purchase of the traders a few items of clothing, sufficient to last perhaps until the next hunting time. From the soil they derived a scanty supply of corn, barely enough to furnish them with gah-no-ha-nah [hominy] and this was obtained by the labor of women and grey headed men, for custom would have it that it was disgraceful for a young man to be seen with a hoe in his hand, except on particular occasions.[72]

Here, once again, he assumes that the "introduction of light and intelligence has struck a mortal blow to the superstitious practices of the Cherokees, and by the aid of that light, a new order of things is introduced, and it is to be hoped will now eradicate the vestiges of older days." The fact that dances, and other traditions as well, were still being performed by a substantial portion of the Cherokee population at that time means that he either refused to recognize this aspect of Cherokee society or had lost touch with it entirely. His disdain for the traditional ways of other tribal peoples was even more pronounced. The Plains Indians, for instance, were primitive "American Arabs" in his opinion, and he repeatedly stressed in his editorials that the "civilized" Cherokees should not be compared with them or any other groups of "savage" Indians.[73] Furthermore, he and the administration both regarded the reports on the progress of the Cherokee reform movement as models for other American Indian communities, as the change in name of the paper from *Cherokee Phoenix* to *Cherokee Phoenix, and Indians' Advocate* as of the February 11, 1829, issue makes clear.

Since it was Boudinot's foremost concern to depict the Cherokees as a civilized people, he vehemently attacked any conduct that might have provided proremoval advocates with additional grounds for slander. In one editorial he lamented the occurrence of crime in the nation, warning that "these frequent thefts and murders will go to confirm the world in the opinion that we are all savages."[74] His most vigorous moral campaign, as might be expected, was against intemperance. He was a member of the executive committee of the Cherokee Temperance Society founded in 1829, and he published numerous editorial tirades against "the curse of mankind" along with related writings borrowed elsewhere (i.e., tracts, sketches, news items). With typical reformist bombast, Boudinot liked to draw parallels among Christianity, patriotism, and the fight against intemperance, not hesitating thereby to appeal to the Cherokee warrior ethos even though he had maintained earlier with equal vehemence that the very term "warrior" was a "Savage appellation":

> We would sincerely hope, while so much is doing abroad to arrest the progress of intemperance, the citizens of this nation will not be inattentive to the call of their country — the call is imperious — it cannot be misunderstood. The call is to the Christian and to the patriot. If an enemy were to come among us in a warlike attitude, and commence, unprovoked, a work of destruction with our women and children, our property, and with our most sacred rights, what patriot is there who would countenance the enemy, and remain an idle spectator? But fellow citizens, we have an enemy among us, a far more dangerous enemy, because its progress is unobserved, and because it insinuates itself as a friend, but mark ye, deaths by violence, deaths by diseases and deaths by accidents, sickness and famine, profanity and indecencies, and a host of other evils, are its trophies and triumphs.[75]

Boudinot rarely expressed his views on manumission (in contrast to the Ridges and many other Cherokee leaders, including John Ross, he did not own slaves), which, after all, was a major source of embarrassment for local Protestant missionaries and antiremoval sympathizers. The official proslavery position of the Cherokee administration undoubtedly made it difficult for him to confront the issue openly in the *Phoenix*, and what little he either wrote himself or included on African Americans and slavery (usually pietistic sketches with titles like "The High-Minded Slave") remains ambiguous at best.[76] In reply to an editorial in the *Milledgeville Recorder*, which forecast that Georgia would rank as one of the great states once it appropriated Cherokee lands, Boudinot countered that before it could hope to rival New York, Pennsylvania, or Ohio it would first "have to overcome one great obstacle before [it] becomes a great state — slavery." Occasionally he also included abolitionist material, such as the lengthy "Memoranda of the Slave Trade and Slavery" outlining the history of abolitionist laws in England and a feature on the struggle against slavery in Mexico. Boudinot seems to have favored the policy of removing freedmen to Africa, as did many of his fellow Presbyterians, since he ran a few articles on the American Colonization Society and its activities.[77] Nevertheless, slavery had extremely negative connotations for him because he did not want to have it associated in any way whatsoever with the current situation of Indians:

> It is a matter of rejoicing to the philanthropist and the republican, there is yet in America, but one class of slaves. Those red men of the west are not yet slaves — their judgement and freedom of speech are not yet muzzled by some proud and earthly master. That they are not thus brought down to the level of negro slaves, but rather that they enjoy and exercise their right of speaking in their defence, and contradicting misrepresentations which have so long imposed on the credulity of the public, is a cause of much chagrin to the Athenian [editor of a Georgia newspaper] and his brethren.[78]

As might be expected from his close identification with the mixed-blood proto-elite, Boudinot was also an ardent promoter of Cherokee nationalism. "While he possesses a national character," he argued, "there is hope for the Indian. But take his rights away, divest him of the last spark of national pride, and introduce him to a new order of things, invest him with oppressive laws, grievous to be borne, he drops like the fading flower before the noon day sun."[79] It is not surprising, therefore, that the problem of removal, which had reached a critical point when the Cherokee national newspaper began to appear, and the resulting conflict with the state of Georgia should become his primary concern as a writer and an editor.

Georgia's legislature reacted to the adoption of the Cherokee Constitution in 1827 by passing a resolution in which it proclaimed that it had absolute title to all territory within its boundaries. It also claimed the right to take possession of lands occupied by the Cherokees by any means necessary and gave the federal government a deadline to comply with the compact of 1802.[80] By this time frontier proremoval sentiment had already permeated the Adams administration as it began to exert political and economic pressure on southeastern Indians to emigrate. On May 6, 1828, a delegation of Arkansas Cherokees signed a treaty with the federal government agreeing to give up their present location in exchange for lands farther west, which also contained an article promising material benefits to any eastern Cherokee volunteering to accompany them. The treaty itself, which Boudinot reprinted in the *Phoenix*, seemed to confirm the Cherokee government's suspicions concerning removal because it made clear that voluntary emigration was obviously no guarantee against further white encroachments. "A blanket has lost its former value with us," he wrote in one of several blistering editorials directed against the Arkansas compact; "so has the rifle and the kettle, and the mention of five pounds of tobacco in a treaty, where the interest of a nation of Indians is supposed to be concerned, looks to us, too much like jesting."[81] When it became known that government agents had even bribed two members of the Arkansas delegation to try and convince parties of eastern Cherokees to emigrate, Boudinot immediately exposed them in his paper. "We are sorry that there are self-interested men in all Indian tribes," he decried, "who will not scruple to sacrifice the interest of their people, and that of the United States, instead of discountenancing, will enter into treaties with them, contrary to the feelings of the rest of their brethren. If such a course is pursued, there is no hope for the Indians."[82]

The discovery of gold in the Cherokee Nation during the spring of 1829 brought matters to a head. Bolstered by the recent election of Andrew Jackson and his promise to press the issue of removal in his first annual message to Congress on December 8, 1829, the General Assembly of Georgia passed legislation on December 20, 1828, and December 19, 1829, incorporating large portions of Cherokee territory within its bounds as separate counties and declaring all Cherokee laws null and void as of June 1, 1830. It also nullified contracts with Indians that had not been witnessed by at least two whites, prohibited Indians from testifying against whites in Georgia courts, and threatened those who promoted antiremoval sentiment with immediate arrest. And, of course, Georgia laws also made it illegal for Cherokees to extract gold from their own mines. Boudinot repeatedly pointed out the obvious discrepancies between the repressive acts of Georgia, which were receiving increasing support from other state representatives in Congress, and the civilization program that had been advocated since the days of the Washington administration. Like all other Cherokee patriots and their remaining supporters among the general public, he felt that removal policy was in effect a reversal, if not a betrayal, of everything the Cherokees had been taught to regard as "progress" by the American nation's own founding fathers:

Why were we not told long ago, that we could not be permitted to establish a government within the limits of any state? Then we could have borne disappointment much easier than now. The pretext for Georgia to extend her jurisdiction over the Cherokees has always existed. The Cherokees have always had a government of their own. Nothing, however, was said when we were governed by savage laws, when the abominable law of retaliation carried death in our midst, when it was a lawful act to shed the blood of a person charged with witchcraft, when a brother could kill a brother with impunity, or an innocent man suffer for an offending relative. At that time it might have been a matter of charity to have extended over us the mantle of Christian laws & regulations. But how happens it now, after being fostered by the U. States, and advised by great and good men to establish a government of regular law; when the aid and protection of the General Government have been pledged to us; when we, as dutiful "children" of the President, have followed his instructions and advice, and have established for ourselves a government of regular law; when everything looks so promising around us, that a storm is raised by the extension of tyrannical and unchristian laws, which threatens to blast all our rising hopes and expectations?[83]

Early in 1830 Georgia further prohibited the Cherokees from holding council, except to cede lands, and required a special license and an oath of allegiance from all whites residing within Cherokee territory. To make matters worse, after a long and heated debate Congress made its proremoval stance final by passing the Indian Removal Act on May 28 of that same year. Alabama and Mississippi eventually followed Georgia's example and imposed their own laws on Indian communities within their borders.[84] This all-out legal campaign to disfranchise southeastern Indians, which demanded no less than the total dissolution of the Cherokee Nation, was reinforced by the strong-arm tactics of Jackson who, for instance, ordered the Cherokee agent to cease paying the annuities due to the Cherokee government by former treaty obligations. In the meantime, Cherokee citizens were being regularly terrorized by "intruders" (gold prospectors and squatters), a band of horse thieves known as the "pony club," and an infamous vigilante force created by Georgia in 1830, the Georgia Guard. Although the federal government was charged by law (i.e., the Indian Trade and Intercourse Act of 1793) and by treaties (the Treaty of Hopewell, 1785, and the Treaty of Holston, 1791) with the responsibility of removing all "intruders" from the Cherokee Nation, Jackson maintained that he would not protect the Cherokees and, consequently, incursions were generally allowed to go unchecked as a further inducement to the Cherokees to move voluntarily.[85]

At one point the Cherokees tried to take matters into their own hands when the Council ordered Major Ridge to lead the Lighthorse Guard to expel intruders near the Georgia border. When the patrol departed, an armed party of Georgians retaliated by beating four intoxicated Cherokees so severely that one of them died from his injuries. The eviction of intruders by the Cherokees raised a storm of protest among Georgians, and both Major Ridge and the principal chief, John Ross, were publicly threatened with murder.[86] Boudinot expressed grim satisfaction at the fact that the first casualty of the conflict with Georgia was a Cherokee and not the other way around, and he further counseled the Cherokees not to allow themselves to be provoked into committing acts of violence in reprisal. "If our word will have any weight with our countrymen in this trying time," he wrote in the Cherokee paper, "we would say, *forebear, forebear* — revenge not but leave vengeance to him to whom vengeance belongeth."[87]

The Cherokees instead maintained their commitment to nonviolent action, sending regular delegations to plead their case in Washington and hiring top lawyers to challenge Georgia's acts in American courts. Aware that a removal bill brought before the Senate on February 22 would probably be passed in the House by a slim majority in spite of heated debate among the representatives (it was finally adopted on May 26 by a vote of 102 to 97), Boudinot wrote an editorial in which he clearly identified the Cherokee's last source of hope for justice:

> Very soon the House of Representatives will decide, if it has not already decided, on this important question. It is much to be feared the Representatives of the people will not respond to the views and feelings of their constituents, but deliver their weak allies to their enemies. Be that as it may — let both Houses of Congress decide as they may, we confidently think justice will be done, even if the Cherokees are not in the land of the living to receive it — posterity will give a correct verdict. But we are not now making such an appeal — we hope we are not yet at the end of our row — we hope there is yet a

tribunal where our injured rights may be defended and protected, and where self interest, party and sectional feelings have nothing to do. — Let then the Cherokees be *firm* and *united* — Fellow citizens, we have asserted our rights, we have defended them thus far, and we will defend them yet by all lawful and peaceable means. — We will no more beg, pray and implore; but we will *demand* justice, and before we give up and allow ourselves to despondency we will, if we can, have the solemn adjudication of a tribunal, whose province is to interpret the treaties, *the supreme law of the land.* Let us then be *firm* and *united.*[88]

Other than lobbying — the Cherokees were supported by influential anti-Jackson politicians like Henry Clay, Daniel Webster, Theodore Freling-huysen, Edward Everett, and David Crockett — the most effective and promising counteroffensive of the Cherokee administration actually took place in the Supreme Court of the United States. As the Cherokees and their lawyers were well aware, the judiciary was then under the supervision of Chief Justice John Marshall, a staunch Federalist with very little sympathy for the Jackson administration.[89] The Cherokee Council also wisely enlisted the services of capable anti-Jackson lawyers like William Wirt, attorney general of the United States from 1817 to 1829 and presidential candidate on the Anti-Masonic ticket in 1832; and John Sargeant, National Republican candidate for the vice-presidency in the same election year. The first opportunity to take the issue to court occurred in the fall of 1830, when a Cherokee by the name of George Tassel was arrested for murder in Georgia. Wirt applied to the Supreme Court for a release of the condemned man on a writ of error based on the argument that Georgia had no jurisdiction over crimes within the Cherokee Nation, but the Georgia authorities bluntly circumvented the issue by expediting the execution. "If such proceedings are sanctioned by the majority of the people of the U. States," Boudinot prognosticated, "the Union is but a tottering fabric, which will soon fall and crumble into atoms."[90] Thus the first of the Cherokee Nation cases in the Supreme Court, *Cherokee Nation* v. *State of Georgia,* was not heard until early in 1831, when Wirt filed an injunction against Georgia's laws for infringing upon the sovereignty of the Cherokee Nation as guaranteed by federal treaties. It was reluctantly dismissed by the Supreme Court on July 18, 1831, for want of jurisdiction on the grounds that the Cherokee Nation was not a foreign state within the meaning of the Constitution but a "domestic, dependent nation . . . in a state of pupilage."[91] The Cherokees and their lawyers interpreted the status of "domestic, dependent nation" as implying that the tribe was recognized legally as a political entity capable of managing its own affairs and consequently continued to seek litigation against Georgia's incursions and to call upon the federal government to assume its treaty responsibilities. Boudinot expressed the Cherokee sentiments in a very realistic assessment of the case in the *Phoenix*:

> It is said by some that the case is "settled," forever put to rest, and a hope is entertained, that nothing more will be said on the subject. Now we apprehend this is doing injustice to the Supreme Court. The case is not settled for the great question at issue between the State of Georgia and the Cherokees was not before that tribunal. The only question before it was, whether it had original jurisdiction — whether the Cherokee nation was a foreign state in the sense of the constitution, & the decision went no further than to say, as we understand it, that the Court has *not* original jurisdiction, and that the Cherokee nation was *not* a foreign state in the sense of the constitution. How such a decision can be understood and construed as sustaining the pretensions of Georgia and the views of the President of the United States, we are not able to say. . . . It is true the Court says that it cannot protect the Cherokees *as a nation*, but does it say that they are not entitled to the protection of the Gen. Government? The opinion plainly intimates that it is the duty of the Executive and Congress of the United States to redress the wrongs, and to guard the rights of the Cherokees if they are oppressed. The whole responsibility is thus thrown, by a judicial decision, upon those branches of the Government. The rights of the Cherokees are as plain, as sacred, as they have been, and the duty of the Government to secure those rights is as binding as ever. What will the Cherokees do under such circumstances? What else can they do but remain peaceably where they are and continue to call upon the *people* of the United States to fulfill their engagements, their solemn promises which have been repeatedly made and which have always been regarded until the commencement of Mr. Eaton's "new era." We see nothing to alter their determination to remain and to maintain their rights by all suitable measures. The land is theirs — their right to it is "unquestionable," and it cannot be taken away from them without great injustice to them and everlasting infamy to the United States.[92]

The second Cherokee Nation case, *Worcester v. State of Georgia*, was opened in the summer of 1831, after ABCFM missionaries Samuel Worcester and Dr. Elizur Butler were arrested for refusing to take an oath of allegiance to Georgia and sentenced to four years of hard labor. Georgians had long suspected the missionaries residing in the Cherokee Nation of promoting antiremoval sentiments among their charges, allegedly to retain their own lucrative positions. But the brutal treatment of the missionaries upon arrest by the Georgia Guard, which Boudinot capitalized on in several issues of the *Phoenix*, was publicly condemned even by many Georgians who otherwise favored removal.[93] With the sanction of the ABCFM, Worcester and Butler took their case before the Supreme Court on the general contention that Georgia's Cherokee Code was unconstitutional. Boudinot recognized that this particular case would be a turning point in the history of Indian–white relations. He wrote: "An important crisis in Indian affairs has indeed arrived — and it is now with the people of this great American Republic to decide the future destiny of those tribes within the limits of the United States. — Both the means and the power are at their disposal."[94]

In late February 1832, Marshall rendered his epoch-making decision that the Cherokee Nation was a "distinct community, occupying its own territory," and that the laws of Georgia were null and void because they had no application without the express consent of the Cherokees.[95] When it became clear that the Jackson administration was not going to enforce the Supreme Court's decision, the prospects for the Cherokees in the removal controversy appeared bleak indeed.[96] Georgia's legislature reacted at once by passing an act in April authorizing the survey of Cherokee lands in preparation for their distribution to white citizens by a lottery system. As Rennard Strickland has observed, the "inability of the United States Supreme Court to uphold that faith shook the very basis of the Cherokee's belief in laws."[97] This, and the fact that Jackson was reelected that same year, provided the primary impetus for the formation of a proremoval faction at this time.

Up until this turn the Ridges and Boudinot had been at the very forefront of the Cherokee antiremoval effort. While Boudinot was busy slashing away at the policy in his editorials, Major Ridge and his son were both active in Cherokee politics. The former was appointed counselor to the principal chief during the fall of 1828, and the latter, who acted as clerk of the General Council in 1829, was elected president of the National Committee in 1830. All three faithfully supported the policies of principal chief John Ross, who was elected in 1827 and would serve in that capacity until his death in 1866.

The biography of John Ross (1790–1866), figurehead of the antiremoval effort and still honored today as the paragon of Cherokee patriotism (or the antithesis of Boudinot and the Ridges), illustrates perfectly the fallacies of the mixed-blood stereotype.[98] Ross was the son of a Scottish trader and a mixed-blood Cherokee. He received instruction from private tutors hired by his father and then attended an academy in Kingston, Tennessee. Even though he was "only" one-eighth Cherokee, could hardly speak or write the Cherokee language, and stood apart from the great majority of his fellow tribesmen in terms of occupation and wealth (he was a successful merchant and planter who owned up to fifty slaves before the outbreak of the Civil

War), John Ross fully identified himself with the Cherokee Nation and was widely respected as a leader as early as 1811, when he became a member of the standing committee. He joined the first delegation to Washington in 1816 and, by mid-1818, was elected to the presidency of the National Committee. Ross was also a delegate to the Cherokee constitutional convention and is thought to have played a substantial role in its formulation. His reputation as a man of integrity was firmly established among the Cherokees in 1823, when he publicly rejected a bribe offered by William McIntosh, the Creek leader and a party to Georgia's machinations who was executed by his own people two years later for signing an unauthorized treaty relinquishing Creek lands and accepting removal.[99] In contrast to Boudinot and John Ridge, Ross also reinforced his ties to the tribe by taking a Cherokee wife, even though he did eventually marry a white Quaker from Delaware after the death of his first spouse. But Ross, who was converted to Methodism in 1829, had as little inclination to preserve Cherokee traditions as his subsequent opponents in the removal issue. He believed and publicly proclaimed, as the Ridges and Boudinot did, that under the "fostering care" of the United States the Cherokees "have merged from the darkness of ignorance and superstition to [their] present degree of advancement in civilized improvement."[100] What led to the quasi-mythical association between Ross and the traditionalists is the simple fact that he held out against removal a few years longer, a stance that obviously conformed to the will of the greater majority of Cherokees at the time.

While the Ridges and John Ross applied their diplomatic talents both at home and in the nation's capital to try to stop Georgia's legal incursions between 1828 and 1832, Boudinot functioned as the public voice of the Cherokee nationalists, and as such he orchestrated a relentless barrage against removal in the pages of the *Phoenix*. As editor and editorialist he proved adept at finding various leads to support the progressive policies of the Cherokee administration and at exposing the fallacies behind the increasingly common contention that only emigration westward could "save" the Indian. In one of his early editorials, for example, he responded to an estimate of the costs of removal by Thomas L. McKenney, then director of the Office of Indian Affairs, by contrasting it to his own detailed calculations for the removal of the Cherokees alone (a grand total of $2,229,662) and then posing the question whether such a sum might not be applied more advantageously in the field of education. "If we fail to improve under such efforts," he challenged, "we will then agree to remove."[101] In answer to an Alabama senator's contention in 1830 that the Cherokees were in a miserable situation with some of them allegedly subsisting "on sap and roots" and therefore much better off moving to the West, Boudinot countered with an ironic proposal to allow the economic statistics of the Cherokee Nation for the coming year to speak for themselves: "We beg our compassionate friends, therefore, not to put their benevolent purposes into effect right away, but to permit us a little longer to subsist on sap and roots. We are endeavoring to procure something more substantial. But if, with the aid of providence, we shall fail, we will then go to a land flowing with milk and honey, where, we presume, our kind friends intend we shall have every thing to our hearts' content without any exertion on our part."[102]

The main gist of his antiremoval discourse, however, echoed the formal objections that were presented orally or in memorials by Cherokee delegations in Washington, namely, that removal would only undo all of the promising efforts made so far to civilize and christianize the Cherokees and that it would also bring shame to the American people since its constitutionality was highly questionable on the grounds that it ran counter to stipulations made in previous treaties, or "the supreme law of the land." In one of his last editorials, written during the period in which the Cherokees were anxiously awaiting the outcome of Worcester's and Butler's appeal to the Supreme Court, he drew a lengthy and dispirited résumé of the protracted conflict. It merits quotation at some length because it is a concise documentation of the Cherokee patriots' standpoint and Boudinot's identification with it at this late stage in the controversy:

> With a commendable zeal the first Chief magistrate of the United States undertook to bring the Cherokees into the pale of civilization, by establishing friendly relations with them by treaties, and introducing the mechanic arts among them. He was indeed a "father" to them — They regarded him as such — They placed confidence in what he said, and well they might, for he was true to his promises. Of course the foundation for the improvement which the Cherokees have since made was laid under the patronage of that illustrious man. His successors followed his example and treated their "red children" as human beings, capable of improvement, and possessing rights derived from the source of all good, and guaranteed by compacts as solemn as a great Republic could make. The attempts of those good men were attended with success, because they believed those attempts were feasible and acted accordingly.
>
> Upon the same principle have acted those benevolent associations who have taken such a deep interest in the welfare of the Indians, and who may have expended so much time and money in extending the benign influence of religion. Those associations went hand in hand with the Government — it was a work of co-operation. God blessed their efforts. The Cherokees have been reclaimed from their wild habits — Instead of hunters they have become the

cultivators of the soil—Instead of wild and ferocious savages, thirsting for blood, they have become the mild "citizens," the friends and brothers of the white man—Instead of the superstitious heathens, many of them have become the worshippers of the true God. Well would it have been if the cheering fruits of those labors had been fostered and encouraged by an enlightened community! But alas! no sooner was it made manifest that the Cherokees were becoming strongly attached to the ways and usages of civilized life, than was aroused the opposition of those from whom better things ought to have been expected. No sooner was it known that they had learned the proper use of the earth, and that they were now less likely to dispose of their lands for a mess of pottage, than they came into conflict with the cupidity and self-interest of those who ought to have been their benefactors—Then commenced a series of obstacles hard to overcome, and difficulties intended as a stumbling block, and unthought of before. The "Great Father" of the "red man" has lent his influence to encourage those difficulties. The *guardian* has deprived his *wards* of their rights—The sacred obligations of treaties and laws have been disregarded—The promises of Washington and Jefferson have not been fulfilled. The policy of the United States on Indian affairs has taken a different direction, for no other reason than that the Cherokees have so far become civilized as to appreciate a regular form of Government. They are now deprived of rights they once enjoyed—A neighboring power is now permitted to extend its withering hand over them—Their own laws, intended to regulate their society, to encourage virtue and to suppress vice, must now be abolished, and civilized acts, passed for the purpose of expelling them, must be substituted.—Their intelligent citizens who have been instructed through the means employed by former administrations, and through the efforts of benevolent societies, must be abused and insulted, represented as avaricious, feeding upon the poverty of the common Indians—the hostility of all those who want the Indian lands must be directed against them. That the Cherokees may be kept in ignorance, teachers who had settled among them by the approbation of the Government, for the best of all purposes, have been compelled to leave them by reason of laws unbecoming any civilized nation—Ministers of the Gospel, who might have, at this day of trial, administered to them the consolations of Religion, have been arrested, chained, dragged away before their eyes, tried as felons, and finally immured in prison with thieves and robbers.

Is not here an array of *difficulties?*—The truth is, while a portion of the community have been, in the most laudable manner, engaged in using efforts to civilize and christianize the Indian, another portion of the same community have been busy in counteracting those efforts. Cupidity and self-interest are at the bottom of these difficulties—A desire to *possess* the Indian land is paramount to a desire to see him *established* on the soil as a *civilized* man.[103]

Under Boudinot's editorship, the *Cherokee Phoenix* evolved as a highly effective propaganda organ of the Cherokee Nation. The principal chief was greatly pleased with its success, stating that, in conjunction with the act of hiring "able lawyers" and sending delegations to Washington, "the wide circulation of the Cherokee Phoenix throughout the United States, have had a very salutary & happy effect in counteracting the misrepresentations which are fabricated against us for the purpose of aiding the unjust policy of our oppressors, by enlightening the great mass of the people of the United States upon the Indian Cause."[104] Its editorials were reprinted in newspapers all over the United States, and it was widely read and cited by antiremoval statesmen and humanitarians. It must thus have been a permanent thorn in the side of Georgia's legislature. During the fall of 1831 Boudinot was even hauled before the commander of the Georgia Guard for printing "falsehoods" (he had previously accused the Guard of beating Cherokee women) and threatened with arrest and corporal punishment. Once again, he did not fail to capitalize on the event in subsequent editorials.[105] Under the subtle title "Civilized Correspondence," he also printed several menacing letters he had received from Georgia citizens, including the reproduction of a drawing depicting his hanging, which is underscored by the caption, "Death to the Rebell."[106]

During his confrontation with the Georgia Guard, Boudinot found himself called upon as well to record and refute occasional contentions that Worcester or some other white missionary was the author of the editorials in the *Phoenix*. In one issue he dutifully reprinted statements of that nature made by the commander of the Guard, who described him as a "peaceable, passive, inoffensive and an ignorant sort of man, and as not possessing sufficient talents to write the editorial articles in the Phoenix," and then added his usual caustic postscript to the allegations in the next:

> I was not, certainly, in the least offended when he informed me that I was considered by them as an ignorant man. I knew they were welcome to their own opinions, and in regard to that one in particular, I was sensible they were correct. I was conscious of ignorance myself, besides I had never placed myself before the public as a man of information. The intimation as to the part which the Missionaries have taken in conducting the Cherokee Phoenix, that is, in writing the editorial articles, is too foolish to demand any attention. I have said as much on that subject as I intend to say, unless any person, who believes or makes the assertion, will come out and attempt to prove that I have only been a tool in the hands of the Missionaries. I do not wish, however, to disguise the truth, that I entertain the highest regard for these persecuted men. I consider them to be men of the strictest integrity and veracity. Among them I have the honor to number some of my best and nearest friends, but they have as little desire to interfere with my duties as editor as to interfere with any other person.[107]

When a similar contention appeared in a Tennessee Methodist newspaper during the first year of his editorship, Boudinot had retorted dryly: "It has already been stated to the public that the Phoenix was under Cherokee influence. It has never been, nor was it ever intended to be, under the influence of any Missionary or White man."[108]

By the fall of 1831 the frozen annuity and impounded gold mines were beginning to take their intended toll on the Cherokee treasury. An application to Congress for a loan had been rejected earlier that year, and the bankrupt Cherokee Nation consequently became entirely dependent upon the support of its wealthier citizens and the solidarity of non-Cherokee sympathizers in order to maintain its ongoing costs, such as lawyers' fees in its legal campaign against Georgia and the operation of its national paper. At a meeting held in October of that year the Council authorized Elias Boudinot, who pledged to keep up the circulation of the *Phoenix* at his own expense during his absence, to undertake another journey throughout the United States in order "to solicit donations in money from all individuals disposed to . . . aid the Cherokee Nation."[109] Thus, in January of the following year, he started his second fund-raising lecture tour for the benefit of the nation, which took him once again to eastern centers of pro-Cherokee sentiment like Philadelphia, New York, New Haven, Hartford, Salem, and Newport. John Ridge, who had been appointed previously as a member of a delegation to Washington charged with the duty of conveying to Jackson the Cherokee Nation's resolution to "never consentingly abandon this country to remove west of the Mississippi River," accompanied his cousin as official secretary.[110] Boudinot entrusted his younger brother, Stand Watie, with the editorship of the *Phoenix* while he was away.

Although he was undoubtedly frustrated by the turn of events in the Cherokee case, Boudinot remained steadfast in his antiremoval stance up until the day of his departure. "The public press is a source of vital importance to our National interest," John Ross stated at the close of his annual message delivered on October 24, 1831, "and it is gratifying to state that the circulation of the Cherokee Phoenix has given increased confidence in the American public as to the improving condition, character and stability of the Cherokee people. Much credit is due to the Editor for the ability and integrity manifested by him in conducting the paper; particularly is much credit due in reference to the honorable course of conduct pursued in his narration of facts &c, under the pressure of circumstances peculiarly offensive."[111] As late as the January 28, 1832, issue of the *Phoenix*, Boudinot was still writing his usual antiremoval diatribes:

And if the Executive does not interfere, will Congress remain silent, connive at such a robbery and consent to the violation of their compacts with the Indians and with Georgia? Whatever may be the conduct of the Executive and congress on this question, it cannot, to the least, effect the determination of the Cherokees. They have taken their stand, and there they will stand! Let the crisis arrive, and it is better that it should come soon. We will test the government to the last, so that we may know what to depend upon hereafter.[112]

At some point before his return from the lecture tour in the spring of 1832, however, Boudinot must have developed serious doubts about the political course hitherto pursued by the Cherokee government with his full support. He and his cousin were in Boston when they first heard the news of John Marshall's favorable decision in *Worcester* v. *Georgia*, and for both it then seemed fairly certain that the Cherokees had finally attained their longed-for objective. Two days later Boudinot wrote an elated letter to his brother, but in it he also pointed out that the matter was now entirely in the hands of the federal government:

You will, before this reaches you, have heard of the decision of the Supreme Court of the United States, in favor of Mr. Worcester and Butler and against the State of Georgia. It is a glorious news. The laws of the State are declared by the highest judicial tribunal in the Country null and void. It is a great triumph on the part of the Cherokees so far as the question of their rights were concerned. The question is forever settled as to who is right and who is wrong, and the controversy is exactly where it ought to be. It is not now before the great state of Georgia and the poor Cherokees, but between the U.S. and the State of Georgia, or between the friends of the judiciary and the enemies of the judiciary. We can only look and see whoever prevails in this momentous crisis.[113]

Almost a full month later John Ridge wrote a letter to Stand Watie from Washington, where he had made an appointment with President Jackson in order to sound out the latter's intentions, expressing similar reservations about the ultimate outcome of the case:

That it has been a day of rejoicing with patriots of our Country on hearing the glorious decision of the Supreme Court, I can readily perceive and congratulate them upon the momentous event. But you are aware and ought to advise our people that the contest is not over and that time is to settle the matter either for us and all the friends of the Judiciary or against us all! We have gained a high standing and consideration in the interests and best affections of the community from which we can never be removed. But Sir, the Chicken Snake General Jackson has time to crawl and hide in the luxuriant grass of his nefarious hypocracy until his responsibility is fastened upon by an execution of the Supreme Court at their next session. Then we shall see how strong the links are to the chain that connect the states to the Federal Union. . . . Now before the explained laws are carried into effect, it will, I fear, first be necessary to cut down this Snake's head and throw it down in the dust.[114]

In view of Boudinot's and Ridge's pessimistic assessment of the situation in these letters, Georgia's failure to release the two missionaries as required by the Supreme Court's decision and Jackson's subsequent refusal to enforce it must have dampened considerably whatever hopes they may still have entertained for a propitious solution to the problem with Georgia if the Cherokees continued to insist on remaining where they were. Although Boudinot had never actually veered from the antiremoval line of argument in any of his editorials, he had nevertheless occasionally intimated that such a course might not always prove tenable under certain adverse circumstances.[115] That all of his expectations were pinned to the outcome of the Cherokee Nation cases in the Supreme Court is evident, for instance, in remarks he made in the *Phoenix* with reference to an editorial on the removal bill published in the *Nashville Banner*: "We are also glad to find that the determination of the Cherokees to bring their case before the Supreme Court meets with his [the editor's] approbation. We will merely say that if the highest judicial tribunal in the land will not sustain our rights and treaties we will give up, and quit our murmurings."[116]

When John Ridge also began to manifest signs of losing faith — perhaps after his frustrating meeting with "Chicken Snake" Jackson in April in which Jackson made it clear that he would definitely not shield the Cherokees from Georgia's incursions — Boudinot's will to resist removal must have worn thinner. The previous signing of a removal treaty by a delegation of Creeks may also have fueled their mutual disillusionment, because the subsequent problems faced by the Creeks were later used by them as a proremoval argument.[117] But what must have depressed them most was the abrupt about-face among many of the Cherokees' most ardent white supporters as soon as it became evident that Marshall's decision would not be enforced. That same month, for instance, Senator Frelinghuysen and Associate Justice John McLean, both of whom had hitherto been outspoken champions of the Cherokee cause, advised John Ridge to consider negotiating with the federal government because removal now seemed inevitable. Sometime in late March or early April, Ridge parted company with Boudinot to rejoin his fellow delegates in Washington for an April 16 meeting with Secretary of War Lewis Cass, who proposed a removal treaty to them on terms that were apparently liberal enough to arouse their interest. Then, in early May, Ridge received a communication from David Greene of the ABCFM informing him that further resistance was deemed futile by most of the "friendly" congressmen and urging him to "make the best terms you can, & go."[118] Although the Cherokee delegates tried to keep their negotiations secret for fear of reprisals, by the time they returned to the Cherokee Nation, on May 15, rumors of their illicit dealings had already leaked out to the public.

For Boudinot the ABCFM's defection from the Cherokee cause must have been the single most conclusive factor behind his decision to join the minority proremoval faction. Not that long before, on December 29, 1830, the ABCFM's representatives among the Cherokees had signed an antiremoval manifesto together with other local Protestant missionaries, which was published in various missionary journals as well as in a special one-page edition of the *Phoenix*.[119] But by spring of the following year Boudinot had received a disconcerting letter from Isaac Proctor and Daniel Butrick of the ABCFM, in which they expressed their doubts about whether the Cherokees would be able to remain in Georgia if Jackson should refuse to comply with the Supreme Court's decision.[120] By the fall of 1832, after any remaining hopes for a change of policy in the executive had been dashed to pieces by Jackson's reelection, almost all of the Cherokee missionaries withdrew from the antiremoval struggle and henceforth limited their attention to strictly religious concerns. On December 25, 1832, the Prudential Committee of the ABCFM advised Worcester and Butler, who were still serving time in prison, to appeal to Georgia for a pardon. The committee's argument that further litigation would only place an additional strain on the Union in the face of the nullification crisis apparently convinced the recalcitrant reformists, as they finally complied with the organization's advice on January 7, 1833. Two days after the Prudential Committee had written to the imprisoned missionaries, it also sent a communication to John Ross recommending that he initiate removal negotiations.[121]

One of the earliest testimonials to Boudinot's change of heart is found in a letter addressed to him by John Ross in the spring of 1832. Here the principal chief expresses his concern about a press statement by a Georgia congressman announcing that the Cherokee delegation in Washington had at last consented to recommend removal to their people, which Stand Watie had reproduced in the *Phoenix*.[122] Since Boudinot was still giving his brother instructions by mail concerning what should appear in the Cherokee national paper, it is very likely that he was directly responsible for the publication of this statement. Perhaps, as Thurman Wilkins has intimated, he intended it as a "trial balloon" to test the Cherokees' response to a new, proremoval policy.[123] Boudinot felt that at least the possibility of considering a removal treaty should be discussed openly before the Cherokee public, in accordance with the principles of democracy. Ross, who regarded the *Phoenix* as "the public property of the Nation," maintained that it should not contain any information that might hinder the Cherokee people's struggle against removal. Although he also believed that "[in] other respects, the liberty of the press should be as free as the breeze that glides upon the surface," Ross's censorship of the *Phoenix* was absolutely legal in terms of the Cherokee Constitution, which, in contrast to its American counterpart, did not guarantee freedom of speech and the press.[124] On the other hand, Boudinot and John Ridge viewed Ross's refusal to allow a forum on removal as an act of "tyranny," because this contradicted the spirit of the Cherokee republican government. The confrontation came to a head at a special council held in the late summer of 1832, when the Cherokee government decided to postpone the scheduled national elections for an indefinite period because of the uncertain situation resulting from Georgia's repressive legislation. This controversial measure did not sit well with either Boudinot or Ridge, especially as the latter may also have harbored plans to run against Ross for the position of principal chief.[125] At the same gathering, U.S. Commissioner Elisha Chester also spoke to the Cherokees, trying to convince them that removal at this stage would prevent much suffering in the future. Boudinot, John Ridge, Andrew Ross (John Ross's brother), and other leading Cherokees openly demonstrated an interest in Chester's arguments and thereby planted the seed for the development of a proremoval faction (later known as the "Treaty Party" or "Ridge Party") in opposition to the Ross administration and its antiremoval followers ("National Party" or "Ross Party"). Shortly thereafter, on July 28, Boudinot wrote an editorial in the *Phoenix*, which reveals the full extent of his disenchantment with the situation at the time:

> What do the good people of the United States think of the distressed condition of the Cherokees? Is their attention so completely engrossed in their own private affairs that they cannot even find time to shed a tear at the recollection of such accumulated oppressions heaped upon their fellow creatures? Has the cause of the Indians been swallowed up in other questions, such as the tariff, the bank &c.? For how can we account for the silence which pervades the public in regard to the conduct of the General Government and the state of Georgia towards the Cherokees? . . . But what signifies to tell all this! They *glory* in their shame — *triumph* over their own laws, and SMILE at the cries of

the subjects of their cruelty. What signifies to tell it, when the complaints of the oppressed are *unheeded* by those in high places, and *regarded* by the people only in *silence*![126]

Anticipating the inevitable consequences, Boudinot tendered his resignation to John Ross in a letter dated August 1, 1832, which he subsequently made public in the *Phoenix*. In the five points listed in the public version of his resignation, Boudinot maintained that the Cherokee paper had fulfilled its purpose, namely, "the defence of our *rights*, and the proper representation of our *grievances* to the people of the United States," but now the matter would have to be settled elsewhere because the decision of the Supreme Court had "forever closed the question of our conventional rights." This being the case, and in view of the fact that the Cherokee Nation was in dire need of funds, he could no longer see the need "to continue the *expenses* in supporting it." His primary reason for giving up the editorship of the Cherokee national paper, however, is listed under point 3:

> Were I to continue as editor, I should feel myself in a most peculiar and delicate situation. I do not know whether I could, at the same time, satisfy my own views, and the views of the authorities of the nation. My situation would then be as embarrassing as it would be peculiar and delicate. I do conscientiously believe it to be the duty of every citizen to reflect upon the dangers with which we are surrounded; to view the darkness which seems to lie before our people — our prospects, and the evils with which they are threatened; to talk over all these matters, and, if possible, come to some definite and satisfactory conclusion, while there is time, as to what ought to be done in the last alternative. I could not consent to be the conductor of the paper without having the right and privilege of discussing these important matters; and from what I have seen and heard, were I to assume that privilege, my usefulness would be paralyzed by being considered, as I have already been, an enemy to the interests of my country and people. I love my country and I love my people, as my own heart bears me witness, and for that very reason I should deem it my duty to tell them the whole truth, or what I believe to be the truth. I cannot tell them that we will be reinstated in our rights, when I have no such hope, and after our leading, active, and true friends in Congress, and elsewhere, have signified to us that they can do us no good.

Under the last two points he further mentioned that the "arduous duties" involved in editing the *Phoenix* over the past four years had not been beneficial to his "health and happiness" and that his "scanty salary of $300" would not have been sufficient to support him in his "situation" (he had six children to feed) in any case.[127]

Ross, who thought that the paper should be continued at all costs, formally accepted Boudinot's resignation in the same issue of the *Phoenix* and further outlined his clear-cut guidelines for its future editorial policy. "The *views of the public authorities* should continue," Ross declared, "and ever be in accordance with the *will of the people*; and the *views of the Editor of the national paper* be the same. The toleration of *diversified views* to the columns of such a paper would not fail to create fermentation and confusion among our citizens."[128]

Boudinot volunteered to carry on with the paper until a replacement could be found, and early in September the editorship was turned over to Elijah Hicks (the first issue under his name appeared September 8, 1832), brother-in-law and devoted follower of John Ross. Hicks chose to blast Boudinot's motives for resigning in the September 29 issue, dismissing the whole matter with an offhand comment that "However valuable the services of this *once* devoted *patriot*, we must bear the *loss*. The *loss* is but a drop in the bucket."[129] Unfortunately for the paper, he was unable to match Boudinot's editorial and managerial talents because the *Phoenix* began to falter shortly after he took over, though its downfall may also have been expedited by the more adverse economic and political conditions he had to contend with. By the time the last issue left the press, on May 31, 1834, the *Phoenix* had long ceased to appear on a regular basis, and its contents had failed to hold the interest of a wider readership. In October 1835 the Georgia Guard seized the Cherokee press with the assistance of Stand Watie and thereby terminated the existence of the first bilingual North American Indian newspaper.[130]

In the period between the close of 1832 and 1835 the rift between the two contending parties led by John Ridge and John Ross widened as the former tried repeatedly to obtain a hearing at council meetings and the latter consistently blocked any such efforts.[131] During the fall council of 1832, John Ridge, acting as president of the National Committee, proposed to send delegates to Washington to discuss the possibility of removal with Jackson. But the National Council resolved instead to send a delegation of antitreaty men with John Ross as their chief counselor, who eventually rejected a government offer of three million dollars to remove, much to the annoyance of the protreaty faction. When this delegation returned from Washington in the spring of 1833, Boudinot, John Ridge, and Major Ridge signed a petition of protest against the course hitherto followed by the Ross administration, which had been written by Ross's own nephew, William Shorey Coodey. Frustrated by their failure to make any headway at the following fall council, Boudinot, the Ridges, and a number of protreaty

Cherokees enrolled for emigration. Major Ridge and Boudinot soon after joined a small deputation (lampooned in the *Phoenix* as "Kitchen Chiefs" in allusion to Jackson's notorious cabinet) to Washington to present their own point of view.[132] Confronted with the presence of the emigration faction at the capital, John Ross felt that he at least had to demonstrate his willingness to discuss the possibility of a treaty with Jackson and even went so far as to propose that, should the Cherokees agree to give up part of their lands to Georgia, they be allowed to live on the remaining portion of their eastern territory under the jurisdiction of the respective states until they were prepared to amalgamate as U.S. citizens.[133] At the same time, however, a few members of the emigration deputation (including John Ross's brother, Andrew Ross) signed a preliminary removal treaty on their own account, much to the consternation of both parties. When this minority treaty was made public before a special council called in August by John Ross, who wisely remained silent about his own compromise proposal, the entire protreaty faction was held responsible. Most of the Cherokees' wrath was directed at the Ridges and Boudinot, who were regarded as the principal leaders of the protreaty faction. Their official exemption from the Georgia lottery, which had wreaked tremendous havoc in the Cherokee Nation after the fall of 1832 (even John Ross's estate was annexed in the spring of 1834), obviously did not help their reputation among those affected by it. A petition for the impeachment of the Ridges and David Vann, another protreaty councilman, was duly adopted by the Council, and they were ordered to appear at the next meeting to answer public charges. But even before the Council was officially adjourned, a member of the emigrant delegation, John Walker, Jr., was murdered as he made his way home from the gathering, the first of many casualties in the ensuing factionalist dispute over removal. The Ridges and Boudinot were also threatened on numerous occasions, and their constant fear of reprisals further increased their dependence upon the federal government and Georgia's authorities for protection.[134]

John Ross, who was anxious to present a united Cherokee front against the removal lobby, apparently made efforts to reconcile with the protreaty faction just before the October council. "It is sincerely to be hoped, that every honorable and patriotic man will under existing state of things unite in recommending and exerting an influence among the people with the view of cultivating harmony among one another," he appealed in a letter to John Ridge, "and to suppress as far as practicable all causes tending to unnecessary excitement and evil. The general welfare of our much oppressed and suffering people requires it at our hands, and their peace & happiness demands it of us — therefore every course calculated to produce strife among the people from partyism, should be discarded. Our country and our people, should be our motto, and their will should direct our steps in the path of duty."[135] The impeachment charges against the Ridges and David Vann were not brought before the Council, however, even though all three had earnestly requested a public trial in order to assist their acquittal. As a consequence of this they called their own meeting at Running Waters on November 27, 1834, and officially founded the Treaty (or Ridge) Party at John Ridge's home. The ad hoc council named a panel of delegates, including John Ridge and Boudinot, to represent the Treaty Party's cause in Washington. A special committee headed by John Ridge and Boudinot prepared a draft of the Treaty Party's resolutions "as to the present condition and future prospects of the Nation," which was signed by fifty-seven Cherokees. The first two of a total of ten resolutions summed up the party members' reasons for considering emigration:

> *Resolved*, That it is our decided opinion, founded upon the melancholy experience of the Cherokees within the last two years, and upon facts which history has furnished us in regard to other Indian nations, that our people cannot exist amidst a white population, subject to laws which they have no hand in making, and which they do not understand; that the suppression of the Cherokee Government, which connected this people in a distinct community, will not only check their progress in improvement and advancement in knowledge, but, by means of numerous influences and temptations which this new state of things has created, will completely destroy every thing like civilization among them, and ultimately reduce them to poverty, misery, and wretchedness.

> *Resolved*, That, considering the progress of the States authorities in this country, the distribution and settlement of the lands, the organization of the counties, the erection of county seats and Courthouses, and other indications of a determined course on the part of the surrounding States, and considering, on the other hand, the repeated refusal of the President and Congress of the United States to interfere in our behalf, we have come to the conclusion that this nation cannot be reinstated in its present location, and that the question left to us and to every Cherokee, is, whether it is more desirable to remain here, with all the embarrassments with which we must be surrounded, or to seek a country where we *may* enjoy our own laws, and live under our own vine and fig-tree.

The Treaty Party, acting under the firm but nevertheless erroneous conviction "that a large majority of the Cherokee people would prefer to remove, if the true state of their condition was properly made known to them," then sent its resolutions to Washington, where they were presented to Congress early in the following year by Edward Everett and Henry Clay, two former opponents of removal.[136]

In February two rival delegations representing the irreconcilable Treaty and National parties were in Washington simultaneously to plead their cases separately before the U.S. government. As might be expected, the representatives of the Treaty Party were shown preferential treatment by the Jackson administration. In the course of their dealings, John Ridge apparently revised his opinion of the "Chicken Snake" president enough to name his newborn son Andrew Jackson.[137] Pressured once again by the presence of a delegation willing to negotiate, John Ross repeated the offer he had made to Jackson in the previous year. The War Department dismissed his proposal as stalling tactics, however, and decided to deal directly with the Treaty Party delegation, appointing the Reverend John F. Schermerhorn as its commissioner for that purpose. When Schermerhorn and the Treaty Party delegates reached a tentative financial agreement for a removal treaty, the National Party delegation responded by making an alternative proposition offering to give up the Cherokee lands outright for the sum of twenty million dollars and, as this was promptly rejected, it agreed to whatever sum the Senate might find justifiable. At the same time, Ross was apparently seriously considering a rather adventurous plan according to which the Cherokees were to accept a cash indemnity for their eastern lands and then settle in Mexico.[138] Writing to his brother from Washington, Boudinot confidently predicted a positive outcome to the crisis after all:

> Our proceedings have finally so frightened Mr. Ross so that he made several propositions lately, all of which have been rejected promptly except the last, which is, to agree to take the gross amount in money which the Senate shall say will be sufficient. His intention is to get the money and hunt out a country for himself. This the President is willing should be laid before the Cherokee people, also a proposition giving the same amount if they will go to the west. The question is to be submitted to the Senate to-day. I have not time to enlarge — but I can tell you our rights are fully secured. I am sure the Cherokees, when they find out that they are to remove at all events will not think of going to a Country of which they know nothing. Where will Ross take them to? But here is a country to which they can go with the same pecuniary advantages — a country already obtained and near by. . . . We have some new prospects of a speedy termination to our perplexities. Be firm to our cause and we shall yet succeed in saving a majority of our people.[139]

His optimism proved to be somewhat premature, however, as the Senate's subsequent recommendation of a payment of five million dollars for the

Cherokee lands was duly rejected by the National Party delegation in early March. Schermerhorn was then directed by Congress to make a provisional agreement with the Treaty Party delegation for the same amount, which was to be presented for ratification by the Cherokee people at their coming annual October council. "The U. States will never have any thing more to do with John Ross," John Ridge reported to his father. "Thus it becomes selfish men."[140]

At a special council meeting called on May 18, Ross spoke out against the provisional treaty agreed upon by "certain unauthorized individuals," calling on the Cherokee representatives at hand "to express a decisive & unequivocal disapprobation against such conduct & proceedings; and also to adopt by Resolution an expression of their determination never to give their assent to any measure that will trifle away the rights & interests of the people; that their *occupant right* in the land will be respected & guarded; and should ever any future arrangement take place between the proper authorities of the nation and of the United States Government for the adjustment of existing difficulties, that no arrangement touching those rights & interests will be made without their consent and providing amply for the same."[141] The Ridges attempted to sway public sentiment in their favor by sponsoring a traditional green corn dance in late August, a rather unusual tactic for a progressive Indian political party.[142] Nevertheless, Ross's agitation against the Treaty Party found attentive ears, and the provisional treaty was firmly rejected by a majority of the Cherokees present at the October council. Even though they obviously had no intention of giving up their plans for removal, Boudinot and the Ridges also voted against the treaty at this time, either because they were momentarily cowed by the vehemence of the antiremoval sentiment expressed by the Cherokees on the occasion or, as Grace Woodward has maintained, to disguise their real intentions for fear of reprisals.[143] The Council thereupon resolved to send another delegation to resume negotiations in Washington, which was to be made up of members of both the National and Treaty parties in a calculated demonstration of Cherokee unity. For some reason Boudinot, who had been appointed as one of the delegates along with John Ridge, declined to go and suggested to Ross that Stand Watie take his place.[144] In mid-December, while the delegation was in Washington, Boudinot, Major Ridge, and four or five hundred Cherokees joined a council that had been called by Schermerhorn in reaction to the fiasco at the October meeting. Both Boudinot and Major Ridge spoke out eloquently in favor of the treaty on this occasion, and on December 29 a committee that included both of them and eighteen other

Cherokees signed the notorious Treaty of New Echota at Boudinot's home. John Ridge and Stand Watie wrote a letter of protest to the secretary of war upon first hearing of the illicit treaty. But when the maverick committee subsequently arrived in Washington with Schermerhorn, they decided to join its ranks and assist in formulating a supplementary treaty on March 1, 1836, with somewhat more favorable conditions.[145] In spite of a storm of protest from the Cherokees (Ross is said to have produced almost 16,000 signatures in opposition, or nearly the entire Nation) as well as numerous congressmen (John Quincy Adams referred to it as an infamous treaty that would bring "eternal disgrace upon the country"), it was ratified in the Senate by a "majority" of one vote on May 17, 1836, and promptly declared law by Jackson on May 23. The federal government then gave the Cherokees until May 26, 1838, to leave their ancestral homelands permanently and join their relatives west of the Mississippi.[146]

The Treaty Party had thus successfully collaborated with white pro-removal interest groups to sell the Cherokee lands against the will of the majority of Cherokees and without the required consent of the Cherokee administration. In terms of American law the "infamous" treaty, though illegal, was viewed as a moral and political embarrassment at worst. According to a Cherokee law, however, which had originally been proposed by none other than Major Ridge and then put into writing by John Ridge in October 1829, it was a capital crime. The Treaty Party members were fully aware of this fact when they set their signatures to it. Major Ridge is reported to have said that he "signed [his] death warrant" as he made his mark on the treaty, and John Ridge made a similar statement elsewhere: "I may yet die by the hand of some poor infatuated Indian. . . . I am resigned to my fate, whatever it may be."[147] In a somewhat melodramatic speech recorded by a white onlooker at the December council in New Echota, Boudinot also made it clear that he had no illusions whatsoever about the probable consequences of his weighty decision:

> I know I take my life in my hand, as our fathers have also done. We will make and sign this treaty. Our friends can then cross the great river, but Tom Foreman and his people will put us across the dread river of death! We can die, but the Great Cherokee Nation will be saved. They will not be annihilated; they can live. Oh, what is a man worth who will not dare to die for his people? Who is there that would not perish, if this great nation may be saved?[148]

Life among their own people became dangerous for the Ridges and Boudinot thereafter, and they wasted little time making preparations to migrate westward. Major Ridge left in the spring of 1837 to settle in the vicinity of Honey Creek, on the border between Missouri and Arkansas, and was followed in the late fall by John Ridge, Boudinot, and their respective families. Shortly before his departure, in the fall of 1836, Boudinot's wife had died, and he was remarried soon after to Delight Sargeant from Pawlet, Vermont, who had taught school at the Brainerd mission.[149] The Ridges had managed to obtain a substantial remuneration for their "improvements" in the Cherokee Nation East and were thus in a position to set themselves up comfortably as merchant-farmers and stock raisers in the Cherokee Nation West. Boudinot, who eventually settled near Park Hill (in present-day Oklahoma) in order to resume his collaboration with Samuel Worcester, was so impoverished when he arrived that Worcester had to request money from the ABCFM to help him erect a modest home for his large family.[150] Boudinot and the Ridges tried to maintain a low profile in the Cherokee Nation West, but the arrival of Ross and his followers late in 1838 soon drew them back into the political arena.

By the time the federal government's deadline for removal had come to pass, only about one-eighth of the Cherokee population had emigrated west. The rest still held on to the desperate hope that the Ross Party would somehow succeed in annulling the Treaty of New Echota. John Ross continued relentlessly to lobby in Washington and to mobilize public sentiment against the fraudulent treaty and its signatories in countless personal letters to government officials and memorials to Congress, two of which were underscored by the signatures of several thousand Cherokees.[151] But the American public and its representatives in Congress now regarded the whole matter as "settled" and were preoccupied instead with their own domestic problems, such as the depression of 1837. Reformers, on the other hand, now focused their whole attention on the debate over slavery. In the spring of 1838 the Jackson administration ordered General Winfield Scott to supervise the enforcement of the Cherokee removal. In a last desperate attempt, Ross proposed a treaty of removal on May 18, 1838, that would have at least provided the Cherokees with a higher remuneration for their lands, but to no avail. Finally, in mid-1838, Ross also gave up and requested funds from the U.S. government so that the Cherokee administration might manage the rounding up of the Cherokee people and thus spare them the degradation of being removed by military force.[152] Beginning in December of that year, approximately thirteen thousand Cherokees made the difficult trek to the northeastern part of present-day Oklahoma in the dead of a hard winter, losing several thousand people along the tragic Trail of Tears before they finally arrived there in the spring of 1839.[153] Only about a thousand Cherokees managed to escape into the rugged mountains of North Carolina and Tennessee, where they eventually became known as the Eastern Cherokees.[154]

The close to one thousand "Treaty" people who had moved to the Cherokee Nation West earlier had voluntarily placed themselves under the rule of the existing government of "Old Settlers," then numbering about eight thousand. When more than twice as many "Late Immigrants" arrived with the intention of reestablishing their former government in the western territory, however, a conflict of interests was unavoidable. At a council called in June of 1839, John Ross attempted to orchestrate an act of union with the Old Settlers but failed due to opposition from the majority of the Old Settlers themselves and the allied Treaty people. On June 22, 1839, Boudinot, Major Ridge, and John Ridge were killed at different locations by unidentified bands of Cherokees.[155] A regular civil war erupted in the Cherokee Nation West immediately thereafter, which was not terminated until the opposing parties reached a temporary agreement on August 6, 1846, after the U.S. government had threatened to take concrete steps toward establishing two separate Cherokee nations.[156] Although John Ross denied any involvement of the Cherokee administration in the killings, it is nevertheless quite likely that they were perpetrated by supporters of his faction. As Ross himself assumed, it is probable that Boudinot and the Ridges were regularly "executed" for various crimes committed according to traditional Cherokee legal understanding: for the lives lost during the Trail of Tears under the ancient law of clan revenge, which had been officially abolished in 1808 and 1810 but never entirely abandoned; and for illegally selling Cherokee lands under the law of 1829, which stated clearly that "any person or persons, citizens of this nation, may kill him or them so offending, in any manner most convenient, within the limits of this nation, and shall not be held accountable for the same."[157] Political motives also played a role in the killings as the victims were held responsible for the discord between Old Settlers and Late Immigrants following the abortive June council. In order to give the assassinations further semblance of legality, a special Cherokee council headed by Ross passed a decree on July 7, 1839, which provided amnesty for all crimes committed in the Cherokee Nation West up to that date, on the one hand, and outlawed all those who threatened to avenge the late killings on the other.[158]

The irony behind this tragic event is that Boudinot, the Ridges, and Ross essentially shared identical views concerning what they thought best for

Cherokee development. All four were active members of a highly influential, progressive, mixed-blood proto-elite who had fully accepted the civilization policies set forth by early U.S. administrations and who, by virtue of their own incumbent position of economic and political power within the Cherokee Nation, sought to impose these on the vast majority of more conservative Cherokees. They were thus digits of the same administrative hand which tried to guide its Cherokee constituents through a difficult period of massive sociocultural change and political stress.

It has been intimated that some members of the Treaty Party, including John Ridge, were part of a frustrated middle class who resented the political and economic power of the Cherokee upper class and, correspondingly, their opposition to the Ross Party may have been prompted by careerism. Not a single document has been revealed so far, however, that would suggest that Boudinot had acted out of disreputable ulterior motives when he signed the minority treaty.[159] His fateful decision was neither more nor less conscientious than, for instance, Worcester's and Butler's professed anxiety over the state of the Union in their resolution to seek a pardon from the Georgia authorities. Worcester himself, who considered the treaty to be a "fraudulent and wicked transaction," still had no doubts as far as Boudinot's integrity was concerned: "his extreme anxiety to save his people from the threatening union led him to unite with a small minority of the nation in forming a treaty with the United States: an act, in my view, entirely unjustifiable, yet, in his case, dictated by good motives."[160]

In claiming the unorthodox right for himself to make political decisions over the heads of the Cherokee populace, Boudinot was acting in accordance not only with the elitist Anglo-Protestant social standards taught to him by his Presbyterian mentors but also with the patronizing stance of the Cherokee mixed-blood proto-elite as savants of a new and better way of life. The only marked difference between Boudinot and Ross, other than Boudinot's having signed a treaty without the required sanction of the Cherokee government, was the precise point in time at which he changed his mind about removal. Three years after the Treaty Party's "capitulation," John Ross also concluded a removal agreement with the U.S. government even though the majority of the Cherokees were undoubtedly still against it (not to mention his earlier proposals, which had also been made without a public referendum). In a letter he wrote to his brother from Washington in the spring of 1838, he legitimized his acquiescence in removal with words that seem to echo Boudinot's sentiments following Jackson's refusal to enforce Marshall's decision in 1832: "Finding it impossible to get justice extended to our Nation, so as to ensure a quiet, permanent, and happy continuance upon the land of our Fathers — the Delegation are now satisfied that the only alternative left us, in the last resort for an adjustment of the affairs is to negotiate a Treaty on the basis of a Removal."[161]

This controversial issue inevitably brings up the purely hypothetical question of whether or not the signing of the minority Treaty of New Echota ultimately thwarted the Ross Party's efforts to stay removal, or whether American expansionism would ever have permitted the greater part of the Cherokees to remain in their homelands in the first place. If the latter were true, then a well-planned and voluntary removal at an earlier date, as Boudinot and the Ridges had in mind, might have proven to be less traumatic. Examples of successful eastern Indian resistance to removal are few and far between. The Cherokees who hid in the mountains of North Carolina were eventually granted a reservation in 1868, but their numbers and the size of the territory they retained were minute in comparison to the former Cherokee Nation East. The same applies to their northern linguistic relatives, the approximately two thousand Senecas of New York. They experienced a very similar fissure into pro- and antiemigration factions, but with the assistance of the Society of Friends (Quakers) and the guiding example of Cherokee lobbying activities they actually managed in 1842 to have the fraudulent removal treaties of 1826 and 1838 renegotiated and were thus able to hold on to at least a fraction of their original territory.[162] It seems highly unlikely, however, that Georgia, a southern state considering secession at the time, would ever have given up its claims on Cherokee lands even if the federal government had tried to enforce the Supreme Court decision. As Walter Conser, Jr., has suggested, the Cherokee resistance movement simply lacked "sufficient political or economic leverage" to defeat the American removal campaign in the long run.[163] Further speculation on this matter, however, would not lead to a better understanding or a legitimation of either Boudinot's or Ross's position on removal, especially under the fairly plausible premise that both men followed a course they sincerely felt to be the best for the Cherokee people. In contrast to Ross, Boudinot simply made a major error in judgment when he assumed that a majority of the Cherokees would have favored removal "if the true state of their condition was properly made known to them." It is thus more a matter of political shortsightedness on his part than a question of morality, which, if it has any validity at all in this historical context, would have to be directed instead at the role of the United States government in the tragic affair.

If Boudinot's reputation as a Cherokee patriot is contradictory at best, his achievement as an Indian man of letters remains unchallenged. Alexander Posey, the noted Creek journalist and humorist of turn-of-the-century Indian Territory, praised him as a "gifted sage" in his poem honoring Sequoyah.[164] Other than his editorials for the *Phoenix* and occasional contributions to other newspapers, Boudinot published an address on Cherokee progress and a collection of documents and commentaries related to the Treaty of New Echota, and he has been credited (albeit erroneously) with the authorship of a popular religious tract. As founding member of the Moral and Literary Society of the Cherokee Nation and editor of the *Cherokee Phoenix*, which had a special poetry column on the fourth page and regularly included other writing as well, Boudinot had to keep abreast of current literary trends. His own views and style were undoubtedly influenced by the same salvationist-reformist impulses that shaped the works of his New England contemporary, William Apess. Boudinot was particularly fond of Washington Irving, for example, whom he quoted repeatedly in his published address and whose "Traits of Indian Character" he serialized in the *Phoenix*. But he was also quite familiar with others who wrote on Indian topics or took up the Cherokee cause, such as Jeremiah Evarts and his widely circulated "William Penn" essays, which were featured in several issues of the Cherokee paper.[165] Since he maintained a regular exchange with other newspapers and journals for items to reprint in the *Phoenix*, Boudinot must also have been exceptionally well informed on all sorts of contemporary issues. The *Phoenix* even reported unusual Indian events abroad, such as a speech delivered in London by Canada's noted Ojibwa missionary, Peter Jones.[166]

An Address to the Whites, his best-known publication, is a sixteen-page pamphlet containing the speech he gave at the First Presbyterian Church in Philadelphia on May 26, 1826, during his first official fund-raising tour of the northeastern states. It is a promotional piece in defense of Indian "character" and the practicality of "civilization" programs and is thus very similar in style, content, and purpose to an antiremoval address published by the Dartmouth-educated Seneca leader Maris Bryant Pierce in 1838 titled *Address on the Present Condition and Prospects of the Aboriginal Inhabitants of North America.*[167]

Beginning with the popular developmentalist premise that Indians are essentially as capable of "progress" as the once "savage" Britons were, he sets out to prove his point by describing the advancements hitherto made by the Cherokees with the aid of comparative statistical data he obtained from two censuses conducted at the Cherokee Nation, one by order of U.S. Indian agent Return J. Meigs in 1810 and the other by the Cherokee Council in 1824. Other than current American reformist texts, he may also have been inspired by the two pieces on Cherokee progress that had been written earlier by his fellow students at the Foreign Mission School: David Brown's report to Secretary of War Thomas L. McKenney titled "Views of a Native Indian, as to the Present Condition of His People," which he wrote following an extended tour through the Cherokee Nation in 1825 and had published that same year in *Niles' Weekly Register* and the *Missionary Herald*; and John Ridge's "short account of the Cherokee Nation, its present state of Civilization, and the manner of its introduction," written in February/March 1826 at the request of Albert Gallatin, who intended to send it to Baron Alexander von Humboldt for publication in Europe.[168] As his predecessors did in their promotional essays, Boudinot points to improvements made in agriculture, trade, religion, morality, and education as evidence for his contention that all efforts to civilize the Cherokees had borne fruit. Of particular relevance for Boudinot are the invention of the Cherokee syllabary by Sequoyah, the translation of the New Testament into Cherokee (he is referring here to the first translation by David Brown and George Lowry in 1825), and the organization of the Cherokee constitutional government. Backed by such strong evidence of Cherokee progress, Boudinot goes on to enumerate the "three important truths" that can be drawn from it: "First, that the means which have been employed for the christianization and civilization of this tribe, have been greatly blessed. Second, that the increase of these means will meet with final success. Third, that it has now become necessary, that efficient and more than ordinary means should be employed."[169] With the third "truth" he is, of course, alluding to the practical purpose of his address, namely, the generation of funds for the seminary and press. Perhaps exaggerating somewhat as far as the number of Cherokees supposedly able to read Cherokee and English is concerned, he proposes (quite realistically, as it turned out) that the establishment of a bilingual Cherokee newspaper "could not fail to create much interest in the American community, favourable to the aborigines, and to have a powerful influence on the advancement of the Indians themselves."[170] Such a newspaper would, in his opinion, provide an alternative and more accurate inside perspective on the "traits of Indian character" expounded on by so many contemporary white authors. Boudinot thus sounds an early, if still modest, call for a national Indian literature:

> How can the patriot or the philanthropist devise efficient means, without full and correct information as to the subjects of his labour. And I am inclined to think, after all that has been said of the aborigines, after all that has been written in narratives, professedly to elucidate the leading traits of their character, that the public knows little of that character. To obtain a correct and complete knowledge of these people, there must exist a vehicle of Indian intelligence, altogether different from those which have heretofore been employed. Will not a paper published in Indian country, under proper and judicious regulations, have the desired effect? I do not say that Indians will produce learned and elaborate dissertations in explanation and vindication of their own character; but they may exhibit specimens of their intellectual efforts, of their eloquence, of their moral, civil and physical advancement, which will do quite as much to remove prejudice and to give profitable information.[171]

If the Cherokees were also granted their second request for "the means of civilization," the establishment of a seminary within the Cherokee Nation, then Boudinot predicts "glorious" prospects for the Cherokees, which he describes in the conventional rhetoric of the reform movement: "Yes, methinks I can view my native country, rising from the ashes of her degradation, wearing her purified and beautiful garments, and taking her seat with the nations of the earth. I can behold her sons bursting the fetters of ignorance and unshackling her from the vices of heathenism. She is at this instant, risen like the first morning sun, which grows brighter and brighter, until it reaches its fulness in glory."[172] Boudinot concludes that Indians have but two alternatives: "they must either become civilized and happy, or sharing the fate of many kindred nations, become extinct." Closing his address with Irving's famous "they will vanish like a vapour from the face of the earth" phrase, he leaves the prospects for a more positive alternative up to his audience's Christian generosity.

Boudinot's second major publication, *Letters and other Papers Relating to Cherokee Affairs*, was first published in 1837 in Athens, Georgia, by the press of the *Southern Banner*. The forty-three-page pamphlet is made up of a collection of previously written documents and personal letters delineating the Treaty Party's standpoint before and during the aftermath of the signing of the Treaty of New Echota, or what he refers to as "the controversy among the Cherokees themselves." He published it in response to a number of widely circulated memorials and letters written by John Ross in which he and John Ridge were severely criticized for signing the Treaty of New Echota.[173] Boudinot's defense was in turn used for propaganda purposes by Governor Lumpkin of Georgia, who had approximately four hundred copies printed in 1838 under the title *Documents in Relation to the*

Validity of the Cherokee Treaty of 1835 and distributed to members of the Senate. Together with a very similar publication produced three years later in conjunction with the Seneca removal issue, Nathan T. Strong's *Appeal to the Christian Community on the Condition and Prospects of the New York Indians*, it is a unique sample of Indian proremoval discourse.[174]

Boudinot's protreaty manifesto can be subdivided into three sections: The first is made up of material relative to his resignation as editor of the *Phoenix*; the second contains documents bearing on the Treaty Party's proremoval platform; and the third is a lengthy letter addressed to John Ross, refuting the latter's accusations in sundry antitreaty writings. The material he compiled also provides valuable insight into his personal motives in the controversy. He prefixes his collection of documents with a commentary on what he considers to be "the great cause" behind the controversy they are supposed to elucidate, namely, the "want of proper information among the people." On the basis of this supposed ignorance he tries to justify the Treaty Party's minority position with an elitist argument: "If one hundred persons are ignorant of their true situation, and are so completely blinded as not to see the destruction that awaits them, we can see strong reasons to justify the action of a minority of fifty persons to do what the majority *would do* if they understood their condition — to save a *nation* from political and moral degradation."[175] Since the greater majority of the Cherokees were against removal and Boudinot must have been aware of this, his pleading here sounds rather contrived.

In the first section, which also includes his statement of resignation as editor and Ross's acceptance of it, Boudinot reproduces a letter he had written to Elijah Hicks on October 2, 1832, in response to Hicks's derogatory comments in the *Phoenix*. Here Boudinot tries to legitimize removal as the lesser of "three evils":

> I have come to the unpleasant and most disagreeable conclusion (whether that conclusion be correct is another question) that our lands, or a large portion of them, are about to be seized and taken from us. Now, as a friend of my people, I cannot say *peace, peace*, when there is no peace. I cannot ease their minds with any expectations of a calm, when the vessel is already tossed to and fro, and threatened to be shattered to pieces by an approaching tempest. If I really believe there is danger, I must act consistently, and give the alarm; tell my countrymen our true, or what I believe to be our true, situation. In the case under consideration, I am induced to believe there is danger, "immediate and appalling," and that it becomes the people of this country to weigh the matter rightly, act wisely, not rashly, and choose a course that will come nearest benefitting the nation. When we come to the last crisis, (and my opinion is,

that we are at that point), one of three things *must* be chosen. 1. Nature's right of all nations to resist and fight in the defence of our lands. But this we must do with a certainty of being annihilated. 2. Submit and peaceably come under the dominion of the oppressor, and suffer, which we most assuredly must if we make that choice, a *moral death*! 3. Avoid the two first by a removal.

If time should prove him wrong, Boudinot concludes, then it would be "an error of *judgment*, not of the *heart*."[176]

The second section reproduces the official proremoval resolutions of the Treaty Party made in November of 1834 and then juxtaposes two sets of proposals presented by the rival parties as they attempted to reach some kind of working agreement in October of the following year. In a succeeding letter "addressed to a friend" and dated May 16, 1836, Boudinot presents a rather confusing disputation against the Ross Party's contentions that the Treaty Party had violated this tentative agreement, accusing the former of accomplishing "their object by a system of delusion" and thereby virtually forcing the latter to take independent action.

In the third section, made up of a wordy communication to John Ross dated November 25, 1836, Boudinot first counters charges the principal chief had leveled against him and other Treaty Party members — "In these there is an evident attempt to present my character to the public in an obnoxious light" — and then tries to turn the tables with a muckraking review of Ross's personal role in the Cherokee controversy. He denies vehemently any implications of his having been "*bought* or *bribed*" in the affair, pointing out testily that while Ross himself was busy making "great preparations, which have now turned out to be a pecuniary advantage to you," he was "toiling, at the most trying time of our difficulties, for the defence of our rights, in an arduous employment, and with a nominal salary of three hundred dollars only, entirely neglecting my own pecuniary interest."[177] He further accuses Ross of having "attempted to produce an impression not in accordance with facts" in his dealings with the Cherokee people, the mass of whom, in his estimation, "have NOT intelligence enough, or 'correct knowledge' of the extent of their difficulties to guide them in these matters." The treaty, he declares, was "the best that can be done for the Cherokees, under present circumstances; a treaty that will place them in a *better* condition than they *now* are." That it was signed only by a minority is relatively irrelevant as far as he is concerned, because this "is no new thing in Cherokee negotiations, as some of the signers of your [Ross's] memorials can testify."[178]

The main thrust of Boudinot's criticism, however, is that the Ross Party was allegedly more concerned about "the pecuniary aspect of this nation's affairs" (with reference to Ross's attempt to obtain a higher remuneration) than it was with the "moral condition of this people." He closes his letter to Ross with an assessment of the present situation among the Cherokees that blatantly contradicts his earlier optimism:

> How can you persist in deluding our people with phantoms, and in your opposition to that which alone is practicable, when you see them dying a moral death? . . . To be sure, from your account of the condition and circumstances of the Cherokees, the public may form an idea different from what my remarks seem to convey. When applied to a portion of our people, confined mostly to whites intermarried among us, and the descendants of whites, your account is probably correct, divesting it of all the exaggeration with which you have encircled it; but look at the mass, look at the entire population as it now is, and say, can you see any indication of a progressing improvement, anything that can encourage a philanthropist? You know that it is almost a dreary waste. I care not if I am accounted a slanderer of my country's reputation; every observing man in this nation knows that I speak the words of truth and soberness. In the light that I consider my countrymen, not as mere animals, and to judge of their happiness by their condition as such, which, to be sure, is bad enough, but as moral beings, to be affected for better or for worse by moral circumstances, I say their condition is wretched.

Perhaps in self-conscious recognition of this turncoat perspective, Boudinot finally returns to his favorite symbol of the rising phoenix to indicate his continued belief in Cherokee progress, albeit in "another country, and under other circumstances," far away from the influence of Georgia's "worthy" citizenry:

> Removal, then, is the only remedy, the only *practicable* remedy. By it there *may be* finally a renovation; our people *may* rise from their very ashes, to become prosperous and happy, and a credit to our race. Such has been and is now my opinion, and under such a settled opinion I have acted in all this affair. My language has been, "fly for your lives"; it is now the same. I would say to my countrymen, you among the rest, fly from the moral pestilence that will finally destroy our nation.[179]

When John Ross finally deigned to respond to Boudinot's invective in a letter addressed to the editors of the *National Intelligencer* early in 1838, he dismissed the "sickening subject" as "a mere farrago of personalities" produced by "an unfriendly individual not employed in any public trust by our Indian nation." He would still have "treated it with utter & silent indifference" if Governor Lumpkin had not been busy at the time convincing the members of the House of Representatives to reissue the "little pamphlet" which, as Ross saw it, "affords some very startling evidences of the danger of confiding in a lampoon as grave authority for a grave assembly upon momentous matters."[180]

The earliest publication attributed to Boudinot, *Poor Sarah*, is a typical example of a popular form of early nineteenth-century American tract literature in which some marginal individual (usually an African American slave) with a faulty command of English gives a first-person account of an exemplary Christian life. "Poor Sarah" is thus one more variation on a standard protagonist in abolitionist literature who attained immortality with Harriet Beecher Stowe's "Uncle Tom" in 1851–52. On the basis of this piece, Boudinot has been regarded as the first Indian author to produce a work of fiction.[181] The text first appeared anonymously in the *Religious Intelligencer* on January 1, 1820, when he was still at the Foreign Mission School in Cornwall and was then reproduced by various newspapers and tract publishers throughout the United States before Boudinot finally made use of it in 1823, probably in connection with his translating work for the ABCFM. Since Boudinot's other publications made concrete reference to his Indian origins, it seems highly unlikely that this popular tract (it went through at least six editions between 1820 and 1822) would have remained anonymous if he had actually been the author.[182] Elias Boudinot's namesake, who was president of the American Tract Society, also wrote vernacular pieces such as the poem titled "Indian Hymn," which Apess included in the appendix of *A Son of the Forest*. Herein might lie a possible clue for the source of confusion, as Boudinot was certainly aware of his benefactor's writings as well as the literature produced by the American Tract Society.

In the excellent introduction to her collection of Boudinot's writings, Theda Perdue has suggested that he was a "tragic figure" not only because of his fatal error in judgment but also for his inability to "accept his people, his heritage, or himself."[183] Boudinot had indeed incorporated the lessons taught by his Moravian and Presbyterian schoolmasters and emulated their way of life. But, in spite of the traumatic experiences that may have led him to modify his political outlook, there is little evidence in Boudinot's writings of a problem pertaining to his self-understanding either as a Christian or as a member of the Cherokee Nation. Instead, he appears to have considered himself to be a very privileged sort of Cherokee: "But I am not as my fathers were—broader means and nobler influences have fallen upon me." He obviously identified with the Cherokee proto-elite, "the intelligence of the country" as he referred to it, who had wrought such radical changes in early nineteenth-century Cherokee life. Even though he had a white ancestor and was the father of mixed-blood children, he nevertheless felt that he was more of a "Cherokee" than John Ross, whose deficiency in the Cherokee language he derided on several occasions.[184] He was part of a culturally and racially mixed Cherokee minority, no doubt, but one that identified itself as Cherokee and nothing else. His conviction that his special qualifications gave him the right and responsibility to make decisions for the benefit of the entire Cherokee Nation appears to have been as much a characteristic of the Cherokee proto-elite as it was of the more conservative Old Light missionaries who influenced his life. For progressives like himself, the survival of the Cherokee Nation in the early nineteenth-century contact environment called for the ability to adapt to new ways. The moments of crisis in Boudinot's life, the racist uproar that accompanied his marriage to Harriet Gold and the failure of the U.S. legal system to adhere to its most sacrosanct principles, led him to the conclusion that the dream he shared with the young chiefs of an independent Cherokee Nation "taking her seat with the nations of the earth" could no longer be fulfilled east of the Mississippi. Right or wrong, it was a decision based on rational political reflection rather than subconscious impulses of a disturbed personality. Thus, other than the temporal question of removal itself, Boudinot the "traitor" was really not much farther away from or closer to Cherokee tradition than John Ross the "patriot" at the moment he made his fatal decision.

6

George Copway, Canadian Ojibwa Methodist and Romantic Cosmopolite

GEORGE COPWAY, THE most widely acclaimed Indian writer of the antebellum era, is something of a paradox.[1] The ups and downs in the erratic career of this transcultural migrant were channeled by his own eccentric nature and the ideological fluctuations that shaped Indian policy in the course of mid-nineteenth-century American expansionism. By virtue of his birth and upbringing he is a Canadian Indian writer, but in terms of authorial genesis he occupies a definite space in the history of early United States Indian literature. Nevertheless, the writings he produced are intrinsically tied to his Southeastern Ojibwa heritage and subsequent education under Canadian Methodist missionaries. The first half of his life in British Canada thus provided him with the experiences from which he fashioned his existence as an author-orator in the United States. Copway's frustrating attempt to shape his identity according to his audience's whims, however, forced him to undergo various personality transformations that finally broke his spirit.

"Ojibwa" is a misleading term applied to a number of distinct Indian groups of the Great Lakes region, whose interconnectedness was based on cultural and linguistic (Central Algonquian) similarities rather than tribal or political ties.[2] Known variously as Saulteaux, Mississaugas, Chippewas (in the United States) and Ojibways (in Canada), the Anishinabes (various spellings, meaning something like "first" or "real" people), as they generally refer to themselves, once occupied the entire territory between the lower peninsula of Michigan, adjacent parts of Ontario, and the plains region of eastern Saskatchewan. They had close historical ties with the Ottawas and Potawatomies, with whom they formed a loose association known as the "three fires."[3] Numbering as many as 50,000 people at the time of contact

and eventually gaining control over more territory than any other Indian
group in North America, the Ojibwas came to play as important a role in
American history as the Six Nations or the Cherokees.[4] For the sake of
clarity, scholars have subdivided the heterogeneous Ojibwas of the postcontact era into four main groups: the Northern Ojibwas (or Saulteaux)
occupying the Laurentian uplands to the north of the Great Lakes; the
Plains Ojibwas (or Bungees) living in southern Saskatchewan and Man-
itoba; the Southwestern Chippewas of Wisconsin and Michigan; and the
Southeastern Ojibwas residing in southern Ontario and the lower peninsula
of Michigan.[5]

Although the Ojibwas had already obtained European trade goods
through Huron middlemen at an earlier date, direct contact between them
and Europeans did not occur until the early seventeenth century, when
they met the first French exploration parties at Sault Ste. Marie. By 1648
Sault Ste. Marie had emerged as a cultural and economic center for various
Ojibwa bands, and their ways of life were beginning to change rapidly in
response to French colonial interests. During the French period (ca. 1640–
1760), the Ojibwas were drawn into the international fur trade and were
deeply affected by it until well into the first half of the nineteenth century.[6]
By the mid-eighteenth century they had become dependent upon European
products and were thus forced to adapt to the demands of the transatlantic
market. Ojibwa settlement patterns first shifted from small, scattered autonomous bands to larger and more permanent villages located near trading
centers, and then fragmented once again into "composite hunting-trapping
bands" as depletion of local furbearing animals necessitated continuous
expansion into new productive trapping areas.[7] On the organizational level,
the position of certain band leaders was enhanced by their direct connections to traders and eventually resulted in the centralization of authority in a
hereditary form of chieftainship. Economic relations with Europeans also
furthered the uniformity of culture and religion among the formerly distinct
Central Algonquian groups, thus giving rise to the notion of a homogeneous
Ojibwa Nation.[8] Finally, extensive Indian-European contact encouraged by
the fur trade resulted in frequent intermarriages in the Great Lakes area
between the 1660s and 1830s, which eventually produced a substantial
population of Indians with European ancestry.[9]

Competition for hunting and trapping territory strained the relations
between Ojibwas and their competing neighbors. By 1701 they and their
allies managed to oust the formidable Iroquois (who had displaced the
Hurons in 1648–50) from the northern shores of Lakes Erie and Ontario.[10]

Beginning in the 1730s, they waged a relentless war against the Sioux, which finally resulted in the latter's withdrawal from the western edge of Lake Superior by the end of the century and left the Ojibwas as the most powerful group of Indians in the entire Great Lakes region.[11] Of less advantage to them was their participation in the imperial struggle between France and England, which led to armed conflict in 1752 and ended the French hegemony in the Great Lakes region in 1760–61 as the British began to occupy French fortifications in the area following their victory at Montreal. The advent of British colonial rule in turn marked the beginning of the end for Ojibwa sovereignty, even though they prospered economically as never before during the late eighteenth century and their territorial expansion continued as late as the 1820s. Needless to say, beginning with the French period the Ojibwas also became acquainted with virgin soil epidemics and the usual negative side effects of a colonial situation.[12]

The British period, which lasted from 1760 to 1796 in the United States and somewhat longer in Canada (1860), brought few alterations in the political status between Ojibwas and Anglo-Americans/Anglo-Canadians during its initial stages as the fur trade continued to dominate all interaction until the 1830s.[13] However, the defeat of the French meant that the Ojibwas were no longer essential as allies to the British, and consequently the latter curtailed the established practice of gift making and ceased to lower the prices arbitrarily for European goods. The Ojibwas now found that they could obtain the commodities they had come to depend upon only in exchange for cash crops such as high-quality furs. This forced Ojibwa trappers to look for new sources of beaver, and their conflicts with competing Indian groups, especially the Eastern Dakotas (Santee Sioux), increased accordingly. Moreover, the British were interested in expanding their own settlements and exploiting other natural resources like timber and minerals, which resulted in increasing pressure on the Ojibwa land base and a long series of Ojibwa land cessions beginning in the early 1760s. Indian dissatisfaction with these changes erupted in Pontiac's uprising (or Beaver War) of 1763, in which many Ojibwas took an active part.[14]

The crown's attempt to control the tide of settlers invading Indian territory under the statutes of the Royal Proclamation of 1763 proved to be ineffective, and therefore most Indians of the Great Lakes area (Sauks and Fox excepted) willingly joined the British campaign against the rebelling colonies. The second Treaty of Paris (1783) set up an international borderline between the United States and Canada and thus bisected the Ojibwa territory politically and historically. In 1785 the Ojibwas signed their first

George Copway. Frontispiece of George Copway, *The Life, History, and Travels of Kah-ge-ga-gah-bowh*, 2nd ed. (Philadelphia: James Homstead, 1847).

armistice and land-cession treaty with the United States at Fort McIntosh. British influence in the American Great Lakes area continued, however, until they finally removed their garrisons under the Jay Treaty of 1784. The following year, the Ojibwas ceded a section of their timberlands in the United States under the Treaty of Greenville, and their relatives in the North were forced to make room for displaced Indian and European Loyalists. Many Ojibwas attempted once again to stem American expansion by joining Tecumseh's confederacy — his second-in-command was an Ojibwa leader from Ontario — and siding with the British in the War of 1812. With the defeat and death of Tecumseh at the Battle of the Thames in the fall of 1813 and the truce concluded between the United States and England at Ghent the following year, the era of Ojibwa sovereignty had finally come to an end.[15]

Whatever economic benefits the Ojibwas may still have managed to gain from their trade in furs with the Hudson's Bay Company (which had swallowed the North West Company in 1821) in Canada and the American Fur Company in the United States ceased almost entirely by the end of the century with the depletion of beaver throughout the Great Lakes region. The situation was further aggravated by the severe depopulation of deer and other large game animals, as well as the beginning of commercial fishing at Sault Ste. Marie in the 1830s. At the same time, the immigrant population in Upper Canada (as the former province of Quebec became known in 1791) increased tenfold, from about 95,000 to 952,000, in the period between the War of 1812 and the 1850s. New land-cession agreements with the U.S. government after the armistice at Spring Wells in 1815 and additional surrenders to the colony of Upper Canada ate away a great portion of Ojibwa territory on both sides of the border.[16] Their relative prosperity began to ebb quickly, and individual families had to disperse to remote areas where they could still manage to find a few furbearing animals, rely increasingly on local small game and fish, or move onto the plains farther west to subsist on buffalo. Others chose instead to comply with new trends in American and British Indian policy and settled in small villages in what still remained of their former territory, where they hoped to learn the White Man's ways from missionaries and their Ojibwa assistants.[17]

The Ojibwas on the southern side of the border were subjected to removal policies during the 1830s and 1840s and had to give up additional tracts of land in northern Illinois and parts of the territory now comprising Michigan, Wisconsin, and Minnesota. Political pressure for total removal of the Ojibwas increased following the discovery of copper deposits along the southern shores of Lake Superior and lasted until 1850, when a presidential order required Wisconsin Ojibwa bands to emigrate to the headwaters of the Mississippi. With the signing of the Treaty of La Pointe in 1854, the Ojibwas finally agreed to relinquish their remaining lands in exchange for permanent reservations in present-day Michigan, Wisconsin, and Minnesota. At this point the federal government also began to promote the allotment of land to individual Ojibwas, long before this practice became part of its official Indian policy in 1887.[18]

Their relatives north of the border fared somewhat better in their relations with British Canadians, at least for the time being. Following the demilitarization of the Great Lakes region under the Rush–Bagot Convention of 1817, the British Indian Department abandoned the policies embodied in the Royal Proclamation of 1763 in favor of an assimilationist program. In order to reduce expenditures, Indian lands were now acquired in exchange for annuities and their former occupants concentrated in "reserves" situated near settled areas, where they could be more easily subjected to proselytization, education in day schools, and instruction in agriculture. In 1830, just six years after the Office of Indian Affairs was created within the Department of War in the United States, Great Britain transferred jurisdiction over Indian affairs from military to civil authorities. Encouraged by British postabolitionist humanitarian organizations such as the Aborigines Protection Society (founded 1836), the success of earlier missionizing activities in Upper Canada under the supervision of the American-based Methodist Episcopal Church and their Ojibwa converts (more on this later), and the desire of many Ojibwas to learn new ways in which to deal with their present problems, the Indian Department initiated a number of halfhearted "civilizing" experiments in Coldwater, the narrows between Lakes Simcoe and Couchiching, and the upper St. Clair River between 1830 and 1837. This assimilationist policy was temporarily interrupted in 1836, when the new lieutenant governor of Upper Canada, Sir Francis Bond Head, proposed to remove Canadian Indians to Manitoulin Island to live as they pleased without white interference. His plan was thwarted only by the loud protest coming from British humanitarians, missionary societies, and the Indians themselves, all of whom pointed to the failures of U.S. removal policy as a deterrent.[19]

Following the guidelines set by the Bagot Commission in 1842, British Indian policy took on a more pronounced protectionist tenor (i.e., acknowledging Indian rights of "occupancy" as guaranteed by the Royal Proclamation of 1763), but at the same time it also stepped up earlier or existing assimilationist policies. In education, for example, residential manual labor schools were given precedence over local day schools. Here the students were expected to spend a half-day in the classroom and a half-day in the field or in shops, with the ultimate goal of terminating government responsibilites for those who managed to become self-sufficient. Mining expeditions to the eastern and northern shores of Lake Superior in the 1840s provoked a conflict with Indians in the area and led to new legislation. The Robinson treaties of 1850 (Robinson-Huron, Robinson-Superior) forced the remaining Ojibwas to accept reserves, and two additional acts protected Indian property rights in Lower and Upper Canada (united as the Province of Canada in 1845). The act pertaining to the Indians in Lower Canada, or Canada East as it was now known, also formulated the first government-imposed definition of "Indian" in Canadian history. In 1857, with the passage of the Gradual Civilization Act, those Indians who could meet the requirements of a special board were to be "enfranchised" and given title to twenty hectares (ca. fifty acres) of land.[20]

In contrast to the earlier efforts to promote civilization among the Ojibwas, the accelerated assimilationist course after the 1840s met with increasing resistance from native leaders and led to a rapid decline in missionizing activity as it usurped Ojibwa community sovereignty and ran astray of their own notions of necessary adaptations, especially in matters of land ownership. The assimilationist thrust was continued by the Dominion of Canada after its formation in 1867, which passed an Enfranchisement Act two years later creating the controversial categories of "status" and "nonstatus" Indians and eschewing responsibilities for the latter. Whereas British Canadian legislation during the first half of the nineteenth century may have been somewhat more liberal at the outset than American policies, the end result for the Ojibwas was just about the same: rapid loss of lands, confinement to reserves, and loss of political autonomy — in other words, dependent status as internal colonies.[21]

Kahgegagahbowh ("Standing Firm") was born in the fall of 1818, as a member of a band of Southeastern Ojibwas living in the vicinity of Rice Lake, just north of Coburg on Lake Ontario.[22] His father, a band leader and medicine man, belonged to the Crane clan, and his mother was a member of the Eagle clan. His grandfather had been among the first group of Ojibwas who migrated southward into present-day southern Ontario around 1700 and wrested the bountiful hunting territory from the Iroquois. European settlers then began to apply the name Mississaugas ("river with several outlets") to most of the Southeastern Ojibwas.[23] Kahgegagahbowh's life began precisely at that critical period in which the Southeastern Ojibwas' hunting-trapping-fishing-gathering days of plenty were coming to an end. The year he was born, agents of the Indian Department purchased most of the Ojibwa territory in the Rice Lake area and thus opened the way for several thousand Irish settlers in the mid-1820s, who appropriated additional lands and ultimately left the Ojibwas in a destitute and demoralized state. Many, including his own father, tried to find solace in alcohol:

> The Ojibway nation, that nation unconquered in war, has fallen prey to the withering influence of intemperance. Their buoyant spirits would once mount the air as on the wings of a bird. Now they have no spirits. They are hedged in, bound, and maltreated, by both the American and British governments. They have no other hope than that some day they will be relieved from their privations and trials by death. The fire-water has rolled towards them like the waves of the sea. Alas, alas! my poor people! The tribe became dissipated, and consequently improvident, and often suffered intensely.[24]

Nevertheless, Kahgegagahbowh still experienced a relatively orthodox Ojibwa upbringing, according to his own account. From his father he learned the skills of hunting and trapping and acquired knowledge of Ojibwa social and religious practices. At the age of twelve he experienced a successful vision quest, when a wind manito appeared to him in a dream and taught him a spiritual song. Through this transfer of spiritual power he was regarded among his people as having been fortunate enough to acquire an "identity." His father then interpreted the dream-vision as portending a long and well-traveled life.[25] He was also introduced to the native art of healing with herbs and minerals by his father, and apparently he was even initiated into the secret rites of the Midewiwin Society, or "Grand Medicine Lodge," which was one of the most important ceremonial events among the Ojibwas.[26] But the young Ojibwa was also confronted with the extreme hardships of life in the Great Lakes area as game became increasingly scarce, relating at one point in his autobiography how his entire family had nearly starved to death during an unsuccessful winter hunting expedition. On the whole, however, Kahgegagahbowh recalled his early days with romantic nostalgia: "Fancy's pictures are not needed in my life to represent the past. The realities stare at me, and the days which I have spent in the forest yet cause a momentary joy, and give life's wheel smoothness in their passage to the grave."[27]

The transformation of Kahgegagahbowh from "one of Nature's children," as he liked to regard himself, into the neophyte George Copway commenced sometime in the fall of 1826, when a group of Christian Ojibwas from Credit River and the Bay of Quinte (where Apess had his transcendental vision) went to attend a religious conference in the vicinity of Coburg. His father and about thirty other Rice Lake Mississaugas came to the meeting to hear the Christian Indians' exhortations on abstinence and their arguments in favor of establishing European-oriented Indian farming communities. Most of the Rice Lake visitors converted that very same day, including his father (henceforth John Copway) and the principal chief of the band, George Paudash, who was purportedly Kahgegagahbowh's grandfather. His mother followed suit that summer.[28] Methodism had thus successfully penetrated the Credit River band, and it soon began to effect permanent changes in their life styles. The Reverend James Evans started a Methodist mission school at Rice Lake in 1828, which Kahgegagahbowh attended together with about fifty other Ojibwa children.

Of all Christian denominations vying to fill the growing spiritual vacuum among Indians in Upper Canada at the turn of the nineteenth century, the most successful by far was the American-based Methodist Episcopal Church, whose missionaries began to arrive in the area during the 1790s and then branched off into an independent Canadian Methodist Conference in 1828.[29] One of the keys to the widespread popularity of Methodism among Canadian Indians was the willingness of this religious body to train native preachers and to entrust them with important missionary duties, a liberal policy they had already implemented successfully among Indians in the United States, as the life history of William Apess well illustrates. In Upper Canada this fruitful relationship led to the emergence of a group of bilingual Ojibwa Methodist missionaries, who also produced a substantial body of English and Algonquian literature: Nahnebahwequay (Catherine Sutton, 1824–65); Sowengisik (the Reverend Henry Bird Steinhauer, ca. 1818–84); Keghezowinninne (the Reverend David Sawyer, ca. 1812–89); Shahwundais (the Reverend John Sunday, ca. 1795–1875); Pahtahsega (the Reverend Peter Jacobs, ca. 1807–90); Sahgahgewagahbaweh (John Summerfield, ca. 1815–36); Maungwudaus (George Henry, ca. 1811–88); and Thayendanegea (John Jones, 1798–1847).[30] Another prominent member of this early-nineteenth-century "Canadian Methodist Ojibwa school" was Kahgegagahbowh's adopted Ottawa cousin, Enmegahbowh (the Reverend John Johnson, ca. 1808–1902), who also emigrated to the United States and eventually joined the Episcopalians there to serve as a missionary to the Southwestern Ojibwas.[31] The driving force behind this Indian literary renaissance in Upper Canada was Kahkewaquonaby (the Reverend Peter Jones, 1802–56) of the Mississauga Credit River band, who was related to several of the individuals named above and whose exemplary life as a missionary affected them all, the younger Kahgegagahbowh not excluded.[32]

Kahkewaquonaby ("Sacred Waving Feathers") was the mixed-blood offspring of a Mississauga chief's daughter and a Welsh-Canadian trader. Since his father was officially married to and lived with a Mohawk woman, he and his older brother John remained under the care of their Ojibwa family until 1816. In keeping with Ojibwa patrilineal lines of descent, however, his membership in the band was not actually formalized until he was nine years old, at which time one of the band's leaders officially adopted him in the place of his own deceased son. In the fourteen years he lived with the Credit River Mississaugas, Kahkewaquonaby also learned to master the skills of a hunter and was introduced to many of the band's customs and ceremonials, knowledge he would later incorporate into his history of the Ojibwa people. In contrast to Kahgegagahbowh, however, Kahkewaquonaby failed to obtain an "identity" at this time. "In all my fastings I never had any vision or dream," he writes, "and, consequently, obtained no familiar god, nor a spirit of the rank of a pow-wow."[33] At one point he carelessly misplaced a number of sacred objects (a war club and a bunch of eagle's feathers representing the thunder manitos) connected with his naming ceremony, another important ceremonial transfer of "identity" among the Ojibwas. Years later he used this particular incident to illustrate his general disregard for traditional Indian beliefs. "I long lost both," he comments sarcastically, "and consequently became powerless and wingless!"[34] Accordingly, his recollections of an "uncertain mode of Indian life" also differed markedly from the euphoric overtones in Kahgegagahbowh's renditions. As far as Kahkewaquonaby was concerned, "the miseries of savage life" had very little to offer and, after he became a missionary, he would never again look beyond the Gospel for spiritual guidance. "I cautioned them against trusting to dreams or visions for fear of being led into error and superstition," he writes about his confrontations with skeptical traditionalists, "and reminded them that God had revealed his will clearly in the Bible, from whence we must derive all our religious knowledge and rule for our conduct."[35]

In 1816 Augustus Jones decided to take charge of his two Mississauga children and bring them to the Grand River reserve to live on his farm together with his Iroquois family. Thus Kahkewaquonaby remained until 1824 among the Iroquois, who eventually adopted him under the name Desagondensta. It was here that he eventually acquired his new "identity" as Peter Jones, learning from his father how to manage a farm and obtaining instruction in the English language at a nearby school. In compliance with his father's request he was baptized by the Church of England in 1820, but his decision then was not entirely dictated by spiritual concerns: "The principle motives which induced me to acquiesce with this wish, were, that I might be entitled to all the privileges of the white inhabitants, and a conviction that it was a duty I owed to the Great Spirit, to take upon me the name of a Christian, as from reading a Sermon, I began to think that the Christian religion was true."[36] Instead, Peter Jones labored as a bricklayer in order to obtain sufficient funds with which to improve his education, hoping that he might launch a worldly career in the Canadian fur trade as a clerk. His ambitions changed abruptly on June 5, 1823, when he had a standard conversion experience during a Methodist camp meeting:

> The love of God being shed abroad in my heart, I loved Him intensely, and praised Him in the midst of the people. Every thing now appeared in a new light, and all the works of God seemed to unite with me in uttering the praises of the Lord. The people, the trees of the woods, the gentle winds, the warbling notes of the birds, and the approaching sun, all declared the power and goodness of the Great Spirit. . . . My heart was now drawn out in love and compassion for all people, especially for my parents, brothers, sisters, and countrymen, for whose conversion I prayed, that they might also find this great salvation. I now believed with all my heart in God the Father, Son, and Holy Ghost, and gradually renounced the world, the flesh, and the devil.[37]

Peter Jones now became an active member of a newly established native Christian community at Grand River known as Davisville, where he taught Sunday school and helped to found the first local Methodist Indian church in the spring of 1824. Here he also gradually developed his speaking talents. He gained formal recognition as a Methodist exhorter in 1825 and was ordained as an itinerant preacher two years later. The year before his ordination he had moved back to his home territory to help set up what would soon become a model village for all Christian Indians of Canada, the Credit River mission. With this project he successfully implemented his notions of selective adaptation: security of ownership of lands, sufficient arable land to establish farming communities, access to a solid education, and acquisition of the basic civil rights enjoyed by British citizens. His progressive views were undoubtedly influenced by widespread missionary reports of the advancements made by the Cherokee Nation, whose achievements he openly admired.[38]

Besides functioning as the principal agent of religious transformation among the Indians of Upper Canada, Jones also turned out to be a capable leader of his own band under a newly adopted political system. In response to pressure from the Indian Department, the Ojibwas had by this time expanded their former system of informal interband council meetings into a Grand Council attended regularly by elected chiefs and their assistants, the so-called second and third chiefs.[39] On January 1, 1829, Jones was elected as one of the three Credit River band chiefs, and in this official capacity he then functioned as a mediator in all their dealings with the British government. He enjoyed widespread respect among other Indian communities of Upper Canada as well, having been entrusted with the duties of an agent by the Ojibwas of Munceytown, the Delawares of Moraviantown, and the Iroquois of Grand River. His missionary and administrative activities took him on extensive travels throughout Canada and the northeastern United States, as well as on three official journeys to England in 1831–32, 1837–38, and 1844–46. Of course, Peter Jones's leadership was not entirely devoid of controversy, not even within his own community. His uncompromising policy of total adaptation to European ways eventually brought him into conflict with conservative Mississaugas during the 1830s and 1840s. His decision in 1847 to relocate the Credit River mission to the Grand River reserve also met with vehement opposition and ultimately resulted in permanent factionalism within the band. However, he demonstrated the same sort of irreproachable personal integrity that characterized the career of Samson Occom. At the time of his conversion the Credit River Mississaugas, like their Rice Lake neighbors, had nearly succumbed to the colonial situation. The revival started by Jones and other Ojibwa Methodists brought a certain stability to the various Christian Indian communities and thus helped them to find ways in which to adapt to the exigencies of the early-nineteenth-century contact environment.

It was none other than Peter Jones who had led these Christian Indians to the religious conference at which so many of the Rice Lake band had converted to Methodism. His extraordinary career as a missionary undoubtedly made a deep impression on young Kahgegagahbowh. According to Copway's own account, on February 27, 1830, his dying mother advised her children "to be good Christians, to love Jesus, and meet her in heaven." He began to comply with her final wishes in the summer, when he left a Methodist camp meeting as George Copway:

> I still groaned and agonised over my sins. I was so agitated and alarmed that I knew not which way to turn in order to get relief, and while kneeling down with the rest I found relief, as though a stream had been let loose from the skies to my heart. Joy succeeded this knowledge, and, were I to live long, I never can forget the feelings with which I arose and spoke the following first

English words — "*Glory to Jesus.*" . . . The next morning, my cousin, George Shawney, and myself, went out into the woods to sing and pray. As I looked at the trees, the hills, and the valleys, O how beautiful they all appeared! I looked upon them, as it were, with new eyes and thoughts. . . . When we reached our homes at Rice Lake, everything seemed to me as if it wore a different aspect; everything was clothed with beauty.[40]

This orthodox conversion experience which, as he claims, changed his entire perspective on the world must have occurred, if we are to believe his own words, at just about the same period in his life (in 1830 he would have been twelve years old) that he had his visionary encounter with the wind manito. Bearing in mind the expectations of his Protestant readers, he downplays his native spiritual experiences in his autobiography, observing here that "little reliance can be placed in dreams." But he immediately counters with the question whether it might not be possible for the Great Spirit to "take this method, sometimes, to bring about some good results." A decade later, in the spring of 1840, he had another "singular dream" in which he foresaw the death of his cousin Thomas Khezig. Copway visualized his cousin's ascension to an orthodox Christian version of heaven but, in accordance with Ojibwa tradition, the deceased first had to cross a black and golden river before he was allowed to turn into an "angel" on the other side. "It is but a dream," he conceded at the conclusion of his lengthy description, "and I wish it to go for what it is worth, and no more." He also narrates a wondrous story about how his family managed to escape starvation because his father had a dream in which a manito directed him to where beaver could be caught.[41] His obvious reluctance to disregard dreams as a meaningful spiritual experience would seem to imply that his conversion to Methodism was probably no less sincere than Peter Jones's but never as absolute. Whenever circumstances required, he could express disdain for Ojibwa "superstition" as readily as his Mississauga elder: "In the days of our ignorance we used to dance around the fire. I shudder when I think of those days of our darkness. I thought the Spirit would be kind to me if I danced before the old men; and day after day, or night after night, I have been employed with others in this way. I thank God that those days will never return."[42] With Copway, however, passages such as these sound somehow contrived and have the hollow ring of a mere perfunctory bow to salvationist literary conventions. He consistently acted out both systems of belief in the course of his various public guises, one as Kahgegagahbowh, "Chief of the Ojibwa Nation," and the other as the Reverend George Copway, "Missionary to His People." This he continued to do even after both of these self-proclaimed titles had long since ceased to have any semblance of legitimacy. It was a form of cultural doubleness which, in his case at least, brought about an acute conflict of personality once his projected images failed to attract a paying audience.

Following his conversion, Copway resumed his studies at the Rice Lake school "with a new and different relish." At one point he was so moved by an exhortation delivered by John Sunday, band chief of the Credit River Mississaugas and Methodist preacher, that he decided to become a missionary himself and "instruct the children in the truths of religion."[43] In 1834 the American Methodist Episcopal Church requested Copway, his uncle John Taunchey, and his cousin Enmegahbowh to assist in its efforts to convert the Ojibwas of Lake Superior. They agreed and thereupon spent the winter at the Keewenaw mission on the southeastern shore of said lake and, in the winter of the following year, transferred to the La Pointe mission in Wisconsin, where they remained until 1836. Here Copway helped the Reverend Sherman Hall of the ABCFM to translate the Gospel of Luke and the Acts of the Apostles into Ojibwa.[44] Between 1836 and 1837 he, his cousin, and another Ojibwa named Peter Marksman established a Methodist mission at Lac Court Oreille. Their superiors were obviously pleased with the results as they agreed to furnish all three with a stipend to improve their education and prepare themselves for ordination at the Ebenezer Manual Labor School near Jacksonville, Illinois. Copway attended this institution from the fall of 1837 until his graduation late in 1839, where he "passed some of the happiest seasons of [his] life" and "learned to read the word of God."[45]

Instead of returning to Canada as planned, Copway apparently decided to test his father's prognostication as he undertook an extensive tour through the northeastern United States, to "the great cities, of which [he] had read so much at school": Chicago, Detroit, Buffalo, Rochester, Albany, New York, Boston, and Syracuse. He attended several conferences along the way and was flattered by all the attention the Americans paid to "a solitary Indian," as he now described himself. In Boston, while viewing the city from atop the statehouse, Copway had a progressivist Indian vision of the "American dream":

> It was from this point that I saw the works of the white man. The steeples, vessels arriving, and others spreading their sails for distant lands. The wharves were filled with merchandise. A few steamboats were running here and there, breathing out fire and smoke. On my left I noticed several towns. The steam cars from Worcester rolled on from the west; others were starting for Provi-

dence, and whizzed along the flats like a troop of runaway horses. Here were factories in different directions. As I saw the prosperity of the white man, I said, while tears filled my eyes, "Happy are thou, O Israel; who is like unto thee, O *people saved by the Lord*!"

What he saw during his tour of the booming eastern urban centers obviously affected him deeply, because he closes this spirited eulogy on Yankee ingenuity with a topical elegy on "vanishing Indians," which he allegedly composed at a later period in his life:

> Once more I see my fathers' land
>   Upon the beach, where oceans roar;
> Where whitened bones bestrew the sand,
>   Of some brave warrior of yore.
> The *groves*, where once my fathers roamed —
>   The *rivers*, where the beaver dwelt —
> The *lakes*, where angry waters foamed —
>   Their *charms*, with my fathers, have fled.
>
> O! tell me, ye "Palefaces," tell
>   Where have my proud ancestors gone?
> Whose smoke curled up from every dale,
>   To what land have their free spirits flown?
> Whose wigwam stood where cities rise;
>   On whose war-paths the steam-horse flies;
> And ships, like mon-e-doos in disguise,
>   Approach the shore in endless files.[46]

Copway returned to Canada in November of 1839. At Peter Jones's house he met Elizabeth Howell, daughter of an immigrant English gentleman farmer from Yorkshire, and "after an intimate acquaintance of some six months" wedded her on June 1, 1840. Her relatives were apparently not happy about the union as most of them refused to be present at the wedding ceremony officiated by Jones. Canadian views on miscegenation were not much different from those in the United States, as Peter Jones and his own English-born wife, Eliza Field, discovered after their marriage in New York in 1833. They had been slandered by the local press, and some of the racist articles were reissued in Upper Canada. Whatever Copway may have felt or thought concerning white attitudes toward intermarriage, he never mentioned it in his writings. He did find the nosy, roundabout questions frequently posed by whites in connection with his marriage to Elizabeth "exceedingly annoying," however. Since his young bride was well versed in

English literature and a proficient writer herself, it is more than likely that she played a key role in her husband's subsequent literary career.[47]

Immediately after their marriage the Copways embarked upon a strenuous 2,000-mile tour to join the American Upper Mississippi Mission in present-day Wisconsin and Minnesota. Along the way they visited the thrice-removed New England Christian Indian towns of Stockbridge and Brothertown near Green Bay. "Their lands are good," he noted condescendingly, "and it is to be hoped that they will continue to conduct themselves well." Somewhere along the Mississippi, his wife and sister-in-law discovered several "Indian deities, made of stone," and, oblivious to the ethnological fever beginning to spread in America at the time, unceremoniously pushed them over into the river. "Their worshippers must have been astounded and mortified when they returned," Copway mused at this demonstration of missionary zealousness, "and discovered that their gods had vanished." They arrived in November at the Upper Mississippi Mission, which was situated in a dangerous no-man's-land between hostile parties of Southwestern Ojibwas and Santee Dakotas.[48]

The task of preaching Christianity to the conservative Ojibwas of the Lake Superior and Upper Mississippi region, who had no social ties whatsoever with the Rice Lake Mississaugas (Copway felt he was "surrounded by savages"), was probably arduous enough. But teaching his traditional enemies, the Sioux, must have been an exasperating experience for the ambitious young missionary. Many years later he could still vividly recall his harrowing confrontations with a Sioux sense of good fun:

> [T]he Sioux tried to intimidate me by pointing their guns at my breast, and by flourishing their war clubs about my head; they would say, "I wish you had *longer hair*, so that I could take a good hold of it and scalp you." I often went to see them in their tepees (wigwams); this was good policy. They frequently showed me some of the scalps of the Ojibways, and danced the scalping dance. What awful noises they made, as they danced in their fantastic dresses, with their faces painted black. They reminded me much of his Satanic and fiendish majesty, rejoicing over a damned spirit entering hell.[49]

To make matters worse, it appears that his relations with fellow missionaries also became strained. One of them described him as a vain, self-confident person with a disposition to be headstrong.[50] However, if one recalls the experiences of Occom, Johnson, Fowler, and Apess in the field, this could simply mean that the bilingual Ojibwa missionary was only trying to assert himself against his colleagues' racist arrogance. Copway's seven-point proposal for terminating the century-old enmity between the Sioux and Ojibwas, which he included in his autobiography because he felt that it was soundly based on his "long experience and close observations among the Sioux and Ojibways," indicates that he had dedicated some thought to the task at hand and may thus have had the audacity to offer his white colleagues some professional advice. On the whole, his recommendations were quite sensible: Increase efforts to christianize and educate both groups, find suitable interpreters to assist the missionaries in this endeavor, locate the missions in neutral territory between the two hostile groups, assure the Indians that these missions would be permanent, limit one denomination to each mission, urge more cooperation among the missionaries themselves, and put an end to denominational dogmatism.[51] That Copway had given serious consideration to the "Indian problem" at this time can also be gleaned from his eyewitness account of the conclusion of a treaty between the United States and Southwestern Ojibwas at La Pointe in 1842, by which the Ojibwas gave up their "mineral regions" in Wisconsin and the upper peninsula of Michigan in exchange for an annuity. Having already witnessed several such annuity payments, he predicted that the unqualified transfer of cash indemnities to "Poor untutored red men" would only leave them at the mercy of unscrupulous white opportunists because they had no previous experience with financial matters. His reasoning here closely reflects the paternalistic misgivings of American reformers:

> What benefit can the many thousands of dollars, which are paid annually, be to Indians, if they are not capable of exercising any judgement in relation to a proper use of money? The fact is that, at the end of every year, they are sunk into deeper degradation. I would now ask, what are millions of money without education? I do not mean that an *equivalent* should not be given for lands ceded to the Government. No; but I do mean that this equivalent should be appropriated in such a way as to produce the greatest benefits and the happiest results. If a certain amount had been given in cash, another amount in cattle and farming utensils, another in clothing, another in houses and schoolhouses, and the like; and with these, if a few mechanics, farmers, and teachers had been sent among them, the Indians might have become industrious, intelligent, and useful citizens. One-third of each annual payment would be sufficient to educate, and to supply the wants of their children. It may be supposed by some, that the white people settled near them give them good advice, and urge upon them the propriety and necessity of appropriating their money in the manner just suggested. Yet this is not only *not the case*, but these very whites, at least a large majority of them, are continually laying plans by which they can extort from those unlettered and ignorant Indians whatever they possess.[52]

In the fall of 1842, Copway gladly complied with Peter Jones's invitation to assist him with his missionary activities in Canada and left the United States to teach school at the Credit River mission until the end of that year. His talents in the field had been recognized by the Wesleyan Methodists, who accepted him as an itinerant preacher and, early in 1843, sent him on a three-month fund-raising tour of Canada West (as Upper Canada was now known) in the company of the Reverend William Ryerson. When he returned in April he labored briefly at the Saugeen mission on Lake Huron and was then transferred to his native community at Rice Lake. The following year he joined Peter Jones and Chief Joseph Sawyer of the Credit River band to attend a conference with the governor general in Montreal to discuss the prospects of establishing a manual labor school for Indians.

It appears that by this time Copway's personal ambitions were rapidly overtaking his spiritual concerns. Peter Jones, who thought a great deal of his younger colleague, noted after their joint venture in Montreal that he lacked the "judgement to carry out any great undertaking" and further complained of his neglect "to seek the advice of those who have older and wiser heads than his own."[53] While at Saugeen, Copway had actually considered abandoning his missionary post for financial reasons which, considering the common practice of underpaying native preachers, may have been a legitimate source of frustration for him, especially since he now had a wife and child to feed. "I met with difficulties," he complains in familiar tones, "for I could obtain nothing without money; and even when a request was made, it was not met by the Society. I could not be convinced that it was my duty to starve, and, therefore, concluded I must leave."[54] Despite this incident, Copway returned to his missionary work among the Saugeen Ojibwas in 1845 and obviously managed to gain their confidence as he was elected vice-president of the Grand Council of the Methodist Ojibwas of Canada West in the summer of the following year. He was also entrusted by them with the duty of collecting and managing funds for the establishment of a manual labor school. This task, however, proved to be the stumbling block that terminated his relatively successful but brief missionary career. Later that year the Saugeen band accused him of having misappropriated their funds. A similar charge was brought before the Indian Department early in the following year by the Rice Lake band, who had also entrusted him with tribal business matters. Copway was eventually jailed for a few weeks in Toronto on the charge of embezzlement and for debts he had incurred. The Indian Department decided not to press charges against him, but soon after his release he was expelled by the Canadian Conference of the Wesleyan

Methodist Church. This ignominious event has, of course, been omitted in his autobiography, which ends just short of his fall from missionary grace.[55]

It is not known what actually became of the tribal money Copway allegedly embezzled, whether he deliberately appropriated a certain amount for his personal use or inadvertently "mismanaged" them due to his own lack of administrative expertise, a mishap which, by the way, also befell respectable white Indian agents like Henry Rowe Schoolcraft.[56] At any rate, his remaining life was as beset with financial problems as that of all of his predecessors in the missionary business. Making a decent living as an Indian evangelist was obviously not easy, but the situation in Canada was made worse by the fact that, as Peter Schmalz has pointed out, there were more educated Indians around at the time than the various Ojibwa communities could possibly support.[57] All this made it very difficult for the highly ambitious convert to gain the kind of prestige that was normally expected of a young Ojibwa. But Copway was certainly not just an innocent victim of social injustice, as he did not shy away from employing rather dubious tactics when it came to promoting his own interests. This happened in 1845, for instance, when he went on a missionary journey to Walpole Island on Lake St. Clair and surreptitiously told his unsuspecting Ojibwa audience there that the governor general wanted all Indians to become Methodists, most probably in order to pad his own record of evangelist "coups."[58] Whatever really happened at this time, Copway ultimately paid dearly for his objectionable (but understandable?) "improvidence" because it left him stranded among whites without a source of income.

Contrary to the pattern of flight in slave narratives, Copway opted for a southern route, from Canada to the United States, to escape his social plight and eventually emerge from anonymity as a recognized ethnic writer. By coincidence, his involuntary exodus took place at about the same time that Peter Jones was preparing to remove voluntarily with his people to New Credit in the southwest corner of the Six Nations' reserve on the Grand River. Copway must have been in dire financial straits by then because he even requested the ABCFM to send him back to the Lake Superior area in spite of his harrowing memories. He boldly informed the organization that he was dissatisfied with the Methodists and that his present position as government agent for his tribe did not give him sufficient opportunity to "labor for the spiritual good" of his people.[59] At the same time, however, he must have been quite busy writing down his memoirs and editing his missionary notes because, on December 9, 1846, he registered *The Life, History, and Travels of Kah-ge-ga-gah-bowh (George Copway)* at the clerk's office in Albany, New York. Copway, and whoever the "friend" was who edited his manuscript, had picked the perfect time and place for such a publication. The betrayal of the Cherokees and the other "civilized" tribes still weighed heavily on the American reformists' conscience, and they were consequently grateful for any indication that their policies had also borne fruit. Furthermore, the eclipsing American romantic movement still left a profitable forum for flesh-and-blood noble savages.[60] The intellectual urban centers of the northeastern United States, which were far removed in time and space from any conflictive interaction with Indians, thus proved to be a highly fertile ground upon which to plant this idealized personal narrative of a converted "child of the forest." The first edition appeared in Albany in 1847, and it was succeeded by numerous reprints before the year came to a close.

The success of Copway's first publication enabled him to launch a career as public speaker and brought him to the attention of leading members of the New York literary circle, thus opening new and seemingly unlimited venues for his ambitions. Between 1847 and 1850 he traveled up and down the Atlantic seaboard delivering talks on topical Indian subjects like "superstitions and legends," manners and customs, origins, advances in Christianity, and problems of intemperance. He also found an appreciative audience among romantic naturists with his extemporizations on "America: Its Elements of Greatness and Its Scenery," which, according to his account, was the topic most often requested of him.[61] The American public of the late 1840s was quite receptive to the stage presence of a "Noble Indian Christian convert," to borrow Donald Smith's titular pun, perhaps because for many Copway seemed to personify the two predominant strands in liberal white attitudes toward Indians: romantic primitivism (the vanishing act) and benevolent reformism (the transformation act). Positive reviews of his lectures in local newspapers, which Copway collected and frequently quoted in his own publications, often highlighted his physical appearance and dramatic style of delivery, very much as if they were describing a masterful performance in one of the many Indian plays that had been sweeping the American stage since the 1830s. A fragment from an article originally published in the *Charleston Courier* and reprinted in later editions of Copway's autobiography well illustrates the point:

> Much even of his English was singularly idiomatic. Biting satire — pungent anecdote, set off with most expressive Indian gesticulation — strokes of wit and humour — touches of pathos — bursts of vehement declamation, after the manner now of a Forest, or a Cooper, and now of a zealous western

preacher — slip-shod conversational talk — most poetic descriptions of nature, fearless statement, off-hand, calm, Indian independence, altogether formed a compound of a rather rare and inimitable nature.[62]

High-ranking American literati were attracted by Copway's pious demeanor and outward appearance. The chief American exponent of the noble savage image, Henry Wadsworth Longfellow, met and befriended Copway on February 26, 1849. "Kah-ge-ga-gah'-bowh an Ojibwa preacher and poet came to see us," he wrote in his journal, "announced and attended by 'Prince Eugene.' I missed their visit, being a[t] Spark's; but met them on my way homeward. The Indian a good-looking young man promises to come and see me on Wednesday. He left me a book of his — an autobiography." He must have been quite impressed with the "Ojibwa preacher and poet" because, on April 12, Longfellow went to Boston to hear Copway lecture. "A rambling talk; gracefully delivered, with a fine various voice," he noted on this occasion, "and a chief's costume, with little bells jangling upon it, like the bells and pomgranites [sic] of the Jewish priests." Two days later Copway spoke on "The Religion, Poetry, and Eloquence of the Indian," and Longfellow attended once again, observing that it was "a lecture more rambling than ever, though not without good passages."[63] Even Francis Parkman, whose own feelings about Indians were mixed at best, remarked following a brief encounter with Copway in Boston a few weeks earlier that he "liked him much and wanted to see more of him, but he [Copway] had his hands full of letters [of recommendation] and everybody was running after him."[64]

After just a few years of residence in the United States Copway had obviously digested the first great "moment of crisis" in his life and managed to carve out a modest place for himself in American society as orator and man of letters. It is quite apparent, however, that he also had little compunction about styling himself an "Indian chief" and "native preacher" to attain such a position, even though he did occasionally add a qualifying "former" in public announcements for his speaking engagements. Perhaps, as Donald Smith has suggested, he had come to identify himself entirely with the popular stage interpretations of the life of Pocahontas who, according to Copway's own estimation of her character in a letter addressed to a Boston newspaper in 1849, was unexcelled "in point of disinterested benevolence" and had "suffered wrongfully" when she was "partially disowned by her nation."[65] He was certainly not at a loss for words when it came to finding plausible explanations for his "free-lance" missionary status, as an article in a Liverpool newspaper commenting on a lecture he delivered there in late July 1850 demonstrates:

> He was formerly a Methodist preacher, but, in advocating his plan, had not placed himself under the direction of any religious society. If he had, he must have gone to any place the society chose to send him; and he was desirous that the cause which he advocated should not rest on the narrow ground of religious sectarianism, but on the broad basis of humanity and justice. It was that which had given him so many friends in his own country. He would not disparage any religious society, but he wished to act independently of any particular one, though he would receive the support of all.[66]

The "plan" mentioned in this article refers to a grand scheme he developed around 1847–48, which he expanded into a major promotional campaign by the close of the decade. Ostracized from his own native community and denied the possibility of engaging in practical missionary work, Copway found himself compelled to experiment with more abstract reformist ideas in his new and self-appointed role as pan-Indian spokesman. His goal was ambitious: "I want to make the great family of the Indians ONE, should I live long enough — *one* in interest, *one* in feeling, *one* while they live, and *one* in a better world after death."[67] Since there can be little doubt that he was familiar with the public debate on the issue of removal, it is not surprising that he lit upon an idea that had already been propagated in the 1820s by removal advocates like Jedediah Morse and Isaac McCoy, namely, the establishment of a western Indian territory and its eventual incorporation into the Union as a state.[68] Various proposals of that nature were actually introduced in Congress during the first half of the nineteenth century but were never ratified. The most significant of these with regard to Copway's own ideas on the subject was Indian Commissioner Hartley T. Crawford's call for the establishment of an Indian Territory in the Old Northwest in 1840, which found the approval of the Whig administration. In the following year, the Indian Office authorized Governor James Duane Doty of Wisconsin Territory to negotiate treaties to that effect with the Sioux inhabitants of the area. He was able to induce them to sign away thirty million acres of land in what is now northwestern Iowa, Minnesota, and the Dakotas, provided that all of the ceded land north of the present Iowa-Minnesota border and south of the 46th parallel would eventually form a territory open only to people of "Indian blood." The treaty, however, failed to be passed by the Senate despite President John Tyler's strong support of it.[69] Similar ideas had been expressed by Indians long before

Copway took them up, such as John Ridge's plea for a Cherokee state in his Charleston speech of 1822. Canadian Ojibwas had also formulated plans for a permanent Indian territory in the Old Northwest during the 1845 Saugeen council meeting at which Copway himself had functioned as vice-president.[70] Thus, even though the federal government began to shift gradually toward a policy of establishing scattered reservations or "colonies" and allotting lands to individual Indians in the second half of the 1850s, with the expansion of U.S. territory from coast to coast after the annexation of Texas in 1845, the settling of the Oregon boundary question in 1846, and the acquisition of the Southwest and southern California by the Treaty of Guadalupe Hidalgo in 1848, the possibility of establishing some kind of remote semiautonomous Indian Territory must have seemed more plausible at that time than ever before, and not only to George Copway. In 1851, almost a year after Copway had presented his own plan to Congress in writing, James Duane Doty addressed a letter to President Millard Fillmore in which he suggested once again the creation of an Indian state in the "country lying *west* of the Territory of Minnesota, between the Coteau du Prairie and Missouri River," approximately the same region Copway had in mind. As late as 1876–77, Lewis H. Morgan was still recommending the policy of setting aside for Indians large lands which might someday be incorporated as Indian states of the Union.[71]

In 1850, when Zachary Taylor authorized the immediate and complete removal of the Ojibwas in Michigan and Wisconsin to unoccupied territory in central Minnesota, the prospect of establishing a permanent Indian land base became especially relevant for Copway.[72] The proposal to furnish Indians with "a territorial or district government, so that they may represent their own nation," is first mentioned in Copway's autobiography in conjunction with a number of other suggestions he made to improve the Indians' situation. In the same chapter he also describes the 1845 Saugeen council and cites the petition signed by the Ojibwa chiefs on that occasion, under which they had requested "that the reserve (now known as the Indian Territory) be a perpetual reserve; as a future refuge for a general colonization of the Ojibway nation, comprising the scattered tribes in Canada West."[73] On March 31, 1848, he disclosed his plan to petition the U.S. government for the creation of a "Kah-ge-ga Indian Territory" ("Ever-to-be Indian Territory," according to his own translation) to an attentive audience in Philadelphia.[74] That the intended Indian state was to bear the first part of his own name is, of course, an indication that Copway's self-estimation had already risen to somewhat dizzy heights and was fast approaching the level of megalomania. As Smith has properly observed, in the following two years Copway demonstrated all of "the directness and aggressiveness of a successful American promoter" in advocating his Indian real estate project.[75] In the tried pose of "Rev. George Copway, Chief of the Ojibways," he transmitted his plans orally to captivated audiences all over the eastern United States and then carried them across the ocean to England and Scotland. He also pleaded his case before the legislatures of several states, managing thereby to enlist the official support of numerous prominent American politicians, especially those connected with the nativist movement of the 1840s and 1850s, whom he subtly baited with calculated appeals to their narcissistic patriotism.[76] Not the man to leave anything untried, he even addressed a personal letter to President Zachary Taylor on the matter while he was in the nation's capital in early March 1849.[77] On his own accord, he conducted an "investigative" tour through Wisconsin, Minnesota, Iowa, and Missouri territory in the summer of 1849, making the rather doubtful contention later that he interviewed "no less than 17,000 Indians" who were "beginning to be alive to their interests" and who supposedly approved of his removal scheme.[78] Copway first outlined his plans in writing in an article for the *American Whig Review* in 1849 and then had his official petition to Congress printed by a press in New York the following year as a thirty-two-page promotional tract titled *Organization of a New Indian Territory, East of the Missouri River.*[79]

Copway's Kah-ge-ga Indian Territory was to be located in "the unsettled land, known as the North-west Territory, between the territories of Nebraska and Minnesota, on the eastern banks of the Missouri." As Smith has pointed out, this would have placed it within the hunting grounds of the Sioux, who were probably not among the thousands of Indians he allegedly interviewed.[80] Here, then, the tribes of the Old Northwest—Copway "would not be understood as thinking or legislating for the civilized portion" of the Old Southwest, whom he considered "by far the most enlightened of the American Indians"—were to find permanent homes and be gradually introduced to civilization under the guidance of an omnipotent (presumably white) governor appointed by the president of the United States, who would in turn be assisted by "a resident Indian to be styled Lieutenant Governor" with an annual salary of "two thousand five hundred dollars, which shall be in full of all charges, allowances, and emoluments of whatever nature or kind." Although he refrained from mentioning any specific candidate for said position, it does not seem far-fetched under the circumstances to assume that he had himself in mind as the most likely choice. Individual tribes were to be allowed to "establish and maintain such government for the regulation of their own internal affairs, as to them may seem proper; not inconsistent with the Constitution of the United States, or the laws thereof." Collectively they would elect a "general Council," which would convene annually "to make all needful regulations respecting the intercourse among the several tribes, to preserve peace, to provide for their common safety, and generally to enact such laws as the welfare of the confederation shall demand." However, decisions by the council had to be submitted to the governor for final approval, who also had the power to adjourn this body at any time. Eventually Kah-ge-ga was "to be erected into a Territorial Government" until that day that "it shall be competent for the said confederate tribes to elect in such a manner as the general Council shall prescribe, a delegate or commissioner to the Congress of the United States."

Copway was quite certain about the practicability of his project. The U.S. government could "influence" the tribes to move by issuing their annuities in the new territory, a tactic it had already employed in its previous attempt to move the Ojibwas to Minnesota, and by guaranteeing that they would never be removed again. As far as the Indians were concerned, Copway argued that they were "a social race" who "would rather live in large bodies than in small ones." Furthermore, he argued that the Ojibwa language, "being the great family language of all the Algonquin tribes west," was "peculiarly adapted for such a state of society." Once they entered the new territory, the tribes would automatically get rid of their hereditary chiefs and frame laws founded on republican ideals. "The hereditary chiefship must cease to exist," Copway demanded in his proposal, "before they can make any rapid advancement; for when you allow the meritorious only to rule, there will be found a great many who will study hard to improve in general information, and fit themselves for statesmen and divines." Lastly, he bolstered his arguments with a long list of advantages that would accrue to both the federal government (primarily lower costs) and Indians (permanent homes, better education) if his plans were carried out.[81]

In spite of all his pen-and-pulpit promotional efforts and the support of numerous influential Americans, Copway's grandiose plan finally met with the same fate as all of the previous proposals — it was never seriously considered by Congress. "His scheme of settling the Indians is a flash in the pan," a skeptical Francis Parkman wrote to one of Copway's benefactors, "or rather he has no settled scheme at all, and never had any. I had a letter from him dated at Council Bluffs [Iowa] which was I believe the farthest limit of his travels. He had a great deal to say about the forest gentlemen, nature's noblemen, etc., but very little about the regeneration of the tribes."[82] Nevertheless, he must still have been brimming with confidence and creative energy in 1850, the year that proved to be the zenith of his literary career. In addition to his proposal, he also published an epic poem in New York titled *The Ojibway Conquest*, which gave rise to his widespread reputation as a "poet" even though it is almost certain that it was written by someone else (more on this later); two new, expanded editions of his autobiography were printed in New York and London; and the first edition of his *Traditional History and Characteristic Sketches of the Ojibway Nation* appeared in London as well.[83] During the late summer he also received an impromptu invitation from Elihu Burritt, a leading figure in the American peace movement and founder of the League of Universal Brotherhood (1846), to represent the "Christian Indian of America" at the Third World Peace Congress convening in Frankfurt am Main, Germany, in August of that same year.[84] The portentous traveler dream-vision of Kah-ge-ga-gah-bowh, a "child of the forest," thus acquired global dimensions as George Copway, ex-cleric and cosmopolite, made preparations to carry his utopian vision of a new Indian territory to the Old World.

Armed with letters of recommendation from American men of letters such as Longfellow and Parkman and showered with the blessings (most likely of a pecuniary nature as well) of wealthy philanthropists like Amos Lawrence, Copway sailed forth from Boston to Liverpool the day after President Zachary Taylor died, on July 10, 1850. He arrived in England about two weeks later and, finding that he had some time to spare before his scheduled crossover to the mainland, immediately plunged into a bustle of social calls and public speaking engagements. Conscious of his role as model Christian Indian, Copway determined to abide by a number of self-imposed rules of behavior during his English sojourn: "I will uphold my race—I will endeavor never to say nor do anything which will prejudice the mind of the British public against my people—In this land of refinement I will be an Indian—I will treat everybody in a manner that becomes a gentleman—I will patiently answer all questions that may be asked of me—I will study to please the people, and lay my own feelings to one side." And, in keeping with the protocol for Indian visitors since the days of Lady Rebecca, the "tall, well-proportioned, and handsome man, with the manners and graceful dignity of a perfect gentleman," was in turn lionized by local reporters and the cream of British society. His weekly schedule of appointments with various lords and ladies reads like an excerpt from a veteran socialite's itinerary: "Sabbath morning—go to Mr. Gambardilli. Evening—at Under Secretary's house, Dr. Wiseman to be there. Monday evening—Tea at Mr. S——, New Broad street. Tuesday—Dine at E. Saunders', George Street—a celebrated Dentist. Wednesday—Hampton Court, with Mrs. Gibson's Pic-nic party. Thursday, August 8th—To Breakfast with R. Cobden, at 9 ½ o'clock. Evening—Dine at Lord Brougham's. Friday—Dine with Lady Franklin and her brother, Sir Simpkinson, 21 Bedford Square." Like all visiting dignitaries, he was also accorded the privilege of sitting in on a session in the House of Commons, where he witnessed a memorable debate between Richard Cobden and Disraeli. Finally, in keeping with his new status as a man of the world with intimate acquaintance with the latest fashion, he also joined the swelling ranks of Jenny Lind worshipers after hearing the "Swedish Nightingale" warble in a Liverpool concert hall shortly before his departure for Germany.[85]

On August 19, Copway and other delegates of the Peace Congress sailed on a steamer from Dover to Calais and proceeded to Frankfurt by rail and riverboat, arriving there three days later. The Third World Peace Congress convened from the twenty-second to the twenty-fourth of August and was attended by several hundred delegates representing countries from all over the globe. Even though it failed to produce any substantial results during times of pronounced inter-European belligerence and widespread social repression—its delegates were frequently pooh-poohed as self-aggrandizing, starry-eyed chatterers in the media—it was still a major political event of its day.[86] George Copway, a "solitary Indian" before an international forum, became one of the main public attractions. During the third sitting, on August 24, he had the honor of proposing the fifth resolution of the Congress, and he then delivered a lengthy speech which received much applause from the audience and mixed reviews in the international press.[87] The correspondent of the London *Times*, one of those who viewed the Congress with skepticism, found little to praise in Copway's presentation:

A great sensation was created by the appearance in the tribune of the Ojibbeway [*sic*] Chief, whose oration has, from the first opening of the Congress, been anticipated as an extraordinary *morceau*. He was dressed in a dark blue frock, with a scarf across his shoulder, after the old French Republican fashion, and the metallic plates round his arm gave a peculiar character to his costume. He began to talk something after a style which may be called "Cooperish," and was abundant in his allusions to the "Great Spirit"—his "pale-faced brethren," and so forth. Soon, however, he dropped the purely national style, and launched out into general morals and literature, stating how, while walking around Frankfurt, he had reflected on the miseries of war, and linking together as eminent men of mind the German poet Schiller and the American poet Longfellow. His oration was delivered in a grandiloquent style, but its effect was rather on the eye than the ear, the great point being the unwrapping of a mysterious implement which he had carried about, and which in the eyes of the peacemakers looked marvelously like a sword. When he deliberately took off the linen wrapper, and discovered something which looked rather like a cat-o'-nine-tails, and which he declared to be an Indian banner of peace, the acclamations were tremendous. This was his grand scenic effect. He should have stopped here, but he did not, and produced an anti-climax. A very wholesome regulation, published by the Congress, limits the time during which a speaker is allowed to "keep the floor" to 20 minutes, but the "stoic of the woods," luxuriating in the sound of his own voice, doubled the time. This profusion of words caused a reaction, and the venerable Dr. Jaup, the most urbane President in the world, mildly limited every future speech to a quarter of an hour.[88]

Copway, who quoted extensively from the *Times* in his account, was probably referring to this article when he expressed his anger at "a fair specimen of English raillery which has been heard by us and read."[89] Another sarcastic summation of the part played by "un honnête homme d'Indienne de la tribu des Ojibeways" was published in the Paris-based *Journal des Débats Politiques et Littéraires*, whose correspondent concluded that "it was decidedly the Indian who turned out to be the lion of the Congress; he overshadowed all the lions of London and Paris. How can one compete with a great chief who speaks of the Great Spirit, and of pale-faced brothers!"[90] Elihu Burritt described the talk in his diary as "a long, windy, wordy speech, extremely ungrammatical and incoherent."[91] Even Copway himself was far from pleased with his performance on that momentous day of his life. "The last of the Congress is about over," he admitted in his journal, "and I have made my poorest speech." The pipe-wielding "Ojibwa Chief," who consciously played the part of the noble savage in this controversial gathering, was obviously viewed by critics of the Congress as a tractable symbol for the visionary nature of the entire peace movement of the mid-nineteenth century. Thus, in playing out his worn-out role in a scenario dominated by seasoned veterans of the international political arena at a time in which liberal idealism and romantic enthusiasm were giving way to disillusioned realism and power politics in Europe, Copway had finally come face to face with his own intellectual limitations:

> For never in my life did I speak to such disadvantage. The people had already heard Girardin, the French orator, Cobden, and a host of others. The speeches of these men had given a commonplace character to the speeches which were to come after them. The people had become tired of listening, and seemed to

have no desire for anything new. Besides this, no new feature could be brought forward in support of the great cause of Peace, and all the arguments had been worn threadbare. The good speeches had preceded me, and the very best, which was to be delivered by the Rev. E. H. Chapin, of New York city, was just at my heels. In this predicament I could not look upon myself with any degree of confidence, nor as being in a very enviable situation.[92]

The enthusiastic reception accorded him by the German audience, for whom a live Christian Indian was still a most welcome novelty, must have assuaged his battered vanity somewhat. Here in Frankfurt Copway's "Cooperish" style still found appreciative ears among an audience who were experiencing the transition between two great German literary movements, *Romantik* and *Realismus*. The fervent dream of national unification and political reform had but recently been dashed by force of arms, and this caused many German intellectuals to look to the United States as a model democracy and to regard the apocryphal Indian of contemporary American literature as the very embodiment of their own yearning for individual freedom and social harmony. Translations of American authors, particularly Cooper's novels, were widely read together with German travel literature of the 1830s and 1840s (i.e., Prince Paul Wilhelm of Württemberg, Prince Maximilian of Wied, Friedrich Gerstäcker). The period was also witnessing the birth of a whole new national genre, the "Indianerroman." Thus, while the Indian as an imaginary panacea for social maladies was being gradually phased out elsewhere, in Germany he was just making his literary debut in the face of ascending social realism. Images of the noble enlightened savages would eventually touch even rational thinkers like Friedrich Engels and would finally culminate in a veritable national mania at the turn of the century under the prolific pen of Karl May.[93]

Reports of "Higaga-Bu, Häuptling der Chipawakis," in the local press were predominantly favorable, if not outright euphoric. The correspondent of the Leipzig *Illustrierte Zeitung*, for instance, gave a glowing account of Copway's speech, which stands in marked contrast to the sarcastic report in the London *Times*:

> A truly uplifting scene took place during the final session. Copway, the Indian Chief, takes the floor. A man in his forties, of light copper complexion, with shiny and straight black hair, nearly beardless, the eyes dark and full of compassion, his build slim and proportional. In a speech delivered in an English which often manifests lyrical qualities, he correlates his own noble wish for peace with the peace found in God, as taught by the Gospel. Still wandering about as a savage among the Indians of his tribe 15 years ago, he is tangible

proof for the advancement of civilization. And he also tells how he ascertained that in Frankfurt, where shady green trees now grow and children play under a canopy of flowers, there once stood embrasures, towers, ramparts, and the instruments of war. He had come from far away in the West, but he did not regret having floated across the great water to present Europeans with a symbol of reconciliation from the sons of the red Cain, a pipe of peace. As he uncovers it and hands it over ceremoniously to the president as representative for the nations here assembled, the men wave their hats, the women salute with their scarves, and a thundering applause erupts which will not cease.[94]

Copway's theatrical presentation of the peace pipe, which was the uncontested highlight of the Congress, has since become part of Frankfurt's permanent historical heritage.[95] A renowned local sculptor captured his noble Indian features in bronze, and another ardent admirer set about translating "his" epic poem on the "Odschibwäh."[96] German dignitaries were as keen to make his acquaintance as their British counterparts had been. According to Copway's account, Prince Frederick (later Kaiser Frederick III), who was commanding Prussian occupation forces in Frankfurt at the time, insisted on meeting the exotic peace messenger on the last day of the Congress, "at 7 o'clock, masonically."[97] After the Congress adjourned, Copway and a number of other American delegates were taken on a brief tour to Heidelberg, Wiesbaden, Düsseldorf, and Cologne, where he was warmly received by several members of the German intellectual elite. Following up on a recommendation by Longfellow, he met the poet Hermann Ferdinand Freiligrath in Düsseldorf on August 28. "It was indeed a great satisfaction to me to receive a red man under my roof," Freiligrath reported back to Longfellow, "and moreover: to see a red man, full of talents and intellectual power, burning and struggling for that civilization, which we men of the old world almost loathe and consider to be one of the sources of many of those evils which harass us." The disenchanted reformist was so inspired by Copway's presence that he requested the latter to stand godfather to his youngest son. "When the dusky brow of the Indian was stooping to the white face of the Teutonic baby," Freiligrath continued, "it was — as it were — a symbol to me of the fraternity of all nations, of the peace and the happiness to come after all the struggles and the battles of these our wonder-working times."[98] Copway also spent "a merry night" in Cologne with Freiligrath and a number of German scholars from Bonn, who did their best to introduce their "dusky" companion to the customary *Gemütlichkeit* on this occasion and were undoubtedly quite disappointed with the latter's demonstration of puritanical temperance. "Though this is a very strange way of showing their friendship," Copway observed later, "they are nevertheless friends — such inconsistencies do the customs of society subject us to!"[99]

Early next morning Copway made his way back to London. In the interim before his return trip to Boston on December 7, he delivered dozens of speeches on temperance and other Indian-related topics throughout England and Scotland, taking every opportunity to promote his own Kah-ge-ga scheme. On one such occasion he informed a London audience that immediately after his return to America he would "call out" two of his "elder brethren" to drum up support for the project in the East and West while he would make the rounds in the South, and that he would personally lay his plan before both houses of Congress on February 15, 1851. It will probably never be known how much money Copway managed to collect in Great Britain or what he did with it. He evidently had so many "appointments" that he had to rent "an office at the Strand." Nevertheless, the mixed responses to his presentation at the Frankfurt Peace Congress may have inhibited his customary prodigality with words after all. "Some applaud and some condemn the speeches," he now readily admitted with reference to reviews in the British press.[100] That his promotional talents did not always produce the desired results is evident from a bitter complaint he lodged against the Aborigines Protection Society, whose members may have been aware of his dark Canadian past: "I endeavored to seek the aid and countenance of the so-called 'Aboriginal Protection Society' — and instead of being any benefit I had to just leave off everything when so many obstacles were thrown in my way. . . . I had made a false high estimation of this body. A great name indeed without power. A body without a knowing aim, and less energy of purpose."[101] He delivered his last lecture "with a heart too full" at a farewell tea party given "by the ladies of Glasgow" on December 5. The next day he departed for Liverpool, whence he was due to sail back to America. In the spring of 1851 he published his travel notes in New York under the title *Running Sketches of Men and Places*, his lengthiest and most pompous publication, but also the least accomplished.

Copway continued to press his Indian Territory plans after his return from Europe, delivering lectures on the subject and even founding a special organization for the purpose, the American Christian Association for Protective Justice to North American Indians.[102] But since Kah-ge-ga was obviously turning out to be the predicted flash in the pan by the summer of 1851 in spite of all his efforts, he concocted an alternative promotional scheme at that time, namely, the establishment of his very own news organ. He apparently had some previous experience as the editor of *Pearl*, a New York magazine devoted to women's temperance associations.[103] Once again he managed to sell his idea to well-known writers like James Fenimore Cooper, Washington Irving, William Cullen Bryant, William Gilmore Simms, John Neal, Nathaniel Willis, Francis Parkman, Henry R. Schoolcraft, Lewis H. Morgan, Thomas L. McKenney, and Edward Everett, all of whom provided him with enthusiastic letters of support to include in the first issue of his paper.[104] For some unknown reason Henry Wadsworth Longfellow, whom he had always regarded as a "friend," was not included among this illustrious groups of well-wishers, even though Copway had specifically requested an endorsement from him.[105]

The first isssue of *Copway's American Indian* appeared in New York City on July 10, 1851.[106] Copway introduced his editorial plans in a "Prospectus" much like Boudinot's earlier one, which opens with the expected apologetic "vanishing Indian" appeal to American benevolence:

> Kah-ge-ga-gah-bowh, better known to the white man as George Copway, a Christianized Indian, and a Chief of the Ojibway nation, proposes to publish a Newspaper with the above title, devoted entirely to subjects connected with the past and present history and condition of the people of his own race. It certainly is a novelty in the literary history of the United States, that an Indian should propose to conduct a paper devoted to the cause of the Indian; and indeed it may by many be deemed a presumptuous undertaking on the part of one whose education, it is truly confessed, has been but limited. If the control of the paper rested on the proprietor alone, he is ready at once to say that he would shrink from the responsible situation in which he proposes to place himself; but he has such assurances of aid, and proposes to make such arrangements, that he believes the paper will not disappoint the reasonable expectations of those who are friendly to the unfortunate race of the red man. That race is fast vanishing away; a few years more and its existence will be found only in the history of the past: may not an Indian, then, hope countenance and support in a modest and unambitious effort to preserve, while yet he may, the still lingering memorials of his own people, once numerous and strong, and interesting alike to Christian, the philanthropist, the philosopher, and the general reader?

He then proceeded to outline the twelve prospective highlights of the paper, including topical focal points such as tribal demographics, advances in civilization, material culture, means of subsistence, languages, manners and customs, traditions, biographies of remarkable Indians, comparisons with other ethnic groups, and reviews of new books on Indian subjects. On a separate page of the same issue, under the rubric "Plain Talk to the Wise," he further specified his editorial policy with an additional twelve-point program. Among other things, he proposed here to include two or three columns in the Algonquian language, "in the shape of familiar letters to an aged and honored father, of events in the eastern country as well as the old world." He also announced that one page would be devoted entirely to advertisements and predicted confidently that this would be tantamount to a guarantee of excellence for the product because, as he contended, "we go on the principle to court no one's favor for his money, but the good that he might do, as well as the good we may be doing in recommending those that we may accept." Moreover, he wanted to assure his readers that he was not merely making an appeal to their charity with this new project but offering them a high-quality publication in return for their modest investment. "We desire all who read our paper to know that we ask no one to subscribe for it on the score of benevolence," he maintained under point 6 of his editorial postscript, "but solely on the merits of its articles, and the themes, as a general thing, will be of an attractive nature." *Copway's American Indian* would cost three dollars per annum, "payable in advance," and could be delivered gratuitously, "if necessary," to all missionaries employed among Indians anywhere and to all tribes operating an English school.[107]

Copway promised much more than he was ever able to deliver in the ensuing issues of his newspaper. His initial supporters were apparently not prepared to contribute anything more substantial than an occasional article, if even that much.[108] The proposed Algonquian column never advanced beyond two brief letters titled "To My Father" in the second and third issues, and only a fraction of his envisioned twelve Indian subject areas actually received significant coverage. His own editorials, usually included under the subtitle "Copway's American Indian," often dealt with dull and contrived topics like "Women as they might be, and as they are" or "The Pleasures of a Country Ramble." With few exceptions, those articles that actually touch upon Indian-related subjects were simply excerpted from his previous publications. Even the scope of his editorship remains somewhat uncertain as he was represented in absentia at least once during the weekly's brief existence.[109] His paper failed to draw sufficient subscribers, advertisers, or benefactors to cover costs, and Copway had to cease production less than three months later, the thirteenth and final issue appearing on October 4. And yet, neither the short duration nor the textual deficits of the paper can detract from the fact that the realization of Copway's rather intrepid project is a remarkable demonstration of journalistic entrepreneurship. Even though it was preceded by the *Cherokee Phoenix* (1828–34) and the *Cherokee Advocate* (1844–53), *Copway's American Indian* is still one of the few nontribal newspapers to be published singlehandedly by an Indian, an achievement that would not be duplicated in the history of American Indian journalism until 1916, when Carlos Montezuma inaugurated his famous personal monthly newsletter, the *Wassaja* (1916–22).[110]

Copway's borderline fame began to fade rapidly by the close of 1851. As Robert Berkhofer has indicated, most American writers and their more sophisticated audiences were becoming bored with noble savages, and even the spectacular success of Longfellow's *Song of Hiawatha* (1855) could not stem the tide. Thoreau's transition from the romantic primitivism of his college days to the more "realistic" views he acquired as a result of his personal contact with Maine Indians in the 1850s is exemplary for the new trend in American literature during the second half of the nineteenth century, in which Indians no longer played a substantial role. The exceptions to this, like John Brougham's immensely popular burlesque, *Metamora; or, The Last of the Pollywogs* (1847) and *Po-ca-hon-tas; or, The Gentle Savage* (1855), only made the public's weariness with romantic characters more apparent.[111] Copway, who had capitalized on the noble savage image, found himself stranded once again in the new cultural scenario.

Copway's reputation among his New York literary acquaintances also began to tarnish in direct proportion to his dwindling income, especially since he had already made himself unpopular with some because of his habit of soliciting "loans" from them. Perhaps this is what Longfellow had in mind when he referred to him as "Kopfweh" (headache) in a postscript to his previously mentioned letter of introduction to Freiligrath.[112] Francis Parkman was more direct about the delicate matter in a letter to Charles Eliot Norton: "I accompanied it [a previous note of recommendation] with a hint that he was not to trouble you with any applications, direct or indirect, for pecuniary aid. You know his weakness on that point. I myself have experienced its effects."[113] Freiligrath, who had been so enthralled with Copway, was apparently also having second thoughts by 1853. In a delayed response to Longfellow's complaint that Copway had failed to deliver certain books the German poet had entrusted him with, he commented sardonically, "Speaking of that worthy [Kahgegagahbowh], I was very vexed indeed to hear, that he had never delivered to you the books and music I had entrusted to his care. Tell me if the war-whoop you intended to raise has frightened him and brought into your hands the volumes in question? If not so, I shall be happy to make up the loss, — swearing, of course, at the same time most awfully at the inexactitude of that *red vagabond and peace-*

monger."[114] Longfellow himself, who had originally commended Copway to Freiligrath as "my friend Kah-ge-ga-gah-bowh," began to lose patience with the "Ojibwa preacher and poet" at some point. More than eight years later he informed Freiligrath that "Kahgegahgabow [*sic*] is still extant. But I fear he is developing the Pau-Puk-Keewis element rather strongly."[115]

With his prospects rapidly dimming, Copway turned from the moribund Whig Party, which had lent support to his project, to the burgeoning American nativist movement. As Dale Knobel has pointed out in his detailed study of Copway's relations with the American Party, the ultranationalistic members of nativist secret societies regarded Indians from a reversed environmentalist perspective, as "native Americans" who had naturally imbibed "healthy American" virtues in their close relationship with the North American habitat. Nativists had thus appropriated a common Indian stereotype as an ideological antidote to the "unhealthy un-American" habits being imported to the United States by an exploding number of European (particularly Irish Catholic) immigrants. Copway's frequent eulogies on nature and patriotic exclamations — "America! America! I adore thee! Land of intelligence, of industry, and the profits thereof" — found appreciative audiences among nativists, and he was even accorded membership in the New York chapter of the Order of United Americans early in 1852.[116] Since his patriotic inclinations were rather flexible — in England he was "proud to say that he was born a British subject," and in the United States he stressed that he was "a native American" — the Ojibwa cosmopolite must have had more pragmatic reasons for affiliating himself with a nationalistic movement.[117] Whereas the reformists had well nigh forsaken the "Indian problem" in their more immediate concern with the slavery issue, nativist politicians continued to criticize the government's Indian policies and to champion their rights in Congress and the media. This demonstration of solidarity might explain why Copway, who had expressed strong abolitionist sentiments on at least one occasion ("Would to God slavery was abolished!"), tied his political interests and, by association, those of Indians in general to the platform of an avowedly racist and antiabolitionist party. Nevertheless, there was also pronounced opposition to his membership in nativist circles. At one point he felt himself called upon to answer some slanderous remarks made by "some malicious person" in the *New York Times*. In a brief letter addressed to the editors of said paper dated September 5, 1856, he tried to legitimize his affiliation with the American Party. As the letter contains an interesting interpretation of his past as well as an explanation for his present political standpoint, it is worth quoting to some extent here:

I deny I am "a subject of Great Britain" in toto. I was quite young in years, when my father was called to preside over the Indians of Canada, having gone from Michigan from the Chippewas, and was not of age when in 1834, 16th July, embarked with the missionaries for the shores of Lake Superior, and in 1843 called back to preside over the General Council of our Nation, on the shores of Lake Huron, from whence I came to New York in 1847, and ever since connected myself with the Indians of the Northwest, and not the Indians of Canada; and my main object why I have lived in Washington and New York has been to carry out the great project of colonizing and concentrating the Indian tribes in one spot, where our American friends might encourage them to the arts of agriculture. Having failed to get the attention of the Democratic Administration of Gen. Pierce, I turned naturally to a people who had a conservative character, therefore I could go for none but Millard Fillmore, because in his administration he was kind to the Indians.

The interest of the Indians identically belongs to the American Party. I leave the public to judge who has been a consistent advocate to the American cause between us. I was a Whig before the American Party came into existence. I was a Fillmore man before the American Party nominated Mr. Fillmore for the Presidency (and if you have had the Negro interest in your ears), as Americans we still try and do what we can for the Indians, which is the crowning mission of the American Party in this country.[118]

His personal reasons for adopting a more conservative stance on the question of African American emancipation also surfaces in one of the speeches he reprinted in the first issue of *Copway's American Indian,* in which he basically echoes John Ridge's earlier lamentations on the frustrating legal status of educated Indians in American society:

Yes, because a few years back the colored man has received some little civil power, and the sight of going and voting for your officers — that is the reason why there is so much agitation and torchlights all over the country. They would be glad to disseminate all kinds of destruction to their people. Why is it? It is because the colored man has got some little power in the ballot box. That is the reason so many politicians are full of philanthropy. An Indian may stand there, who may have gone through the colleges of your country, and become a gentleman, a polished man, an orator in your assemblies; but there he stands isolated, perfectly alone, without any power, without any means to make himself tell upon the community. Just because these things have been denied to the red man, because these privileges have been withheld, and we have been laid aside, we, as a people, have only been men when it suits the paleface, and we have been nothing when it suits us to be so in our own country.[119]

It is understandable, from Copway's point of view at least, that he should seek support for his shelved Kah-ge-ga project from a party that publicly demanded that only native-born Americans be allowed to hold public office. As a living representative of the most "naturally" naturalized of all "native" Americans, he may even have speculated on some kind of official position in conjunction with his project if Millard Fillmore were reelected as the American Party's presidential candidate. Furthermore, the artificial distinction made between British and American citizenship in the "native American" context was certainly meaningless from an Ojibwa standpoint. Unfortunately for Copway, however, the nativist movement also faded out after the 1856 elections, leaving him totally bereft of a forum for his ideas.

Only sparse information is available on Copway's activities and whereabouts during the second half of the 1850s.[120] Beset by personal tragedy (three of his four children died in the fall/winter season of 1849–50) and domestic problems (separation from his wife, 1856–58), outlawed among his own people, snubbed by his former literary "friends," ignored by the American public, and facing bankruptcy, it is not surprising if Copway either began "to lose all touch with reality," as Smith has intimated, or simply resorted to somewhat less "noble" survival tactics. Although he continued on the lecture circuit until 1855, he also tried to supplement his income and, perhaps, catch the public's interest again with a series of more or less dubious exploits. In 1852 he and a white undertaker removed Red Jacket's remains from a threatened Indian cemetery in Buffalo, probably a well-intentioned act which nevertheless aroused the anger of the Senecas, whom he had failed to inform beforehand.[121] In 1858 he may have forged the signatures of several "chiefs" and "warriors" in a petition for federal funds to defray costs for the "promotion of civilization" among Indians in Kansas and Nebraska territories. That same year he is also on record as having volunteered to go to Florida in order to convince the remaining Seminoles there to remove peacefully to Indian Territory in present-day Oklahoma, and as having been arrested for debt in Boston.

It appears that Copway also developed a drinking habit. In a desperate soliciting letter addressed to Erastus Corning, president of the New York Central Railway, he assured his hoped-for benefactor that he had ceased taking "firewater." He further complained that his domestic problems had almost driven him to ruin — his wife had "been led astray in an evil hour" — and that he needed to borrow the sum of $100 for six weeks in order to return to England, where he thought he could earn money lecturing. From there he planned to visit the Holy Land, a popular destination for contemporary American writers of travel literature, perhaps having another publication in mind. Curiously enough, he named Freiligrath, who was in England then, as his creditor. "Fred Freilegrath [*sic*] Esqr a Poet and the Presedent [*sic*] of the Swiss Bank No 2 Royal Exchange London," he assured Corning, "is to be the kind man who will supply me with all the money I may want — he has been writing to me several times and has sent word by his friends for me to come — for when I saw him in Germany he named his only son after my Indian name."[122]

John Johnson said that his adoptive cousin died at Pontiac, Michigan, around 1863, a statement that was accepted as fact by Copway's early biographers. But, as Donald Smith has discovered, his name reappeared in 1864, when he and his brother David were trying to make money by recruiting Canadian Indians as cannon fodder for the Union army. Considering that Johnson had taken a very firm stand against similar illicit doings among the Gull Lake mission Ojibwas in 1862, he may well have preferred to think of his shameless relative as having departed from the world of the living.[123] Copway's name crops up once again in 1867 in two advertisements for "healing services" in the *Detroit Press*, indicating that he had not forgotten the skills his father had taught him so long ago. In the summer of 1868 he was back in Canada, at the Lake of Two Mountains Catholic mission near Montreal. Here he established a reputation for himself as a healer among the resident Algonquians and Iroquois and vehemently opposed the efforts of local Methodist missionaries. His wife and only surviving child had apparently left him for good by this time (or the other way around) to live with their white relatives at Port Dover, Ontario. Finally, on January 17, 1869, "Kakikekapo," or "Doctor Copway," converted to Roman Catholicism under the name Joseph-Antoine. A few days later the fifty-one-year-old Kahgegagahbowh, alias George Copway, alias Joseph-Antoine, passed away. In contrast to Peter Jones, who spent his final days surrounded by friends and relatives in the comfort of his classical revival–style country villa near New Credit and whose funeral was attended by a great crowd of Indians and whites, Copway died in total obscurity, so close and yet so unbridgeably far from his own home community. His childhood dream-vision had been fulfilled, however, as he had led a well-traveled life.[124]

If one compares George Copway with Peter Jones, who never deviated from the missionary path and actively attended to the welfare of his own native community until his death, Copway can easily appear in a less propitious light. His cousin John Johnson also adhered faithfully to his calling after they parted company in 1839. He continued to do missionary work for the American Methodists in the upper Mississippi area until they abandoned the field in 1844, and he then rejoined the Episcopalians in the same capacity. He was finally ordained by this religious body in 1858 and became a respected religious leader of the Gull Lake mission in Minnesota.[125] But not all of Peter Jones's Ojibwa Methodist contemporaries turned out to be so persistent in their profession. After a successful twenty-year career as a missionary in the Hudson's Bay Company territory, Peter Jacobs, a Mississauga orphan who had been adopted into the Credit River band, suddenly took to alcohol and was expelled from the Methodist Conference in 1858. He also tried to solicit funds in the United States without the official sanction of a church organization before finally returning to the Rama Reserve in Canada, where he barely managed to scrape together a living as a schoolteacher, interpreter, merchant, fisherman, and guide.[126] George Henry, regarded by the Methodists as one of their most promising converts, chose to leave the organization in 1844 to found a professional Indian dance troupe. That same year he accompanied his troupe to Europe, where they eventually joined up with George Catlin's traveling "Indian Collection" in Paris in 1845 and toured with him through England, France, and Belgium until the following year. They remained in Europe until 1848 and then returned to perform in Canada and the United States. While in England he even converted to Roman Catholicism temporarily, much to the disgust of his pronounced "antipapist" half-brother, Peter Jones. George Henry had thus given up his religious calling to make an early incursion into what would soon become a fairly common source of employment for remnant "hostile" Indians, the "Wild West" of American show business.[127]

Copway's life story is unique, however, if it is regarded in the broader context of transculturation. While Peter Jones and his disciples opted for a somewhat more secure mediating position as missionaries in a rapidly shrinking Ojibwa social environment, Copway essayed instead to penetrate the White Man's cultural sanctuary to become nothing less than a recognized member of the American literary elite. Like the legendary Pau-Puk-Keewis Longfellow identified him with, who transformed himself into various animals so that he could take part in their mysterious ways of life, Copway also put on various cultural guises in the course of his quixotic journey through the White Man's strange world.[128] Even though he frequently displayed all the wiliness of a seasoned trickster, he failed in the long run to recognize that he was just playing a standard role in a worn-out plot. He tried to ascend (and was lured) to a position that was simply not available to an Indian in antebellum American society, even if he had actually manifested the talents required to fill it. His desperate maneuvers along the way to his envisioned status as the Indian's "Great Red Father" in the White

Man's realm, were as often ludicrous as they were tragic. Finally, consumed by the shame of defeat in the approaching winter of his life, he may have succumbed to psychic stress and temporarily developed symptoms of what has been termed "windigo psychosis" in anthropological literature.[129] With his self-esteem seriously threatened by the recognition of his failure as a provider and a leader, two principal Ojibwa criteria for male success, he may have been possessed by a "cannibalistic" urge to turn against his own immediate family, his Methodist fraternity, and, finally, himself. But if there is an element of buffoonery in Copway's life, he was certainly no fool. His perseverance and entrepreneurship, his imaginative survival tactics, his rational assessment of the contemporary Indian situation, his literary output, and, last but not least, his capacity to dream still leave him with a respectable place in the history of American Indian literature.

George Copway produced an impressive body of writing: an autobiography, a promotional pamphlet, a "borrowed" epic poem, a tribal history, a European travel account, thirteen issues of a newspaper, dozens of articles, and, if we take his word for it, some "hundreds of letters every year."[130] Some of his work is still being read today outside of specialized scholarly circles. His autobiography and history have been reprinted as recently as 1970 and 1978 respectively, legends and other excerpts from his writings have been featured in several modern anthologies, and at least one of his articles was reproduced in a major contemporary American magazine.[131]

Even though he is clearly a product of the Second Great Awakening like Apess and Boudinot, his affinity with the American romantic age encouraged him to demonstrate a degree of pride and interest in Indian traditions that is uncommon for salvationist authors of his day. "No living writer, nor historian has done so much justice to the noble traits of our people," he wrote of Cooper, and he paid a very personal tribute to Longfellow by naming his last-born daughter Minnehaha.[132] Copway was a satellite member of New York City's literary circle, which included notable writers such as Washington Irving, William Cullen Bryant, John Neal, and Nathaniel P. Willis, and he associated with other representatives of nineteenth-century American regionalist literature like William Gilmore Simms. Even though he appears to have had few connections with Boston's transcendentalists, his enthusiasm for Ojibwa history was probably fueled by the popular writings of New England's great romantic historians: George Bancroft, William Prescott, and, without doubt, Francis Parkman. But, other than his obvious debt to the romantic age, Copway profited most from the ethnological interest generated by the publications of the American antiquarians, which blossomed in the 1840s after the establishment of the American Ethnological Society in 1842 and the Smithsonian Institution in 1848.[133] In New York he had direct contact with respected antiquarian scholars associated with the American Ethnological Society and the New York Historical Society such as Albert Gallatin, Ephraim George Squier (who supported his Kah-ge-ga project), Henry Rowe Schoolcraft, and Lewis H. Morgan. At the same time, it does not seem unreasonable to assume that Copway provided some of his literary acquaintances — especially Longfellow and School-craft — with invaluable firsthand information on the Ojibwas and may thus have influenced their work as well.

Copway's *Life, History, and Travels of Kah-ge-ga-gah-bowh* was a best seller in its own day and went through at least six editions in the first year of its publication. Two expanded versions of his autobiography appeared in 1850, one in London as *Recollections of a Forest Life* and the other in New York as *The Life, Letters, and Speeches of Kah-ge-ga-gah-bowh*.[134] Like Apess's earlier autobiography, it is a typical salvationist narrative with its unilinear development from "savagism" to the pulpit. In this sense it is also comparable to the missionary journals written by his fellow Canadian Ojibwa Methodists, Peter Jacobs's *Journal of the Reverend Peter Jacobs* (1857) and Peter Jones's *Life and Journals of Kah-ke-wa-quo-na-by* (1860), as well as the autobiographical sketches produced by John Johnson, which were not published until 1902 and 1904. But Copway's lengthier and much more personal narrative, which is a full-fledged autobiography like Apess's rather than a missionary journal with an autobiographical preface like Jacobs's and Jones's, distinguishes itself from all of these because a good third of the original version is made up of a fairly detailed account of his life prior to conversion. In contrast, Jones quickly skims over the "miseries of savage life" in his introductory chapter titled "Brief Account of Kah-ke-wa-quo-na-by" as if he were in a hurry to get on with the more important business of his spiritual transformation. "No wonder the Indians pine away and die; their life is after all a hard one," he concludes. Jacobs reduces the "very cruel and wicked" days of his youth "when Indians made the women do all the work" to a mere paragraph in the cropped autobiographical entry to his journal titled "Peter Jacobs' History of Himself." And Johnson, who was initiated into the Grand Medicine Lodge like his cousin and claims that he can still remember all of its teachings, does not bother to waste many words on "heathenism" in the brief letter sketching out his life because, as he sees it, it would just "take too much time." All three appear to take pains to assure their readers that their conversion to Christianity has liberated them from a totally degraded way of life.[135] Though Copway also interjects a pious comment here and there about the "days of our darkness," these are always overshadowed by his primitivist outbursts:

> I was born in *Nature's wide domain*! The trees were all that sheltered my infant limbs — the blue heavens all that covered me. I am one of Nature's children; I have always admired her; she shall be my glory; her features — her robes, and the wreath about her brow — the seasons — her stately oaks, and the evergreen — her hair, ringlets over the earth — all contribute to my enduring love of her; and whenever I see her, emotions of pleasure roll in my breast, and swell and burst like waves on the shores of the ocean, in prayer and praise to Him who has placed me in her hand. It is thought great to be born in palaces, surrounded with wealth — but to be born in Nature's wide domain is greater still! . . . Is this dear spot, made green by the tears of memory, any less enticing and hallowed than the palaces where princes are born? I would much more glory in this birthplace, with the broad canopy of heaven above me, and the giant arms of the forest trees for my shelter, than to be born in palaces of marble, studded with pillars of gold! Nature will be Nature still, while palaces shall decay and fall in ruins. Yes, Niagara will be Niagara a thousand years hence! The rainbow, a wreath over her brow, shall continue as long as the sun, and the flowing of the river — while the work of art, however impregnable, shall in atoms fall![136]

He fills the first five chapters of his book with various episodes from his distinctly happy childhood days, embellishing his account with fairly detailed descriptions of Ojibwa material culture, means of subsistence, religious beliefs, oral traditions, and warfare before finally proceeding to relate the circumstances of his conversion and subsequent missionary activities. Copway thus not only supplements the conventional salvationist framework of his autobiographical narrative with a topical naturist-nativist tribute to the American wilderness but also takes into full account the rising public interest in North American ethnology. In so doing, he introduces the "inside informant" perspective in Indian autobiography, a genre hitherto dominated entirely by the relativist approach of converts whose spiritual journals always counterpose "savagism" and "civilization." Aware of the contemporary scholarly interest in "legendary" material and sharing the common belief that Indian ways of life were doomed to disappear in the immediate future, Copway is also one of the first Indian authors to recognize the significance of oral traditions in the context of Indian history and to urge native literates to record such knowledge from the elders while there is still time: "The *traditions* handed down from father to son were held sacred; one half of these are not known by the white people, however far their researches may have extended. There is an unwillingness, on the part of Indians, to communicate many of their traditions. The only way to come at these is to educate the Indians, so that they may be able to write out what they have heard, or may hear, and publish it."[137]

Nevertheless, as a firm believer in the superiority of the written over the spoken word and convinced as he is of the inevitable triumph of "civilization," he fails, of course, to take into account the self-protective censure mechanisms (ethnic barriers) behind the Indian reluctance to transmit sacred knowledge to outsiders. But regardless of which current trends may have influenced Copway's multifaceted convictions — antiquarianism, romanticism, or nativism — he still brings an important introspective shift to Indian literature. In his autobiography, the culturally dismembered Indian convert begins to look back nostalgically for something that may have been irretrievably lost, rather than given up voluntarily. "Thank heaven I am an Indian," he proclaims in a speech he appended to the expanded versions of his autobiography. "Yes; were I to be the last to stand on the peaks of the Rocky Mountains, I would still raise my hand to the world as a part of a noble specimen of humanity, the representative of the Indians who once lived in this country."[138] This melodramatic appeal to vanishing-noble-savages sentiment, if read from a modern perspective, is still a concrete manifestation of ethnic consciousness expressed in the orthodox language of a mid-nineteenth-century Indian missionary gone romantic. It is one more indication that Copway's conversion experience was a developmental phase of life and not a finite process of personality transformation. In Jamesian terms, the "habitual center of his personal energy" was never taken up permanently by Christianity, and consequently his spiritual identity remained open to fluctuations between traditional Ojibwa beliefs and succeeding "peripheral" Protestant religious ideas.

Copway's worldly views on the "Indian problem" are more consistent. In his autobiography he makes four practical recommendations to "those whose benevolent feelings lead them to commiserate the condition of the aborigines of America," which conform closely to Peter Jones's principles of selective adaptation:

1. They should establish missions and high schools wherever the whites have frequent intercourse with them.
2. They should use their influence, as soon as the Indians are well educated, and understand the laws of the land, to have them placed on the same footing as the whites.

3. They should procure for them a territorial or district government, so that they may represent their own nation.
4. They should obtain for them deeds of their own lands; and, if qualified according to law, urge their right to vote.[139]

In the course of his subsequent promotional speaking tours he expanded his views on Indian policy and committed them to writing in the 1849 article for the *American Whig Review*, which he reprinted the following year in his *Organization of a New Indian Territory*. Here, as a prelude to his plan "to save the Indians from extinction," Copway lists "a few reasons why they have not materially improved, and why their numbers have been greatly lessening." The explanations he provides — contact with immoral frontier society, predilection for a nomadic hunter's life, fear of further removals, lack of good schools, overabundance of hunting lands, intertribal and imperial wars, diseases and alcohol — are all borrowed from the re-formist repertoire of scholarly officials like McKenney, Schoolcraft, Squier, Gallatin, Morgan, and others, with whose writings Copway was probably well acquainted. With respect to the "mode generally adopted for the intro-duction of Christianity among Indians," however, he expresses sentiments that are undoubtedly founded upon his own experiences as a missionary in Canada. Aware that he is treading "on delicate ground" with this particular issue, he nevertheless points an accusing finger at clerical dogmatism, com-menting that the services of "men of *liberal education* as well as of devoted piety" would be of much greater benefit to Indians in the long run. In addition, he shares Jedediah Morse's earlier opinion that the common prac-tice of translating biblical texts into native languages is counterproductive to Indian mental development:

I have tried to convince the different missionaries that it is better to teach the Indians in English, rather than in their own language, as some have done and are now doing. A great amount of *time* and *money* have been expended in the translation of the Bible into various languages, and afterward the In-dian has been taught to read; when he might have been taught English in much less amount of time and with less expenditure of money. Besides this, the few books that have been translated into our language are the *only books* which they *can* read, and in this are perpetuated his views, ideas and feelings; whereas, had he been taught English, he would have been introduced into a wide field of literature; for so *very* limited would be the literature of his own language, that he could have no scope for his powers; consequently, the sooner he learned the almost universal English and forgot the Indian, the better.[140]

The "three most requisite things for an Indian youth to be taught," Copway maintains further, perhaps remembering when he assisted Peter Jones's efforts to establish a manual labor school for Canadian Ojibwas, "are a good mechanical trade, a sound code of morality, and a high-toned literature."[141]

After having defined the various causes behind the "Indian problem," Copway goes on to clarify his reasons for wanting to establish a permanent Indian Territory in the Old Northwest. Once again, he presents run-of-the-mill arguments used previously by philanthropists and politicians to legitimize removal, which would eventually become part and parcel of allotment philosophy during the latter part of the nineteenth century: irreversible displacement by western emigration, occupation of more land than is required for an agricultural economy, inevitable sale of lands to the government for annuities, and rapidly diminishing resources. More remarkable in this context is his accurate forecasting of the costly Plains Indian wars that took place from the 1860s to the 1880s as a direct consequence of displacement and the wanton destruction of buffalo. "Desperation will drive the Indian to die at the cannon's mouth," he predicted, "rather than 'remove' beyond the Rocky Mountains."[142]

Copway's rather ignominious debut as a poet in 1850 with *Ojibway Conquest* is of interest primarily as a trivial curiosity in publishing history, and perhaps as a testimonial to his keen awareness of going trends in the literary market. "His" epic poem actually failed to find many readers, but it nevertheless preceded Longfellow's similar lyrical best seller by a full five years. Although he entered this publication under his name at the clerk's office of the Court of the United States for the Southern District of New York in 1850, authorship was claimed in 1888 by Julius Taylor Clark, a former Indian agent, who said that he had permitted Copway to publish it under his name and to share in the royalties for use in his missionizing efforts among Indians. According to Clark, Copway had told him that the poem would sell only if he could publish it in his own name. After granting permission, Clark never heard from Copway again and only found out about the publication of the poem many years later, when he discovered an unopened copy while rummaging through a package of old letters and documents. His version has been accepted as the truth by Copway's biographers. Perhaps Copway did send Clark a copy, which the latter somehow mislaid, but he certainly failed to reveal or credit his "ghostwriter." His modest reputation as a poet thus rests solely upon deception, unless one counts the rather contrived poem dedicated to his wife at the beginning of *Ojibway Conquest*, the authorship of which has not yet been contested. In addition, Copway revised the twenty-two ethnographic endnotes to the poem, the last one of which assures the reader that "Never will a true Indian stoop to low cunning and meanness which characterizes the higher state of pretended civilized life of other nations."[143]

It is known, for instance, that Copway borrowed as freely from Schoolcraft's "fanciful stories" as Longfellow did, but just how, if at all, he (and indirectly Clark) may have contributed to *The Song of Hiawatha* can only be a matter of speculation. Since Copway himself was also interested in Ojibwa legends and published a number of them in his own tribal history, it is quite likely that he imparted some of his firsthand knowledge on the subject during his conversations with Longfellow. He also sent Longfellow a brief extract from "his" *Ojibway Conquest* late in 1849 and personally delivered a copy of the published poem to Longfellow's home six months later.[144] While Longfellow's debt to Elias Lönrott's Finnish folk epic, *Kalevala*, which he read in the summer of 1854, is a matter of historical record, it may still be that the Ojibwa epic poem Copway published under his name earlier also fed the idea to transcribe North American Indian legendary material into meter. There are parallels between the two pieces, such as the melodramatic love story about an adopted Sioux warrior and an Ojibwa maiden in one, and the equally sentimental but tribally reversed connection between an Ojibwa culture-hero and a Sioux maiden in the other. Longfellow himself suggested a direct tie between Copway and his own epic poem by identifying the former with Pau-Puk-Keewis, "the handsome Yenadizzi" who embodies some of the less heroic but certainly more authentic attributes of Nanabozho, which he carefully avoided in his (and Schoolcraft's) counterfeit culture-hero-trickster figure of Hiawatha, who is actually of Iroquois origins. After all, Copway's appropriation of Clark's manuscript does have the touch of first-rate prankishness about it if one just considers who was actually "copping" from whom in the marketing of Indian legendary material in the first place.[145]

Copway's contention that his *Traditional History and Characteristic Sketches of the Ojibwa Nation* was "the first volume of Indian history written by an Indian" is inaccurate as it was preceded by David Cusick's *Sketches of Ancient History of the Six Nations* (1827), which had gone through its third edition by 1848. In fact, Copway must have been aware of Cusick's work because he borrowed freely from it for his own speeches on Indian religious beliefs.[146] In contrast to Cusick's *Sketches*, which is based entirely on oral sources, Copway's tribal history was patterned after early structural models for American ethnological studies. It basically follows the framework of special questionnaires prepared in the 1820s by Lewis Cass, then superintendent of Indian affairs, to be sent out to Indian agents for the systematic collection of data. These provided a practical set of questions on specific topics such as history, tribal organization, forms of government, language, manners and customs, subsistence methods, religious beliefs, state of civilization, and so on. This structure was subsequently expanded by Schoolcraft and perfected by Morgan, who has often been designated as the "father of American anthropology" for his highly systematic approach to ethnological practice and theory. Since Copway included a very similar questionnaire prepared by Schoolcraft in the first issue of his newspaper, it is quite likely that he used similar guidelines for his own research on the Ojibwa.[147] His *Traditional History* appeared at a time when there was a pronounced public interest in Indian history and authors like Drake, Heckewelder, Schoolcraft, Gallatin, McKenney, Catlin, Morgan, and others were being widely read. Copway credits most of these early American historians in his own works, and he knew several of them personally.[148] Moreover, the period just before the Civil War (1850–61) was a turning point not only for American ethnology but also in the production of Ojibwa autohistoriography with the completion of two additional tribal histories: Peter Jones's *History of the Ojebway Indians*, which he wrote around 1843 and which was published posthumously in 1861; and William Whipple Warren's *History of the Ojibways*, which was partially serialized in the *Minnesota Democrat* in 1851, finished as a manuscript in the winter of 1853–54, and published by the Minnesota Historical Society long after Warren's death, in 1885.[149]

Traditional History was not quite as popular in its day as Copway's autobiography, but it turned out to be his most enduring and most frequently cited contribution to Indian literature. Its reception, however, has been mixed both then and since. Even as Copway was preparing to publish it in New York, Francis Parkman confided to George Squier that he had "no great faith" in the work because "Copway is endowed with a discursive imagination and facts grow under his hands into a preposterous shape and dimensions." More recently, Donald Smith feels that "the book does not really work" because one-third of it is made up of verbatim excerpts from other sources and thus lacks the "unity and the content" found in Warren's and Jones's work. On the other hand, historian Leroy Eid shares Elémire Zolla's earlier view that Copway succeeds quite well "in telling a coherent historical account" in his article supporting the "Ojibwa Thesis" based on oral traditions collected by Copway, Jones, Warren, and other native historians, which contends that, contrary to most historical accounts, the "invincible" Iroquois were soundly thrashed by the combined forces of Ojibwas, Ottawas, Potawatomies, and remnant Hurons (Wyandots) in the seventeenth century and were thereby prevented from expanding farther into the Great Lakes area.[150]

Whereas Warren focuses his attention on oral accounts of the protracted Ojibwa–Sioux conflict, Copway and Jones cover a much wider spectrum of Ojibwa ethnography. Their affinity with contemporary American ethnological methodology is evident, for instance, in their nearly identical topical framework patterned closely after the questionnaires mentioned above. Both favor the modern Bering Strait theory of Indian origins whereas Warren still adheres to the anachronistic biblical connection with the Hebrews.[151] Copway and Jones also have a similar developmentalist point of departure, namely, to demonstrate that there is sufficient evidence of merit in traditional Ojibwa ways of life to legitimize the continuing missionary efforts among them. They interpret Ojibwa history from a relativist Christian moral standpoint and are thus at pains to point out similarities between Ojibwa society and their adopted occidental ideals — namely, worship of one Supreme Being, notions of good and evil, democratic form of government, individual ownership of hunting territories, and so on.

On the whole, however, Copway's history is more attuned to the New England romantic "literary history" tradition than either of his contemporaries, which is made evident in his frequent use of flamboyant language and his efforts to "salvage" the Ojibwa past. In this latter context, at least, Peter Jones is once again unable to diverge from his rigid missionary assumption of Anglo-Saxon superiority. "From experience of my early life," he writes in his introductory chapter, "I can truly say, that their imaginary bliss is so mixed up with everything that is abominable and cruel, that it would be vain to look for real happiness among savage tribes." In contrast, Copway finds, "much, very much that is interesting and instructive in that nation's actions" to record for posterity before, as he opines, it should "pass away" with its people.[152]

A particularly interesting part of Copway's approach to Ojibwa history is that he tries to develop a methodological model with which to grade the historical dependability of oral traditions. "The history of the Ojibways," he begins in a romantic vein, "like that of other Indian tribes, is treasured up in traditional lore. It has been passed down from age to age on the tide of a song; for there is much poetry in the narrative of the old sage as he dispenses his facts and fancies to the listening group that throngs around him." But in order to distinguish between "facts" and "fancies" for the benefit of his more critical antiquarian audience, Copway proposes to strain his orally transmitted information through a rather ingenious "scientific" sieve:

> In listening to the traditions of the Indians in their wigwams, the traveller will learn that the chiefs are the repositories of the history of their ancestors. With these traditions there are rules to follow by which to determine whether they are true or false. By these rules I have been governed in my researches. The first is to inquire particularly into the leading points of every tradition narrated. The second is to notice whether the traditions are approved by the oldest chiefs and wise men. . . . Such are more likely to be true, and if places and persons are mentioned, additional clue is given to their origin and proof obtained of their truth or falsity. . . . The chiefs have generally been those who have at all times retained a general history of their nation.[153]

Another unique feature of his history is the transcription of traditional oral tales into a short-story format, which foreshadows the numerous collections of "legendary" material published by Indian historians and anthropologists after the close of the century. His inclusion of several graphic representations of birchbark characters in a chapter immediately succeeding the transcribed legends with the provocative title "Their Language and Writings" might be an intimation on his part that, from an Ojibwa standpoint at least, the gap between orality and chirography is not so great after all.[154]

Copway also broaches subjects in his history that would eventually be of general interest in Algonquian ethnology. His scholarly attention to orally transmitted knowledge (together with Jones's and Warren's) did help to set the record straight on Ojibwa–Iroquois interaction in the Great Lakes area. He was also the first to discuss the notion of property rights among Ojibwa bands in conjunction with hunting and trapping territories. In the debate that ensued after Frank G. Speck published his "pioneering" observations on this particular issue among the Algonquian Montagnais in 1914–15, Copway's modest but earlier contribution to this controversial topic has been ignored altogether.[155]

The erratic life of its author does not really detract from the value of *Traditional History* as a primary autoethnographic source on the Ojibwas. At the time he published it, the bilingual Ojibwa historian could look back on the twelve years he lived at Rice Lake and another dozen years of experience in the field as a missionary among Indians in the Great Lakes region. Much of his ethnographic and historical information, which is more carefully edited here than in his earlier autobiography, is apparently no less accurate or "authentic" than Jones's or Warren's accounts, neither of which differs markedly in factual detail. If Warren is correct in maintaining that his Ojibwa ancestry, bilinguality, and personal experiences distinguish his history from the "mainly superficial" information collected by "transient sojourners" with inadequate knowledge of Indian customs and languages, then Copway has no less right to the claim. "Though I cannot wield the pen of a *Macaulay* or the graceful word of an *Irving* with which to delineate an Indian's life," he writes in his typically bumptious manner, "yet I move a pen guided by an intimate knowledge of the subject it traces out, the joys and the sorrows it records."[156] He is one of the first American historians to join the oral, historical, and biographical into a homogeneous autohistoric portrait of an Indian tribe. If Copway's work shows traces of dilettantism it should be remembered that such a complex literary-historical approach was not successfully (in terms of critical acclaim) achieved by an Indian author until Momaday's *Way to Rainy Mountain* appeared in 1969.[157]

Copway's *Running Sketches of Men and Places* is his least accomplished work because, among other things, approximately half of it is made up of lengthy, boring passages taken verbatim from contemporary British travel guides and periodicals, poetic citations, and excerpts from his own previous publications.[158] The book has the appearance of having been patched together haphazardly for the sake of bulk, and the reader is thus required to sift through redundant pages in order to find the scattered passages with personal impressions. Copway had obviously taken his cue from American travel literature, a popular genre of the day in which a number of his literary "friends," such as Irving, Cooper, Bryant, Willis, Neal, and Longfellow, were represented. One of the main purposes of antebellum American travel literature, other than entertaining its readers with glowing accounts of famous individuals and historical sites in the Old World, was to demonstrate the moral, political, and physical superiority of the New World and its inhabitants.[159] Apocryphal accounts attributed to real or imagined Indian travelers, or "rational savages" who cast a critical eye on European customs, were first published in sixteenth-century France (e.g., Montaigne's account of the Tupinambás in Rouen) and reappeared more frequently in eighteenth-century French literature (e.g., Lahontan's "Adario," Voltaire's "L'Ingénu," Drévetière's "Arlequin"). They made their debut in England (if one excludes Dryden's earlier "Montezuma," which was set in the New World) in the early issues of the *Spectator* and became a fairly common genre in English letters thereafter.[160] Thus, while the idea itself was not entirely new, an authentic first-hand account by a flesh-and-blood Indian "tourist" in mid-nineteenth-century Europe must have been as enticing a publishing venture then as it would be now. And yet, this seemingly unique literary endeavor was preceded by the work of another Ojibwa traveler, George Henry (Maungwudaus), who published three short pamphlets in England and the United States in 1847–48, in which he relates his European impressions while touring with his Ojibwa–Ottawa dance troupe.[161] Nor was the role of the observant "ethnic voyager" limited to Indians. Several African American writers were also traveling in Europe at this time, usually as representatives of reformist or abolitionist organizations, and some of them eventually published their travelogues as well.[162]

Henry's compressed account (nine pages of a sixteen-page pamphlet) lies entirely within the eighteenth-century European "rational savage" tradition with its pretended naiveté and seemingly harmless observations of continental society delivered in a (purposely?) faulty "Indian" English.[163] One example among many is his description of a visit to Queen Victoria's palace:

> Mr. Harris took us into the Queen's house. She is a small woman but handsome. There are many women handsomer than she. Prince Albert is a handsome and well built man. Her house is large, quiet country inside of it. We got tired before we went through all the rooms in it. Great many warriors with their swords and guns stands outside watching for the enemy. We have been told that she has three or four other houses in other places as large. The one we saw they say is much too small for her, and they are building a much larger one on one side of it.

If it were not for the somber fact that the text is undermined by personal disaster — seven members of the group fell ill and died while in Europe, including Henry's wife and three of his children — it could just be regarded as an example of Indian "innocents abroad" wit. "At Glasgow, two of my children died," he writes without the slightest indication of pathos, "another in Edinburgh; buried them in the burying ground of our friends the Quakers; and after we visited other towns at the North and South, we went to England again; my wife died at Newark."[164] The juxtaposition of mild satire and rancorless tragedy, however, takes Henry's travel account beyond the artificial scope of the invented "rational savage." In an unassuming and yet most effective manner, Henry's little booklet manages to transmit some of the irony and pain of Indian existence in a stereotypical guise in the dawning age of the Wild West show.

It is particularly interesting to read Henry's travelogue together with George Catlin's parallel account of the same events. Catlin was aware of the fact that, "though they looked with unenlightened eyes, they saw and correctly appreciated many things in London and Paris which the eyes of Londoners and Parisians scarcely see." In his estimation, for example, their presentation to the kings and queens of France and Belgium must have been the "grandest epoch of the poor fellows' lives," and of which they would "be sure to make their boasts as long as they live." George Henry, however, devoted no more than a cursory paragraph to this particular episode:

> Shook hands with Louis Phillippe and all his family in the Park, called St. Cloud; gave them little war dance, shooting with bows and arrows at a target, ball play; also rowed our birch bark canoe in the artificial lake, among swans and geese. There were about four thousand French ladies and gentlemen with them. We dined with him in the afternoon in his Palace. He said many things concerning his having been in America when he was a young man. He gave us twelve gold and silver medals; he showed us all the rooms in his house.

What Henry did register with his "unenlightened eyes" and described in more vivid detail were the incongruities of European civilization, such as the presence of "many very rich, and many very poor," the ignoble spectacle of a public execution, or the dissection ("same as we do with venison") of thirty bodies in an anatomy class by "medicine men."[165] Catlin himself began to doubt whether the practice of "sending parties [of Indians] to foreign countries to see all that can be seen and learned in civilized life" was really beneficial, and not only because of the frequent deaths. "They have witnessed and appreciated the virtues and blessings, and at the same time the vices and miseries and degradations of civilized life," he concluded, "the latter of which will doubtless have made the deepest impressions upon their minds, and which (not unlike some *more distinguished travellers than themselves*) they will comment and enlarge upon, and about in equal justice to the nation they represent and are endeavouring to instruct."[166]

Copway's book, written in carefully edited English and replete with literary name dropping, is much blunter in its obsequious appeal to American nativist chauvinism. "I have thought that I love my native land," he declares as he is about to depart for Europe, "but I realize it more to-day than ever; and all that is lovely is magnified. . . . I may see other countries equally beautiful and grand in scenery, yet let me be an enthusiast for my own dear native land."[167] The American reader knows, of course, that he is not going to come across anything truly comparable in all of his prospective travels. In the midst of an effusive soliloquy on the Rhine — "O thou river of majestic beauty, and grandeur!" — with ostentatious allusions to a long string of German historians and bards "who have all left something as a memento of their fond love for this river" and the inevitable citation from Byron's *Childe*

Harold, Copway slows down just long enough to set the folks back at home at ease:

> Poetry and song. Over this river each sweet strain has exhausted itself. The Germans rightly think there is only one Rhine in the world. We give them credit for love of country, and we ask them the same, when we say it would take twenty-five or thirty such rivers to make one Mississippi! . . . When any nation comes to boasting of rivers, we have one too that could swallow all the German rivers at once.[168]

In keeping with the egalitarian principles embodied in the noble-rational-savage image, he also points an accusing finger at the gap between rich and poor and laments the absence of American gallantry in relations with the fairer sex. Like George Henry, he frowns at the mien of certain classes of European women. But, whereas Henry and his companions find that some of the "eighty thousand common wives of the City of London" whom they encounter at a British officers' ball are good for kissing only, Copway launches into a spirited disputation on womanhood after having observed some rustic German peasant women at work in their fields with the more "enlightened eyes" of a connoisseur:

> The hardy race of women are in the fields performing the duties of husbandmen, while their husbands, sons, and brothers are stationed at the frontier towns of the north, ready for war. These German women are short and portly and have ruddy complexions. With their sun-burnt faces they may compare to advantage, as far as redness is concerned, with any of our squaws in America; and like them they are serviceable at home and in the field. But of course there are *ladies* for the parlor in Germany as well as in every other civilized country. To grace saloons and drawing-rooms, women must be converted into butterflies, joined in the middle by a thread, ornamented with a variety of hues, formed to flutter and fly about, and to live on sickening sweets, such as their counterparts, the flowers of the boudoir, may offer. There is more heart in a German peasant woman, and more soul in a simple-minded squaw, than in a thousand toys that are formed only for ornaments and playthings. Doubtless either extreme is to be deprecated, and the noble gentlewoman is a medium between the two, free from coarseness on the one hand and from frailty on the other.[169]

Unfortunately, passages such as these (however one may wish to take them) are too few and far between in Copway's text to save it from the tedious banalities of plagiarized touristic trivia. With the possible exception of the historically relevant sections on the Third World Peace Congress, which were also to a great extent copied directly from English newspaper reports, its main point of interest is simply as a nonsalvationist curiosity of nineteenth-century American Indian literature. With his usual quick nose for fashionable literary trends, he concludes his account with new plans for a prospective journey to the Holy Land in order "to seek the footprints of the Savior." American travel literature might have been enriched by another unusual Indian "innocents abroad" tale if Copway's intended journey to this highly popular tourist destination of the time had actually materialized. In this case, however, his dream-vision had apparently played itself out.

George Copway's life and works mark the close of the salvationist epoch in American Indian literature. He began his role as cultural mediator in the conventional position of a Protestant missionary within the Indian community and then abruptly crossed the spiritual–secular border to establish himself in American society as an independent organ of pan-Indianism. In the end he failed to realize his own aspirations to grandeur as an Indian leader and author, partly because of inherent weaknesses in his character and limited literary talents but primarily as a result of the fickleness of a late-romantic American audience grown weary of Indian stories, who first lured him into the limelight as an exotic curiosity and then abruptly let him fall into oblivion. Even though the "Protestant ethic" would continue to shape the lives of Indian authors for many generations to come, Copway's immediate successors in the literary field would orient themselves toward more worldly matters. Indian missionary-writers became an exception rather than the rule by the second half of the nineteenth century, and it was Copway, the traveler, who took the first difficult step in a new direction.

7

The Transition of American Indian Literature from Salvationism to Modernity

DURING THE EARLY 1850s, when George Copway's borderline literary fame in the East had already begun to fade, an expatriate Cherokee managed to establish himself as a professional writer in distant California. If Copway's life and works mark the conclusion of the salvationist period in the history of American Indian literature, then the career of journalist-poet-novelist John Rollin Ridge (Yellow Bird, 1827–67), the eldest son of John Ridge, embodies its transition into the modern era.[1] He also had to abandon his native community as a young adult and seek his fortune in the White Man's world. His adventurous journey into literary being in the Far West was shaped by the explosive political tensions that characterized both Cherokee and American society on the eve of the Civil War, rather than by any concern with rewards or punishments in the hereafter. Like his father, John Ridge, Yellow Bird never took up a religious vocation even though he was educated by a Protestant missionary. Instead, after having to abandon the Cherokee Nation for killing a man, he first tried in vain to make a strike in the gold fields of California and then became a very successful journalist. As a political editorialist, he was a staunch Douglas Democrat, joining the Union (or Peace) Democrats when the Civil War broke out. He was also an antiabolitionist and identified closely with the "Young America" movement and its filibustering activities. He shared his father's hope that someday the Cherokee Nation would become "an integral part of the United States, having Senators and Representatives in Congress, and possessing all the attributes, first of a territorial government, and then of a sovereign state."[2] John Rollin Ridge personifies a new development in American Indian literature for the simple reason that he is the first writer of the salvationist period who managed to break away entirely from the missionary mold. He always identified himself as an author of Cherokee descent and was regarded as such by his audience, but he also traveled farther along the "White Man's road" than any of his predecessors. His assimilationist views clearly foreshadowed the more secularized federal Indian policies of the postbellum era.

Ridge not only managed to make a relatively comfortable living as a journalist in American society, and this at a time in which the vocation itself was hardly a lucrative prospect for anyone regardless of background, but was also a successful poet and novelist. His popular romantic verses, a few of which also had Indian themes, appeared in major California journals alongside prominent "frontier" authors like Bret Harte, Cincinnatus Hiner Miller, Charles Warren Stoddard, and Samuel Clemens. With the publication of his *Life and Adventures of Joaquín Murieta* in 1854, he created the legendary character of a California social bandit whose exploits have since been retold in numerous pirated editions and formed the basis for two Hollywood films.[3] Although Indians are not directly involved, there are nevertheless many parallels with Ridge's own traumatic experiences in the aftermath of the Cherokee removal. This blood-and-thunder tale of a Mexican mestizo's retaliation against the injustices committed by American miners during the California gold-rush days has all of the characteristics of an ethnic protest novel in which the racist mechanisms of colonial exploitation are consciously exposed by the author. Ridge's fictional interpretation of Murieta's escapades as a heroic struggle against Yankee oppression gained the full approbation of the Hispanic community. In the United States the account was celebrated in late-nineteenth-century Mexican American *corridos* (narrative ballads), serialized in Spanish-language newspapers of the same period, adapted for use on stage in the Hispanic theater of the 1920s and 1930s, and finally provided Rodolfo ("Corky") Gonzales with the leitmotif for *I Am Joaquín*, the epic poem that launched the modern period of Chicano literature in 1967.[4] Mexican author Ireneo Paz was inspired to produce a widely read "historical" novel about Murieta in 1908, and Chilean poet Pablo Neruda wrote an antiimperialism play based on the tale in 1966 that was staged for eleven weeks in Santiago the following year.[5]

The missionary imperative of the salvationist period would persist among generations of Indian writers to come, but henceforth their lives and works would be increasingly affected by politics and the vicissitudes of a booming publishing industry rather than the fickle benevolence of sectarian societies. Indian exhorters, who could once astonish an Anglo audience with mere demonstrations of English diction from the pulpit, ceased to be a novelty during the second half of the nineteenth century. Although the ministry continued to draw educated Indians into its fold and even produced a few authors, the predominance of the missionary-writer in American Indian letters was over. At a time in which American society sought to solve its problems in the political arena rather than depending upon religious or philanthropical organizations, the calling had, as Emerson concluded when he quit the ministry in 1832, become "antiquated."[6] The careers of Ely S. Parker (1828–95) and Elias C. Boudinot (1835–90), which have several parallels and yet took an altogether different course, well illustrate the expanding professional possibilities for Indian intellectuals after the 1850s.

Born on the Seneca Tonawanda Reservation in New York, Ely Parker was first instructed at a local Baptist mission school and then attended Yates and Cayuga academies in the same state until he was eighteen.[7] While still in school he began to gain political expertise by accompanying tribal delegations to Washington as an interpreter. In 1852 he was nominated grand sachem of the tribe. His people's immediate concern was to save the Tonawanda Reservation rather than having to move to Kansas according to earlier treaty stipulations. Parker and his fellow delegates accomplished this by 1857, when the government allowed them to buy back their reservation with money granted them for relinquishment of their claims in Kansas. After trying in vain to enter the legal profession — he was refused admission to the bar on the grounds that he was not a citizen — he launched a very successful career in civil engineering. Parker managed to overcome racial prejudice in the army and obtain a commission as captain of the engineers in 1863. He served as Ulysses S. Grant's staff officer during the Civil War and finally resigned from the army in 1869 with the rank of brigadier general. He held the post of commissioner of Indian affairs from 1869 to 1871, when he resigned in the wake of charges made against him of defrauding the government, even though he had been acquitted previously by a special committee of the House of Representatives. Disappointed, he abandoned his public career to try his hand as a private businessman without much success and then took up various minor positions with the police department of New York City.

Even though Parker had fought hard to save the Tonawanda Reservation and knew enough about Iroquois traditions to become Lewis Morgan's primary informant, he was still a firm believer in the policy of assimilation and even supported the end of the treaty-making process on the grounds that the "advantages and the power of execution are all on one side."

However, he was very critical of the policies hitherto followed by the missionary societies. In his estimation, "Indian civilization has been a failure then, because in his case the cart was placed before the horse. He has been required first to change his religion and then to become civilized, first to walk before he had learned to creep."[8] In an 1867 report on Indian affairs addressed to Grant, who was secretary of war at the time, he presented an alternative four-point plan which proposed to transfer the Bureau of Indian Affairs back to the War Department (the BIA was transferred to the Department of the Interior in 1849 under 9 U.S. Stat. 395), to abolish private trade with Indians, to consolidate tribes in a number of districts under a territorial government, and to create a permanent commission "composed of such white men as possessed in large degree the confidence of their country, and a number of the most reputable educated Indians, selected from different tribes," whose duty it would be to "explain to the various tribes the advantages of their consolidation upon some common territory, over which Congress shall have extended the aegis of good, wise, and wholesome laws for their protection and perpetuation."[9]

Elias Cornelius Boudinot, son of Elias Boudinot, was born at New Echota in the Cherokee Nation East but brought up in New England by his stepmother's family after his father's assassination in 1839.[10] He attended Burr Seminary in Vermont and the Gunnery, a preparatory school in Connecticut. After teaching school in Vermont until 1853, he moved to Fayetteville, Arkansas, to study law. By 1859 he was a practicing lawyer and also part owner and editor of the Fayetteville *Arkansian*. When Arkansas left the Union in 1861 Boudinot joined his uncle Stand Watie's Cherokee Confederate forces and rose to the rank of lieutenant colonel. He soon gave up the commission, however, to serve as the Cherokee delegate in the Confederate Congress in Richmond. After the war he headed the southern Cherokee delegation in Washington and tried without success to have the Cherokee Nation divided into a northern and southern sector. Privately, he and his uncle operated a tobacco factory in the Cherokee Nation which was seized by federal agents in 1869 for failure to pay federal excise taxes. Boudinot maintained that the factory was exempted from taxation according to a treaty signed with the Cherokees in 1866 and the dispute ended up in the Supreme Court where the seizure was affirmed in the Cherokee Tobacco case of 1871, an important decision that initiated a series of legal measures extending federal jurisdiction over Indian domestic affairs.[11] During the 1870s and 1880s Boudinot was busy lobbying in Washington for the incorporation of Indian Territory as an official territory of the United States. He also turned to professional lecturing at this time, speaking widely on various Indian subjects such as "The Manners, Customs, Traditions, and Present Condition of the Civilized Indians in the Indian Territory," as well as advocating the formation of a "Territory of Oklahoma" in Indian Territory, the private allotment of Indian lands, and the granting of citizenship to all Indians. "I would hail the sectionizing and division of the lands in severalty," he wrote in a promotional pamphlet published in 1874, "the sale of surplus lands to actual white settlers, and the merging of *Indian* citizenship into *American* citizenship, as the greatest blessings, for my race."[12] His radical views brought him into direct conflict with William Potter Ross, editor of the *Cherokee Advocate* and John Ross's successor as principal chief, and soon made him just as unpopular among the conservative majority of the Cherokees as his father had been.[13] He started his own newspaper, the Muskogee *Indian Progress*, in 1875 and, when the Creeks forced him to close it down because they disagreed with his political views, continued to publish it in Vinita until the spring of 1876. Boudinot also wrote a letter to the editor of the *Chicago Times* in 1879 asserting that millions of acres in Indian Territory had been ceded to the government and were thus open to homestead laws, a false rumor that helped to get the boomer movement started and certainly did not improve his reputation among Indians. In 1885 Boudinot, who had long been a supporter of the Democratic Party, came very close to being nominated commissioner of Indian affairs. When his aspirations to the post were dashed by the new Cleveland administration he abandoned his highly controversial political career and returned to Arkansas to practice law for the remainder of his days.

Indian policy after the Civil War changed more in detail and matters of administration than it did in principle. It can be roughly characterized as the juridic-legislative enforcement of earlier assimilationist policies upon a conquered peoples whose vestiges of sovereignty were now being rapidly curtailed by a powerful nation that had completely engulfed them within its boundaries. In the decades just before and immediately after the Civil War, Americans swarmed to every "unoccupied" corner of the nation, and the appropriation of "surplus" Indian lands was, as always, the essential purpose of legal transactions between the original inhabitants and an increasingly centralized administration. The Plains Indians, who stood directly in the way of western expansion, mounted a desperate armed defense against white encroachments in a series of "Indian Wars" lasting from the 1840s to the 1880s. Once "pacified," they were concentrated on a number of geographically segregated reservations which could, as the policy intended, be further whittled down in size if the inhabitants learned how to sustain themselves as farmers and ranchers on individually owned parcels of land. It was expected that they would soon give up all vestiges of their former ways of life and eventually become self-reliant American citizens. The magic formula for such wholesale transformation was not new: European-style agriculture and housing, private property, and education.[14]

The secularization of Indian policy was a gradual process. Beginning with Grant's "Peace Policy" in 1869, Protestant and Roman Catholic missionaries were regularly appointed as reservation agents and superintendents in an effort to curb corruption in the Indian service. Active laymen also dominated the Board of Indian Commissioners, which was established by Grant in the same year to exercise joint control with the secretary of the interior over the BIA and to supervise the distribution of congressional funds. According to Parker, however, "religious bigotry, intolerance and jealousies by the various Christian bodies at home and between the agents sent out" ultimately thwarted this plan.[15] In contrast to the short-lived Peace Policy, which was eventually abandoned after Grant's presidency terminated in 1877, the Board of Commissioners continued to function in its advisory capacity until 1933.[16] Missionaries also maintained their former influence as instructors in numerous sectarian contract schools, which were started in 1869 and continued to operate until the government closed them at the end of the century, after positions in the Indian school service had been brought under civil service protection.[17]

Nevertheless, by the 1870s the U.S. government began to assume more and more direct responsibility over Indian affairs. Federal authority was cemented with the passage of the Indian Appropriation Act of 1871 (16 U.S. Stat. 544, 566), which stipulated that henceforth no Indian group would be "acknowledged or recognized as an independent nation, tribe or power with whom the United States may contract by treaty." All subsequent "agreements" could practically be concluded by Congress without the consent of Indians. Besides eroding Indian sovereignty and land holdings with a series of congressional acts and Supreme Court decisions during the last quarter of the nineteenth century, the federal government also tightened its control over Indian education.[18] Starting in the 1870s, it began to appropriate increasing sums for this specific purpose and to sponsor a growing number of nonsectarian "government" schools. Initially the Indian service favored the manual labor boarding school (or training school) model because it removed children from the supposedly "negative" influence of their native environment. An early institution of this type was Hampton Institute in Virginia, a special school for African American freedmen, which also opened its doors to Indian students in 1878.[19] The first, and most famous, manual labor boarding school exclusively for Indians was Carlisle Indian Industrial School, founded in Pennsylvania in 1876 by Richard Henry Pratt, whose oft-cited slogan "Kill the Indian and save the man!" epitomized the educational philosophy of the era. It was followed in rapid succession by the Forest Grove School in Oregon (1880), Chilocco School in Indian Territory (1884), Genoa Industrial School for Indian Youth in Nebraska (1884), and Haskell Institute in Kansas (1884). The other common type of federally funded institution was the reservation day school, which became more popular at the turn of the century as administrators eventually came to the conclusion that Indian students could also have a "positive" influence in their communities. By the end of the century the federal government was spending about $2.7 million (in contrast to $20,000 in 1877) for education and operating approximately 290 boarding and reservation day schools with an average enrollment of some 20,000 Indian students.[20] Finally, during the 1890s, there was also a gradual shift toward subsidizing Indian children in local public schools.

The curriculum in government Indian schools, which was standardized after 1898, included the basic academic courses taught at white schools along with religious and vocational training. English as the sole language of instruction was strictly enforced by the administration, even in the sectarian contract schools. Boys learned "practical" skills primarily related to agricultural activities, such as carpentry, blacksmithing, masonry, wheelwrighting, or harness making, while girls were taught sewing, cooking, laundering, and other "domestic sciences." Basically, then, these institutions still closely reflected the educational philosophy of seventeenth- and eighteenth-century mission schools, with the notable exception that preparing Indian missionaries for the field was no longer of primary concern.

An important change, however, which was to affect the development of Indian literature, was the dramatic increase in the number of Indian students, especially after the government authorized the commissioner to enforce school attendance of Indian children in 1891 (26 U.S. Stat. 1014). By the 1920s approximately 90 percent of Indian children were already enrolled in either government or public schools. Since most of these children were being recruited from the recently conquered tribes of the West, educated Plains Indians eventually began to challenge the hegemony of mission-trained authors from the East in American Indian literature after the turn of the century. A steady growth, as well, in the number of female students attending these new schools resulted in the increasing prominence of Indian women in the letters.[21]

Even though the percentage of Indian children in school was still relatively small (under 10 percent) during the last quarter of the nineteenth century and standards in government-sponsored institutions were generally geared toward lower-class menial labor, a few exceptionally talented individuals still managed to obtain a higher education and enter more prestigious professional fields such as medicine, law, or business. By the turn of the century there emerged a small but highly influential urban Indian middle class, or national proto-elite, which began to formulate and propagate a distinctly pan-Indian consciousness. Largely through the efforts of a prominent white sociologist and reformer, Fayette A. McKenzie, six of these allotment-era prototypes of the "successful" Indian got together in Columbus, Ohio, on April 3–4, 1911, and founded the American Indian Association. The preamble to their statement of purpose on the occasion read: "The Temporary Executive Committee of the American Indian Association declares that the time has come when the American Indian race should contribute, in a more united way, its influence and exertion with the rest of the citizens of the United States in all lines of progress and reform, for the welfare of the Indian race in particular, and humanity in general." This core group quickly enlarged its membership and, in cooperation with leading white reformers, called together a "National Conference" in Columbus on October 12–17 of that same year to hear talks about and participate in discussions on various aspects of the "Indian problem." During a separate business session attended by Indians only, the name of the organization was permanently changed to Society of American Indians (SAI). Membership was to consist of United States Indians (actives), Indians from other parts of the Americas (Indian associates), and interested persons of "non-Indian blood" (associates). Only the first two categories entailed the right to hold office and to vote. In January of 1913, the SAI began to publish its own periodical, the *Quarterly Journal* (1913–15), later renamed the *American Indian Magazine* (1915–20).[22]

The political platform of the SAI essentially adhered to earlier and contemporary reformist policies. The Reverend Sherman Coolidge, Arapaho minister and one of the founders of the SAI, outlined the organization's original seven-point statement of objectives in a later issue of the *Quarterly Journal*:

First. To promote and co-operate with all efforts looking to the advancement of the Indian in enlightenment which leave him free as a man to develop according to the natural laws of social evolution.

Second. To provide through our open conferences the means for a free discussion on all subjects bearing on the welfare of the race.

Third. To present in a just light the true history of the race, to preserve its records and emulate its distinguishing virtues.

Fourth. To promote citizenship and to obtain the rights thereof.

Fifth. To establish a legal department to investigate Indian problems and to suggest and to obtain remedies.

Sixth. To exercise the right to oppose any movement that may be detrimental to the race.

Seventh. To direct its energies exclusively to general principles and universal interests, and not allow itself to be used for any personal or private interest.[23]

Its active members hoped to have a direct say in the formulation of future Indian policy by means of promotional-educational campaigns and lobbyist activities in Washington, D.C., where they decided to set up their headquarters. In the long run, however, the SAI lacked the financial means, political clout, and community roots to fulfill its role as a national Indian organization. Another factor that undoubtedly contributed to its gradual disintegration in the early 1920s was heated internal squabbling over issues such as the abolition of the BIA or prohibiting the use of peyote in particular Indian ceremonies. Nevertheless, the SAI had set an example, and Indian political organizations became a permanent feature in Indian–white relations thereafter.

Most of the SAI's active members were well educated and, not surprisingly, included several well-known Indian authors of the day. In fact, the sheer number of publications that began to appear after the turn of the century indicates that American Indian literature was experiencing an unprecedented boom. This was largely due to the rise of an erudite urban Indian intellectual elite and, in addition, to a number of interrelated sociocultural trends in the United States, which regenerated public interest in books by and about Indians. One of these was the general resurgence of benevolent concern with the "Indian problem" in 1879–80, when a group of Poncas, who had been removed to Indian Territory, made a tragic attempt to return to their homelands and their widely publicized plight became a *cause célèbre* around which reformist zeal could rally once again. These Friends of the Indian, as they are frequently referred to, joined forces in various lobbyist organizations (Women's National Indian Association, 1879; Indian Rights Association, 1882; Lake Mohonk Conference of the Friends of the

Indian, 1883) to push through the policies that culminated in the passage of the General Allotment Act (Dawes Act) in 1887. Even though reformist zeal began to wane after the 1890s, its public relations activities — notably publications like Helen Hunt Jackson's *Century of Dishonor* (1881) and *Ramona* (1884) — had aroused a broader and more permanent humanitarian concern with Indian affairs. In the realm of popular literature, the local-color movement (1865–90) with its focus on regional settings and local customs formed an additional arena for the exploration of Indian topics. The contemporary back-to-nature movement and its major offshoot, the Boy Scouts of America (1910), also promoted and reflected a marked interest in the woodsmanship of the unchallenged master of the American wilds.[24] In scholarship, the beginning of the "golden age" of American "salvage" anthropology after the establishment of the Bureau of American Ethnology in 1879 had assiduous scholars, who continued to believe Indian ways were on the brink of extinction, scouring reservations for venerable informants who could provide them with data about "disappearing" ways of life. Finally, not to be discounted was the rise of the mass publishing industry during the second half of the nineteenth century, especially the emergence of national magazines that could reach millions of readers such as *Harper's* and *Sunset*, which boosted the market for Indian literature as well. Indian writers now even had access to a variety of specialized literary forums, such as the SAI's *Quarterly Journal*; several periodicals published by manual labor boarding schools like Hampton's *Southern Workman*, Haskell's *Indian Leader*, Carlisle's *Red Man*, Chilocco's *Indian School Journal*, and Chemewa's *Chemewa American*; a rapidly growing number of tribal newspapers, especially in Indian Territory (Oklahoma); and other agency-based publications.[25] Nevertheless, although these developments certainly stimulated Indian literary production, the continued public interest in the Indian as a relic of the past did not motivate Indian authors to develop new themes or to relate traditional Indian ways of life to modern American society. This is in turn reflected in the works of many Indian authors of the allotment era who, after all, wrote primarily (though not entirely) for a non-Indian audience.

The impressive body of literature produced by American Indians between the end of the Civil War and the 1930s is both regionalist (tribal) and nationalist (pan-Indian) in character, with, of course, individual authors moving freely between these two fluid categories. Regionalist authors like Richard Calamit Adams (Delaware, 1864–1921), Andrew J. Blackbird (Ottawa, 1810?–1900), Peter Dooyentate Clarke (Wyandot, n.d.), Elias Johnson

(Tuscarora, n.d.), and Joseph Nicolar (Penobscot, 1827–94) wrote important autohistories of their respective tribes.[26] Prominent among the regionalist writers are Sarah Winnemucca Hopkins (Paiute, 1845?–91); S. Alice Callahan (Creek, 1868–94), Simon Pokagon (Potawatomi, 1830–99), and Alexander Lawrence Posey (Creek, 1873–1908). Sarah Winnemucca wrote a moving narrative autobiography in 1883 titled *Life among the Paiutes,* in which she described her adventures as interpreter and scout in Nevada at the beginning of the reservation period from what might be styled a Victorian feminist perspective. She was extremely critical of the role played by missionaries in the execution of Grant's Peace Policy and shared Ely Parker's sentiments about returning the administration of Indian affairs to the army. It is said that her book, which also advocates the allotment of lands to Indians, helped to effect the passage of the General Allotment Act.[27] Alice Callahan published *Wynema, a Child of the Forest* in 1891, a romance about the education of a young Creek girl who falls in love with the brother of her white Methodist schoolmistress and eventually becomes a teacher herself. It also has interesting details of Creek life in Indian Territory and some critical passages on allotment policies, the massacre at Wounded Knee in 1890, and the problem of intemperance.[28] Simon Pokagon is credited as the author of *Queen of the Woods,* a semiautobiographical Victorian temperance novel incorporating elements from Algonquian oral traditions that was published shortly after his death in 1899. He also authored a series of articles on Potawatomi history and produced a number of curious white birchbark booklets for the 1893 World's Fair in Chicago which have become sought-after collector's items.[29] Alexander Posey was an accomplished journalist, poet, and humorist whose "Fus Fixico Letters" — short dialogues in vernacular Creek-English between a standard set of "full-blood" characters who quip about all sorts of contemporary Indian Territory issues — enjoyed national and international recognition for their unique language and biting political satire. In contrast to most of his contemporaries, Posey wrote primarily for local newspapers and an appreciative Indian audience. Together with John Rollin Ridge, he is also one of the first Indian authors effectively to combine Indian oral traditions and Western literary conventions in his romantic poetry.[30] Finally, Indian regionalism can be said to have reached a high point with the advent of professional Indian anthropologists like Francis La Flesche (Omaha, 1860?–1932), John Napoleon Brinton Hewitt (Tuscarora, 1859–1937), William Jones (Sac-Fox, 1871–1909), and Arthur Caswell Parker (Seneca, 1881–1955), who penetrated yet another hitherto exclusive all-white American academic institution with their extensive and still invaluable autoethnographic contributions.[31]

Foremost among the nationalist writers, whose works deal with more universal pan-Indian issues, are Gertrude Simmons Bonnin (Yankton Sioux, 1876–1938), Charles Alexander Eastman (Wahpeton Sioux, 1858–1939), John Milton Oskison (Cherokee, 1874–1947), Carlos Montezuma (Yavapai, 1867?–1923), and Arthur C. Parker. Although a Canadian Indian by birth, Emily Pauline Johnson (Mohawk, 1861–1913) should also be mentioned in connection with these authors, if only because most of her short stories were published in the United States. With the exception of Johnson, all of these writers were active members of the SAI and played key roles in the formulation of its pan-Indian policies. Charles Eastman (Ohiyesa), the most widely read of all early Indian authors, published nine books with the cooperation of his wife, Elaine Goodale Eastman. These include two autobiographies, *Indian Boyhood* (1902) and *From the Deep Woods to Civilization* (1916); a treatise on Indian spirituality, *The Soul of the Indian* (1911); and an analysis of contemporary Indian affairs, *The Indian To-day* (1915). He was also closely affiliated with American naturalists and wrote many stories and articles on Indian woodsmanship.[32] Gertrude Bonnin (Zitkala-Sa) produced a number of short stories and autobiographical sketches for major U.S. magazines between 1900 and 1901, which she published collectively as *American Indian Stories* in 1921, as well as a collection of traditional Sioux tales under the title *Old Indian Legends* in 1901. She was a highly critical observer of Indian–white relations, and her negative evaluation of her own boarding school experience contrasted markedly with the accounts by her male contemporaries.[33] John Oskison, the least known of the turn-of-the-century authors, was nevertheless a very successful writer in his time who published numerous short stories in national magazines, three novels set in Indian Territory, a fictive biography of Sam Houston, and a history of Tecumseh. He also wrote several articles on Indian policy for the SAI's *Quarterly Journal* and was a staff writer and associate editor for *Collier's Weekly*.[34] Emily Johnson (Tekahionwake) was a fairly successful stage performer and played a major role in the birth of national Canadian literature. Other than her two books of poetry, *The White Wampum* (1895) and *Canadian Born* (1903), and a collection of Squamish legends titled *Legends of Vancouver* (1911), she wrote many short stories for *Boy's World* and *Mother's Magazine*, both based in Elgin, Illinois. In 1913 these were collected in two volumes, *The Shagganappi* and *The Moccasin Maker*.[35]

Carlos Montezuma, physician and publisher of a newsletter, and Arthur Parker, anthropologist and editor of the SAI journal, were the two most brilliant Indian polemicists in the allotment era. Montezuma wanted the immediate abolition of the BIA and the reservation system, while Parker took a more moderate stand advocating gradual adaptation. Their contrary views on future Indian policies frequently clashed openly in the pages of the *Quarterly Journal* and the columns of *Wassaja*.[36]

An especially noteworthy development during this productive era in the history of Indian literature is the blossoming of the short story from the turn of the century until the 1920s. Most of the short fiction published by Indians adhered to the more limited productions of the local-color movement — sentimental stories with a retrospective "informant" focus on ethnographic detail. Nevertheless, a few of the pieces written by Gertrude Bonnin, Charles Eastman, Emily Johnson, and John Oskison, who were the most accomplished in this genre, effectively portray the psychological trauma of deculturation in a colonial situation.[37]

It was precisely this generation of professional Indian writers who, once they were confronted with the false promises of the assimilationist reform movement, began to experience a collective moment of crisis. Symbolically, the public campaign against allotment policies began to crystallize during the early 1920s, when New Mexico threatened to encroach upon the property rights of the Rio Grande Pueblos. These ancient native communities of the American Southwest with their very visible ties to the past and harmonious relationship to the environment appealed to the imagination of a warshocked "lost generation," many of whom had sought spiritual convalescence in this remote area of the nation. One of these, John Collier, organized the American Indian Defence Association in 1923 in order to reverse federal Indian policies. Several of the former SAI activists joined the Committee of One Hundred, an advisory board created by the secretary of the interior that same year in response to growing criticism of the BIA and its allotment program. The committee served as a catalyst for the famous "Meriam Report" prepared by the Brookings Institution in 1926–28, a critical assessment of the contemporary situation on reservations, which in turn prepared the way for "Indian New Deal" policies carried out under the commissionership of John Collier between 1933 and 1945.[38] Woodrow Wilson's formula of "self-determination" for satellite nations and the urban-sociological theorem of "cultural pluralism," both of which gradually edged out the paternalistic "melting pot" dogma of the previous century, now began to shape Indian–white relations. With the exception of a temporary relapse during the 1950s popularly referred to as "termination," and occasional interventions by diehard assimilationist congressmen, these two principles have become the doctrinal pillars of federal Indian policy.[39]

When the Indian Citizenship Act (43 U.S. Stat. 253) was passed in 1924 and all "Indians" were juridically transformed into "Americans" whether they wanted to be or not, Indian "progressives" began to reconsider their ethnic identities. It was certainly not just a matter of caprice when Carlos Montezuma, the "fiery Apache" (*sic*) who had been the foremost Indian advocate of Pratt's radical assimilationist philosophy, chose to spend his remaining days in a brush shelter among the Fort McDowell Yavapais.[40] Nor is there any reason to doubt Luther Standing Bear (Teton Sioux, 1868–1938), one of the first Indians to attend Carlisle and author of four popular books, when he concluded toward the end of his life that "if today I had a young mind to direct, to start on the journey of life, and I was faced with the duty of choosing between the natural way of my forefathers and that of the white man's present civilization, I would, for its welfare, unhesitatingly set that child's feet in the path of my forefathers. I would raise him to be an Indian."[41] Perhaps the most significant expression of autointrospective reflection on Indian–white relations, and yet another turning point in the history of American Indian literature, was the advent of the sophisticated Indian culture-conflict novel of the 1920s and 1930s. In 1927 Mourning Dove (Coleville, 1888–1936) published *Cogewa, the Half-Blood*, which was followed by John Joseph Mathews's (Osage, 1894–1979) *Sundown* in 1934 and D'Arcy McNickle's (Cree-Flathead, 1904–77) *The Surrounded* in 1936. These novels take up and expand on the mixed-blood theme introduced earlier by Bonnin and Johnson. Each one revolves around a transcultural protagonist's quest for a positive identity in a hostile contact environment.[42] It is here, expressed in the creative language of these early Indian novelists and short-story writers, that the moment of crisis experienced by each of their literary forerunners finally became part of the collective American cultural experience. The writings produced by Indians between the 1850s and 1930s, which include several volumes of poetry, short stories, and novels, thus form the transition between the salvationist and modern periods in American Indian literature.

The Protestant missions in antebellum America converted only a fraction of the Indian population, which has led some historians to romanticize them as "a noble experiment that failed."[43] Their dismal record can be attributed to Indian resistance to assimilation on the one hand and segregationist colonial policies on the other, both of which made the integration of christianized Indians on either side of the cultural frontier difficult. But the sheer number of converts says nothing whatsoever about the significance of Christian Indians in the history of Indian–white relations. An obsession with the "traditional" can easily lead to the (de)classification of converted Indians as assimilationists who supposedly forfeited a kind of existence that many still regard (and guard) in terms of the romantic noble savage tradition, as the fulfillment of Western civilization's yearning for harmony between man and nature. The life histories of the Indian missionary-writers outlined in this book should make it clear that the complex subject of Praying Indians requires a much more differentiated point of view, one that takes into full account the nature of the contact environment in which these individuals lived and which does not make unwarranted comparisons with precontact conditions. Daily existence in a colonial situation, in which creative adaptability was as essential for the survival of threatened Indian communities as manifestations of resistance, had very little in common with primitivist fancies or the theoretical constructs of "salvage" ethnology.

Conversion to Christianity among eastern Indians generally occurred after native communities were overwhelmed by the colonial situation. Significantly, the missionary-writers emerged at a time when the European colonists were also reacting to the stress of imperial contentions in the New World, which eventually sparked a widespread evangelical movement in the 1730s that went on intermittently until the Civil War. The extent to which the missionary-writers identified with the two Great Awakenings is made apparent by the fact that each was ordained as a minister of the Gospel by one of the New Light Protestant sects. Personal prestige and economic improvement were certainly important reasons for their voluntary conversion, but there can be little doubt that they were also motivated by the firm conviction that all Indians could benefit from missionary programs. The question that remains to be asked is whether their conversion to Christianity entailed the total negation of Indian cultural values or served them as a point of departure for an effective survival strategy based on selective adaptation. As individuals, each one of the missionary-writers responded to the contact environment in a different fashion. In terms of the synecdochic sense of self, however, they all came to the same conclusion that Indians needed to find ways in which to adapt to the colonial situation and consequently devoted all of their energy toward this goal. As missionaries and writers, they developed a relatively homogeneous survival strategy, an Indian theology of liberation, so to speak, which has retained its political relevance to the present.

In contrast to many contemporary authors and activists of Indian descent, the missionary-writers of the antebellum era were balanced bilinguals who lived and worked within the Indian community. They performed the vital function of cultural mediators for tribal societies varying in size from a few hundred to several thousand individuals. In addition, they were frequently entrusted with other responsibilities normally assigned to sachems, such as officiating at ceremonial gatherings, providing for the needy, settling internal disputes, and carrying on external tribal affairs. Some of the leaders who promoted Christianity among Indians, such as Joseph Brant and John Ross, had already been members of the ruling elite prior to their conversion, while others who were not so well connnected, like Samson Occom and Peter Jones, ascended to leadership positions in their communities after they had converted.

But the careers of the missionary-writers also show that Christian Indians were not just a by-product of the Great Awakening. In the first place, some of the standard practices promoted by the missionary societies, such as European-style farming, were not totally unfamiliar to converts whose ancestors had acquainted the colonists with a long list of indigenous agricultural products. The ethical standards put forward by Protestant missionaries like honesty, generosity, chastity, and cleanliness were not, despite the missionaries' presumptions, new to tribal peoples long accustomed to similar codes of social behavior. Indeed, the climax of the evangelist conversion, the neophyte's moment of "rebirth" with its emphasis on visionary revelation and emotional release, had many counterparts in Indian cultures. Occom's and Copway's preoccupation with dreams and activities as healers, for instance, are indicative of the kinds of cultural crossovers that were probably going on. In their writings, Occom, Aupaumut, Apess, Boudinot, and Copway often pointed out that there were parallels between Indian religions and Christian teachings, a reminder that also functioned to legitimize the very traditions their Protestant mentors wanted them to cast off. Here, perhaps, is the first "hidden" trace of the thread that ties postcontact Indian intellectual history to precontact Indian spirituality, which became more visible in Charles Eastman's *Soul of the Indian* (1911) and finally took shape in Vine Deloria's *God Is Red* (1973).[44]

The missionary-writers, and by inference other Christian Indians as well, were quick to recognize the disjunctions between the preachings and practices of Christianity among the colonists. Occom frequently expressed his doubts in his correspondence and other unpublished writings, and Apess, Boudinot, and Copway were openly critical of dominant society in their published works. All of them came into open conflict with their white "superiors" over matters of professional competence and, with the possible exception of Jones, were denied equal opportunity by the missionary societies they worked for. Discrimination on the basis of race, more than anything else, triggered the moments of crisis in their lives. It was precisely this recognition of the schizophrenic nature of colonialist Indian policy, rather than American expansionary forces alone, that probably induced each one of them (except Apess) finally to seek — either in practice or in writing — the fulfillment of their hybrid Christian-Indian ideals "beyond the pale" of Anglo-Saxon civilization. Those who originated from remnant Coastal Algonquian groups, like Occom, Johnson, and Aupaumut, sought to establish their semiautonomous Christian Indian villages some place far removed from the influence of frontier whites. Those who were born into larger Indian communities, like Boudinot, Ridge, and Copway, envisioned the creation of an independent Indian nation or state in the West that might one day join the American federation. John Ross seriously considered mass emigration to Mexico to preserve the sovereignty of the Cherokee Nation, and Peter Jones counseled his people to move westward in the hope of establishing a permanent homeland there for the Ojibwas of Upper Canada. The missionary-authors' promotion of voluntary removal can thus only be properly understood as integral with their attempts to maintain a way of life they obviously considered to be more desirable than anything American society was prepared to offer at the time. The notion of a separate Indian state or nation continues to draw the attention of modern-day Indian intellectuals.[45]

The missionary-writers' evangelical concern for the welfare of Indian souls in the afterlife did not blind them to the more worldly needs of their people. They were all more or less exponents of a theology of liberation in which Christian and republican principles were joined in a universal indictment of colonial oppression and exploitation. The political goals they wrote about and tried to realize — permanent land base, improved education, legal enfranchisement, control over tribal resources, autonomy in internal affairs — were not that far removed from those agitated for by Indians since the rise of the "Red Power" movement during the 1960s. Their activities ranged from a full-fledged insurrection in the case of Apess to more moderate tactics like petitioning, lobbyism, litigation, and addressing the public in print or on the stage.

An outstanding characteristic of the missionary-writers is the relative ease with which they moved back and forth across the "great divide" between orality and literacy. Their knowledge of English and mastery of the written word were frequently employed by Indian communities to defend themselves against cultural and political incursion, particularly in matters of "interpreting" the White Man's law. Each one was as accomplished at public speaking as they were at writing, and this usually in both languages. It is not surprising, therefore, that a substantial part of literature produced by them is made up of transcribed versions of their sermons and speeches. This marked penchant for what might be called "orature" was also passed on to succeeding generations of Indian writers.

Like many of the mythical voyagers in North American Indian oral traditions, the missionary-writers, all of whom were travelers across great distances in both a physical and philosophical sense, also ventured into unfamiliar terrain where, after having surmounted various obstacles, they attained a new view of the world. Most returned to their native communities to share their visions and to offer their invaluable new skills as cultural brokers in an age of great changes. Only a few ever got "lost" permanently along the way. Understanding this side of the conversion experience also means that we need to reconsider the role of Christianity among the remnant northeastern Indian communities who, in contrast to their more numerous Iroquoian neighbors, have virtually remained "invisible" to the white public eye until very recently. The Baptist-Methodist tradition begun by "Blind Joe" Amos and William Apess among the Mashpees continues to be a driving force behind their unabated efforts to gain federal recognition as a tribe; the Mohegan Church has functioned as that group's center for community life ever since it was founded as a Congregationalist meeting-house in 1831; the members of the Brothertown Nation in Wisconsin identify closely with their New England Christian Indian roots. Examples such as these, in which Christianity has functioned as a basis for the maintenance of intragroup coherence as well as the formation of intergroup religious sodalities, imply that there has been a more subtle (compared to the Southwest) but still visible form of compartmentalization in the Northeast. The legacy of the missionary-writers has been kept alive in many ways.

Notes

CHAPTER ONE

1. Georges Balandier introduced the term "situation coloniale" in his *Sociologie actuelle de l'Afrique noire: dynamique des changements sociaux en Afrique centrale* (Paris: Presses universitaires de la France, 1955), 3–36. See also George W. Stocking, Jr., ed., *Colonial Situations: Essays on the Conceptualization of Ethnographic Knowledge* (Madison: University of Wisconsin Press, 1991), 3–8.

2. See Ronald J. Horvath, "A Definition of Colonialism," *Current Anthropology* 13, no. 1 (February 1972): 45–51.

3. See Everett Hagen, *On the Theory of Social Change* (Homewood, IL: Dorsey Press, 1967), 471.

4. Horvath, "Definition," 47.

5. See Palmer Patterson, "The Colonial Parallel: A View of Indian History," *Ethnohistory* 18, no. 1 (Winter 1971): 1–17; and Darcy Ribeiro, "The Culture-Historical Configuration of the American Peoples," *Current Anthropology* 11, nos. 4–5 (October/December 1970): 403–434.

6. See, for instance, Gary Anders, "The Internal Colonization of Cherokee Native Americans," *Development and Change* 10, no. 1 (January 1979): 41–55; Ward Churchill and Winona La Duke, "Native North America," in M. Annette Jaimes, ed., *The State of Native America: Genocide, Colonization, and Resistance* (Boston: South End Press, 1992), 241–266; Cardell K. Jackobson, "Internal Colonialism and Native Americans: Indian Labor in the United States from 1871 to World War II," *Social Science Quarterly* 65 (1984): 158–171; Robert K. Thomas, "Colonialism: Classic and Internal," *New University Thought* 4, no. 4 (Winter 1966/67): 39–43. On the evolution of the term, see Robert J. Hind, "The Internal Colonial Concept," *Comparative Studies in Societies and History* 26, no. 3 (July 1984): 543–568.

7. Joseph Jorgensen, "A Century of Political Economic Effects on American Indian Society," *Journal of Ethnic Studies* 6, no. 3 (1978): 1–82. See also idem, "Indians and the Metropolis," in Jack O. Wardell and O. Michael Watson, eds., *The American Indian in Urban Society* (Boston: Little, Brown, 1971), 67–113.

8. See Kwame Nkrumah, *Neo-colonialism: The Last Stage of Imperialism*, 2nd ed. (New York: International Publishers, 1966), ix.

9. See Gordon Brotherston, *Book of the Fourth World: Reading the Native Americans through Their Literature* (New York: Cambridge University Press, 1992), 1–6; George Manuel and Michael Posluns, *The Fourth World: An Indian Reality*

(New York: Free Press, 1974); and Roxanne Dunbar Ortiz, "The Fourth World and Indigenism: Politics of Isolation and Alternatives," *Journal of Ethnic Studies* 12, no. 1 (Spring 1984): 79–105.

10. Hind, "Internal Colonial Concept," 565.

11. See Bill Ashcroft, Gareth Griffiths, and Helen Tiffin, *The Empire Writes Back: Theory and Practice in Post-colonial Literatures* (London/New York: Routledge, 1989), 38.

12. Clifford Geertz, *The Interpretation of Culture* (New York: Basic Books, 1973), 89.

13. Ngugi wa Thiong'o, *Decolonizing the Mind: The Politics of Language in African Literature* (London: Currey & Heinemann, 1989), 3.

14. Jorgensen, "A Century of Political Economic Effects," 9.

15. See James Clifford, "Introduction: Partial Truths," in James Clifford and George E. Marcus, eds., *Writing Culture: The Poetics and Politics of Ethnography* (Berkeley: University of California Press, 1986), 1–26; and Milton Singer, "A Survey of Culture and Personality Theory and Research," in Bert Kaplan, ed., *Studying Personality Cross-Culturally* (New York: Harper & Row, 1961), 9–90. For critical views, see Mina D. Caulfield, "Culture and Imperialism: Proposing a New Dialectic," in Dell Hymes, ed., *Reinventing Anthropology* (New York: Random House, 1969), 183–188; and Jorgensen, "Indians and the Metropolis," 67–69.

16. Robert Redfield, Ralph Linton, and Melville J. Herskovitz, "Memorandum for the Study of Acculturation," *American Anthropologist* 38, no. 1 (January/March 1936): 149–152; Fernando Ortiz, *Contrapunteo Cubano del Tobacco y el Azúcar* (1945; rpt., Barcelona: Editorial Ariel, 1973), 129–135.

17. See Raymond Teske, Jr., and Bardin H. Nelson, "Acculturation and Assimilation: A Classification," *American Ethnologist* 1, no. 2 (May 1974): 351–367.

18. Frantz Fanon, *The Wretched of the Earth*, trans. Constance Farrington, 19th ed. (New York: Grove Press, 1978), 24.

19. See H. G. Barnett, L. Broom, B. J. Siegel, E. Z. Vogt, and J. B. Watson, "Acculturation: An Explanatory Formulation," in D. E. Walker, ed., *The Emergent Native Americans* (Boston: Brown, 1972), 19–43.

20. See William L. Leap, "American Indian Languages," in Charles A. Ferguson and Shirley B. Heath, eds., *Language in the USA* (Cambridge/London/New York: Cambridge University Press, 1981), 116–144.

21. See Emanuel J. Drechsel, "'Ha, Now Me Stomany That!' A Summary of Pidginization and Creolization of North American Indian Languages," *Linguistics* 173 (May 23, 1976): 63–81; Garrick Mallery, *Sign Language among North American Indians* (Paris: Mouton, 1972); and Allan R. Taylor, "Indian Lingua Francas," in Ferguson and Heath, *Language in the USA*, 175–195.

22. See Dell Hymes, "Linguistic Problems in Defining the Concept of Tribe," in J. Helm, ed., *Essays on the Problem of Tribe: Proceedings of the American Ethnological Society, 1968* (Seattle: University of Washington Press, 1968), 23–48.

23. Ngugi, *Decolonizing the Mind*, 28.

24. Albert Memmi, *The Colonizer and the Colonized*, trans. Howard Greenfield (London: Earthscan Publications, 1990), 173.

25. Joshua Fishman, *Language and Ethnicity in Minority Sociolinguistic Perspective* (Clevedon/Philadelphia: Multilingual Matters, 1989), 212.

26. See Stephen J. Greenblatt, "Learning to Curse: Aspects of Linguistic Colonialism in the Sixteenth Century," in Fredi Chiappelli, ed., *First Images of America: The Impact of the New World on the Old*, 2 vols. (Berkeley: University of California Press, 1976), 2:561–580; Paul Goetsch, "Linguistic Colonialism and Primitivism: The Discovery of Native Languages and Oral Traditions in Eighteenth-Century Travel Books and Novels," *Anglia* 106, nos. 3–4 (1988): 338–359; and James Sledd, "Bi-dialectalism: The Linguistics of White Supremacy," in Lenard F. Dean, Walker Gibson, and Kenneth G. Wilson, eds., *The Play of Language* (New York: Oxford University Press, 1971), 19–25.

27. Paulo Freire, *Pedagogy of the Oppressed*, trans. Myra B. Ramos (New York: Seabury Press, 1970), 60–61.

28. See Nicholas P. Canny, "The Ideology of English Colonization," *William and Mary Quarterly* 30, no. 4 (October 1973): 575–598.

29. See Jack D. Forbes, "Colonialism and American Education," in Joshua Reichert and Miguel Trujillo, eds., *Perspectives on Contemporary Native American & Chicano Educational Thought* (Davis, CA: D.Q.U. Press, 1973–74), 17–38; and Jorge Noriega, "American Indian Education in the United States: Indoctrination for Subordination to Colonialism," in Jaimes, *State of Native America*, 371–402.

30. U.S. Congress, Senate, Special Subcommittee on Indian Education, *Indian Education: A National Tragedy — a National Challenge* (Washington, DC: Government Printing Office, 1969).

31. Leap, "American Indian Languages," 116.

32. Uriel Weinreich, *Languages in Contact*, 5th ed. (The Hague: Mouton, 1962), 99–102.

33. See Frances Svensson, "Language as Ideology: The American Indian Case," *American Indian Culture and Research Journal* 1, no. 3 (1975): 29–35.

34. Ashcroft, Griffiths, and Tiffin, *The Empire Writes Back*, 38.

35. Fishman, *Language and Ethnicity*, 181.

36. See Edward P. Dozier, "Two Examples of Linguistic Acculturation," *Language* 32 (1956): 146–157.

37. William L. Leap, *American Indian English* (Salt Lake City: University of Utah Press, 1993), 281–282; and idem, "Ethnics, Emics, and the New Ideology: The Identity Potential of Indian English," in Thomas K. Fitzgerald, ed., *Southern Anthropological Society Proceedings*, no. 8 (Athens: University of Georgia Press, 1974), 51–62. See also B. O. Flannigan, *American Indian English* (Ann Arbor: University of Michigan Press, 1986).

38. Dell Hymes, "The Religious Aspects of Language in Native American Humanities," in Bruce T. Grindal and Dennis M. Warren, eds., *Essays in Humanistic Anthropology: A Festschrift in Honor of David Bidney* (Washington, DC: University Press of America, 1979), 102–111.

39. Simon Ortiz, "Towards a National Indian Literature: Cultural Authenticity in Nationalism," *MELUS* 8, no. 2 (Summer 1981): 7–12.

40. For a contrary view, see the cryptanalytic approach in La Van Martineau,

The Rocks Begin to Speak (Las Vegas: KC Publications, 1973). See also the chapter on pictographs as autobiography in Hertha Dawn Wong, *Sending My Heart across the Years: Tradition and Innovation in Native American Autobiography* (New York: Oxford University Press, 1992), 57–87.

41. Walter J. Ong, *Orality and Literacy: The Technologizing of the Word* (London/New York: Methuen, 1982), 85, 179.

42. Ruth Finnegan, *Literacy and Orality: Studies in the Technology of Communication* (Oxford/New York: Basil Blackwell, 1988), 41–42.

43. See Robert A. Williams, Jr., *The American Indian in Western Legal Thought: The Discourses of Conquest* (New York/Oxford: Oxford University Press, 1990).

44. Tzvetan Todorov, *The Conquest of America: The Question of the Other*, trans. Richard Howard (New York: Harper & Row, 1984), 68, 251.

45. James Axtell, *The Invasion Within: The Contest of Cultures in Colonial North America* (New York/Oxford: Oxford University Press, 1985), 14.

46. Jack Goody, "Evolution and Communication: The Domestication of the Savage Mind," *British Journal of Sociology* 24, no. 1 (March 1973): 11.

47. See Dorothy V. Jones, *License for Empire: Colonialism by Treaty in Early America* (Chicago/London: University of Chicago Press, 1982).

48. Article II, section 2, or the so-called Treaty Clause; and Article I, section 8, or the so-called Commerce Clause. Indians are also mentioned in Article I, section 1, regarding the apportionment of taxes. See Nell Jessup Newton, "Federal Power over Indians: Its Sources, Scope, and Limitations," *University of Pennsylvania Law Review* 132, no. 2 (January 1984): 195–288. Seminal works in this field include Felix Cohen, *Handbook of Federal Indian Law* (1942; rpt., Albuquerque: University of New Mexico Press, 1972); and Charles F. Wilkinson, *American Indians, Time and the Law: Historical Rights at the Bar of the Supreme Court* (New Haven: Yale University Press, 1987).

49. Luther Standing Bear, *Land of the Spotted Eagle* (1934; rpt., Lincoln: University of Nebraska Press, 1978), 249.

50. See William Cronon, *Changes in the Land: Indians, Colonists, and the Ecology of New England* (New York: Hill & Wang, 1983), 65–66; and Yasuhide Kawashima, *Puritan Justice and the Indian: White Man's Law in Massachusetts, 1630–1763* (Middletown, CT: Wesleyan University Press, 1986), 43–45.

51. See Russel L. Barsh, "Behind Land Claims: Rationalizing Dispossession in Anglo-American Law," *Law & Anthropology* 1 (1986): 15–50; and Arrell M. Gibson, "Philosophical, Legal, and Social Rationales for Appropriating the Tribal Estate, 1607 to 1980," *American Indian Law Review* 12 (1984): 3–38.

52. See Sidney L. Harring, *Crow Dog's Case: American Indian Sovereignty, Tribal Law, and United States Law in the Nineteenth Century* (New York: Cambridge University Press, 1994), 282–292.

53. Francis Jennings, *The Invasion of America: Indians, Colonialism, and the Cant of Conquest* (New York: W. W. Norton, 1976), 128–145.

54. See Henry W. Bowden, *American Indians and Christian Missions: Studies in Cultural Conflict* (Chicago/London: University of Chicago Press, 1981); and Vine Deloria, Jr., *God Is Red* (New York: Delta Publishing, 1973), esp. 247–287.

55. See Hartley Burr Alexander, *The World's Rim: Great Mysteries of the North*

American Indians (Lincoln: University of Nebraska Press, 1967), 170–197; Ake Hultkrantz, *The Religions of the American Indians,* trans. Monica Seterwall (Berkeley: University of California Press, 1979), 9–139; and Ruth M. Underhill, *Red Man's Religion: Beliefs and Practices of the Indians North of Mexico* (Chicago: University of Chicago Press, 1965), 20–105.

56. See James Axtell, "The Power of Print in the Eastern Woodlands," *William and Mary Quarterly* 44, no. 2 (April 1987): 300–309; rpt. in idem, *After Columbus: Essays in the Ethnohistory of Colonial North America* (New York/Oxford: Oxford University Press, 1988), 86–99.

57. Axtell, *Invasion Within,* 178.

58. See Joseph Jorgensen, *The Sun Dance: Power for the Powerless* (Chicago: University of Chicago Press, 1972).

59. See Gregory E. Dowd, *A Spiritual Resistance: The North American Indian Struggle for Unity, 1745–1815* (Baltimore/London: Johns Hopkins University Press, 1992).

60. William James, *The Varieties of Religious Experience,* in *The Works of William James* (Cambridge/London: Harvard University Press, 1985), 15:162. James writes: "Let us hereafter, in speaking of the hot place in man's consciousness, the group of ideas to which he devotes himself, and from which he works, call it the habitual centre of his personal energy. It makes a great difference to a man whether one set of his ideas, or another, be the centre of his energy; and it makes a great difference, as regards any set of ideas which he may possess, whether they become central or remain peripheral in him. To say that a man is 'converted' means, in these terms, that religious ideas, previously peripheral in his consciousness, now take a central place, and that religious aims form the habitual centre of his energy."

61. See Ward Churchhill, "Literature and the Colonization of the American Indian," *Journal of Ethnic Studies* 10, no. 3 (Fall 1982): 37–56. For additional critical literature on Indian stereotypes, see Louise Barnett, *The Ignoble Savage: American Literary Racism, 1790–1890* (Westport, CT: Greenwood Press, 1975); Robert Berkhofer, Jr., *The White Man's Indian: Images of the American Indian from Columbus to the Present* (New York: Alfred A. Knopf, 1978); Richard Drinnon, *Facing West: The Metaphysics of Indian-Hating and Empire-Building* (New York: Meridian, 1980); Roy Harvey Pearce, *Savagism and Civilization: The Study of the Indian and the American Mind* (1953; rpt., Baltimore: Johns Hopkins University Press, 1967); and Richard Slotkin, *Regeneration through Violence: The Mythology of the American Frontier, 1600–1860* (Middletown, CT: Wesleyan University Press, 1973).

62. See Peter G. Beidler, "The Indian Half-Breed in Turn-of-the-Century Short Fiction," *American Indian Culture and Research Journal* 9, no. 1 (1985): 1–12; Robert E. Bieder, "Scientific Attitudes toward Indian Mixed-Bloods in Early Nineteenth Century America," *Journal of Ethnic Studies* 8, no. 2 (Summer 1980): 17–30; and William J. Scheick, *The Half-Blood: A Cultural Symbol in Nineteenth-Century American Fiction* (Lexington: University Press of Kentucky, 1979).

63. See Finnegan, *Literacy and Orality,* 143.

64. See Willard Walker, "Native American Writing Systems," in Ferguson and Heath, *Language in the USA,* 145–174.

65. See Ives Goddard and Kathleen Bragdon, eds., *Native Writings in Massachusett*, 2 vols. (Philadelphia: American Philosophical Society, 1988), 1:1–23.

66. For a listing of Indian newspapers, see James P. Danky, ed., and Maureen E. Hady, comp., *Native American Periodicals and Newspapers, 1828–1982: Bibliography, Publishing Record, and Holdings* (Westport, CT: Greenwood Press, 1984); Daniel F. Littlefield, Jr., and James W. Parins, *American Indian and Alaskan Native Newspapers and Periodicals, 1826–1924* (Westport, CT: Greenwood Press, 1984); and idem, *American Indian and Alaskan Native Newspapers and Periodicals, 1925–1970* (Westport, CT: Greenwood Press, 1986). On the history of Indian journalism, see James Murphy and Sharon Murphy, *Let My People Know: American Indian Journalism* (Norman: University of Oklahoma Press, 1981).

67. Rupert Costo and Jeanette Henry, eds., *The American Indian Reader: History* (San Francisco: The Indian Historian Press, 1972). 20.

68. Fishman, *Language and Ethnicity*, 216–217.

69. Robert K. Thomas, "Pan-Indianism," in Stuart Levine and Nancy O. Lurie, eds., *The American Indian Today* (Baltimore: Penguin Books, 1970), 128–140.

70. Guillermo Bonfil Batalla, comp., *Utopia y revolucion: El pensamiento politico contempraneo de los Indios en America Latina* (1981; rpt., Mexico: Editorial Nueva Imagen, 1988), 11–53.

71. Fishman, *Language and Ethnicity*, 107, 109.

72. Gerald R. Alfred, *Heeding the Voices of Our Ancestors: Kahnawake Mohawk Politics and the Rise of Nationalism* (Toronto/New York: Oxford University Press, 1995), 14–15.

73. See Ward Churchill, "I Am Indigenist," in idem, *Struggle for the Land: Indigenous Resistance to Genocide, Ecocide, and Expropriation in Contemporary North America* (Monroe, ME: Common Courage Press, 1993), 403–451. On the evolution of the term "indigenism" since the Mexican Revolution, see Instituto Indigenista Interamericano, "El indigenismo: recuento y perspectiva," *América Indigena* 50, no. 1 (January/March 1990): 63–91.

74. M. Estelle Smith, "Governing at Taos Pueblo," *Eastern New Mexico University Contributions in Anthropology* 2, no. 1 (1969): 39.

75. See Fishman, *Language and Ethnicity*, 210–211; and Ribeiro, "Culture-Historical Configuration of the American Peoples," 404.

76. See Milton M. Gordon, "Assimilation in America: Theory and Practice," in Lawrence W. Levine and Robert Middlekauff, eds., *The National Temper: Readings in American Culture and Society* (New York: Harcourt Brace Jovanovich, 1972), 266–284.

77. Fishman, *Language and Ethnicity*, 210–211.

78. Victor Turner, *Dramas, Fields, and Metaphors: Symbolic Action in Human Society* (Ithaca/London: Cornell University Press, 1974), 45, 201–202, 231–233.

79. James A. Clifton, "Alternate Identities and Cultural Frontiers," in idem, ed., *Being and Becoming Indian: Biographical Studies of North American Frontiers* (Chicago: Dorsey Press, 1989), 29. See also idem, "Personal and Ethnic Identity on the Great Lakes Frontier: The Case of Billy Caldwell, Anglo-Canadian," *Ethnohistory* 25, no. 1 (Winter 1978): 69–94.

80. See G. Reginald Daniel, "Beyond Black and White: The New Multiracial

Consciousness," in P. P. Root, ed., *Racially Mixed People in America* (Newbury Park, CA: Sage Publications, 1992), 333–341; and Malcolm McFee, "The 150% Man: A Product of Blackfoot Acculturation," *American Anthropologist* 70, no. 6 (December 1968): 1096–1107.

81. Everett V. Stonequist, *The Marginal Man: A Study in Personality and Culture Conflict* (1937; rpt., New York: Russell & Russell, 1961), 122, 130–131.

82. Marcus Lee Hansen, "The Third Generation in America," *Commentary* 14 (November 1952): 492–500.

83. Fanon, *Wretched of the Earth*, 222–223, 240–241.

84. Jack Forbes feels that American Indian literature is still inhibited by colonialism and that truly native literature can be found only in media used by Indians themselves such as tribal newspapers and Indian-operated presses. See Jack D. Forbes, "Colonialism and Native American Literature: Analysis," *Wicazo Sa Review* 3 (1987): 17–23.

85. James C. Scott, *Domination and the Arts of Resistance: Hidden Transcripts* (New Haven: Yale University Press, 1990), xii.

86. James Axtell, *The European and the Indian: Essays in the Ethnohistory of Colonial North America* (New York/Oxford: Oxford University Press, 1981), 5. See also idem, "Ethnohistory: An Historian's Viewpoint," *Ethnohistory* 26, no. 1 (Winter 1979): 1–13.

87. See, for instance, Michael Dorris, "Native American Literature in an Ethnohistorical Context," *College English* 41, no. 2 (October 1979): 147–162; and Colin Johnson, "White Forms, Aboriginal Content," in Jack Davis and Bob Hodge, eds., *Aboriginal Writing Today* (Canberra: Australian Institute of Aboriginal Studies, 1985), 21–33. I have borrowed the term "autoethnographic expression" from Mary Louise Pratt, *Imperial Eyes: Travel Writing and Transculturation* (London/New York: Routledge, 1992), 6. She uses it to "refer to instances in which colonized subjects undertake to represent themselves in ways that *engage with* the colonizer's own terms." A related term is Sioui's "Amerindian autohistory," an ethical approach to history that studies the persistence of Indian values through their own testimonial. See Georges E. Sioui, *For an Amerindian Autohistory: An Essay on the Foundations of a Social Ethic*, trans. Sheila Fischman (Montreal/Kingston: McGill-Queen's University Press, 1992), 21–23.

88. For a sophisticated theoretical approach combining ethnography and postmodern literary criticism in the analysis of American Indian literature, see Arnold Krupat, *Ethnocriticism: Ethnography, History, Literature* (Berkeley: University of California Press, 1992), 3–45.

89. Pratt, *Imperial Eyes*, 1–11.

90. My approach is certainly not unusual. See Clifton, *Being and Becoming Indian*; R. David Edmunds, ed., *American Indian Leaders: Studies in Diversity* (Lincoln: University of Nebraska Press, 1980); Frances Karttunen, *Between Worlds: Interpreters, Guides, and Survivors* (New Brunswick, NJ: Rutgers University Press, 1994); Margot Liberty, ed., *American Indian Intellectuals*, Proceedings of the American Ethnological Society, 1976 (St. Paul: West Publishing, 1978); L. G. Moses and Raymond Wilson, eds., *Indian Lives: Essays on Nineteenth- and Twentieth-Century Native American Leaders* (Albuquerque: University of New Mexico Press, 1985);

and Margaret C. Szasz, ed., *Between Indian and White Worlds: The Cultural Broker* (Norman/London: University of Oklahoma Press, 1994).

91. For an extensive listing of early American Indian writings since 1772, see Daniel F. Littlefield, Jr., and James W. Parins, *A Biobibliography of Native American Writers, 1772–1924* (Metuchen, NJ: Scarecrow Press, 1981); and idem, *A Bio-bibliography of Native American Writers, 1772–1924: A Supplement* (Metuchen, NJ: Scarecrow Press, 1985). For general reference, see Paula Gunn Allen, ed., *Studies in Native American Literature* (New York: Modern Languages Association, 1982); Arnold Krupat, *The Voice in the Margin: Native American Literature and the Canon* (Berkeley: University of California Press, 1989); Kenneth Lincoln, *Native American Renaissance* (Berkeley and Los Angeles: University of California Press, 1983); David Murray, *Forked Tongues: Speech, Writing, & Representation in North American Indian Texts* (Bloomington: Indiana University Press, 1991); A. La Vonne Brown Ruoff, *American Indian Literatures: An Introduction, Bibliographic Review, and Selected Bibliography* (New York: Modern Languages Association, 1990); Gerald Vizenor, *Narrative Chance: Post-modern Discourse on Native American Indian Literatures* (Albuquerque: University of New Mexico Press, 1989; rpt., Norman: University of Oklahoma Press, 1993); Andrew Wiget, *Native American Literature* (Boston: Twayne Publishers, 1985); and idem, ed., *Dictionary of Native American Literature* (New York/London: Garland Publishing, 1994).

CHAPTER TWO

1. Tzvetan Todorov, *The Conquest of America: The Question of the Other*, trans. Richard Howard (New York: Harper & Row, 1984), 101.

2. See Norma Alarcón, "Traddutora, Traditora: A Paradigmatic Figure of Chicana Feminism," *Cultural Critique* 13 (Fall 1989): 57–87.

3. Cristóbal Colon, *Textos y documentos completos*, ed., Consuelo Varela (Madrid: Alianza Editorial, 1982), 31.

4. See Harald E. L. Prins, "To the Land of the Mistigoches: American Indians Traveling to Europe in the Age of Exploration," *American Indian Culture and Research Journal* 17, no. 1 (1993): 175–195.

5. Ibid.; and Henry S. Burrage, ed., *Early English and French Voyages, 1534–1608* (New York: Charles Scribner's Sons, 1906). See also James Axtell, *The Invasion Within: The Contest of Cultures in Colonial North America* (New York/Oxford: Oxford University Press, 1985), 24–27; Olive P. Dickason, *The Myth of the Savage and the Beginnings of French Colonialism in the Americas* (Edmonton: University of Alberta Press, 1984), 203–229; Samuel G. Drake, *The Book of the Indians of North America* (Boston: Josiah Drake, 1833), Book 2: 1–9; Allan Forbes, *Some Indian Events of New England* (Boston: State Street Trust, 1934), 26–64; Jack D. Forbes, *Africans and Native Americans: The Language of Race and the Evolution of Red-Black Peoples*, 2nd ed. (Urbana/Chicago: University of Illinois Press, 1993), 26–64; and Carolyn T. Foreman, *Indians Abroad, 1493–1938* (Norman: University of Oklahoma Press, 1944). Jack Forbes contends that Indians traveled to Europe and Africa long before the Europeans came to America; see Forbes, *Africans and Native Americans*, 6–25.

6. Prins, "To the Land of Mistigoches," 186–190.

7. See Charles M. Hudson, *The Southeastern Indians* (Knoxville: University of Tennessee Press, 1976), 103–104; John R. Swanton, *The Indians of the Southeastern United States*, Smithsonian Institution, Bureau of American Ethnology Bulletin 137 (Washington, DC: Government Printing Office, 1946), 36–37; and J. Leitch Wright, Jr., *The Only Land They Knew: The Tragic Story of the American Indians in the Old South* (New York: Free Press, 1981), 33–36.

8. See Christian F. Feest, "Virginia Algonquians," in Bruce G. Trigger, ed., *Handbook of North American Indians: Northeast* (Washington, DC: Smithsonian Institution Press, 1978), 15:254; idem, *The Powhatan Tribes* (New York: Chelsea House Publishers, 1990), 17–18; and Carl O. Sauer, *Sixteenth-Century North America: The Land and the People as Seen by the Europeans* (Berkeley: University of California Press, 1971), 222–224.

9. See Drake, *Book of the Indians of North America*, 2:6–8; Forbes, *Some Indian Events of New England*, 31; Neal Salisbury, *Manitou and Providence: Indians, Europeans, and the Making of New England, 1500–1643* (New York: Oxford University Press, 1982), 95–96; and Bert Solwen, "Indians of Southern New England and Long Island: Early Period," in Trigger, *Handbook of North American Indians*, 15:171.

10. Studies of early Indian interpreters have tended to focus upon the Iroquois. See Nancy L. Hagedon, "'A Friend to Go Between Them': The Interpreter as Cultural Broker during Anglo-Iroquois Councils, 1740–70," *Ethnohistory* 35, no. 1 (Winter 1988): 60–80; Yasuhide Kawashima, "Forest Diplomats: The Role of Interpreters in Indian-White Relations on the Early American Frontier," *American Indian Quarterly* 13, no. 1 (Winter 1989): 1–14; and Daniel K. Richter, "Cultural Brokers and Intercultural Politics: New York-Iroquois Relations, 1664–1701," *Journal of American History* 75, no. 1 (June 1988): 40–67. See also Francis Karttunen, *Between Worlds: Interpreters, Guides, and Survivors* (New Brunswick, N.J.: Rutgers University Press, 1994).

11. Prins, "To the Land of the Mistigoches," 185–186; Salisbury, *Manitou and Providence*, 91–92.

12. See Leonard A. Adolf, "Squanto's Role in Pilgrim Diplomacy," *Ethnohistory* 11, no. 3 (Summer 1964): 247–261; Leo Bonfonti, *Biographies and Legends of the New England Indians* (Wakefield, MA: Pride Publications, 1970), 24–32; Drake, *Book of the Indians of North America*, 2:4–42; John H. Humins, "Squanto and Massasoit: A Struggle for Power," *New England Quarterly* 60, no. 1 (March 1987): 54–70; Lincoln N. Kinnicut, "The Plymouth Settlement and Tisquantum," *Massachusetts Historical Society Proceedings* 48 (1915): 103–118; Neal Salisbury, "Squanto: Last of the Patuxets," in David G. Sweet and Gary B. Nash, eds., *Struggle for Survival in Colonial America* (Berkeley: University of California Press, 1981), 228–246; and Frank Shuffelton, "Indian Devils and Pilgrim Fathers: Squanto, Hobomok, and the English Conception of Indian Religion," *New England Quarterly* 49, no. 1 (March 1976): 108–116.

13. Salisbury, "Squanto," 230.

14. Quoted from Samuel Eliot Morison, ed., *Of Plymouth Plantation, 1620–1647, by William Bradford* (New York: Alfred A. Knopf, 1952), 99. See Shuffelton,

"Indian Devils and Pilgrim Fathers," 108; and Humins, "Squanto and Massasoit," 70.

15. Smith quoted from Philip L. Barbour, ed., *The Complete Works of Captain John Smith (1580–1631) in Three Volumes* (Chapel Hill: University of North Carolina Press, 1986), 2:451; Bradford quoted from Morison, ed., *Of Plymouth Plantation*, 114.

16. Salisbury, "Squanto," 243.

17. See Philip L. Barbour, *Pocahontas and Her World: A Chronicle of America's First Settlement in Which Is Related the Story of the Indians and the Englishmen, Particularly Captain John Smith, Captain Samuel Argall, and Master John Rolfe* (Boston: Houghton Mifflin, 1969); Frances Mossiker, *Pocahontas: The Life and the Legend* (New York: Alfred A. Knopf, 1969); and Grace S. Woodward, *Pocahontas* (Norman: University of Oklahoma Press, 1969). On the literary myths surrounding Pocahontas, see Robert S. Tilton, *Pocahontas: The Evolution of an American Narrative* (Cambridge/New York: Cambridge University Press, 1994). See also Marilyn J. Anderson, "The Best of Two Worlds: The Pocahontas Legend as Treated in Early American Drama," *Indian Historian* 12, no. 2 (Summer 1979): 54–59, 64; Rayna Green, "The Pocahontas Perplex: The Image of Indian Women in American Culture," *Massachusetts Review* 16, no. 4 (Autumn 1975): 698–714; Jay B. Hubbell, "The Smith-Pocahontas Story in Literature," *Virginia Magazine of History and Biography* 65 (July 1957): 273–300; and Philip Young, "The Mother of Us All: Pocahontas Reconsidered," *Kenyon Review* 24, no. 3 (Summer 1962): 391–415.

18. See Feest, "Virginia Algonquians" and *Powhatan Tribes*; Helen C. Rountree, *The Powhatan Indians of Virginia: Their Traditional Culture* (Norman: University of Oklahoma Press, 1989); idem, *Pocahontas's People: The Powhatan Indians of Virginia through Four Centuries* (Norman: University of Oklahoma Press, 1990); and idem, ed., *Powhatan: Foreign Relations, 1500–1722* (Charlottesville/London: University Press of Virginia, 1993).

19. For Smith's account, see Barbour, *Complete Works of John Smith*, 2:146–153, 258–262. On the controversy over its authenticity, which began with a skeptical interpretation by Henry Adams published in the *North American Review* in 1867, see Joseph A. Leo Lamay, *Did Pocahontas Save Captain John Smith?* (Athens: University of Georgia Press, 1992), 7–18 (the author tries to prove the veracity of the account). On the persistence of the Pocahontas story among Tidewater Indians, see Christian Feest, "Pride and Prejudice: The Pocahontas Myth and the Pamunkey," *European Review of Native American Studies* 1 (1987): 5–12.

20. Quote from Ralph Hamor's *True Discourse of the Present Estate of Virginia* (1615) is taken from Louis B. Wright, ed., *The Elizabethan's America: A Collection of Early Reports by Englishmen on the New World* (Cambridge: Harvard University Press, 1966), 227–228. See Mossiker, *Pocahontas*, 159.

21. For Rolfe's letter, which was first published in Hamor's *True Discourse of the Present Estate of Virginia* (1615), see Wright, *Elizabethan's America*, 233–237. Smith is quoted from Barbour, *Complete Works of John Smith*, 2:246.

22. Vine Deloria, Jr., *Custer Died for Your Sins: An Indian Manifesto* (New York: Macmillan, 1969), 3.

23. See J. Frederick Fausz, "Opechancanough: Indian Resistance Leader," in

Sweet and Nash, *Struggle for Survival in Colonial America*, 21–37; and Feest, *Powhatan Tribes*, 47–55.

24. See Gary B. Nash, "The Image of the Indian in the Southern Colonial Mind," *William and Mary Quarterly* 29 (1972): 197–230.

25. Alexander Whitaker, *Good News from Virginia* . . . (London: Imprinted by Felix Kingston for William Weley, 1613), 40. For William Strachey's famous description of "wanton" Pocahontas in his *History of Travel into Virginia Britannia* (1612), see Wright, *Elizabethan's America*, 216–217.

26. See James Axtell, *The School upon a Hill: Education and Society in Colonial New England* (New Haven: Yale University Press, 1974), esp. chap. 7. On colonial Indian education, see Evelyn C. Adams, *American Indian Education: Government Schools and Economic Progress* (1946; rpt. New York: Arno Press, 1971), 6–26; Alice C. Fletcher, *Indian Education and Civilization: A Report Prepared in Answer to Senate Resolution of February 23, 1885*, Bureau of Education Special Report, 1888 (Millwood, NY: Kraus Reprint, 1973), 82–104; and Margaret C. Szasz, *Indian Education in the American Colonies, 1607–1783* (Albuquerque: University of New Mexico Press, 1988), 25–45. For an excellent survey of Indian education, see Margaret C. Szasz and Carmelita S. Ryan, "American Indian Education," in Wilcomb E. Washburn, ed., *Handbook of North American Indians: History of Indian-White Relations* (Washington, DC: Smithsonian Institution Press, 1988), 4:284–300.

27. See Axtell, *Invasion Within*, 23–127; Henry W. Bowden, *American Indians and Christian Missions: Studies in Cultural Conflict* (Chicago/London: University of Chicago Press, 1981), 59–95; and John D. Shea, *History of Catholic Missions among the Indian Tribes of the United States, 1529–1854* (1855; rpt. New York: AMS Press, 1973).

28. See W. Stitt Robinson, Jr., "Indian Education and Missions in Colonial Virginia," *Journal of Southern History* 18 (February/November 1952): 152–168.

29. See Axtell, *Invasion Within*, 179–181; Robert H. Land, "Henrico and Its College," *William and Mary Quarterly* 18, no. 4 (October 1938): 453–498; H. C. Porter, *The Inconstant Savage: England and the North American Indian, 1500–1660* (London: Duckworth, 1979), 434–450; and Peter Walne, "The Collections for Henrico College, 1616–1618," *Virginia Magazine of History and Biography* 80 (1972): 259–266.

30. See Francis Jennings, *The Invasion of America: Indians, Colonialism, and the Cant of Conquest* (New York: W. W. Norton, 1976), 54. See also C. E. Hatch, Jr., and T. G. Gregory, "The First American Blast Furnace, 1619–1622," *Virginia Magazine of History and Biography* 70, no. 3 (July 1962): 259–296, esp. 267–268.

31. Jennings, *Invasion of America*, 53.

32. See W. Stitt Robinson, Jr., "Tributary Indians in Colonial Virginia," *Virginia Magazine of History and Biography* 67 (January 1959): 49–64.

33. Robinson, "Indian Education and Missions in Colonial Virginia," 161–166. See also Axtell, *Invasion Within*, 190–196; H. L. Ganter, "Some Notes on the Charity of the Honorable Robert Boyle, Esq.," *William and Mary Quarterly* 15, no. 1 (January 1935): 1–39, and 15, no. 4 (October 1935): 346–384; Szasz, *Indian Education in the American Colonies*, 67–77; and Lyon G. Tyler, *The College of*

William and Mary in Virginia: Its History and Work, 1693–1907 (Richmond: Whittet & Shepperson, 1907).

34. Alexander Spotswood to the Council of Trade, November 17, 1711, in Alexander Spotswood, *The Official Letters of Alexander Spotswood, Lieutenant Governor of the Colony of Virginia*, 2 vols., ed. R. A. Brock (Richmond: Virginia Historical Society, 1882–85), 1:121–123. Quoted in Ganter, "Some Notes on the Charity of Robert Boyle," 366–367.

35. See Robinson, "Tributary Indians in Colonial Virginia," 165; and Szasz, *Indian Education in the American Colonies*, 77.

36. William K. Boyd, ed., *William Byrd's Histories of the Dividing Line betwixt Virginia and North Carolina* (New York: Dover Publications, 1967), 118; Hugh Jones, *The Present State of Virginia* (1724), ed. Richard L. Morton (Chapel Hill: University of North Carolina Press, 1956), 114. Both quoted in Ganter, "Some Notes on the Charity of Robert Boyle," 368–369. See also Axtell, *Invasion Within*, 196; and Robinson, "Indian Education and Missions in Colonial Virginia," 166.

37. For interpretations of Puritan-Indian relations during the seventeenth century I have relied primarily on Axtell, *Invasion Within*, 218–241; Bowden, *American Indians and Christian Missions*, 93–133; Jennings, *Invasion of America*, 228–253; Salisbury, *Manitou and Providence*, 166–202; and Szasz, *Indian Education in the American Colonies*, 101–128. For further references to missionary activities among North American Indians, see James P. Ronda and James Axtell, *Indian Missions: A Critical Bibliography* (Bloomington: University of Indiana Press, 1978).

38. See Jennings, *Invasion of America*, 178–179, 186–227.

39. After the Restoration, in 1661, the New England Company received a new charter as the Company for the Propagation of the Gospel in New England and the Parts Adjacent in America. The standard work on this organization is William Kellaway, *The New England Company, 1649–1776: Missionary Society to the American Indians* (1961; rpt., Westport, CT: Greenwood Press, 1975). See also Frederick L. Weiss, "The New England Company of 1646 and Its Missionary Enterprises," *Publications of the Colonial Society of Massachusetts* 38 (1959): 132–218.

40. James P. Ronda, " 'We Are Well as We Are': An Indian Critique of Seventeenth-Century Christian Missions," *William and Mary Quarterly* 34 (January 1977): 67.

41. See James Axtell, "The White Indians of Colonial America," *William and Mary Quarterly* 32, no. 1 (January 1975): 55–88; idem, *Invasion Within*, 302–327; and Joseph N. Heard, *White into Red: A Study of the Assimilation of White Persons Captured by Indians* (Metuchen, NJ: Scarecrow Press, 1973).

42. On the ideological clash between Puritans and Indians, see James Axtell, "Through a Glass Darkly: Colonial Attitudes toward the Native Americans," *American Indian Culture and Research Journal* 1 (1974): 17–24; David I. Bushnell, Jr., "The Treatment of the Indians in Plymouth Colony," *New England Quarterly* 26 (June 1953): 193–218; Roy H. Pearce, "The 'Ruines of Mankind': The Indian and the Puritan Mind," *Journal of the History of Ideas* 13, no. 2 (1952): 200–217; idem, "The Metaphysics of Indian-Hating," *Ethnohistory* 4, no. 1 (Winter 1957): 27–40; William Simmons, "Cultural Bias in the New England Puritans' Perception of Indians," *William and Mary Quarterly* 38, no. 1 (January 1981): 56–72; G. E. Thomas,

"Puritans, Indians, and the Concept of Race," *New England Quarterly* 48, no. 1 (March 1975): 3–27; Wilcomb E. Washburn, "The Moral and Legal Justifications for Dispossessing the Indians," in James M. Smith, ed., *Seventeenth-Century America: Essays in Colonial History* (Chapel Hill: University of North Carolina Press, 1959), 15–32; and idem, "The Clash of Morality in the American Forest," in Fredi Chiappelli, ed., *First Images of America: The Impact of the New World on the Old*, 2 vols. (Berkeley: University of California Press, 1976), 1:335–350.

43. A primary source on seventeenth-century Praying Indian towns is Daniel Gookin, *Historical Collections of the Indians in New England* (Boston: Apollo Press, by Belknap & Hall, 1792; rpt., n.p.: Towtaid, 1970); also reprinted in *Collections of the Massachusetts Historical Society*, 1st ser. 1 (1806): 141–227; the 1970 ed. is cited here. For additional sources, see Francis Jennings, "Goals and Functions of Puritan Missions to the Indians," *Ethnohistory* 18, no. 2 (Spring 1971): 197–212; Kenneth M. Morrison, " 'That Art of Coyning Christians': John Eliot and the Praying Indians of Massachusetts," *Ethnohistory* 21, no. 1 (Winter 1974): 77–94; Gary B. Nash, "Notes on the History of Seventeenth-Century Missionization in Colonial America," *American Indian Culture and Research Journal* 2, no. 2 (1978): 3–8; Neal Salisbury, "Red Puritans: The 'Praying Indians' of Massachusetts Bay and John Eliot," *William and Mary Quarterly* 31, no. 1 (January 1974): 27–54; and William Simmons, "Conversion from Indian to Puritan," *New England Quarterly* 52, no 2 (June 1979): 197–218.

44. Jennings, "Goals and Functions of Puritan Missions to Indians," 208–209; idem, *Invasion of America*, 245–246. For biographical data on Eliot and Mayhew, see Ola A. Winslow, *John Eliot: "Apostle to the Indians"* (Boston: Houghton Mifflin, 1968); and Lloyd C. M. Hare, *Thomas Mayhew: Patriarch to the Indians, 1593–1682* (1932; rpt., St. Clair Shores, MI: Scholarly Press, 1971). On Mather's praise for Eliot's activities, see Constance Post, "Old World Order in the New: John Eliot and 'Praying Indians' in Cotton Mather's *Magnalia Christi Americana*," *New England Quarterly* 66, no. 3 (September 1993): 416–433.

45. See Axtell, *Invasion Within*, 221–222; Bowden, *American Indians and Christian Missions*, 118; and Jennings, *Invasion of America*, 238–239.

46. Jennings, *Invasion of America*, 241. The act has been reprinted in Charles M. Segal and David Stineback, eds., *Puritans, Indians, and Manifest Destiny* (New York: G. P. Putnam's Sons, 1977), 156–157.

47. Salisbury, "Red Puritans," 50. See also Axtell, *Invasion Within*, 218, 230.

48. Gookin, *Historical Collections of the Indians in New England*, 65–88 (cited from 1970 ed.). See also Norman E. Tanis, "Education in John Eliot's Indian Utopias, 1646–1675," *History of Education Quarterly* 10, no. 3 (Fall 1970): 308–323; and William W. Tooker, "The Significance of John Eliot's Natick," *American Anthropologist* 10, no. 9 (September 1897): 281–287.

49. See Susan L. MacCulloch, "A Tripartite Political System among Christian Indians of Early Massachusetts," *Kroeber Anthropological Society Papers* 34 (Spring 1966): 63–73. Eliot later published his scheme in *The Christian Commonwealth; or, The Civil Policy of the Rising Kingdom of Jesus Christ* (London: Livewell, Chapman, 1659); rpt. in *Collections of the Massachusetts Historical Society*, 3rd ser. 9 (1846): 127–164.

50. Salisbury, "Red Puritans," 32.

51. MacCulloch, "Tripartite Political System," 64–65; Tanis, "Education in Eliot's Indian Utopias," 312. A set of rules for Praying Indians from Concord dated January 1647 has been reprinted in the appendix to Edward H. Spicer, *A Short History of the Indians of the United States* (New York: Van Nostrand, 1969), 174–175.

52. See Axtell, *Invasion Within*, 223.

53. The experiences of Christian Indians after King Philip's War are described in Daniel Gookin, *An Historical Account of the Doings and Sufferings of the Christian Indians in New England, in the Years 1675, 1676, 1677* (1677), in *Archaeologica Americana* (Cambridge: Cambridge University Press, 1836), 2:423–534. See also Salisbury, "Red Puritans," 54; Tanis, "Education in Eliot's Indian Utopias," 320–321; and Thomas, "Puritans, Indians, and the Concept of Race," 6–7, 20–23.

54. For a thorough study of the Natick community, see Jean Maria O'Brian, "Community Dynamics in the Indian-English Town of Natick" (Ph.D. diss., University of Chicago, 1990).

55. See Jennings, "Goals and Functions of Puritan Missions to Indians," 200; Simmons, "Conversion from Indian to Puritan," 215–216; and James P. Ronda, "Generations of Faith: The Christian Indians of Martha's Vineyard," *William and Mary Quarterly* 38, no. 3 (July 1981): 369–394.

56. Axtell, *Invasion Within*, 229–230; Jennings, *Invasion of America*, 230–231; Simmons, "Conversion from Indian to Puritan," 203.

57. See Laura E. Conkey, Ethel Boissevain, and Ives Goddard, "Indians of Southern New England and Long Island: Late Period," in Trigger, *Handbook of North American Indians*, 15:180–181; Jennings, "Goals and Functions of Puritan Missions to Indians," 200; idem, *Invasion of America*, 231; and Gladys Tantaquidgeon, "Notes on the Gay Head Indians of Massachusetts," Museum of the American Indian, Heye Foundation, *Indian Notes* 7, no. 1 (1930): 1–26.

58. See Gary B. Nash, *Red, White, and Black: The Peoples of Early America* (Englewood Cliffs, NJ: Prentice-Hall, 1974), 127.

59. Salisbury, "Red Puritans," 46.

60. See Elise M. Brenner, "To Pray or to Be Prey, That Is the Question: Strategies for Cultural Autonomy of Massachusetts Praying Town Indians," *Ethnohistory* 27, no. 2 (Spring 1980): 135–152; Harold W. Van Lonkhuyzen, "A Reappraisal of the Praying Indians: Acculturation, Conversion, and Identity at Natick, Massachusetts, 1646–1730," *New England Quarterly* 63, no. 3 (September 1990): 396–428; Ronda, "Generations of Faith"; Neil Salisbury, "Religious Encounters in a Colonial Context: New England and New France in the Seventeenth Century," *American Indian Quarterly* 16, no. 4 (Fall 1992): 501–509; and J. William T. Youngs, Jr., "The Indian Saints of Early New England," *Early American Literature* 16, no. 3 (Winter 1981/82): 241–256.

61. On traditional religions in the Northeast, see Denise L. Carmody and John T. Carmody, *Native American Religions: An Introduction* (New York: Paulist Press, 1993), 15–40; John J. Collins, *Native American Religions: A Geographical Survey* (Lewiston/Queenstown: Edwin Mellen Press, 1991): 289–297; and Elisabeth Tooker, ed., *Native North American Spirituality of the Eastern Woodlands* (New York: Paulist Press, 1980).

62. See Roy Hidemichi Akagi, *The Town Proprietors of the New England Colonies* (Philadelphia: University of Pennsylvania Press, 1924), 38–44, 103–104, 110–114.

63. See George P. Castile, "Mau Mau in the Mechanism: The Adaptation of Urban Hunters and Gatherers," *Human Organization* 35, no. 4 (Winter 1976): 394–397; and James C. Scott, *Domination and the Arts of Resistance: Hidden Transcripts* (New Haven: Yale University Press, 1990).

64. Axtell, *Invasion Within*, 285–286.

65. See Allan Forbes, *Other Indian Events of New England* (Boston: State Street Trust, 1941), 2:64–76; and Samuel E. Morison, *Harvard College in the Seventeenth Century* (Cambridge: Harvard University Press, 1936), 340–360.

66. See Morison, *Harvard College in the Seventeenth Century*, 342, 357, 359; Szasz, *Indian Education in the American Colonies*, 175–176.

67. Jennings, *Invasion of America*, 178–179, 298–326. See also Yasuhide Kawashima, *Puritan Justice and the Indian: White Man's Law in Massachusetts, 1630–1763* (Middletown, CT: Wesleyan University Press, 1986), 225–239.

68. See Szasz, *Indian Education in the American Colonies*, 173–189.

69. See Gookin, *Historical Collections of the Indians in New England*, 65–88.

70. Biographies of and dialogues attributed to Praying Indians are found among several early promotional tracts. One of the first is the anonymous *New England's First Fruits, in respect to the progress of learning, in the Colledge at Cambridge in Massachusetts-bay . . .* (1643), in *Collections of the Massachusetts Historical Society*, 1st ser. 1 (1792): 242–250 (Jennings cites Thomas Weld and Hugh Peter as probable authors, in *Invasion of America*, 342). John Eliot's voluminous writings include a collection of invented (and perhaps partially authentic) dialogues between Indians on religious matters: *Indian Dialogues, for their Instruction in that great Service of Christ* (Cambridge, MA, 1671); rpt. in Henry W. Bowden and James P. Ronda, *John Eliot's Indian Dialogues: A Study in Cultural Interaction* (Westport, CT: Greenwood Press, 1980). He and Thomas Mayhew also published a series of Indian confessions in *Tears of Repentance; or, A further Narrative of the Progress of the Gospel Amongst the Indians in New-England* (London: Printed by Peter Cole in Leaden-Hall, 1653); rpt. in *Collections of the Massachusetts Historical Society*, 3rd ser. 4 (1834): 197–260. Occasional biographical sketches are also found in other promotional tracts by Edward Winslow, Henry Whitfield, and Thomas Shepard, which have been reprinted collectively as "Tracts Relating to the Attempts to Convert to Christianity the Indians of New England," *Collections of the Massachusetts Historical Society*, 3rd ser. 4 (1834): i–288. More detailed and numerous accounts were recorded later by Experience Mayhew. See Mayhew, *Indian Converts; or, Some account of the lives and dying speeches of a considerable number of the Christianized Indians of Martha's Vineyard, New England* (London: Printed for Samuel Gerrish, bookseller in Boston, in New England, and sold by J. Osborn, 1727), containing short biographies of thirty Indian preachers or church officeholders, thirty-seven "good men," thirty-nine "good women," and twenty-two "good children"; idem, *Narratives of the Lives of Pious Indian Women who lived on Martha's Vineyard More than One Hundred Years Since* (1727; rpt. Boston: James Loring, 1830); and idem, *Narratives of Pious Indian Children* (1727; rpt., Boston: James Loring, 1829).

71. Thomas Mayhew to Henry Whitfield, September 7, 1650, in Henry Whitfield, *The Light appearing more and more towards the perfect Day; or, A farther Discovery of the present state of the Indians in New-England, Concerning the Progresse of the Gospel amongst them* (London: Printed by T. R. & E. M. for John Bartlet, 1651); rpt. in *Collections of the Massachusetts Historical Society*, 3rd ser. 4 (1834): 100–147 (the letter is on pp. 109–18). See also Ronda, "Generations of Faith," 375–378; Simmons, "Conversion from Indian to Puritan," 204–206; and Youngs, "Indian Saints of Early New England," 244–245.

72. Experience Mayhew basically copied and updated Thomas Mayhew's earlier account. See Mayhew, *Indian Converts*, 1–12 (quote on pp. 1–2).

73. Ibid., 5.

74. Whitfield, *The Light appearing more and more towards the perfect Day*, 116.

75. Eliot and Mayhew, *Tears of Repentance*, 231–232 (p. 8 in the original). Waban's missionary efforts are the subject of the second dialogue in Eliot, *Indian Dialogues*, 94–119. For comparison, see the exhortation by Hiacoomes in Mayhew, *Indian Converts*, 11.

76. Anonymous, *The Day Breaking, If Not The Sun-Rising of the Gospell with the Indians in New-England* (1647), in *Collections of the Massachusetts Historical Society*, 3rd ser. 4 (1834): 3–4. See Jennings, *Invasion of America*, 239–241.

77. See Ives Goddard and Kathleen Bragdon, eds., *Native Writings in Massachusett*, 2 vols. (Philadelphia: American Philosophical Society, 1988); Wolfgang Hochbruck and Beatrix Dudensing-Reichel, " 'Honoratissimi Benefactores': Native American Students and Two Seventeenth-Century Texts in the University Tradition," *Studies in American Indian Literature* 4, nos. 2–3 (Summer/Fall 1992): 35–47; and Walter T. Meserve, "English Works of Seventeenth-Century Indians," *American Quarterly* 8 (Fall 1976): 264–276.

78. See William W. Tooker, *John Eliot's First Indian Teacher and Interpreter: Cockenoe-De-Long Island and the Story of His Career from the Early Records* (New York: Francis P. Harper, 1896). See also Meserve, "English Works of Seventeenth-Century Indians," 267–268; and Szasz, *Indian Education in the American Colonies*, 111–113.

79. John Eliot, *The Indian Grammar Begun; or, An Essay to Bring the Indian Language into Rules, for the Help of Such as Desire to Learn the Same, for the Furtherance of the Gospel among Them* (Cambridge, MA: Printed by Marmeduke Johnson, 1666), 65. Quoted in Tooker, *Eliot's First Teacher and Interpreter*, 13.

80. Several of the preserved writings in Massachusett deal with the transfer of property. See Goddard and Bragdon, *Native Writings in Massachusett*, 13–18.

81. See Tooker, *Eliot's First Teacher and Interpreter*, 17, 25–28, 43. Various land transactions in which Cockenoe acted as intermediary are recorded in this biography. Also quoted in Meserve, "English Works of Seventeenth-Century Indians," 267.

82. Meserve, "English Works of Seventeenth-Century Indians," 267; Tooker, *Eliot's First Teacher and Translator*, 30–31 (quote on pp. 36–37).

83. Gookin, *Historical Account of the Doings and Sufferings of the Christian Indians in New England*, 444. See also Drake, *Book of the Indians of North America*,

2:56–57; Meserve, "English Works of Seventeenth-Century Indians," 266–267; and Szasz, *Indian Education in the American Colonies*, 113–115. Allan Forbes claims that he was a Mohegan; see Forbes, *Other Indian Events of New England*, 76.

84. See Drake, *Book of the Indians of North America*, 2:56–57; George Emery Littlefield, *The Early Massachusetts Press, 1638–1711*, 2 vols. (Boston: Club of Odd Volumes, 1907), 1:77–78; Meserve, "English Works of Seventeenth-Century Indians," 268–268; and Szasz, *Indian Education in the American Colonies*, 115–119.

85. The letter has been reprinted in Forbes, *Some Indian Events of New England*, 84; and Meserve, "English Writings of Seventeenth-Century Indians," 269–270. The captives' release was arranged by three Praying Indians, Tom Nepponit, Peter Conway, and Peter Jethro, who were sent to deal with King Philip as representatives for the Council. See Gookin, *Historical Account of the Doings and Sufferings of the Christian Indians in New England*, 507–508. See also the letter concerning the same event by Peter Jethro in Meserve, "English Writings," 269.

86. John Eliot to Sir Robert Boyle, January 15, 1683. The letter is found in the Boyle Letters, vol. 2, no. 161, Royal Society Archives, London. Also quoted in Drake, *Book of the Indians of North America*, 2:57; Forbes, *Other Indian Events of New England*, 76; and Littlefield, *Early Massachusetts Press*, 77.

87. For a list of Indian books printed by the New England Company during this period, see chap. 6 in Kellaway, *New England Company*; and Weiss, "New England Company of 1649 and Its Missionary Enterprise," 216–218.

88. See James C. Pilling, *Bibliography of Algonquian Languages*, Bureau of American Ethnology Bulletin 13 (Washington, DC: Government Printing Office, 1891).

89. See Drake, *Book of the Indians of North America* 3:8–12; Forbes, *Other Indian Events of New England*, 70–71; William Hubbard, *A Narrative of the Troubles with the Indians in New-England* (Boston: Printed by John Foster, 1677), 13–16; Increase Mather, *A Brief History of the War with the Indians in New-England* (London: Printed for Richard Chiswell, 1676), 2–3; and Jeanne Ronda and James P. Ronda, "The Death of John Sassomon: An Exploration in Writing New England History," *American Indian Quarterly* 1 (1975): 91–102. There may have been another Indian who attended Harvard prior to the establishment of the Indian College, as records mention a Harvard-educated "Privy Councellor" with King Philip, who was supposedly killed during a skirmish with the colonists in July 1675. See Meserve, "English Writings of Seventeenth-Century Indians," 353.

90. Mather, *Brief History of the War with the Indians in New-England*, 2. See Ronda and Ronda, "Death of John Sassomon," 95–100.

91. See Forbes, *Other Indian Events of New England*, 69–70; Gookin, *Historical Collections of the Indians of New England*, 21, 52–53; Hochbruck and Dudensing-Reichel, "Honoratissimi Benefactores," 36–40, 42–44; Meserve, "English Writings of Seventeenth-Century Indians," 265; Morison, *Harvard College in the Seventeenth Century*, 354–356; and Szasz, *Indian Education in the American Colonies*, 123–125.

92. See Robert C. Black III, *The Younger John Winthrop* (New York: Columbia University Press, 1966), 307–308. Joel is also said to have written several sermons; see Forbes, *Other Indian Events of New England*, 68.

93. Boyle Letters, vol. 2, no. 12, Royal Society Archives. Hiacoomes's piece, which is not found among the Boyle Letters, has yet to be located. Caleb's letter has been reproduced in Hochbruck and Dudensing-Reichel, "Honoratissimi Benefactores," 37; and Morison, *Harvard College in the Seventeenth Century*, 355. Hochbruck's and Dudensing-Reichel's translation into English (38–39) is reprinted with the kind permission of Wolfgang Hochbruck. Thanks also to Willy Fangmann for providing me with an additional translation for cross-reference.

Honoratissimi benefactores

Referunt historici, de Orpheo musico et insigni Poeta quod ab Apolline Lyram accepterit eaque tantum valuerit, ut illius Cantu sylvas saxumque moverit et Arbores ingentes post se traxerit, ferasque ferocissimas mitiores rediderit imo, quod accepta Lyrâ ad infernos descenderit et Plutonem et Proserpinam suo carmine demulsuerit, et Eurydicen uxorem ab infernis ad superos evexerit: Hoc symbolum esie statuunt Philosophi Antiquissimi, ut ostendant quod tanta et vis et virtus doctrinae et politioris literaturae ad mutandum Barborum Ingenium: qui sunt tanquam arbores, saxa, et bruta animantia: et eorum quasi matephorisin efficiendam, eosque tanquam Tigres Cicurandos et post se trahendos.

Deus vos delegit esse patronos nostros, et cum omni sapientiâ, intimâque Commiseratione vos ornavit, ut nobis Paganis salutiferam opem feratis, qui vitam progeniemque a majoribus nostris ducebamus, tam animo quam corporeque nudi fuimos, et ab omni humanitate alieni fuimus, in deserto huc et illuc variisque erroribus ducti fuim[us].

O terque, quaterque ornatissimi, amantissimique viri, quas quantasque quam maximas, immensasque gratias vobis tribuamus: eo quod omnium rerum Copiam nobis suppetitaveritis propter educationem nostram, et ad sustentationem corporum nostrorum: immensas, maximasque expensas effudistis.

Et praecipuè quas quantasque, Gratias Deo Opt.[imo] M[a]x.[imo] dabimus qui sanctas scripturas nobis revelavit, Dominumque Jesum Christum nobis demonstravit, qui est via veritatis et vitae. Praeter haec omnia, per viscera misericordiae divinae, aliqua spes relicta sit, ut instrumenta fiamus, ad declarandum, et propogandum evangelium Cognatis nostris Conterraneisque: ut illi etiam Deum Cognoscant: et Christum.

Quamvis non posumus par pari redere vobis, reliquisque Benefactoribus nostris, veruntamen speramus. nos non defuturos apud Deum supplicationibus importunis exorare pro illis pijs miserercordibus viris, qui supersunt in vetere Angliâ, qui pro nobis tantam vim auri, argentique effuderunt ad salutem animarum nostrarum procurandam et pro vobis etiam, qui instrumenta, et quasi aquae ductus fuistis omnia ista beneficentia nobis Conferendi.

Vestre Dignitati devotissimus:

Caleb Cheeshahteaumauk.

94. See Forbes, *Other Indian Events of New England*, 70; and Morison, *Harvard College in the Seventeenth Century*, 356–357.

95. The unsigned petition is preserved in the Public Record Office in London, England (COI/37-174 XC16394).

96. See Forbes, *Other Indian Events of New England*, 70; Hochbruck and Dudensing-Reichel, "Honoratissimi Benefactores," 40–42; and Morison, *Harvard College in the Seventeenth Century*, 357.

97. Cotton Mather, *Magnalia Christi Americana; or, The Ecclesiastical History of New England; From Its First Planting in the Year 1620, unto the Year of Our Lord 1698* (London: Parkhurst, 1702), 3:153. Morison (*Harvard College in the Seventeenth Century*, 357, n. 2) points out that an English paraphrase in heroic couplets was published by "Philo Muses" in *American Magazine & Historical Chronicle* (Boston) 1 (1744): 166–170. The translation in the text is also provided by Hochbruck and Dudensing-Reichel, "Honoratissimi Benefactores" (Meserve has a slightly different version; see "English Works of Seventeenth-Century Indians," 196–197, n. 5).

> In obitum Viri verè Reverendi
> D. Thomae Thacheri
> Qui Ad
> Dom. ex hâc Vitâ migravit, 18.8.1678
> Tentabo Illustrem, tristi memorare dolore
>   Quem Lacrymis repetunt Tempora, nostra, Virum.
> *Memnona* sic Mater, Mater ploravit Achillem,
>   Justis cum Lacrymis, cumque Dolore gravi
> Mens stupet, ora silent, justum nunc palmo recusat
>   Officium: Quid? Opem Tristis Apollo negat?
> Ast Thachere Tuus conabor dicere laudes
>   Laudes Virtutis, quae super Astra volat.
> Consultis Rerum Dominis, Gentique togatae
>   Nota fuit virtus, ac tua Sancta Fides.
> Vivis post Funus; Faelix post Fata; *Jaces Tu?*
>   Sed *Stellas* inter *Gloria* nempe *Jaces*
> Mens Tua jam caelos repetit; Victoria parta est:
>   Iam Tuus est Christus, quod meruitque tuum.
> Hic Finis Crucis; magnorum haec meta malorum;
>   Ulterius non quo progrediatur erit.
> Crux jam cassa manes; requiescunt ossa Sepulchro;
>   Mors moritur; Vitae Vita Beata redit
> Quum tuba per Densas sonitum dabit ultima Nubes,
>   Cum Domino Rediens Ferrea Sceptra geres.
> Caeles tum scandes, ubi Patria Vero piorum
>   Praevius hanc patriam nunc tibi *Jesus* adit.
> Illic vera Quies; illic sine fine voluptas;
>   Gaudia & Humanis non referenda sonis.
> Σῶμ' ἔχει ἡ κονίν, ἐπί γῆς τ' ὄνομ' οὔποτ' ὀλεῖται,
>   Κλεινὸν ἐν ἡμετέροις κ' ἐσομενοῖσι χρόνοις

ψυχὴ δ' ἐκ ρεθέων πταμένη, βῆ οὔρανον αἰπύν,
Μιχθεῖσ' ἀθάνατος πνεύμασιν ἀθανάτοις.

98. See J. L. Sibley, *Biographical Sketches of Graduates of Harvard University* (Cambridge: Harvard University Press, 1873–1932), 1:202–203; Clifford K. Skipton, *Biographical Sketches of Those Who Attended Harvard College*, 13 vols. (Cambridge: Harvard University Press, 1935–75), 6:142–144; and Szasz, *Indian Education in the American Colonies*, 175–176.

99. See Kenneth Silvermann, ed., *Selected Letters of Cotton Mather* (Baton Rouge: University of Louisiana Press, 1971), 150–151.

100. Hochbruck and Dudensing-Reichel, "Honoratissimi Benefactores," 42–44.

101. "Letter from King Philip to Governor Prince," n.d., in *Collections of the Massachusetts Historical Society*, 1st ser. 2 (1793): 40 (brackets mine).

102. For similar texts in Massachusett, see Goddard and Bragdon, *Native Writings in Massachusett*, 1:173, 175, 179, 181, 225, 373.

103. The full letter is reprinted "word for word" in Gookin, *Historical Account of the Doings and Sufferings of the Christian Indians in New England*, 483.

104. See Axtell, *Invasion Within*, 276.

CHAPTER THREE

1. Most of Occom's writings are found among the papers of Eleazar Wheelock, Special Collections, Baker Library, Dartmouth College (hereafter cited as Wheelock Papers). These include his correspondence from 1756 to 1774, fourteen sermons, his journals from 1743 to 1790 (also in typescript, 3 vols.), and miscellaneous materials. Additional writings are preserved among the Samson Occum holdings of the Connecticut Historical Society (79998), which contains original and related correspondence from 1727 to 1808, a diary from 1787, and several sermons (hereafter cited as Samson Occom Papers). The material found at the Baker Library is available in microfilm under the title "The Papers of Eleazar Wheelock together with the Early Archives of Dartmouth College & Moor's Indian Charity School and Records of the Town of Hanover, New Hampshire, through the year 1779" from University Microfilm International, Ann Arbor (16 reels; reel 14 has most of the Occom writings); the Samson Occom Papers of the Connecticut Historical Society can also be obtained on microfilm directly from the society (79998, 1 reel, which I have used for reference here). Two full-length biographies have been written: William De Loss Love, *Samson Occom and the Christian Indians of New England* (Boston: Pilgrim Press, 1899) — in spite of its early publication date and ethnocentric bias, this is still the most comprehensive and perceptive account of his life; and Harold Blodgett, *Samson Occom* (Hanover, NH: Dartmouth College Publications, 1935). Letters relating to Occom's England journey have been published in Leon B. Richardson, ed., *An Indian Preacher in New England* (Hanover, NH: Dartmouth College Publications, 1933). See also R. Pierce Beaver, *Church, State, and the American Indians: Two and a Half Centuries of Partnership in Missions between Protestant Churches and Government* (St. Louis: Concordia Publishing House, 1966), 153–183; Samuel Buell, *A Sermon*

Preached at East-Hampton, August 29, 1759; at the Ordination of Mr. Samson Occum, A Missionary among the Indians (New York: Printed by James Parker, 1761), iii–xvi; Belle M. Brain, "Samson Occom, the Famous Indian Preacher of New England," Missionary Review of the World 33 (1910): 913–919; Earnest Edward Eells, "Indian Missions on Long Island, part V, Samson Occom," Journal of the Department of History of the Presbyterian Church in the U.S.A. 19, no. 3 (September 1940): 99–109; John C. Huden, "Samson Occom, Indian Missionary," Long Island Forum, November 1941, 259–260, 262; idem, "Occum's Report on Montauks," Long Island Forum, July 1947, 127–128; Nathaniel Miles, Samson Occom, the Mohegan Indian Teacher, Preacher, and Poet, with a Short Sketch of His Life (Madison: By the author, 1888); Will Ottery and Rudi Ottery, A Man Called Sampson (Camden, ME: Penobscot Press, 1989), 34–49; A. La Vonne Brown Ruoff, "Introduction: Samson Occom's Sermon Preached by Samson Occom . . . at the Execution of Moses Paul, an Indian," Studies in American Indian Literature 4, nos. 2–3 (Summer/Fall 1992): 75–81; William B. Sprague, Annals of the American Pulpit (New York) 3 (1858): 192–195; and Margaret C. Szasz, "Samson Occom: Mohegan as Spiritual Intermediary," in idem, ed., Between Indian and White Worlds: The Cultural Broker (Norman: University of Oklahoma Press, 1994), 61–78.

2. For a historical survey of this era I have relied on Arrell M. Gibson, The American Indian: Prehistory to the Present (Lexington, MA: D. C. Heath, 1980), 218–248; William T. Hagan, American Indians (Chicago: University of Chicago Press, 1979), 1–30; D'Arcy McNickle, They Came Here First: The Epic of the American Indian (New York: Harper & Row, 1975), 134–158; Gary B. Nash, Red, White, and Black: The Peoples of Early America (Englewood Cliffs, NJ: Prentice-Hall, 1974), 239–275; Francis P. Prucha, American Indian Policy in the Formative Years: The Indian Trade and Intercourse Acts, 1790–1834 (Lincoln: University of Nebraska Press, 1970), 5–25; and Richard White, The Middle Ground: Indians, Empires, and the Republics in the Great Lakes Region, 1650–1815 (New York: Cambridge University Press, 1991), 223–523.

3. Prucha, American Indian Policy in the Formative Years, 2, 26–50. See also George D. Harmon, Sixty Years of Indian Affairs: Political, Economic, and Diplomatic, 1789–1850 (Chapel Hill: University of North Carolina Press, 1941); Reginald Horsman, Expansion and American Indian Policy, 1783–1812 (East Lansing: Michigan State University Press, 1967); idem, "United States Indian Policies, 1776–1815," in Wilcomb E. Washburn, ed., Handbook of North American Indians: History of Indian-White Relations (Washington, DC: Smithsonian Institution Press, 1988), 4:29–39; and Walter H. Mohr, Federal Indian Relations, 1774–1778 (Philadelphia: University of Philadelphia Press, 1933).

4. Quoted in McNickle, They Came Here First, 153.

5. Quoted in Alice C. Fletcher, Indian Education and Civilization, Bureau of Education Special Report, 1888 (Millwood, NY: Kraus Reprint, 1973), 102.

6. See Beaver, Church, State, and the American Indians. A list of the major missionary societies is in J. D. McCallum, ed., Letters of Eleazar Wheelock's Indians (Hanover, NH: Dartmouth Publications, 1932), 299–313.

7. See Cedrick B. Cowing, The Great Awakening and the American Revolution: Colonial Thought in the 18th Century (Chicago: Rand McNally, 1971); Edwin S.

Gaustad, *The Great Awakening in New England* (New York: Quadrangle Books, 1957); Stephen A. Marini, "The Great Awakening," in Charles H. Lippy and Peter W. Williams, eds., *Encyclopedia of the American Religious Experience: Studies in Traditions and Movements* (New York: Charles Scribner's Sons, 1988), 2:775–798; and Richard Warck, "The Shepherd's Tent: Education and Enthusiasm in the Great Awakening," *American Quarterly* 30, no. 2 (Summer 1978): 177–198. On the effects of the Great Awakening on Indians, see John F. Freeman, "The Indian Convert: Theme and Variation," *Ethnohistory* 12, no. 2 (Spring 1965): 113–128; William S. Simmons, "The Great Awakening and Indian Conversion in Southern New England," in *Papers of the Tenth Algonquian Conference*, ed. William Cowan (Ottawa: Carleton University Press, 1979), 25–36; and idem, "Red Yankees: Narragansett Conversion in the Great Awakening," *American Ethnologist* 10, no. 2 (May 1983): 253–271.

8. See Clarence C. Goen, *Revivalism and Separatism in New England, 1740–1800* (New Haven: Yale University Press, 1962); Gaustad, *Great Awakening in New England*, 66–67, 105–107; and David S. Lovejoy, *Religious Enthusiasm in the New World: Heresy to Revolution* (Cambridge: Harvard University Press, 1985), 180–187.

9. See Robert F. Berkhofer, Jr., "Protestants, Pagans, and Sequences among the North American Indians, 1760–1860," *Ethnohistory* 10, no. 3 (Summer 1963): 201–232; idem, "Model Zions for the American Indian," *American Quarterly* 15, no. 2 (Summer 1963): 176–190; Henry W. Bowden, *American Indians and Christian Missions: Studies in Cultural Conflict* (Chicago/London: University of Chicago Press, 1981), 134–163; and Margaret C. Szasz, *Indian Education in the American Colonies, 1607–1783* (Albuquerque: University of New Mexico Press, 1988), 191–217.

10. *A Letter from the Revd Mr. Sargeant of Stockbridge to Dr. Colman of Boston; Containing Mr. Sargeant's Proposal of a more effectual Method for the Education of Indian Children; to raise 'em if possible into a civil and industrious People; by introducing the English Language among them, and thereby instilling into their Minds and Hearts, with a more lasting Impression, the Principles of Virtue and Piety* (Boston: Printed by Rogers and Fowle for D. Henchman in Cornhill, 1743). See James Axtell, *The Invasion Within: The Contest of Cultures in Colonial North America* (New York/Oxford: Oxford University Press, 1985), 196–204.

11. *Collections of the Massachusetts Historical Society*, 6th ser. 1 (1886): 401–402; quoted in Bowden, *American Indians and Christian Missions*, 136.

12. John Eliot to Sir Robert Boyle, April 22, 1684, Boyle Letters, vol. 2, nos. 165 and 171, Royal Society Archives, London.

13. Wheelock outlined the history of his school in nine promotional pamphlets published between 1763 and 1775. The first and most important is *A Plain and Faithful Narrative of the Original Design, Rise, Progress and Present State of the Indian Charity School in Lebanon* (Boston: Richard and Samuel Draper, 1763). The subsequent publications were titled *A Continuation of the Narrative of the State, &c, of the Indian Charity-School, at Lebanon, In Connecticut . . .* (Boston, 1765; London, 1766; London, 1767; London, 1769; Hartford, 1771; Portsmouth, 1773; Hartford, 1773; Hartford, 1775) (hereafter cited as *Wheelock Narratives*). For a

biography of Wheelock, see David McClure and Elijah Parish, *Memoirs of the Rev. Eleazar Wheelock* (Newburyport, MA: Edward Little, 1811); and James D. McCallum, *Eleazar Wheelock, Founder of Dartmouth College* (Hanover, NH: Dartmouth College Publications, 1939). See also Frederick Chase, *A History of Dartmouth College and the Town of Hanover, New Hampshire (to 1815)* (Brattleboro: Vermont Publishing, 1928); and Love, *Samson Occom*, 56–81. For a critical assessment, see James Axtell, "Dr. Wheelock's Little Red School," in idem, *The European and the Indian: Essays in the Ethnohistory of Colonial North America* (New York/Oxford: Oxford University Press, 1981), 87–109.

14. *Wheelock Narratives* (1763), 11, 14–15.

15. Ibid., 15.

16. See McCallum, *Letters of Wheelock's Indians*. For a critical review of some of these writings, see Laura Murray, " 'Pray Sir, Consider a Little': Rituals of Subordination and Strategies of Resistance in the Letters of Hezekiah Calvin and David Fowler to Eleazar Wheelock, 1764–1768," *Studies in American Indian Literature* 4, nos. 2–3 (Summer/Fall 1992): 48–64.

17. I have relied primarily on John W. De Forest, *History of the Indians of Connecticut: From the Earliest Known Period to 1850* (Hartford: W. J. Hamersley, 1851; rpt., Hamden, CT: Shoestring Press, 1964); Melissa Jayne Fawcett, *The Lasting of the Mohegans: The Story of the Wolf People* (Uncasville, CT: Mohegan Tribe, 1995); Steven F. Johnson, *Ninnuock [The People]: The Algonquian People of New England* (Marlborough, MA: Bliss Publishing, 1995), 225–236; and Benjamin Trumbull, *A Complete History of Connecticut* (Hartford: Hudson & Goodwin, 1797). See also A. Holmes, "Memoir of the Mohegans," *Collections of the Massachusetts Historical Society*, 1st ser. 9 (1804): 77–90; Froelich G. Rainey, "A Compilation of Historical Data Contributing to the Ethnography of Connecticut and Southern New England Indians," *Bulletin of the Archaeological Society of Connecticut* 3 (April 1936): 1–90; Frank G. Speck, "Notes on the Mohegan and Niantic Indians," *Anthropological Papers of the American Museum of Natural History* 3 (1909): 183–210; idem, "Native Tribes and Dialects of Connecticut: A Mohegan-Pequot Diary," in *Forty-third Annual Report of the Bureau of American Ethnology, 1925–26* (Washington, DC: Government Printing Office, 1928), 199–287; and Anthony F. C. Wallace, "Political Organization and Land Tenure among the North Eastern Indians, 1600–1830," *Southwestern Journal of Anthropology* 13, no. 4 (Winter 1957): 301–321.

18. Trumbull, *Complete History of Connecticut*, 28. See also Lloyd C. M. Hare, "Mohegan-Pequot Relationships," *Bulletin of the Archaeological Society of Connecticut* 21 (1947): 26–34; and Arthur L. Peale, *Uncas and the Mohegan-Pequot* (Boston: Meador Publishing, 1939). Melissa Fawcett, the Mohegan tribal historian, feels that the name "Pequot" was adopted by the Mohegans after they had migrated from New York to Connecticut. Fawcett, *Lasting of the Mohegans*, 10–11.

19. James Kendall Hosmer, ed., *Winthrop's Journal, 1630–1649*, 2 vols. (New York: Charles Scribner's Sons, 1908), 2:134–136. See also Fawcett, *Lasting of the Mohegans*, 14–15; Francis Jennings, *The Invasion of America: Indians, Colonialism, and the Cant of Conquest* (New York: W. W. Norton, 1976), 266–268; and Wilcomb E. Washburn, "Seventeenth-Century Indian Wars," in Bruce G. Trigger,

ed., *Handbook of North American Indians: Northeast* (Washington, DC: Smithsonian Institution Press, 1978), 15:90–91.

20. See E. Edwards Beardsley, "The Mohegan Land Controversy," *Papers of the New Haven Colony Historical Society* 3 (1882): 205–225; Francis M. Caulkins, *History of Norwich, Connecticut: From Its Possession by the Indians, to the Year 1866* (1845; Chester, CT: Pequot Press, 1976), 261–270; De Forest, *History of the Indians of Connecticut*, 303–346, 447–489; Carroll Alton Means, "Mohegan-Pequot Relationships, as Indicated by the Events Leading to the Pequot Massacre of 1637 and Subsequent Claims in the Mohegan Land Controversy," *Bulletin of the Archaeological Society of Connecticut* 21 (December 1947): 26–34; and Joseph Henry Smith, *Appeals to the Privy Council from the American Plantations* (New York: Columbia University Press, 1956), 422–444.

21. On the legal significance of the Mohegan case, see Bruce Clark, *Native Liberty, Crown Sovereignty: The Existing Aboriginal Right of Self-Government in Canada* (Montreal/Kingston: McGill-Queen's University Press, 1991), 39–45. In October of 1994, after the Mohegans had been granted federal recognition, they finally agreed to give up their land claims against the state, which they based on a violation of the 1790 Trade and Intercourse Act. See Fawcett, *Lasting of the Mohegans*, 32–33.

22. Fawcett, *Lasting of the Mohegans*, 17–18.

23. See Love, *Samson Occom*, 24–34.

24. "Samson Occom's account of himself, written September 17, 1768," is included in his journals, Wheelock Papers, and cited in segments of Love, *Samson Occom*, and Blodgett, *Samson Occom*. It has been reprinted in its entirety more recently in Bernd C. Peyer, ed., *The Elders Wrote: An Anthology of Early Literature Written by North American Indians, 1768–1934* (Berlin: Dietrich Reimer Verlag, 1982), 12–18; and (together with Occom's sermon at the execution of Moses Paul) in Paul Lauter et al., eds., *The Heath Anthology of American Literature* (Lexington, MA: Heath, 1990), 1:730–751. On Occom's youth, see also Blodgett, *Samson Occom*, 27–36; Helen C. Knight, *Lady Huntington and Her Friends* (New York: American Tract Society, 1853), 150–156; Love, *Samson Occom*, 21–41; and Ottery and Ottery, *A Man Called Sampson*, 34–35.

25. See Harry S. Stout and Peter Onuf, "James Davenport and the Great Awakening in New London," *Journal of American History* 70, no. 3 (December 1983): 556–578.

26. See Blodgett, *Samson Occom*, 28–29; De Forest, *History of the Indians of Connecticut*, 334–335; and Love, *Samson Occom*, 21–23.

27. Love, *Samson Occom*, 37.

28. Buell, *Sermon Preached at East-Hampton*, vii.

29. See Blodgett, *Samson Occom*, 37–53; and Love, *Samson Occom*, 42–55.

30. See *Wheelock Narratives* (1763), 16–18, 26, 29, 41.

31. The illegible date is probably February 7, 1759; Occom Journal, Wheelock Papers. This fragment clearly reflects the highly emotional style of Jonathan Edwards's famous sermon "Sinners in the Hands of an Angry God," delivered at Enfield, Connecticut, on July 8, 1741: "O Sinner! Consider the fearful danger you

are in: it is a great furnace of wrath, a wide and bottomless pit, full of the fire of wrath, that you are held over."

32. Occom Journal, June 28–September 25, 1757, Wheelock Papers. Quote from Buell, *Sermon Preached at East-Hampton*, ix. See also Blodgett, *Samson Occom*, 48–50; and Love, *Samson Occom*, 49–53.

33. David Fowler (Montauk, ca. 1735–1807), one of Wheelock's most successful pupils, was also instrumental in establishing Brothertown. See McCallum, *Letters of Wheelock's Indians*, 85–113; and Murray, "Pray Sir, Consider a Little." On Occom's mission among the Oneidas, see Blodgett, *Samson Occom*, 55–68; and Love, *Samson Occom*, 82–104. The mission is also described in detail in an unpublished manuscript by William De Loss Love titled "An Account of the Christian Indians Who Were Associated with Rev. Samuel Kirkland in His Indian Missions," typescript, Special Collections, Baker Library, Dartmouth College (the original is in the Hamilton College Library). Love writes here that Fowler was probably born about 1745 (p. 8).

34. Samson Occom to Eleazar Wheelock, September 8, 1764, Wheelock Papers (ms. 764508.3). Cited in Blodgett, *Samson Occom*, 73; and Szasz, *Between Indian and White Worlds*, 66.

35. Entry made June 14, 1761, in Occom Journal, May 30–July 7, 1761, Wheelock Papers. Quoted in Blodgett, *Samson Occom*, 57; and Love, *Samson Occom*, 88.

36. See McClure and Parish, *Memoirs of Eleazar Wheelock*, 45.

37. *Wheelock Narratives* (1767), 27 (italics mine). Quoted in Blodgett, *Samson Occom*, 63–64; and Love, *Samson Occom*, 93.

38. Mentioned in Johnson, *Ninnuock*, 231. For details on the conflict, see Blodgett, *Samson Occom*, 69–83; and Love, *Samson Occom*, 119–129.

39. Wheelock to George Whitefield, October 10, 1764. Quoted in Blodgett, *Samson Occom*, 78–79; and Love, *Samson Occom*, 125.

40. Wheelock to Whitefield, May 4, 1765; and Wheelock to John Brainerd, January 14, 1765, Wheelock Papers (mss. 765304 and 765114.3). Reprinted in Richardson, *Indian Preacher in England*, 26–27, 29–32.

41. Minutes of the Connecticut Correspondents, March 12, 1765. Reprinted in Blodgett, *Samson Occom*, 79–80; Love, *Samson Occom*, 127; and Richardson, *Indian Preacher in England*, 28–29.

42. Caulkins, *History of Norwich*, 269 (the date given here, 1754, is obviously incorrect as the decision was handed down in 1771; perhaps the original letter read 1774). Quoted in Beardsley, "The Mohegan Land Controversy," 223; Blodgett, *Samson Occom*, 77; and Love, *Samson Occom*, 123.

43. Occom recorded his voyage in his journal from November 21, 1765, to July 22, 1766, Wheelock Papers. See Blodgett, *Samson Occom*, 84–104; Love, *Samson Occom*, 130–151; and Richardson, *Indian Preacher in England*, 81–87, 100–109.

44. Charles Jeffrey Smith to Wheelock, March 30, 1764. Reprinted in Richardson, *Indian Preacher in England*, 19–20; quoted in Blodgett, *Samson Occom*, 84.

45. Solomon Williams to Wheelock, January 9, 1765, in Richardson, *Indian Preacher in England*, 24.

46. See Chase, *History of Dartmouth College*, 48–53. Occom apparently met with one of the Masons in London and loaned him money. This was probably Samuel Mason, who was imprisoned for debt. See Robert Keen to Nathaniel Whitaker, September 10, 1767, in Richardson, *Indian Preacher in England*, 295–296. There is also a letter extant from John Mason to Occom, February 18, 1768, Samson Occom Papers (0089–0090).

47. Occom to Wheelock, December 6, 1765, Wheelock Papers (ms. 765656.2), in Richardson, *Indian Preacher in England*, 75–76.

48. Hayden White, *Tropics of Discourse: Essays in Cultural Criticism* (Baltimore: Johns Hopkins University Press, 1978), 191. Quoted in David Murray, *Forked Tongues: Speech, Writing, & Representation in North American Indian Texts* (Bloomington: Indiana University Press, 1991), 35–36.

49. Sprague, *Annals of the American Pulpit*, 194–195. Wheelock gives a much more positive description of his oratorical talents: "his deportment in the pulpit commanded attention and respect. His compositions were easy, figurative, and impressive. With a modest assurance, he appeared impressed with the importance of his subject. He usually wrote his sermons, but could extemporize with readiness." Quoted from McClure and Parish, *Memoirs of Eleazar Wheelock*, 45. Samuel Buell noted that although he "uses great Plainness of Speech . . . Those, who have had Opportunity to observe, take Notice, that his Manner of Expression, when he preaches to the *Indians*, is vastly more natural and free and eloquent, quick and powerful, than 'tis wont to be, when he preaches to others. As an Instructor of the *Indians*, he makes frequent Use of apt and significant Similitudes, to convey and illustrate Truth: Such a Method of conveying *Ideas*, you know, Sir, is natural to *Indians* in general, and therefore, doubtless, as pleasing as 'tis natural." Buell, *Sermon Preached at East-Hampton*, viii–ix. Quoted in Blodgett, *Samson Occom*, 35–36.

50. Wheelock to Whitaker, November 28, 1767, Wheelock Papers (ms. 767628.1), in Richardson, *Indian Preacher in England*, 320–322.

51. Quoted in Blodgett, *Samson Occom*, 95.

52. Wheelock to Occom, August 15, 1771, Wheelock Papers (ms. 771465).

53. Wheelock to John Thornton, August 25, 1768, in Richardson, *Indian Preacher in England*, 351–352. Quoted in Blodgett, *Samson Occom*, 107.

54. Thornton to Wheelock, February 28, 1772, in Richardson, *Indian Preacher in England*, 358–359. Cited in Blodgett, *Samson Occom*, 127.

55. Quote from Occom Journal, August 30, 1786, Wheelock Papers. There are several indications in Occom's journal that he had assumed the negative Puritan association with the concept of "wilderness."

56. One letter of confession dated January 4, 1769, is found among the Wheelock Papers (ms. 769104); the other, an almost verbatim copy, n.d., is in the Samson Occom Papers (0105). The report of the Suffolk Presbytery is cited in Love, *Samson Occom*, 163–164.

57. Occom to Wheelock, March 17, 1769, Wheelock Papers (ms. 769217.2). See Blodgett, *Samson Occom*, 110–112; Love, *Samson Occom*, 162–165; and Richardson, *Indian Preacher in England*, 353, 357.

58. Occom to Wheelock, July 24, 1771, Wheelock Papers (ms. 771424). The

letter is reprinted in full in Blodgett, *Samson Occom*, 122–124. Hezekiah Calvin, a Delaware and former student of Wheelock's, also voiced similar misgivings concerning the latter's educational plans. See Edward Deake to Wheelock, June 21, 1768, in McCallum, *Letters of Wheelock's Indians*, 65.

59. See Chase, *History of Dartmouth College*, 32–35, 46, 90 ff., 217 ff.; Love, *Samson Occom*, 157–162; and Leon B. Richardson, "The Dartmouth Indians, 1800–1893," *Dartmouth Alumni Magazine*, June 1930, 524–525.

60. Jere R. Daniell II, "Eleazar Wheelock and the Dartmouth College Charter," Dartmouth College Bicentennial, Baker Library, 1969 (italics mine). The article also appeared in *Historical New Hampshire* 24, no. 4 (Winter 1969): 3–44. Cited in Axtell, "Dr. Wheelock's Little Red School," 108.

61. The Scottish fund remained available to Dartmouth until 1922, when it was channeled to other purposes. The reason given, which basically follows Wheelock's earlier reasoning, was the lack of "qualified" Indian candidates. See "Petition of the Society in Scotland for Propagating Christian Knowledge to Settle Scheme for Application of Trust-Funds" (Edinburgh: T. & A. Constables, 1922). Only three Indians graduated in the eighteenth century: Daniel Simons (Narragansett, class of 1777); Sir Peter Pohquonnoppet (Stockbridge, class of 1780), and Lewis Vincent (Huron, class of 1781). The most famous among Dartmouth's early graduates, the Sioux author Charles Alexander Eastman (class of 1887), paid tribute to Occom in his second autobiography and also acted out the part of the "Pious Mohegan" in a tableau for the sixth earl of Dartmouth during exercises at the laying of the cornerstone of the new Dartmouth Hall on October 26, 1904. See Eric P. Kelly, "The Dartmouth Indians," *Dartmouth Alumni Magazine*, December 1929, 122–125; and Leon B. Richardson, "The Dartmouth Indians," 524–527. It should be pointed out here that Dartmouth has officially renewed its commitment to Indian education since the 1970s and now operates one of the most successful Native American Studies programs in the country. The college is also in the process of reestablishing Wheelock's original ties with New England Indian communities, including Occom's Mohegan descendants.

62. *Wheelock Narratives* (1771), 18–21.

63. Wheelock to Occom, February 24, 1772, Wheelock Papers (ms. 772174.1); quoted in Blodgett, *Samson Occom*, 126–127. Occom to Wheelock, June 1, 1773, Wheelock Papers (ms. 773351); quoted in Love, *Samson Occom*, 159. See also David McClure to Wheelock, May 21, 1770, in Richardson, *Indian Preacher in England*, 354–355.

64. Occom to John Bailey, May 1783, Samson Occom Papers (0307–0310); quoted in part in Love, *Samson Occom*, 159–160, and idem, "Account of the Christian Indians," 25. See also Occom to Wheelock, January 27, 1772; July 13, 1772; June 1, 1773; and Wheelock to Occom, July 21, 1773; February 6, 1774, Wheelock Papers (mss. 772127.1, 772413.2, 773351, 773421.2, 774156.1). On the final correspondence between Occom and Wheelock, see also Richardson, *Indian Preacher in England*, 349–362.

65. Occom, undated and unaddressed letter, Samson Occom Papers (0339–0340). Occom mentions an article in a newspaper dated November 3, 1791, which implies that it was written late in 1791 or early in 1792.

66. See De Forest, *History of the Indians of Connecticut*, 472–474. Melissa Fawcett feels that Occom and other Mohegans left the funeral services as a protest against Ben Uncas's burial at the royal Mohegan burial ground in Norwich because they felt he was not a legitimate sachem. She also maintains that the sachemship was then outlawed by the Connecticut Colony. Fawcett, *Lasting of the Mohegans*, 17–18, 40. Steven Johnson believes that the walkout occurred as a protest against the presence of the English at the funeral, which Occom considered to be hypocritical. Johnson, *Ninnuock*, 233–234.

67. The fragment by Occom, dated April 28, 1778, is found among the Samson Occom Papers (0112–0113). Zachary Johnson to Richard Law, May 30, 1781, Samson Occom Papers (0301). Johnson also accuses certain Indians whom he designates as not being true Mohegans of allowing stock to wander over their pastures and removing fences, Samson Occom Papers (0114–0115). Another undated letter, which may have been written by Occom, contains complaints about Ben Uncas being a "tool" of the overseers and of illegally selling land and timber to the English. It also claims that the tribe has the right to make its own decisions concerning the sachemship according to ancient customs; Samson Occom Papers (0030–0032).

68. See Bernard W. Sheehan, *Seeds of Extinction: Jeffersonian Philanthropy and the American Indian* (New York/London: W. W. Norton, 1974), 244–245.

69. See Blodgett, *Samson Occom*, 146–199; Ottery and Ottery, *A Man Called Sampson*, 34–49; Love, *Samson Occom*, 207–230; and idem, "Account of the Christian Indians," 32–39. In a letter to Susanna Wheatley dated September 21, 1773, Occom wrote: "Tuesday after I left Boston, I preach'd at Natick in the forenoon to a large Aditory, for Short-Notice, the Indians there are almost extinct"; Wheelock Papers (ms. 773521). Reprinted in Blodgett, *Samson Occom*, 148.

70. Quoted in Love, "Account of the Christian Indians," 31.

71. Occom Journal, Tuesday, August 16, 1787, Samson Occom Papers. Quoted in Blodgett, *Samson Occom*, 194. After 1772 he also received a pension of fifty pounds from the trustees of the London fund. See Chase, *History of Dartmouth College*, 245.

72. All three answering speeches of the Oneidas delivered January 21, 22, 24 are contained in the Wheelock Papers (ms. 774121). Reprinted in McCallum, *Letters of Wheelock's Indians*, 167–172. Quoted in Blodgett, *Samson Occom*, 152; and Love, *Samson Occom*, 212–220.

73. Occom Journal, July 8, 1774–August 14, 1774, and December 19, 1774–February 9, 1775, Wheelock Papers. The Oneida deed is found in Love, *Samson Occom*, 222–223; and mention of the Oneida "Declaration of Neutrality" is on p. 226.

74. Occom to Beloved Brethren, n.d., Samson Occom Papers (0274–0275). It is reprinted in Love, *Samson Occom*, 228–229; and in the *Journal of Presbyterian History* 52, no. 4 (Winter 1974): 414–415.

75. Occom Journal, October 4–December 4, 1785, Wheelock Papers (italics mine). Quoted in Blodgett, *Samson Occom*, 184; Love, *Samson Occom*, 252. See also Ottery and Ottery, *A Man Called Sampson*, 46–47. The name "Brothertown" was probably borrowed from the Delaware Christian Indian community founded by John Brainerd near Trenton, New Jersey (1758–1801). See Susanne Banta Hayes,

"John Brainerd and the First Indian Reservation," *Indian Historian* 12, no. 4 (Winter 1979): 20–21.

76. The request is in the Samson Occom Papers (0327–0328). Reprinted in Blodgett, *Samson Occom*, 196–197. A second request presented jointly by the Brothertowns and New Stockbridges is dated November 28–29, 1787, Samson Occom Papers (0329–0330). Reprinted in Love, *Samson Occom*, 276; Occom is quoted from a 1792 letter cited on p. 282.

77. Occom Journal, September 20–December 5, 1787, and December 10, 1787–August 10, 1788, Wheelock Papers.

78. Occom's version of the dispute is in an undated letter probably addressed to the governor of New York, Samson Occom Papers (0359–0361); and in Occom to the Most Honorable Assembly in the State of New York, n.d., Samson Occom Papers (0362–0364). Love believes that the first letter must have been written in the summer of 1792. See Love, "Account of the Christian Indians," 36.

79. The entry, dated 1791, reads: "For several months past they have been in a most unhappy divided state, & their spirit of resentment towards each other so great as to break up the peace of the settlement & threatens its ruin. . . . Their present unhappy divisions & animosities are greatly attributed to Mr. O——m." See Samuel Kirkland, *The Journal of Samuel Kirkland: 18th-Century Missionary to the Iroquois, Government Agent, Father of Hamilton College*, ed. Walter Pilkington (Clinton, NY: Hamilton College, 1980), 211. See also Blodgett, *Samson Occom*, 205–210; Love, *Samson Occom*, 283–298; and Ottery and Ottery, *A Man Called Sampson*, 47–49. Another survey of Brothertown's beginnings is in Thomas Commuk, "Sketch of the Brothertown Indians," *Wisconsin Historical Collections* 4 (1859): 291–298. Curiously, the latter mentions only David Fowler as a founding father.

80. Occom Journal, December 10, 1787–August 10, 1788, Wheelock Papers. Quoted in Blodgett, *Samson Occom*, 200.

81. Occom Journal, October 13, 1789, and January 10, 1790, Wheelock Papers. Quoted in Blodgett, *Samson Occom*, 205.

82. Kirkland, *Journal*, 222–224. Cited in part in Blodgett, *Samson Occom*, 211; and Love, *Samson Occom*, 296–297.

83. The site, where David Fowler is buried, was forgotten until 1893 when William De Loss Love was able to find it again. He suggested then that it should be preserved as a memorial. See Love, *Samson Occom*, 298–299. A more detailed five-page account is appended to idem, "Account of the Christian Indians." The Dartmouth class of 1911 also proposed a monument, and a group of American Indian students at the institution made a similar suggestion in 1971. Descendants of Occom's from Brothertown have recently visited the cemetery, which is located on private property about a quarter-mile from the Bogusville Hill Road, off State Route 12B, just north of Deansboro. There is a historical marker at the edge of the road. I thank Dorothy E. McConnell, historian of the town of Marshall, and Linda Welch, academic assistant at NAS Dartmouth, for the information on the current situation of the site.

84. See George Selement, "Publication and the Puritan Minister," *William and Mary Quarterly* 37, no. 2 (April 1980): 219–241.

85. For a listing of Occom's journals, see Blodgett, *Samson Occom*, 33, n. 12;

and Love, *Samson Occom*, 38, no. 36. It is very probable that sections of the journal have been lost.

86. Blodgett, *Samson Occom*, 33.

87. See Steven E. Kagle, *American Diary Literature, 1620–1799* (Boston: Twayne Publishers, 1979), 16; William Mathews, *American Diaries* (Berkeley: University of California Press, 1945), ix; and Daniel B. Shea, *Spiritual Autobiography in Early America* (Princeton: Princeton University Press, 1968), x.

88. The section on the Oneida mission is excerpted in Love, *Samson Occom*, 87–90; the section describing his English tour has been included in Richardson, *Indian Preacher in England*, 81–87, 100–109; the section on his travels between Mohegan and Brothertown is contained in part in Blodgett, *Samson Occom*, 169–205, and Love, *Samson Occom*, 249–275.

89. H. David Brumble III, *American Indian Autobiography* (Berkeley: University of California Press, 1988), 21–47. See also Hertha Dawn Wong, *Sending My Heart across the Years: Tradition and Innovation in Native American Autobiography* (New York: Oxford University Press, 1992), 25–26.

90. Occom Journal, January 23–April 26, 1786, Wheelock Papers.

91. Arnold Krupat, *The Voice in the Margin: Native American Literature and the Canon* (Berkeley: University of California Press, 1989), 141.

92. The letter is in Wheelock Papers (ms. 7656281). Reproduced in Richardson, *Indian Preacher in England*, 70–71.

93. Murray, *Forked Tongues*, 57.

94. Ibid., 63; and James C. Scott, *Domination and the Arts of Resistance: Hidden Transcripts* (New Haven: Yale University Press, 1990), xii.

95. Samson Occom, "An Account of the Montauk Indians, on Long Island," *Collections of the Massachusetts Historical Society*, 1st ser. 1, 10 (1809): 105–111.

96. See William S. Simmons, *Spirit of the New England Tribes: Indian History and Folklore, 1640–1984* (Hanover/London: University Press of New England, 1986), 73.

97. *Ten Indian Remedies: From Manuscript Notes on Herbs and Roots, by Rev. Samson Occom as Compiled in the Year 1754* (n.p.: Printed by Edward C. Lathem, 1964), Special Collections, Baker Library, Dartmouth College (DCH E 98 M35 04). The original list is kept by the New London County Historical Society.

98. The letter by Moses Paul is reproduced in Blodgett, *Samson Occom*, 139–140.

99. See Ronald A. Bosco, "Lectures at the Pillory: The Early American Execution Sermon," *American Quarterly* 30, no. 2 (Summer 1978): 156–176; Daniel A. Cohen, "In Defense of the Gallows: Justifications of Capital Punishment in New England Execution Sermons, 1674–1825," *American Quarterly* 40, no. 2 (June 1988): 147–164; and, especially, Wayne C. Minnick, "The New England Execution Sermon, 1639–1800," *Speech Monographs* 35, no. 1 (March 1968): 77–89.

100. See Yasuhide Kawashima, "Jurisidiction of the Colonial Courts over the Indians in Massachusetts, 1689–1773," *New England Quarterly* 42, no. 4 (December 1969): 532–550.

101. See Kathleen J. Bragdon, "Crime and Punishment among the Indians of

Massachusetts, 1675–1750," *Ethnohistory* 28, no. 1 (Winter 1981): 23–32; and Minnick, "New England Execution Sermon," 85–86.

102. Quoted from the 1773 edition printed by S. and E. Hall of Salem.

103. Occom was an unusually well-read man. His correspondence is full of references to books he either read or would have liked to obtain. He is said to have owned an "extensive and valuable library," which was bequeathed to his son-in-law Paul Menona. See Hiel Hollister, *Pawlet for One Hundred Years* (Pawlet, VT: Pawlett Historical Society, 1976), 215–216. Thanks to John Moody for this information, which he received from Dorothy Offensend of Wells, Vermont. The latter feels that Paul Menona might be identical with Anthony Paul (b. 1758), the husband of Occom's daughter Christiana and son of Moses Paul. Since both are said to have been preachers in the vicinity of Lake George, she may well be right. See Love, *Samson Occom*, 355.

104. See Love, *Samson Occom*, 169–176. It has been reprinted recently in *Studies in American Indian Literature* 4, nos. 2–3 (Summer/Fall 1992): 82–105; and Lauter et al., *Heath Anthology of American Literature*, 736–751. The original full title was *A Sermon Preached at the Execution of Moses Paul, an Indian who was executed at New Haven on the 2nd of September 1772 for the Murder of Mr. Moses Cook, late of Waterbury, on the 7th of December 1771 / Preached at the Desire of Said Paul by Samson Occom, minister of the gospel and missionary to the Indians, New Haven, 1772.* Twenty-three copies are found in Special Collections, Baker Library, Dartmouth College. The Welsh version, also in the Baker Library, is titled *Pregeth ar Ddihenyddiad Moses Paul, Indian, yr hwn a gefwyd yn euog o Lofruddiaeth* (Cerrfryrddin: Argraphwyd gan John Daniel, yn Heol-y-Brenin, 1789).

105. The broadside, of uncertain authorship, is reproduced by R. Pierce Beaver, "Protestant Churches and the Indians," in Washburn, *Handbook of North American Indians*, 4:434; and Ola E. Winslow, *American Broadside Verse from Imprints of the 17th and 18th Centuries* (New Haven: Elliots Books, 1930). An excerpt is included in Olive W. Burt, *American Murder Ballads and Their Stories* (1958; rpt., New York: Citadel Press, 1964), 150–151.

106. Sylvanus Conant, *The Blood of Abel and the Blood of Jesus* (Boston: Edes & Gill, 1765), 20. Quoted in Bosco, "Lectures at the Pillory," 172–173; and Minnick, "New England Execution Sermon," 84.

107. Samuel Danforth, *The Woful Effects of Drunkenness* (Boston: B. Green, 1710). Danforth argues, as Occom does, that drink will ruin a man's health and consequently waste his estate, leave his family in poverty, and deprive him of honor and esteem among his people. See Minnick, "New England Execution Sermon," 86.

108. Amos Whiting to Occom, May 2, 1773, Samson Occom Papers (0179–0180).

109. A similar interpretation of Occom's sermon based on the broadside version is given in Rayna D. Green, "The Only Good Indian: The Image of the Indian in American Vernacular Culture" (Ph.D. diss., Indiana University, 1973; Ann Arbor, MI: University Microfilms 74-9426, 1973), 72–73.

110. See Murray, *Forked Tongues*, 34–48.

111. The full title is *A Choice Collection of Hymns and Spiritual Songs; In-*

tended for the Edification of Sincere Christians, of All Denominations. By Samson Occom (New London, CT: Printed and sold by Timothy Green, 1774). See Love, *Samson Occom,* 176–187. Another Indian collection of hymns was published by Thomas Commuck, a Narragansett from Brothertown (Wisconsin), under the title *Indian Melodies,* harmonized by Thomas Hastings (New York: G. Lane & C. B. Tippett, 1845). It contains a hymn on p. 31 that is either attributed to or named in honor of Samson Occom. Commuck, as was pointed out earlier (n. 79 above), did not include Occom as founder in his sketch of Brothertown, perhaps in order not to undermine his own false claim in the preface that "no son of the forest, to his knowledge, has ever undertaken a task of the kind"; *Indian Melodies,* v. Interestingly, he also dedicates one hymn to Apes[s] (p. 28).

112. Blodgett, *Samson Occom,* 145; Love, *Samson Occom,* 180–181. Among the Wheelock Papers there is a list of twenty-six hymns attributed to Occom.

113. The former is reprinted in Charles Seymour Robinson, *A Selection of Spiritual Songs with Music for Use in Social Meetings* (New York: Scribner, 1879), 83. The latter, dated 1801, is contained in Albert Christ-Janer, Charles W. Hughes, and Carleton Sprague Smith, *American Hymns Old and New* (New York: Columbia University Press, 1980), 553. Love, who includes both versions in his biography, feels that Occom is the author of each, though they were published after his death. See Love, *Samson Occom,* 183–187. Miles notes that one of Occom's hymns became a standard (hymn no. 167) in the prayer book of the Presbyterian Church. See Miles, *Samson Occom,* 6–7.

114. Lois Marie Hunter, *The Shinnecock Indians* (Islip, NY: Buys Brothers, 1950), 31–33. This is an allusion to a tradition among the Narragansetts that a certain tune was known among them and other Coastal Algonquians long before the arrival of Europeans and that they immediately recognized it upon first hearing services in a Plymouth church. Commuck, a Narragansett, has incorporated it under the title "Old Indian Hymn" in his *Indian Melodies.* See Love, *Samson Occom,* 177.

115. Occom Journal, January 23–April 27, 1786, Wheelock Papers. Quoted in Blodgett, *Samson Occom,* 187.

116. See Speck, "Native Tribes and Dialects of Connecticut," 274–275. On the importance of dreams in the Indian conversion experience, see Robert F. Berkhofer, Jr., *Salvation and the Savage: An Analysis of Protestant Missions and American Indian Response, 1787–1862* (Lexington: University of Kentucky Press, 1965), 116–117.

117. See Regina Flannery, *An Analysis of Coastal Algonquian Culture* (Washington, DC: Catholic University of America Press, 1939), 32–33; and Daniel G. Brinton, *The Myths of the New World: A Treatise on the Symbolism and Mythology of the Red Race of America* (1876; rpt., New York: Hashell House, 1968), 159–162, 288–290.

118. Brumble, *American Indian Autobiography,* 44.

119. See Peter W. Williams, *America's Religions: Traditions and Cultures* (New York: Macmillan, 1990), 170.

120. The essay on Occom, dated January 18, 1984, was written by Everett R. Carson and is available along with other posthumous data used here in the Samson Occom Vertical File, Wheelock Papers. Dartmouth's best-known literary exponents

of Indian descent, Michael Dorris and Louise Erdrich, also make a brief ironic reference to Occom ("that jewel in the college's crown; its very own American Indian preacher/recruiter/fund-raiser, the first in a procession of salaried aboriginal tokens") in their novel, *The Crown of Columbus* (New York: Harper-Collins, 1991), 136–137.

121. Entry dated Thursday, October 18, 1787, Occom Journals, September 20–December 7, 1787, Wheelock Papers.

122. The proposal was made public in the *Montauk Pioneer*, August 16, 1969. Quote from the *East Hampton Star*, June 25, 1970. In an article in the *Long Island Press*, June 14, 1970, Karl Grossman refers to Occom as "an Indian revolutionary 200 years before his time." The above material is available in the Samson Occom Vertical File, Wheelock Papers.

123. See Melissa Fawcett Sayet, "Sociocultural Authority in Mohegan Society," *Artifacts* 16 (1987): 40–41; and Fawcett, *Lasting of the Mohegans*, 32–34. In a recent conversation, Melissa Fawcett informed me that Occom's name was still "good" for propaganda purposes and highly cherished but that the most respected elder of the contemporary Mohegan community at Uncasville is his sister Lucy Tantaquidgeon (1731–1830), who chose to remain in Connecticut and helped to found the Mohegan Church. Her descendant, the noted scholar and traditionalist Gladys Tantaquidgeon (b. 1889), was still operating the Tantaquidgeon Indian Museum (founded in 1931) in 1995.

124. See Jack Campisi, *The Brothertown Indian Nation of Wisconsin: A Brief History*, pamphlet (Woodruff, WI: Brothertown Indian Nation, 1991). See also Ottery and Ottery, *A Man Called Sampson*, 43–53.

125. Brant produced a "Mohawk Prayer Book" in 1786 together with Daniel Claus, a translation. He apparently hoped to write a history of the Six Nations in English but never completed it. See Douglas W. Boyce, "A Glimpse of Iroquois Culture History through the Eyes of Joseph Brant and John Norton," *Proceedings of the American Philosophical Society* 117, no. 4 (August 1973): 286–294. On the life of Brant, see Isabel T. Kelsay, *Joseph Brant, 1743–1807: Man of Two Worlds* (Syracuse, NY: Syracuse University Press, 1984); and William L. Stone, *Life of Joseph Brant: Thayendanegea*, 2 vols. (New York: A. V. Blake, G. Dearborn, 1838; rpt., New York: Kraus Reprint, 1969). There is, however, a long line of Iroquoian historians beginning with David Cusick (Tuscarora) and Elias Johnson (Tuscarora) in the nineteenth century and culminating with prominent early-twentieth-century anthropologists like Arthur C. Parker (Seneca) and J. N. B. Hewitt (Tuscarora). See "Books by Iroquois Authors (Mohawk, Seneca, Cayuga, Tuscarora, Oneida, Onondaga)," *American Indian Quarterly* 6, nos. 3–4 (Fall/Winter 1982): 358–376. One might also mention John Norton, Joseph Brant's adopted "nephew," who wrote a journal in 1816 with accounts of Iroquois, Cherokee, and other eastern woodland Indians' cultures. See Carl F. Klinck and James J. Talman, eds., *The Journal of Major John Norton, 1816* (Toronto: Champlain Society, 1970).

126. Quoted from a fragment in Samson Occom Papers (0403–0407). About eighteen sermons written between 1760 and 1766 (a few are not dated) are found among the Wheelock Papers. Several more are preserved in the Samson Occom Papers (0397–0483).

127. Undated mss., Samson Occom Papers (0474, 0456). The first is cited in Love, *Samson Occom*, 176. During the 1770s abolitionism was a common issue among many New Light preachers, such as Jonathan Edwards. In 1774 Connecticut passed a law forbidding the importation of Indian, black, or mulatto slaves. See Lorenzo J. Greene, "Slave-Holding New England and Its Awakening," *Journal of Negro History* 13, no. 4 (October 1928): 492–533.

128. See Julian D. Major, Jr., ed., *The Poems of Phillis Wheatley* (Chapel Hill: University of North Carolina Press, 1981), 6–7; and William H. Robinson, *Phillis Wheatley and Her Writings* (New York/London: Garland Publishing, 1984), 44. Phillis Wheatley Peters (1753–84), an African slave purchased by the Wheatley family when she was about seven, taught herself how to write and eventually became a fairly well-known poet. One of her first writing efforts was a letter addressed to Samson Occom around 1765–66, who was well acquainted with the Wheatleys. Occom was probably instrumental in getting the countess of Huntingdon to support the publication of her *Poems on Various Subjects, Religious and Moral* (London: A. Bell, 1773) and helped to sell the collection in Connecticut. See Susanna Wheatley to Occom, March 29, 1773, Samson Occom Papers (0171–0173). The responding letter Phillis Wheatley wrote to Occom on February 11, 1774, a rare documentation of her own antislavery sentiments, was published in various local newspapers and is included in most modern collections of her work. A clipping from the Goodspeed Book Shop's dealer catalogue also mentions a copy of Eliot's Bible that was purchased from Occom by the African American Methodist preacher and author Lemuel Haynes (1753–1833), indicating some association between them as well.

129. See Murray, *Forked Tongues*, 44–47.

130. Entry of Wednesday, February 8, 1786, Occom Journal, January 23–April 26, 1786, Wheelock Papers. Occom's personal library also contained a signed copy of *Acts and Laws Passed by the General Court or Assembly of His Majesty's English Colony of Connecticut in New England, in America* (1769), which has been preserved in the Baker Library, Dartmouth College. See Blodgett, *Samson Occom*, 186, n. 8.

131. Joseph Johnson's diary, two autobiographical sketches, several sermons, and a number of letters are found among the Wheelock Papers; a diary fragment, about a dozen of his letters, and ten sermons are also preserved among the Samson Occom Papers. A number of his letters and addresses have been reprinted in McCallum, *Letters of Wheelock's Indians*, 122–199. See also Love, *Samson Occom*, 64–66, 207–230; and idem, "Account of the Christian Indians," 30–35.

132. Samuel Kirkland to Wheelock, December 29, 1768 in McCallum, *Letters of Wheelock's Indians*, 140–141.

133. Joseph Johnson to Wheelock, December 29, 1767, Wheelock Papers (ms. 767679.2). In McCallum, *Letters of Wheelock's Indians*, 125–127.

134. Johnson to Wheelock, February 11, 1768, Wheelock Papers (ms. 768302). See also McCallum, *Letters of Wheelock's Indians*, 127–129, 135–136.

135. See McCallum, *Letters of Wheelock's Indians*, 108–109; and Murray, "Pray Sir, Consider a Little," 57–64. In the long run, Kirkland remained a close and faithful friend of the Christian Indians and broke off relations with Wheelock at about the same time that Occom did. Kirkland agreed with Occom that the English

fund should have been applied for the benefit of Indian students. He founded the Oneida Academy in 1793, which became Hamilton College in 1810. See Samuel K. Lothrop, *Life of Samuel Kirkland: Missionary to the Indians* (Boston: Little, Brown, 1848).

136. See McCallum, *Letters of Wheelock's Indians*, 136–142.

137. Wheelock Papers (ms. 773480). In McCallum, *Letters of Wheelock's Indians*, 150.

138. The original is found among the Wheelock Papers. There is also what appears to be a fragment of a diary from the same period, dated November 1771–January 2, 1772 (ms. 772102). Another fragment dated May 24, 1772, is preserved among the Samson Occom Papers (0484–0485).

139. He probably read the abridged version of Baxter's *Saints' Everlasting Rest; or, A Treatise on the Blessed State of Souls in their Enjoyment of God in Heaven*, prepared by Benjamin Fawcett in 1764, which was frequently used by Protestant missionaries in North America. See Richardson, *Indian Preacher in England*, 286, n. 2.

140. Diary fragment, May 24, 1772, Samson Occom Papers (0484–0485).

141. The license is contained among the Wheelock Papers (ms. 774475.1). Reproduced in McCallum, *Letters of Wheelock's Indians*, 177–178.

142. Joseph Johnson, "To all Enquiring friends, or to all Strangers that may Cast their Curious but dying eyes upon these lines," Wheelock Papers (ms. 772900.2). Also in McCallum, *Letters of Wheelock's Indians*, 146–148.

143. Wheelock Papers (ms. 773674.1). In McCallum, *Letters of Wheelock's Indians*, 158–160. The document contains the names of six other Indians, but there is no doubt that Johnson is the author. A similar letter dated October 13, 1773, is preserved among the Samson Occom Papers (0201–0202).

144. Johnson to the Provincial Congress of the Colony of New York, August 26, 1775, Samson Occom Papers (0270–0273).

145. Johnson to Occom, May 25, 1774, Samson Occom Papers (0248–0250).

146. Wheelock Papers (mss. 774120, 774121). In McCallum, *Letters of Wheelock's Indians*, 160–172. Copies are also found among the Samson Occom Papers (0227–0230). Johnson's speech in English was apparently translated for the Oneidas by Edward Johnson.

147. See A. M. Drummond and Richard Moody, "Indian Treaties: The First American Drama," *Quarterly Journal of Speech* 39, no. 1 (February 1953): 15–24; and Lawrence C. Wroth, "The Indian Treaty as Literature," *Yale Review*, July 1928, 749–766.

148. Joseph Johnson to William Johnson, July 8, 1774, Wheelock Papers (ms. 774408).

149. George Washington to Joseph Johnson, February 20, 1776, Wheelock Papers (ms. 776170.1). Among the papers are two letters, a recommendation, and a passport (mss. 775372.2, 776116.1, 776116.2, 776170). See also McCallum, *Letters of Wheelock's Indians*, 191–192, 194–196, 198. Mention of a meeting between Johnson and Washington is made in Johnson to John Phillips, March 19, 1776, Samson Occom Papers (0270–0273).

150. Charles Evans, ed., *The American Bibliography: A Chronological Direc-*

tory of All Books, Pamphlets and Periodical Publications Printed in the USA, 1639–1800 (New York: P. Smith, 1941–1957), 15392. The letter has been reprinted in Peyer, *The Elders Wrote*, 19–24. In a postscript to his letter to William Johnson, July 8, 1774, Joseph Johnson mentions *"two small Pieces*, which I composed, and got Printed." Wheelock Papers (ms. 774408; italics mine). Mention of another letter that was "reprinted in Boston" is made in Joseph Johnson to Occom, October 10, 1773, Samson Occom Papers (0203–0204).

151. "A Discourse by Jos. Johnson," Farmington, November 7, 1773; and "discourse to My Indian Brethren," Kanoarohare, January 22, 1774, Wheelock Papers (mss. 773607, 774122). Nine sermons written at Farmington between August 28, 1772 and June 14, 1774, and another at Dartmouth dated August 22, 1774, are also included among the Samson Occom Papers (0486–0620, erroneously listed as Occom's sermons).

152. See H. B. Tanner, "History of Kaukauna's Revolutionary Hero," *Kaukauna Wisconsin Times*, August 1926; and Jeanne Ronda and James P. Ronda, " 'As They Were Faithful': Chief Hendrick Aupaumut and the Struggle for Stockbridge Survival, 1757–1830," *American Indian Culture and Research Journal* 3, no. 3 (1979): 43–55. His role as U.S. emissary to the western tribes is discussed in Katherine C. Turner, *Red Men Calling on the Great White Father* (Norman: University of Oklahoma Press, 1951), 3–27.

153. See Jeremy Belknap and Jedediah Morse, "Report on the Oneida, Stockbridge, and Brotherton Indians" (1796), Museum of the American Indian, Heye Foundation, *Indian Notes and Monographs* 54 (1955); idem, eds., "The Report of a Committee of the Board of Correspondents of the Scots Society for Propagating Christian Knowledge, Who Visited the Oneida and Mohekunuh Indians," *Collections of the Massachusetts Historical Society*, 1st ser. 5 (1816): 12–32; Ted J. Brasser, *Riding the Frontier's Crest: Mahican Indian Culture and Culture Change*, Publications in Ethnology, no. 13 (Ottawa: National Museum of Man, 1974); idem, "Mahican," in Trigger, *Handbook of North American Indians*, 15: 198–212; Patrick Frazier, *The Mohicans of Stockbridge* (Lincoln: University of Nebraska Press, 1992); Electa Jones, *Stockbridge, Past and Present; or, Records of an Old Mission Station* (Springfield, MA: Samuel Bowles, 1854); Marion J. Mochon, "Stockbridge-Munsee Cultural Adaptations: 'Assimilated Indians,' " *Proceedings of the American Philosophical Society* 112 (1968): 191–194; and Alanson B. Skinner, "Notes on Mahikan Ethnology," *Bulletin of the Public Museum of the City of Baltimore* 2, no. 3 (1925): 87–116.

154. See Colin G. Calloway, *The American Revolution in Indian Country: Crisis and Diversity in Native American Communities* (New York: Cambridge University Press, 1995), 85–107.

155. Wayne E. Stearns, "Hendrick," in Dumas Malone, *Dictionary of American Biography* (New York: Charles Scribner's Sons, 1932), 532–533. "King" Hendrick was probably a born Mahican; he served as sachem and representative of the Six Nations at councils with the English. At the Albany Congress of 1754 he made a famous speech that was published in London's *Gentlemen's Magazine*, June 1755, 254. He died in battle during the French and Indian War.

156. Aupaumut and John Quinney translated "The Assembly's Shorter Cate-

chism" into Mahican around 1818. See Willard Walker, "Native American Writing Systems," in Charles A. Ferguson and Shirley B. Heath, eds., *Language in the USA* (Cambridge: Cambridge University Press, 1981), 154. Electa Jones also mentions that he sent a written Mahican speech to his people in New York requesting them to move to White River in Indiana; *Stockbridge, Past and Present*, 120.

157. For an overview of the political issues leading up to the War of 1812, see Reginald Horsman, *The Diplomacy of the New Republic, 1776–1815* (Arlington Heights, IL: Harlan Davidson, 1985); and White, *Middle Ground*, 366–523.

158. "A Narrative of an Embassy to the Western Indians from the Original Manuscript of Hendrick Aupaumut, with Prefatory Remarks by Dr. B. H. Coates," *Memoirs of the Pennsylvania Historical Society* 2 (1827): 61–131. The exact date when it was written is not known, but it was probably completed in 1793 as a report to Henry Knox. The original narrative is in the Pickering Papers, reel 59, Massachusetts Historical Society. It has been reproduced in part in Lauter, *Heath Anthology of American Literature*, 752–756.

159. Aupaumut, "Narrative," 130. See Tanner, "History of Kaukauna's Revolutionary Hero," 6; and Turner, *Red Men Calling on the Great White Father*, 25–26.

160. Aupaumut, "Narrative," 99–100.

161. Hendrick Aupaumut to John Sargeant, Jr., n.d., *Missionary Herald* 1, no. 9 (February 1809): 426. This letter is followed by another dated March 27, 1808, in which he describes how the "Prophet's followers have done much mischief already, on the frontiers." The first, probably also written in 1808, is quoted in Ronda and Ronda, "As They Were Faithful," 50.

162. Aupaumut, "Narrative," 127. Compare with Benjamin Lincoln, "Journal of a Treaty Held in 1793, with the Indian Tribes North-West of the Ohio, by Commissioners of the United States," *Collections of the Massachusetts Historical Society*, 3rd ser. 5 (1836): 109–176. The latter, which also mentions Aupaumut's parallel activities at the Miami Rapids, contains an interesting address to the Commissioners of the United States dated August 16, 1793. It is an eloquent illustration of the "hostile" point of view held by leaders like Brant and Red Jacket, with whom Aupaumut was conferring at the time:

"Brothers, money to us is of no value, and to most of us unknown; and as no consideration whatever can induce us to sell our lands, on which we get sustenance for our women and children, we hope we may be allowed to point out a mode by which your settlers may be easily removed, and peace thereby obtained.

"Brothers, we know that these settlers are poor, or they would never have ventured to live in a country which has been in continual trouble ever since they crossed the Ohio. Divide therefore this large sum of money, which you have offered to us, among these people; give to each also a portion of what you say you would give us annually, over and above this very large sum of money; and we are persuaded they would most readily accept of it in lieu of the lands you sold to them. If you add also the great sums you must expend in raising and paying armies with a view to force us to yield you our country, you will certainly have more than sufficient for the purposes of repaying these settlers for all their labor and improvements.

"Brothers, you have talked to us about concessions. It appears strange that you should expect any from us, who have only been defending our just rights against your invasions. We want peace. Restore to us our country, and we shall be enemies no longer."

163. Aupaumut, "Narrative," 128.

164. Ronda and Ronda, "As They Were Faithful," 45.

165. Jones, *Stockbridge, Past and Present*, 15–23. Reproduced in Peyer, *The Elders Wrote*, 25–33. An abridged version titled "Extract from an Indian History" is in the *Collections of the Massachusetts Historical Society* 9 (1804): 99–102. Ronda and Ronda mention yet another slightly different version in Jedediah Morse, ed., *First Annual Report of the American Society for Promoting the Civilization and General Improvement of the Indian Tribes in the United States* (New Haven, 1824), 42–45.

166. Aupaumut's close involvement with Mahican culture is further corroborated by his efforts to write down oral traditions, which have been included in part in Jones, *Stockbridge, Past and Present*; Skinner, "Notes on Mahikan Ethnology"; and John G. E. Heckewelder, "An Account of the History, Manners, and Customs of the Indian Nations, Who Once Inhabited Pennsylvania and the Neighbouring States," *Transactions of the Committee of History, Moral Science, and General Literature of the American Philosophical Society* 1 (Philadelphia, 1819). Mentioned in Brasser, "Mahican," 212.

167. Aupaumut, "Narrative," 128.

168. Hendrick Aupaumut, "Extracts from the Journal of Rev. John Sargeant," *Missionary Herald* 1 (November 1805): 270–272, 316–317. Cited in part in Ronda and Ronda, "As They Were Faithful," 46. See also his speeches dated October 7, 1804, and May 30, 1805, in "Extracts from Mr. Sargeant's Journal," *Missionary Herald* 1, no. 7 (December 1808): 367–368, and 1, no. 10 (March 1806): 464–465.

169. See Ronda and Ronda, "As They Were Faithful," 53.

170. Ibid., 44.

171. John W. Quinney (1797–1855), who was related to Aupaumut through the latter's marriage to Lydia Quinney, acquired a three-year education in New York, along with Solomon Hendrick, and became one of the most illustrious leaders in the history of the Stockbridge Indians. It was chiefly through his efforts that the Stockbridge Indians were able to emerge through the first half of the nineteenth century as a distinct group with their own land base. See Levi Konkapot, Jr., "The Last of the Mohicans," *Wisconsin Historical Collections* 4 (1858): 303–307, and the miscellaneous materials, which include a speech and some writings, in Ibid., 309–333. He was educated at Orangedale Academy in New Jersey, according to Belknap and Morse, "Report on the Oneida, Stockbridge, and Brotherton Indians," 25.

172. See Brasser, "Mahican," 210–211; Marion J. Mochon, "History of the Wisconsin Stockbridge Indians," *Wisconsin Archaeologist*, n.s. 49 (1968): 81–95; and Ronda and Ronda, "As They Were Faithful," 54.

CHAPTER FOUR

1. William Apess published five books: *A Son of the Forest* (New York: By the author, 1829), revised as *A Son of the Forest: The Experience of William Apes, a Native of the Forest* (New York: By the author; G. F. Bunce, Printer, 1831); *The*

Increase of the Kingdom of Christ: A Sermon (New York: By the author, G. F. Bunce, Printer, 1831); *The Experiences of Five Christian Indians of the Pequot Tribe; or, An Indian's Looking-Glass for the White Man* (Boston: By the author; James B. Dow, Printer, 1833), reprinted as *Experience of Five Christian Indians of the Pequot Tribe* in 1837; *Indian Nullification of the Unconstitutional Law of Massachusetts Relative to the Marshpee Tribe; or, The Pretended Riot Explained* (Boston: Jonathan Howe, 1835; rpt., Stanfordville, NY: Earl M. Coleman, 1979); and *Eulogy on King Philip* (Boston: By the author, 1836; rpt., 1837). The books have been published collectively in Barry O'Connell, ed., *On Our Own Ground: The Complete Writings of William Apess, A Pequot* (Amherst: University of Massachusetts Press, 1992). This valuable publication also includes an excellent and extensive introduction on Apess's life and works. An early study which acknowledges Apess's historical connection with reformism is Kim McQuaid's "William Apes, Pequot: An Indian Reformer in the Jackson Era," *New England Quarterly* 50, no. 4 (December 1977): 605–626. His involvement in the Mashpee rebellion is described in Donald M. Nielsen, "The Mashpee Indian Revolt of 1833," *New England Quarterly* 58, no. 3 (September 1985): 400–420. Apess's writings (primarily his two autobiographies) have been analyzed in Arnold Krupat, *The Voice in the Margin: Native American Literature and the Canon* (Berkeley: University of California Press, 1989), 132–201; idem, "Native American Autobiography and the Synecdochic Self," in Paul J. Eakin, ed., *American Autobiography: Retrospect and Prospect* (Madison: University of Wisconsin Press, 1991), 171–194, reprinted in Arnold Krupat, *Ethnocriticism: Ethnography, History, Literature* (Berkeley: University of California Press, 1992), 201–231; David Murray, *Forked Tongues: Speech, Writing, & Representation in North American Indian Texts* (Bloomington: Indiana University Press, 1991), 49–64; and A. La Vonne Brown Ruoff, "Three Nineteenth-Century American Indian Autobiographers," in A. La Vonne Brown Ruoff and Jerry W. Ward, eds., *Redefining American Literary History* (New York: MLA, 1990), 251–269. The mystery of Apess's death is cleared up in Barry O'Connell, "William Apess and the Survival of the Pequot People," *Algonkians of New England: Past and Present*, Dublin Seminar for New England Folklife, *Annual Proceedings* 16 (1991): 89–100. Apess's ideological debt to Methodism is discussed in Karin M. Tiro, "Denominated 'Savage': Methodism, Writing, and Identity in the Works of William Apess, a Pequot," *American Quarterly* 48, no. 4 (December 1996): 653–679. Earlier tributes to Apess's significance are found in Ernest S. Bates, "William Apes," in Allen Johnson and Dumas Malone, eds., *Dictionary of American Biography* (New York: Charles Scribner's Sons, 1928, 7:323; Stanley J. Kunitz and Howard Haycraft, *American Authors, 1600–1900: A Biographical Dictionary of American Literature* (New York: H. W. Wilson, 1938), 35; and Elémire Zolla, *The Writer and the Shaman: A Morphology of the American Indian*, trans. Raymond Rosenthal (New York: Harcourt Brace Jovanovich, 1969), 231. See also Randall Moon, "William Apess and Writing White," *Studies in American Indian Literature* 5, no. 4 (Winter 1993): 44–54.

2. N. Scott Momaday, "The Man Made of Words," in *Indian Voices: The First Convocation of American Indian Scholars* (San Francisco: Indian Historian Press, 1970), 49–62.

3. Michael P. Rogin, *Fathers and Children: Andrew Jackson and the Subjugation of the American Indian* (New York: Alfred A. Knopf, 1975), 307.

4. See Francis P. Prucha, *American Indian Policy in the Formative Years: The Indian Trade and Intercourse Acts, 1790–1834* (Lincoln: University of Nebraska Press, 1970); idem, "United States Indian Policies, 1815–1860," in Wilcomb E. Washburn, ed., *Handbook of North American Indians: History of Indian-White Relations* (Washington, DC: Smithsonian Institution Press, 1988), 4:40–50; and, especially, Ronald N. Satz, *American Indian Policy in the Jacksonian Era* (Lincoln: University of Nebraska Press, 1975). Rogin's *Fathers and Children* offers an interesting psychological perspective on this period.

5. See Annie H. Abel, *The History of Events Resulting in Indian Consolidation West of the Mississippi* (1908; rpt., New York: AMS Press, 1972). The text to the Removal Act is found in Wilcomb B. Washburn, ed., *The American Indian and the United States: A Documentary History*, 4 vols. (New York: Random House, 1973), 2169–2171.

6. Johnson v. M'Intosh, 21 U.S. (8 Wheat.) 543 (1823), in Washburn, *American Indian and the United States*, 2537–2553. On the importance of this case in legal history, see Robert A. Williams, Jr., *The American Indian in Western Legal Thought: The Discourses of Conquest* (New York/Oxford: Oxford University Press, 1990), 287–323.

7. See Prucha, *American Indian Policy in the Formative Years*, 51–65; Satz, *American Indian Policy in the Jacksonian Eras*, 143; and Washburn, *American Indian and the United States*, 2172–2182.

8. Cherokee Nation v. Georgia, 30 U.S. (5 Pet.) 1 (1831); Worcester v. Georgia, 21 U.S. (6 Pet.) 515 (1832). See Washburn, *American Indian and the United States*, 2554–2602, 2603–2648.

9. On the ideological background of the removal era, see Robert F. Berkhofer, Jr., *The White Man's Indian: Images of the American Indian from Columbus to the Present* (New York: Alfred A. Knopf, 1978), 33–69, 157–166; Roy Harvey Pearce, *Savigism and Civilization: The Study of the Indian and the American Mind* (Baltimore: Johns Hopkins University Press, 1953), 53–236; and Bernard W. Sheehan, *Seeds of Extinction: Jeffersonian Philanthropy and the American Indian* (New York/London: W. W. Norton, 1974).

10. On the application of Locke's notions of property to obtain Indian lands after the Revolution, see Williams, *American Indian in Western Legal Thought*, 233–286; on Vattel's principles as a means of justifying removal, see Albert K. Weinberg, *Manifest Destiny: A Study of Nationalist Expansionism in American History* (Baltimore: Johns Hopkins University Press, 1935), 77–99.

11. See Hoxie N. Fairchild, *The Noble Savage: A Study in Romantic Naturalism* (New York: Columbia University Press, 1928); Leslie A. Fiedler, "The Indian in Literature in English," in Washburn, ed., *Handbook of North American Indians*, 4:573–581; and Albert Keiser, *The Indian in American Literature* (New York: Oxford University Press, 1933).

12. See Ray Allen Billington, *Land of Savagery, Land of Promise: The European Image of the American Frontier in the Nineteenth Century* (1981; rpt., Norman: University of Oklahoma Press, 1985).

13. See Brian W. Dippie, *The Vanishing American: White Attitudes and U.S. Indian Policy* (Middletown, CT: Wesleyan University Press, 1982).

14. Pearce, *Savagism and Civilization*, 58.

15. See Roy H. Pearce, "The Significance of the Captivity Narrative," *American Literature* 19 (1947/48): 1–20; and Richard Slotkin, *Regeneration through Violence: The Mythology of the American Frontier, 1600–1860* (Middletown, CT: Wesleyan University Press, 1973), 94–145.

16. See Louise Barnett, *The Ignoble Savage: American Literary Racism, 1790–1890* (Westport, CT: Greenwood Press, 1975), 129–142; and Richard Drinnon, *Facing West: The Metaphysics of Indian-Hating and Empire-Building* (New York: Meridian, 1980), 137–164.

17. See Reginald Horsman, "Scientific Racism and the American Indian in the Mid-Nineteenth Century," *American Quarterly* 27, no. 2 (May 1972): 152–169; and idem, *Race and Manifest Destiny: The Origins of American Racial Anglo-Saxonism* (Cambridge: Harvard University Press, 1981), 189–207.

18. Horsman, *Race and Manifest Destiny*, 205.

19. See Lee Eldridge Huddleston, *Origins of the American Indians: European Concepts, 1492–1729* (Austin: University of Texas Press, 1967), 128–143; and Robert Wauchope, *Lost Tribes and Sunken Continents: Myth and Method in the Study of American Indians* (Chicago: University of Chicago Press, 1962), 50–68. See also Berkhofer, *White Man's Indian*, 34–38; and Pearce, *Savagism and Civilization*, 61–62.

20. James Adair, *The History of American Indians . . .* (London: Printed for E. C. Dilly, 1775); Elias Boudinot, *A Star in the West; or, A Humble Attempt to Discover the Long Lost Tribes of Israel . . .* (Trenton, NJ: Fenton, Hutchinson, & Dunham, 1816); Lydia Sigourney, *Traits of the Aborigines of America* (Cambridge, MA, 1822).

21. See Abel, *Events Resulting in Indian Consolidation*, 370–381; and Washburn, *American Indian and the United States*, 1017–1187.

22. See Sydney E. Ahlstrom, *A Religious History of the American People* (New Haven: Yale University Press, 1972), 415–428; Richard D. Birdsall, "The Second Great Awakening and the New England Social Order," *Church History* 39, no. 3 (September 1970): 345–364; John B. Boles, *The Great Revival, 1787–1805* (Lexington: University of Kentucky Press, 1972); Winthrop S. Hudson, *Religion in America: An Historical Account of the Development of American Religious Life*, 3rd ed. (New York: Charles Scribner's Sons, 1981), 134–203; Donald G. Mathews, "The Second Great Awakening as an Organizing Process, 1780–1830: An Hypothesis," *American Quarterly* 21, no. 1 (Spring 1969): 23–43; William W. Sweet, *The Story of Religion in America* (New York: Harper & Row, 1930), 233–242; and Peter W. Williams, *America's Religions: Traditions and Cultures* (New York: Macmillan, 1990), 166–174.

23. See Mary K. Cayton, "Social Reform from the Colonial Period through the Civil War," in Charles H. Lippy and Peter W. Williams, eds., *Encyclopedia of the American Religious Experience: Studies in Traditions and Movements* (New York: Charles Scribner's Sons, 1988), 3:1429–1440; and Williams, *America's Religions*, 174–183.

24. See Ahlstrom, *Religious History of the American People*, 422; Cayton, "Social Reform from the Colonial Period through the Civil War," 1431–1434; Clifford S. Griffin, *Their Brothers' Keepers: Moral Stewardship in the United States, 1800–1865* (New Brunswick, NJ: Rutgers University Press, 1960); Charles Foster, *An Errand of Mercy: The Evangelical United Front, 1790–1837* (Chapel Hill: University of North Carolina Press, 1960); Timothy L. Smith, *Revivalism and Social Reform in Mid-Nineteenth Century America* (New York: Abingdon Press, 1957); and Williams, *America's Religions*, 174–183.

25. See Cedric C. Goen, *Broken Churches, Broken Nation: Denominational Schisms and the Coming of the American Civil War* (Macon, GA: Mercer University Press, 1985).

26. See Linda K. Kerber, "The Abolitionist Perception of the Indian," *Journal of American History* 62, no. 2 (September 1975): 271–295; and Robert W. Mardock, "The Anti-slavery Humanitarians and the Indian Policy Reform," *Western Humanities Review* 7 (Spring 1958): 131–146.

27. On Indian slavery, see Donald Grinde, Jr., "Native American Slavery in the Southern Colonies," *Indian Historian* 10, no. 2 (Spring 1977): 38–42; and Almon W. Lauber, *Indian Slavery in Colonial Times within the Present Limits of the United States* (1913; rpt., Williamstown, MA: Corner House Publications, 1979), 25–47. On Indian indenture, see Yasuhide Kawashima, "Indian Servitude in the Northeast," and Peter H. Wood, "Indian Servitude in the Southeast," in Washburn, *Handbook of North American Indians*, 4:404–406, 407–409. On the topic of Indian slaveholders, see Annie Heloise Abel, *The American Indians as Slaveholders and Secessionists*, 3 vols. (Cleveland: A. H. Clark, 1915; rpt., Lincoln: University of Nebraska Press, 1992); Laurence Foster, *Negro-Indian Relationships in the Southeast* (1928; rpt., Philadelphia: University of Pennsylvania Press, 1935); Rudi Halliburton, *Red over Black: Black Slavery among the Cherokee Indians* (Westport, CT: Greenwood Press, 1977); Daniel F. Littlefield, Jr., *Africans and Seminoles: From Removal to Emancipation* (Westport, CT: Greenwood Press, 1977); idem, *The Cherokee Freedman: From Emancipation to American Citizenship* (Westport, CT: Greenwood Press, 1978); idem, *Africans and Creeks: From the Colonial Period to the Civil War* (Westport, CT: Greenwood Press, 1979); idem, *The Chicasaw Freedmen: A People without a Country* (Westport, CT: Greenwood Press, 1980); and Theda Perdue, *Slavery and the Evolution of Cherokee Society, 1540–1866* (Knoxville: University of Tennessee Press, 1979).

28. See Robert T. Lewit, "Indian Missions and Anti-slavery Sentiment: A Conflict of Evangelical and Humanitarian Ideals," *Mississippi Valley Historical Review* 50, no. 1 (June 1963): 39–55; Kerber, "Abolitionist Perception of the Indian," 282–285; and William G. McLoughlin, "Indian Slaveholders and Presbyterian Missionaries, 1837–1861," *Church History* 42 (December 1973): 535–551.

29. See D'Arcy McNickle, *They Came Here First: The Epic of the American Indian* (New York: Harper & Row, 1975), 177–188.

30. On the post–Civil War period, see Robert Winston Mardock, *The Reformers and the American Indian* (Columbia: University of Missouri Press, 1971).

31. See Charles I. Foster, "Colonization of Free Negroes in Liberia," *Journal of Negro History* 38, no. 1 (January 1953): 41–66; Floyd J. Miller, *The Search for*

a Black Nationality: Black Emigration and Colonization, 1787–1863 (Urbana: University of Illinois Press, 1975); Philip J. Staudenraus, *The African Coloniza-tion Movement, 1816–1865* (New York: Columbia University Press, 1961); and David M. Streifford, "The American Colonization Society: An Application of Re-publican Ideology to Early Antebellum Reform," *Journal of Southern History* 45, no. 2 (May 1979): 201–220.

32. Dippie, *The Vanishing American*, 77.

33. See Anne C. Loveland, "Evangelism and Immediate Emancipation in Ameri-can Anti-slavery Thought," *Journal of Southern History* 32 (May 1966): 172–188.

34. In contrast to the issue of slavery in the Southeast, social relations between Indians and blacks in America have received relatively little scholarly attention. See Jack D. Forbes, *Africans and Native Americans: The Language of Race and the Evolution of Red-Black Peoples*, 2nd ed. (Urbana/Chicago: University of Illinois Press, 1993); James H. Johnson, "Documentary evidence of the Relations of Ne-groes and Indians," *Journal of Negro History* 14, no. 1 (January 1929): 21–43; Gary B. Nash, *Red, White, and Black: The Peoples of Early America* (Englewood Cliffs, NJ: Prentice-Hall, 1974), 290–297; Kenneth W. Porter, "Relations between Negroes and Indians within the Present Limits of the United States, 1789–1837," *Journal of Negro History* 17, no. 3 (July 1932): 287–367; Carter G. Woodson, "The Relation of Negroes and Indians in Massachusetts," *Journal of Negro History* 5, no. 1 (January 1920): 45–57; and J. Leitch Wright, Jr., *The Only Land They Knew: The Tragic Story of the American Indians in the Old South* (New York: Free Press, 1981), 248–278.

35. See Kevin Mulroy, *Freedom on the Border: The Seminole Maroons in Flor-ida, the Indian Territory, Coahuila, and Texas* (Lubbock: Texas Technological Uni-versity Press, 1993), 6–34; Kenneth W. Porter, "Florida Slaves and Free Negroes in the Seminole War, 1835–1842," *Journal of Negro History* 28, no. 4 (October 1943): 390–421; idem, "Negroes and the Seminole War, 1817–1818," *Journal of Negro History* 36, no. 3 (July 1951): 249–280; idem, "Negroes and the Seminole War, 1835–1842," *Journal of Southern History* 34, no. 4 (November 1964): 427–450; and J. Leitch Wright, Jr., "A Note on the First Seminole War as Seen by Indians, Negroes, and Their British Advisors," *Journal of Southern History* 34 (November 1968): 565–567.

36. On Pequot history, see especially Laurence M. Hauptman and James D. Wherry, eds., *The Pequots in Southern New England: The Fall and Rise of an American Indian Nation* (Norman: University of Oklahoma Press, 1990). See also John W. De Forest, *History of the Indians of Connecticut: From the Earliest Known Period to 1850* (1851; rpt., Hamden, CT: Shoestring Press, 1964; Paul Marodia, "Puritan and Pequot," *Indian Historian* 3, no. 3 (Summer 1970): 9–15; and J. Dyne-ley Prince and Frank G. Speck, "The Modern Pequots and Their Language," *Ameri-can Anthropologist* 5, no. 2 (April/June 1903): 193–212.

37. See Drinnon, *Facing West*, 46–61.

38. The above information is taken from a leaflet handed out at Foxwoods in 1995 titled "The Mashantucket Pequot Nation."

39. Apess, *Experiences of Five Christian Indians*, 53 (155). I am using the 1833 edition printed in Boston by James B. Dow. The page numbers in parentheses refer

to O'Connell's collected works (*On Our Own Ground*), which is more readily available to the reader.

40. Apess gives two different dates for his birth: In *A Son of the Forest* it is January 31, 1798; in *Experiences of Five Christian Indians* it is January 30, 1798. I have opted for the spelling "Apess," which appeared in later editions of his publications, with due deference to O'Connell's research. The change may have been Apess's reaction to common nineteenth-century racist associations between apes and African Americans. See Winthrop Jordan, *White over Black: American Attitudes toward the Negro, 1550–1812* (Chapel Hill: University of North Carolina Press, 1968), 29–32, 235–239, 491–497.

41. Apess, *A Son of the Forest*, 7–9 (3–4). I am using the second, revised edition printed by G. F. Bunce in New York in 1831. Page numbers in parentheses are in O'Connell, *On Our Own Ground*.

42. On the problems of race classification, see Jack D. Forbes, "The Evaluation of the Term Mulatto: A Chapter in Black-Native American Relations," *Journal of Ethnic Studies* 10, no. 2 (Summer 1982): 45–66; idem, "Mulattoes and People of Color in America: Implications for Black-Indian Relations," *Journal of Ethnic Studies* 12, no. 2 (Summer 1984): 17–61; and idem, "The Manipulation of Race, Caste, and Identity: Classifying Afroamericans, Native Americans, and Red-Black People," *Journal of Ethnic Studies* 17, no. 4 (Winter 1990): 1–51. Forbes has expanded his views on the subject in his *Africans and Native Americans*.

43. O'Connell, *On Our Own Ground*, xxvii–xxviii, n. 17. His primary source is Barbara W. Brown and James M. Rose, *Black Roots in Southeastern Connecticut, 1650–1900* (Detroit: Gale Research, 1980), 9–11. The latter mention that a Captain Joseph Taylor of Colchester had an Indian servant in the 1790s and a black slave woman by the name of Candace Apes. They conclude that William, an ex-soldier who had been living in Stonington and Groton, came to Colchester and married Candace sometime prior to purchasing land there in 1811 (p. 11).

44. See De Forest, *History of the Indians of Connecticut*, 356–357, 443, 445; Lorenzo J. Greene, *The Negro in Colonial New England, 1620–1776* (New York: Columbia University Press, 1942), 95–96; and Porter, "Relations between Negroes and Indians," 312. See also chap. 8 in U.S. Department of Commerce, Bureau of the Census, *A Century of Population Growth, 1790–1909* (Washington, DC: Government Printing Office, 1909).

45. See Greene, *Negro in Colonial New England*, 294.

46. Paul Cuffee, *Narrative of the Life and Adventures of Paul Cuffee, a Pequot Indian* (Vernon, CT: Printed by Horace N. Bill, 1839). See Carter Woodson, "Paul Cuffee," *Journal of Negro History* 8, no. 1 (January 1923): 153–232. Okah Tubbee, *A Thrilling Sketch of the Life of the Distinguished Chief Okah Tubbee, Alias Wm. Chubbee, Son of the Head Chief, Mosholeh Tubbee, of the Choctaw Nation of Indians* (New York, 1848). See H. David Brumble, *American Indian and Eskimo Autobiographies* (Lincoln: University of Nebraska Press, 1981), 141–142; Charles Dougall, "Okah Tubbee," *Dictionary of Canadian Biography* (Toronto: University of Toronto Press, 1985), 3:898–899; and Daniel F. Littlefield, Jr., "Introduction," in idem, ed., *The Life of Okah Tubbee* (Lincoln: University of Nebraska Press, 1988),

vii–xliv; and Sylvester Long, *Long Lance: The Autobiography of a Blackfoot Indian Chief* (New York: Cosmopolitan Book, 1926). See Hugh A. Dempsey, "Long Lance," in Margot Liberty, ed., *American Indian Intellectuals*, Proceedings of the American Ethnological Society, 1976 (St. Paul: West Publishing, 1978); 197–205; Donald B. Smith, *Long Lance: The True Story of an Impostor* (Toronto: Macmillan, 1982); and idem, "From Sylvester Long to Chief Buffalo Child Long Lance," in James A. Clifton, ed., *Being and Becoming Indian: Biographical Studies of North American Frontiers* (Chicago: Dorsey Press, 1989), 183–203.

47. Apess, *A Son of the Forest*, 9 (5).

48. The records show that William, an Indian boy, was given medical assistance by the town of Colchester in 1802 and was probably one of the children bound out by the town selectmen that same year. See Brown and Rose, *Black Roots in Southeastern Connecticut*, 11.

49. Apess, *A Son of the Forest*, 22 (10). See Margaret Szasz, *Indian Education in the American Colonies, 1607–1783* (Albuquerque: University of New Mexico Press, 1988), 1–24.

50. Apess, *A Son of the Forest*, 14 (7).

51. Ibid., 21 (10), 23 (11).

52. O'Connell points out that they may have been members of the Christian Church, dissenting Methodists who had separated themselves from the main body in 1793. *On Our Own Ground*, 12, n. 6.

53. Apess, *A Son of the Forest*, 26 (12).

54. Ibid., 26–28 (12–13).

55. Apess, *Experiences of Five Christian Indians*, 8 (123).

56. Ibid., 10 (124).

57. Apess, *A Son of the Forest*, 37–41 (18–19); *Experiences of Five Christian Indians*, 11–12 (125–126).

58. Apess, *A Son of the Forest*, 41 (19), 45 (21); *Experiences of Five Christian Indians*, 14 (127), 16 (129).

59. Apess, *A Son of the Forest*, 48–49 (22), 54–55 (25); *Experiences of Five Christian Indians*, 18 (131). See also Brown and Rose, *Black Roots in Southeastern Connecticut*, 11. O'Connell includes a transcription of Apess's enlistment and service record in which he is recorded as having deserted on September 14, 1815. O'Connell, *On Our Own Ground*, xxxii, n. 25.

60. Apess, *A Son of the Forest*, 69–70 (32–33).

61. Ibid., 75 (35).

62. Ibid., 79–80 (37–38); *Experiences of Five Christian Indians*, 18–19 (131).

63. Apess, *A Son of the Forest*, 90 (42).

64. Ibid., 92–93 (43–44); *Experiences of Five Christian Indians*, 20 (132).

65. Apess, *A Son of the Forest*, 97 (46).

66. Ibid., 98 (46). Mary's own autobiography is included in Apess, *Experiences of Five Christian Indians*, 22–36 (133–144). As O'Connell points out, Mary Wood may well have been of African-Indian-Spanish descent because the native population in the Spanish Caribbean islands was primarily mestizo at that time, a supposition that is corroborated by Apess's mention of having joined a "colored" religious

group just prior to meeting her. O'Connell, *On Our Own Ground*, 46, n. 45. According to the Salem vital records, the wedding took place on December 13, 1821. See Brown and Rose, *Black Roots in Southeastern Connecticut*, 11.

67. Apess, *A Son of the Forest*, 107 (51).

68. There is some variance on dates here. In *A Son of the Forest*, 107, he writes that he made a renewed application three months after his rejection; in *Experiences of Five Christian Indians*, 20, he claims to have left the Methodist Episcopal Church on April 11, 1829.

69. O'Connell has provided a valuable "Textual Afterword" in which the deviations between the first edition of 1829 and the second of 1831 are listed and commented upon. *On Our Own Ground*, 311–324.

70. See Donald G. Mathews, *Slavery and Methodism: A Chapter in American Morality, 1780–1845* (Princeton, NJ: Princeton University Press, 1965).

71. See Lewis V. Baldwin, *"Invisible" Strands in African Methodism: A History of the African Union Methodist Protestant and Union American Methodist Episcopal Churches, 1805–1980* (Metuchen, NJ: American Theological Library Association and Scarecrow Press, 1983); Harry Richardson, *Dark Salvation: The Story of Methodism as it Developed among Blacks in America* (Garden City, NY: Doubleday, 1976); Milton C. Sernett, *Black Religion and American Evangelicalism: White Protestants, Plantation Missions, and the Flowering of Negro Christiantiy, 1787–1865* (Metuchen, NJ: Scarecrow Press, 1975), esp. chaps. 5 and 6; and James Beverly Ford Shaw, *The Negro in the History of Methodism* (Nashville: Parthenon Press, 1954).

72. George White, *A Brief Account of the Life, Experiences, Travels, and Gospel Labours of George White, an African: Written by Himself, and Revised by a Friend* (New York: John C. Totten, 1810). See William L. Andrews, *To Tell a Free Story: The First Century of African-American Autobiography, 1760–1865* (Urbana/Chicago: University of Illinois Press, 1986), 52–56. Racial discrimination within the church is also a main topic in Richard Allen, *The Life, Experience, and Gospel Labors of the Rt. Rev. Richard Allen to which Is Annexed the Rise and Progress of the African Methodist Church in the United States of America* (Philadelphia: Martin & Boden, 1833). See Patrick C. Kennicot, "Black Preachers in the Antislavery Movement," *Speech Monographs* 37, no. 1 (March 1970): 15–24.

73. Charles Yrigoyen, Jr., "United Methodist," in Lippy and Williams, *Encyclopedia of the American Religious Experience*, 539–553 (esp. 544–546).

74. O'Connell, *On Our Own Ground*, 323.

75. Ibid., xxxiv–xxxv. Quote taken from Apess, *Indian Nullification*, 172. I am using the version included in O'Connell's anthology.

76. See Hauptman and Wherry, *Pequots in Southern New England*, 125–127.

77. Apess, *Indian Nullification*, 247–248.

78. This statement appears in the 1837 edition of *Experiences of Five Christian Indians*. Quoted in O'Connell, *On Our Own Ground*, 151, n. 13.

79. Apess kept a detailed record of his activities at Mashpee in his *Indian Nullification*. The best modern source for the Mashpee "rebellion" and Apess's role in it is Nielsen, "Mashpee Indian Revolt of 1833." See also Jack Campisi's "Introduction" to the 1979 edition of Apess's *Indian Nullification*, vii–x; McQuaid, "William

Apes, Pequot," 614–622; and O'Connell's "Introduction" to *On Our Own Ground*, xxxv–xxxviii. For a general history of the Mashpees, see Francis G. Hutchins, *Mashpee: The Story of Cape Cod's Indian Town* (West Franklin, NH: Amarta Press, 1979); and the autoethnography by Russell M. Peters, *The Wampanoags of Mashpee: An Indian Perspective on American History* (n.p.: Nimrod Press, 1987). The contemporary Mashpees and their bid for federal recognition are described in Paul Brodeur, *Restitution: The Land Claims of the Mashpee, Passamaquoddy, and Penobscot Indians of New England* (Boston: Northeastern University Press, 1985), 3–65; Jack Campisi, *The Mashpee Indians: Tribe on Trial* (Syracuse: Syracuse University Press, 1991); and James Clifford, "Identity in Mashpee," in idem, *The Predicament of Culture: Twentieth-Century Ethnography, Literature, and Art* (Cambridge: Harvard University Press, 1987), 277–346.

80. Quoted in Brodeur, *Restitution*, 14.

81. Clifford, "Identity in Mashpee," 297–298, 306–307. For a critical view of the term "triracial isolates" and its application to Indian communities filing for federal recognition, see Susan Greenbaum, "What Is in a Label? Identity Problems of Southern Indian Tribes," *Journal of Ethnic Studies* 19, no. 2 (Summer 1991): 107–126.

82. Apess, *Indian Nullification*, 170–173.

83. Ibid., 175. The petition is reproduced in Peters, *Wampanoags of Mashpee*, 32–33. See also Campisi, *Mashpee Indians*, 99–118; McQuaid, "William Apes, Pequot," 617–618; and Nielsen, "Mashpee Indian Revolt of 1833," 408–409.

84. Apess, *Indian Nullification*, 177.

85. Ibid.

86. See Greene, *Negro in Colonial New England*, 124–143, 160–161.

87. See also Joseph C. Carrol, *Slave Insurrections in the United States, 1800–1865* (1938; rpt., New York: New American Library, 1969); and Eugene D. Genovese, *From Rebellion to Revolution: Afro-American Slave Revolts in the Making of the Modern World* (Baton Rouge: Louisiana State University Press, 1979), 82–137.

88. Apess, *Indian Nullification*, 179.

89. Ibid., 180.

90. See Nielsen, "Mashpee Indian Revolt of 1833," 413.

91. See Kerber, "Abolitionist Perception of the Indian," 282.

92. *Barnstable Patriot*, February 5, 1834. Quoted in Apess, *Indian Nullification*, 227.

93. Apess, *Indian Nullification*, 194, 242–246.

94. Ibid., 205. Jeremiah Evarts (1781–1831), secretary of the American Board of Commissioners for Foreign Missions, was strongly opposed to removal and wrote a series of articles against it in the *National Intelligencer* under the pseudonym "William Penn," which were published collectively in 1829 as *Essays on the Present Crisis in the Conditions of the American Indians* in Boston and then passed out to congressmen in a condensed version. Apess, who includes a letter to the editor of the *Boston Advocate* by "William Penn" in *Indian Nullification* (214–216), was undoubtedly influenced by Evarts's legalistic rhetoric. Evarts's address was published in the *Cherokee Phoenix and Indians' Advocate*, July 24, 1830. It is reprinted in Francis P. Prucha, ed., *Cherokee Removal: The "William Penn" Essays and Other Writings by*

Jeremiah Evarts (Knoxville: University of Tennessee Press, 1981), 253–262. See John A. Andrew, *From Revivals to Removals: Jeremiah Evarts, the Cherokee Nation, and the Search for the Soul of America* (Athens: University of Georgia Press, 1992).

95. Apess, *Indian Nullification*, 206.

96. See McQuaid, "William Apes, Pequot," 621–622; and Nielsen, "Mashpee Indian Revolt of 1833," 416–419.

97. The jury argued that, although there was sufficient evidence that it had functioned as a tribe in 1834 and 1842, this was not recognizable in 1790, 1869, 1870, and 1976! The Mashpees attempted a second lawsuit (Mashpee II) in 1981, but it was dismissed in 1982. The 1978 decision was affirmed by the First Circuit appellate court in May 1983, and in October of that year the Supreme Court refused to hear the case. See Brodeur, *Restitution*, 59–65; Campisi, *Mashpee Indians*, 9–65; and Clifford, "Identity in Mashpee," 333–336.

98. Apess, *Indian Nullification*, 166.

99. *Boston Daily Advocate*, December 27, 1833. Quoted in Nielsen, "Mashpee Indian Revolt of 1833," 416. Nielsen also provides some additional citations indicating Apess's decline in popularity (418–419).

100. O'Connell, *On Our Own Ground*, xxxviii, lxxx–lxxxi.

101. See O'Connell, "Apess and the Survival of the Pequot People," 92, n. 5.

102. O'Connell, *On Our Own Ground*, xliii.

103. Rufus B. Anderson, ed., *Memoirs of Catherine Brown, a Christian Indian of the Cherokee Nation* (Philadelphia: American Sunday School Union, 1824; rpt., Boston: Massachusetts Sabbath School Union, 1832). An abstract from her memoirs was published in the *Missionary Herald* 21, no. 7 (July 1825): 193–200. Catherine Brown (ca. 1800–23) attended the Brainerd mission school, Cherokee Nation, in 1817–19 and then taught at the Creek Path mission school. Her total devotion to Christiantiy made her the darling of Protestant missionary circles. She contracted tuberculosis while caring for her afflicted brother John and died on July 18, 1823. Her death was a much publicized event. Several of her pious letters were also published in missionary journals: to David Brown, February 21, 1821, *Missionary Herald* 17, no. 8 (August 1821): 258–259; to David Brown, August 10, 1821, *Religious Remembrancer* 9, no. 8 (October 13, 1821): 30; no name, February 16, 1822, *Religious Remembrancer* 9, no. 37 (May 4, 1822): 146–147. See John F. Freeman, "The Indian Convert: Theme and Variation," *Ethnohistory* 12, no. 2 (Spring 1965): 118–120; and Mary A. Higginbotham, "The Creek Path Mission," *Journal of Cherokee Studies* 1, no. 2 (Fall 1976): 72–86.

104. The first to point out the connections between Apess's autobiography and slave narratives was Ruoff, "Three Nineteenth-Century American Indian Autobiographers," 252–255.

105. For information on slave narratives I have relied on Andrews, *To Tell a Free Story*; Stephen Butterfield, *Black Autobiography in America* (Amherst: University of Massachusetts Press, 1974); Charles T. Davis and Henry Louis Gates, "Introduction: The Language of Slavery," in idem, eds., *The Slave's Narrative* (Oxford/New York: Oxford University Press, 1985), xi–xxxiv; Frances Smith Foster, *Witnessing Slavery: The Development of Ante-Bellum Slave Narratives* (Westport, CT: Greenwood Press, 1979); Charles H. Nichol, *Many Thousand Gone: The Ex-Slaves'*

Account of Their Bondage and Freedom (Leiden: E. J. Brill, 1963); Sidonie Smith, *Where I'm Bound: Patterns of Slavery and Freedom in Black American Autobiography* (Westport, CT: Greenwood Press, 1974); and Marion W. Starling, *The Slave Narrative: Its Place in American History* (Washington, DC: Howard University Press, 1988).

106. See Andrews, *To Tell a Free Story*, 7; Butterfield, *Black Autobiography in America*, 3, 32; and Foster, *Witnessing Slavery*, 45. On Brainerd's influential memoirs, see Freeman, "The Indian Convert," 121–125; and Steven E. Kagle, *American Diary Literature, 1620–1799* (Boston: Twayne Publishers, 1979), 38–46. Apess acknowledges his debt to Brainerd in the introduction to his "Appendix" in *A Son of the Forest*, 113 (52).

107. Krupat, "Native American Autobiography and the Synechdochic Self," 176.

108. See Andrews, *To Tell a Free Story*, 5; and Butterfield, *Black Autobiography in America*, 32.

109. In his appendix to *A Son of the Forest*, Apess quotes extensively from Elias Boudinot's *Star in the West*, and copies almost verbatim all of Washington Irving's popular essay, "Traits of Indian Character," which first appeared in *Analectic Magazine* 3 (February 1814): 145–156, and was reprinted in his widely read *Sketchbook* of 1819.

110. See Andrews, *To Tell a Free Story*, 14.

111. Apess, *A Son of the Forest*, 7 (34). I am using the version of the sermon in O'Connell, *On Our Own Ground*, 101–115.

112. Apess, *Experiences of Five Christian Indians*, 60 (160).

113. See Davis and Gates, *The Slave's Narrative*, xxviii; O'Connell, *On Our Own Ground*, xlv; Smith, *Where I'm Bound*, 24. See also Richard M. Huber, *The American Idea of Success* (New York: McGraw-Hill, 1971), 15–22.

114. Olaudah Equiano, *The Interesting Narrative of the Life of Olaudah Equiano, or Gustavus Vassa, the African*. Written by Himself (London: By the author, 1789); William Grimes, *Life of William Grimes, the Runaway Slave*. Written by Himself (New York: By the author, 1825); White, *Brief Account*.

115. See Andrews, *To Tell a Free Story*, 9, 26; Davis and Gates, *The Slave's Narrative*, xxviii; Smith, *Where I'm Bound*, 15, 45.

116. See Janet Duitsman Cornelius, *"When I Can Read My Title Clear": Literacy, Slavery, and Religion in the Antebellum South* (Columbia: University of South Carolina Press, 1991); and Karen C. Chambers Dalton, " 'The Alphabet Is an Abolitionist': Literacy and African Americans in the Emancipation Era," *Massachusetts Review* 32, no. 4 (Winter 1991/92): 545–580.

117. See Andrews, *To Tell a Free Story*, 5; and Smith, *Where I'm Bound*, 13–14.

118. Apess, *Experiences of Five Christian Indians*, 10 (124); *A Son of the Forest*, 50 (24).

119. Gilbert H. Barnes, *The Anti-Slavery Impulse, 1830–1844* (1933; rpt., New York: Harcourt, Brace and World, 1964), 43, 51. See also Butterfield, *Black Autobiography in America*, 40–46.

120. C. G. Jung, "On the Psychology of the Trickster Figure," in Paul Radin, *The Trickster: A Study in American Indian Mythology* (London: Routledge & Kegan

Paul, 1956): 195–211. On African-Indian connections, see Alan Dundes, "African Tales among the North American Indians," *Southern Folklore Quarterly* 29, no. 3 (September 1965): 207–219; William G. McLoughlin, "A Note on African Sources of American Indian Racial Myths," *Journal of American Folklore* 89, no. 353 (July/September 1976): 331–336; and Mac Linscott Ricketts, "The North American Indian Trickster," *History of Religions* 5, no. 2 (Winter 1966): 327–350. On the trickster figure as a source of covert defiance, see James C. Scott, *Domination and the Arts of Resistance: Hidden Transcripts* (New Haven: Yale University Press, 1990), 162–166.

121. Apess, *A Son of the Forest*, 48 (22), 76 (36); *Eulogy on King Philip*, 42 (304). I am using the second edition of *Eulogy*, published in Boston in 1837 (page numbers in parentheses refer to O'Connell, *On Our Own Ground*). See Alex Lichtenstein, " 'That Disposition to Theft, with which They Have Been Branded': Moral Economy, Slave Management, and the Law," *Journal of Social History* 21, no. 3 (Spring 1988): 413–440.

122. O'Connell, *On Our Own Ground*, lxxiv.

123. David Walker, *Walker's Appeal, in Four Articles; Together with a Preamble, to the Coloured Citizens of the World, but in Particular, and Very Expressly, to those of the United States of America. Written in Boston, State of Massachusetts, September 28, 1829* (Boston: D. Walker, 1829; rpt., New York: Arno Press, 1969). Walker's quasi-insurrectionist pamphlet went through three editions within one year, and it is highly unlikely that Apess was not aware of it. He may also have read Robert Alexander Young's *Ethiopian Manifesto, Issued in Defense of the Blackman's Rights, in the Scale of Universal Freedom*, which appeared in New York early in 1829 and in which the author predicts the advent of a "colored" Messiah.

124. Quote from the preface of the 1831 edition of *A Son of the Forest*. As O'Connell has pointed out, Apess replaced "An Indian's Looking-Glass for the White Man" with a much shorter and milder sketch titled "An Indian's Thought" in the second, 1837 edition of *Experiences*. Here he calls on white Christians to teach Indians by example and to help them. See O'Connell, *On Our Own Ground*, 161, n. 16.

125. See Andrews, *To Tell a Free Story*, 77–81.

126. O'Connell, *On Our Own Ground*, 106–107, 111, 113–115. Apess's mention here of "twelve hundred church members in the woods of Canada" may well be a reference to the Methodist revival led by Peter Jones. Jones had appeared together with an Indian children's choir at the tenth anniversary of the Methodist Missionary Society in New York City on May 4, 1829. As Apess deposited copyright title to *A Son of the Forest* in New York around this time, he may well have attended this major Methodist event. Jones also remained briefly in New York before his departure from there to England on March 24, 1831, the year *Increase of the Kingdom of Christ* was published. See Donald B. Smith, *Sacred Feathers: The Reverend Peter Jones (Kahkewaquonaby) & the Mississauga Indians* (Lincoln/London: University of Nebraska Press, 1987), 112–129.

127. As Apess mentions an upcoming lengthier version of his autobiography in this text, O'Connell feels that the shorter version may have been written prior to the manuscript for *A Son of the Forest*. O'Connell, *On Our Own Ground*, 120, n. 1.

128. Apess, *Experiences of Five Christian Indians*, 38 (145).

129. Ibid., 55–57 (157–158).

130. See Jordan, *White over Black*, 175, 471–472; and Nash, *Red, White, and Black*, 287.

131. Apess, *Experiences of Five Christian Indians*, 59–60 (159–160).

132. O'Connell, *On Our Own Ground*, 273.

133. The controversy has its origins in a copy of the book once owned by Samuel G. Drake and now in possession of the Mashpee Historical Society, in which Drake jotted down that it had been written by Snelling at the request of Apess. See O'Connell, *On Our Own Ground*, xliii–xliv, n. 38.

134. Calhoun, then vice-president under Jackson, drafted a document titled "Exposition and Protest" in conjunction with South Carolina's protest against the "tariff of abominations" in 1828 in which he defended a state's right to nullify acts of Congress deemed unconstitutional. Georgia's nullification of Cherokee laws in turn posed a political dilemma for Andrew Jackson, who feared that if federal priorities in this case were enforced according to the Supreme Court decision of 1831 it would cause Georgia to side with South Carolina in the crisis and ultimately pose a threat to the Union. See William W. Freehling, *Prelude to the Civil War: The Nullification Controversy in South Carolina, 1816–1836* (New York: Harper & Row, 1966); and Edwin A. Miles, "After John Marshall's Decision: *Worcester* v. *Georgia* and the Nullification Crisis," *Journal of Southern History* 39, no. 4 (November 1973): 519–544.

135. O'Connell, *On Our Own Ground*, 212–214.

136. Ibid., 230. See Paulo Freire, *Pedagogy of the Oppressed*, trans. Myra B. Ramos (New York: Seabury Press, 1970), 60–61.

137. Albert Memmi, *The Colonizer and the Colonized*, trans. Howard Greenfield (London: Earthscan Publications, 1990), 139; O'Connell, *On Our Own Ground*, 230.

138. O'Connell, *On Our Own Ground*, 230–231.

139. Ibid., 274.

140. Ibid., lxxiv.

141. Merton L. Dillon, *The Abolitionists: The Growth of a Dissenting Minority* (DeKalb, IL: Northern Illinois University Press, 1974), 76.

142. Washington Irving, "Philip of Pokanoket," *Analectic Magazine* 3 (June 1814): 502–515. See William L. Hedges, *Washington Irving: An American Study, 1802–1832* (Baltimore: Johns Hopkins University Press, 1965), 114–115; Robert L. Hough, "Washington Irving, Indians, and the West," *South Dakota Review* 6 (Winter 1968/69): 27–39; and Keiser, *The Indian in American Literature*, 52–64.

143. Lydia Maria Child, *The First Settlers of New England; or, Conquest of the Pequods, Narragansets and Pokanokets: as Related by a Mother to Her Children, and Designed for the Instruction of Youth* (Boston: Munroe & Francis, 1828). Child had previously published a novel set at the time of King Philip's War, *Hobomok, a Tale of Early Times* (Boston: Cummings, Hilliard, 1824). See Carolyn Karcher's introduction to her edition of Child's writings, *Hobomok & Other Writings on Indians* (New Brunswick, NJ: Rutgers University Press, 1986).

144. John August Stone, *Metamora; or, The Last of the Wampanoags* (1829), in

William Coyle and Harvey Damaser, eds., *Six Early American Plays, 1798–1890* (Columbus, OH: Charles Merrill, 1968), 47–95. See B. Donald Grose, "Edwin Forrest, *Metamora*, and the Indian Removal Act of 1830," *Theatre Journal* 37, no. 2 (May 1985): 181–191.

145. Apess, *Eulogy on King Philip*, 41 (304).

146. Ibid., 37–38 (301).

147. Ibid., 41–42 (304).

148. O'Connell, *On Our Own Ground*, 306.

149. See also Jackson's Second Annual Message, December 6, 1830, both in James D. Richardson, *A Compilation of the Messages and Papers of the Presidents* (Washington, DC: Government Printing Office, 1896–99), 2:457–459, 521–523.

150. Apess, *Eulogy on King Philip*, 46 (307).

151. Ibid., 14–15 (286). Compare, for instance, with the "National Day of Mourning" declaration made by the United American Indians of New England in 1970. In Thomas E. Sanders and Walter W. Peek, eds., *Literature of the American Indian* (New York: Glencoe Press, 1973), 519–520.

152. Carlos Montezuma (1865?–1923), erroneously known as the "Fiery Apache," was born a Yavapai (Mohave-Apache), captured as a youth by Pimas, and then sold to and adopted by an Italian immigrant. He became a physician in adult life and one of the foremost advocates of Indian adaptation. He established his own newsletter, *Wassaja* (1916–22), in which he demanded the abolition of the Bureau of Indian Affairs and the reservation system. A column in the newsletter with caustic political commentary was titled "Arrow Points." Later in life he became a vital figure in the political affairs of the Fort McDowell Yavapais, as well as the Pimas and Papagos, helping them to retain their remaining lands. When his health began to fail, he returned to McDowell to die among his people. See Peter Iverson, *Carlos Montezuma and the Changing World of American Indians* (Albuquerque: University of New Mexico Press, 1982).

153. See Krupat, "Native American Autobiography and the Synecdochic Self," 176, 185.

154. James H. Cone, *Black Theology of Liberation* (Philadelphia/New York: J. B. Lippincott, 1970), 11, 17, 34–49, 54–55, 212–219.

155. See Brodeur, *Restitution*, 16; and Peters, *Wampanoags of Mashpee*, 32–33, 35.

156. Quote from the first edition. See O'Connell, *On Our Own Ground*, 310.

157. Apess, *Experiences of Five Christian Indians*, 17 (130).

CHAPTER FIVE

1. Published primary sources: *An Address to the Whites, Delivered in the First Presbyterian Church on the 26th of May, 1826* (Philadelphia: William F. Geddes, 1826), reprinted in Paul Lauter et al., eds., *The Heath Anthology of American Literature* (Lexington, MA: Heath, 1990), 1:1761–1769; "Prospectus for Publishing at New Echota, in the Cherokee Nation, a Weekly Newspaper, to be Called the *Cherokee Phoenix*," broadside, 1827 (copy available in the Newspaper Collection

of the Oklahoma Historical Society and the Gilcrease Institute of American History and Art); numerous editorials in the *Cherokee Phoenix* (later *Cherokee Phoenix and Indian Advocate*) from February 21, 1828, to August 11, 1832 (available in microfilm from the American Antiquarian Society); *Letters and Other Papers Relating to Cherokee Affairs; Being in Reply to Sundry Publications Authorized by John Ross. By E. Boudinot, Formerly Editor of the Cherokee Phoenix* (Athens, GA: Southern Banner, 1837), reprinted in *Documents in Relation to the Validity of the Cherokee Treaty of 1835 . . . Letters and Other Papers Relating to Cherokee Affairs: Being a Reply to Sundry Publications Authorized by John Ross* (Washington, DC: Blair & Rives, 1838 as Senate Document 121, 25th Cong. 2nd sess.); and Boudinot's personal correspondence in Edward E. Dale and Gaston L. Litton, eds., *Cherokee Cavaliers: Forty Years of Cherokee History as Told in the Correspondence of the Ridge-Watie-Boudinot Family* (Norman: University of Oklahoma Press, 1939); see also Edward E. Dale, "Letters of the Two Boudinots," *Chronicles of Oklahoma 6* (1928): 328–347. His two pamphlets, a few newspaper articles, the "Prospectus," and several editorials from the *Cherokee Phoenix* have been collected along with an excellent introduction and detailed editorial comments in Theda Perdue, ed., *Cherokee Editor: The Writings of Elias Boudinot* (Knoxville: University of Tennessee Press, 1983). Unpublished primary sources: Ridge and Boudinot Family Papers, 1835–90, in Stand Watie Miscellaneous Files, Cherokee Nation Papers, 1801–1982, Western History Collections, University of Oklahoma Library. Published secondary sources: Ralph Henry Gabriel, *Elias Boudinot, Cherokee, and His America* (Norman: University of Oklahoma Press, 1941), a biography focusing on his sojourn at Cornwall and marriage to Harriet Gold; Mary Boudinot Church, "Elias Boudinot," *Magazine of History* 17, no. 6 (December 1913): 209–221, a brief biography by a relative; and Barbara F. Luebke, "Elias Boudinot, Indian Editor: Editorial Columns from the *Cherokee Phoenix*," *Journalism History* 6, no. 2 (Summer 1979): 48–53. Although it concentrates on the Ridge family, there is invaluable information pertaining to Boudinot in Thurman Wilkins, *Cherokee Tragedy: The Story of the Ridge Family and the Decimation of a People* (New York: Macmillan, 1970). Unpublished secondary sources: Barbara F. Luebke, "Elias Boudinot, Indian Editor: The Father of American Indian Journalism" (Ph.D. diss., University of Missouri, 1981).

2. Literature on the Cherokees is too extensive to be outlined here. Of particular relevance to the transitional period in which Boudinot lived are Henry Thomas Malone, *Cherokees of the Old South: A People in Transition* (Athens: University of Georgia Press, 1956); William G. McLoughlin, *Cherokees and Missionaries, 1789–1839* (New Haven: Yale University Press, 1984); idem, *Cherokee Renascence in the New Republic* (Princeton: Princeton University Press, 1986); Rennard Strickland, *Fire and the Spirits: Cherokee Law from Clan to Court* (Norman: University of Oklahoma Press, 1975); and, especially, Wilkins, *Cherokee Tragedy*. Useful general histories of the Cherokees include Marion L. Starkey, *The Cherokee Nation* (New York: Alfred A. Knopf, 1946; rpt., New York: Russell & Russell, 1972), and Grace Woodward, *The Cherokees* (Norman: University of Oklahoma Press, 1969). For additional literature, see Raymond A. Fogelson, *The Cherokees: A Critical Bibli-*

ography (Bloomington: Indiana University Press, 1978); and George P. Murdock and Timothy J. O'Leary, *Ethnographic Bibliography of North America*, 4th ed. (New Haven: Human Relations Area Files Press, 1975), 4:166–184.

3. McLoughlin, *Cherokee Renascence*, 4.

4. Ibid., 3–32; Malone, *Cherokees of the Old South*, 2–36. See also David H. Corkran, *The Cherokee Frontier, 1740–1762* (Norman: University of Oklahoma Press, 1962); Gary C. Goodwin, *Cherokees in Transition: A Study of Changing Culture and Environment Prior to 1775*, University of Chicago, Department of Geography, Research Paper no. 181 (Chicago, 1977), 82–146; Tom Hatley, *The Dividing Paths: Cherokees and South Carolinians through the Era of Revolution* (New York: Oxford University Press, 1993); and John Phillip Reid, *A Better Kind of Hatchet: Law, Trade, and Diplomacy during the Early Years of European Contact* (University Park: Pennsylvania State University Press, 1976). On Cherokee population statistics, see Russell Thornton, *American Indian Holocaust and Survival: A Population History since 1492* (Norman/London: University of Oklahoma Press, 1987), 114–118; and idem, *The Cherokees: A Population History* (Lincoln/London: University of Nebraska Press, 1990), 19–46.

5. Strickland, *Fire and the Spirits*, 40–52. See also Fred O. Gearing, *Priests and Warriors: American Social Structures for Cherokee Politics in the 18th Century*, Anthropological Association Memoir 93 (Menasha, WI: American Anthropological Association, 1962); and V. Richard Persico, Jr., "Early Nineteenth-Century Cherokee Political Organization," in Duane H. King, ed., *The Cherokee Indian Nation: A Troubled History* (Knoxville: University of Tennessee Press, 1979), 92–109.

6. McLoughlin, *Cherokee Renascence*, 20–21; Woodward, *The Cherokees*, 88–116.

7. Malone, *Cherokees of the Old South*, 46–47.

8. McLoughlin, *Cherokees and Missionaries*, 11; idem, *Cherokee Renascence*, 3–4; and Strickland, *Fire and the Spirits*, 40–49. For a detailed study of Cherokee demographic shift, see Thornton, *The Cherokees*.

9. See McLoughlin, *Cherokees and Missionaries*, 8; and Strickland, *Fire and the Spirits*, 41–45.

10. McLoughlin, *Cherokees and Missionaries*, 25. See also Malone, *Cherokees of the Old South*, 55–56; Strickland, *Fire and the Spirits*, 50; and Woodward, *The Cherokees*, 120.

11. McLoughlin, *Cherokees and Missionaries*, 124–149; idem, *Cherokee Renascence*, 65–67, 301, 326–349. For a discussion of the role of classes in Cherokee society during removal, see Theda Perdue, "The Conflict Within: Cherokees and Removal," in William L. Anderson, ed., *Cherokee Removal: Before and After* (Athens: University of Georgia Press, 1991), 55–74.

12. See McLoughlin, *Cherokee Renascence*, 109–145, 156–157; and Woodward, *The Cherokees*, 127–128.

13. Woodward, *The Cherokees*, 131.

14. Quoted in Francis P. Prucha, "United States Indian Policies, 1815–1860," in Wilcomb E. Washburn, ed., *Handbook of North American Indians: History of Indian-White Relations* (Washington, DC: Smithsonian Institution Press, 1988): 4:43.

15. See William G. McLoughlin, "Thomas Jefferson and the Beginning of Cherokee Nationalism," *William and Mary Quarterly* 32 (October 1975): 562–580. A letter written by Washington dated 1796 and addressed to the Cherokees on the topic of "civilization" was reprinted in one of the earliest issues of the *Cherokee Phoenix* 1, no. 5 (March 20, 1828): 1, cols. 4, 5; 2, col. 1.

16. Article 14 quoted in McLoughlin, *Cherokee Renascence*, 24. See also Charles C. Royce, "The Cherokee Nation of Indians: A Narrative of Their Official Relations with the Colonial and Federal Government," in Smithsonian Institution, *Bureau of American Ethnology, Fifth Annual Report, 1883–1884* (Washington, DC: Government Printing Office, 1887), 158–169.

17. On missionary activities among the Cherokees in the early nineteenth century, see Malone, *Cherokees of the Old South*, 91–117; and McLoughlin, *Cherokees and Missionaries*. For a brief survey of nineteenth-century missionary activities with reference to the Cherokees, see Henry W. Bowden, *American Indians and Christian Missions* (Chicago: University of Chicago Press, 1981), 164–197. An analysis of the fundamental principles behind missionary educational policies at this time with reference to the Cherokees is found in Robert F. Berkhofer, Jr., "Model Zions for the American Indian," *American Quarterly* 15, no. 2 (Summer 1963): 176–190; and idem, *Salvation and the Savage: An Analysis of Protestant Missions and American Indian Response, 1787–1862* (Lexington: University of Kentucky Press, 1965).

18. McLoughlin, *Cherokees and Missionaries*, 35–53. On Moravian missions, see Edmund Schwarze, *History of the Moravian Missions among the Southern Indian Tribes of the United States* (Bethlehem, PA: Times Publishing, 1923).

19. See Berkhofer, "Model Zions for the American Indian," 178–181; and McLoughlin, *Cherokees and Missionaries*, 54–81.

20. McLoughlin, *Cherokees and Missionaries*, 102–123. See also Robert S. Walker, *Torchlights to the Cherokees: The Brainerd Mission* (New York: Macmillan, 1931). On the ABCFM, see William E. Strong, *The Story of the American Board* (Boston: Pilgrim Press, 1910); and Joseph Tracy, *History of the American Board of Commissioners for Foreign Missions* (New York: M. W. Dodd, 1842).

21. See Berkhofer, "Model Zions for the American Indian," 176–178.

22. See McLoughlin, *Cherokees and Missionaries*, 150–179; and Woodward, *The Cherokees*, 140.

23. On Cherokee resistance to Christianity, see McLoughlin, *Cherokees and Missionaries*, 82–101; and idem, "Cherokee Anti-mission Sentiment, 1824–1828," *Ethnohistory* 21, no. 4 (Fall 1974): 678–703. On the Cherokee "ghost dance," see James Mooney, "The Ghost Dance Religion," in Smithsonian Institution, *Bureau of American Ethnology, 14th Annual Report, 1892–93*, pt. 2 (Washington, DC: Government Printing Office, 1896); William G. McLoughlin, "New Angles of Vision on the Cherokee Ghost Dance Movement," *American Indian Quarterly* 5 (November 1979): 317–346; and idem, *Cherokee Renascence*, 168–185.

24. See Malone, *Cherokee of the Old South*, 87; and Strickland, *Fire and the Spirits*, 219.

25. See Anderson, *Cherokee Removal*; and Louis Filler and Allen Gutman, eds., *The Removal of the Cherokee Nation: Manifest Destiny or National Dishonor?*

(Lexington, MA: D. C. Heath, 1962). For a historical survey of removal in the Southeast, see Annie H. Abel, *The History of Events Resulting in Indian Consolidation West of the Mississippi* (1908; rpt., New York: AMS Press, 1972); and Grant Foreman, *Indian Removal: The Emigration of the Five Civilized Tribes of Indians* (Norman: University of Oklahoma Press, 1932; rev. ed., 1986). See also James R. Christianson, "Removal: A Foundation for the Formation of Federalized Indian Policy," *Journal of Cherokee Studies* 10 (Fall 1985): 215–229; Kenneth Penn Davis, "The Cherokee Removal, 1835–1838," *Tennessee Historical Quarterly* 32 (Winter 1975): 311–330; and Donald Grinde, Jr., "Cherokee Removal and American Politics," *Indian Historian* 8, no. 3 (Summer 1975): 33–42, 56.

26. Alexis de Tocqueville, *Democracy in America*, ed. Phillips Bradley, 2 vols. (New York: Vintage Books, 1945), 1:369.

27. Paul L. Ford, ed., *The Writings of Thomas Jefferson*, 10 vols. (New York: G. P. Putnam's Sons, 1893–99), 8:243–244. Quoted in Brian W. Dippie, *The Vanishing American: White Attitudes and U.S. Indian Policy* (Middletown, CT: Wesleyan University Press, 1982), 56.

28. Quoted in Malone, *Cherokees of the Old South*, 65–66.

29. See Robert F. Berkhofer, Jr., *The White Man's Indian: Images of the American Indian from Columbus to the Present* (New York: Alfred A. Knopf, 1978), 158–159; Francis P. Prucha, *American Indian Policy in the Formative Years: The Indian Trade and Intercourse Acts, 1790–1834* (Lincoln: University of Nebraska Press, 1970), 226–229; and Royce, "The Cherokee Nation of Indians," 238–240. On Cherokee participation in the Creek War, see R. S. Cotterill, *The Southern Indians: The Story of the Five Civilized Tribes before Removal* (Norman: University of Oklahoma Press, 1954), 176–190; and James Mooney, "Myths of the Cherokees," in Smithsonian Institution, *Bureau of American Ethnology, 19th Annual Report, 1897–98*, pt. 1 (Washington, DC: Government Printing Office, 1900), 88–97.

30. See McLoughlin, *Cherokees and Missionaries*, 240; idem, *Cherokee Renascence*, 260–276; Mooney, "Myths of the Cherokees," 102; Malone, *Cherokees of the Old South*, 68–71; Royce, "The Cherokee Nation of Indians," 212–219; and Woodward, *The Cherokees*, 131.

31. Walter H. Conser, Jr., "John Ross and the Cherokee Resistance Campaign, 1833–1838," *Journal of Southern History* 44, no. 2 (May 1978): 191–212.

32. See Malone, *Cherokees of the Old South*, 74–90; McLoughlin, *Cherokee Renascence*, 146–167, 277–301, 326–349; Strickland, *Fire and the Spirits*, 53–119; Persico, "Early Nineteenth-Century Cherokee Political Organization," 92–109; and Woodward, *The Cherokees*, 139–156. The early laws are recorded in Cherokee Nation, *Laws of the Cherokee Nation: Adopted by the Council at Various Periods, Printed for the Benefit of the Nation* (Tahlequah, Cherokee Nation: Office of the Advocate, 1852), hereafter cited as *Cherokee Laws*. A summary of Cherokee resolutions from 1808 to 1829 is found in Strickland, *Fire and the Spirits*, 211–226.

33. See Persico, "Early Nineteenth-Century Cherokee Political Organization," 101–102; Strickland, *Fire and the Spirits*, 65, 227–236. The Cherokee Constitution is reprinted in Emmet Starr, *History of the Cherokee Indians and Their Legends and Folk Lore* (1921; rpt., New York: Kraus Reprint, 1969), 53–65; and in Strickland, *Fire and the Spirit*, 227–236. For a comparative study of constitutional govern-

ments established by four of the Five Civilized Tribes, see Duane Champagne, *Social Order and Political Change: Constitutional Governments among the Cherokee, the Choctaw, the Chickasaw, and the Creek* (Stanford: Stanford University Press, 1992).

34. See McLoughlin, *Cherokees and Missionaries*, 213–238; idem, *Cherokee Renascence*, 109–110, 163, 388–410; and, especially, Theda Perdue, "Traditionalism in the Cherokee Nation: Resistance to the Constitution of 1827," *Georgia Historical Quarterly* 66 (1982): 159–170.

35. *Cherokee Laws*, 4–53, 79, 119, 136–141.

36. One of the earliest accounts of Sequoyah was published in the *Cherokee Phoenix* 1, no. 24 (August 13, 1828): 2, cols. 1–2, under the initials "G. C." Boudinot also wrote a piece on Sequoyah for the *American Annals of Education*, April 1, 1832. Reproduced in Perdue, *Cherokee Editor*, 48–58. On Sequoyah's life, see Grant Foreman, *Sequoyah* (Norman: University of Oklahoma Press, 1938); George E. Foster, *Se-Quo-Yah: The American Cadmus and Modern Moses* (Philadelphia: Office of the Indian Rights Association, 1885); and Jack F. Kilpatrick, *Sequoyah, of Earth and Intellect* (Austin: Encino Press, 1965). Foreman vehemently objects to Foster's earlier contention that Sequoyah's father was an itinerant German peddler named George Gist. For a more controversial presentation of Sequoyah's life, see Traveller Bird, *Tell Them They Lie: The Sequoyah Myth* (Los Angeles: Western Lore Publishers, 1971). Compare the latter with Raymond D. Fogelson, "On the Varieties of Indian History: Sequoyah and Traveller Bird," *Journal of Ethnic Studies* 2, no. 1 (Spring 1974): 105–112. For a description of Sequoyah's syllabary, see Willard Walker, "Notes on Native Writing Systems and the Design of Native Literacy Programs," *Anthropological Linguistics* 11, no. 5 (May 1969): 148–166.

37. Estimates of Cherokee literacy vary considerably: from 3,914 readers (ca. 20 percent) of Cherokee, according to a census in 1835, to 90 percent literacy in the late 1830s. See William G. McLoughlin and Walter H. Conser, Jr., "Cherokees in Transition: A Statistical Analysis of the Federal Cherokee Census of 1835," *Journal of American History* 64, no. 3 (December 1977): 678–703 (esp. 693); and Walker, "Notes on Native Writing Systems," 151.

38. See Carmelita L. Monteith, "Literacy among the Cherokee in the Early Nineteenth Century," *Journal of Cherokee Studies* 9, no. 2 (Fall 1984): 56–73. For samples of the variety of applications for Sequoyah's syllabary, see Jack F. Kilpatrick and Anna Gritts Kilpatrick, eds., *The Shadow of Sequoyah: Social Documents of the Cherokees, 1862–1964* (Norman: University of Oklahoma Press, 1976).

39. For Worcester's role in the promotion of Sequoyah's syllabary and the Cherokee press, see Althea Bass, *Cherokee Messenger* (1936; rpt., Norman: University of Oklahoma Press, 1968); and Jack F. Kilpatrick and Anna G. Kilpatrick, eds., *New Echota Letters: Contributions of Samuel A. Worcester to the "Cherokee Phoenix"* (Dallas: Southern Methodist University Press, 1968).

40. John Arch (Atsi), missionary and interpreter, translated the third chapter of the Gospel of John into the Cherokee syllabary in 1821. He died of tuberculosis at Brainerd on June 18, 1825. His memoirs were published as *Memoir of John Arch, a Cherokee Young Man, Compiled from Communications of Missionaries in the Cherokee Nation*, 2nd ed. (Boston: Massachusetts Sabbath School Union, 1832). David Brown (ca. 1802–29), or A-with, was the brother of the previously men-

tioned Catherine Brown. He attended the Foreign Mission School with Boudinot from 1820 to 1823 and then studied at Andover Theological Seminary. Together with his father-in-law, George Lowery, he translated the New Testament directly from the Greek into Cherokee in 1825. Both also prepared an official compilation of Cherokee laws for the Cherokee Council. It is said that he assisted Sequoyah on a portion of the Cherokee syllabary. David Brown served as secretary of the Cherokee Council, lectured widely on Cherokee progress, and also traveled throughout the Cherokee Nation to make a report on the current situation for Secretary of War Thomas L. McKenney. His report, in the form of a letter addressed to the editor of the *Family Visitor*, dated September 2, 1825, was published in two missionary journals: "The Cherokee Indians," *Niles' Register* 5, no. 7 (October 15, 1825): 105–107; "Cherokees: View of a native Indian, as to the present condition of his people," *Missionary Herald* 21, no. 11 (November 1825): 354–355. It is also included in Walter Lowie et al., eds., *American State Papers, Indian Affairs*, 2 vols. (Washington, DC: Gales & Seaton, 1832–34), 2:651. Some of his letters were published in the *Religious Remembrancer* 9, no. 8 (October 13, 1821): 30; 9, no. 21 (January 12, 1822): 82; 10, no. 8 (October 19, 1822): 36. See Mary A. Higginbotham, "The Creek Path Mission," *Journal of Cherokee Studies* 1, no. 2 (Fall 1976): 72–86.

41. *Cherokee Laws*, 47. Quoted in Perdue, *Cherokee Editor*, 67; and Woodward, *The Cherokees*, 143–144.

42. *Cherokee Laws*, 84–86. Quoted in Strickland, *Fire and the Spirits*, 219.

43. See Bass, *Cherokee Messenger*, 69–89; Strickland, *Fire and the Spirits*, 219–220; and Woodward, *The Cherokees*, 144. The Cherokee Nation produced a great quantity of material in syllabary between 1828 and 1907. For bibliographical references to Cherokee publications, see Carolyn T. Foreman, *Oklahoma Imprints (1835–1907): A History of Printing in Oklahoma before Statehood* (Norman: University of Oklahoma Press, 1936); and Lester Hargrett, *Oklahoma Imprints, 1835–1890* (New York: R. R. Bowker for the Bibliographical Society of America, 1951).

44. For different perspectives on the history of the *Cherokee Phoenix*, see George E. Foster, "Journalism among the Cherokee Indians," *Magazine of American History* 18, nos. 1–5 (July 1887): 65–70; Henry T. Malone, "The Cherokee Phoenix: Supreme Expression of Cherokee Nationalism," *Georgia Historical Quarterly* 34, no. 3 (September 1950): 163–188; Robert G. Martin, "The Cherokee Phoenix: Pioneer of Indian Journalism," *Chronicles of Oklahoma* 25, no. 2 (Summer 1947): 102–118; James Murphy and Sharon Murphy, *Let My People Know: American Indian Journalism* (Norman: University of Oklahoma Press, 1981), 20–33; and Theda Perdue, "Rising from the Ashes: The *Cherokee Phoenix* as an Ethnohistorical Source," *Ethnohistory* 24, no. 3 (Summer 1977): 207–217.

45. See Church, "Elias Boudinot," 209; Perdue, *Cherokee Editor*, 3–5; and Wilkins, *Cherokee Tragedy*, 6–7, 32–35. A genealogical chart of the Ridge-Boudinot-Watie family is found in Dale and Litton, *Cherokee Cavaliers*.

46. The main source on the Ridge family is Wilkins, *Cherokee Tragedy*. See also Thomas L. McKenney and James Hall, *History of the Indian Tribes of North America, with Biographical Sketches and Anecdotes of the Principal Chiefs* (Edinburgh: John Grant, 1934), 1:368–369, 2:326–332.

47. Edwin Welles Dwight, ed., *Memoirs of Henry Obookiah; a Native of the*

Sandwich Islands, Who Died at Cornwall, Connecticut, February 17, 1818, aged 26 (New Haven, 1819; rpt., Elizabeth Town, NJ: Edson Hart, J & E Sanderson, 1819). See Carolyn T. Foreman, "The Foreign Mission School at Cornwall, Connecticut," *Chronicles of Oklahoma* 7, no. 3 (September 1929): 242–259.

48. Quoted in Berkhofer, *Salvation and the Savage*, 28; and Church, "Elias Boudinot," 210.

49. The letter, dated January 8, 1821, was published in the *Missionary Herald* 17, no. 8 (August 1821): 257; reprinted in Gabriel, *Elias Boudinot*, 53–54; and Perdue, *Cherokee Editor*, 43–44. David Brown's somewhat more polished letter of thanks to the baron, dated January 6, 1821, is also published in the same issue of the *Missionary Herald* (pp. 257–258) along with a letter addressed to him by his sister Catherine dated February 21, 1821 (pp. 258–259).

50. *Religious Remembrancer* 9, no. 8 (October 13, 1821): 31. The undated letter was addressed to the Reverend Nicholas Patterson of Baltimore. See Perdue, *Cherokee Editor*, 44–45, 59 (n. 6).

51. Extract from an undated and unaddressed letter by "Kub-la-ga-nah" in the *Religious Remembrancer* 9, no. 21 (January 12, 1822): 82. It was probably written late in 1821 and addressed to the Reverend Nicholas Patterson. In a letter dated October 1822, David Brown mentioned that he and "Brother B——" intended to stay at Andover for one year. Brown remained at the institution after Boudinot left. *Religious Remembrancer* 10, no. 8 (October 19, 1822): 36.

52. Elias Boudinot to a clergyman in the vicinity of Charleston, South Carolina, January 24, 1823, *Religious Remembrancer* 10, no. 33 (April 5, 1823): 129; extract of a letter from Boudinot, March 3, 1823, *Religious Remembrancer* 10, no. 38 (May 10, 1823): 152; copy of a letter from Boudinot, April 9, 1823, *Religious Remembrancer* 10, no. 41 (May 31, 1823): 164.

53. See the following publications by John Ridge: "The Cherokee War path," ed. Carolyn T. Foreman, *Chronicles of Oklahoma* 9, no. 3 (September 1931): 233–263; "John Ridge on Cherokee Civilization in 1826," ed. William C. Sturtevant, *Journal of Cherokee Studies* 6, no. 2 (Fall 1981): 79–91, reprinted as "Essay on Cherokee Civilization," in D. McQuade et al., eds., *Harper Anthology of American Literature* (New York: Harper & Row, 1987), 730–737; "Sequoyah and the Cherokee Alphabet," in Charles Hamilton, ed., *Cry of the Thunderbird: The American Indian's Own Story* (Norman: University of Oklahoma Press, 1972), 241–242, originally from a speech quoted in Peter Jones, *History of the Ojebway Indians: With Especial Reference to Their Conversion to Christianity* (London: A. W. Bennett, 1861), 187–188. Ridge also wrote frequently for the *Cherokee Phoenix* and had a number of articles printed in religious papers like the *Christian Herald* and *Boston Recorder*, as well as regional papers such as the *Arkansas Gazette*. Most of his writings have not been published and are found in the Western History Collections, University of Oklahoma Library; Georgia Department of Archives and History; Manuscript Division, University of Texas; and John Howard Payne Papers, Ayer Collection, Newberry Library. Two of his poems have been printed in Wilkins, *Cherokee Tragedy*, 123–124.

54. The letter is contained in the Ayer Collection, Newberry Library. Quoted in excerpts in Wilkins, *Cherokee Tragedy*, 129.

55. "Indian Address," *Religious Remembrancer* 10, no. 18 (December 21, 1822): 70.

56. For details on the Ridge-Northrup and Boudinot-Gold marriages and the reaction to them, see Gabriel, *Elias Boudinot*, 57–92; Church, "Elias Boudinot," 210–217; and Wilkins, *Cherokee Tragedy*, 131–134, 146–153.

57. Perdue, *Cherokee Editor*, 10–11.

58. *Christian Herald* 10, no. 15 (December 20, 1823): 467–468. Quoted in part in Wilkins, *Cherokee Tragedy*, 147.

59. Wilkins, *Cherokee Tragedy*, 192–193.

60. See Perdue, *Cherokee Editor*, 227, n. 12; and Wilkins, *Cherokee Tragedy*, 161–162. The Cherokees did not establish their own schools until after removal to what is now Oklahoma. Here, in 1851, they founded a Female Seminary and Male Seminary which operated until 1856 and then again from 1871 and 1875, respectively, until 1910. See Brad Agnew, "A Legacy of Education: The History of the Cherokee Seminaries," *Chronicles of Oklahoma* 63, no. 2 (Summer 1985): 128–147.

61. The constitution of the society drawn up by Ridge is under the rubric "Cherokee Nation," *Boston Recorder and Telegraph* 10, no. 11 (March 12, 1825): 44, cols. 3–4; and Boudinot's appeal is under the heading "From the Cherokee Nation," *Boston Recorder and Telegraph* 10, no. 31 (July 29, 1825): 124, cols. 2–3. The first is quoted at length in Wilkins, *Cherokee Tragedy*, 162–163. The latter is reproduced in Perdue, *Cherokee Editor*, 45–47.

62. The treaty with the Creeks was concluded January 24, 1826, and John Ridge claimed $15,000 for his services as secretary (ultimately he received $10,000). On the other hand, the Cherokee Council appropriated $1,500 for a press from the donations collected by Boudinot, of which 8 percent would have been a grand total of $120. On Ridge's activities among the Creeks, see Wilkins, *Cherokee Tragedy*, 154–185.

63. See Murphy and Murphy, *Let My People Know*, 25; Perdue, *Cherokee Editor*, 87; Starkey, *Cherokee Nation*, 92–93; and Wilkins, *Cherokee Tragedy*, 193.

64. See Foreman, *Sequoyah*, 29.

65. Quoted in Bass, *Cherokee Messenger*, 252, 256; and Gabriel, *Elias Boudinot*, 114. Boudinot and Worcester translated *Cherokee Hymns Compiled from Several Authors and Revised* (New Echota, Cherokee Nation, 1829); *The Gospel According to Matthew* (New Echota, 1829); *The Acts of the Apostles* (New Echota, 1833); *The Gospel of Jesus Christ According to John* (Park Hill, Cherokee Nation, 1838). Boudinot may also have helped Worcester translate texts that were published after his death in 1839. See Perdue, *Cherokee Editor*, 36, n. 32.

66. He later published the "Prospectus" in the *Cherokee Phoenix* 1, no. 2 (February 28, 1828): 3, cols. 2–3. The "Prospectus" is reproduced in Perdue, *Cherokee Editor*, 89–90. See also Foster, "Journalism among the Cherokee Indians," 65–66; Malone, "Cherokee Phoenix," 166; and Wilkins, *Cherokee Tragedy*, 198, 367 (n. 32).

67. *Cherokee Phoenix* 1, no. 1 (February 21, 1828): 3, cols. 2–4 (italics mine). Reprinted in Perdue, *Cherokee Editor*, 91–95.

68. *Cherokee Phoenix* 1, no. 40 (December 3, 1828): 2, col. 3. See Foster,

"Journalism among the Cherokee Indians," 65–66; Luebke, "Elias Boudinot, Indian Editor: Columns," 48–53, esp. n. 3; Martin, "Cherokee Phoenix," 108–114; Perdue, *Cherokee Editor*, 85–153; and Wilkins, *Cherokee Tragedy*, 199.

69. *Cherokee Phoenix* 1, no. 15 (June 4, 1828): 2, col. 4. Quoted in Malone, "Cherokee Phoenix," 169; and Perdue, *Cherokee Editor*, 11.

70. See Perdue, "Rising from the Ashes," 213.

71. *Cherokee Phoenix* 1, no. 22 (July 30, 1828): 3, col. 1; *Cherokee Phoenix* 1, no. 49 (February 18, 1828): 2, col. 5. The latter is in Perdue, *Cherokee Editor*, 107–108.

72. *Cherokee Phoenix* 1, no. 45 (January 21, 1829): 2, cols. 3–4 (brackets mine). In Perdue, *Cherokee Editor*, 102–103 (she gives a translation of *gah-no-ha-nah* on p. 148, n. 26).

73. *Cherokee Phoenix* 2, no. 26 (September 30, 1829): 3, cols. 1–2. See also ibid., 1, no. 21 (July 21, 1828): 2, cols. 1–2 (a disassociation from the Creeks); 2, no. 39 (January 6, 1830): 3, col. 3 (disassociation from New York Indians); and 3, no. 1 (April 21, 1830): 2, cols. 4–5 (Cherokees more "civilized" than other Indians).

74. *Cherokee Phoenix* 1, no. 7 (April 3, 1828): 2, col. 5. In Perdue, *Cherokee Editor*, 97–98. See also Malone, "Cherokee Phoenix," 175–176.

75. *Cherokee Phoenix* 1, no. 31 (October 1, 1828): 2, cols. 3–4; 1, no. 14 (May 28, 1828): 3, col. 1. In Perdue, *Cherokee Editor*, 17, 102–103. As of the March 25, 1829, issue, the *Phoenix* frequently carried a special column titled either "Temperance" or "Intemperance."

76. *Cherokee Phoenix* 2, no. 27 (October 14, 1829): 4, col. 5.

77. *Cherokee Phoenix* 2, no. 13 (July 1, 1829): 2, col. 4 (quoted in Martin, "Cherokee Phoenix," 109; reprinted in Perdue, *Cherokee Editor*, 110–111); *Cherokee Phoenix* 1, no. 52 (March 11, 1829): 4, cols. 2–3; 4, no. 33 (March 3, 1832): 4, cols. 1–3; 1, no. 32 (October 8, 1828): 3, col. 3; 3, no. 2 (May 1, 1830): 4, cols. 2–3.

78. *Cherokee Phoenix* 2, no. 41 (January 27, 1830): 3, cols. 2–3 (brackets mine).

79. *Cherokee Phoenix* 1, no. 46 (January 28, 1829): 2, cols. 4–5. In Perdue, *Cherokee Editor*, 103–106.

80. See Kenneth Penn Davis, "Chaos in Indian Country: The Cherokee Nation, 1828–1835," in King, *Cherokee Indian Nation*, 129–147; and Carl J. Vipperman, " 'Forcibly If We Must': The Georgia Case for Cherokee Removal, 1802–1832," *Journal of Cherokee Studies* 3, no. 2 (Spring 1978): 104–111.

81. *Cherokee Phoenix* 1, no. 20 (July 9, 1828): 2, cols. 1–3. Boudinot reprinted the treaty in ibid., 1, no. 21 (July 21, 1828): 1, cols. 1–5.

82. *Cherokee Phoenix* 1, no. 25 (August 20, 1828): 2, col. 1. Quoted in Perdue, *Cherokee Editor*, 24.

83. *Cherokee Phoenix* 2, no. 11 (June 17, 1829): 2, cols. 3–4. In Perdue, *Cherokee Editor*, 108–109.

84. See Annie H. Abel, *The History of Events Resulting in Indian Consolidation West of the Mississippi* (1908; rpt., New York: AMS Press, 1972), 370–412.

85. See Prucha, *American Indian Policy in the Formative Years*, 139–212.

86. See McLoughlin, *Cherokee Renascence*, 431–432; and Wilkins, *Cherokee Tragedy*, 212–213. See also John Ross to Boudinot, February 13, 1830, *Cherokee Phoenix* 2, no. 44 (February 17, 1830): 2, col. 4; 3, cols. 1, 2.

87. *Cherokee Phoenix* 2, no. 43 (February 10, 1830): 2, cols. 4–5. In Perdue, *Cherokee Editor*, 112–113 (see also pp. 113–114); quoted in Gabriel, *Elias Boudinot*, 129; and Wilkins, *Cherokee Tragedy*, 213. Boudinot also pleads nonviolence in *Cherokee Phoenix* 2, no. 45 (February 24, 1830): 2, cols. 4–5; and 3, no. 12 (July 10, 1830): 3, col. 2.

88. *Cherokee Phoenix* 3, no. 4 (May 15, 1830): 2, col. 5. In Perdue, *Cherokee Editor*, 117–118.

89. On the legal and historical significance of the Cherokee Nation cases, see Joseph C. Burke, "The Cherokee Cases: A Study in Law, Politics, and Morality," *Stanford Law Review* 21, no. 3 (February 1969): 500–531; Vine Deloria, Jr., and Clifford Lyttle, *American Indians, American Justice* (Austin: University of Texas Press, 1983), 27–33; Allen Guttman, ed., *States' Rights and Indian Removal: The Cherokee Nation v. The State of Georgia* (Boston: D. C. Heath, 1965); Richard Peters, *The Case of the Cherokee Nation against the State of Georgia* (Philadelphia: John Grigg, 1831); and William F. Swindler, "Politics as Law: The Cherokee Cases," *American Indian Law Review* 3 (1975): 7–20. See also G. Edward White, *The Marshall Court and Cultural Change, 1815–35* (New York: Macmillan, 1988), esp. chap. 10.

90. *Cherokee Phoenix* 3, no. 33 (January 8, 1831): 2, col. 2. In Perdue, *Cherokee Editor*, 120–121. On the Tassel case, see Sidney L. Harring, *Crow Dog's Case: American Indian Sovereignty, Tribal Law, and United States Laws in the Nineteenth Century* (New York: Cambridge University Press, 1994), 25–56.

91. Cherokee Nation v. Georgia, 30 U.S. (5 Pet.) 1 (1831). See Wilcomb B. Washburn, ed., *The American Indian and the United States: A Documentary History*, 4 vols. (New York: Random House, 1973), 2554–2602.

92. *Cherokee Phoenix* 3, no. 45 (April 16, 1831): 3, cols. 3–4. In Perdue, *Cherokee Editor*, 125–127. John Henry Eaton (1790–1856) was secretary of war under Jackson.

93. The arrest is commented on by Boudinot in various issues from March 19 to September 24, 1831. See Bass, *Cherokee Messenger*, 115–160; Gabriel, *Elias Boudinot*, 120–133; McLoughlin, *Cherokees and Missionaries*, 239–265; idem, *Cherokee Renascence*, 428–447; and Perdue, *Cherokee Editor*, 122–123, 128–130.

94. *Cherokee Phoenix* 4, no. 26 (January 14, 1832): 2, cols. 1–2.

95. Worcester v. Georgia, 21 U.S. (6 Pet.) 515 (1832). See Washburn, *American Indian and the United States*, 2603–2648.

96. For different interpretations of Jackson's role in Indian removal, see Anton-Hermann Chroust, "Did President Jackson Actually Threaten the Supreme Court with Nonenforcement of Its Injunction against the State of Georgia?" *American Journal of Legal History* 5 (January 1960): 76–78; Edwin A. Miles, "After John Marshall's Decision: *Worcester v. Georgia* and the Nullification Crisis," *Journal of Southern History* 39, no. 4 (November 1973): 519–544; Francis P. Prucha, "Andrew Jackson's Indian Policy: A Reassessment," *Journal of American History* 54, no. 3 (December 1969): 527–539; Michael P. Rogin, *Fathers and Children: Andrew Jackson and the Subjugation of the American Indian* (New York: Alfred A. Knopf, 1975), 165–205; Ronald N. Satz, *American Indian Policy in the Jacksonian Era* (Lincoln: University of Nebraska Press, 1975), 39–63; and idem, "Rhetoric versus

Reality: The Indian Policy of Andrew Jackson," in Anderson, *Cherokee Removal*, 29–54.

97. Strickland, *Fire and the Spirits*, 78. See also Foreman, *Indian Removal*, 236. On the lottery system, see Douglas C. Wilms, "Georgia's Land Lottery of 1832," *Chronicles of Oklahoma* 52 (1974): 52–60; and idem, "Cherokee Land Use in Georgia before Removal," in Anderson, *Cherokee Removal*, 9–13.

98. Two full-length biographies have been published: Rachel Eaton, *John Ross and the Cherokee Indians* (Menasha, WI: George Banta, 1914; rpt., Chicago: University of Chicago Press, 1921); and Gary E. Moulton, *John Ross, Cherokee Chief* (Athens: University of Georgia Press, 1978). See also Conser, "Ross and the Cherokee Resistance Campaign"; Gary Moulton, "John Ross," in David R. Edmunds, ed., *American Indian Leaders: Studies in Diversity* (Lincoln: University of Nebraska Press, 1980), 88–106; and Theda Perdue's review essay, "John Ross and the Cherokees," *Georgia Historical Quarterly* 70, no. 3 (Fall 1986): 456–476. The writings of John Ross (letters and public documents) have been collected in Gary Moulton, ed., *The Papers of Chief John Ross*, vol. 1, *1807–1839*; vol. 2, *1840–1866* (Norman: University of Oklahoma Press, 1985). The first volume also includes two letters written by Elias Boudinot and five by John Ridge.

99. On William McIntosh (ca. 1775–1825), see Benjamin W. Griffith, Jr., *McIntosh and Weatherford, Creek Indian Leaders* (Tuscaloosa: University of Alabama Press, 1988).

100. John Ross, Annual Message, October 14, 1829, in Moulton, *Papers of John Ross*, 1: 169.

101. *Cherokee Phoenix* 1, no. 12 (May 14, 1828): 3, cols. 1–2. In Perdue, *Cherokee Editor*, 99–100. See also Malone, *Cherokees of the Old South*, 153–170.

102. *Cherokee Phoenix* 4, no. 4 (July 16, 1831): 3, cols. 2–3. In Perdue, *Cherokee Editor*, 128–131.

103. *Cherokee Phoenix* 4, no. 18 (November 12, 1831): 2, cols. 1–2. In Perdue, *Cherokee Editor*, 140–143. See also Ross, Annual Message, October 24, 1831, in Moulton, *Papers of John Ross*, 1: 224–231. For an "ethnocritical" interpretation of the Cherokee antiremoval writings and the language of the Removal Act, see Arnold Krupat, *Ethnocriticism: Ethnography, History, Literature* (Berkeley: University of California Press, 1992), 129–163.

104. Ross to the Cherokees, April 14, 1831, in Moulton, *Papers of John Ross*, 1: 215–219 (quote on p. 217).

105. Boudinot had written a fragment titled "Cherokee Women Beware," *Cherokee Phoenix* 4, no. 4 (July 16, 1831): 3, col. 3, which was the source of offense. He reported his arrest under the title "Liberty of the Press" in ibid., 4, no. 8 (August 20, 1831): 2, col. 5; 3, col. 1; and 4, no. 9 (August 27, 1831): 2, cols. 3–4. He printed the commander's response along with his own sarcastic comments in the ibid., 4, no. 12 (September 17, 1831): 3, cols. 2–4. See also Malone, "Cherokee Phoenix," 182–185; Perdue, *Cherokee Editor*, 22–23, 132–140; and Wilkins, *Cherokee Tragedy*, 226.

106. *Cherokee Phoenix* 4, no. 7 (August 12, 1831): 3, cols. 1–2.

107. *Cherokee Phoenix* 4, no. 8 (August 20, 1831): 2, col. 5; 3, col. 1; and 4, no. 9 (August 27, 1832): 2, cols. 3–4. Quoted in Malone, "Cherokee Phoenix," 185; and Perdue, *Cherokee Editor*, 134.

108. *Cherokee Phoenix* 1, no. 37 (November 12, 1828): 2, col. 4. In Perdue, *Cherokee Editor*, 19.

109. Quoted in Woodward, *The Cherokees*, 168.

110. See Ross to John Martin, John Ridge, and William S. Coodey, December 1, 1831, in Moulton, *Papers of John Ross*, 1: 232–233. See also Wilkins, *Cherokee Tragedy*, 230.

111. Ross, Annual Message, October 24, 1831, in Moulton, *Papers of John Ross*, 1: 224–231 (quote on p. 230).

112. *Cherokee Phoenix* 4, no. 28 (January 28, 1832): 2, col. 4.

113. Boudinot to Stand Watie, March 7, 1832, Cherokee Nation Papers, box 149, F1. In Dale and Litton, *Cherokee Cavaliers*, 4–7. Quoted in Wilkins, *Cherokee Tragedy*, 235–236.

114. John Ridge to Watie, April 6, 1832, in Dale and Litton, *Cherokee Cavaliers*, 7–10.

115. Boudinot expressed the possibility of removing in *Cherokee Phoenix* 2, no. 15 (July 15, 1829): 2, col. 2 ("We do not undertake to say that they will remain here at all hazards, for 'persecution — what will it not accomplish?' as the *Journal of Commerce* remarks. We know, however, the feelings of many individuals — in regard to them, we speak with confidence when we say, *coercion alone will remove them to the western country alloted for the Indians*"); and ibid., 4, no. 24 (December 21, 1831): 3, cols. 2–3 ("Be their course as it may it cannot effect the determination of the Cherokees. They have taken their stand and are contending for vital principles — They have counted the cost, and *if the long protracted controversy between them and Georgia must end in the loss of their beloved country it must be so*"). In Perdue, *Cherokee Editor*, 110, 144 (italics mine).

116. *Cherokee Phoenix* 3, no. 11 (July 3, 1830): 2, cols. 4–5; 3, col. 1 (brackets mine). Quoted in Strickland, *Fire and the Spirits*, 78, n. 38.

117. See Boudinot, *Letters Relating to Cherokee Affairs*, 12; also in Perdue, *Cherokee Editor*, 177; and Wilkins, *Cherokee Tragedy*, 236–237. A Choctaw delegation had already agreed to remove under the Treaty of Dancing Rabbit Creek on September 27, 1830. The Seminoles signed a removal treaty on May 9, 1832, as did the Chicasaws on October 20 of that same year. See Foreman, *Indian Removal*, 27–29, 110–111, 197–198, 320–321; and Woodward, *The Cherokees*, 161. During the fall of 1832 John Ridge himself advised the Creek Council to remove and thereby helped indirectly to foment what turned out to be a regular civil war between proremoval and antiremoval parties in Creek territory. See Mary E. Young, *Redskins, Ruffleshirts, and Rednecks: Indian Allotments in Alabama and Mississippi* (Norman: University of Oklahoma Press, 1961), 73–113.

118. David Greene to John Ridge, May 3, 1832, ABCFM Archives, Houghton Library. Quoted in Wilkins, *Cherokee Tragedy*, 240 (see also pp. 238–241, 253).

119. *Cherokee Phoenix-Extra*, January 1, 1830. This date is an original printing error as it should read 1831. See McLoughlin, *Cherokees and Missionaries*, 255–257; idem, *Cherokee Renascence*, 440–441; and Wilkins, *Cherokee Tragedy*, 225–226.

120. Isaac Proctor and Daniel Butrick to Boudinot, April 15, 1831, Payne Papers. Quoted in McLoughlin, *Cherokees and Missionaries*, 260.

121. Benjamin Wisner to Ross, December 27, 1832, ABCFM Archives, Houghton Library. Mentioned in McLoughlin, *Cherokees and Missionaries*, 310, n. 25. See Bass, *Cherokee Messenger*, 157–159; McLoughlin, *Cherokees and Missionaries*, 265; idem, *Cherokee Renascence*, 445–447; and Miles, "After Marshall's Decision," 526–527.

122. Ross to Boudinot, May 17, 1832, in Moulton, *Papers of John Ross*, 1: 244. The reference is to a statement by General Daniel Newman, which was printed in the *Cherokee Phoenix* 4, no. 45 (May 26, 1832): 2, col. 3.

123. Wilkins, *Cherokee Tragedy*, 238. Boudinot probably also sent Stand Watie information on the removal negotiations conducted by two renegade Cherokee leaders, Walker and Starr, which Watie reported in the *Cherokee Phoenix* 4, no. 43 (May 12, 1832): 2, col. 5.

124. Ross, Annual Message, October 13, 1828, in Moulton, *Papers of John Ross*, 1: 141. Quoted in Martin, "Cherokee Phoenix," 104–105.

125. Ross, Annual Message, October 10, 1832, in Moulton, *Papers of John Ross*, 1: 251. See Eaton, *Ross and the Cherokee Indians*, 59–60; Perdue, *Cherokee Editor*, 231, n. 53; idem, "The Conflict Within," 70; and Wilkins, *Cherokee Tragedy*, 243. Gary Moulton, however, implies that both Major Ridge and John Ridge actually proposed that the elections be postponed. See Moulton, "John Ross," 95–96.

126. *Cherokee Phoenix* 4, no. 48 (July 7, 1832): 2, cols. 2–3.

127. Boudinot to Ross, August 1, 1832, in Moulton, *Papers of John Ross*, 247–248; and *Cherokee Phoenix* 4, no. 52 (August 11, 1832): 2, col. 3. He later reprinted his resignation in his *Letters Relating to Cherokee Affairs*, 3–4. In Perdue, *Cherokee Editor*, 162–164. Curiously, the fifth point listed in the *Phoenix* is absent in his original letter of resignation to John Ross as well as the version included in his *Letters Relating to Cherokee Affairs*.

128. Ross to the General Council, August 4, 1832, in Moulton, *Papers of John Ross*, 1: 249–250; *Cherokee Phoenix* 4, no. 52 (August 11, 1832): 2, cols. 4–5. Also included in Boudinot's *Letters Relating to Cherokee Affairs*, 4–5. See Malone, "Cherokee Phoenix," 185–186; and Perdue, *Cherokee Editor*, 164–166.

129. Boudinot, *Letters Relating to Cherokee Affairs*, 7–10. In Perdue, *Cherokee Editor*, 169–174. Quoted in Wilkins, *Cherokee Tragedy*, 246.

130. See Ross to John F. Schermerhorn and Benjamin F. Currey, August 22, 1835, and Ross to the Senate, March 8, 1836, in Moulton, *Papers of John Ross*, 1: 352, 403–404. The latter states that Richard Fields had been appointed as editor to replace Hicks. The captured Cherokee press was apparently briefly employed to produce protreaty propaganda. Worcester established a new press, the Park Hill Mission Press, at Tahlequah (Oklahoma) in 1835 and began to print the *Cherokee Almanac* in 1836. On October 25, 1843, the Cherokee Council authorized the establishment of a national press and newspaper. The *Cherokee Advocate*, the second Cherokee national newspaper, appeared from September 26, 1844, to September 28, 1853. It has been reissued since 1976. See Bass, *Cherokee Messenger*, 178–197; Foster, "Indian Journalism among the Cherokee Indians," 67–70; Malone, "Cherokee Phoenix," 185–188; Martin, "Cherokee Phoenix," 115–118; Murphy and Murphy, *Let My People Know*, 29–35; and Woodward, *The Cherokees*, 172, 184–185.

131. A detailed account of this phase in the conflict is in Wilkins, *Cherokee Tragedy*, 242–290. See also Bass, *Cherokee Messenger*, 161–177; Davis, "Chaos in Indian Country," 129–147; Foreman, *Indian Removal*, 238–250, 264–278; McLoughlin, *Cherokees and Missionaries*, 300–334; Royce, "The Cherokee Nation of Indians," 272–283; and Woodward, *The Cherokees*, 173–190.

132. *Cherokee Phoenix* 5, no. 44 (April 5, 1834): 3, col. 3. See Wilkins, *Cherokee Tragedy*, 259.

133. Ross to Andrew Jackson, March 28, 1834, in Moulton, *Papers of John Ross*, 1: 282–283.

134. See Wilkins, *Cherokee Tragedy*, 271–272; and Woodward, *The Cherokees*, 181.

135. Ross to John Ridge, September 12 [and 15], 1834, in Moulton, *Papers of John Ross*, 1: 302–304. See Conser, "Ross and the Cherokee Resistance Campaign," 195; and Woodward, *The Cherokees*, 178–179.

136. The resolutions and Boudinot's comments on the impeachment charges are found in his *Letters Relating to Cherokee Affairs*, 10–13. See Perdue, *Cherokee Editor*, 174–178; and Wilkins, *Cherokee Tragedy*, 265–266.

137. See Wilkins, *Cherokee Tragedy*, 269.

138. Ross to Lewis Cass, February 14, 25, 27, and 28, 1835; Ross to Friedrich Ludwig Von Roenne, March 5, 1835; and Ross to Joaquin Maria Del Castillo y Lanzas, March 22, 1835, in Moulton, *Papers of John Ross*, 1: 321–323, 324–328, 330, 334–336. See Conser, "Ross and the Cherokee Resistance Campaign," 100–103; Moulton, *John Ross*, 62; Wilkins, *Cherokee Tragedy*, 285; and Woodward, *The Cherokees*, 179–180.

139. Boudinot to Watie, February 28, 1835, Cherokee Nation Papers, box 149, F2. In Dale and Litton, *Cherokee Cavaliers*, 10–11.

140. John Ridge to Major Ridge and others, March 10, 1835, in Dale and Litton, *Cherokee Cavaliers*, 12–14.

141. Ross to the General Council, May 18, 1835, in Moulton, *Papers of John Ross*, 1: 337–338. See Moulton, *John Ross*, 60–63; and Perdue, *Cherokee Editor*, 229–230, n. 41.

142. See Wilkins, *Cherokee Tragedy*, 276–278.

143. Woodward, *The Cherokees*, 187.

144. Ross to Boudinot, November 23, 1835, and Boudinot to Ross, November 25, 1835, in Moulton, *Papers of John Ross*, 1: 375–376.

145. See Perdue, *Cherokee Editor*, 231, n. 58.

146. Adams is quoted in Woodward, *The Cherokees*, 193. On the content of the treaty itself, see Royce, "The Cherokee Nation of Indians," 253–257; and Starr, *History of the Cherokee Indians*, 85–101. See also Robert A. Rutland, "Political Background of the Cherokee Treaty of New Echota," *Chronicles of Oklahoma* 27, no. 4 (December 1949): 389–406.

147. *Cherokee Laws*, 136–137. See Ross to the Senate and House of Representatives, April 30, 1846, in Moulton, *Papers of John Ross*, 2: 292 (Ross states: "a law voted for and carried through by Ridge himself, and under the authority of which he himself killed the celebrated Double Head"). John Ridge's statement was made in

the *Arkansas Gazette*, October 2, 1839. Quoted in Strickland, *Fire and the Spirits*, 77, n. 35.

148. J. W. Underwood in the *Carterville Courant*, March 26, 1885. Quoted in Perdue, *Cherokee Editor*, 27; and Wilkins, *Cherokee Tragedy*, 287. Tom Foreman was an opponent of the treaty who had publicly voiced a threat against those who had signed it.

149. Boudinot described the sad event in a letter to his in-laws dated August 16, 1836. "The Death of Harriet Gold Boudinot," *Journal of Cherokee Studies* 4, no. 2 (Spring 1979): 102–107. See also Higginbotham, "The Creek Path Mission," 82.

150. See Grant Foreman, *The Five Civilized Tribes* (1984; rpt., Norman: University of Oklahoma Press), 284; Gabriel, *Elias Boudinot*, 176; and Wilkins, *Cherokee Tragedy*, 308–315.

151. "To the Senate and House of Representatives," June 21 and September 28, 1836; and "To the Senate and House of Representatives," February 22, 1837, in Moulton, *Papers of John Ross*, 1: 458–461, 470–474.

152. See Moulton, *John Ross*, 60–61; idem, "John Ross," 96–97; and Royce, "The Cherokee Nation of Indians," 291–292.

153. For different angles on the tragic episode, see Duane H. King and E. Raymond Evans, eds., "The Trail of Tears: Primary Documents on the Cherokee Removal," *Journal of Cherokee Studies* 3 (Summer 1978), special issue; Theda Perdue, "Cherokee Women and the Trail of Tears," *Journal of Women's History* 1 (Spring 1989): 14–30; Ronald N. Satz, "Cherokee Traditionalism, Protestant Evangelism, and the Trail of Tears," *Tennessee Historical Quarterly* 44 (Fall/Winter 1985): 285–301, 380–401; idem, "The Cherokee Trail of Tears: A Sesquicentennial Perspective," *Georgia Historical Quarterly* 73 (Fall 1989): 431–466; and Russell Thornton, "The Demography of the Trail of Tears: A New Estimate of Cherokee Population Losses," in Anderson, *Cherokee Removal*, 75–95.

154. See John R. Finger, "The Impact of Removal on the North Carolina Cherokees," in Anderson, *Cherokee Removal*, 96–111; idem, *The Eastern Band of Cherokees, 1819–1900* (Knoxville: University of Tennessee Press, 1984); William H. Gilbert, *The Eastern Cherokees*, Smithsonian Institution, Bureau of American Ethnology Bulletin 133, Anthropological Paper no. 23 (Washington, DC: Government Printing Office, 1943), 169–413; and Duane H. King, "The Origin of the Eastern Cherokees as a Social and Political Entity," in idem, *Cherokee Indian Nation*, 164–180.

155. For accounts of the killings, see Bass, *Cherokee Messenger*, 255–256; Grant Foreman, ed., "The Murder of Elias Boudinot," *Chronicles of Oklahoma* 12 (March 1934): 19–24; Mooney, "Myths of the Cherokees," 134–135; and Wilkins, *Cherokee Tragedy*, 329–339. Boudinot's brother, Stand Watie, survived the "conspiracy" and carried on the family feud with the Ross Party until he made a temporary truce with John Ross in 1846. The feud resumed during the Civil War, in which Stand Watie came to play a counterrole to that of the Seneca Union general Ely S. Parker, going down in history as the last Confederate general to surrender. See Kenny Franks, *Stand Watie and the Agony of the Cherokee Nation* (Memphis: Memphis State University Press, 1979).

364 / Notes to Pages 213–216

156. See Foreman, *The Five Civilized Tribes*, 281–310, 321–351; William G. McLoughlin, *After the Trail of Tears: The Cherokees' Struggle for Sovereignty, 1839–1880* (Chapel Hill/London: University of North Carolina Press, 1992), 34–48; Gerard Reed, "Postremoval Factionalism in the Cherokee Nation," in King, *Cherokee Indian Nation*, 148–163; Royce, "The Cherokee Nation of Indians," 298–334; Morris Wardell, *A Political History of the Cherokee Nation, 1838–1907* (Norman: University of Oklahoma Press, 1963), 3–75; Wilkins, *Cherokee Tragedy*, 329–339; and Woodward, *The Cherokees*, 219–237.

157. See Ross to Joel R. Poinsett, January 3, 1840; Ross to the Senate and House of Representatives, February 28, 1840, and April 30, 1846, in Moulton, *Papers of John Ross*, 2: 4, 10, 292. The blood-law text is found in the Payne Papers. Quoted in Wilkins, *Cherokee Tragedy*, 209. A thorough study of traditional clan revenge law is in John Philip Reid, *A Law of the Blood: The Primitive Law of the Cherokee Nation* (New York: New York University Press, 1970).

158. See Foreman, *The Five Civilized Tribes*, 300; Wardell, *Political History of the Cherokee Nation*, 23–25; and Wilkins, *Cherokee Tragedy*, 341.

159. See Perdue, "The Conflict Within." Boudinot is absolved of illicit doings in Foreman, *The Five Civilized Tribes*, 423; and Wilkins, *Cherokee Tragedy*, 251. A more negative interpretation of Boudinot's role is given in Woodward, *The Cherokees*, 182–191.

160. Quoted in Gabriel, *Elias Boudinot*, 176; and Bass, *Cherokee Messenger*, 218.

161. John Ross to Lewis Ross, April 5, 1838, in Moulton, *Papers of John Ross*, 1: 622–624. Quoted in Conser, "Ross and the Cherokee Resistance Campaign," 211.

162. See Thomas S. Abler and Elizabeth Tooker, "Seneca," in Bruce G. Trigger, ed., *Handbook of North American Indians: Northeast* (Washington, DC: Smithsonian Institution Press, 1978), 15:505–517; and Anthony F. C. Wallace, *The Death and Rebirth of the Seneca* (1970; rpt., New York: Vintage Books, 1972), 321–330. See also Ross et al. to the Seneca Delegation, April 14, 1834, in Moulton, *Papers of John Ross*, 1: 284–287.

163. Conser, "Ross and the Cherokee Resistance Campaign," 212.

164. Alexander Lawrence Posey, "Ode to Sequoyah," in Lauter et al., *Heath Anthology of American Literature*, 2: 492.

165. Boudinot serialized Irving's "Traits of Indian Character" in the following issues of the *Cherokee Phoenix*: March 6, March 13, and April 3, 1828. He also included Irving's essay "Character of Columbus" in the May 14, 1828, issue. Evarts's "William Penn" essays appeared regularly in the *Cherokee Phoenix* from September 16, 1829, to February 17, 1830.

166. "Speech of Peter Jones," *Cherokee Phoenix* 4, no. 9 (August 27, 1831): 1, cols. 3–5. Delivered before the London Tract Society, May 15, 1831.

167. The full title of the address originally given at the Buffalo Baptist Church on August 28, 1838, is *Address on the Present Condition and Prospects of the Aboriginal Inhabitants of North America, with Particular Reference to the Seneca Nation. By M. B. Pierce, a Chief of the Seneca Nation, and a Member of Dartmouth College* (New York: Steele's Press, 1838). Pierce (1811–74), a key figure in the Seneca strug-

gle to maintain a land base in New York and in the subsequent "Seneca Revolution" of 1848, is also the author of an unpublished journal, "A Book of Memorandum" (1840), describing his experiences at Dartmouth and a trip to Washington and Philadelphia as a member of a Seneca delegation. The original is at the Buffalo Historical Society. For background on Pierce, see H. A. Vernon, "Maris Bryant Pierce: The Making of a Seneca Leader," in L. G. Moses and Raymond Wilson, eds., *Indian Lives: Essays on Nineteenth- and Twentieth-Century Native American Leaders* (Albuquerque: University of New Mexico Press, 1985), 19–42.

168. Wilkins, *Cherokee Tragedy*, 190–193 (see nn. 40 and 53).

169. Boudinot, *Address to the Whites*, 11 (75). Page numbers in parentheses refer to Perdue, *Cherokee Editor*.

170. Ibid., 13 (76). John Ridge claims that one-third of the Cherokees could "read & write in the English Language" and a "large majority" could "read and write in George Guess' syllabic character." See Sturtevant, "Ridge on Cherokee Civilization," 87.

171. Boudinot, *Address to the Whites*, 13 (76–77).

172. Ibid., 14 (77).

173. See Ross to the Senate, March 8, 1835; Ross to the Senate and House of Representatives, June 21, 1836; Letter from John Ross . . . in Answer to Inquiries from a Friend, July 2, 1836; Ross to the Senate and House of Representatives, September 28, 1836; Ross to the Senate and House of Representatives, February 22, 1837; and Letter from John Ross . . . to a Gentleman of Philadelphia, May 6, 1837, in Moulton, *Papers of John Ross*, 1: 394–413, 427–444, 444–456, 458–461, 470–474, 490–503. John Howard Payne, who was a staunch supporter of Ross, assisted the latter in formulating and circulating antitreaty material. See Moulton, *John Ross*, 82.

174. The full title of Strong's pamphlet is *Appeal to the Christian Community on the Condition and Prospects of the New York Indians, in Answer to a Book, Entitled The Case of the New York Indians, and Other Publications of the Society of Friends. By Nathaniel T. Strong, a Chief of the Seneca Tribe* (New York, 1841). Strong's views are diametrically opposed to those expressed by his fellow Seneca chief, Maris B. Pierce (see above, n. 167).

175. Boudinot, *Letters and Other Papers Relating to Cherokee Affairs*, 2 (162). I am using here the 1838 version of the manifesto on public record as Senate Document 121, 25th Cong., 2nd sess. Page numbers in parentheses refer to Perdue, *Cherokee Editor*.

176. Ibid., 9–10 (173).

177. Ibid., 29 (203). The complete statement reads as follows: "It is well known that while you [Ross] were adding one farm after another, and stretching your fences over hills and dales, from river to river, and through swamps and forests, no doubt, (for I can conceive no other substantial reason for such unusual conduct,) with a view to these very times; I say, while you were making these great preparations, which have now turned out to be a pecuniary advantage to you, I was here, toiling, at the most trying time of our difficulties, for the defence of our rights, in an arduous employment, and with a nominal salary of three hundred dollars only, entirely neglecting my own pecuniary interest. You know it is so; it is too notorious

to call for denial; and yet you would present me as being actuated, in this affair, by interested motives!"

178. Ibid., 37 (215–216), 41 (222).

179. Ibid., 42–43 (223–225).

180. Ross to Francis P. Blair and John C. Rives, February 8, 1838, in Moulton, *Papers of John Ross*, 1: 590–593.

181. See Geary Hobson, "Remembering the Earth," in idem, ed., *The Remembered Earth: An Anthology of Contemporary Native American Literature* (Albuquerque: Red Earth Press, 1979), 5; and Andrew Wiget, "Elias Boudinot, Elisha Bates, and *Poor Sarah*: Frontier Protestantism and the Emergence of the First Native American Fiction," *Journal of Cherokee Studies* 8 (Spring 1983): 4–21.

182. It was published as "Religion Exemplified in the Life of Poor Sarah," in the *Religious Intelligencer*, January 1 and 8, 1820; *Boston Recorder*, March 11, 1820; and *Connecticut Mirror*, March 6 and 13, 1820. I am grateful to Kristin Herzog, who first pointed this out to me in 1982. It also appeared as a pamphlet under various titles between 1820 and 1822, before Boudinot published it as *Poor Sarah; or, Religion Exemplified in the Life and Death of a Pious Indian Woman* (Mount Pleasant, OH: Elisha Bates, 1823). An entry at the Library of Congress under "Elias Boudinot" states that it was probably a reprint of tract 128 published by the American Tract Society and that it is thought to be the true story of a Mrs. Sarah Rogers (d. 1810), an Indian woman who lived in Connecticut.

183. Perdue, *Cherokee Editor*, 33.

184. Quotes from Boudinot, *Address to the Whites*, 4 (69); idem, *Letters and Other Papers Relating to Cherokee Affairs*, 20 (189). Boudinot refers to Ross's linguistic deficiency in ibid., 18–19 (186–187).

CHAPTER SIX

1. Despite his renown, relatively little has been written about Copway. The primary source on his life are his own four books: *The Life, History, and Travels of Kah-ge-ga-gah-bowh (George Copway), a Convert to the Christian Faith, and a Missionary to His People for Twelve Years; with a Sketch of the Present State of the Ojebwa Nation, in Regard to Christianity and Their Future Prospects* (Albany: Weed & Parsons, 1847) (unless otherwise stated, I will be referring to the 1851 edition published in London by C. Gilpin under the title *Recollections of a Forest Life: or, The Life and Travels of Kah-ge-ga-gah-bowh, or, George Copway, Chief of the Ojibway Nation*); *Organization of a New Indian Territory, East of the Missouri River. Arguments and Reasons Submitted to the Honorable the Members of the Senate and House of Representatives of the 31st Congress of the United States: By the Indian Chief Kah-ge-ga-gah-bowh, or Geo. Copway* (New York: S. W. Benedict, 1850); *The Traditional History and Characteristic Sketches of the Ojibway Nation* (London: C. Gilpin, 1850) (unless otherwise stated, I will be referring to the 1851 edition published in Boston by Benjamin B. Mussey); and *Running Sketches of Men and Places, in England, France, Germany, Belgium, and Scotland* (New York: J. C. Riker, 1851). Copway's work was first considered in Elémire Zolla, *The Writer and the Shaman: A Morphology of the American Indian* (New York: Harcourt Brace

Jovanovich, 1969), 237–240. The best secondary sources are Donald B. Smith, "Kahgegagahbowh," *Dictionary of Canadian Biography* (hereafter cited as *DCB*) (Toronto: University of Toronto Press, 1976), 9:419–421; and, especially, idem, "The Life of George Copway or Kah-ge-ga-gah-bowh (1818–1869) — and a review of his writings," *Journal of Canadian Studies* 23, no. 3 (Autumn 1988): 5–38. Further information on Copway is in Donald B. Smith, *Sacred Feathers: The Reverend Peter Jones (Kahkewaquonaby) & the Mississauga Indians* (Lincoln: University of Nebraska Press, 1987). Copway's autobiography is analyzed in A. La Vonne Brown Ruoff, "George Copway: Nineteenth-Century American Autobiographer," *Auto/Biography* 2, no. 1 (1987): 617; and idem, "Three Nineteenth-Century American Indian Autobiographers," in A. La Vonne Brown Ruoff and Jerry W. Ward, eds., *Redefining American Literary History* (New York: MLA, 1990), 251–269. Gerald Vizenor comments on Copway's life and works in his "Three Anishinaabeg Writers," in idem, *The People Named the Chippewa* (Minneapolis: University of Minnesota Press, 1984), 56–74. His relationship with Longfellow is discussed in Ernest J. Moyne, "Longfellow and Kah-ge-ga-gah-bowh," in J. Chesley Mathews, ed., *Henry W. Longfellow Reconsidered: A Symposium* (Hartford: Transcendental Books, 1970), 48–52. Copway's reliability as historian is discussed in Leroy V. Eid, "The Ojibway-Iroquois War: The War the Five Nations Did Not Win," *Ethnohistory* 26, no. 4 (Fall 1979): 297–324; and D. Peter MacLeod, "The Anishinabeg Point of View: The History of the Great Lakes Region to 1800 in Nineteenth-Century Mississauga, Odawa, and Ojibwa Historiography," *Canadian Historical Review* 73, no. 2 (June 1992): 194–210. His relations with the American nativistic movement are covered in Dale T. Knobel, "Know-Nothings and Indians: Strange Bedfellows?" *Western Historical Quarterly* 15 (April 1984): 175–198. See also the earlier biographical sketches in Frederick Dockstader, *Great North American Indians: Profiles in Life and Leadership* (New York: Van Nostrand Reinhold, 1977), 59; George Harvey Genzmer, "Copway, George," *Dictionary of American Biography* (New York: Charles Scribner's Sons, 1930), 4:433; and William Jones, "Copway, George," in F. W. Hodge, ed., *Handbook of American Indians North of Mexico*, Smithsonian Institution, Bureau of American Ethnology Bulletin 30 (Washington, DC: Government Printing Office, 1907–1910), 347.

2. Literature on the Ojibwas is extensive. A recent and comprehensive work on the Southeastern Ojibwas is Peter S. Schmalz, *The Ojibwa of Southern Ontario* (Toronto: University of Toronto Press, 1991). The Ojibwas on the American side are covered in Edmund Danziger, Jr., *The Chippewas of Lake Superior* (Norman: University of Oklahoma Press, 1978). Shorter accounts are Robert E. Ritzenthaler, "Southwestern Chippewa," and E. S. Rogers, "Southeastern Ojibwa," both in Bruce G. Trigger, ed., *Handbook of North American Indians: Northeast* (Washington, DC: Smithsonian Institution Press, 1978), 15:743–759, 760–771. I have also relied on Harold Hickerson, *The Southwestern Chippewa: An Ethnohistorical Study*, American Anthropological Association Memoir 92 (Menasha, WI, 1962); and idem, *The Chippewa and Their Neighbors: A Study in Ethnohistory* (New York: Holt, Rinehart & Winston, 1970); Ruth Landes, *Ojibway Sociology* (New York: Columbia University Press, 1969); idem, *Ojibway Religion and the Midéwiwin* (Madison: University of Wisconsin Press, 1969); and Christopher Vecsey, *Traditional Ojibwa Religion and*

Its Historical Changes (Philadelphia: American Philosophical Society, 1983). Besides Copway's *Traditional History*, two more histories were written by contemporary Ojibwas: Peter Jones, *History of the Ojebway Indians: With Especial Reference to Their Conversion to Christianity* (London: A. W. Bennett, 1861; rpt., Freeport, NY: Books for Libraries, 1970); and William Whipple Warren, *History of the Ojibways, Based upon Traditions and Oral Statements*, Minnesota Historical Collections, 5 (1885): 21–394; reprinted as *History of the Ojibway Nation* (Minneapolis: Ross & Haines, 1970; rpt., St. Paul: Minnesota Historical Society, 1984). In subsequent citations to Warren, I use the 1970 edition, except as noted. For additional literature, see George P. Murdock and Timothy J. O'Leary, *Ethnographic Bibliography of North America*, 4th ed. (New Haven: Human Relations Area Files Press, 1975), 2:217–241; and Helen H. Tanner, *The Ojibwas: A Critical Bibliography* (Bloomington: Indiana University Press, 1976). On Great Lakes Indian history, see Ives Goddard, "Central Algonquian Languages," and Lyle M. Stone and Donald Chaput, "History of the Upper Great Lakes Area," both in Trigger, *Handbook of North American Indians*, 15: 583–587, 602–609; W. Vernon Kinietz, *Indians of the Great Lakes* (Ann Arbor: University of Michigan Press, 1940); George I. Quimby, *Indian Life in the Upper Great Lakes, 11,000 B.C. to A.D. 1800* (Chicago: University of Chicago Press, 1960); Robert E. Ritzenthaler and Pat Ritzenthaler, *The Woodland Indians of the Western Great Lakes* (1970; rpt., Milwaukee: Milwaukee Public Museum, 1983); Helen H. Tanner, ed., *Atlas of Great Lakes Indian History* (Norman: University of Oklahoma Press, 1987); and, especially, Richard White, *The Middle Ground: Indians, Empires, and the Republics in the Great Lakes Region, 1650–1815* (New York: Cambridge University Press, 1991).

3. Ritzenthaler, "Southwestern Chippewa," 743.

4. Schmalz, *Ojibwa of Southern Ontario*, 4; and Ritzenthaler, "Southwestern Ojibwa," 743.

5. Hickerson, *Southwestern Chippewa*, 2–3.

6. Danziger, *Chippewa of Lake Superior*, 26–52; Quimby, *Indian Life in the Upper Great Lakes*, 122–127; Stone and Chaput, "History of the Upper Great Lakes Area," 602–606; Tanner, *Atlas of Great Lakes History*, 39–47; Vecsey, *Traditional Ojibwa Religion*, 26–30; White, *Middle Ground*, 1–222. On the Great Lakes fur trade, see Carolyn Gilman, *Where Two Worlds Meet: The Great Lakes Fur Trade* (St. Paul: Minnesota Historical Society, 1982); and Arthur J. Ray, *Indians in the Fur Trade: Their Role as Hunters, Trappers, and Middlemen in the Lands Southwest of Hudson Bay, 1660–1870* (Toronto: University of Toronto Press, 1974). For a case study of the Ojibwas and the fur trade, see Charles A. Bishop, *The Northern Ojibwa and the Fur Trade: An Historical and Ecological Study* (Toronto: Holt, Reinhart & Winston of Canada, 1974).

7. See Hickerson, *Southwestern Chippewa*, 88–89; idem, "The Chippewa of the Upper Great Lakes: A Study in Sociopolitical Change," in Eleanor B. Leacock and Nancy O. Lurie, eds., *North American Indians in Historical Perspective* (New York: Random House, 1971), 169–199.

8. Ritzenthaler, "Southwestern Ojibwa," 743–744; Rogers, "Southeastern Ojibwa," 762; and Stone and Chaput, "History of the Upper Great Lakes Area," 605.

9. See Harriet Gorham, "Families of Mixed Descent in the Western Great Lakes Region," in Bruce Alden Cox, ed., *Native People, Native Lands: Canadian Indians, Inuit and Metis* (Ottawa: Carleton University Press, 1987), 37–55.

10. See Eid, "Ojibwa-Iroquois War"; and Schmalz, *Ojibwa of Southern Ontario*, 18–34. See also the autohistorical accounts in Copway, *Traditional History*, 73–96; Jones, *History*, 111–133; and Warren, *History of the Ojibway Nation*, 146–154.

11. See Hickerson, *Southwestern Chippewa*, 12–29; idem, *The Chippewa and Their Neighbors*, 64–79; Tanner, *Atlas of Great Lakes History*, 42–43. This war also forms the bulk of the second half of Warren's *History of the Ojibway Nation*. See also Copway, *Traditional History*, 55–67.

12. On epidemics in the Great Lakes region, see Tanner, *Atlas of Great Lakes History*, 169–174.

13. On the British period, see Danziger, *Chippewas of Lake Superior*, 53–67; Stone and Chaput, "History of the Upper Great Lakes Area," 606–607; Tanner, *Atlas of Great Lakes History*, 55–56; Vecsey, *Traditional Ojibwa Religion*, 14–16; and White, *Middle Ground*, 223–365.

14. Pontiac was said to be of Ottawa-Ojibwa descent. See Schmalz, *Ojibwa of Southern Ontario*, 63–84; Tanner, *Atlas of Great Lakes History*, 48–53; and White, *Middle Ground*, 269–314.

15. See Schmalz, *Ojibwa of Southern Ontario*, 86, 116–118; Tanner, *Atlas of Great Lakes History*, 121; and White, *Middle Ground*, 366–523. See also J. R. Miller, *Skyscrapers Hide the Heavens: A History of Indian-White Relations in Canada* (Toronto: University of Toronto Press, 1989), 83–98.

16. See Robert J. Surtees, "Indian Land Cessions in Upper Canada, 1815–1830," in A. L. Getty and Antoine S. Lussier, eds., *As Long as the Sun Shines and the Water Flows: A Reader in Canadian Native Studies* (Vancouver: Nakoda Institute and University of British Columbia Press, 1983), 56–64.

17. See Danziger, *Chippewas of Lake Superior*, 68–90; Ritzenthaler, "Southwestern Ojibwa," 745; Rogers, "Southeastern Ojibwa," 763–764; Schmalz, *Ojibwa of Southern Ontario*, 85–119, 120–146; Stone and Chaput, "History of the Upper Great Lakes Area," 607–609; and Tanner, *Atlas of Great Lakes History*, 155–161.

18. Tanner, *Atlas of Great Lakes History*, 162–168; and Vecsey, *Traditional Ojibwa Religion*, 16–19. On Ojibwa removal, see James A. Clifton, "Wisconsin Death March: Explaining the Extremes in Old Northwest Indian Removal," *Transactions of the Wisconsin Academy of Sciences, Arts, and Letters* 75 (1987): 1–39.

19. Miller, *Skyscrapers Hide the Heavens*, 99–115; and Schmalz, *Ojibwa of Southern Ontario*, 132–135, 162–164. On Canadian Indian policy at this time, see George F. G. Stanley, "As Long as the Sun Shines and Waters Flow: An Historical Comment," John L. Tobias, "Protection, Civilization, Assimilation: An Outline History of Canada's Indian Policy," and John S. Milloy, "The Early Indian Acts: Developmental Strategy and Constitutional Change," all in Getty and Lussier, *As Long as the Sun Shines and the Water Flows*, 1–28, 29–38, 39–55; Robert J. Surtees, "The Development of an Indian Reserve Policy in Canada," *Ontario History* 61, no. 2 (June 1969): 87–98; L. F. S. Upton, "The Origins of Canadian Indian Policy," *Journal of Canadian Studies* 8 (1973): 51–61; and Paul Williams, "Canada's Laws

about Aboriginal Peoples: A Brief Overview," *Law & Anthropology* 1 (1986): 93–120.

20. The titles of the acts were: "An Act for the better protection of the Lands and Property of Indians in Lower Canada" and "An Act for the Protection of the Indians in Upper Canada from imposition, and the property occupied or enjoyed by them from trespassing and injury." See Miller, *Skyscrapers Hide the Heavens*, 108–111; and Tobias, "Protection, Civilization, Assimilation," 15–16.

21. On the present state of Indian legal rights in Canada, see Bruce Clark, *Native Liberty, Crown Sovereignty: The Existing Aboriginal Right of Self-Government in Canada* (Montreal/Kingston: McGill-Queen's University Press, 1991); and Jack Woodward, *Native Law* (Toronto: Caswell, 1989).

22. Copway, *Recollections*, 1–51. The only source on Copway's early life is his own autobiography.

23. See Rogers, "Southeastern Ojibwa," 769; Donald B. Smith, "The Dispossession of the Mississauga Indians: A Missing Chapter in the Early History of Upper Canada," *Ontario History* 73, no. 2 (June 1981): 67–87; and idem, *Sacred Feathers*, 17–33.

24. Copway, *Recollections*, 32–33.

25. Ibid., 39–40; Copway, *Traditional History*, 149–150. Power, or medicine, emanated from a host of spirits, the manitos, who could appear in the form of plants, animals, minerals, or natural phenomena. This power could be transferred through visions or dreams to fortunate individuals, who were thereby said to have acquired an identity. The Ojibwas consequently placed great importance upon the vision quest and the interpretation of dreams, particularly in the case of adolescent males. Those lacking the favor of a spirit were in turn considered to be very unfortunate because, according to Ruth Landes, they would remain "empty, fearful, and cowardly" for the rest of their lives. See Landes, *Ojibway Religion*, 21–41, esp. 35–37; and Vecsey, *Traditional Ojibwa Religion*, 121–143. On the importance of dreams among the Ojibwas, see Frances Densmore, *Chippewa Customs*, Smithsonian Institution, Bureau of American Ethnology Bulletin 86 (Washington, DC: Government Printing Office, 1929), 78–86; Alfred I. Hollowell, "The Role of Dreams in Ojibwa Culture," in Gustave E. von Grunebaum and Roger Caillois, eds., *The Dream and Human Societies* (Berkeley: University of California Press, 1966), 267–292; and Landes, *Ojibway Sociology*, 115–117. For a very poetic account of the vision quest, see Basil Johnston, *Ojibway Ceremonies* (Lincoln: University of Nebraska Press, 1982), 43–44.

26. Copway, *Recollections*, 29–31; idem, *Traditional History*, 169–175. It is not clear whether the midewiwin (various spellings), a ceremony performed by a secret curative society, is of pre- or postcontact origin. For a postcontact dating, see Hickerson, *The Chippewa and Their Neighbors*, 51–63; Landes, *Ojibway Religion*, 71–204; and Vecsey, *Traditional Ojibwa Religion*, 174–190. For a precontact dating, see Walter James Hoffman, "The Midéwiwin, or 'Grand Medicine Society' of the Ojibwa," in *Bureau of American Ethnology, Seventh Annual Report, 1885–86* (Washington, DC: Government Printing Office, 1891), 143–300; and Warren, *History of the Ojibway Nation*, 65–67, 77–80.

27. Copway, *Recollections*, 2.

28. Ibid., 56–65. Copway's date for the meeting (1827) is uncertain. Donald B. Smith dates it in late August 1826 but claims elsewhere that it took place when Copway was about ten (1827–28). Peter Jones records his first visit to the Rice Lake area in June 1826. See Smith, *Sacred Feathers*, 95; idem, "Kahgegagahbowh," 419; idem, "Life of George Copway," 8; and Peter Jones, *Life and Journals of Ka-ke-wa-quo-na-by (Rev. Peter Jones), Wesleyan Missionary* (Toronto: Anson Green, 1860), 69.

29. See Vecsey, *Traditional Ojibwa Religion*, 26–58, esp. 30–32. On missionary activities in Canada, see Elizabeth Graham, *Medicine Man to Missionary: Missionaries as Agents of Change among the Indians of Southern Ontario* (Toronto: Peter Martin Associates, 1975); and John W. Grant, *Moon of Wintertime: Missionaries and the Indians of Canada in Encounter since 1534* (Toronto: University of Toronto Press, 1984).

30. See G. S. French, "Pahtahsega," *DCB* 11 (1982): 660–661; idem, "Shah-Wun-Dais," *DCB* 10 (1972): 647–648; Peter Jacobs, *Journal of the Reverend Peter Jacobs, Indian Wesleyan Missionary, from Rice Lake to the Hudson's Bay Territory, and Returning, Commencing May, 1852* (New York: By the author, 1857; Isaac Khilisile Mabindisa, "The Praying Man: The Life and Times of Henry Bird Steinhauer" (Ph.D. diss., University of Alberta, 1984); Krystyna Z. Sieciechowicz, "Steinhauer, Henry Bird," *DCB* 11 (1982): 848–849; Donald B. Smith, "Nahnebahwe-quay," *DCB* 9 (1976): 590–591; idem, "Kezhegowinninne," *DCB* 11 (1982): 473–474; idem, "Jones, John," *DCB* 7 (1988): 455–456; and Conrad Vandusen (Enemikeese), *The Indian Chief: An Account of the Labours, Losses, Sufferings, and Oppression of Ke-zig-ko-e-ne-ne (David Sawyer), a Chief of the Ojibway Indians in Canada West* (London: J. Hatchard, 1867). For samples of their writings, see Penny Petrone, ed., *First People, First Voices* (Toronto: University of Toronto Press, 1983).

31. See John Johnson, "The Story of Enmegabowh's Life," in Henry Benjamin Whipple, *Lights and Shadows of a Long Episcopate* (New York: Macmillan, 1902), 497–510; and idem, *En-me-gah-bowh's Story: An Account of the Disturbances of the Chippewa Indians at Gull Lake in 1857, and Their Removal in 1868* (Minneapolis: Women's Auxiliary, St. Barnabas Hospital, 1904). See also "Enmegahbowh," in Hodge, *Handbook of American Indians North of Mexico*, 425.

32. Other than his *Life*, which contains a brief autobiographical sketch (pp. 1–16), and *History of the Ojebway*, which is also prefaced with an autobiographical account (pp. 1–23), Jones is also the author of numerous articles, sermons, and translations. On his life and works, see Smith, *Sacred Feathers*; and idem, "Jones, Peter," *DCB* 8 (1985): 439–443. His translations are listed in James C. Pilling, *Bibliography of Algonquian Languages*, Bureau of American Ethnology Bulletin 13 (Washington, DC: Government Printing Office, 1891), 266–272.

33. Jones, *History of the Ojebway*, 91. See also Smith, *Sacred Feathers*, 15, 35.

34. Jones, *Life*, 2. On the importance of Ojibwa naming ceremonies, see Johnston, *Ojibway Ceremonies*, 13–30.

35. Jones, *Life*, 136.

36. Ibid., 7.

37. Ibid., 13.

38. Jones, *History*, 217–218. See also Smith, *Sacred Feathers*, 183–184, 238.

Jones mentions John Ridge in his history (p. 187), and his own niece was named Catherine Brown Sunegoo, after the well-known Cherokee convert. See Smith, *Sacred Feathers*, 114–115.

39. Rogers, "Southeastern Ojibwa," 765–766. Copway describes what he calls a "General Council" in *Recollections*, 153–164. See also Landes, *Ojibway Sociology*, 1–4; Ritzenthaler, "Southwestern Ojibwa," 753; and Schmalz, *Ojibwa of Southern Ontario*, 11.

40. Copway, *Recollections*, 67–69.

41. Ibid., 34–36, 117–122. He also relates another lengthy story of a young Ojibwa girl's dream in *Traditional History*, 154–164, which he reprinted as "Influence in Dreams" in *Copway's American Indian* 1, no. 2 (July 19, 1851): 2, cols. 4, 5, 6. On Ojibwa notions of death and an afterworld, see Vecsey, *Traditional Ojibwa Religion*, 59–71; Jones, *History*, 101–104; and Warren, *History of the Ojibway Nation*, 72–74.

42. Copway, *Recollections*, 26.

43. Ibid., 69–70. See also Smith, "Life of George Copway," 8–16.

44. *Minuajimouin Gainajimot au St. Luke. Anishinabe enuet Giizhianikvnotabivng au S. Hall, mekvdeuikonaie; Gaie au George Copway, anishinabe gvgikueinini* (Boston: Printed for the ABCFM by Crocker & Brewster, 1837); *Odizhijigeuiniua igiu gaanoninjig. Anishinabe Enuet Anikvnotabivng au Sherman Hall, gaie au George Copway* [Acts of the Apostles in the Ojibwa language] (Boston: Printed for the ABCFM by Crocker & Brewster, 1838). Found in British Library, London, 3070 b12, 3070 b5.

45. Copway, *Recollections*, 97–98. Copway's accounts of his education are somewhat confusing as at this point in his autobiography he claims that before attending the Ebenezer school he "could neither speak nor read five words correctly" and that his two years there provided him with "all the education (little as it is) which I now possess" (97). In his preface to the 1851 edition he states that he "received but three years' schooling" and that he had begun to speak the English language only a few years ago (xi); and in the preface to his 1850 London edition of *Traditional History* he writes, "Twenty months passed in a school in Illinois has been the sum-total of my schooling" (vi).

46. Copway, *Recollections*, 102–108. Quotes on pp. 107–108.

47. Ibid., 116, 122–123. See Smith, "Life of George Copway," 12–14 (see also p. 30, n. 40). On Jones's marriage, see idem, "The Transatlantic Courtship of the Reverend Peter Jones," *Beaver* 308, no. 1 (Summer 1977): 4–13; idem, "Eliza and the Reverend Peter Jones," *Beaver* 308, no. 2 (Autumn 1977): 40–46; and idem, *Sacred Feathers*, 130–149.

48. Copway, *Recollections*, 122–144. Quotes on pp. 125–126.

49. Ibid., 138.

50. See Smith, "Life of George Copway," 14 (see also p. 32, n. 49).

51. Copway, *Recollections*, 142–143.

52. Ibid., 146–147.

53. Quoted in Smith, "Life of George Copway," 16.

54. Copway, *Recollections*, 149.

55. See Smith, "Life of George Copway," 16–17.

56. Copway claimed to have spent some of the money for the education of Moses Alexander, son of the Saugeen chief. See Smith, "Life of George Copway," 33 n. 58. Schoolcraft was removed from his government position as Indian agent in 1840 on charges of graft and misappropriation of Indian funds, which he denied and attributed to the political machinations of his opponents. In 1841 he moved to New York where, like Copway, he embarked upon a new life as a writer. See Robert E. Bieder, *Science Encounters the Indian, 1820–1880: The Early Years of American Anthropology* (Norman: University of Oklahoma Press, 1986), 171–172.

57. Schmalz, *Ojibwa of Southern Ontario*, 156.

58. Smith, "Life of George Copway," 16.

59. Ibid., 17.

60. See Lucy Maddox, *Removals: Nineteenth-Century American Literature & the Politics of Indian Affairs* (New York: Oxford University Press, 1991).

61. Copway, *Running Sketches*, 325; for written samples of his talks, see "Superstitions of the Indians and Their Legends" and "The Evangelization of the North American Indians," 128–147, 304–324. A summary of a lecture he delivered in England on American nature, which originally appeared in the *Yorkshireman*, is reprinted in *Running Sketches*, 325–332. See also "Speech" in *Copway's American Indian* 1, no. 1 (July 10, 1850): 2, cols. 2–6. Copway apparently had a circular printed in Boston in 1849 titled "The Lectures of Kah-ge-ga-gah-bowh (or G. Copway, the Indian Chief) . . . on Monday, Feb. 26, and on Wednesday, Feb. 28, 1849." Mentioned in Daniel F. Littlefield, Jr., and James W. Parins, *A Biobibliography of Native American Writers, 1772–1824* (Metuchen, NJ: Scarecrow Press, 1981), 35.

62. Copway, *Recollections*, 238–248 (quote on p. 247). See also *Running Sketches*, 222–224.

63. Longfellow's Journal, February 26, April 12, and April 14, 1849 (ms., Houghton Library, Harvard University). See Samuel Longfellow, ed., *Life of Henry Wadsworth Longfellow with Extracts from his Journals and Correspondence*, 2 vols. (Boston: Ticknor, 1886), 2:135. Quoted in Moyne, "Longfellow and Kah-ge-ga-gah-bowh," 48.

64. Francis Parkman to Charles Eliot Norton, March 3, 1849, and Parkman to Ephraim George Squier, March 15, 1849, in Wilbur R. Jacobs, ed., *Letters of Francis Parkman*, 2 vols. (Norman: University of Oklahoma Press, 1960), 1:59–61 (brackets mine). Quoted in Smith, "Life of George Copway," 20–21. On Parkman's views on Indians, see David Levin, *History as Romantic Art: Bancroft, Prescott, Motley, and Parkman* (Stanford: Stanford University Press, 1959), 126–141.

65. The letter, titled "James River — Smith and Pocahontas," is dated July 15, 1850, and included along with four others in Copway, *Recollections*, 228–233. See Smith, "Life of George Copway," 22.

66. "The Indians of the Western Continent of America," *Liverpool Mercury*, July 30, 1850, 5, cols. 2, 3. The paper also advertises a forthcoming lecture by "The Reverend George Copway, — Kah-ge-ga-gah-bowh, a North American Indian, *formerly* a Chief of the Ojibway nation" (1, col. 2; italics mine). Similar reviews of this talk are found in the *Liverpool Standard*, July 30, 1850, 8, col. 4; and the *Liverpool Times*, August 1, 1850, 2, cols. 1, 2. The former states "that he had ceased to continue officially as a preacher in the Wesleyan body, on the ground that he might

do more good by appealing to the people on the broad basis of humanity and justice." It is interesting to note that Copway omitted this when he quoted from the *Standard* in his first edition of *Traditional History*, 284–292, and from the *Mercury* in his *Running Sketches*, 58–65.

67. Copway, "The American Indians," *American Whig Review* 9 (June 1849): 631–638; reprinted in Bernd C. Peyer, ed., *The Elders Wrote: An Anthology of Early Literature Written by North American Indians, 1768–1934* (Berlin: Dietrich Reimer Verlag, 1982), 75–86. See also Copway, *Organization,* 17.

68. See Annie H. Abel, "Proposals for an Indian State, 1778–1878," *Annual Report of the American Historical Association for the Year 1907* (Washington, DC: Government Printing Office, 1908), 1:87–104; and George A. Schulz, *An Indian Canaan: Isaac McCoy and the Vision of an Indian State* (Norman: University of Oklahoma Press, 1972).

69. See Ronald N. Satz, *American Indian Policy in the Jacksonian Era* (Lincoln: University of Nebraska Press, 1975), 224–227; and Alice E. Smith, *James Duane Doty: Frontier Promoter* (Madison: State Historical Society of Wisconsin, 1954), 257–262.

70. See Smith, "Life of George Copway," 19–20.

71. James Duane Doty to Millard Fillmore, January 20, 1851, in Abel, "Proposals for an Indian State," 103–104. See also Carl Resek, *Lewis H. Morgan, American Scholar* (Chicago: University of Chicago Press, 1960), 43. On early U.S. reservation policies, see John M. Findley, "An Elusive Institution: The Birth of Indian Reservations in Gold Rush California," in George P. Cortille and Robert L. Bell, eds., *State and Reservation: New Perspectives on Federal Indian Policy* (Tucson: University of Arizona Press, 1992), 13–37; and Robert A. Trennert, Jr., *Alternative to Extinction: Federal Indian Policy and the Beginnings of the Reservation System, 1846–1851* (Philadelphia: Temple University Press, 1975).

72. See Danziger, *Chippewas of Lake Superior,* 86–88.

73. Copway, *Recollections,* 157–158, 161.

74. Ibid., 187; Copway, *Organization,* 18.

75. Smith, "Life of George Copway," 21.

76. See Knobel, "Know-Nothings and Indians." Among those who supported Copway's plans were Benjamin F. Butler and George Briggs, governors of Massachusetts; Alexander Ramsey, governor of Minnesota, senator, and secretary of war; Charles Manly, governor of North Carolina; Edward Everett, congressman and noted orator; Ephraim G. Squier, chargé d'affaires to Central America, archaeologist; Kenneth Rayner, congressman; William F. Havemeyer, mayor of New York; John P. Bigelow, editor of the *New York Evening Post*; Benjamin Silliman, noted Yale scientist; and Asa Whitney, the railroad promoter. Copway included their letters of support at the end of his *Organization,* 26–32.

77. George Copway to Zachary Taylor, March 7, 1849; mentioned in Smith, "Life of George Copway," 21.

78. Cited in "The American Indians," *Liverpool Standard* (July 30, 1850), 8, col. 4.

79. Versions of this plan are also found in Copway, *Recollections,* 184–209,

211–215; idem, *Traditional History*, 240–266; and idem, "New Indian Republic," *Indian Advocate* 5 (September 1850): 4.

80. Copway, *Organization*, 13; Smith, "Life of George Copway," 20.

81. Copway, *Organization*, 13–15, 18–23; idem, "The American Indians," 636–637.

82. Parkman to Squier, November 18, 1849, in Jacobs, *Letters of Francis Parkman*, 65–67 (brackets mine).

83. *The Ojibway Conquest, a Tale of the Northwest* (New York: George P. Putnam, 1850); reprinted in Edwin C. Guillet, *The Valley of the Trent* (Toronto: Champlain Society, 1957), 442–462. The New York edition of his autobiography was published by S. W. Benedict under the title *The Life, Letters, and Speeches of Kah-ge-ga-gah-bowh, or, G. Copway, Chief of the Ojibway Nation*.

84. For background on Burritt and the World Peace Congress, see Merle Curti, ed., *The Learned Blacksmith: The Letters and Journals of Elihu Burritt* (New York: Wilson-Erickson, 1937), 28–39; and Chas. Northend, ed., *Elihu Burritt; A Memorial Volume Containing a Sketch of his Life and Labors, with Selections from His Writings and Lectures, and Extracts from His Private Journals in Europe and America* (New York: D. Appleton, 1879), 101–108.

85. Copway, *Running Sketches*, 55, 98–113, 122–126, 148–152. The description of his appearance is taken from an article in the *Liverpool Standard* which Copway quoted in the same publication on p. 54.

86. Times were not opportune for the ideal of universal peace and brotherhood. The nationalistic and social movements surging in central Europe in 1848 had been crushed by professional Prussian, Austrian, and Russian armies by 1850. The Danish-German War (1848–50) was still going on, and armed conflict between Prussia and Austria seemed imminent. Even the site of the Congress itself, the Paulskirche (Church of St. Paul), seat of the Nationalversammlung (General Assembly), of which Carl Jaup (1781–1860) was president and which was the symbol of German democratic aspirations, was not free of controversy. It was here, in April of the previous year, that the powerless delegates had offered the imperial crown to the king of Prussia. Only a few days after the Congress disbanded, on September 1, Austria and Prussia withdrew their representatives and soon after reestablished the old conservative order. The presence at the Congress of Austrian General Julius von Haynau (1786–1853), known in England as the "Hyena" for his cruelty in repressing the Hungarian revolution, was viewed by many as an ironic symbol of the impotence of the peace movement. Major European journals like the London *Times* and the Paris *Journal des Débats Politiques et Littéraires* were consequently highly critical of the event. Later, the Crimean War (1854–55) added to the frustrations of the international peace movement. See Veit Valentin, "Der Erste Internationale Friedenskongreß auf Deutschen Boden 1850," in Hans-Ulrich Wehler, ed., *Veit Valentin: Von Bismarck zur Weimarer Republik: Sieben Beiträge zur deutschen Politik* (Köln: Kiepenheuer & Witsch, 1979): 27–37.

87. The fifth resolution was: "This Congress acknowledging the principle of nonintervention, recognizes it to be the sole right of every state to regulate its own affairs." Copway describes the Peace Congress in some detail in *Running Sketches*,

208–253. Much of his information was taken directly from the London *Times* and the minutes of the Congress, which were published the following year in English and German. See *Report of the Proceedings of the Third General Peace Congress, held in Frankfort, on the 22nd, 23rd, and 24th August, 1850* (London: C. Gilpin, 1851); and *Verhandlungen des dritten allgemeinen Friedenskongresses, gehalten in der Paulskirche zu Frankfurt a/M., am 22., 23., und 24. August 1850* (Frankfurt am main: J. D. Sauerländer's Verlag, 1851).

88. "The Peace Congress," *Times* (London), August 28, 1850, 5, cols. 2, 3.

89. Copway, *Running Sketches*, 252. The *Times* was also highly critical of William Wells Brown's abolitionist speech at the Peace Congress in Paris the previous year. See Paul Jefferson, ed., *The Travels of William Wells Brown* (New York: Markus Wiener, 1991), 17, n. 9.

90. *Journal des Débats Politiques et Littéraires* (Paris), September 2, 1850, 1, cols. 1, 2 ("c'est décidément l'Indienne qui a été le lion du Congrès; il rejeté dans l'ombre tous les lions de Londres et de Paris. Comment lutter avec une grande-chef qui parle du grand esprit, e des frères à la face pâle!").

91. The Burritt statement is from a diary entry dated August 24, 1850, Burritt's Diaries, New Britain, Connecticut, Public Library. Quoted in Smith, "Life of George Copway," 24.

92. Copway, *Running Sketches*, 221. The reference is to Emile de Girardin (1806–81), eminent French journalist; Richard Cobden (1804–65), British statesman and champion of the British Anti-Corn-Law League; and the Reverend Edwin Hubbell Chapin (1814–80), American Universalist clergyman and noted orator.

93. See Preston A. Barba, *Cooper in Germany* (Bloomington: Indiana University Press, 1914); Hartmut Lutz, *"Indianer" und "Native Americans": Zur sozial- und literaturhistorischen Vermittlung eines Stereotyps* (Hildesheim: Olms-Verlag, 1985), 244–446; and Hans Plischke, *Von Cooper bis Karl May: Eine Geschichte des völkerkundlichen Reise- und Abenteuerromans* (Düsseldorf: Droste Verlag, 1951).

94. *Illustrierte Zeitung* (Leipzig), September 21, 1850, 183–184: "Einen wirklich erhebenden Anblick bot die letzte Sitzung dar. Copway, der indianische Häuptling, besteigt die Rednerbühne. Ein Mann in den Vierzigern, von einer leichten Kupferfarbe, mit glänzend schwarzen und schlichten Haaren, fast bartlos, das Auge dunkel und verständig, der Wuchs schlank und proportioniert. In einer englischen, sich oft zur Poesie erhebenden Rede erkennt er sein erhabeneres Motiv für den Frieden, als den Frieden in Gott, wie ihn das Evangelium lehrt. Vor 15 Jahren noch als Wilder unter den Indianern seines Stammes umherirrend, zeigt er an sich die Fortschritte der Zivilization. Auch habe man ihm gesagt, daß in Frankfurt, wo jetzt schattige Bäume grünen und Kinder unter Blumen spielen, ehemals Schießscharten, Thürme, Wälle und Waffen gestanden hätten. Weit von Westen sei er gekommen, es reue ihn nicht, den großen See durchschwommen zu haben, um den Europäern von den Söhnen des roten Kain das Symbol der Versöhnung, die Friedenspfeife zu bringen. Als er sie aus ihrer Umhüllung heraus nimmt und dem Präsidenten als Räpresentanten der hier anwesenden Nationen feierlich überreicht, da schwenken die Männer ihre Hüte, da grüßen die Frauen mit den Tüchern, da erschallt ein Beifallssturm, der nicht enden will." Other positive reviews of his talk are found in *Frankfurter Oberpostamts-Zeitung*, August 24, 1850, 2, cols. 1, 2, 3; and *Allge-*

meine Zeitung (Augsburg), August 27, 1850, 1, col. 1. Interestingly, the German minutes of the Peace Congress contain a much more detailed rendition of his speech than the English version does. Compare *Report of the Proceedings of the Third General Peace Congress*, 42, and *Verhandlungen des dritten allgemeinen Friedens-kongresses*, 41–43. An appendix in the latter has additional news about Copway and clarifies the fallacy behind the title "Chief" in the local press (97–98). Not all German journalists were thus impressed, however. The Berlin-based satirical weekly, *Kladderadatsch* (September 1, 1850), ridiculed Copway and the Congress with a caricature showing the "retired savage and cannibal, Hi Ge Ga Gah Bowh," in a silly costume offering a Bavarian-style "peace" pipe and "peace" cigars to President Jaup — who was also the president of the powerless German General Assembly at the time it was being usurped by Prussia and Austria — and promising to refrain henceforth from regarding his pale-faced brothers as "beefsteaks."

95. The peace pipe itself has apparently been lost, but the event was brought up again relatively recently in *Frankfurter Allgemeine Zeitung*, December 3, 1986, 41. It was also featured in a display commemorating the city's 1,200th anniversary ("FFM 1200 — Traditionen und Perspektiven einer Stadt," May 17, 1994).

96. His bust, cast by Eduard Schmidt von der Launitz (1797–1869), was probably destroyed during World War II, but a black-and-white photograph of the plaster mold is still found in the Frankfurt archives (Nachlass Launitz, S 1/80, Box 1-4, Stadtarchiv Frankfurt). See Isolde Schmidt, *Eduard Schmidt von der Launitz, 1797–1869: Ein Beitrag zur Skulptur des 19. Jahrhunderts in Frankfurt am Main* (Frankfurt: Verlag Waldemar Kramer, 1992), 140–143, 206, 253. See also R. Adler, trans., *Die Besiegung der Odschibwäh* (Frankfurt: Brönner, 1851). A second translation was prepared by Karl Cloos of Cologne, but I have not been able to determine whether it was ever published.

97. Copway, *Running Sketches*, 254. The reference must be to Frederick Wilhelm III (1831–88), son of Wilhelm I, who was crowned kaiser of Germany and king of Prussia just before his death. He is said to have been a man of liberal ideas.

98. Hermann Ferdinand Freiligrath to Henry Wadsworth Longfellow, June 19, 1851, in James Taft Hatfield, "The Longfellow-Freiligrath Correspondence," *Publications of the Modern Language Association* 48, no. 4 (December 1933): 1269–1273. Quoted in Moyne, "Longfellow and Kah-ge-ga-gah-bowh," 49. Freiligrath (1810–76), who translated Longfellow's *Song of Hiawatha* [Der Sang von Hiawatha] in 1857, was a representative of an informal literary group known as Das Neue Deutschland (ca. 1830–50) which participated in the reform movements of 1848. He emigrated to England in 1851 and did not return to Germany until 1868.

99. Copway, *Running Sketches*, 268.

100. Ibid., 297, 304–324. He also includes a list of twenty-nine speaking engagements between November 7 and December 5 (pp. 302–303).

101. Ibid., 278.

102. See Knobel, "Know-Nothings and Indians," 179–181.

103. Moyne, "Longfellow and Kah-ge-ga-gah-bowh," 52, n. 18. Moyne, who has gleaned this information from *Rode's New York City Directory*, states that Copway is listed as editor for the winter season, 1850–51. He assumes the magazine in question was *The Pearl: A Ladies' Weekly Literary Gazette*. The *National*

Union Catalog lists a *New York Washingtonian and Ladies' Pearl* (1846–48) as a weekly devoted to the advocacy of the various ladies' total abstinence associations.

104. Among the other supporters whose letters are included in the first issue of *Copway's American Indian* were Anson Burlingame (1820–70), congressman; George P. Morris (102–64), editor of the *New York Mirror* and poet; Joseph P. Chandler (1792–1880), journalist and congressman; and Alfred B. Street (1911–81), lawyer and poet.

105. Copway to Longfellow, June 12, 1851; mentioned in Moyne, "Longfellow and Kah-ge-ga-gah-bowh," 50.

106. A complete collection of *Copway's American Indian* is found in the Newspaper Library of the British Library at Colindale, London, under the reference A. misc. 148.

107. *Copway's American Indian* 1, no. 1 (July 10, 1851): "Prospectus," 1, col. 1; "Plain Talk to the Wise," 3, col. 1.

108. Only Morgan and Irving contributed more than one article, and Parkman and Everett provided one each. The others apparently made no contribution at all.

109. He credits a Mr. Thomas Frére with the editorship of the third (July 26) issue: 2, col. 5.

110. Copway's paper was also preceded by the family-operated *Choctaw Telegraph* (1848–50), which then became the *Intelligencer* (1850–52). See James Murphy and Sharon Murphy, *Let My People Know: American Indian Journalism* (Norman: University of Oklahoma Press, 1981), 16–38. On Montezuma's *Wassaja*, see Peter Iveson, *Carlos Montezuma and the Changing World of American Indians* (Albuquerque: University of New Mexico Press, 1982), 106–111, 170–173.

111. Robert F. Berkhofer, Jr., *The White Man's Indian: Images of the American Indian from Columbus to the Present* (New York: Alfred A. Knopf, 1978), 95. See also Werner Sollors, *Beyond Ethnicity: Consent and Descent in American Culture* (New York: Oxford University Press, 1986), 131–141; and Gaile McGregor, *The Noble Savage in the New World Garden: Notes Toward a Syntactics of Place* (Toronto: University of Toronto Press, 1988), 26–27. On Thoreau's shifting attitudes toward Indians, see Robert F. Sayre, *Thoreau and the American Indians* (Princeton: Princeton University Press, 1977).

112. Longfellow to Freiligrath, June 12, 1850, in Andrew Hilen, ed., *The Letters of Henry Wadsworth Longfellow* (Cambridge: Belknap Press of Harvard University Press, 1972), 3:258–259. Also in Hatfield, "Longfellow-Freiligrath Correspondence," 1268. Longfellow's postscript read: "You send me Anarchy (Anneke), and I send you Kopfweh (Copway)!" His other pun was in reference to a reformist Prussian officer, Fritz Anneke, who had emigrated to the United States.

113. Parkman to Norton, November 10, 1850, in Jacobs, *Letters of Francis Parkman*, 78–79. Longfellow is also on record for having "lent" five dollars to Copway in April of 1854. He filed it in his account book for 1840–82 as "Not to be called for" (ms., Houghton Library). Mentioned in Moyne, "Longfellow and Kah-ge-ga-gah-bowh," 52, n. 23.

114. Freiligrath to Longfellow, September 25, 1853, Houghton Library (italics mine). Quoted in Moyne, "Longfellow and Kah-ge-ga-gah-bowh," 50. On July 16, 1851, Longfellow had written: "But the precious books you sent he has not yet

delivered. I have written to him lately about them, and if they are not forth-coming, I shall raise such a war-whoop, that it will frighten him. If they are lost, I shall never forgive him." Copway called on Longfellow on August 29, 1851, and, not finding him at home, first helped himself to one of Longfellow's cigars and then wrote him a note complimenting him on his nice domicile and blaming his own wife for not having brought the books from London. He promised that he would send for all his trunks and deliver the books as soon as they arrived. Apparently he never did so. See Longfellow to Freiligrath, June 12, 1851, in Hatfield, "Longfellow-Freiligrath Correspondence," 1273–1274; also in Hilen, ed., *Letters of Henry Wadsworth Longfellow*, 3: 302–304; and Moyne, "Longfellow and Kah-ge-ga-gah-bowh," 50.

115. Longfellow to Freiligrath, December 14, 1858, in Hilen, *Letters of Henry Wadsworth Longfellow*, 4: 108–109. Pau-Puk-Keewis is the mischiefmaker in his *Song of Hiawatha*. Quoted in Moyne, "Longfellow and Kah-ge-ga-gah-bowh," 50.

116. Quote in Copway, *Recollections*, 214; idem, "My Country," *Copway's American Indian* 1, no. 2 (July 19, 1851): 2, cols. 2, 3. See Smith, "Life of George Copway," 24. Indian intellectuals were attracted to secret Masonic orders up until the 1930s. Members included notable individuals like Ely S. Parker, Arthur C. Parker, Carlos Montezuma, Henry Roe Cloud, and Charles Eastman. See Arthur C. Parker, *American Indian Freemasonry* (Albany: Buffalo Consistory, 1919).

117. Quotes in "The American Indians," *Liverpool Standard,* July 30, 1850, 8, col. 4; and Copway, *Recollections*, 208.

118. "Letter from George Copway," *New York Times*, September 8, 1856, 3, col. 3. It was written in response to a previous letter in the *Times* titled "Anti-Copway" in which the writer states that he is "insulted" by having "to listen to one of his character . . . without reference to other objections, which ought to exclude him from any American rostrum. . . . he is now, and always has been, a British subject." *New York Times*, September 3, 1856, 5, col. 2. Copway had delivered several speeches at the American Party convention at Albany, including the ratification meeting for George Briggs's nomination to Congress at the Knickerbocker Hall on August 30. See also Copway, *Recollections*, 222; and Knobel, "Know-Nothings and Indians," 186.

119. "Speech," *Copway's American Indian* 1, no. 1 (July 10, 1851): 2, cols. 2–6.

120. Most of the information is found in Smith, "Life of George Copway," 25–28.

121. See William C. Bryant to Ely S. Parker, June 25, 1884, in Arthur C. Parker, *The Life of General Ely S. Parker: Last Grand Sachem of the Iroquois and General Grant's Military Secretary* (Buffalo: Buffalo Historical Society, 1919), 204–206. Bryant thought the perpetrators "should be acquitted of any intentions to do wrong" and mentioned that the articles buried with the body were found intact. Red Jacket's remains were reinterred ceremonially that year with the assistance of Bryant and the Buffalo Historical Society. Mentioned in Smith, "Life of George Copway," 26.

122. Copway to the Honorable Erastus Corning, January 24, 1860, Autograph Collection of Simon Gratz, Historical Society of Pennsylvania. Mentioned in Moyne, "Longfellow and Kah-ge-ga-gah-bowh," 52, n. 24. In the letter Copway also claims to have obtained funds for his son to enroll at Dartmouth, but no Copway, or Ojibwa for that matter, is listed as an Indian student in the Dartmouth rolls at that time.

123. In his autobiographical sketch Johnson wrote the following on the matter of recruiting Indians: "It is true I could make one or two thousand dollars in a few days. But to go and sell my poor people to get Money! Oh, no! I cannot do it." See Johnson, *En-me-gah-bowh's Story*, 11–18.

124. See Smith, "Life of George Copway," 28; idem, "Jones, Peter," 442; and idem, *Sacred Feathers*, 215–249.

125. See "Enmegahbowh," in Hodge, ed., *Handbook of American Indians North of Mexico*, 425.

126. See French, "Pahtahsega," 660–661.

127. Catlin recorded his experiences with Henry's troupe in Europe in his *Notes of Eight Years' Travels and Residence in Europe, with His North American Indian Collection* (London: By the author, 1848), 278–310. See also Allan Forbes, *Some Indian Events of New England* (Boston: State Street Trust, 1934), 66–74; Carolyn Foreman, *Indians Abroad, 1493–1938* (Norman: University of Oklahoma Press, 1944), 193–195; Christopher Mulvey, "Among the Sag-A-Noshes: Ojibwa and Iowa Indians with George Catlin in Europe, 1843–1848," in Christian F. Feest, ed., *Indians in Europe: An Interdisciplinary Collection of Essays* (Aachen: Rader Verlag, 1987), 253–275; and Smith, *Sacred Feathers*, 187–188, 200–202, 217–219, 317 (n. 78).

128. On Pau-Puk-Keewis, see Mentor L. Williams, ed., *Schoolcraft's Indian Legends* (East Lansing: Michigan State University Press, 1956), 97–105.

129. Wiitiko (or windigo) psychosis is a somewhat controversial term applied to a form of mental disorder involving obsessive cannibalism, resulting from starvation anxieties. It is also related to the fear of individual failure in success-oriented Ojibwa society. See Charles A. Bishop, "Northern Algonkian Cannibalism and Windigo Psychosis," *World Anthropology* (The Hague, 1975), 23:237–248; and Seymour Parker, "The Wiitiko Psychosis in the Context of Ojibwa Personality and Culture," *American Anthropologist* 62, no. 4 (August 1960): 603–623.

130. Copway, "The Pen," *Copway's American Indian* 1, no. 7 (August 23, 1851): 2, col. 1. He claims to have written five books of 266, 100, 260, 364, and 37 pages, respectively. Unfortunately, Copway's letters are spread far and wide in public and private collections. Some are available at the Library of Congress (Miscellaneous Manuscripts Collection, box 57, George Copway materials), Minnesota Historical Society (Grace Lee Nute Papers), Pennsylvania Historical Society (six letters written between January 12, 1846, and January 24, 1860), Chicago Historical Society, Massachusetts Historical Society, and National Archives of Canada.

131. See Copway, *Recollections of a Forest Life* (Toronto: Canadiana, 1970), and *Indian Life and Indian History* (New York: AMS Press, 1978). His autobiography has also been excerpted in Paul Lauter et al., eds., *The Heath Anthology of American Literature* (Lexington, MA: Heath, 1990), 1: 1453–1466. Shorter writings are included in Kent Gooderham, ed., *I Am an Indian* (Toronto: J. M. Dent, 1969), 133–134; Charles Hamilton, ed., *Cry of the Thunderbird: The American Indian's Own Story*, 2nd ed. (Norman: University of Oklahoma Press, 1972), 27–31, 42–43, 46–48, 52, 60–63, 75–76; Abraham Chapman, ed., *Literature of the American Indians: Views and Interpretations* (New York: New American Library, 1975), 30–52; Petrone, *First People, First Voices*, 106–110; and Peyer, *The Elders*

Wrote, 75–86. Excerpts from one of his letters to the editor of the *Saturday Evening Post* dated March 30, 1850, were reprinted as "The End of the Trail" in a special bicentennial issue of the *Post*, 248, no. 5 (July/August 1976): 25.

132. *Copway's American Indian* 1, no. 2 (July 19, 1851): 2, col. 4. Reprinted in *Studies in American Indian Literature* 4, nos. 2–3 (Summer/Fall 1992): 196–197. See also Smith, "Life of George Copway," 27. On the romantic age and the imagery of the American wilderness and Indians, see Roderick Nash, *Wilderness and the American Mind*, rev. ed. (New Haven: Yale University Press, 1974), 67–83; and G. Harrison Orians, "The Rise of Romanticism, 1805–1855," in Harry Hayden Clark, ed., *Transitions in American Literary History* (Durham, NC: Duke University Press, 1953), 163–244.

133. Robert E. Bieder and Thomas G. Tax, "From Ethnologists to Anthropologists: A Brief History of the American Ethnological Society," in John V. Murra, ed., *American Anthropology: The Early Years*, 1974 Proceedings of the American Ethnological Society (St. Paul: West Publishing, 1976), 11–22; and Curtis M. Hinsley, Jr., *Savages and Scientists: The Smithsonian Institution and the Development of American Ethnology, 1846–1910* (Washington, DC: Smithsonian Institution Press, 1981).

134. The full title is *The Life, History, and Travels of Kah-ge-ga-gah-bowh (George Copway), a Young Indian Chief of the Ojebwa Nation, a Convert to the Christian Faith, and a Missionary to His People for Twelve Years; with a Sketch of the Present State of the Ojebwa Nation, in Regard to Christianity and Their Future Prospects. Also an Appeal; with All the Names of the Chiefs now Living, Who Have Been Christianized, and the Missionaries Now Living Among Them. Written by Himself.* This 158-page edition was expanded in 1850 by the inclusion of an address he gave before the legislature of Pennsylvania in 1849, five letters he had addressed to Boston papers in 1849, a letter to the *Chicago Tribune* from 1849, and three press notices of his speeches on his Indian Territory project. For a listing of the various editions, see American Library Association, *National Union Catalog pre-1956 Imprints* (London: Mansell, 1970), 122:349–350; and Littlefield and Parins, *Biobibliography of Native American Writers*, 34–37.

135. Jacobs, *Journal*, 3–6; Jones, *Life*, 1–16; Johnson, "Story of Enmegahbowh's Life," 497–510; idem, *En-me-gah-bowh's Story*, 10.

136. Copway, *Recollections*, 10–12.

137. Ibid., 44.

138. Ibid., 208.

139. Ibid., 163.

140. Copway, "The American Indians," 633–634; idem, *Organization*, 8–9. In 1822 Morse had stated "let Indians forget their own languages, in which nothing is written, and nothing of course can be preserved, and learn ours, which will at once open to them the whole field of every kind of useful knowledge." Jedediah Morse, *Report to the Secretary of War . . .* (1822; rpt. New York: Kelley, 1970), 357.

141. Copway, "The American Indians," 633; idem, *Organization*, 7.

142. Copway, "The American Indians," 635; idem, *Organization*, 12.

143. [Copway], *The Ojibway Conquest*, 10, 91, See the preface to Julius Taylor Clark, *The Ojibue Conquest: An Indian Episode. With Other Waifs of Leisure*

Hours (n.p., 1898), v–vi. Mentioned in Moyne, "Longfellow and Kah-ge-ga-gah-bowh," 51, n. 7. See also Smith "Life of George Copway," 21.

144. Copway to Longfellow, November 29, 1849, Houghton Library. See Moyne, "Longfellow and Kah-ge-ga-gah-bowh," 48. He also delivered a copy to Parkman in June. Both presentation copies are now in the Houghton Library. See Smith, "Life of George Copway," 21, 35 (nn. 81, 82).

145. Copway refers to Schoolcraft's collection of legends as "fanciful stories" in his *Traditional History*, 97. The peace pipe episode in the first canto and the winter starvation scene in the twentieth canto, for instance, are also reminiscent of Copway's autobiography. On Longfellow's sources, see Newton Arvin, *Longfellow: His Life and Work* (Boston: Little, Brown, 1963), 154–180; and Stith Thompson, "The Indian Legend of Hiawatha," *Publications of the Modern Language Association* 27 (1922): 128–140.

146. See Copway, *Traditional History*, xi. David Cusick's third edition of *Sketches* was printed in Lockport, NY, by Turner & McCallum, 1848. Compare with Copway's speech on Indian religious beliefs in *Running Sketches*, 135–143. Here Copway mentions the same Iroquois legendary beings as Cusick (Flying Heads, Stonish Giants, a huge mosquito), and in a paragraph on witchcraft (p. 138) he copies Cusick's text nearly verbatim. See the latest edition of Cusick's history (New York: AMS Press, 1976), 29.

147. For a sample of the questionnaire, see William N. Fenton, "Answers to Governor Cass' Questions by Jacob Jameson, a Seneca (ca. 1821–1825)," *Ethnohistory* 16, no. 2 (Spring 1969): 113–139. For Schoolcraft's version, see "Brief Memorandum of Topics," *Copway's American Indian* 1, no. 1 (July 10, 1850): 2, col. 6.

148. In Copway's opinion McKenney, "the *undoubted* friend of the red man" to whom he dedicated "his" epic poem, had written the "best work upon the Indians." Schoolcraft he considered to be the historian "who has studied the [Ojibwa] language more than any other person." See Copway, *Recollections*, 165; idem, *Traditional History*, 123 (brackets mine). Copway also mentions Samuel Gardner Drake as a source (*Recollections*, 165).

149. See Jones, *History*, 245. William Whipple Warren (1825–53) was the mixed-blood son of trader Lyman Marcus Warren and Mary Cadotte. He attended mission school at La Pointe on Madeline Island and subsequently made a living as interpreter and farmer. In 1851, when he began to work on his history, he was elected to the state House of Representatives in St. Paul. He had plans to write additional books on Ojibwa culture and religion but died before he could do so, at the age of twenty-eight. See J. Fletcher Williams, "Memoir of William W. Warren," in Warren, *History of the Ojibway Nation* (Minneapolis: Ross & Haines, 1970), 9–20; and W. Roger Buffalohead, "Introduction," in Warren, *History of the Ojibway Nation* (St. Paul: Minnesota Historical Society, 1984), ix–xvii. See also the brief account in Vizenor, "Three Anishinaabeg Writers," 56–59. Mention should also be made in this context of the three articles by the Canadian Ottawa historian, Francis Assikinack: "Legends and Traditions of the Odahwah Indians," "Social and Warlike Customs of the Odahwah Indians," and "The Odahwah Indian Language," *Canadian Journal of Industry, Science, and Art* 3, no. 14 (March 1858): 115–125; 3, no.

16 (July 1858): 297–309; 3, no. 18 (November 1858): 481–485. On the life of this fellow "three-fires" historian, see Douglas Leighton, "Assikinack, Francis," *DCB* 9 (1976): 10–11.

150. Parkman to Squier, November 18, 1848, in Jacobs, *Letters of Francis Parkman*, 65–66. See Eid, "Ojibwa-Iroquois War," 314; Francis Jennings, *The Ambiguous Iroquois Empire* (New York: W. W. Norton, 1984), 20–24, 205–208; Smith, "Life of George Copway," 23; and Zolla, *The Writer and the Shaman*, 238. The "Ojibwa Thesis" is corroborated by two other nineteenth-century native historians. See Assikinack, "Social Customs of the Odahwah Indians"; and Peter Dooyentate Clarke, *Origin and Traditional History of the Wyandotts, and Sketches of Other Indian Tribes of North America* (Toronto: Hunter, Rose, 1870).

151. See William W. Warren, "Traditions of Descent," in William McClements, ed., *Native American Folklore in the Nineteenth Century* (Athens, OH: Shallow Press/University of Ohio Press, 1986), 253–263.

152. Copway, *Traditional History*, vii–viii; Jones, *History*, 28.

153. Copway, *Traditional History*, x–xi, 28. Both Jones and Warren also acknowledge their debts to oral traditions. See Jones, *History*, 31; and Warren, *History of the Ojibway Nation*, 23–27.

154. Copway, *Traditional History*, 123–139. Also in Chapman, *Literature of the American Indians*, 43–52. Copway and Jones were preceded in their analysis of the Ojibwa language by another native scholar: John Summerfield, *Sketch of Grammar of the Chippeway Language, to Which is Added a Vocabulary of Some of the Most Common Works, by John Summerfield, alias Sahgahgewagahbaweh* (Cazenovia, NY: J. F. Fairchild and Son, 1834).

155. Copway, *Recollections*, 13–14; and idem, *Traditional History*, 33–48, 81–88. See Harvey A. Feit, "The Construction of Algonquian Hunting Territories: Private Property as Moral Lesson, Policy Advocacy, and Ethnographic Error," in George W. Stocking, Jr., ed., *Colonial Situations: Essays on the Contextualization of Ethnographic Knowledge* (Madison: University of Wisconsin Press, 1991), 109–134.

156. Copway, *Traditional History*, viii; Warren, *History of the Ojibway Nation*, 24. Copway's reference to Macaulay, whose immensely successful *History of England* first appeared in two volumes in 1849, is another indication of his own preference for popular historiography. D. Peter MacLeod feels that Copway's, Jones's, and Warren's histories are quite similar as they are all based on inquiries among elders and have a specifically native point of view. MacLeod, "The Anishinabeg Point of view," 204–210.

157. N. Scott Momaday, *The Way to Rainy Mountain* (Albuquerque: University of New Mexico Press, 1969); originally appeared as *The Journey of Tai-me* (Santa Barbara, CA: Privately printed, 1967). See Mick McAllister, "The Topology of Remembrance in *The Way to Rainy Mountain*," *Denver Quarterly* 12, no. 4 (1977–78): 19–31.

158. Most of his information on and descriptions of European cities, amounting to ca. fifty pages of his text, was quoted directly from the widely used English travel guides put out by the publishers Adam Black and Charles Black. These and the poetic citations may have been selected with the help of his wife, who accompanied

him on part of the journey. See Copway, *Running Sketches*, 66–80, 86–88, 162–164, 166–168, 172–191.

159. See Bruce Greenfield, *Narrating Discovery: The Romantic Explorer in American Literature* (New York: Columbia University Press, 1992); and Robert E. Spiller, *The American in England during the First Half Century of Independence* (1926; rpt., Chicago: Porcupine Press, 1976).

160. See the fictive accounts of the Iroquois sachem, "King Sa Ga Tean Qua Rash Tow" written by Addison in the *Spectator* 1, no. 50 (April 27, 1711), and no. 56 (May 4, 1711). Reprinted in Donald F. Bond, *The Spectator* (Oxford: Clarendon Press, 1965), 211–221, 236–240. See also Benjamin Bissel, *The American Indian in English Literature of the Eighteenth Century* (1925; rpt., Hamden, CT: Shoestring Press, 1968); and, especially, Anthony Pagden, "The Savage Critic: Some European Images of the Primitive," *Yearbook of English Studies* 13 (1983): 32–45.

161. Maungwudaus, *Remarks concerning the Ojibway Indians, by One of Themselves Called Maungwudaus, Who Has Been Travelling in England, France, Belgium, Ireland, and Scotland* (Leeds: C. A. Wilson, 1847); idem, *An Account of the Chippewa Indians, Who Have Been Travelling in the United States, England, Ireland, Scotland, France, and Belgium; with Very Interesting Incidents in Relation to the General Characteristics of the English, Irish, Scotch, French, and Americans, with Regard to Their Hospitality, Peculiarities, etc.* (Boston: By the author, 1848); idem, *An Account of the North American Indians, Written for Maungwudaus, a Chief of the Ojibway Indians Who Has Been Travelling in England, France, Belgium, Ireland, and Scotland* (Leicester: T. Cook, 1848). The Boston edition is reprinted in Peyer, *The Elders Wrote*, 66–74. In the context of nineteenth-century Indian travel literature mention should also be made of Jones's notes on his three voyages to England in his *Life and Journals*, 294–346, 392–408, 410–411.

162. See, for instance, Jeremiah Asher, *An Autobiography, with Details of a Visit to England . . .* (Philadelphia: By the Author, 1862); William Wells Brown, *Three Years in Europe; or, Places I Have Seen and People I Have Met* (London: C. Gilpin, 1852), reprinted in Jefferson, *Travels of William Wells Brown*, 71–235; and David F. Dorr, *A Colored Man Round the World. By a Quadroon* (Cleveland: By the author, 1858).

163. Catlin wrote that Henry "spoke and wrote the English language very correctly." Catlin, *Notes of Eight Years' Travels in Europe*, 299. See also the letter by Maungwudaus to Peter Jones, October 19, 1845 in Jones, *History*, 219 (erroneously dated 1854). Reproduced in Foreman, *Indians Abroad*, 194–195; and Smith, *Sacred Feathers*, 201–202.

164. Maungwudaus, *Account of the Chippewa Indians*, 4, 8–9 (I am using the 1848 Boston ed.).

165. Ibid., 3, 6–8.

166. Catlin, *Notes of Eight Years' Travels in Europe*, 290, 306–307, 309 (italics in the original).

167. Copway, *Running Sketches*, 11–12.

168. Ibid., 199–200.

169. Ibid., 41, 165–166, 256. Compare with Maungwudaus, *Account of the Chippewa Indians*, 3, 5–6, 11.

CHAPTER SEVEN

1. Primary sources on John Rollin Ridge's life include an autobiographical sketch in the preface to his posthumous *Poems. By John R. Ridge* (San Francisco: Henry Payot, 1869), 4–9; and his correspondence in the Ridge and Boudinot Family Papers, 1835–90, in Stand Watie Miscellaneous Files, Cherokee Nation Papers, 1801–1982, Western History Collections, University of Oklahoma Library. Some of these letters have been included in Edward E. Dale and Gaston L. Litton, eds., *Cherokee Cavaliers: Forty Years of Cherokee History as Told in the Correspondence of the Ridge-Watie-Boudinot Family* (Norman: University of Oklahoma Press, 1939), 35–39, 64–68, 71–72, 81–87. See also Edward E. Dale, "John Rollin Ridge," *Chronicles of Oklahoma* 4, no. 4 (1926): 312–321. A number of his writings on American Indians are available in David Farmer and Rennard Strickland, eds., *A Trumpet of Our Own: Yellow Bird's Essays on the North American Indian* (San Francisco: Book Club of California, 1981). The main secondary source is James W. Parins, *John Rollin Ridge: His Life & Works* (Lincoln: University of Nebraska Press, 1991). A shorter biography is in Angie Debo, "John Rollin Ridge," *Southwest Review* 17, no. 1 (1931): 59–71. Ridge's journalistic career in California is covered briefly in Carolyn T. Foreman, "Edward W. Bushyhead and John Rollin Ridge, Cherokee Editors in California," *Chronicles of Oklahoma* 14, no. 3 (1936): 295–311; David E. Gordon, "Early California Journalism, John Rollin Ridge," *Overland Monthly* 44 (August 1904): 128–131; and M. A. Ranck, "John Rollin Ridge in California," *Chronicles of Oklahoma* 10, no. 4 (December 1932): 560–569.

2. John Rollin Ridge, "The Cherokees: Their History — Present Condition and Future Prospects," in Farmer and Strickland, *A Trumpet of Our Own*, 49–53 (quote on p. 52). The original article appeared in the Clarksville (Texas) *Northern Standard*, January 20, 1849.

3. John Rollin Ridge, *The Life and Adventures of Joaquín Murieta, the Celebrated California Bandit, by Yellow Bird* (San Francisco: William B. Cooke, Booksellers and Stationers, 1854; rpt., Norman: University of Oklahoma Press, 1955). The first pirated version appeared in the *California Police Gazette* 1, nos. 34–43 (September 3–November 5, 1859). The most successful edition, which borrowed freely from both versions and also served as a basis for the Hollywood script, was Walter Noble Burns, *The Robin Hood of El Dorado* (New York: Coward-McCann, 1932). Its publication history is discussed in the introduction to the new edition by Joseph H. Jackson (pp. xi–l). See also Franklin Walker, *San Francisco's Literary Frontier* (New York: Alfred A. Knopf, 1934), 45–54; and idem, "Ridge's Life of Joaquín Murieta, the First and Revised Edition Compared," *California Historical Society Quarterly* 16, no. 3 (September 1937): 257–280. For interpretations of the novel, see John Lowe, "Space and Freedom in the Golden Republic: Yellow Bird's *The Life and Adventures of Joaquin Murieta, the Celebrated California Bandit,*" *Studies in American Indian Literature* 4, nos. 2–3 (Summer/Fall 1992): 106–122; and Louis Owens, *Other Destinies: Understanding the American Indian Novel* (Norman/London: University of Oklahoma Press, 1992), 32–40.

4. Rodolfo ("Corky") Gonzales, *I Am Joaquín* (New York: Bantam Books, 1972), first published in the Denver *El Gallo* 1 (1967). A version of the "Corrido de

Joaquín Murieta," is found in Antonia Castañeda Shular, Tomás Ybarra-Frausto, and Joseph Summer, eds., *Literatura Chicana: Texto y contexto/Chicano Literature: Text and context* (Englewood Cliffs, NJ: Prentice-Hall, 1972), 66. The story was serialized by an anonymous author under the title "Las aventuras de Joaquín Murieta," in the Santa Barbara *La Gaceta*, June 4–July 23, 1881. Brígido Caro, a Mexican American playwright, wrote a popular play, *Joaquín Murieta*, that was performed by various Hispanic theater groups in 1927. See Nicolás Kanellos, *A History of Hispanic Theatre in the United States: Origins to 1940* (Austin: University of Texas Press, 1990), 45–46.

5. Pablo Neruda, *Fulgor y Muerte de Joaquín Murieta: Bandido chileno injusticiado en California el 23 de julio de 1853* (Santiago: Zig Zag, 1966), reprinted as *Splendor and Death of Joaquin Murieta*, trans. Ben Belitt (New York: Farrar, Straus & Giroux, 1972); Ireneo Paz, *Vida y aventuras del más celébre bandido sonorense Joaquín Murieta. Sus grandes proezas en California*, 4th ed. (Mexico City: Tipografía y encuadernación de I. Paz, 1908), reprinted as *Life and Adventures of the Celebrated Bandit Joaquin Murieta*, trans. Frances P. Belle (Chicago: Regan, 1925). The *California Police Gazette* version was reprinted in Spain, translated into French, retranslated into Spanish by the Chilean diplomat Roberto Hyenne as *El bandido Chileno*, in turn plagiarized by a certain "Professor Acigar" in Spain as *El Caballero Chileno*, and then finally reimported to Mexico.

6. *The Journals and Miscellaneous Notebooks of Ralph Waldo Emerson*, vol. 4, ed. Alfred R. Ferguson (Cambridge: Belknap Press of Harvard University Press, 1964), 27. Indian preachers certainly did not disappear entirely from Indian intellectual circles. Sherman Coolidge (Arapaho), Henry Roe Cloud (Winnebago), Philip Gordon (Ojibwa), and Joseph K. Griffis (Osage), for instance, were all active members of the Society of American Indians. Gordon edited two newspapers: the Lawrence, Kansas, *War Whoop* in 1916; and the Reserve, Wisconsin, *A-ni-shi-na-bwe E-na-mi-ad* in 1918. Griffis is the author of an autobiography: *Tahan: Out of Savagery into Civilization* (New York: Doran, 1915).

7. See William H. Armstrong, *Warrior in Two Camps: Ely S. Parker, Union General and Seneca Chief* (Syracuse, NY: Syracuse University Press, 1978); and Arthur C. Parker, *The Life of General Ely S. Parker: Last Grand Sachem of the Iroquois and General Grant's Military Secretary* (Buffalo: Buffalo Historical Society, 1919; rpt., New York: AMS Press, 1985). See also Elizabeth Tooker, "Ely S. Parker," in Margot Liberty, ed., *American Indian Intellectuals*, Proceedings of the American Ethnological Society, 1976 (St. Paul: West Publishing, 1978), 15–30. Some of his writings, including a brief autobiographical sketch, have been collected in "Writings of General Parker," *Proceedings of the Buffalo Historical Society* 8 (1905): 520–536.

8. Parker, "Writings," 529, 532.

9. "Letter from the Secretary of War, addressed to Mr. Schenck, chairman of the Committee on Military Affairs, transmitting a report by Colonel Parker on Indian affairs," U.S. House of Representatives, 39th Cong., 2nd sess., Misc. Doc. no. 37 (Washington, DC: Government Printing Office, 1867).

10. See John P. Adams, *Elias Cornelius Boudinot* (Chicago: Rand, McNally, 1890); Thomas B. Colbert, "Visionary or Rogue: The Life and Legacy of Elias

Cornelius Boudinot," *Chronicles of Oklahoma* 65, no. 3 (Fall 1987): 268–281; idem, "Elias Cornelius Boudinot, 'The Indian Orator and Lecturer,'" *American Indian Quarterly* 13, no. 3 (Summer 1989): 248–259; and Muriel H. Wright, "Notes on Colonel Elias C. Boudinot," *Chronicles of Oklahoma* 41 (Winter 1963–64): 382–407. Two dissertations have been written: Lois Elizabeth Forde, "Elias Cornelius Boudinot" (Ph.D. diss., Columbia University, 1951); and Thomas B. Colbert, "Prophet of Progress: The Life and Times of Elias Cornelius Boudinot" (Ph.D. diss., Oklahoma State University, 1982).

11. See Robert K. Heimann, "The Cherokee Tobacco Case," *Chronicles of Oklahoma* 41 (Fall 1963): 299–322.

12. Elias C. Boudinot, *Remarks of Elias C. Boudinot, of the Cherokee Nation, in Behalf of the Bill to Organize the Territory of Oklahoma, Before the House Committee on Territories, May 13, 1874* (Washington, DC: McGill & Witherow, 1874), 7. He also published numerous articles, speeches, pamphlets, and memorials to Congress. See Daniel F. Littlefield, Jr., and James W. Parins, *A Biobibliography of Native American Writers, 1772–1924* (Metuchen, NJ: Scarecrow Press, 1981), 19–21; and idem, *A Biobibliography of Native American Writers, 1772–1924: A Supplement* (Metuchen, NJ: Scarecrow Press, 1985), 17–18.

13. William Potter Ross (1820–91), nephew of John Ross, graduated with honors from Princeton in 1842 and became editor of the *Cherokee Advocate* in 1844. He served as principal chief from 1873 to 1875 and was opposed to congressional plans for the establishment of Oklahoma Territory. He is the author of numerous articles, speeches, and memorials to Congress. See *The Life and Times of Hon. William P. Ross of the Cherokee Nation*, ed. Mrs. William P. Ross (Fort Smith: AR: Weldon & Williams, 1893). For a list of his publications, see Littlefield and Parins, *Biobibliography of Native American Writers*, 156–157.

14. Much has been written about this dramatic period in Indian–white relations. See especially Henry E. Fritz, *The Movement for Indian Assimilation, 1860–1890* (Philadelphia: University of Pennsylvania Press, 1963; rpt., Westport, CT: Greenwood Press, 1981); Frederick E. Hoxie, *A Final Promise: The Campaign to Assimilate the Indians, 1880–1920* (Lincoln: University of Nebraska Press, 1984); and Francis P. Prucha, *American Indian Policy in Crisis: Christian Reformers and the Indian, 1865–1900* (Norman: University of Oklahoma Press, 1976). An earlier but still useful study is Loring B. Priest, *Uncle Sam's Stepchildren: The Reformation of the United States Indian Policy, 1865–1887* (New Brunswick, NJ: Rutgers University Press, 1942; rpt., New York: Octagon Books, 1969). For an excellent survey, see William T. Hagan, "United States Indian Policies, 1860–1900," in Wilcomb E. Washburn, ed., *Handbook of North American Indians: History of Indian-White Relations* (Washington, DC: Smithsonian Institution Press, 1988), 4:51–65.

15. Parker, "Writings," 535.

16. On missionaries and the Peace Policy, see Robert H. Keller, Jr., *American Protestantism and United States Indian Policy, 1869–1882* (Lincoln: University of Nebraska Press, 1983); Robert W. Mardock, *The Reformers and the American Indian* (Columbia: University of Missouri Press, 1971); and Peter J. Rahill, *The Catholic Indian Missions and Grant's Peace Policy, 1870–1884* (Washington, DC: Catholic University of America Press, 1953).

17. See Francis P. Prucha, *The Churches and the Indian Schools, 1888–1912* (Lincoln: University of Nebraska Press, 1979).

18. See Evelyn C. Adams, *American Indian Education: Government Schools and Economic Progress* (1946; rpt., New York: Arno Press, 1971), 47–65; Alice C. Fletcher, *Indian Education and Civilization*, Bureau of Education Special Report, 1888 (Millwood, NY: Kraus Reprint, 1973), 161–195; and Estelle Fuchs and Robert Havighurst, *To Live on This Earth: American Indian Education* (Garden City, NY: Doubleday, 1972), 222–245.

19. See Alice Littlefield, "Learning to Labor: Native American Education in the United States, 1880–1930," in John H. Moore, ed., *The Political Economy of North American Indians* (Norman: University of Oklahoma Press, 1993), 43–59. On Indian enrollment at Hampton, see also Wilbert H. Ahern, "The Returned Indians: Hampton Institute and Its Indian Alumni, 1879–1893," *Journal of Ethnic Studies* 10, no. 4 (Winter 1983): 101–124; and Abraham Makofsky, "Experience of Native Americans at a Black College: Indian Students at Hampton Institute, 1878–1923," *Journal of Ethnic Studies* 17, no. 3 (Fall 1989): 31–46.

20. See William N. Hailmann, *Education of the Indian*, in Nicholas M. Butler, ed., *Monographs on Education in the United States*, no. 19 (Albany, NY: J. B. Lyon, 1900), 8, 29; and Margaret C. Szasz and Carmelita S. Ryan, "American Indian Education," in Washburn, *Handbook of North American Indians*, 4: 293.

21. See Gretchen M. Bataille, ed., *Native American Women: A Biographical Dictionary* (New York: Garland Publishing, 1993).

22. The major source on the SAI is Hazel W. Hertzberg, *The Search for an Indian Identity: Modern Pan-Indian Movements* (Syracuse: Syracuse University Press, 1971), 31–209 (quote on p. 36). See also idem, "Indian Rights Movement, 1887–1973," in Washburn, *Handbook of North American Indians*, 4:305–323; and Wilcomb E. Washburn, "The Society of American Indians," *Indian Historian* 3, no. 1 (Winter 1970): 21–23. The minutes of the first conference were published under the title *Report of the Executive Council on the Proceedings of the First Annual Conference of the Society of American Indians* (Washington, DC: Society of American Indians, 1912). The collected writings of the SAI are available on microfilm: John W. Larner, Jr., ed., *The Papers of the Society of American Indians, 1906–1946* (Wilmington, DE: Scholarly Resources, 1986) (10 rolls).

23. Sherman Coolidge, "The Function of the Society of American Indians," *Quarterly Journal* 2, no. 1 (January/March 1914): 186–190.

24. Two major Indian authors wrote specifically for the Boy Scouts: Charles Alexander Eastman, *Indian Scout Talks: A Guide for Boy Scouts and Camp Fire Girls* (Boston: Little, Brown, 1914), reprinted as *Indian Scout Craft and Lore* (New York: Dover, 1974); and Arthur C. Parker, *The Indian How Book* (New York: George H. Doran, 1927; rpt., New York: Dover, 1975).

25. See James Murphy and Sharon Murphy, *Let My People Know: American Indian Journalism* (Norman: University of Oklahoma Press, 1981), 39–69.

26. See Richard C. Adams, *A Brief History of the Delaware Indians*, U.S. Congress, Senate, 59th Cong., 1st sess., Senate Doc. no. 501, serial no. 4916 (Washington, DC: Government Printing Office, 1906); Andrew J. Blackbird, *History of the Ottawa and Chippewa Indians of Michigan* (Ypsilanti, MI: Ypsilanti Job Publishing

House, 1887), revised as *Complete Both Early and Late History of the Ottawa and Chippewa Indians, of Michigan, a Grammar of Their Language, Personal and Family History of Author* (Harbor Springs, MI: Babcock & Darling, 1897); Peter Dooyentate Clarke, *Origin and Traditional History of the Wyandotts, and Sketches of Other Indian Tribes of North America* (Toronto: Hunter, Rose, 1870); Elias Johnson, *Legends, Traditions, and Laws of the Iroquois, or Six Nations, and a History of the Tuscarora Indians* (Lockport, NY: Union Printing and Publishing, 1881; rpt., New York: AMS Press, 1978); and Joseph Nicolar, *The Life and Traditions of the Red Man* (Bangor, ME: C. H. Glass, 1893).

27. Sarah Winnemucca, *Life among the Paiutes: Their Wrongs and Claims* (Boston: Cuppler, Upham, 1883; rpt., Reno: University of Nevada Press, 1994). A short version was published earlier as "The Pah-Utes," *The Californian* 6 (1882): 252–256. Several biographies are available. See Gae Whitney Canfield, *Sarah Winnemucca of the Northern Paiutes* (Norman: University of Oklahoma Press, 1983); and Katherine Gehm, *Sarah Winnemucca* (Phoenix, AZ: O'Sullivan Woodside, 1975). See also George F. Brimlow, "The Life of Sarah Winnemucca: The Formative Years," *Oregon Historical Quarterly* 53, no. 2 (1952): 103–134; and Catherine S. Fowler, "Sarah Winnemucca," in Liberty, *American Indian Intellectuals*, 33–42. For interpretations of her autobiography, see H. David Brumble III, *American Indian Autobiography* (Berkeley: University of California Press, 1988), 60–71; Brigitte Georgi-Findlay, "The Frontiers of Native American Women's Writing: Sarah Winnemucca's *Life among the Paiutes*," in Arnold Krupat, ed., *New Voices in Native American Literary Criticism* (Washington/London: Smithsonian Institution Press, 1993), 222–252; and A. La Vonne Brown Ruoff, "Three Nineteenth-Century American Indian Autobiographers: William Apes, George Copway, and Sarah Winnemucca," in A. La Vonne Brown Ruoff and Jerry Ward, eds., *Redefining American Literary History* (New York: MLA, 1990), 251–269.

28. S. Alice Callahan, *Wynema, A Child of the Forest* (Chicago: H. E. Smith, 1891; rpt., Lincoln: University of Nebraska Press, 1990). See Annette Van Dyke, "An Introduction to *Wynema, A Child of the Forest*, by Sophia Alice Callahan," *Studies in American Indian Literature* 4, nos. 2–3 (Summer/Fall 1992): 123–128; and Carolyn T. Foreman, "S. Alice Callahan: Author of *Wynema, A Child of the Forest*," *Chronicles of Oklahoma* 33, no. 3 (Autumn 1955): 306–315.

29. Simon Pokagon, *O-gî-mäw-kwĕ Mit-i-gwä-kî (Queen of the Woods). Also Brief Sketch of the Algaic Language* (Hartford, MI: C. H. Engle, 1899; rpt., Berrien Springs, MI: Hardscrabble, 1972). See Cecilia B. Buechner, "The Pokagons," *Indiana Historical Society Publications* 10, no. 5 (1933): 279–340; rpt., Berrien Springs, MI: Hardscrabble, 1976; James Clifton, *The Pokagons, 1683–1983: Catholic Potawatomi of the St. Joseph River Valley* (Washington, DC: Potawatomi Nation and University Press of America, 1984); John Cumming, "Pokagon's Birch Bark Books," *American Book Collector* 18, no. 8 (1968): 14–17; and David H. Dickason, "Chief Simon Pokagon: 'The Indian Longfellow,' " *Indiana Magazine of History* 57, no. 2 (1961): 127–140.

30. His poems were published posthumously by his wife as *The Poems of Alexander Lawrence Posey* (Topeka: Crane, 1910). The "Fus Fixico Letters" have been made available in Daniel F. Littlefield, Jr., and Carol A. Petty Hunter, eds., *The Fus*

Fixico Letters: Alexander Posey (Lincoln: University of Nebraska Press, 1994). See Daniel F. Littlefield, Jr., *Alex Posey: Creek Poet, Journalist, and Humorist* (Lincoln: University of Nebraska Press, 1992). As far as regionalist Indian literature is concerned, Indian Territory and later the state of Oklahoma proved to be an extraordinarily fertile ground for what is probably the closest thing to an American "métis" literature with highly successful mixed-blood authors who wrote primarily on non-Indian themes like Will Rogers (Cherokee, 1879–1935), the poet and playwright Rolla Lynn Riggs (Cherokee, 1899–1954), and mystery novel author Todd Downing (Choctaw, 1902–74).

31. See Hartley B. Alexander, "Francis La Flesche," *American Anthropologist*, n.s. 35 (1933): 328–331; Marie L. B. Baldwin, "John N. B. Hewitt, Ethnologist," *Quarterly Journal* 2, no. 2 (April/June 1914): 146–151; William Fenton, *Parker on the Iroquois* (Syracuse: Syracuse University Press, 1968); Margot Liberty, "Native American 'Informants': The Contribution of Francis La Flesche," in John V. Murra, ed., *American Anthropology: The Early Years*, Proceedings of the American Ethnological Society, 1974 (St. Paul: West Publishing, 1976), 99–100; H. N. Rideaut, *William Jones* (New York: Frederick A. Stockes, 1912); and Barbara Stoner, "Why Was William Jones Killed?" *Field Museum of Natural History Bulletin* 42, no. 8 (September 1971): 10–13.

32. Charles A. Eastman, *Old Indian Days* (New York: McClure, Phillips, 1907; rpt., New York: Dover, 1971); idem, *The Soul of the Indian* (Boston: Houghton Mifflin, 1911; rpt., Lincoln: University of Nebraska Press, 1980); idem, *The Indian To-day: The Past and Future of the First American* (Garden City, NY: Doubleday, Page, 1915; rpt., New York: AMS Press, 1975); idem, *From the Deep Woods to Civilization* (Boston: Little, Brown, 1916; rpt., Lincoln: University of Nebraska Press, 1977). See Marion W. Copeland, *Charles Alexander Eastman (Ohiyesa)*, Boise State University Western Writers Series (Boise: Boise State University, 1978); and Raymond Wilson, *Ohiyesa: Charles Eastman, Santee Sioux* (Urbana: University of Illinois Press, 1983).

33. Gertrude Bonnin, *Old Indian Legends* (Boston: Ginn, 1901; rpt., Lincoln: University of Nebraska Press, 1985); idem, *American Indian Stories* (Washington, DC: Hayworth Press, 1921; rpt., Lincoln: University of Nebraska Press, 1985). See also Gertrude Bonnin, Charles F. Fabens, and Mathew K. Sniffen, *Oklahoma's Poor Rich Indians: An Orgy of Graft and Exploitation of the Five Civilized Tribes — Legalized Robbery* (Philadelphia: Office of the Indian Rights Association, 1924). No major biography has been published on this extremely interesting Indian writer. See Dexter Fisher, "The Transformation of Tradition: A Study of Zitkala-Sa and Mourning Dove, Two Transitional American Indian Writers" (Ph.D. diss., City University of New York, 1979); and Deborah Sue Welch, "Zitkala-Sa: An American Indian Leader, 1876–1938" (Ph.D. diss., University of Wyoming, 1985). For interpretations of her work, see Dexter Fisher, "The Transformation of Tradition: A Study of Zitkala Sa and Mourning Dove, Two Transitional American Indian Writers," in Andrew Wiget, ed., *Critical Essays on Native American Literature* (Boston: G. K. Hall, 1985), 202–211; David L. Johnson and Raymond Wilson, "Gertrude Bonnin, 1876–1938: 'Americanize the First American,'" *American Indian Quarterly* 12, no. 1 (Winter 1988): 27–40; and Dorothea M. Susag, "Zitkala-Sa (Ger-

trude Bonnin), a Power(full) Literary Voice," *Studies in American Indian Literature* 5, no. 4 (Winter 1993): 3–24. It is interesting to compare Bonnin's negative accounts of her education with the more positive depictions in Eastman's autobiography and Francis La Flesche, *The Middle Five: Indian Schoolboys of the Omaha Tribe* (1900; rpt., Lincoln/London: University of Nebraska Press, 1978).

34. John M. Oskison, *Wild Harvest* (New York: D. Appleton, 1925); idem, *Black Jack Davy* (New York: D. Appleton, 1926); idem, *A Texas Titan: The Story of Sam Houston* (Garden City, NY: Doubleday, Doran, 1929); idem, *Brothers Three* (New York: Macmillan, 1935); idem, *Tecumseh and His Times* (New York: G. P. Putnam's Sons, 1938). See Arney L. Strickland, "John Milton Oskison: A Writer of the Transitional Period of the Oklahoma Indian Territory," *Southwestern American Literature* 2, no. 3 (Winter 1972): 125–134; and Gretchen Ronnow, "John Milton Oskison, Cherokee Journalist: A Singer of the Semiotics of Power," *Native Press Research Journal* 4 (Spring 1987): 1–14.

35. Emily P. Johnson, *The White Wampum* (London: John Lane, 1895), and idem, *Canadian Born* (Toronto: George N. Morang, 1903), published collectively as *Flint and Feather* (Toronto: Mousson, 1912; rpt., Markham, Ont.: PaperJacks, 1973); idem, *Legends of Vancouver* (Vancouver: Sunset Publishing, 1911; rpt., Toronto: McClelland, 1961); idem, *The Shagganappi* (Toronto: William Briggs, 1913); idem, *The Moccasin Maker* (Toronto: William Briggs, 1913; rpt., Tucson: University of Arizona Press, 1987). See Betty Keller, *Pauline: A Biography of Pauline Johnson* (Douglas & McIntyre, 1981); and Marcus Van Steen, *Pauline Johnson: Her Life and Work* (Toronto: Mousson, 1965).

36. On Montezuma, see Peter Iverson, *Carlos Montezuma and the Changing World of American Indians* (Albuquerque: University of New Mexico Press, 1982). On Parker, see Hazel W. Hertzberg, "Arthur C. Parker, Seneca, 1881–1955," in Liberty, *American Indian Intellectuals*, 129–138; and idem, "Nationality, Anthropology, and Pan-Indianism in the Life of Arthur C. Parker," *Proceedings of the American Philosophical Society* 123, no. 1 (1979): 47–72.

37. See Bernd C. Peyer, ed., *The Singing Spirit: Early Short Stories by North American Indians* (Tucson: University of Arizona Press, 1989), especially Johnson's "Red Girl's Reasoning," 18–34, and Bonnin's "Soft-Hearted Sioux," 78–85.

38. John Collier (1884–1968) was employed in the immigrant wards of New York City from 1907 to 1919 and then moved to California to do social work among migrant workers. After losing his job in 1920, he went to New Mexico where he became fascinated by Pueblo community life and its apparent contrast to the evils of modern American individualism. See Lawrence C. Kelly, *The Assault on Assimilation: John Collier and the Origins of Indian Policy Reform* (Albuquerque: University of New Mexico Press, 1983); Kenneth R. Philip, *John Collier's Crusade for Indian Reform, 1920–1954* (Tucson: University of Arizona Press, 1977); and Graham Taylor, *The New Deal and Native American Tribalism* (Lincoln: University of Nebraska Press, 1980).

39. See Donald L. Fixico, *Termination and Relocation: Federal Indian Policy, 1945–1960* (Albuquerque: University of New Mexico Press, 1986).

40. See Iverson, *Carlos Montezuma*, 173.

41. Luther Standing Bear, *Land of the Spotted Eagle* (Lincoln: University of

Nebraska Press, 1978), 258–259 (originally Boston: Houghton Mifflin, 1934). See also idem, *My People the Sioux* (Boston: Houghton Mifflin, 1928; rpt., Lincoln: University of Nebraska Press, 1975), in which he makes a critical appraisal of his experiences at Carlisle; and idem, *My Indian Boyhood* (Boston: Houghton Mifflin, 1931), written for children along with *Stories of the Sioux* (Boston: Houghton Mifflin, 1934). On his life and works, see Richard N. Ellis, "Luther Standing Bear," in L. G. Moses and Raymond Wilson, eds., *Indian Lives: Essays on Nineteenth- and Twentieth-Century Native American Leaders* (Albuquerque: University of New Mexico Press, 1985), 139–158; and Frederick Hale, "Acceptance and Rejection of Assimilation in the Works of Luther Standing Bear," *Studies in American Indian Literature* 5, no. 4 (Winter 1993): 24–41.

42. Mourning Dove [Christine Quintasaket], *Cogewea, the Half-Blood: A Depiction of the Great Montana Cattle Range* (Boston: Four Seas, 1927; rpt., Lincoln: University of Nebraska Press, 1981); John Joseph Mathews, *Sundown* (New York: Longmans, Green, 1934; rpt., Norman: University of Nebraska Press, 1988); D'Arcy McNickle, *The Surrounded* (New York: Dodd, Mead, 1936; rpt., Albuquerque: University of New Mexico Press, 1978). These novels are discussed in Charles R. Larson, *American Indian Fiction* (Albuquerque: University of New Mexico Press, 1978); Priscilla Oakes, "The First Generation of Native American Novelists," *MELUS* 5, no. 1 (1978): 57–65; and Owens, *Other Destinies*. See also John Lloyd Purdy, *Word Ways: The Novels of D'Arcy McNickle* (Tucson: University of Arizona Press, 1990). For an excellent biography of McNickle, see Dorothy R. Parker, *Singing an Indian Song: A Biography of D'Arcy McNickle* (Lincoln: University of Nebraska Press, 1992). On Mathews, see Terry P. Wilson, "Osage Oxonian: The Heritage of John Joseph Mathews," *Chronicles of Oklahoma* 59, no. 3 (1981): 254–293. On Mourning Dove, see Susan K. Bernardin, "Mixed Messages: Authority and Authorship in Mourning Dove's *Cogewea, The Half-Blood: A Depiction of the Great Montana Cattle Range*," *American Literature* 67, no. 3 (September 1995): 487–509; and Jay Miller, ed., *Mourning Dove: A Salishan Autobiography* (Lincoln: University of Nebraska Press, 1990).

43. Samuel E. Morison, *Harvard College in the Seventeenth Century* (Cambridge: Harvard University Press, 1936), 359.

44. Vine Deloria, Jr., *God Is Red* (New York: Delta, 1973); Eastman, *The Soul of the Indian.*

45. See Ward Churchill, *Struggle for the Land: Indigenous Resistance to Genocide, Ecocide, and Expropriation of Contemporary North America* (Monroe, ME: Common Courage Press, 1993), 403–451; and Vine Deloria, Jr., *Behind the Trail of Broken Treaties: An Indian Declaration of Independence* (New York: Delta, 1974), 161–186.

Index

Abenakis, 22, 24

abolitionists, 125–127, 148, 152–153, 156, 163–164, 189, 229, 330 n.127; and Boudinot, 189; connections with Indian removal, 125–127; influence on Apess, 148, 152–153, 163–164; literature by, 152–153, 189; and New Light preachers, 330 n.127; protest anti-miscegenation laws in Massachusetts, 156

aborigines, 3

Aborigines Protection Society (1836), 229, 254; Copway on, 254

acculturation (as term), 4

Acoma Pueblo, 9

Adair, James, *History of the American Indian* (1775), 123

Adams, Henry, 306 n.19

Adams, John, 119

Adams, John Quincy, 119, 185, 190, 211; favored by Cherokees, 185; and removal, 119, 190; on Treaty of New Echota, 211

Adams, Richard Calamit (Delaware), 287

African Americans, 59, 92, 93, 95, 100, 119, 124, 125–127, 130–131, 138, 141, 143–144, 148–153, 156, 158, 164, 188–189, 222, 259, 274, 283–284, 330 n.128, 340–341 n.46, 342 n.72, 346 n.123; African-Indian writers, 130–131, 340–341 n.46; antebellum authors, 148–153, 274, 342 n.72, 346 n.123; anti-miscegenation laws, 156; Apess on, 158; attend Occom's sermon, 92, 95; "Black Theology," 164; and Boudinot, 188–189, 222; colonization in Africa, 119, 126, 189; connections with Occom, 100, 330 n.128; Copway on, 259; execution of Bristol (1764), 93; and Great Awakening,

59; influence on Apess, 148–153, 164; and Methodists, 138, 342 n.72; relations with Indians, 125–127, 130–131, 141, 143–144, 283–284, 330 n.128; and Second Great Awakening, 124, 138; slave revolts, 143–144. *See also* abolitionists; slavery

African Methodist Episcopal Church (1816), 138

African Methodist Episcopal Zion Church (1821), 138

Alfred, Gerald (Mohawk), 15

Algonquian, 13, 42, 44, 47, 71, 74, 106, 129, 164, 165, 248, 255–256, 272, 288; Copway on, 248, 255–256, 272; groups, 129, 165; language, 71, 74, 106, 248, 255–256; literacy, 13, 42, 44, 47; oral traditions in Pokagon's *Queen of the Woods,* 288; rumor that Occom is unable to speak it, 74; scholarship, 272. *See also* Central Algonquians; Coastal Algonquians

Allen, Richard, 342 n.72

Amadas, Philip, 22

American Bible Society (1816), 125

American Board of Commissioners for Foreign Missions (ABCFM, 1810), 124, 172, 176, 177, 178, 179, 184, 194–195, 203, 212, 222, 237, 242; Boudinot translates for, 222; Copway requests employment from, 242; Copway translates for, 237; establishes Brainerd mission, 172; opposes removal, 124; preference for Pickering's Cherokee orthography, 176; provides funds for Boudinot, 212; publishes Boudinot's and Brown's letters in *Missionary Herald,* 179; reverses anti-

American Board of Commissioners for Foreign Missions (*cont.*)
removal stance, 203; selects Boudinot, Brown, and Ridge for Foreign Mission School, 178; supports Cherokee press, 177, 184; and *Worcester v. State of Georgia,* 194–195, 203

American Colonization Society (1816), 126, 189; Boudinot runs articles on, 189; and removal, 126

American Ethnological Society (1842), 264; Copway associates with members of, 264

American Fur Company, 228

American Indian Association, 285. *See also* Society of American Indians

American Indian Defence Association (1923), 290

Amerian Indian English, 8–9, 274; in George Henry's *Account,* 274; as language accommodation, 8–9

American Indian Historical Society (1964), 14

American Indian literature, 19–20, 286–290; definition, 19–20; historical phases, 20, 286–290

American Party, 258–260, 379 n.118; and Copway, 258–260, 379 n.118

American Revolution, 57, 84–85, 105, 107–108, 110, 111, 125, 126, 128, 131, 141, 156–157, 160, 164, 167; and Apess's rhetoric, 156–157, 160, 164; and Cherokees, 167; Christian Indians promote neutrality, 84–85, 108; Indians fight on British side, 57; Joseph Johnson on, 107; and Mashpees, 141; militia massacres Moravian Mahicans, 111; Occom on, 84–85; and Pequots, 128; role of Joseph Johnson in, 107–108; and Stockbridge Indians, 110

American Sunday School Union (1824), 125

American Temperance Union (1826), 125

American Tract Society (1826), 125, 222

American Whig Review (New York), 247, 267

Amherst, Jeffrey, 70

Amoret (Abenaki), 22

Amos, Daniel (Mashpee), 146, 147

Amos, Joseph (Blind Joe, Mashpee), 141, 146, 295; leads Baptist revival at Mashpee, 141; legacy of, 295; organizes Free and United Church with Apess, 146

Andover Theological Seminary (MA), 180

Anishinabes, 224. *See also* Ojibwas

Anneke, Fritz, 378 n.112

Anti-Masonic Party, 193

Apes, Candace (mother of Apess), 130, 340 n.43

Apes, William (Pequot, father of Apess), 130, 340 n.43

Apess, William (Pequot), 117, 123, 128, 129–165, 216, 222, 232, 239, 263, 264, 293–294, 295, 328 n.79, 334–335 n. 1, 340 nn.40, 43, 341 nn.48, 59, 341–342 n.66, 342 nn.68, 69, 345 n.109, 346 nn. 123, 124, 126, 127; 347 n.133; affinity with antebellum African American literature, 148–152, 346 n.123; on amalgamation, 156, 158; arrested, 145; asks to be adopted by Mashpees, 142; beaten by grandmother, 131; on being Indian, 165; on being sold, 133; bibliographical references to, 334–335 n.1; birth of, 129, 340 n.40; bound out, 131–134, 341 n.48; career as preacher, 136–139; on "colored" Christ, 156, 164; conversion experience, 134; critical views on missionaries, 158, 165; critical views on Puritans, 157; death of, 147–148; on designation "Indian," 132; develops drinking habit, 134; *Eulogy on King Philip* (1836), 147, 152, 159–163; *Experiences of Five Christian Indians* (1833), 140, 152, 154–156, 346 n.127; family background, 129–130, 340 n.43; formulates "An Indian's Appeal" (1833), 146; *Increase of the Kingdom of Christ* (1831), 140, 145, 150, 153–154; *Indian Nullification* (1835), 142, 147, 148, 156–159, 347 n.133; "An Indian's Looking Glass for the White Man," 150, 154–156, 346 n.124; on intemperance, 131–132; marries Mary Wood, 137, 341–342 n.66; maturation as author, 152–153; ordained by Methodist Protestant Church, 137–139; paraphrases Jackson's removal speech, 162–163; preacher's license denied, 137–138, 342 n.68; relations with Methodists, 132–133, 134, 135–139, 346 n.126; returns to Connecticut, 135–136; runs away to

Canada, 134, 341 n.59; on slavery, 133, 156, 161–162; *Son of the Forest* (1829, 1831), 137, 138, 139–140, 149–152, 160, 222, 342 n.69, 345 n.109; on Ten Lost Tribes of Israel, 150, 153; wanders about in Canada, 134–135; and Woodland Revolt, 140–147, 164; writes two petitions for Mashpees, 143

Arch, John (Cherokee), 177, 353 n.40; attends Brainerd mission school, 177; biography, 353 n.40

Argall, Samuel, 28

Aristotle, 123

Arkansas Cherokees (Old Settlers), 174, 176, 190; sign removal treaty (1828), 190

Arkansian (Fayetteville), 281

Arminianism, 125

Articles of Confederation, 58

Ashurst, William, 50

Assikinack, Francis (Ottawa), 382–383 nn.149, 150

assimilation (as term), 5

Atkin Report and Plan (1755), 55

Attaculcullah (Little Carpenter, Cherokee), 177

Aubert, Thomas, 22

Aupaumut, Captain Hendrick (Mahican), 101, 110–116, 293, 294, 332 n.152, 332–333 n.156, 333 nn.158, 161, 333–334 n.162, 334 nn.166, 168; addresses Delawares, 112–113, 115, 334 n.168; assumes sachemship of Hudson River Mahicans, 111; attends John Sargeant's school, 111; bibliographical references to, 332 n.152; birth of, 111; death of, 116; "History of the Muh-he-con-nuk Indians" (1854), 114, 334 n.166; moves to Wisconsin, 115–116; "Narrative" (1827), 111–114, 333 n.158, 333–334 n.162; opposes Tecumseh and Tenskwatawa, 113, 333 n.161; participates in American Revolution, 111; serves as U.S. peace emissary, 111–114; writings in Mahican, 332–333 n.156

Axtell, James, 10, 12, 19

Ayllón, Lucas Vásquez de, 23

Aztecs, 21, 23

Bacon's Rebellion (1676), 32

Bagot Commission, 229

Balandier, Georges, 297 n.1

Bancroft, George, 263

Baptists, 124, 127, 131, 133, 141, 172, 280; and Apess, 131, 133; among Cherokees, 172; among Mashpees, 141; and Second Great Awakening, 124, 127; among Senecas, 280

Barber, Jonathan, 64

Barlowe, Arthur, 22

Barnstable Patriot (MA), 145–146

Baron de Campagne, correspondence with Boudinot and Brown, 179–180, 355 n.49

Batalla, Guillermo Bonfil, 15

battles, 111, 113, 116, 117, 134, 228; Fallen Timbers (1794), 111, 113; Horseshoe Bend (1814), 117; Lake Champlain (1814), 134; Thames (1813), 117, 228; Tippecanoe (1811), 116

Baxter, Richard, *Saints' Everlasting Rest* (1764), 104, 331 n.139

Bay of Quinte (Canada), 135, 232; described by Apess, 135

Benevolent Empire, 125

benevolent societies, 125

Bering Strait, 271

Berkhofer, Robert, Jr., 257

Bible, 10, 12–13, 109, 124, 233, 267; and conversion experience, 12–13; Copway on, 267; Joseph Johnson cites from, 109; Peter Jones on, 233; and legal ideology, 10; and Second Great Awakening, 124

Bigelow, John P., 374 n.76

Big Knives, 113, 115; mentioned by Aupaumut, 113

Bird, Robert Montgomery, *Nick of the Woods* (1836), 122

Blackbird, Andrew J. (Ottawa), 287

Blackburn, Gideon, 172

Black Hawk (Sauk), 101

Black Hawk War (1832), 124

Black Theology (as term), 164

Blodgett, Harold, 87, 88, 96

Board of Indian Commissioners (1869), 283

Bonnin, Gertrude Simmons (Zitkala-Sa, Yankton Sioux), 289–291, 391 n.33; *American Indian Stories* (1921), 289; *Old Indian Legends* (1901), 289

Boston (MA), 46, 60, 71, 75, 93, 140, 144, 156, 159, 160, 165, 180, 184, 201, 237, 244, 249, 254, 260, 263

Boston Board of Commissioners (New England Company), 65–66, 67–68, 69, 71, 72, 73, 74–75, 76, 104; appoints Joseph Johnson schoolmaster of Farmington, 104; fails to provide for Occom at Montauk, 67–68; opposed to Occom's journey to England, 74–75; provides stipend for Occom, 65–66; recommends Occom for ordination, 69; strained relations with Wheelock, 72, 75

Boston Courier, 145

Boston Daily Advocate, 145, 147

Boston Latin School, 50

Boston Recorder and Telegraph, 183

Boudinot, Elias, 123, 150, 178, 222, 345 n.109, 348 n.1; bequeaths name to Gallegina, 178; *Star in the West* (1816), 123, 345 n.109; writings included in Apess's *A Son of the Forest,* 150, 222, 345 n.109

Boudinot, Elias (Gallegina, Cherokee), 166, 169, 177–223, 263, 281, 293–294, 348–349 n.1, 355 nn.49, 50, 51, 52, 356 nn.61, 62, 65, 66, 357 n.75, 358 nn.87, 93, 359 n.105, 360 n.115, 361 n.127, 363 n.149, 365–366 n.177, 366 n.182, 184; *Address to the Whites* (1826), 216–218; advocates non-violence, 192, 358 n.87; advocates removal, 206–211, 218–222; at Andover Theological Seminary, 180, 355 n.51; on arrest of missionaries by Georgia Guard, 194, 358 n.93; assassination of, 213; attacks Ross, 220–221, 223, 365–366 n.177, 366 n.184; bibliographical references to, 348–349 n.1; birth of, 177; on *Cherokee Nation v. Georgia,* 194; against clan revenge, 191; and conflict with Georgia, 189–201; confrontation with Georgia Guard, 199, 359 n.105; correspondence with Stand Watie, 201, 209; on death of Harriet Gold, 363 n.149; drafts resolutions of Treaty Party with Ridge, 208; editorials against removal, 191, 192–193, 196–198, 200–201; edits *Cherokee Phoenix,* 183–206; educated by Moravians, 178; on execution of George Tassel, 193; first fund-raising tour, 183, 216–218, 356 n.62; at Foreign Mission school, 178–182, 222; on intemperance, 188, 357 n.75; *Letters and other Papers* (1837), 218–222; marries Delight Sargeant, 212; marries Harriet Ruggles Gold, 181–182, 183; moral issues in *Phoenix,* 186–188; moves to Cherokee Nation West, 211–212; outlines editorial policy, 184–186; *Poor Sarah* (1823), 222, 366 n.182; predicts his own death, 211; promotes "civilization," 182–183, 186–188, 356 n.61; "Prospectus" (1827), 184–185, 186, 356 n.66; published correspondence (1821–1823), 179–180, 355 n.49–52; resigns as editor, 205–206, 219–220, 361 n.127; second fund-raising tour for Cherokee press, 200–203; signs Coodey's petition of protest, 206; signs Treaty of New Echota, 210–211; on slavery, 188–189; teacher at Hightower, 183; translations with Worcester, 182, 184, 356 n.65; wavers on anti-removal stance, 201–205, 360 n.115; on *Worcester v. Georgia,* 195, 201

Boudinot, Elias Cornelius (Cherokee), 280–282; owner of *Indian Progress* (1875–76), 282; promotes assimilationist policies, 281–282

Bourne, Richard, 140

Boy Scouts of America (1910), 287, 388 n.24; Eastman and Parker write for, 388 n.24; promote interest in Indians, 287

Boyle, Sir Robert, 32–33, 41, 47–49, 51–52; addressed by Caleb Cheeshateaumauk and Joel Hiacoomes, 48–49, 51, 52; Boyle Fund established after death of, 32, 51; Boyle School established at William and Mary, 33; correspondence with Eliot, 47

Boy's World (Elgin, IL), 289

Bradford, William, 26

Brafferton Hall (Boyle School), 33

Brafferton Manor (England), 32

Brainerd, David, 149, 324–325 n.75, 345 n.106; founds Delaware Christian Indian community, 324–325 n.75; *Memoirs* (1822), 149; mentioned by Apess, 345 n.106

Brainerd Mission School (Cherokee Nation), 172, 177, 180, 212; attended by John Arch and David Brown, 177; established by Cyrus Kingsbury, 172; visited by Boudinot, 180

Brant, Joseph (Mohawk), 99–100, 108,
293, 329 n.125; leads Mohawks to Canada, 99–100; pupil at Wheelock's school,
99; translates "Mohawk Prayer Book"
(1786), 329 n.125
Briggs, George, 374 n.76, 379 n.118
Brinton, Daniel, 97
British Indian Department (Canada), 229,
231, 234, 241; does not press charges
against Copway, 241; promotes assimilation, 229; purchases land from Ojibwas,
231
Brodeur, Paul, 164
Brothertown (NJ), 324–325 n.75
Brothertown (NY), 84–85, 87, 89, 111,
128–129; founded, 84–85; New Stockbridge founded in vicinity of 85, 111; Occom moves to, 87; Occom travels to and
from, 84–85, 89; Pequots move to, 128–
129
Brothertown (WI), 239
Brothertown Indians, 84–85, 86–87, 116;
conflict with Oneidas, 86–87; establish
government, 84–85; factionalism over
land leases, 86–87; join Stockbridge Indians in Wisconsin, 116
Brothertown Indian Nation of Wisconsin,
99, 295; seeks federal recognition, 99
Broughman, John, *Metamora* (1847) and
Po-ca-hon-tas (1855), 257
Brown, Catherine (Cherokee), 148, 344
n.103, 355 n.49, 371–372 n.38; biography, 344 n.103; correspondence with
David Brown, 344 n.103, 355 n.49; Peter
Jones names daughter after, 371–372
n.38; *Memoirs* (1824), 148
Brown, Charles Brockden, *Edgar Huntly*
(1799), 122
Brown, David (Cherokee), 177, 178, 183,
217, 344 n.103, 353–354 n.40, 355
nn.49, 51; attends Andover Theological
Seminary, 180, 355 n.51; attends Brainerd mission school, 177; attends Foreign
Mission School, 178–179; biography,
353–354 n.40; co-founds Moral and Literary Society, 183; correspondence with
the baron de Campagne (1821), 179, 355
n.49; translates New Testament with
George Lowry, 217; "Views of a Native
Indian" (1825), 217, 353–354 n.40

Brown, William Wells, 376 n.89
Brookings Institution, 290
Brumble, David, III, 89, 97
Bryant, William Cullen, 255, 263, 273, 379
n.121; Copway associates with, 263; on
Copway's removal of Red Jacket's body,
379 n.121; supports *Copway's American
Indian,* 255; and travel literature, 273
Buell, Rev. Samuel, 65, 69, 70, 76, 322
n.49; admonishes Occom to remain humble, 76; extolls Occom as "ornament to
the Christian religion," 69; on Occom's
progress as student, 65; on Occom's public speaking abilities, 322 n.49; provides
Occom with funds, 70
Buffalo Baptist Church, 364–365 n.167
Bureau of American Ethnology (1879), 287
Bureau of Indian Affairs (BIA, Office of Indian Affairs), 116, 120, 163, 196, 229,
245, 281, 283, 286, 290; approves
Stockbridge-Munsee tribal constitution,
116; Board of Indian Commissioners to
exercise control over, 283; created within
Department of War, 120, 229; criticized
by Carlos Montezuma, 163; Ely Parker
proposes return to Department of War,
281; mounting public criticism of, 290;
SAI debates abolition of, 286; transferred
to Interior, 281
Burlingame, Anson, 378 n.104
Burritt, Elihu, 249, 251; criticizes Copway's
speech, 251; invites Copway to Third
World Peace Congress, 249
Burr Seminary (VT), 281
Butler, Benjamin F., 374 n.76
Butler, Dr. Elizur, 194, 197, 201, 203, 214;
arrested by Georgia Guard, 194; men-
tioned by Boudinot, 201; seeks pardon
from Georgia, 203, 214; and *Worcester v.
State of Georgia,* 194, 197, 201, 203
Butrick, Daniel, 203
Byrd, William, *History of the Dividing Line*
(1728), 33
Byron, Lord George Gordon, 275

Cabot, Sebastian, 22
Cain, 253
Caldwell, Charles, *Thoughts on the Original Unity of the Human Race* (1830),
123

Caleb, Hannah (Pequot), 154; biography by
Apess, 154
Calhoun, John C., 120, 157, 347 n.134;
creates BIA, 120; "Exposition and Pro-
test" (1828), 157, 347 n.134
Callahan, S. Alice (Creek), *Wynema* (1891),
288
Calvin, Hezekiah (Delaware), 323 n.58
Calvinism, 98, 125
Cambridge Grammar School, 41, 46, 48;
attended by Caleb Cheeshahteaumauk
and Joel Hiacoomes, 48; Indian students
at, 41; possibly attended by James
Printer, 46
Campbell, Thomas, 121
Canada East, 230
Canada West, 241
Canadian Conference of the Wesleyan
Methodist Church (1828), 232, 241–
242, 262; established, 232; expells Cop-
way, 241–242; expells Jacobs, 262
Canadian Indian Studies, 20
Cape Cod (MA), 26, 53, 140
Cape Verde Islanders, 141
captivity narratives, 91, 122, 149; as anti-
Indian literature, 122; execution sermons
as popular as, 91; surpassed in popularity
by slave narratives, 149
Carlisle Indian Industrial School (PA), 284,
291; attended by Luther Standing Bear,
291; founded by Pratt, 284
Caro, Brígido, 386 n.4
Carson, Everett R., 328 n.120
Cartier, Jaques, 22
Cass, Lewis, 202, 270; issues questionnaires
to Indian agents, 270; proposes removal
treaty to Cherokee delegation, 202
Cassasinamon, Robin (Pequot sachem),
128
Catholics, 30, 258, 261, 262, 283; convert
Copway, 261; convert George Henry,
262; and Grant's "Peace Policy," 283
Catlin, George, 262, 270, 274–275, 384
n.163; account of Ojibwas in Europe,
274–275; on George Henry, 384 n.163;
with "Indian Collection in Europe," 262
Cayuga Academy (NY), 280
Cayugas, 84
Central Algonquian, 224, 225; linguistic
ties among Ojibwas, 224; relations with

Europeans further uniformity of culture,
225
Cerberus, 97
Challoung, Henry, 24
Champlain, Samuel de, 23
Chandler, Joseph P., 378 n.104
Chapin, Emile Hubbell, 252, 376 n.92
Charles I, 49
Charles V, 23
Charles IX, 23
Charleston Courier, 243–244
Chateaubriand, René de, 121
Chauncy, Charles, 41, 92
Cheeshahteaumauk, Caleb (Wampanoag),
41, 48–49, 51, 52, 314 n.93; attends
Cambridge Grammar School, 48; attends
Harvard Indian College, 41, 48; authen-
ticity of address questioned, 51; "Hono-
ratissimi benefactores" (1663), 48–49,
51, 52, 314 n.93
Chemewa American, 287
Cherokee Advocate (Tahlehquah), 256,
282, 361 n.130
Cherokee Almanac (Tahlequah), 361 n.130
Cherokee Nation West, 212, 213, 281–
282; Boudinot and the Ridges move to,
212; conflict between Old Settlers and
New Immigrants, 213; incorporation
into Territory of Oklahoma, 281–282
Cherokee Nation v. State of Georgia
(1831), 120, 193–194; Boudinot on,
194; and Indian sovereignty, 120, 193
Cherokee Phoenix (New Echota), 177,
183–206, 207, 216, 219, 256, 361
n.130; ceases to exist, 206, 361 n.130; established, 177, 183–185; Elijah Hicks
editor of, 206; lampoons pro-treaty delegation, 207; name changed to *Cherokee
Phoenix, and Indians' Advocate,* 188;
notice on Peter Jones's speech in London,
216; Stand Watie interim editor of, 200;
as voice of Cherokee Nation under
Boudinot, 183–205. *See also* Boudinot,
Elias; Hicks, Elijah; Ross, John; Watie,
Stand
Cherokee Temperance Society (1829), 188
Cherokee Tobacco Case (1871), 281
Cherokees, 55, 69, 119, 120, 143, 146,
157, 166–223, 225, 234, 243, 247, 278–
279, 281–282, 294, 347 n.134, 352–353

n.33, 353 n.37, 354 n.43, 356 n.60, 361
n.130, 365 n.170, 371–372 n.38; admired by Copway, 247; admired by Peter
Jones, 234, 371–372 n.38; censuses, 187,
217; and Cherokee Nation Cases, 120,
192–195, 200–203; and clan revenge,
175, 191; codify laws in English,
174; conflict with Georgia, 173–174,
185, 189–196, 200–204; constitution
(1827), 173, 175, 184, 189, 204, 352–
353 n.33; devastated by epidemics, 167;
discovery of gold in Cherokee Nation,
190–191; establish constitutional government, 174–176, 217; establish national press and *Cherokee Phoenix,* 177,
183–184, 361 n.130; first phase of postcontact transformation, 166–169; General Council of, 175, 176, 177, 182–184,
186; history of relations with Euro-
Americans, 166–177; influence of missionaries, 172–173; influence of mixed-
bloods, 170–171, 172, 214–215, 223;
institutionalize Sequoyah's syllabary,
176–177, 184, 354 n.43; internal conflicts in Cherokee Nation West, 213,
281–282; laws nullified by Georgia,
190–191; literacy, 176, 353 n.37, 365
n.170; National Committee of, 171, 175,
178, 182, 196, 206; National Council of,
169, 171, 172, 173, 174–175, 177, 193,
200, 206, 207–208, 217; and the nullification crisis, 157, 347 n.134; petition for
impeachment of the Ridges, 207–208;
postpone elections, 204; problems with
intruders, 191–192; reject provisional removal treaty, 210; removal of, 173–177,
212–213; second phase of post-contact
transformation (Cherokee Nation), 166,
169–176; seminaries, 182, 217–218, 356
n.60; sign protest against Treaty of New
Echota, 211; on Trail of Tears, 212–213
Chester, Elisha, 204
Chicago Times, 282
Chicago World's Fair (1893), 288
Chickamaugans (Five Lower Towns), 167–
169, 174; remove to Arkansas, 174; separate from main body of Cherokees,
167–169
Chickasaws, 119, 167, 360 n.117
Chicora, Francisco de (Yamasee), 23

Chief Bowles (Cherokee), 174
Child, Lydia Maria, 126, 160, 347 n.143;
Hobomok (1824), 347 n.143; opposes
removal, 126; *The First Settlers of New
England* (1828), 160
Chilocco School (Indian Territory), 284
Chinook Jargon, 6
Choctaws, 55, 119, 360 n.117
Choctaw Telegraph (Indian Territory), 378
n.110
Christian Herald (Plattsburgh), 182
Christian Indians, 12–13, 33–53, 57, 60–
61, 82–87, 96, 108, 110–111, 140–141,
164, 231–235, 239, 291–295, 311 n.70,
313 n.85, 328 n.114, 332–333 n.156,
353–354 n.40, 371 n.32, 372 n.44, 386
n.6; biographies of, 42–53, 311 n.70;
found Brothertown and New Stockbridge
(NY), 82–87; and hymns, 96, 328 n.114;
letter by Christian Indians of Wamesit
(1675), 53; at Mashpee, 140–141;
among Ojibwas, 231–235; problems
with Oneidas, 86–87; relations with
seventeenth-century Puritans, 33–53;
role in American Revolution, 57, 84,
108, 110–111; as scribes for Metacom,
46–48, 51–52, 313 n.85; significance in
Indian-white relations, 291–295; and
stereotype of sellout, 160; at Stockbridge
(MA), 60–61, 110–111; survival strategies, 38–40, 44, 292–295; as translators
of the Gospel, 44–47, 217, 237, 332–
333 n.156, 353–354 n.40, 371 n.32, 374
n.44; vernacular literacy, 13, 52; and voluntary removal, 294
Church of England, 234
Civil War (1861–1865), 20, 121, 148, 195–
196, 270, 278, 280, 282, 287, 292, 363
n.155; Ely Parker in, 280, 363 n.155;
Stand Watie in, 363 n.155
Clark, Julius Taylor, 268–269; claims authorship of *Ojibway Conquest,* 268
Clarke, Peter Dooyentate (Wyandot), 287,
383 n.150; and "Ojibwa Thesis," 383
n.150
Clay, Henry, 193, 209; presents resolutions
of Treaty Party to Congress, 209; supports Cherokees, 193
Clelland, Robert, 73, 97; conflict with Occom, 73

Clemens, Samuel, 279
Cleveland, Grover, 282
Clifford, James, 141
Clifton, James, 17
Cloud, Rev. Henry Roe (Winnebago), 379 n.116, 386 n.6
Coastal Algonquians, 27, 39, 66, 91, 97–98, 127, 130, 294, 328 n.114; competitive leadership, 27; intermarriages with African Americans, 130; not affected by removal, 127; similarities with Christianity, 39, 97–98, 328 n.114; socio-linguistic network, 66
Cobden, Richard, 250, 251, 376 n.92; debate with Disraeli witnessed by Copway, 250; speech mentioned by Copway, 251
Coburg (Canada), 230, 232
Cockenoe-de-Long Island (Montauk), 44–45, 47, 52; biography, 44–45; deeds written by (1661), 45, 52; deserves credit for "Indian Library," 47
Colden, Cadwallader, 70
Coleman, Benjamin, 60
Collacot, Richard, 44
College of William and Mary, 32–33; charter mentions christianization of Indians, 32; Indian students at Boyle School, 32–33
Collier, John, 290, 391 n.38; biography, 391 n.38; commissioner of Indian affairs, 290
Collier's Weekly (New York), 289
colonialism (as term), 1–2
colonial situation (as term), 1, 297 n.1
Columbus, Christopher, 14, 22
Commission of the United Colonies of New England, 45
Committee of One Hundred, 290
Commuck, Thomas (Narragansett), 325 n.79, 328 nn.111, 114; Indian Melodies (1845), 328 n.79
Conant, Sylvanus, Blood of Abel, and Blood of Jesus (1765), 93
Cone, James H., 164
Confederate Congress, 281
Congregationalists, 65, 69, 141, 142, 172, 179, 295; among Cherokees, 172; establish ABCFM, 172; joined by Boudinot, 179; Mohegan Church, 295
Congress (U.S.), 58, 59, 162, 170, 171, 173, 190–191, 200, 205, 212, 245, 247–248, 278, 281, 283; affirms "utmost good faith," 58; establishes civilization fund, 59, 171; and establishment of an Indian state, 245, 247–248; and Indian Appropriation Act (1871), 283; and Indian Trade and Intercourse Acts, 171; Ely Parker on, 281; petitioned by Copway, 248; petitioned by John Ross, 212; and removal, 170, 173, 190–191, 200, 205, 212, 245
Connecticut Board of Commissioners (SSPCK), 72, 73–74; enlists Occom, 72; forces Occom to withdraw from Mason Controversy, 73–74
Connecticut River, 62
Conser, Walter, Jr., 215
Constitution (U.S.), 10, 58, 119, 126, 143, 171, 173, 175, 248, 300 n.48; and abolitionists, 126; Cherokees model constitution after, 171, 175; cited by Apess, 143; Indians mentioned in, 10, 58, 300 n.48; Jefferson proposes amendment to, on removal, 173; mentioned by Copway, 248; and "natural rights of man," 119
contact zone (as term), 19
Continental Congress, 57–58
Conway, Peter (Algonquian scribe), 313 n.85
Coodey, William Shorey (Cherokee), 206
Cooke, William, 33
Coolidge, Rev. Sherman (Arapaho), 285, 386 n.6; outlines objectives of SAI, 285
Coombs, Isaac (Mashpee), 146
Cooper, James F., 122, 160, 243, 252, 255, 263, 273; Copway on, 263; supports Copway's American Indian, 255; Wept of Wish-Ton-Wish (1829), 160
Copeland, Rev. Patrick, 31
Copway, David (Ojibwa, brother of George), 261
Copway, George (Kahgegagahbowh, Ojibwa), v, 224, 230–277, 278, 293–294, 366–367 n.1, 372 nn.41, 44, 45, 373 nn.56, 61, 373–374 n.66, 374 n.76, 375–376 n.87, 376–377 n.94, 377 nn.95, 96, 100, 379 n.118, 380 n.130, 381 nn.131, 134, 382 nn.145, 146, 383–384 n.158; accused of mismanagement, 241, 373 n.56; affinity with Romantic Movement, 231, 263, 265, 266, 271; as-

sociation with American nativist movement, 247, 258–260, 275, 379 n.118; attends Peace Congress in Frankfurt, 250–253, 254, 375–376 n.87, 376–377 n.94; on being Indian, 266; bibliographical references to, 366–367 n.1, 380–381 nn.130, 131, 134; birth of, 230; career in the U.S., 242–249; conflict with missionaries, 239, 241–242; connections to American ethnology, 263–265, 269–270, 271; conversion experience, 231–232, 235–237; converts to Roman Catholicism, 261; death of, 261; decline of, 257–261, 260–261; develops drinking habit, 260; on dreams and visions, 231, 236, 372 n.41; editorial policy, 255–256; editor of *Copway's American Indian,* 254–257; education of, 232, 236, 255, 372 n.45; in Europe, 245, 249–254, 275–277; expelled by Canadian Methodists, 241–242; founds Association for Protective Justice to Indians, 254; *History* (1850), 249, 263, 269–273; on Indian education, 266–268; on intemperance, 231; lectures, 243–244, 250–252, 254, 259, 260, 373 n.61, 373–374 n.66, 377 n.100; letter to *New York Times* (1856), 258–259, 379 n.118; *Life* (1846), 231, 235–236, 237–238, 239, 240, 242–244, 246, 263, 264–267, 270, 381 n.134; marriage to Elizabeth Howell, 238–239, 260–261; on missionaries, 267; missionary activities in Canada, 241–242; *Ojibway Conquest* (1850), 249, 253, 268–269, 377 n.96; on oral traditions, 265–266, 271; *Organization of a New Indian Territory* (1850), 247–248, 267–268; poem on "vanishing Indians," 238; reception in Germany, 252–254, 376–377 n. 94, 377 n. 95–96; *Running Sketches* (1851), 249–254, 273–277, 382 n.146, 383–384 n.158; scheme for "Kah-ge-ga Indian Territory," 245–249, 253, 264, 374 n.76; in Scotland, 254; on slavery, 258; and *Song of Hiawatha,* 269, 382 n.145; translates Gospel, 237, 372 n.44; travels in America, 237; tributes to America, 237–238, 243, 258, 265, 275–276; at Upper Mississippi Mission, 239–240; views on the "Indian problem,"

240, 266–278; on women, 256, 276. *See also* Jones, Peter; Longfellow, Henry Wadsworth; Parkman, Francis
Copway, John (Ojibwa, father of George), 230, 232
Copway, Minnehaha (Ojibwa, daughter of George), 263
Copway's American Indian (New York), 254–257, 259, 378 nn.104, 106; supporters of, 378 n.104
Cornelius, Elias, 178
Corning, Erastus, 260–261; solicited by Copway, 260–261
Cornwall (CT), 178, 180, 181, 222
corridos, 279
Cortereal, Gaspar, 22
Cortés, Hernán, 21, 23
Cortlet, Elijah, 41, 46. *See also* Cambridge Grammar School
Costo, Rupert (Cahuilla), 14
Cotton, John, 43
Council of Massachusetts, 142, 143
Crawford, Hartley T., 245
Credit River (Canada), 232
Credit River band (Ojibwas), 232–235, 262
Credit River Mission (Canada), 234, 235, 241; Copway teaches school at, 241; as model Christian Indian village, 234; relocated to Grand River reserve, 235
Creek Path (Cherokee Nation), 174
Creek Path Conspiracy (1819–22), 174
Creek Path Mission School (Cherokee Nation), 180, 344 n.103
Creeks, 55, 119, 167, 174, 196, 202, 282, 288, 360 n.117; close down E. C. Boudinot's *Indian Progress,* 282; sign removal treaty, 202, 360 n.117; subject of Callahan's *Wynema,* 288; subject of Posey's "Fus Fixico Letters," 288
Creek War (1812–14), 174, 178
Crockett, David, 193
Cuffee, Paul, Sr., 130
Cuffee, Paul, Jr. (Pequot), *Narrative of the Life and Adventures of* (1839), 130
cultural brokers, 16–18
culture hero, 16, 269
Cusick, David (Tuscarora), 269, 329 n.125, 382 n.146; Copway borrows from his *Sketches* (1827), 269, 382 n.146

Daily Commercial Gazette (Boston), 146

Dale, Sir Thomas, 28, 31

Danforth, Samuel, 91, 94, 327 n.107; *Cry of Sodom Enquired Into* (1675), 91; *Woful Effects of Drunkenness* (1710), 94, 327 n.107

Daniell, Jere, 80

Dartmouth College, 58, 61, 79–80, 96, 98, 104, 216, 323 n.61, 328–329 n.120, 379 n.122; Indian students attending, 80, 216, 323 n.61, 379 n.122; ordination of Joseph Johnson, 104

Davenport, Rev. James, 61; converts Occom, 61

Declaration of Independence, 119

Delawares, 55, 57, 112–113, 115, 235, 324–325 n.75, 334 n.168; addressed by Aupaumut, 112–113, 115, 334 n.168; Peter Jones agent for, 235; treaty with U.S., 57

Deloria, Vine, Jr. (Standing Rock Sioux), 155, 293; *God Is Red* (1973), 293

Democratic Party, 282

Department of War, 209

Dermer, Thomas, 23, 25

De Soto, Hernán, 166, 177

Detroit Press, 261

diglossia (as term), 8

Dippie, Brian, 126

Disraeli, Benjamin, 250

Domagaia (Iroquois), 22

Dominion of Canada, 230

Don Diego Colón (Taino), 22

Dorris, Michael (Modoc), 328–329 n.120

Doty, James Duane, 245–246; letter to Fillmore on Indian state, 246; treats with Sioux, 245

Doublehead (Cherokee), 170, 178; The Ridge and execution of, 178

Democratic Party, 259

Douglas Democrats, 278

Downing, Todd (Cherokee), 390 n.30

Drake, Samuel G., 122, 270, 347 n.133, 382 n.148; claims Snelling is author of Apess's *Nullification,* 347 n.133; mentioned by Copway, 382 n.148

Drévetière, François Delisle de la, 273

Dryden, John, 273

Dunster, Henry, 40

Eastburn, James Wallis (and Robert Charles Sand), *Yamoyden* (1820), 160

Eastern Cherokees, 213, 214

Eastern Dakotas. *See* Santee Sioux

East India Company, 31

East Indian School, 31

Eastman, Charles Alexander (Ohiyesa, Wahpeton Sioux), 289, 290, 293, 323 n.61, 379 n.116, 388 n.24; *From the Deep Woods to Civilization* (1916), 289; *Indian Boyhood* (1902), 289; *The Indian To-day* (1915), 289; pays tribute to Occom, 323 n.61; *The Soul of the Indian* (1911), 289, 293; writes for Boy Scouts, 388 n.24

Eastman, Elaine Goodale, 289

Easton, John, 48

Eaton, John Henry, 194, 358 n.92

Ebenezer Manual Labor School (Jacksonville, IL), 237

Edwards, Jonathan, 59, 64, 109, 149, 320–321 n.31, 330 n.127; edition of *Memoirs of the Reverend Davis Brainard* (1822), 149; leads Great Awakening, 59, 64; style of exhortation, 109, 320–321 n.31

Eid, Leroy, 270

Eleazar (Harvard scholar), 41, 50–51, 52, 315–316 n.97; poem on Rev. Thacher (1679), 50–51, 315–316 n.97

Eliot, Andrew, 92

Eliot, John, 34–37, 40, 43, 44–48, 60, 61, 83, 89, 96, 311 n.70; establishes Praying Indian towns in Massachusetts, 36–37; and Indian translators, 44–48; learns Massachusett language, 35; records Indian confessions, 89, 311 n.70; on teaching in English, 60; on Waban, 43

Emerson, Ralph Waldo, 280

Enfranchisement Act (1869), 230

Engels, Friedrich, 252

Enlightenment, 60, 119, 122, 124–125, 149, 164; and Apess, 164; and Indian education, 60; and Second Great Awakening, 124–125; and slave narratives, 149

Environmentalism, 120–121

Epenow (Capawake sachem), 23, 24, 25

Episcopalians, 73, 261–262; joined by John Johnson, 261–262; Occom threatens to deflect to, 73

Equiano, Olaudah, 150

Erdrich, Louise (Ojibwa), 328–329 n.120

Esopus Indians, 110

ethnicity (as term), 15

ethnic nationalism (as term), 15

ethnic proto-elite (as term), 16

ethnohistory (definition), 19

Evans, Rev. James, 232

Evarts, Jeremiah (William Penn), 126, 146, 156, 216, 343–344 n.94, 364 n.165; Apess influenced by, 146, 156, 343–344 n.94; author of "Address of the Cherokees" (1830), 146; biography, 343 n.94; opposes removal, 126; serialized in *Cherokee Phoenix*, 364 n.165; "William Penn" essays, 146, 216, 343–344 n.94, 364 n.165

Everett, Edward, 193, 209, 255, 374 n.76, 378 n.108; contributes to *Copway's American Indian*, 255, 378 n.108; opposes removal, 193; presents resolutions of Treaty Party to Congress, 209; supports Copway's Indian territory plan, 374 n.76

execution sermons, 91–95, 108–109; Johnson's letter to Moses Paul, 108–109; as literature, 91–92; Occom's sermon to Moses Paul, 92–95

Fanon, Frantz, 5, 18

Farmington (CT), 83, 107, 109

Fawcett, Melissa (Mohegan), 319 n.18, 324 n.66, 329 n.123

Ferdinand and Isabella, 22

Fields, Richard (Cherokee), 361 n.130

Fillmore, Millard, 246, 259–260; supported by Copway, 259–260

Finnegan, Ruth, 9

Finney, Charles Grandison, 139

First Nations (Canada), 3

First Presbyterian Church, 216

First Seminole War (1817), 127

Fish, Rev. Phineas, 141–144, 147; conflict with Mashpees, 141–144; invites Apess to preach, 142; leaves Mashpee, 147

Fishman, Joshua, 7, 8, 15

Fiske, John, 144–145

Fitch, Rev. James, 63

Five Civilized Tribes, 119, 124, 125–126, 127, 145, 181, 247; and abolitionists, 126, 145; Copway on, 247; participate in slave trade, 125; and removal, 124; John Ridge on, 181

Forbes, Allan, 50

Forbes, Jack D., 303 n.84, 304 n.5

Foreign Mission School (Cornwall, CT), 178–182, 222; attended by David Brown, Boudinot, and John Ridge, 179–182, 222; criticized for Ridge-Northrup marriage, 181; forced to close after Boudinot-Gold marriage, 181–182; goals of, 179

Foreman, Tom (Cherokee), 211, 363 n.148

Forest Grove School (OR), 284

Forrest, Edwin, 160, 243

Fort McDowell Reservation (AZ), 291

Fourth World (as term), 3, 15

Fowler, David (Montauk), 70–71, 72, 82–85, 102, 107, 239, 321 n.33, 325 nn.79, 83; biography, 321 n.33; founds Brothertown (NY) with Occom and Johnson, 82–85; among the Oneidas, 70–71, 102, 107; strained relations with Samuel Kirkland, 102

Fowler, Mary (Montauk, wife of Occom), 66

Fox Indians, 226

Foxwoods High Stakes Bingo and Casino Resort, 128

Frankfurt (Germany), 250–253, 377 n.95

Franklin, Benjamin, 106, 150; *Autobiography* (1817–18), 150; prints Indian treaties, 106

Freiligrath, Hermann Ferdinand, 253, 257–258, 260–261, 377 n.98; asks Copway to stand as godfather to his son, 253; complains to Longfellow about Copway, 257–258

Freire, Paulo, 7, 157

Frelinghuysen, Theodore, 193, 202

Freneau, Philip, 122

French and Indian War (1754–63), 55, 70, 110, 167; Occom among the Oneidas during, 70; participation of Cherokees, 167; participation of Stockbridge Indians, 110

Frére, Thomas, 378 n.108

Friends of the Indian, 286–287

Froebel, Friedrich, 66

Gallatin, Albert, 122, 217, 264, 267, 270; promotes article by John Ridge, 217; supports Copway's "Kah-ge-gah" project, 64

Gambold, Anna and Rev. John, 178

Garrison, William Lloyd, 145, 149–150, 152, 160; and African American writers, 149–150; and Apess's writings, 152; champions Mashpees, 145; mobbed in Boston, 160

Gay Head Indians, 38, 53, 99

Geerz, Clifford, 3

General Allotment Act (Dawes Act, 1887), 287

General Assembly of Georgia, 190, 195; declares Cherokee laws null and void, 190

General Assembly of New York, 86, 101; passes "Act for relief" (1791) of Christian Indians, 86

General Court of Connecticut, 62–64, 65, 83; approves Ben Uncas's appointments, 65; favorable to removal of Christian Indians, 83; and Mason Controversy, 62–64

General Court of Massachusetts, 35, 36, 141, 145; declares blasphemy a capital crime, 35; and Mashpee revolt, 141, 145; sets aside lands for Christian Indians, 36

General Court of Plymouth Colony, 141

Genesis, 121, 176

George II, 63

George III, 72, 75, 101, 141

George, Sally (Pequot), 136, 154; Apess with, 136; biography of, by Apess, 154

Georgia Compact (1802), 173–174

Georgia Guard, 192, 194, 199; arrests Butler and Worcester, 194; confronts Boudinot, 199

Georgia Lottery, 195, 207; Boudinot and Ridges exempted from, 207

Gerstäcker, Friedrich, 252

ghost dance movement (Cherokee 1811–13), 173

Gilbert, Raleigh, 23

Girardin, Emile de, 251, 376 n.92

Gist, Nathaniel, 176

Gold, Harriet Ruggles (wife of Boudinot), 181–182, 183, 212, 223, 363 n.149

Gomez, Estévan, 22

Gonzales, Rodolfo "Corky," *I Am Joaquín* (1967), 279

Goody, Jack, 9, 10

Gookin, Daniel, 45–46, 48; on Joel Hiacoomes, 48; on Job Nesuton, 45

Gookin, Daniel (younger), 60

Gordillo, Francisco, 22, 23

Gordon, Rev. Philip (Ojibwa), 386 n.6

Gorges, Ferdinando, 24, 25

Gospel, 12, 20, 60, 63, 69, 70, 96, 100, 108, 114, 124, 136, 138, 154, 163, 176, 198, 237, 292, 353–354 n.40; Apess on, 136, 154, 163; Boudinot on, 198; and Great Awakening, 124, 138, 292; Indians trained as ministers of, 20, 69; Occom on, 70, 96, 114; translating of, 12, 60, 176, 237, 353–354 n.40; Washington on, 108; Wheelock on, 100

Gradual Civilization Act (1857), 230

Grand Council of the Methodist Ojibwas of Canada West, 235, 241, 246, 259; elects Copway vice-president, 241, 246; mentioned by Copway, 259

Grand River reserve (Canada), 233, 234, 235, 242

Grant, Ulysses S., 280, 281, 282, 288; and "Peace Policy," 282, 288

Great Awakening, 42, 59–60, 64, 97, 98, 124, 292, 293; characteristics of, 59–60; and Jonathan Edwards, 59; and Indian missionary-writers, 292–293; and Mohegans, 64; and Occom, 98; Second Great Awakening as continuation of, 124; and George Whitefield, 59, 97

Great Lakes, 224–231, 271, 272

Green, Bartholomew, 46–47

Green, Samuel, 46, 93

Green, Thomas, 93

Green Bay (WI), 116, 239

green corn dance, 210

Greene, David, 203

Grenville, Richard, 22

Griffis, Rev. Joseph K. (Tahan, Osage), 386 n.6

Grimes, William, 150, 153

Groton (CT), 83, 128, 135

Gull Lake Mission (MI), 261, 262

Hall, Rev. Sherman, 237

Hallett, Benjamin, 145

Hamilton Academy (NY), 331 n.135

Hammon, Jupiter, 148

Hamor, Ralph, 28
Hampton Institute (VA), 283–284
Handsome Lake (Seneca), 115
Hansen, Marcus Lee, 18
Harlow, Edward, 23
Harper's (NY), 287
Harrison, William, 113
Harte, Bret, 279
Harvard College, 40–41, 44, 46–51, 141, 143, 313 n.89; appoints Fish as minister to Mashpees, 141; chapter of, and Indians, 40–41; Harvard College Press, 41, 46; Harvard Indian College, 41, 44, 47–51, 313 n.89; Mashpees address petition to, 143
Haskell Institute (KS), 284
Hassanamesitt (Grafton, MA), 46, 49
Havemeyer, William F., 374 n.76
Haynau, Julius von, 375 n.86
Haynes, Lemuel, 148, 330 n.128
Head, Sir Francis Bond, 229
Heckewelder, John G. E., 122
Hendrick, "King" (Mohawk-Mahican), 111, 332 n.155; biography, 332 n.155; possible grandfather of Aupaumut, 111
Hendrick, Solomon (Mahican, son of Aupaumut), 116, 334 n.171
Henrico College, 30–32
Henry II, 23
Henry VII, 22
Henry, George (Maungwudaus, Ojibwa), 232, 262, 274–276, 384 n.163; abandons Methodists to form Indian dance troupe, 262; account of travels with Catlin in Europe, 274–275; letter to Peter Jones, 384 n.163
Hessians, 141
Hewitt, John Napoleon Brinton (Tuscarora), 288, 329 n.125
Hiacoomes (Wampanoag), 37–38, 42–43, 48, 312 n.75; biography, 42–43; confession of (1653), 43; converted by Mayhew, Jr., 37–38; in Eliot's *Indian Dialogues,* 312 n.75
Hiacoomes, Joel (Wampanoag), 41, 48, 52; death of, 48; at Harvard Indian College, 41
Hiawatha (Iroquois), 269
Hicks, Charles (Cherokee), 178
Hicks, Elijah, 206, 219; assumes editorship
of *Phoenix,* 206; Boudinot responds to diatribe by, 219
hidden transcript (as term), 18
Hightower (Cherokee Nation), 183, 184
Hillhouse, Judge William, 133
Hispanics, 279
Hiwassee (Cherokee Nation), 177
Hiwassee River, 172
Hobbamock (Wampanoag), 26–27
Hobson, Nicholas, 23, 24
Honey Creek (Cherokee Nation West), 212
Hopkins, Sarah Winnemucca (Paiute), *Life among the Paiutes* (1883), 288
Horsman, Reginald, 123
Horton, Azariah, 66
Housatonic River, 110
Housatonic Valley Indians, 60, 110; Mahicans seek refuge with, 110; Sargeant, Sr., missionary of, 60
House of Commons (England), 250
House of Representatives (U.S.), 58, 192, 221, 280; acquits Parker, 280; Boudinot on, 192; House Committee on Indian Affairs, 58; Ross on, 221
Houston, Sam, 289
Howell, Elizabeth (wife of Copway), 238–239, 260; marriage to Copway, 238–239; separation from Copway, 260
Hubbard, William, 47–48, 160; account of King Philip's War, 160; on Sassomon's death, 47–48
Hudson's Bay Company, 228, 262
Humbolt, Alexander von, 217
Hunt, Thomas, 24
Huntingdon, Selina, countess of, 75, 330 n.128; hosts Occom in England, 75
Hurons (Wyandots), 23, 55, 225, 271; displaced by Iroquois, 225; and the "Ojibwa Thesis," 271
Hyenne, Roberto, 386 n.5
Hymes, Dell, 8

Illustrierte Zeitung (Leipzig), 252–253, 376 n.94
immediatists, 126
Indian (as term), 14–15
Indian Appropriation Act (1871), 283
Indian Citizenship Act (1924), 291
Indian education, 7, 30–33, 40–44, 53, 59–61, 95, 172–173, 229, 230, 283–285;

Indian education (*cont.*)
among Cherokees, 172; in colonial Massachusetts, 40–44; in colonial Virginia, 30–33; Copway on, v, 266–268; as federal policy, 283–285; during Great Awakening, 59–61, 172–173; as instrument of colonization, 7; and missionaries, 53, 283; Occom on, 95; among Ojibwas, 229, 230; report of Special Subcommittee on (1969), 7; Sargeant, Sr. on, 60–61; Wheelock's "Grand Design," 61
Indian Leader (Haskell), 287
Indian policy, 54–59, 119–121, 123–124, 148, 166, 170, 171–175, 177, 191, 206–213, 216, 224, 225–230, 245–246, 248, 258, 268, 278, 282–287, 288, 290–291, 293–294; allotment, 229, 246, 268, 283–287; British, 54–57, 226–230, 293–294; civilization fund, 59, 171; civilization program, 58, 119, 166, 170, 177, 191, 216, 230; early American, 57–59, 171–173, 226–228, 293–294; French, 225–226; Grant's Peace Policy, 283, 288; Indian New Deal, 290; removal, 119–121, 123–124, 148, 173–174, 175, 206–213, 228–229, 245–246, 248, 268; self-determination, 290–291; termination, 290–291
Indian Progress (Muskogee-Vinita), 282
Indian Rights Association (1882), 286
Indian School Journal (Chilocco), 287
Indian Territory (OK), 216, 260, 281–282, 286, 287, 288, 289, 389–390 n.30; E. C. Boudinot promotes incorporation as "Territory of Oklahoma," 281–282; as literary center, 389–390 n.30; in Posey's "Fus Fixico Letters," 288; in Oskison's fiction, 289
Indian Trade and Intercourse Acts (1790–1834), 58, 120, 171, 192, 320 n.21
indigenism (as term), 15
intemperance, 69, 78, 92, 94–95, 124, 131–132, 147–148, 155, 188, 231, 260, 262, 288; and Apess, 131–132, 147–148, 155; Boudinot on, 188; and Copway, 231, 260; as "Indian" vice, 92; and Peter Jacobs, 262; and Occom, 69, 78, 94–95; Pokagon's temperance novel, 288; as revivalist issue, 124
internal colonialism (as term), 2
Iroquoian, 106

Iroquois (Six Nations), 55, 70, 77, 83, 108, 111–112, 225, 230, 233, 235, 242, 269, 270–271, 272, 295, 329 n.125, 382 n.146; autohistory, 329 n.146; and council at Newton (NY), 111–112; Joseph Johnson as mediator among, 108; Peter Jones agent for, 235; and the "Ojibwa Thesis," 225, 230, 270–271, 272
Irving, Washington, 150, 160, 216, 218, 255, 263, 273, 345 n.109, 364 n.165, 378 n.108; contributes to *Copway's American Indian*, 255; Copway on, 273; excerpted in *A Son of the Forest*, 150, 160, 345 n.109; "Philip of Pokanoket" (1814), 160; serialized in *Cherokee Phoenix*, 216, 364 n.165; *Sketch Book* (1819), 160; "Traits of Indian Character" (1814), 150, 160, 216, 345 n.109, 364 n.165

Jackson, Andrew, 119, 162–163, 173, 174, 185, 190, 191, 192, 193, 195, 201–203, 207, 209, 211, 212, 214, 347 n.134; annual message to Congress (1829), 190; campaign against Creeks, 174; declares Treaty of New Echota as law, 211; election of, 190; fails to enforce Supreme Court decision, 195, 203, 214; and nullification crisis, 347 n.134; orders enforced removal of Cherokees, 212; orders payments to Cherokees stopped, 191; paraphrased by Apess, 162–163; refuses to protect Cherokees from intruders, 192, 202; John Ridge on, 201–202, 209; shows preference for Treaty Party, 209; as speculator, 173; and treaties, 119
Jackson, Helen Hunt, *Century of Dishonor* (1881) and *Ramona* (1884), 287
Jacobs, Rev. Peter (Pahtahsega, Ojibwa), 232, 262, 264–265; expelled by Methodists, 262; *Journal* (1857), 264–265
James, William, 13, 266, 301 n.60; on conversion experience, 13, 301 n.60
James (Massachusett Indian), 40
James I, 28
Jamestown Massacre, 29
Jaup, Carl, 251, 375 n.86, 377 n.94
Jefferson, Thomas, 116, 119, 145, 171, 173, 198; Boudinot on, 198; and civilization program, 171; influence on Apess,

145; meeting with Aupaumut, 116; proposes amendment to Constitution, 173; on removal, 119, 173

Jehovah, 43, 93, 155; Apess on, 155; Hiacoomes on, 43; Occom on, 93

Jennings, Francis, 12, 32, 33–34, 41, 159

Jesuits, 23

Jesus Christ, 29, 70, 85, 94, 100, 104, 109, 135, 136, 156, 164, 180; Apess on, 135, 156, 164; Boudinot on, 180; Joseph Johnson on, 104, 109; Occom on, 70, 85, 94, 100

Jethro, Peter (Algonquian scribe), 52, 313 n.85

Jewett, Rev. David, 64, 73–74, 82, 97; conflict with Occom, 73–74

Job, 163

Johnson, Elias (Tuscarora), 287–288, 329 n.125

Johnson, Emily Pauline (Tekahionwake, Mohawk), 289, 290, 291; *Canadian Born* (1903), 289; *Legends of Vancouver* (1911), 289; *The Moccasin Maker* (1913), 289; *The Shagganappi* (1913), 289; *The White Wampum* (1895), 289

Johnson, John (Enmegahbowh, Ojibwa), 232, 237, 261–262, 264–265, 380 n.123; autobiographical sketches by (1902, 1904), 264–265, 380 n.123; gives wrong date for Copway's death, 261; missionary activities for Methodists, 261; missionary among Ojibwas of Lake Superior, 237; ordained by Episcopalians, 261–262

Johnson, Joseph (Mohegan), 82, 83, 101–110, 111, 112, 116, 135, 148, 153, 239, 294, 330 n.131, 331 n.149, 332 n.150–151; address to Oneidas (1774), 106; on American Revolution, 107; bibliographical references to, 330 n.131, 332 n.150–151; correspondence with Occom, 105; correspondence with Wheelock, 102–103; death of, 108; diary of (1771–1772), 103–105; emissary of peace in American Revolution, 107–108, 331 n.149; letter to Moses Paul (1772), 108–109; marries Tabitha Occom, 104; message to Christian Indians, 105; at Moor's Indian Charity School, 101; ordained at Dartmouth College, 104; role in founda-

tion of Brothertown, 105–107; schoolmaster among the Oneidas, 102; sermons by, 109, 332 n.150–151; sketch of whaling experience, 103

Johnson, Marmeduke, 46

Johnson, Sir William, 70, 78, 84, 105, 106; intercedes for Christian Indians among Oneidas, 84, 105, 106; introduces Occom to Oneidas, 70; withdraws support from Charity School, 78

Johnson, Steven, 324 n.66

Johnson, Zachary (Mohegan), 82, 101, 324 n.67; conflict with Occom, 82, 324 n.67

Johnson's and Graham's Lessee v. William McIntosh (1823), 120

Jonathan (Massachusett), 40

Jones, Augustus (father of Peter), 233

Jones, Hugh, *Present State of Virginia* (1724), 33

Jones, John (Thayendanega, Ojibwa), 232

Jones, Peter (Kahkewaquonaby-Desagondensta, Ojibwa), 216, 232–235, 238, 241, 242, 261, 262, 264–265, 266, 268, 270–273, 293, 294, 346 n.126, 364 n.166, 371 n.32, 371–372 n.38; biography, 232–235; conversion experience, 234; on Copway, 241; death of, 261; on dreams and visions, 233; *History* (1861), 270–273; *Life* (1860), 264–265; marriage to Eliza Field, 238; mentioned in *Cherokee Phoenix*, 216, 364 n.166; moves to New Credit, 242, 294; notions of selective adaptation, 234, 266; promotes manual labor school for Ojibwas, 241, 268; travels to England, 235

Jones, William (Sac-Fox), 288

Jorgensen, Joseph, 2, 4

Journal des Débats Politiques et Littéraires (Paris), 251, 376 n.90

Kansas Territory, 260

Keewenaw Mission, 237

Khezig, Thomas (Ojibwa), 236

Kickapoos, 55

King George's War (1740–48), 55, 167

King Philip's War (1675), 37, 41, 42, 46, 47, 49, 64, 121, 140, 160; and Christian Indians, 37, 41; and image of Indians, 121; and image of Metacom, 160; Job Nesuton dies in, 46; Mashpees remain

King Philip's War (*cont.*)
   netural, 140; Mohegans in, 64; James
   Printer in, 46; sparked by Sassomon's
   murder, 47
Kingsbury, Cyrus, 172
King William's War (1689–97), 55
Kirkland, Rev. Samuel, 71, 87, 88, 89, 102,
   325 n.79, 330–331 n.135; breaks with
   Wheelock, 330–331 n.135; on Joseph
   Johnson, 102; on Occom, 87, 88, 325
   n.79; preaches funeral sermon for Oc-
   com, 88
Knobel, Dale, 258
Knox, Henry, 112, 119, 333 n.138
Krupat, Arnold, 90, 149

La Flesche, Francis (Omaha), 288, 391 n.33
Lahontan, Louis-Armnand Baron de, 273
Lake Champlain, 110
Lake Erie, 57, 225
Lake Huron, 241, 259
Lake Mohonk Conference of the Friends of
   the Indian (1883), 286–287
Lake of Two Mountains Mission (Canada),
   261
Lake Ontario, 225, 230
Lake Superior, 226, 228, 230, 237, 239,
   242, 259
Lancastrian system, 66
Langston, Gideon, 33
Langston, John, 33
language (in colonial situation), 7–9
Lantern Hill reservation (CT), 128
La Pointe Mission (WI), 237, 240
Larnell, Benjamin, 41, 51, 52; at Harvard
   Indian College, 41; poem by, in three lan-
   guages, 51
Las Casas, Bartolomé de, 123
Late Immigrants, 213
Launitz, Eduard Schmidt von der, 253, 377
   n.96
Lawrence, Amos, 249
League of Universal Brotherhood (1846),
   249
Leclerc, Georges Louis comte de Buffon,
   121
Leverett, John, 50
Liberator (Boston), 145, 152
Lighthorse Guard (Cherokee), 174, 178,
   192

Lincoln, Governor Levi, 144
Lind, Jenny, 250
Liverpool (England), 245, 249, 250, 254
local color movement, 287
Locke, John, *Two Treatises of Government*
   (1690), 121
London (England), 249, 251, 254, 264,
   275, 276
Long, Sylvester (Catawba), *Long Lance*
   (1926), 130–131
Longfellow, Henry Wadsworth, 244, 249–
   250, 253, 255, 257–258, 262, 264, 269,
   273, 377 n.98, 378–379 nn.112, 113,
   114, 382 n.145; Copway names daughter
   in honor of, 262; on Copway, 244, 257,
   258, 262, 269, 378–379 nn.112, 113,
   114; Copway on, 249–250; fails to sup-
   port *Copway's American Indian,* 255;
   recommendations for Copway, 249, 253,
   257; *Song of Hiawatha* (1855), 257, 269,
   377 n.98, 382 n.145
Long Island Presbytery, 69
Long Parliament, 34
Lönrott, Elias, *Kalevala,* 269
Lord Dunmore's War (1774), 55
Lord Kames, Henry Homes, 123
Louisiana Purchase (1803), 118, 173
Love, William De Loss, 65, 84, 96, 325
   n.83, 328 n.113
Lowell, James Russell, 126
Lower Town Cherokees, 170
Lowry, George (Cherokee), 217
Loyalists (Tories), 170, 228
Lumpkin, Governor Wilson, 218, 221
Lundy, Benjamin, 126

Macaulay, Thomas Babington, 273, 383
   n.156
Madison, James, 174
Mahicans, 99, 110–111, 112, 114; rela-
   tions with Euro-Americans, 110–111,
   114
malinchismo, 21
Malintzin (La Malinche, Doña Marina), 21
Mamohet (Mohegan), 63
Maneddo (Abenaki), 22
Manifest Destiny, 119, 173
manitos, 233
Manly, Charles, 374 n.76
Manteo (Lord Roanoke), 22

Maoris, 3
marginal man (as term), 17–18
Marksman, Peter (Ojibwa), 237
Marshall, Chief Justice John, 120, 193, 195, 201, 202, 214; and Cherokee Nation Cases, 120, 195, 201, 202, 214; and Jackson, 193
Martha's Vineyard (MA), 23, 37, 43, 48, 53
Martyr, Peter, 23
Mashantucket Pequot Indian Land Claims Settlement Act (1983), 128
Mashantucket Pequots, 64, 128. *See also* Pequots
Mashpee Historical Society, 347 n.133
Mashpees (Wampanoags), 53, 139, 140–147, 152, 156–159, 164, 295, 344 n.97; petition for federal recognition, 295, 344 n.97; relations with Euro-Americans, 140–142; Woodland Revolt, 141–147, 156–159, 164
Mason, John (overseer), 62
Mason, John (Puritan), 127
Mason, John, Jr., 75, 322 n.46
Mason, Captain John, 64
Mason, Samuel, 75, 322 n.46
Mason Controversy, 62–63, 64, 72–74; Occom's role in, 72–74
Massachusett Bible, 46
Massachusett Indians, 26, 34–37, 40; and John Eliot, 34–37
Massachusett language, 36, 46, 141
Massachusetts Bay Company, 33, 34, 35
Massachusetts House of Representatives, 146; Apess presents petition to, 146
Massasoit (Wampanoag sachem), 25–27, 44; and Squanto, 25–27
Mather, Cotton, 35, 50, 51, 60, 92; Eleazar's poem in *Magnalia Christi Americana* (1702), 50; on Indian languages, 60; praises John Eliot, 35; sends Larnell's poem to William Ashurst, 51
Mather, Increase, 47–48, 92, 160; on death of Sassomon, 47–48; on Metacom, 160
Mathews, John Joseph (Osage), *Sundown* (1934), 291
Mau Mauing (as term), 40
Maximilian, Prince of Wied, 252
May, Karl, 252
Mayan, 21
Mayhew, Experience, 42, 89, 311 n.70; collects Indian conversion testimonies, 89, 311 n.70; on Hiacoomes, 42; *Indian Converts* (1727), 42
Mayhew, Thomas, Sr., 37–38, 60, 61, 96
Mayhew, Thomas, Jr., 34–35, 37–38, 42–43, 60, 61, 96, 311 n.70; establishes Christian Indian towns, 37–38; and Hiacoomes, 42–43; *Light appearing more and more towards the perfect Day* (1651), 42; more liberal than Eliot, 38; publishes Indian confessions with Eliot, 311 n.70
McCoy, Rev. Isaac, 245
McGillivray, Alexander (Creek), 55
McHenry, James, 122
McIntosh, William (Creek), 196
McKenney, Thomas L., 196, 217, 255, 267, 270, 354 n.40, 382 n.148; Boudinot responds to, 196; David Brown reports to, 217, 354 n.40; Copway on, 382 n.148; influence on Copway, 267, 382 n.148; supports *Copway's American Indian*, 255
McKenzie, Fayette A., 285
McLaughlin, William G., 171, 175
McLean, John, 202
McLuhan, Marshal, 9
McNickle, D'Arcy (Cree-Flathead), *The Surrounded* (1936), 291
McQuaid, Kim, 147
Meigs, Return J., 217
Melville, Herman, *Moby Dick* (1851), 128
Memmi, Albert, 6–7, 158
Menominees, 116
Menona, Paul (Anthony Paul Mohegan), 327 n.103
Meriam Report (1928), 290
Messamoet (Micmac), 23
Meserve, Walter, 48
Metacom (King Philip, Wampanoag sachem), 40, 44, 46, 47–48, 52, 62, 129, 159–163; in antebellum American literature, 160; Apess claims relationship to, 129; Apess's eulogy on, 159–163; joined by Christian Indians, 40, 46, 52; and murder of Sassomon, 47–48; requests ransom for Mary Rowlandson, 46
Methodist Book Concern, 137
Methodist Episcopal Church, 137–139, 152, 229, 232, 237; Apess breaks with,

Methodist Episcopal Church (*cont.*) 137–139, 152; in Canada, 229, 232; enlists Copway's services, 237; internal problems, 138–139

Methodist Protestant Church, 137–139; ordains Apess, 137–138

Methodists, 117, 124–125, 127, 132–134, 135, 138–139, 153, 172, 196, 200, 224, 229, 232–233, 236–237, 241–242, 261, 262, 263, 264, 288; and African Americans, 124, 127, 138; and Apess, 132–134, 135, 153; in Callahan's *Wynema,* 288; among Canadian Ojibwas, 224, 229, 232–233; and Canadian Ojibwa writers, 232–233, 264; among Cherokees, 172, 196; and Copway, 224, 236–237, 241–242, 261, 263; and George Henry, 262; and Great Awakening, 124, 127; internal squabbles, 138–139; and Peter Jacobs, 262, 264; and John Johnson, 261; and Peter Jones, 234–235, 236, 264; and John Ross, 196; and Second Great Awakening, 124–125

Miamis, 55, 115–16

Miantonomo (Narragansett sachem), 44, 62; murdered by Uncas's Mohegans, 62

Micmacs, 23

Midewiwin Society (Grand Medicine Lodge), 231, 264, 370 n.26; Copway initiated into, 231; John Johnson initiated into, 264

Milledgeville Recorder (GA), 189

Miller, Cincinnatus Hiner, 279

Minnesota Democrat, 270

Minnesota Historical Society, 270

Missionary Herald (Boston), 176, 179, 217

Mississaugas, 230, 232, 235–237, 239, 262; origin of name 230. *See also* Ojibwas

Mississippi River, 55, 119, 122, 173, 174, 181, 200, 211, 223, 239

Missouri River, 246, 247

Mobilian Jargon (Choctaw-Chickasaw trade language), 6

Moctezuma, 21, 23

Mohawks, 15, 72, 84, 110, 233; and Peter Jones, 233; relations with Mahicans, 110

Mohegan (CT), 72, 76, 83, 89, 102, 135

Mohegan Indians v. Connecticut (1743), 63. *See also* Mason Controversy

Mohegans, 61–64, 71, 72–74, 77, 81–82, 97, 99, 103–104, 114, 127, 141, 295, 319 n.18, 320 n.21, 323 n.61, 324 nn.66, 67, 329 n.123; conflict with Occom, 81–82, 324 nn.66, 67; and dreams, 97; gain federal recognition (1994), 99, 320 n.21; at Mashpee, 141; and Mason Controversy, 62–63, 72–74; and Mohegan Church, 295, 329 n.123; and Pequots, 127, 319 n.18; reintegrate John Johnson, 103–104; relations with Euro-Americans, 61–64

Momaday, N. Scott (Kiowa), 117, 274; *Way to Rainy Mountain* (1969), 274

Monroe, James, 119, 174

Montagnais, 272

Montaigne, Michel Eyquem de, 23, 273

Montauk Historical Society, 99; proposes Samson Occom Day, 99

Montauks, 66–68, 69, 71, 77, 90–91, 99, 114, 141; among Mashpees, 141; Occom's account of, 90–91, 114; relations with Occom, 66–68, 69, 71

Montezuma, Carlos (Yavapai), 163, 257, 289, 290, 291, 348 n.152, 379 n.116; biography, 348 n.152; dies among Yavapais, 291; favors abolition of BIA and reservations, 163, 290; publisher of *Wassaja,* 257

Montour, John, 33

Montreal (Canada), 134, 226, 241

Moor's Indian Charity School, 61, 70, 74, 75, 78–81, 101, 109, 318–319 n.13; closed down, 79; founded by Wheelock, 61; David Fowler at, 70; Joseph Johnson at, 101, 109; moved from Lebanon to Hanover, 78–81; Occom's benefit tour for, 74

Moral and Literary Society of the Cherokee Nation, 183, 216

Moravians (United Brethern), 111, 172, 178, 184, 222; Boudinot educated by, 178, 184, 222; among Cherokees, 172, 178, 222; massacre at Gnadenhütten (OH), 111

Morgan, Lewis H., 246, 255, 264, 267, 270, 280, 378 n.108; advocates Indian state, 246; contributes to *Copway's*

American Indian, 255, 378 n.108; cooperates with Ely Parker, 280
Morris, George P., 378 n.104
Morse, Rev. Jedediah, 245, 267, 381 n.140; advocates removal, 245; on teaching Indians English, 267, 381 n.140
Morton, Samuel George, *Crania Americana* (1839), 123
Mother's Magazine (Elgin, IL), 289
Mourning Dove (Christal Quintasket, Coleville), *Cogewea* (1927), 291
Munsee dialect, 110
Murieta, Joaquin, 279
Murphey, Charles, 33
Murray, David, 90

Nahuatl, 21
Namaskets, 47
Nanabozho, 269
Nantucket Indians, 48
Nantucket Island (MA), 37
Narragansetts, 25, 62, 99, 127, 141, 328 n.114; conflict with Mohegans, 62; and Indian hymns, 328 n.114; among Mashpees; and Pequot War, 127; Wampanoags tributaries to, 25
Nashville Banner, 202
Natick (MA), 35–36, 37, 46, 47, 83
National American Education Society, 125
national ethnos (as term), 16
National Intelligencer (Washington, DC), 221
National Party. *See* Ross Party
Neal, John, 255, 263, 273; supports *Copway's American Indian,* 255
Nebraska Territory, 260
neocolonialism (as term), 3
Nepponit, Tom (Algonquian scribe), 52, 313 n.85; mentioned in letter written for Metacom, 52
Neruda, Pablo, 279
Nesuton, Job (Massachusett), 45–46, 47; dies in King Philip's War, 46; translates Gospel for Eliot, 45
New Credit (Canada), 242, 261
New Echota (New Town, Cherokee Nation), 175, 177, 182, 184, 281
New England Company (1649), 34, 41, 43, 59, 65–66, 76, 87, 308 n.39; ceases to operate in U.S., 87; created by Long Par-

liament, 34; pays for Hiacoomes's services, 43; provides funds for Harvard Indian College, 41; provides stipend for Occom, 65–66. *See also* Boston Board of Commissioners
New England townships, 40, 83; and Christian Indians, 40; Occom familiar with, 83
New Hampshire House of Representatives, 108; letter of introduction for Joseph Johnson, 108
New Haven (CT), 91, 200
New Lights, 59, 97, 292; and Great Awakening, 59; and Indian missionary-writers, 292; Occom's ties to, 97
New London (CT), 63, 64, 65, 93, 101, 127, 133
New Stockbridge (NY), 85, 86–87, 88, 111, 115–116
New Testament, 65, 104, 217; Joseph Johnson reads, 104; Occom on, 65; translated into Cherokee by David Brown and George Lowry, 217
New York Annual Conference of the Methodist Protestant Church, 139, 140; Apess participates as Pequot delegate, 140; appoints Apess to preach among Pequots, 139
New York Central Railway, 260
New York City, 134, 137, 140, 200, 237, 238, 243, 249, 251, 254, 255, 257, 259, 263, 264, 268, 270
New York Historical Society, 264
New York Times, 258–259, 379 n.118; "Anti-Copway" letter, 379 n.118; letter by Copway, 258–259
Newfoundland Company, 25
Ngugi wa Thiong'o, 3–4, 6
Niantic (Nahantuk, CT), 83
Niantics, 71, 99
Nicolar, Joseph (Penobscot), 288
Niles' Weekly Register (Philadelphia), 217
Nonantum, 36
Northrup, Sarah Bird (wife of John Ridge), 181
North West Company, 228
Northwest Confederacy, 55
Northwest Ordinance (1787), 58, 118
Northwest Territory (Old Northwest), 58, 113, 117, 127, 245, 247, 259, 268; Aupaumut as emissary in, 113; Copway

Northwest Territory (*cont.*)
on, 259; and Copway's "Kah-ge-gah"
project, 247, 268; Indian commissioner's
call for establishment of Indian state in,
245; Indian wars in, 58, 117
Norton, Charles Eliot, 257
Norton, John, "Journal" (1816), 329 n.125
Nullification Crisis (1832), 157, 203, 347
n.134; and Apess, 157; and Calhoun's exposition, 157, 347 n.134; and Cherokee
removal, 203

Obookiah, Henry (Sandwich Islander),
Memoirs (1819), 179
Occom, Christiana (Mohegan, daughter of
Occom), 327 n.103
Occom, Samson (Mohegan), 54, 61, 63,
64–101, 102, 103, 104, 105, 108, 109,
114, 116, 134, 144, 148, 153, 159, 163,
235, 239, 293, 294, 316–317 n.1, 322
nn.49, 55, 324 nn.66, 67, 325 nn.79, 83,
327 nn.103, 104, 327–328 n.111, 328–
329 n.120, 329 nn.122, 123, 126, 330
nn.128, 130; "Account of the Montauk
Indians" (1761), 90–91; appointed minister by New Stockbridge community,
85; attends Wheelock's school, 65–66;
autobiographical letter (1765), 90; autobiographical sketch (1768), 64–65, 67,
68, 89–90; "Awaked by Sinai's Awful
Sound," 96; on being Indian, 68; bibliographical references to, 316–317 n.1;
birth of, 64; on Brothertown's "Body
Politick," 85; collects £11,000 for Charity School, 76; confession of intemperance, 78; confession related to Mason
Controversy, 73–74; conflict with John
Sargeant, Jr., 87; connections to Phillis
Wheatley and Lemuel Haynes, 330
n.128; conversion experience, 64–65;
correspondence with Wheelock, 75, 78–
79, 81; criticizes Dartmouth, 78–79, 81;
death of, 88; dream of George Whitefield,
97; founds Brothertown (NY), 82–85;
Hymns (1774), 96, 327–328 n.111; Indian remedies (1754), 91; initiates revival at Mohegan, 104; involvement in
Mason Controversy, 72–74; as itinerant
preacher, 85–86, 89; journal (1743–
1790), 69, 70, 84, 85, 87, 88, 88–89,

101; journey to Great Britain, 74–76; on
immoral behavior of English, 70; legacy
among northeastern Indian communities,
98–99; library of, 327 n.103, 330 n.130;
among the Montauks, 66–68; among the
Oneidas, 70–71, 89; petitions New York
Assembly, 86–87; problems with Mohegans, 81–82, 324 n.67; relationship with
Wheelock deteriorates, 76–81; report
to Wheelock on Oneidas, 71; Samson
Occom Day (1970), 99, 329 n.122; selected as Mohegan councilor, 65; *Sermon*
(1772), 91–96, 327 n.104; sermons by,
329 n.126; settles in New Stockbridge,
87; site of grave, 325 n.83; on slavery,
100; speech on Indian neutrality, 84–85
Occom, Tabitha (Mohegan, wife of Joseph
Johnson), 104
Ockham, Joshua (Mohegan, father of Occom), 64
O'Connell, Barry, 130, 138
Odeon, 159
Ohio River, 57
Ohio Valley, 55, 111
Ojibwa Nation, 225
Ojibwas (Anishinabe), 55, 216, 224–242,
244, 246–248, 250, 251, 253, 259, 261–
275, 294, 370 n.25, 380 n.129, 382–383
n.149, 384 n.154; and allotment, 229;
autohistory, 270–273, 382–383 n.149,
384 n.154; British period, 226–228; defeat Iroquois, 225, 270–271, 272; and
dreams and visions, 231, 370 n.25; end
of sovereignty, 228; French period, 225;
and fur trade, 226–228; and missionaries, 228–230; notions of property, 272;
relations with Euro-Americans, 224–
230; and removal, 228–229, 246, 248;
U.S.–Canadian period, 228–230; wars
with Sioux, 226, 240, 271. *See also* Mississaugas
Ojibwa Thesis, 270–271, 272
Old Lights, 59, 223; and Great Awakening,
59
Old Settlers (Arkansas Cherokees), 174,
213; conflict with New Immigrants, 213;
origin of name, 174
Old Southwest, 117, 119, 124, 127
Oneidas, 57, 58, 70–71, 78, 79, 83–85,
86–87, 99, 102, 105–108, 109, 111,

115; adopt Christian Indians into Covenant Chain, 83; Declaration of Neutrality (1775), 84; grand lands to Christian Indians, 83–85, 105–108, 111; problems with Christian Indians, 86–87, 115; relations with Occom, 70–71; withdraw children from Charity School, 78
Ong, Walter, 9
Onondagas, 84
Oothcaloga (Cherokee Nation), 177
Opechancanough (Wampanoag), 26, 29, 32
Order of United Americans, 258
Ortiz, Fernando, 4
Ortiz, Simon (Acoma Pueblo), 8–9
Oskison, John Milton (Cherokee), 289, 290
Ottawas, 55, 224, 271
Oweneco (Mohegan sachem), 62

Paiutes, 288
Pake Ponesso (Wampanoag), 42–43
pan-Indianism (as term), 15
Paris (France), 22, 23, 251, 262, 275
Parker, Arthur Caswell (Seneca), 288, 289, 329 n.125, 379 n.116, 388 n.24; advocates gradual adaptation, 290; writes for Boy Scouts, 388 n.24
Parker, Ely S. (Seneca), 280–281, 283, 288, 363 n.155, 379 n.116; biography, 280; criticizes missionaries and agents, 283; report on Indian affairs (1867), 281
Park Hill (Cherokee Nation West), 212
Park Hill Mission Press, 361 n.130
Parkman, Francis, 244, 248–249, 253, 257, 263, 270, 378 n.108, 382 n.144; contributes to *Copway's American Indian,* 255; on Copway, 244, 248–249, 257, 270
Paucatuck Pequots, 128. *See also* Pequots
Paudash, George (Ojibwa), 232
Paul, Moses (Mohegan), 91–96, 108–109; addressed by Joseph Johnson, 108–109; addressed by Occom (1772), 91–96
Paulding, James Kirke, 122
Pawtuxets, 24, 25, 27
Payne, John Howard, 365 n.173
Paz, Ireneo, 279
Pearce, Roy Harvey, 122
Pearl (New York), 254–255, 377–378 n.103
Penn, William. *See* Jeremiah Evarts
Pequit, Alice (Wampanoag), 130

Pequots, 33–34, 61–62, 99, 117, 127–129, 131–132, 139, 140, 154; Apess's biographies of Pequot women, 154; appoint Apess delegate to Methodist Conference, 140; letters attesting Apess's character, 140; and Mohegans, 61–62; relations with Euro-Americans, 33–34, 127–129; situation during Apess's youth, 131–132
Pequot War (1636–37), 33–34, 44, 62, 128; Cockenoe-de-Long Island captured during, 44; Pequots consolidate after, 128; as prelude for missionizing activities, 33–34; Uncas joins English side, 62
Perdue, Theda, 182, 222
Philadelphia, 200, 216, 246
Phillippe, Louis, 275
Pickering, John, 176
Pierce, Franklin, 259
Pierce, Maris Bryant (Seneca), 216, 364–365 n.167, 365 n.174; *Address* (1838), 216, 364–365 n.167; biography, 364–365 n.167
Pilgrims. *See* Puritans
Plains Indians, 6, 15, 188, 268, 282–283, 284–285; Boudinot on, 188; and concept of pan-Indianism, 15; Copway on, 268; and Indian literature, 284–285; and reservation policy, 282–283; sign language of, 6
Plains Ojibwas (Bungees), 225. *See also* Ojibwa
Plymouth Rock, 162
Pocahontas (Matoka, Lady Rebecca; Pamunkey), 24, 27–29, 31, 75, 244, 249, 306 n.19; Copway on, 244; as cultural broker, 27–29; in England, 31, 75, 249
Pohquonnopet, Sir Peter (Stockbridge), 323 n.61
Pokagon, Simon (Potawatomi), *Queen of the Woods* (1899), 288
polygenesis, 122–123
Pomeroy, Rev. Benjamin, 65
Poncas, 286
Pontiac (Ottawa), 101, 369 n.14
Pontiac's War (Beaver War, 1763), 55, 70, 110, 226; and Ojibwas, 226; and Stockbridge Indians, 110
pony club, 192
Poosepatucks, 66
Popham, Sir George, 23, 24

Posey, Alexander Lawrence (Creek), 155,
216, 288; on Boudinot, 216; "Fus Fixico
Letters," 288
Potawatomis, 55, 115, 224, 271, 288;
Pokagon on, 288; and Stockbridge In-
dians, 115
Powhatan (Pamunkey sachem), 27–29, 44
Pratt, Mary Louise, 303 n.87
Pratt, Richard Henry, 284
Praying Indians. See Christian Indians
Presbyterian General Assembly, 172
Presbyterians, 69, 85, 172, 179, 184, 189,
214, 222; and Boudinot, 179, 184, 189,
214, 222; among Cherokees, 172; ordain
Occom, 69
Prescott, William, 263
primitivism, 121, 265, 273–275, 292; and
apocryphal Indian travelers, 273–275;
and Copway, 265; European tradition of,
121
Prince, Thomas, 52
Pring, Martin, 22
Printer, James (Wowaus, Nipmuck), 46–47,
52; biography, 46–47; letter to Governor
Leverett (1676), 46, 52
Privy Council (London), 75
Proctor, Isaac, 203
progressives (as term), 16–17
proto-ethnos (as term), 16
Province of Canada, 230
Provincial Congress of New York, 108; let-
ter of introduction for Joseph Johnson,
108
Providence (RI), 137, 237–238
Prudential Committee of the ABCFM, 184,
203; reverses anti-removal stance, 203
Pueblo Indians, 8
Puritans, 22, 25–27, 33–53, 128, 154,
157, 159–163; and Apess's criticism of,
157, 159–163; and Christian Indians,
34–42; conquest of Pequots, 33–34; and
Squanto, 25–27; views on Indians, 34
Quakers (Society of Friends), 124, 196,
215, 274
Quarterly Journal (American Indian Maga-
zine), 285, 287, 289, 290; founded, 285;
Montezuma and Parker write for, 290;
Oskison writes for, 289
Queen Anne, 62
Queen Anne's War (1702–13), 55

Queen Victoria, 274
Quexós, Pedro de, 22, 23
Quinney, John W. (Stockbridge sachem),
116, 332–333 n.156, 334 n.171; biogra-
phy, 334 n.171; translation with
Aupaumut, 332–333 n.156

Raleigh, Sir Walter, 22, 24
Rama Reserve (Canada), 262
Ramsey, Alexander, 374 n.76
Rawson, Rev. Grindell, 50
Rayner, Kenneth, 374 n.76
Realismus, 252
Red Jacket (Seneca), 260, 379 n.121
Red Man (Carlisle), 287
Red Power, 294
Reese, Susanna (Cherokee, mother of
Boudinot), 177
Religious Intelligencer (New Haven),
222
Religious Remembrancer (Philadelphia),
179
Removal Act (1830), 119, 127, 192–193;
Boudinot on, 192–193
Ribeiro, Darcy, 2
Rice Lake (Canada), 230, 231, 235, 241,
272
Rice Lake band (Ojibwas), 232, 235, 239,
241
Ridge, Andrew Jackson (Cherokee), 209
Ridge, John (Skahtlelohskee, Cherokee),
178–183, 188, 195, 196, 200–204, 206–
212, 213–214, 217, 218, 246, 259, 278,
294, 355 n.53, 356 nn.61, 62, 360 n.117,
371–372 n.38; accompanies Boudinot
on fund-raising tour, 200–201; advises
Creeks to remove, 360 n.117; advocates
removal, 206–211; assassination of, 213;
drafts resolutions of Treaty Party with
Boudinot, 208; educated by Moravians,
178; elected president of National Committee, 195; at Foreign Mission School,
179–182; joins Cherokee delegates in
Washington, 202–203; legal advisor to
Creeks, 183, 356 n.62; letter to Christian
Herald on prejudice (1822), 182, 259;
letter to Monroe on Cherokee progress
(1822), 180; letter to Stand Watie on
"Chicken Snake" Jackson, 201–202;
marriage to Sarah Bird Northrup, 181;

mentioned in Jones's *History,* 355 n.53, 371–372 n.38; moves to Cherokee Nation West, 211–212; publications by, 355 n.53; "Short Account of the Cherokee Nation" (1826), 217; signs Coodey's petition of protest, 206; signs final draft of Treaty of New Echota, 211; speech at Circular Church in Charleston (1822), 181, 246; writes constitution of Moral and Literary Society (1825), 183, 356 n.61

Ridge, John Rollin (Yellow Bird, Cherokee), 278–279, 288, 385–386 nn.3, 4, 5; biography, 278–279; *Joaquin Murieta* (1854), 279, 385–386 nn.3, 4, 5; romantic poetry by, 288

Ridge, The (Major Ridge, Kahnungdatlageh, Cherokee), 177–178, 188–189, 192, 195, 206–212, 213; advocates removal, 206–211; appointed counselor to principal chief, 195; assassination of, 213; and civilization program, 177–178; leads Lighthorse Guard against intruders, 192; moves to Cherokee Nation West, 210–211; against removal, 195; role as Cherokee leader, 178; signs Coodey's petition of protest, 206; signs Treaty of New Echota, 210–211; as slave owner, 188–189

Ridge, Nancy (Cherokee), 178

Ridge Party (Treaty Party), 204, 208–211, 214, 218–220; and Cherokee middle class, 214; founded at John Ridge's home, 208; resolutions of, 208–209

Riggs, Rolla Lynn (Cherokee), 390 n.30

Rio Grande Pueblos, 290

River Indian Confederacy, 115

Rocky Mountains, 266, 268

Rogers, John, 92

Rogers, Will (Cherokee), 390 n.30

Rogin, Michael, 119

Rolfe, John, 28

romantic movement, 243, 252, 263, 266, 271, 277; influence on Copway, 263, 266, 271, 277

Ronda, James P., 34, 114, 116

Ronda, Jeanne, 114, 116

Ross, Andrew (Cherokee), 204, 207; signs preliminary removal treaty, 207

Ross, John (Cherokee), 183, 188, 192, 195–196, 198–199, 200, 203–212, 213, 214–215, 218–223, 282, 293, 294, 359 n.98, 361 n.122, 362 n.147, 363 n.155; accepts Boudinot's resignation, 205–206; attempts reconciliation with Ridge Party, 207–208; bibliographical references to, 359 n.98; biography, 195–196; censors entry in *Phoenix,* 203–204, 205, 361 n.122; co-founds Moral and Literary Society, 183; compromise proposals for removal, 207, 209, 212; considers removal to Mexico, 209, 294; on death penalty, 362 n.147; denounces Treaty Party, 218; elected principal chief, 195; on his decision to remove, 214–215; opposes removal, 203–212; praises *Phoenix* and its editor, 199, 200; response to Boudinot's *Letters,* 221–222; threatened with murder, 192; tries to unite Cherokee Nation West, 213, 363 n.155

Ross Party (National Party), 204, 209–210, 212, 214, 215, 220–221, 363 n.155; criticized by Boudinot, 220–221; in Washington, 209–210, 212

Ross, William Potter (Cherokee), 282, 387 n.13; biography, 387 n.13; editor of *Cherokee Advocate,* 282

Rowlandson, Mary, 46

Royal Proclamation (1763), 55–56, 82, 226, 228, 229

Royal Society of London, 48

Running Waters (Cherokee Nation), 208

Rush-Bagot Convention (1817), 229

Ryerson, Rev. William, 241

Sale Creek (Cherokee Nation), 172

Salisbury, Neal, 24, 27, 35

Saltonstall, Nathaniel, 48

Samoset (Wampanoag), 25

Sampson, John, 33

Sampson, Sarah (Mashantucket Pequot, mother of Occom), 64, 65; arranges meeting with Wheelock, 65

Sampson, Thomas, 33

Sand, Robert Charles. *See* James Wallis Eastburn

Santee Sioux (Eastern Dakotas), 226, 239; Copway on, 239

Sargeant, Delight (wife of Boudinot), 212

Sargeant, John (National Republican), 193

Sargeant, John, Sr., 60, 97, 110, 172, 179; founds Christian Indian community at Stockbridge (MA), 110; on Indian education, 60

Sargeant, John, Jr., 87, 97, 113, 115, 334 n.168; letter from Aupaumut, 113; Occom on, 87; as pastor of New Stockbridge (NY), 87; records speeches by Aupaumut, 115, 334 n.168

Sassacomoit (Assacomit, Abenaki), 22, 23, 24; adventures precede Squanto's, 24

Sassacus (Mohegan sachem), 61

Sassamon, John (Massachusett), 41, 47–48; at Harvard, 41; murder of, 47–48

Saugeen band (Ojibwa), 241

Saugeen Mission (Canada), 241

Sauks, 226

Saulteaux (Northern Ojibwas), 224, 225. See also Ojibwas

Sault Ste. Marie (Canada), 225, 228

Savignon (Huron), 23

Sawyer, Rev. David (Keghezowinninne, Ojibwa), 232

Sawyer, Chief Joseph (Ojibwa), 241

Schermerhorn, Rev. John F., 209–211

Schiller, Friedrich, 250

Schmalz, Peter, 242

Schoolcraft, Henry Roe, 122, 242, 255, 264, 267, 269, 270, 373 n.56, 382 nn.145, 148; accused of mismanagement, 242, 373 n.56; contributes to Copway's American Indian, 255, 270; Copway on, 269, 382 nn.145, 148; influence on Copway, 264, 267, 269, 270

scientific racism, 122–123, 150

Scott, James, 18, 40, 90

Scott, General Winfield, 212

Second Great Awakening, 124–125, 127, 132, 138, 159, 172, 263, 292; African American-Indian interaction during, 127; and Apess, 132, 159; characteristics of, 124–125; and Cherokees, 172; and Copway, 263; and Indian missionary-writers, 292

Second Seminole War (Florida War, 1835), 124, 127; and abolitionists, 127

Seminoles, 119, 260, 360 n.117; and Copway, 260

Senate (U.S.), 192, 209, 211, 218–219, 245; Boudinot on, 209; Boudinot's Let-

ters distributed to, 218–219; Doty's treaty with Sioux not ratified by, 245; ratifies Treaty of New Echota, 211; and removal, 192, 209, 211, 218–219

Senecas, 84, 215, 219, 260, 280, 364–365 n.167; angry over removal of Red Jacket's remains, 260; and Ely Parker, 280; Marys Pierce and the Seneca Revolution, 364–365 n.167; resist removal, 215, 280; Nathan T. Strong for removal of, 219

Separatists, 25

Sepúlveda, Juan Ginés de, 123

Sequestered Lands, 62. See also Mason Controversy

Sequoyah (George Gist, Cherokee), 13, 176–177, 182, 184, 217, 353 n.36, 355 n.53; awarded silver medal by General Council, 176, 182; biography, 176, 353 n.36; and Boudinot, 184, 217; and Cherokee syllabary, 13, 176–177, 182, 184, 355 n.53; John Ridge on, 355 n.53

Sewall, Samuel, 50

Shattuck, Tobias (Narragansett), 75

Shawnees, 55, 167

Shinnecocks, 66, 96, 99; honor Occom, 96, 99

Silliman, Benjamin, 374 n.76

Silva, Peter, Jr. (Shinnecock), 99; address honoring Occom, 99

Simms, William Gilmore, 255, 263

Simons, Daniel (Narragansett), 323 n.61

Sioux, 239–240, 245, 247, 269, 271; Copway on, 239–240, 269; negotiate treaties with James Doty, 245; Warren on, 271

Skicowaros (Abenaki), 22–23

Slany, John, 24

slavery, 100, 123, 124, 125–127, 133, 138, 143–144, 149–152, 156, 161–162, 188–189, 212, 242, 258, 330 n.127; Apess on, 133, 156, 161–162; Boudinot on, 188–189; Copway on, 258; among Indians, 125–127, 188–189; and Methodists, 138; and New Light preachers, 330 n.127; Occom on, 100; and racism, 123; and reformers, 212; slave codes, 144; slave insurrections, 143–144; slave narratives, 149–152, 242

Smith, Donald, 243, 244, 247, 260, 270

Smith, Captain John, 24, 26, 27–28; on Pocahontas, 27–28; on Squanto, 24, 26

Smith, Samuel Stanhope, 123
Smithsonian Institution (1848), 264
Snelling, William G., 157, 347 n.133
Society for the Propagation of the Gospel
among the Indians and Others in North
America (1787), 87, 141; enlists John
Sargeant, Jr., 87; and Mashpees, 141
Society for the Propagation of the Gospel in
Foreign Parts (SPG, 1701), 59
Society in Scotland for Propagating Christian Knowledge (SSPCK, 1709), 59, 69–
70, 72, 80, 323 n.61; plans to send Occom
among the Cherokees, 69; sends Occom
on mission to Oneidas, 70; withholds
funds from Charity School, 80, 323 n.61
Society of American Indians (SAI, 1911),
285–287, 289, 290; founding of, 285;
and Indian authors, 289, 290; internal
disagreement, 286; objectives of, 285–
286; preamble of American Indian Asso-
ciation, 285; publishes journal, 285
Solemnization of Marriage Act (1786), 156
Southeastern Ojibwas, 224, 225, 230–231.
See also Ojibwas
Southern Banner (Athens, GA), 218
Southern Indian Confederation, 55
Southern Workman (Hampton Institute),
287
Southwestern Ojibwas, 224, 225, 239, 240.
See also Ojibwas
Spanish, 21, 23, 24
Special Subcommittee on Indian Education
(report 1969), 7
Speck, Frank G., 97, 272
Spectator (London), 273, 384 n.160
spiritual autobiography, 149
Spotswood, Alexander, 32–33
Spring Place (Cherokee Nation), 172, 178
Squanto (Tisquantum, Pawtuxet), 24–27,
29; as cultural broker among Puritans,
24–27
Squier, Ephraim George, 264, 267, 270,
374 n.76; and Copway, 264, 267, 374
n.76; letter from Parkman on Copway,
270
Stamp Act (1765), 75
Standing Bear, Luther (Teton Sioux), 10–
11, 291; on being Indian, 291; on the
written word, 10–11
St. Clair, Anthony, 111

Steinhauer, Rev. Henry Bird (Sowengisik,
Ojibwa), 232
Stockbridge (MA), 60, 84, 85, 110, 113–
114
Stockbridge (WI), 239
Stockbridge Indians, 58, 60–61, 84–85,
86–87, 110–116; conflict with Oneidas,
86–87; factionalism over Occom's role as
preacher, 87; found New Stockbridge
(NY), 85, 111; provide refuge for Broth-
ertown Indians, 84–85; removal to Indi-
ana, 115–116; removal to Wisconsin,
116; and John Sargeant, Sr., 60–61, 110;
treaty with U.S., 58
Stockbridge-Munsees, 116
Stoddard, Charles Warren, 279
Stone, John Augustus, *Metamora* (1829),
160
Stonequist, Everett, 17–18
Stowe, Harriet Beecher, 222
Street, Alfred B., 378 n.104
Strickland, Rennard, 195
Strong, Nathan, 92
Strong, Nathan T. (Seneca), 219, 365
n.174; *Appeal* (1841), 219
Stroughton, Dr. John, 40
Suffolk Presbytery, 78; Occom's letter of
confession to, 78
Summerfield, John (Sahghahgewagahbaweh,
Ojibwa), 232, 383 n.154
sun dance, 12
Sunday, Rev. John (Shahwundais, Ojibwa),
232, 237; inspires Copway, 237
Sunegoo, Catherine Brown (Ojibwa,
daughter of Jones), 371–372 n.38
Sunset (Menlo Park, CA), 287
Supreme Court, 193–195, 197, 201–203,
281, 283; and Cherokee Nation Cases,
193–194, 197, 201–203; and Cherokee
Tobacco case, 281; and Indian policy,
283
Sutton, Catherine (Nahnebahwequay,
Ojibwa), 232

Tahanedo (Dehamada, Abenaki), 22
Taignoagny (Iroquois), 22
Tantaquidgeon, Gladys (Mohegan), 329
n.123
Tantaquidgeon, Lucy (Mohegan), 329
n.123

Tantaquidgeon Indian Museum, 329 n.123
Taos Pueblo, 16
Tassel, George (Cherokee), 193
Taunchey, John (Ojibwa), 237
Taylor, Zachary, 246, 247, 249; letter from
    Copway, 247
Tecumseh (Shawnee), 55, 101, 113, 116,
    228, 289; and Aupaumut, 113, 116; and
    Ojibwas, 228; and pan-Indian front, 55;
    subject of novel by Oskison, 289
Ten Commandments, 114
Ten Lost Tribes of Israel, 123, 150, 153,
    271; American authors on, 123; Apess
    on, 150, 153; Warren on, 271
Tenskwatawa (Shawnee), 113, 333 n.161;
    Aupaumut on, 113, 333 n.161
Thacher, Rev. Thomas, 50–51; eulogy on,
    by Eleazar, 50–51
Thanksgiving, 26
Third World Peace Congress (1850), 249,
    250–253, 254, 276, 375 n.86, 375–376
    n.87, 376–377 n.94; Copway invited to,
    249; Copway speaks at, 250–253, 254,
    376–377 n.94; and Copway's Running
    Sketches, 276, 375–376 n.87; failures of,
    375 n.86; minutes published, 375–376
    n.87
Thomas, Robert (Cherokee), 15
Thoreau, Henry, 257
Thornton, John, 77, 85; defends Occom in
    letter to Wheelock, 77; provides funds for
    Occom, 85
three fires, 224
Tidewater Indians, 27–29
Times (London), 250–251
Tocqueville, Alexis de, 173
Todorov, Tzvetan, 9–10, 21
Tonawanda Reservation (NY), 280
traditionalists (as term), 15–17
Trail of Tears, 166, 212–213; and assas-
    sination of Boudinot and the Ridges, 213
transcendentalists, 135, 263
transculturation (as term), 4
treaties, 55, 57, 86, 111, 113, 117, 127,
    169, 171, 178, 192, 211, 212, 215, 218,
    226, 228; Dancing Rabbit Creek (1830),
    360 n.117; Fort McIntosh (1785), 228;
    Fort Schuyler (1788), 86; Fort Wayne
    (1803, 1809), 113; Ghent (1814), 117,
    228; Greenville (1795), 111, 113, 228;
    Guadalupe Hidalgo (1848), 246; Hart-
    ford (1638), 127; Holston (1791), 171,
    192; Hopewell (1785), 169, 192; as in-
    struments of colonialism, 10–11; Jay
    (1784), 228; La Pointe (1854), 229; New
    Echota (1835), 178, 211, 212, 215, 216,
    218; Paris I (1763), 55; Paris II (1783),
    57, 226; Robinson-Huron/Robinson Su-
    perior (1850), 230; Spring Wells, 228
treaty literature, 106, 112–113, 333–334
    n.162; and Aupaumut, 112–113; and
    Joseph Johnson, 106
Treaty Party. See Ridge Party
trickster, 16, 152, 262, 269; and Apess's
    humor, 152; and Copway, 262, 269; as
    cultural broker, 16
Tubbee, Laah Ceil Manatoi Elaah
    (Delaware-Stockbridge), 130
Tubbee, Okah, A Thrilling Sketch of the
    Life of (1848), 130
Tunxis, 99
Tupinambás, 23, 273
Turner, Nat, 144
Turner, Victor, 17
Tuscaroras, 32–33, 57, 58, 84, 108, 167;
    children as hostages at College of Wil-
    liam and Mary, 32–33; remain neutral
    during American Revolution, 57, 108
Tuscarora War (1711), 32–33
Tyler, John, 245

Uncas (Mohegan sachem), 61–64
Uncas, Major Ben (Mohegan sachem), 63
Uncas, Ben II (Mohegan sachem), 63, 64, 65
Uncas, Ben III (Mohegan sachem), 72–73,
    81, 324 nn.66–67; complains about Oc-
    com, 73
Uncas, Isiah (Mohegan), 82
Uncas, John (Mohegan), 82
Uncasville (CT), 99
Underhill, John, 127
Union Democrats (Peace Democrats), 278
United Colonies, 41
Upper Mississippi Mission, 239
Upper Canada, 228–230, 234–235, 241,
    294
Upper Town Cherokees, 172

vanishing Indian, 122, 153, 158, 161, 238,
    255, 287; and Apess, 153, 158, 161; and

Copway, 238, 255; and "salvage" anthropology, 287

Vann, David (Cherokee), 178, 207–208

Vattel, Emerich von, *Droit de gens* (1758), 121

Velasco, Luis de (Don Luis, Algonquian), 23

Vincent, Lewis (Huron), 323 n.61

Virginia Company, 30–32

Vizenor, Gerald (Ojibwa), 155

Voltaire, François Marie Arouet de, 132, 273

Waban (Massachusett), 35, 36, 42, 43–44, 312 n.75; appointed Chief Minister of Justice, 35, 44; confession of, 43; converted by Eliot, 35

Walker, David, *Walker's Appeal* (1829), 152, 346 n.123

Walker, John, Jr. (Cherokee), 207

Wampanoags (Pokanokets), 25–27, 37–38, 42–43, 47, 62, 141, 147, 160; and Mashpees, 141, 147; and Praying Indians of Martha's Vineyard, 37–38, 42–43; relations with Squanto, 25–27

Wampy, Anne (Pequot), 154; biography of, by Apess, 154

Wampy, Elijah (Tunxis), 83, 86, 107; leads Brothertown faction wanting to lease lands, 86; sent as representative of Christian Indians to Oneidas, 83, 107

Wanape, 23

Wanchese, 22

Wappinger Indians, 110

War of 1812, 58, 113, 115, 119, 121, 126, 228; and American literature, 121; and Aupaumut, 113; and Indian policy, 58; and Manifest Destiny, 119

Warren, William Whipple (Ojibwa), 270–273, 382 n.149; biography, 382 n.149; *History* (1885), 270–273

Washington, George, 108, 111, 119, 171, 197–198, 331 n.149, 351 n.15; Boudinot on, 197–198; and civilization program, 119, 171; encourages Cherokees to form a nation, 171; and Joseph Johnson, 108, 331 n.149; letter by, in *Cherokee Phoenix,* 351 n.15; promotes Aupaumut to Captain, 111

Wassaja (Chicago), 257, 290

Watie, David (Oowatie, Cherokee, father of Boudinot), 177–178

Watie, Stand (Cherokee), 200, 201, 203, 210–211, 281, 361 n.123, 363 n.155; as Confederate general, 281, 363 n.155; escapes assassination, 363 n.155; interim editor of *Phoenix,* 200, 203, 361 n.123; in Washington for Boudinot, 210–211

Watts, Isaac, 96

Watuspaquin (Massachusett), 47

Wayne, Anthony, 111

Webster, Daniel, 193

Weinreich, Uriel, 8

Weld, Daniel, 41

Weld, Theodore Dwight, 139

Wesley, John, 138

Weymouth, George, 22, 24

Wheatley, Phillis, 100, 148, 330 n.128; correspondence with Occom, 100, 330 n.128

Wheelock, Eleazar, 61, 64, 65, 66–67, 70–83, 88, 90, 97, 99, 100, 101–104, 172, 179, 318 n.13, 322 n.49; on advantage of Indian missionaries, 66–67; correspondence with Occom, 81, 83; death of, 81; on failure of Indian missionaries, 80; founds Connecticut Board of Commissioners for the SSPCK, 72; founds Dartmouth College, 79; founds Moor's Indian Charity School, 61; and "Grand Design," 61, 70, 72, 77, 80, 318 n.13; impressed by Occom's success, 66; manipulates Dartmouth College charter, 79–80; meets Occom, 65; moves Charity School to Hanover, 78–81; *Narratives* of (1763–1775), 66–67, 80, 318 n.13; and Occom's fund-raising trip to England, 74–76; and Occom's mission among Oneidas, 70–71; on Occom's public speaking abilities, 322 n.49; regards Occom's success in England with suspicion, 76–77; relations with Joseph Johnson, 101–104; stigmatizes Occom as alcoholic, 76; supports Occom's Brothertown project, 83

Whig Party, 245, 258–259; relations with Copway, 258–259

Whitaker, Rev. Alexander, *Good News from Virginia* (1613), 29

Whitaker, Rev. Nathaniel, 74–76; journey to England with Occom, 74–76

White, Rev. George, 138, 150

White, Hayden, 75

Whitefield, George, 59, 64, 72, 75, 79, 97; and Great Awakening, 59, 64; hosts Occom in England, 75; Occom on, 79, 97; refuses to provide funds for Occom and Fowler, 72

White Path Rebellion (1827), 175

Whitney, Asa, 374 n.76

Wilhelm, Frederick III, 253, 377 n.97

Wilhelm, Prince Paul of Würtenberg, 252

Wilkins, Thurman, 203

Williams, William, 133

Willis, Nathaniel, 255, 263, 273; supports *Copway's American Indian*, 255

Wilson, Woodrow, 290

Windham Association of Connecticut, 69; examines Occom, 69

windigo psychosis, 263, 380 n.129

Winnebago Rebellion (1827), 124

Winthrop, John, Jr., 48

Wirt, William, 193

Women's National Indian Association (1879), 286

Wompowess, John (Nipmuck), 41, 49–50; letter to King Charles I (ca. 1675), 49

Wood, Mary (wife of Apess), 137, 154, 341–342 n.66; autobiography in Apess's *Experiences*, 154; marries Apess, 137

Woodland Revolt, 143–147. *See also* Mashpees

Woodward, Grace, 210

Worcester, Rev. Samuel, 176–177, 182, 184, 194–195, 197, 201, 203, 212, 214, 353 n.39, 356 n.65, 361 n.130; arrested by Georgia Guard, 194; and *Cherokee Phoenix*, 177, 184, 186; establishes Park Hill Mission Press, 361 n.130; exonerates Boudinot, 214; helps Boudinot after removal, 212; mentioned by Boudinot, 201; seeks pardon from Georgia, 203, 214; and Sequoyah's syllabary, 176, 353 n.39; translations with Boudinot, 182, 184, 356 n.65

Worcester v. State of Georgia (1832), 120, 194–195, 201

Wounded Knee Massacre (1890), 288

Wyandots. *See* Hurons

Yale, 65

Yamasees, 55

Yamasee War (1715), 55

Yates Academy (NY), 280

Yavapais, 291

Yeardley, Governor George, 30

Young, Robert Alexander, *Ethiopian Manifesto* (1829), 346 n.123

Young America movement, 278

Zolla, Elémire, 270